THE ROUGH GUIDE TO

Chile

This sixth edition updated by

Anna Kaminski, Shafik Meghji and Rosalba O'Brien

ROUGH
GUIDES

roughguides.com

Contents

INTRODUCTION **4**

Where to go	6	Things not to miss	12
When to go	10	Itineraries	22
Author picks	11		

BASICS **24**

Getting there	25	Spectator sports	37
Getting around	26	Outdoor activities	38
Accommodation	30	National parks and reserves	42
Food and drink	32	Health	43
The media	35	Culture and etiquette	44
Festivals	35	Travel essentials	45

THE GUIDE **52**

1 Santiago and around	52	7 Chiloé	314
2 Valparaíso, Viña and the Central Coast	94	8 Northern Patagonia	346
		9 Southern Patagonia	382
3 El Norte Chico	122	10 Tierra del Fuego	418
4 El Norte Grande	166	11 Easter Island and the Juan Fernández Archipelago	442
5 The Central Valley	216		
6 The Lake District	258		

CONTEXTS **466**

History	467	Books	504
Landscape and the environment	492	Chilean Spanish	509
Chilean music: nueva canción	498		

SMALL PRINT & INDEX **516**

OPPOSITE DEATH VALLEY, SAN PEDRO DE ATACAMA **PREVIOUS PAGE** GRAFFITI, VALPARAÍSO

Introduction to
Chile

A long, narrow sliver of land, clinging to the edge of a continent, Chile has often drawn attention to itself for its wholly implausible shape. Seen in the pages of an atlas, the country's outline strikes you as aberrant and fantastical; 4300km in length (the equivalent of Norway to Nigeria), and with an average width of just 175km, the very idea of it seems absurd. Once you're on Chilean soil, however, these boundaries make perfect sense, and visitors quickly realize that Chile is a geographically self-contained unit. The Andes, the great mountain range that forms its eastern border, are a formidable barrier of rock and ice that cuts the country off from Argentina and Bolivia. The Atacama Desert, a 1000km stretch of parched wasteland, separates it from Peru to the north. And to the west, only a few islands dotted in the Pacific Ocean break the waves that roll onto Chile's coast from Australasia.

All this has created a country distinct from the rest of South America and one that defies many people's expectations of an Andean country. It is developed, relatively affluent and non-corrupt, and – with the exception of the infamous military regime of the 1970s and 1980s – boasts a long tradition of **political stability** and orderly government. It is, without doubt, one of the safest and most relaxing South American countries to travel in. Its buses are comfortable and run on time; its people polite, respectful and discreet; and its **indigenous minorities**, in the main, coexist peacefully alongside the rest of the population.

A country of geographical extremes, Chile's diversity is reflected both in its people – from the alpaca herders of the altiplano and the gauchos of Patagonia to the businessmen of Santiago – and its cuisine, which encompasses the tropical fruit of the arid north as well as king crab from the southern fjords. Above all, though, it is for its remote and dizzyingly beautiful landscapes that visitors head to Chile. With a population of fifteen million largely confined to a handful of major cities, much of the country is made up of vast tracts of scarcely touched wilderness – places where you can be days from the nearest tarred road.

ABOVE EXPEDITION IN THE CHILEAN ANDES

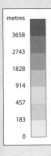

metres	
	3658
	2743
	1828
	914
	457
	183
	0

Easter Island (Chile)

PERU

Arica

Iquique

BOLIVIA

PARAGUAY

Calama

San Pedro
de Atacama

Antofagasta

Copiapó

ARGENTINA

La Serena · Vicuña

Cordoba

Buenos Aires

Los Vilos

Viña del Mar

Mendoza

Valparaíso · SANTIAGO

Buenos Aires

Rancagua

*Juan Fernández
Archipelago (Chile)*

Talca

Chillán

Concepción

PACIFIC

OCEAN

Temuco · Pucón

Valdivia

Osorno

Puerto Varas

Puerto Montt

Ancud

Chiloé Castro

Quellón

*Arch. de los
Chonos*

Chaitén

N

Puerto Aisén

Coyhaique

Golfo de Penas

Cochrane

ATLANTIC

OCEAN

Villa O'Higgins

El Chaltén

Isla Wellington

El Calafate

Puerto Natales

Strait of Magellan

*Tierra
del Fuego*

Punta Arenas

Porvenir

Ushuaia

Puerto
Williams

Cape Horn

0	250

kilometres

Where to go

Few countries can match Chile for the **sheer
diversity of scenery and range of climatic zones**
– from the driest desert in the world to immense
ice-fields and glaciers. Spread between these
extremes is a kaleidoscope of panoramas, taking in
sun-baked scrubland, lush vineyards and orchards,
virgin temperate rainforest, dramatic fjords and
endless **Patagonian steppes**. Towering over it all is
the long, jagged spine of the Andes, punctuated by
colossal peaks and **smouldering volcanoes**.

Given Chile's great length, and the huge distances
that separate the main attractions, it's important to
plan your **itinerary** (see p.22) before you go. The
country splits roughly into two halves, with Santiago
the jumping-off point for both the sunny north, all
vineyards, beaches and desert, and the capricious
south, comprised of glaciers, mountains, forests and
fjords. If you wish to hit both extremes, a LAN air
pass (see p.25) or inexpensive Sky Airline flights
make it possible.

Santiago, though boasting some fine monuments
(including one to Salvador Allende), museums and
restaurants, is not a destination city like Río or
Buenos Aires, but is handy for visiting some of the
country's oldest **vineyards**. Near Santiago, the
quirky port of **Valparaíso** – Chile's other major city
– provides an interesting contrast, with its snaking
alleyways decorated by local street artists, its gritty
vibe and the funiculars allowing splendid views of
the bay from its many hills.

North of Santiago, highlights include the handsome
colonial city of **La Serena** and the lush, deeply rural
Elqui Valley, its hills ideal for horse treks and its distilleries perfect for sampling pisco – a
drink that's the source of great dispute between Chile and Peru. A succession of idyllic
beaches lies spread out along the dazzling fringe of the **Norte Chico**, a region comprising
semi-arid landscapes and hardy vegetation that takes all the moisture it needs from sea mists.
The little mining city of **Copiapó** serves as a springboard for excursions to the white sands
and alluring waters of **Bahía Inglesa**, one of the country's most attractive seaside resorts, and
east into the barely trodden cordillera, where you'll find the mineral-streaked volcanoes of
Parque Nacional Nevado de Tres Cruces and the almost impossibly turquoise **Laguna Verde**.

FACT FILE

• Though Chile lives and breathes **football**, the national team has not had much luck against its mightier neighbour, Argentina. The first ever win over its rivals in 2008 was a cause for national jubilation.

• **17.2 million people** live in Chile, consisting of a fairly homogenous mestizo population with a few indigenous groups: Mapuche in the Lake District (around 650,000), Aymara in the far north (around 54,000), Easter Island's Rapa Nui (around 4300), Yámana (around 1800) and Kawéskar (around 2800) in Patagonia and Tierra del Fuego.

• Chile's **motto** is *Por la razón o la fuerza*' meaning 'By right or by might'.

• One of the most **developed** countries in Latin America, Chile has the steadiest growth in the region and the lowest level of corruption in Latin America.

• In the longest recorded dry spell in Chile's **Atacama Desert**, it didn't rain for over 40 years.

• Chile only legalized **divorce** in 2004.

• Although notorious for **Pinochet's** infamous **military dictatorship** during the 1970s and 1980s, Chile otherwise has a long history of parliamentary democracy.

Further north, the harshly beautiful **Atacama Desert**, stretching over 1000km into southern Peru, presents an unforgettable, moonlike landscape, whose sights number ancient petroglyphs (indigenous rock art), abandoned nitrate ghost towns, a scattering of fertile, fruit-filled oases and a clutch of the world's most powerful telescopes that take advantage of the clear night skies. Tiny **San Pedro de Atacama** makes an ideal base for exploring the arid landscape, sandboarding in Valle de la Luna, visiting high-altitude hot springs and stargazing. Up in the Andes, the vast plateau known as the **altiplano** encompasses snowcapped volcanoes, bleached-white salt flats, lakes speckled pink with flamingos, grazing llamas, alpacas and vicuñas, tiny whitewashed churches and indigenous Aymara communities. The best points to head for up here are **Parque Nacional Lauca** – the highest of Chile's many national parks, and accessible from the city of Arica (home to a superb museum featuring Chinchorro mummies) – and **Parque Nacional Volcán Isluga**, near the busy seafront city of Iquique, popular with surfers and paragliders.

South of Santiago, the lush **Central Valley**, with its swathes of orchards and vineyards, dotted with stately haciendas, invites you to find Chile's best vintage by sampling the offerings of the various vineyards, including Carmenère, the country's signature grape. Further south, the famous, much-visited **Lake District** presents a postcard-perfect landscape of conical volcanoes (including the temperamental **Volcán Villarrica** and the exquisite **Volcán Osorno**), iris-blue lakes, rolling pastureland and dense araucaria forests; the adventure sport capitals of **Pucón** and **Puerto Varas** both offer a welcome injection of adrenaline, with trekking, volcano climbing, mountain biking, whitewater rafting and horseriding to tempt active travellers. A short ferry ride from Puerto Montt, at the southern edge of the Lake District, the **Chiloé** archipelago is a quiet, rural backwater, famous for its rickety houses on stilts, unique wooden churches, rich local mythology and a Polynesian-style regional dish.

Back on the mainland south of Puerto Montt, the **Carretera Austral** – a 1000km-long, partially paved "highway" – carves its way through virgin temperate rainforest and past dramatic fjords, two of which are the embarkation points for boat trips out to the sensational **Laguna San Rafael glacier** – a fast-disappearing landmark. Tiny **Futaleufú** is one of the world's top spots for whitewater-rafting, the region's pristine rivers are also a favourite with fly-fishermen, and the new **Parque Patagonia** gives you the opportunity to hike through gorgeous landscapes for days.

Beyond the Carretera Austral, cut off by the **Campo de Hielo Sur** (Southern Ice-Field), lies **Patagonia**, a country of bleak windswept plains bordered by the magnificent granite spires of the **Torres del Paine** massif, Chile's single most famous sight, its namesake park a magnet for hikers and climbers. Just over the easily crossed border in Argentina are two of the region's star attractions: the **Fitz Roy Sector** in the north of the **Parque Nacional Los Glaciares**, a favourite for trekkers, and, to the south, the awe-inspiring **Glaciar Perito Moreno** – South America's most accessible glacier. Across the Magellan Strait, **Tierra del Fuego**, shared with Argentina, sits shivering at the bottom of the world, a remote land of harsh, desolate beauty, steeped in dreams of a gold rush past, the lively city of **Ushuaia** on the Argentinian side giving easy access to the Beagle Strait, teeming with wildlife, while

CHILE'S WILDLIFE

Chile's diverse **animal kingdom** inhabits a landscape of extremes. The country's formidable natural barriers – the immense Pacific, lofty Andes and desolate Atacama – have resulted in an exceptional degree of **endemism**, with a third of the mammals that live here, such as the shy pudú (pygmy deer), not found anywhere else in the world.

Four species of **camelid** alone are found in the barren altiplano, namely the shaggy, domesticated **llama** and **alpaca** in the north, and their wild cousins – the Patagonia-dwelling **guanaco** and the delicate **vicuña** with its highly prized fur, restricted to the high altitudes. Chile's biggest cat is the elusive **puma**, another Patagonia resident, while smaller wildcats, from the **colo-colo** to the **guiña**, also stalk these grasslands. Endemic rodents, such as the mountain **vizcacha**, are found in the northern highlands, while several species of **fox** can be spotted in the desert, altiplano and coastal forest.

A country seemingly made for birdwatchers, Chile is home to a curious mix of the small and beautiful, such as **hummingbirds** (including the firecrown, endemic to the Juan Fernández islands), while at the other end of the scale is the mighty Andean **condor**, soaring over the mountains. High in the Andes near the Bolivian border, the **Chilean and James's flamingo** gather at remote saltwater lakes, while the long-legged **ñandú** propels itself over the Patagonian steppe. Equally impressive seabirds include the **Humboldt**, **Magellanic** and **king penguins**, while Chile's coastal waters host some spectacular mammals, such as the **blue whale** and several species of **dolphins**.

Chile's southernmost town, **Puerto Williams,** is the gateway to one of South America's toughest treks, the **Dientes de Navarino.**

Finally, there are the country's two Pacific possessions: **Easter Island** – one of the most remote places on earth, famed for its mysterious statues and fascinating Polynesian culture – and the little-visited **Isla Robinson Crusoe**, part of the Juan Fernández Archipelago, the largest marine reserve in Chile, sporting dramatic volcanic peaks covered with dense vegetation and a wealth of endemic wildlife.

ABOVE LLAMA, ALTIPLANO

ADVENTURE SPORTS

If you're looking to experience an adrenaline rush in the great outdoors, you've come to the right place. Chile features some of the best **skiing** in the southern hemisphere and the finest resorts lie just 40km from Santiago, in Valle Nevado and Portillo, while the Termas de Chillán ski centre in the middle of the country allows you to combine the longest run in South America with steaming thermal pools for après-ski relaxation.

Spanning the 4320km length of the country, the hugely ambitious **Sendero de Chile** (Chile Trail; ⓦsenderodechile.cl) currently consists of numerous sections running through

spectacularly varied scenery and skirting some splendid volcanoes. **Volcanoes** are in fact a defining feature of Chile's geography. In the Far North, experienced trekkers can tackle behemoths such as Volcán Parinacota and Volcán Ojos del Salado – the tallest active volcano in the world – while the Lake District's Volcán Villarrica and Volcán Osorno make spectacular day climbs for novices. The most challenging vertical ascents are the giant granite towers at the heart of Torres del Paine National Park. If the mountains aren't high enough, climb aboard a hot-air balloon or **paraglide** above Iquique's giant sand dune – a favourite with sandboarders.

Water junkies will undoubtedly be tempted by Chile's veritable playground of rivers and seas. While Río Trancura and Río Petrohue cater to beginners, Río Futaleufú remains Chile's most challenging river for **whitewater rafting** and **kayaking**, while the northern sector of Parque Pumalín, the Gulf of Ancud, the southern fjords and the turbulent Magellan Strait are all prime **sea-kayaking** territory.

When to go

Given the dramatic variety of Chile's climate (see p.46) and geography, the country can be visited at any time of year, but there is, of course, an **ideal time to visit each region**. Santiago and the surrounding area, northern Chile and the Atacama Desert are year-round destinations, though temperatures tend to be hottest between January and March. Easter Island's climate is mild and warm all year, but February is the time to go to if you want to catch the **island's biggest festival**. If you have your heart set on **skiing** around Santiago or further south, the best time is from July through to September (also the perfect time to go husky sledding in the Lake District), when snow conditions are ideal. The **season for adventure sports** in the Lake District and northern Patagonia tends to be November through to March, when the weather is warmest, though kayaking can be done year-round. Patagonia and Tierra del Fuego are best visited in the warmer months of November to March; from June to September many places are closed and the area is difficult to navigate due to the snow, though it can also be a beautiful time to visit the southern national parks, which you'll have pretty much to yourself.

ABOVE WHITEWATER RAFTING ON THE RÍO TRANCURA

Author picks

Scaling the breathless heights of its lofty national parks, driving some of Chile's most challenging and isolated roads, and enduring the heat of the desert, Rough Guides authors have covered every nook and cranny of this impossibly-shaped country – from the wilds of southern Isla Navarino to the Atacama Desert in the north. Here are their personal favourites:

Best sunrise Chile has numerous contenders for this title, but the mesmerizing sight of the sun rising up behind the fifteen colossal *moai* of Ahu Tongariki (p.453) on Easter Island is hard to beat.

Dawn by canoe Paddle your canoe through Chepu Valley's sunken forest (p.325) at dawn – the best time to see the varied birdlife.

Ghost towns Explore the haunting nitrate towns of Humberstone and Santa Laura (p.193) – once thriving centres of industry, but long-since abandoned to the desert.

Drive that sled Step into the snow-shoes of a musher and bond with your own husky team during a multi-day expedition in the Andes (p.272).

Put your trip in context Santiago's thought-provoking Museo de la Memoria y los Derechos Humanos (Museum of Memory and Human Rights) is dedicated to the many victims of the Pinochet dictatorship (p.70).

Stargazing Make the most of clear night skies and see the universe like you've never seen it before with potent telescopes and engaging astronomers at the mountaintop Del Pangue observatory (p.146).

Hit the road For the ultimate driving challenge, take on Chile's Carretera Austral (p.352) through the land of cowboys and pioneers, admiring the waterfalls plunging down from the mountains around you.

Pristine trekking possibilities Explore the mountains and the valleys of the new Parque Patagonia (see p.375) where you walk alongside almost-tame guanacos.

> Our author recommendations don't end here. We've flagged up our favourite places – a perfectly sited hotel, an atmospheric café, a special restaurant – throughout the guide, highlighted with the ★ symbol.

FROM TOP HUSKY SLEDDING, THE ANDES; *MOAI* STATUES AT SUNRISE

24

things not to miss

It's not possible to see everything Chile has to offer in one trip – and we don't suggest you try. What follows is a selective taste of the country's highlights: outstanding scenery, picturesque villages and dramatic wildlife. All highlights have a page reference to take you into the guide, where you can find out more. Coloured numbers refer to chapters in the Guide section.

1 SOUTHERN PATAGONIA
Page 382
Explore the tip of the Americas, where the country splinters into granite towers, glaciers and fjords.

2 WINE TASTING, COLCHAGUA VALLEY
Page 229
Sample some of the best red wines in the world as you taste your way along the "Ruta del Vino".

3 LAGUNA VERDE
Page 159
Massive active volcanoes surround these richly hued waters, making for an almost surreal landscape that's the perfect spot to enjoy the bubbling lakeside hot springs.

4 PARQUE NACIONAL LAUCA

Page 211

Behold Chile's highest national park, with altitudes between 4000m and 6000m, herds of llamas, remote geysers and altiplano lakes.

5 RODEOS AND HUASOS

Page 221

Witness expert horsemanship and a slice of national culture at the rodeos in the Central Valley.

6 PARAGLIDING IN IQUIQUE

Page 189

Soar over Iquique, one of South America's top paragliding destinations, and enjoy incredible views of the giant sand dune of Cerro Dragón far below.

7 PENGUINS

Page 396

Head to the thriving sanctuaries at Isla Magdalena and Seno Otway for an up-close look at penguins.

8 VALPARAÍSO

Page 96

This remarkable city sits perched by the sea, draped over a jumble of steep hills around a wide bay.

12

9 CURANTO
Page 322

In Chiloé, tuck into this delicious concoction of shellfish, smoked meat and potato dumplings, traditionally cooked in a pit in the ground.

10 CHINCHORRO MUMMIES
Page 209

Gape at these prehistoric, remarkably intact mummies, pulled from a seven-thousand-year-old burial site near Arica.

11 HIKING VOLCÁN VILLARRICA
Page 282

Take a guided hike up this active volcano, the focal point of a park with excellent opportunities for trekking and camping.

12 TRACKING PABLO NERUDA
Pages 71, 104 & 111

The Nobel Prize-winning poet is one of Chile's best-known literary exports. Visit any of the three houses he lived in: La Chascona in Santiago, La Sebastiana in Valparaíso, or the museum in Isla Negra.

13 SURFING IN PICHILEMU
Page 230

Tackle the challenging Punta de Lobos break at Chile's best surfing spot, or learn to surf on beginner-friendly waves in Pichilemu.

14 BAHÍA INGLESA
Page 162

Dip into turquoise waters and soak up rays on the sands of this relatively unspoilt beach.

15 TERMAS DE PUYUHUAPI
Page 363

Isolated and largely inaccessible, the resort here is home to steaming hot springs, and is one of the great getaways along the Carretera Austral.

16 TAPATI, EASTER ISLAND
Page 452

Partake in the remote island's liveliest festival, complete with traditional dancing, woodcarving and surfing competitions, all amid the mysterious *moai* stone statues.

17 PARQUE NACIONAL TORRES DEL PAINE
Page 402

Without a doubt, this spectacular park is what draws most visitors to southern Chile, and it does not disappoint even after all the photos and build-up.

18 SEA LIONS IN THE BEAGLE CHANNEL
Page 438

If you make it all the way down to Tierra del Fuego, a trip through the Channel to see these delightful creatures is a near requisite.

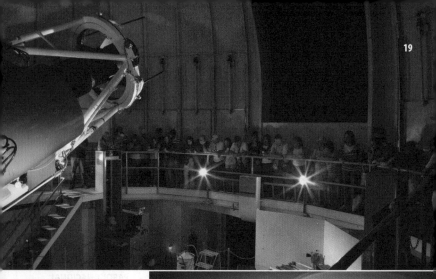

19 THE NIGHT SKY
Page 146

Chile's northern skies are the most transparent in the southern hemisphere, as testified by the many international observatories stationed here. Head to the Elqui Valley's Cerro Mamalluca observatory to play astronomer and gaze up at the stars.

20 PISCO ELQUI
Page 147

Take a tour of a distillery, followed by a taste of a pisco sour, Chile's national cocktail.

21 LAPIS LAZULI
Page 50

For a lovely Chilean souvenir, pick up jewellery made from lapis, the cool blue stone mined throughout the country and sold in local crafts markets.

22 CHURCHES OF CHILOÉ
Pages 320 & 329

The archipelago's beautiful wooden churches rise over the heart of almost every small village.

23 VALLE DE LA LUNA
Page 185

Trek across this aptly named moonscape, just south of San Pedro de Atacama.

24 SAN RAFAEL GLACIER
Page 369

Embark on an exhilarating boat ride alongside this stunning ice formation.

20

21

Itineraries

The following itineraries span the entire length of this incredibly varied country, taking you from the icy fjords and snow-tipped mountains of the south to the fertile wine-growing valleys in the centre and parched desert and highland lagoons of the north. Given the vast distances involved, you may not be able to cover every highlight, but even picking a few from the itineraries below will give you a thrilling window onto Chile's geographical and cultural wonders.

THE GRAND TOUR

Allow at least three weeks if you wish to cover Chile from top to bottom; flying between some of the destinations will allow you to cover vast distances quickly.

❶ **Atacama desert** Visit erupting geysers, crinkly salt plains and emerald lakes in the morning, and deep, mystical valleys by sunset in the driest desert on earth. **See p.168**

❷ **Elqui Valley/stargazing near Vicuna** Take advantage of some of the clearest skies in Chile and look at the universe through some of the world's most powerful telescopes. **See p.143**

❸ **Santiago** Chile's rapidly evolving capital city boasts a vibrant eating out and nightlife scene, several fascinating museums, numerous cultural pursuits and excellent ski resorts. **See p.56**

❹ **Easter Island** Gazing down into the giant crater of the extinct Rano Kau volcano and visiting the magical *moai* at Ahu Tongariki and Rano Raraku truly are once-in-a-lifetime experiences. **See p.444**

❺ **Valparaíso** Valparaíso is a tangle of colourful houses, cobbled streets and bohemian hang-outs spread across a series of undulating hills overlooking the Pacific, with Pablo Neruda's house nearby. **See p.96 & p.104**

❻ **Central Valley wineries** Visit the numerous traditional bodegas around Curicó and Santa Cruz, and try some of Chile's finest vintages. **See p.229 & p.232**

❼ **Chiloé** Sample one of the country's most memorable dishes, admire the *palafitos* (traditional houses on stilts) or hike through temperate rainforest on Chile's mist and legend shrouded island. **See p.314**

❽ **Parque Nacional Torres del Paine** Hike the trails of Chile's most popular – and most spectacular – national park or climb the granite towers that give the park its name. **See p.402**

NATURAL CHILE

Since Chile's varied landscapes span the entire country, allow at least three weeks for this trip.

❶ **Parque Nacional Lauca** Admire the volcanoes, high-altitude lagoons dotted with flamingos and grazing llamas and vicuñas in Chile's highest national park. **See p.211**

❷ **Isla Robinson Crusoe** With its endemic flora and fauna, extensive underwater attractions and demonic peaks, Isla Robinson Crusoe still has the end-of-the-world castaway feel that inspired Daniel Defoe's famous book. **See p.460**

ABOVE CUERNOS DEL PAINE, PARQUE NACIONAL TORRES DEL PAINE

❸ **Lake District hot springs** Relax in the many thermal springs that dot the region and range from rustic soaking pools to resort-style complexes with hotels and excellent restaurants. **See p.277**

❹ **A boat trip around the San Rafael glacier** Head out to the ice-filled lagoon that is Chile's fastest shrinking glacier and get close to the ice in a speedboat. **See p.369**

❺ **Tierra del Fuego** Explore the deserted roads running through steppe and dotted with guanacos and rheas, or fish in the pristine lakes and rivers of the most remote region in Chile. **See p.418**

❻ **Beagle Channel** Take a boat trip in the country's southernmost reaches, in search of penguins, sea lions and the occasional pod of Commerson's dolphins. **See p.438**

❼ **Cape Horn** Fly over some of the world's most treacherous waters or brave a sailing trip to Chile's southernmost group of weather-beaten islands. **See p.430**

ADVENTURE CHILE

With the exception of the treks, all items on this itinerary are doable as day excursions, so a couple of weeks should be sufficient.

❶ **Paragliding/surfing in Iquique** Ilquique's perfect climate makes it one of the best places in the world to soar the skies or dance through waves. **See p.189**

❷ **Adrenaline sports in Pucón** In the Lake District's adventure capital you can skydive, mountain bike or snowboard down the slopes of Volcán Villarrica, or go husky sledding in Parque Nacional Villarrica. **See p.274**

❸ **Climbing Volcán Osorno** Tackle the Lake District's most perfect conical peak in a full-day ascent from Lago Llanquihue, and be rewarded by all-encompassing views of the area. **See p.304**

❹ **Kayaking in Parque Pumalín** Explore the maze of tiny islands in the isolated fjords of Chile's largest private nature reserve as part of a multi-day expedition. **See p.354**

❺ **Whitewater rafting on Río Futaleufú** Ride the waves of the most challenging river in Chile, navigating such rapids as the "Throne Room" and "Inferno". **See p.359**

❻ **Trekking the Dientes de Navarino** Hike one of South America's toughest treks at the very end of the world. **See p.428**

ROAD IN THE ALTIPLANO

Basics

25 Getting there

26 Getting around

30 Accommodation

32 Food and drink

35 The media

35 Festivals

37 Spectator sports

38 Outdoor activities

42 National parks and reserves

43 Health

44 Culture and etiquette

45 Travel essentials

Getting there

Most people fly into Chile, arriving at Santiago's modern international airport, though some travel by land from neighbouring countries, and a handful arrive by sea.

Airfares depend on the **season**. You'll pay the highest fares in the December to February and June to August periods, the southern and northern hemisphere's summer holiday months, respectively. Fares drop slightly during the "shoulder" months – March and November – and you'll generally get the best prices during the low seasons: April, May, September and October.

Flights from the US and Canada

US travellers shouldn't find it too hard to get a fairly convenient flight to Santiago. American Airlines (Ⓦaa.com), Delta (Ⓦdelta.com) and LAN (Ⓦlan .com) offer **non-stop flights** from airports such as **Miami**, **Dallas-Fort Worth** and **Atlanta**. It is also possible to travel via other Latin American countries such as Peru and Brazil. **Typical fares are around** US$1000–1500 in the high season.

Air Canada (Ⓦaircanada.com) – and sometimes LAN – has flights from Toronto to Santiago; typical high season fares are around C$1450–1900. It is often cheaper to fly via the US.

Flights from the UK and Ireland

There are currently no direct flights from either London or Dublin to Chile, so you'll have to travel via **a European, Latin American or US city**; LAN (Ⓦlan.com), Iberia (Ⓦiberia.com), Air France (Ⓦairfrance.com) and TAM (Ⓦtam.com.br) are among the options. In general, high-season fares cost around £900–1100. In addition to price, it's also worth paying attention to the routes used by the different airlines; even the shortest and most convenient ones via Madrid or Buenos Aires entail a total travelling time of over sixteen hours. Flying via the US is longer still (though sometimes cheaper).

Flights from Australia, New Zealand and South Africa

Qantas (Ⓦqantas.com) and LAN (Ⓦlan.com) offer flights from Sydney and Auckland to Santiago. In the high season, expect to pay from around Aus$2600/NZ$3400.

South African Airways (Ⓦflysaa.com) has flights from Johannesburg to Sao Paulo, Brazil, from where there are regular connections to Santiago. It is often cheaper to buy the main flight separately and then book your flight on to Chile. Expect to pay from R15,000 in total.

Round-the-world flights

If Chile is only one stop on a longer journey, consider buying a round-the-world (RTW) ticket. An "off-the-shelf" ticket will have you touching down in about half a dozen cities. An itinerary including Santiago costs from around £1300. Alternatively, you can have a travel agent custom-make a RTW ticket for you, though this is more expensive. Trailfinders (Ⓦtrailfinders.com) and STA Travel (Ⓦstatravel.com) both sell RTW tickets.

Air passes

Air passes are another alternative if you plan to visit several destinations in South America. The **Visit South America** pass (Ⓦoneworld.com) is operated by the Oneworld alliance (which includes LAN, British Airways, Iberia, Qantas and American Airlines). It allows you to plan your own itinerary, with set flight prices depending on the distance travelled between (or within) countries; note that you must use a minimum of three flights. LAN's **South America Airpass** is similar, though generally a little cheaper. However, you may find that promotional fares within Chile are a better option than either of the passes.

If you plan to visit Easter Island, your flight there from Santiago will be far cheaper if it is bought in conjunction with a LAN international flight.

Buses and tours

Several roads **connect Chile with Argentina** – from Santiago or Valparaíso to Mendoza via Los

---

ARRIVAL TAX

Chile levies an **arrival tax** for **Canadian, Australian, Mexican and Albanian** citizens in reciprocation for similar taxes levied on Chilean citizens arriving in these countries. This means you must pay **US$132, US$61, US$23 or US$30 respectively;** at the time of writing there was nevertheless talk of abolishing these fees – check with your Chilean consulate for the latest. The payment is valid for the lifetime of the passport and is not levied when crossing land borders.

A BETTER KIND OF TRAVEL

At Rough Guides we are passionately committed to travel. We believe it helps us understand the world we live in and the people we share it with – and of course tourism is vital to many developing economies. But the scale of modern tourism has also damaged some places irreparably, and climate change is accelerated by most forms of transport, especially flying. All Rough Guides' flights are carbon-offset, and every year we donate money to a variety of environmental charities.

Andes; from Osorno and Puerto Montt to Bariloche and from Puntas Arenas to Río Gallegos – all of which are served by buses. There are other routes, including the Ruta 41 from La Serena, one of the most dramatic, which leads over the mountains from the Elqui Valley before joining other roads to San Juan. The route only opens in the warmer months between October/November and April. All Andean routes, even the road to Mendoza, can be blocked by snow from April onwards. A decent road and regular buses link Chile to Peru from Arica through to Tacna. You can also catch buses from Arica to La Paz in Bolivia; this takes you through the stunning scenery of the Lauca National Park (see p.211), but it does mean travelling from sea level up to 4500m in just a few hours so take plenty of water and expect to feel pretty uncomfortable. Many travellers cross from Uyuni in Bolivia to San Pedro de Atacama via a salt flats tour.

Trains

Chile has **international rail links** between Arica and Tacna in Peru (suspended at the time of writing, though there are plans to reopen it) and between Uyuni in Bolivia and Calama. Plans to construct a railway line between Arica and La Paz in Bolivia have been mooted in the past.

AGENTS AND OPERATORS

Adventure Associates Australia ☎ 02 8916 3000, ⓦ adventureassociates.com.au. Established operator with tours and cruises to Antarctica, Chile and South America as a whole.

Adventures Abroad ☎ 1-800 665 3998, ⓦ adventures-abroad .com. Adventure specialists offering two-week tours to Patagonia, and extended trips throughout Chile and Argentina.

Anglatin Ltd ☎ 1-800 918 8580, ⓦ anglatin.com. A range of tours focusing on topics such as rural life, birdwatching, ancient cultures and even llamas.

Dragoman UK ☎ 01728 861 133, ⓦ dragoman.com. Overland journeys in purpose-built vehicles; shorter camping and hotel-based safaris, too.

Exodus UK ☎ 0845 240 5550, ⓦ exodus.co.uk. Adventure tour operator taking small groups for specialist programmes including hiking, biking, overland and cultural trips.

Explore Worldwide UK ☎ 0870 333 4001, ⓦ explore.co.uk. Small-group tours, treks, expeditions and safaris throughout Chile.

Intrepid Travel UK ☎ 0800 781 1660, ⓦ intrepidtravel.com. Small-group tours with the emphasis on cross-cultural contact and low-impact tourism.

Journey Latin America UK ☎ 020 3603 8965, ⓦ journeylatinamerica.co.uk. Long-established Latin America specialists, with a huge choice of trips (both package and tailor-made) across Chile, including many multi-country tours.

Mountain Travel Sobek ☎ 1-888 831 7526, ⓦ mtsobek.com. Trips include a "Patagonia Explorer" package, featuring hiking and sailing.

Nature Expeditions International ☎ 1-800 869 0639, ⓦ naturexp.com. The 15-day Chile tour takes in Torres del Paine and the Atacama desert.

REI Adventures ☎ 1-800 622 2236, ⓦ rei.com/adventures. Climbing, cycling, hiking, cruising, paddling and multi-sport tours.

Ski.com ☎ 1-800 908 5000, ⓦ ski.com. Package skiing trips to Portillo and Valle Nevado.

South America Travel Centre Australia ☎ 03 9642 5353, ⓦ satc.com.au. Large selection of tours and accommodation packages throughout the region.

Tucan Travel UK ☎ 020 8896 1600, ⓦ tucantravel.com. Backpacker group trips in Chile and neighbouring countries.

Wilderness Travel ☎ 1-800 368 2794, ⓦ wildernesstravel.com. Specialists in hiking, cultural and wildlife adventures.

Wildlife Worldwide UK ☎ 020 8667 9158, ⓦ wildlifeworldwide .com. Customised trips for wildlife and wilderness enthusiasts.

World Expeditions Australia ☎ 02 8270 8400, ⓦ worldexpeditions.com.au, New Zealand ☎ 09 368 4161, ⓦ worldexpeditions.co.nz. Offers a range of adventure holidays.

Getting around

Travelling in Chile is easy, comfortable and, compared with Europe or North America, inexpensive. Most Chileans travel by bus, and it's such a reliable, affordable option that you'll probably do likewise. However, internal flights are handy for covering long distances in a hurry. The country has a good road network, and driving is a quick, relatively stress-free way of getting around. Chile's rail network has fallen into decline and

only limited services are available. South of Puerto Montt, ferry services provide a slow but scenic way of travelling as far as Puerto Natales.

By air

Chile is a country of almost unimaginable distances (it's more than 5000km by road from Arica to Punta Arenas), which makes **flying** by far the quickest and most convenient way of taking in both its northern and southern regions in a single trip. Fares are quite high, though you can find good promotions from time to time.

The leading airline is **LAN** (Ⓦ LAN.com), which besides offering the widest choice of domestic flights, is Chile's principal long-haul carrier and the only one with flights to Easter Island. **Sky Airline** (Ⓦ skyairline.cl) has more limited routings but usually lower prices.

Air taxis and regional airlines operate regular services to smaller destinations between Puerto Montt and Puerto Williams, but they are susceptible to weather delays and won't fly without a minimum number of passengers (usually six). There are also flights from Santiago to Isla Robinson Crusoe (see p.464).

By bus

Chile's **long-distance buses** offer an excellent service, far better than their European or North American counterparts – thanks mainly to the enormous amount of legroom, frequent departures and flexible itineraries. Facilities depend less on individual companies than on the class of bus you travel on, with prices rising according to comfort level. A **pullman** (not to be confused with the large company of the same name) or **clásico** contains standard semi-reclining seats; a **semicama** has seats with twice the amount of legroom that recline a good deal more; and a **salon cama**, at the top of the luxury range, has wide seats (just three to a row) that recline to an almost horizontal position à la first class on a plane. All buses have toilets. Many include meals or snacks, while others stop at restaurants where set meals might be included in the ticket price. DVDs, piped music and bingo games are also common attractions (or irritations). Check out the locations of the screens first and seat yourself appropriately.

Thanks to the intense competition and price wars waged between the multitude of bus companies, **fares** are low. As a rule of thumb, reckon on around

CH$1000–1500 per hour travelled on standard inter-city buses; the most luxurious services are at least four times that. It always pays to compare fares offered by the different companies serving your destination, as you'll almost certainly find one offering a special deal. This price-comparing is easily done at the central terminal used by long-distance buses in most cities, where you'll find separate booking offices for each company (though Tur Bus and Pullman Bus, the two largest companies, often have their own separate terminals). Some towns, however, don't have a **central terminal**, in which case buses leave from their company offices.

Buy your ticket at least a few hours in advance, preferably the day before travelling, especially if you plan to travel on a Friday; book further in advance if you plan to travel over public holidays. An added advantage of buying ahead is that you'll be able to choose a seat away from the toilets, either by the aisle or window and, more importantly, the side of the bus you sit on. Even with a/c, seats on the sunny side can get extremely hot. There is little reason to buy a round-trip ticket unless you are travelling at peak season.

When it comes to **boarding**, make sure that the departure time on your ticket corresponds exactly to the time indicated on the little clock on the bus's front window, as your ticket is valid only on the bus it was booked for. Your luggage will be safely stored in lockers under the bus and the conductor will issue you a numbered stub for each article.

If you're travelling north of Santiago on a long-distance route, or crossing an international border, the bus and all luggage may be searched by Ministry of Agriculture officials at checkpoints, and all sandwiches, fresh fruit and vegetables will be destroyed.

By local bus, colectivo and taxi

Local buses, often called micros, connect city centres with suburbs and nearby villages. These buses are often packed, and travelling with a large rucksack can be difficult. The main points of the route and final destination are displayed on the inside of the front window, but it always helps to carry a street map and be able to point to your intended destination. Buses that leave the city for the countryside normally depart from their own *terminal rural*, usually close to the Mercado Municipal (market building).

Colectivos, which are shared taxis operating along a set route with fixed fares, are normally only slightly more expensive than local buses. Most colectivos look exactly like regular taxis (apart from being all black, not black and yellow) and have their route or final destination marked on a board on the roof, but in some cities colectivos are bright yellow cars, often without a roof-board.

Taxis are normally black with a yellow roof. Foreigners are often overcharged, so check that the meter has been turned on before you start a journey and get an estimate for the fare, if possible in Spanish. Fares should be shown in the windscreen.

By car

While Chile's towns and cities are linked by plenty of buses, most visitors are here for the country's wilderness areas, which are often difficult, and sometimes impossible, to reach on public transport. Many remote attractions are visited by tour companies, but for more independence, your best bet is to **rent a car**. To do this, you need to be at least 21 years old and have a major credit card so you can leave a blank voucher as a guarantee. You're allowed to use your national driver's licence, but you're strongly advised to bring, in addition, an **international licence**. Chile's carabineros (police officers), who frequently stop drivers to check their documents, are often suspicious of unfamiliar foreign licences and are always happier when dealing with international ones. Traffic regulations are rarely enforced, except for speeding on the highways. The **speed limit** is 50km per hour or less in urban areas and 100km per hour on highways; radar speed traps are commonplace. If an oncoming vehicle flashes its headlights, you're being warned of carabineros lurking ahead. If you do get pulled over, exercise the utmost courtesy and patience, and under no circumstances do or say anything that could possibly be interpreted as bribery.

Rental outlets and costs

Several international car-rental companies have offices throughout Chile. In addition to these, you'll find an abundance of local outlets which are often, but by no means always, less expensive than the international firms. Rates can vary quite a lot from one company to another, and it's always worth checking as many as possible online to compare prices. **Basic saloon cars** go from around US$50 per day. Make sure the quoted price includes IVA (the nineteen percent Chilean value added tax), insurance and unlimited mileage. Your rental contract will almost certainly be in (legal and convoluted) Spanish – get the company to take you

through it. In most cases your liability, in the event of an accident, is around the US$500 mark; costs over this amount will be covered in total by the company. Petrol, at the time of writing, costs around US$7 1.15 per litre.

CAR RENTAL AGENCIES

Avis Ⓦ www.avis.cl.
Budget Ⓦ budget.com.
Dollar Ⓦ dollar.com.
Hertz Ⓦ hertz.cl.
Thrifty Ⓦ thrifty.com.

Driving in towns

Most Chilean towns are laid out on a grid plan, which makes navigating pretty easy. However, the country is obsessed with **one-way traffic** systems, and many streets, even in the smallest towns, are one-way only, the direction of traffic alternating with each successive street. The direction is usually indicated by a white arrow above the street name on each corner; if in doubt, look at the direction of the parked cars. **Parking** is normally allowed on most downtown streets (but on one side only), and around the central square. You'll invariably be guided into a space by a wildly gesticulating cuidador de autos – a boy or young man who will offer to look after your car in return for a tip. In larger towns there's a small half-hourly charge for parking on the street, administered by eagle-eyed traffic wardens who slip tickets under your wipers every thirty minutes then pounce on you to collect your money before you leave (a small tip is expected, too). If you can't find a space, keep a look-out for large "estacionamiento" signs, which indicate private car parks.

Driving on highways

The **Panamerican** highway, which runs through Chile from the Peruvian border to the southern tip of Chiloé, is known alternately as Ruta 5, la Panamericana, or el longitudinal, with sur (south) or norte (north) often added on to indicate which side of Santiago it's on. Thanks to a multi-billion dollar modernization project, it is quickly becoming a divided highway, with two lanes in each direction and a toll booth every 30km. This is undoubtedly a major improvement over most single-lane highways in Chile, which are prone to head-on collisions involving buses and trucks.

Backcountry and altiplano driving

You'll probably find that many places you want to get to are reached by dirt road, for which it's essential to rent a suitable vehicle, namely a **Jeep** or **pick-up truck**. On regular dirt roads you rarely need a 4WD vehicle. For **altiplano driving**, however, you should pay extra to have 4WD (with the sturdiest tyres and highest clearance), as you can come across some dreadful roads, hundreds of kilometres from the nearest town. Make sure, too, that you take two spare tyres, not one, and that you always carry a funnel or tube for siphoning, and more than enough petrol. Also pick up several five-litre water jugs – it may be necessary for either the passengers or the engine at some point. It can be difficult to navigate in the *altiplano*, with so much open space and so few landmarks – if you don't have a GPS-enabled device, make a careful note of your kilometre reading as you go along, so you can chart your progress over long roads with few markers. A compass is also helpful. Despite this tone of caution, it should be emphasized that *altiplano* driving is among the most rewarding adventures that Chile offers.

Finally, a general point on **tyre punctures**. This is such a common occurrence in Chile that even the smallest towns have special workshops (bearing signs with a tyre painted white) where they are quickly and cheaply repaired.

Hitching

While we don't recommend hitching as a safe way of getting about, there's no denying that it's widely practised by Chileans themselves. In the summer it seems as though all the students in Chile are sitting beside the road with their thumb out, and in rural areas it's not uncommon for entire families to hitch a lift whenever they need to get into town.

By ferry

South of Puerto Montt, where the mainland breaks up into an archipelago, a network of ferries operates through the fjords, inlets and channels of Chile's far south, providing a more scenic and romantic alternative to flights and long-distance buses. Two ferries in particular are very popular with tourists: one from Puerto Montt to Chacabuco and the San Rafael glacier, the other between Puerto Montt and Puerto Natales. In addition, there are ferry links with Quellón on Chiloé, and with Chaitén, on the Carretera Austral, as well as a number of shorter routes forming a bridge along various points of the Carretera Austral (see p.348). There's also a ferry trip across Lago Todos Los Santos, in the Lake District, connecting Petrohué with Peulla, near the Argentine border (see p.299).

MAIN FERRY ROUTES

Petrohué–Peulla, across Lago Todos Los Santos Five hours; daily crossings (year-round) with Andina del Sud (Ⓦ andinadelsud .com). See p.299.

Puerto Montt–Chacabuco 24 hours; one sailing per week with Navimag (year-round; Ⓦ navimag.com) and TransMarChilay (year-round; Ⓦ transmarchilay.cl). See p.312 & p.368.

Puerto Montt–Chacabuco–Laguna San Rafael Five days, four nights (returning to Puerto Montt); one sailing per week with Navimag (year-round) and two, three or four with TransMarChilay (year-round). See p.312 & p.368.

Puerto Montt–Chaitén Ten hours; one sailing per week with Navimag (Jan & Feb); three or four per week with TransMarChilay (year-round). See p.312 & p.357.

Puerto Montt–Puerto Natales Four days, three nights; one sailing per week with Navimag (year-round). See p.312 & p.398.

Quellón–Chaitén Five hours; three sailings per week with Navimag (Jan & Feb). See p.316 & p.340.

By bike

With the right amount of time and energy, travelling by bike can be incredibly rewarding. Your time is your own and you won't find yourself stuck to rigid timetables or restricted to visiting destinations only served by public buses.

Supplies in Chile can be unreliable so it's best to bring as much as you can from home. A good, sturdy mountain bike is a must, along with the usual locks and chains, strong racks, repair kit, lights, waterproof panniers, jackets and over-trousers. All equipment and clothes should be packed in plastic to protect from dust and moisture. Your major problem will be getting hold of **spares** when you need them – bike shops tend to be found only in Santiago and a few major cities. When on the road, bear in mind that long stretches are bereft of accommodation options and even the most basic services, so you must be completely self-sufficient and prepared for a long wait if you require

ADDRESSES

These are nearly always written with just the street name (and often just the surname, if the street is named after a person) followed by the number; for example, Prat 135. In the case of avenues, however, the address usually starts with the word *avenida*, eg Avenida 21 de Mayo 553. Buildings without a street number are suffixed by s/n, short for *sin número* ("without a number").

assistance. Some bus companies will not transport bicycles unless you wrap frame and wheels separately in cardboard. When you enter the country, you may well find that customs officials enter details of your bicycle in your passport to prevent you from selling it.

The main dangers when cycling on Chile's roads are drivers. Make sure you stand out in the traffic by wearing bright colours, good reflective gear and lights when the visibility is poor. It goes without saying that you should **wear a helmet**; it's actually illegal to ride in Chile without one. Before you set off get your hands on one of the many good guidebooks available on long-distance cycling. Alternately contact the **Cyclists Touring Club** in the UK (☎0844 736 8450, ⓦctc.org.uk).

By train

Chile once possessed a huge network of **railways**, particularly in the far north where hundreds of kilometres of lines transported the region's nitrate ore down to the ports to be shipped abroad. Now the nitrate days are over, no national railway lines operate north of Santiago, and what lines are left south of the capital are unable to compete with the speed, prices and punctuality offered by buses.

Accommodation

On the whole, the standard of accommodation in Chile is reasonable, though many visitors feel prices are high for what they get, especially in mid- and top-range hotels. Bottom-end accommodation starts at around CH$8000 (US$16) for a dorm room, around CH$20,000 (US$40) for a double. You'll have to pay from around CH$35,000 (US$70) for a double or twin with a private bathroom in a decent mid-range hotel, and from CH$50,000 (US$100) for a smarter hotel. There's usually a wide choice in the major tourist centres and the cities on the Panamericana, but in more remote areas you'll invariably have to make do with basic *hospedajes* (modest rooms, often in family homes). Most places include a small breakfast in their rates.

The price of accommodation often increases dramatically in **high season** – January, February and mid-September – particularly in seaside resorts, where it can as much as double or even triple.

Outside high season it's always worth trying to negotiate a discount. A simple *"¿tiene algo un poco mas económico?"* ("do you have anything a little cheaper?") or *"¿me puede dar un descuento?"* ("could you give me a discount?") will often get you a lower price on the spot. It's rarely necessary to make reservations, unless you've got your heart set on a particular hotel, in which case it can be a good idea to phone a few days in advance – especially at weekends, even more so if it's within striking distance of Santiago.

Room rates are supposed to be quoted inclusive of IVA (a Chilean goods and services tax of nineteen percent), but you should always check beforehand (*¿está incluido el iva?*). Many mid- and most upper-range hotels give you the opportunity to pay for your accommodation in US dollars, which exempts you from paying IVA. However, hotels are not always eager to offer this discount – they need to be reminded forcefully. Often, though, if they can't take off IVA, they'll offer you a discount of ten percent if you pay cash.

In 2013 the Chilean government launched a sustainable tourism certification programme for hotels; for a list of establishments which have met the criteria visit ⓦchilesustentable.travel.

Hotels

Chilean hotels are given a one- to five-star rating by Sernatur (the national tourist board), but this only reflects facilities and not standards, which vary widely. In practice, then, a three-star hotel could be far more attractive and comfortable than a four-star and even a five-star hotel; the only way to tell is to go and have a look, as even the room rates aren't a reliable indication of quality.

In general, **mid-range hotels** fall into two main categories: large, old houses with spacious, but sometimes tired, rooms; and modern, purpose-built hotels, usually with smaller rooms, no common areas and better facilities. You'll always get a private bathroom with a shower (rarely a bath), hot water

---

ACCOMMODATION ALTERNATIVES

Useful websites that provide alternatives to standard hotel and hostel accommodation:
Airbnb ⓦairbnb.com.
CouchSurfing ⓦcouchsurfing.org.
onefinestay ⓦonefinestay.com.
Vacation Rentals by Owner ⓦvrbo.com.

ACCOMMODATION PRICES

Except where stated, prices in this book are for the cheapest **double room** in high season. At the lower end of the scale, **single travellers** can expect to pay half this rate, but mid- and upper-range hotels usually charge the same for a single as for a double. Note that the price of accommodation in many tourist centres drops significantly outside January and February. Rough US dollar equivalents are given for rooms costing US$150 and above, according to the exchange rates around the time of publication. All Argentinian accommodation is likewise quoted in US dollars due to the volatility of the peso.

and towels, and generally satellite TV. As the price creeps up there's usually an improvement in decor and space, and at the upper end you can expect room service, a mini-bar (*frigobar*), a safe, a hotel restaurant, private parking and sometimes a swimming pool. The standards of top-end **hotels** can still vary quite dramatically, however – ranging from stylish boutique hotels or charming *haciendas* to grim, impersonal monoliths catering for businessmen.

Motels, incidentally, are usually not economical roadside hotels, but places where couples go to have sex (rooms are generally rented for three-hour periods).

Residenciales

Residenciales are the most widely available, and widely used, accommodation option. As with hotels, standards can vary enormously, but in general they offer simple, modestly furnished rooms, usually off a corridor in the main building, or else in a row arranged around the backyard or patio. They usually contain little more than a bed, a rail for hanging clothes and a bedside table and lamp, though some provide additional furniture, and a few more comforts such as a TV or a thermos for making tea or coffee. Most, but not all, have shared bathrooms.

Where places differ is in the upkeep or "freshness" of the rooms: some are dank and damp, others have good bed linen, walls that are painted every summer, and a clean, swept, feel to them. Some of

the slightly more expensive *residenciales* are very pleasant, particularly the large, nineteenth-century houses. While some *residenciales* cater exclusively to tourists, many, especially in the mining towns of the north, fill mainly with workmen.

Hospedajes and casas de familia

The distinction between a *residencial* and a *hospedaje* or *casa de familia* is often blurred. On the whole, the term **hospedaje** implies something rather modest, along the lines of the cheaper *residenciales*, while a **casa de familia** (or *casa familiar*) offers, as you'd expect, rooms inside a family home. The relationship between the guest and the owner is nevertheless no different from that in a *residencial*. *Casas de familia* don't normally have a sign at the door, and if they do it usually just says "*Alojamiento*" ("lodging"); more commonly, members of the family might go and meet tourists at the bus stations. These places are perfectly safe and you shouldn't worry about checking them out. Sometimes you'll find details of *casas de familia* at tourist offices as well.

Cabañas

Cabañas are very popular in Chile, and you'll find them in tourist spots up and down the country, particularly by the coast. They are basically holiday chalets geared towards families, and usually come with a kitchen, sitting/dining area, one double bedroom and a second bedroom with bunks. They range from the very rustic to the distinctly grand, complete with daily maid service. Note that the price is often the same for two people as it is for four: i.e. charged by cabin rather than per person. That said, as they're used predominantly by Chileans, their popularity tends to be limited to January, February and sunny weekends; outside these times demand is so low that you can normally get a very good discount. Many *cabañas* are in superb locations, right by the ocean, and it can be wonderfully relaxing to self-cater for a few days in the off-season.

FIVE GREAT PLACES TO STAY

Explora Rapa Nui Easter Island. See p.450.
Somerscales Boutique Hotel Valparaíso. See p.107.
Hotel Cumbres San Pedro de Atacama. See p.181.
Ilaia Punta Arenas. See p.392.
The Singular Patagonia Puerto Natales. See p.399.

Refugios

Many of the ranger stations in the national parks have a limited number of bunk beds available for tourists, at a charge from around CH$5000 (US$8.50) per person. Known as **refugios**, these places are very rustic – often a small, wooden hut – but they usually have toilets, hot running water, clean sheets and woollen blankets. Some of them, such as those at the Salar de Surire and Lago Chungará, are in stunning locations. Most *refugios* are open year-round, but if you're travelling in winter or other extreme weather conditions it's best to check with the regional forestry (Conaf) office in advance. While you're there, you can reserve beds in the *refugio*. This is highly advisable if you're relying solely on the *refugio* for accommodation, but if you're travelling with a tent as a back-up, it's not really necessary to book ahead.

Hostels

Hostels are increasingly banding together to provide a link between Chile's major cities. What was until recently a score of isolated bargain spots is now starting to resemble a highly developed hostelling operation such as the one, for example, in New Zealand; some are pretty smart, and a few even style themselves as "boutique hostels". In addition to dorms, most also have a selection of private rooms. Hostels also tend to be among the best informal networks for information about local guides and excursions.

Many hostels are affiliated to Hostelling International (⑨ hihostels.com), and offer discounts for members.

Camping

There are plenty of opportunities for **camping** in Chile, though it's not always the cheapest way to sleep. If you plan to do a lot of camping, equip yourself with the annual Spanish-language camping guide, **Turistel Rutero Camping**, which has maps, prices and information. Even those who don't speak Spanish will find plenty of helpful information, ranging from trail maps to cabins. Official campsites range from plots of land with minimal facilities to swanky grounds with hot showers and private barbecue grills. The latter, often part of holiday complexes in seaside resorts, can be very expensive, and are usually only open between December and March.

It's also possible to camp wild in the countryside, but you'll really need your own transport to do this in remote areas. Most national parks don't allow camping outside designated areas, in order to protect the environment. Instead they tend to have either rustic camping areas administered by Conaf (very common in northern Chile), costing from around CH$5000 (US$8.50) per tent, or else smart, more expensive sites run by *concesionarios* (more common in the south) that charge around CH$20,000 (US$34) for two to four people. As for beaches, some turn into informal, spontaneously erected campsites in summer; on others, camping is strictly forbidden.

If you do end up camping wild on the beach or in the countryside, bury or pack up your excrement, and take all your refuse with you when you leave. Note that butane gas and sometimes Camping Gaz are available in hardware shops in most towns and cities. If your stove takes white gas, you need to buy *bencina blanca*, which you'll find either in hardware stores or, more commonly, in pharmacies.

For details of **camping in Chile's national parks**, see p.43.

Food and drink

Chile boasts a vast range of quality raw produce, but many restaurants lack imagination, offering the same limited menu. That's not to say, however, that you can't eat well in Chile, and the fish and seafood, in particular, are superb. There are also various traditional dishes, often called *comida típica* or *comida criolla*, still served in old-fashioned restaurants known as *picadas*. Furthermore, most cities have increasing numbers of smarter restaurants.

On the whole, eating out tends to be inexpensive. In local restaurants you can expect to pay around CH$3500–5500 for a main course. If you're aiming to keep costs way down, rather than resort to the innumerable **fast-food outlets**, you could head for the **municipal markets** found in most towns; besides offering an abundance of cheap, fresh produce, they are usually dotted with food stalls. The best trick is to join the Chileans and make lunch your main meal of the day; many restaurants offer a fixed-price *menú del día*, always much better value than the à la carte options.

As for the other meals of the day, **breakfast** at most *residenciales* and hotels is usually a disappointing affair of toasted rolls, jam and tea or coffee, though if your hosts are inclined to pamper you, this will be accompanied by ham, cheese and cake. The great tradition of *onces* – literally "elevenses" but served, like afternoon tea, around 5 o'clock – is a light snack consisting of bread, ham, cheese and biscuits when taken at home, or huge fruit tarts and cakes when out in a *salon de té*. Except during annual holidays or at weekends, relatively few Chileans go out to dinner, which leaves most restaurants very quiet through the week. Note, also, that most places don't open for dinner before 8 or 9pm.

Fish and seafood

Chile's fish and seafood rank among the best in the world. To sample the freshest offerings, head to one of the many *marisquerías* (fish restaurants), particularly those along the coasts of the Litoral Central and the Norte Chico.

A note of caution: you should never collect shellfish from the beach to eat unless you know for sure that the area is free of red tide, an alga that makes shellfish toxic, causing death within a few hours of consumption (see p.44). There is little danger of eating shellfish contaminated by red tide in restaurants.

Meat dishes

Chileans are also tremendous carnivores, with beef featuring prominently on most restaurant menus and family dinner tables. The summertime *asado* (barbecue) is a national institution. Always slow, leisurely affairs, accompanied by lots of Chilean wine, *asados* take place not only in back gardens, but also in specially equipped picnic areas that fill to bursting on summer weekends. In the south, where the weather is less reliable, large covered grills known as *quinchos* provide an alternative venue for grilling; animals such as goats are often sliced in half and cooked in *quinchos* on long skewers, Brazilian-style. The restaurant equivalent of an *asado* is the *parrillada* – a mixture of grilled

MINGAS TO MAYOCAN: CHILE'S NOT SO HUMBLE POTATO

The **potato**, a staple in the Chilean diet, has long been the subject of numerous traditions and superstitions. Nowhere is this truer than in Chiloé, where potatoes must be sown during a waning moon in August or September, unless large *macho* specimens are required for seeds, in which case they are sown at the full moon. Neighbours help each other in every aspect of cultivation, a communal labouring tradition known as a *minga*. There are three main *mingas*: *quechatún*, the turning of the earth; *siembra de papa*, the planting; and *cosecha* or *sacadura*, the harvest.

Among the mythology and traditional customs associated with the potato are "magic stones" (*piedras cupucas*), which are found on Cerro Chepu, a hill near Ancud in Chiloé. Believed to have been hidden by witches (*brujos*), these porous silicon stones are carefully guarded until the potato plants bloom, and then the flowers are placed on them and burnt as a sacrifice.

Another potato myth holds that a small silver lizard, *el Lluhay*, feeds on potato flowers, and anyone who can catch one is guaranteed good fortune. Still another maintains that a maggot, *la coipone*, which lives in the potato root ball, will prevent babies from crying when placed under their pillows.

MASH IT UP: POPULAR AND TRADITIONAL POTATO DISHES

Chuchoca Mashed potato mixed with flour and pig fat, plastered onto a long, thick wooden pole (*chuchoquero*) and cooked over an open fire.
Colao Small cakes made from potato, wheat, pork fat and crackling, cooked in hot embers.
Mallo de papas Potato stew.
Mayo de papas Peeled, boiled potatoes mashed with onions, chillies, pepper and pig fat.
Mayocan A potato, seaweed and dried-shellfish stew traditionally eaten for breakfast.
Milcao Small cakes of grated and mashed potato that are steamed like dumplings, baked or deep fried.
Pan de papas Baked flat round cakes of mashed potato mixed with flour, eggs and pig fat.
Papas rellenas Sausage-shaped rolls of mashed potato mixed with flour and filled with meat or shellfish.
Pastel de papas A baked dish with alternating layers of mashed potato and meat or shellfish topped with more potato.

steaks, chops and sausages, sometimes served on a hot grill by your table. Following beef in the popularity stakes is **chicken**, which is usually served fried, but can also be enjoyed oven- or spit-roasted. Chilean chickens are nearly all corn-fed and are delicious when well cooked. Succulent, spit-roasted chicken is widely available and inexpensive in Arica, in the far north, owing to the locally based chicken-breeding industries. In central Chile, *pollo al coñac* is a popular, and very tasty, chicken casserole, served in large clay pots with brandy and cream. Pork also features on many restaurant menus, but lamb (*cordero*) is hardly ever available, except in the Lake District.

Traditional food

There's a wide range of older, traditional dishes – usually a fusion of indigenous and Hispanic influences – that are still very much a part of Chilean home cooking and can, with a little luck, be found in the small, old-fashioned restaurants that survive in the hidden corners of town or out in the countryside. Though recipes vary from region to region, depending on the local produce available, there are a few core staples, including sweetcorn and potatoes. **Sweetcorn** forms the basis of two of the most traditional Chilean dishes: *humitas* – mashed corn, wrapped in corn husks and steamed – and **pastel de choclo**, a pie made of mince or chicken topped by pureed sweetcorn and sugar and then baked in the oven. The **potato**, meanwhile, is such an important staple in the Chilean diet that it has acquired its own mythology and folklore (see box, p.33).

Another great traditional dish (or snack) is the *empanada*, as symbolic as the national flag, although it was introduced by the Spanish and is popular throughout South America. Baked or fried, large or small, sweet or savoury, *empanadas* (which are not unlike Cornish pasties) can be filled with almost anything, but the most traditional filling is *pino*, a mixture of minced beef, loads of onions, a slice of hard-boiled egg, and an olive, with the pit (beware, as this is a good way to lose a tooth in Chile!).

Also very typical are **soups** and **broths**. There are numerous varieties, of which the most famous, cropping up as a starter on many a set meal, is *cazuela*. Named after large Spanish saucepans, *cazuela* is celebrated as much for its appearance as for its taste, with ingredients carefully chosen and cooked to retain their colour and texture: pale yellow potato, orange pumpkin, split rice, green beans, peas and deep yellow sweetcorn swimming in stock, served in a large soup plate with a piece of

> ### TIPPING
> It's customary to leave a ten percent tip in restaurants – service is rarely included in the bill. You are not, however, expected to tip taxi drivers.

meat on the bone, and sprinkled with parsley and coriander. Other favourite one-pot broths include *caldillo*, very similar to *cazuela* but with fish instead of meat, and *escabechado*, a stew made with fish steaks that have been fried then soaked in vinegar. Doubtless because it is so economical, offal enjoys a long (though waning) history in Chilean cookery.

Fast food

All of Chile's towns are well endowed with greasy-spoon cafés and snack bars – usually known as *fuentes de soda* or *schoperías* – serving draught beer and cheap fast food. This usually consists of **sandwiches**, which are consumed voraciously by Chileans – indeed, one variety, the **Barros Luco** (beef and melted cheese), is named after a former president who is said to have devised the combination. **Barros Jarpa** (ham and cheese) is another dietary staple. The choice of fillings is firmly meat-based, with most options revolving around **churrasco** – a thin cut of griddle-fried beef, rather like a minute steak.

Chile is also the unlikely home of a variety of **hot dogs**. Sitting all by itself in a bun, the hot dog is simply called a *vienesa*, but it's called an *especial* when mayonnaise is squeezed along the top, and the addition of tomato, sauerkraut and avocado makes it a *dinámico*. The most popular version is the *italiano* – tomato, mayonnaise and avocado, which together resemble the colours of the Italian flag. It is not until the sausage is buried under extra sauerkraut and chopped tomato that it becomes completely *completo*.

Drinking

Soft **fizzy drinks** can be found everywhere in Chile. Bottled **mineral water**, too, is widely available, both sparkling (*con gas*) and still (*sin gas*). **Coffee**, in Chile, is often instant Nescafé, although it's getting easier to find good, real coffee (ask for *café de grano*). **Herbal teas** are widely available and come in countless flavours. The most popular varieties are *manzanilla* (camomile), *menta* (mint) and *boldo* (a fragrant native plant). Where Chile really comes into its own, though, is with the delicious, freshly squeezed **fruit juices** (*jugos naturales*) available in many bars, restaurants and roadside stalls, especially in the Central Valley, and a few northern oases like Pica. Another home-grown drink is *mote con huesillo*, sold at numerous roadsides throughout the Central Valley and Lake District in summer. *Mote* is boiled or soaked barley grain, and *huesillos* are sun-dried peaches, though this sweet, gooey drink can be made with any fresh soft fruit.

Chilean **beer** doesn't come in many varieties, with Cristal and Escudo dominating the choice of bottled lagers, and Kunstman the only speciality brand to make a national mark.

There's always a good selection of **wine**, on the other hand, though the choice on restaurant lists rarely reflects the vast range of wines produced for export. Regarded as the Chilean national drink, **pisco sour** is a tangy, refreshing aperitif made from pisco (a white brandy created from distilled Moscatel grapes, freshly squeezed lemon juice and sugar – see box, p.148). You may also come across a number of **regional specialities**, including *chicha de manzana* (apple cider), made at home by every *huaso* (see box, p.37) in the Central Valley. Further south, in the Lake District, a traditional element of many drinks is *harina tostada* (toasted maize flour), used by the Mapuche since pre-Spanish days. Today it's still common to see Mapuche sitting around a table with a large jug of frothy coffee-coloured liquid, which is dark beer mixed with *harina tostada*. The flour is also mixed with cheap wine, among other drinks, and is usually stocked by the sackful at local Lake District bars.

The media

Media output in Chile is nothing to get excited about. If you know where to look, journalistic standards can be high but you might find yourself turning to foreign TV channels or papers if you want an international view on events.

Newspapers and magazines

The Chilean **press** has managed to uphold a strong tradition of editorial freedom ever since the country's first newspaper, *La Aurora*, was published by an anti-royalist friar in 1812, during the early days of the independence movement. One year before *La Aurora* folded in 1827, a new newspaper, *El Mercurio* (ⓦemol.com), went to press in Valparaíso, and is now the longest-running newspaper in the

Spanish-speaking world. Emphatically conservative, and owned by the powerful Edwards family, *El Mercurio* is considered the most serious of Chile's dailies, but still has a minimal international coverage. The other major daily is *La Tercera*, which tends to be more sensationalistic. The liberal-leaning *La Nación* is the official newspaper of the state. The online English-language *Santiago Times* (ⓦsantiagotimes.cl) is a good read, though you'll need to subscribe to get full access.

Chile also produces a plethora of racy **tabloids** as well as *¡Hola!*-style clones. For a more edifying read, try the selection of *Private Eye*-style satirical papers, such as *The Clinic* (ⓦtheclinic.cl).

In Santiago you can usually track down a selection of foreign papers, though elsewhere you'll generally have to rely on online editions.

Television and radio

Cable TV is widespread, offering innumerable domestic and international channels. CNN is always on offer, and BBC World is widely available. Of the five terrestrial channels, top choice is Channel 7, the state-owned Televisión Nacional, which makes the best programmes in Chile. Generally, however, soap operas, game shows and, of course, football, predominate.

Voice of America (ⓦvoanews.com) and Radio Canada (ⓦrcinet.ca) can both be accessed but unfortunately the BBC no longer broadcasts its World Service in Chile.

Festivals

Most of Chile's festivals are held to mark religious occasions, or to honour saints or the Virgin Mary. What's fascinating about them is the strong influence of pre-Spanish, pre-Christian rites, particularly in the Aymara communities of the far north and the Mapuche of the south. Added to this is the influence of colourful folk traditions rooted in the Spanish expeditions of exploration and conquest, colonization and evangelism, slavery and revolution.

In the *altiplano* of the **far north**, Aymara herdsmen celebrate Catholic holy days and the feasts of ancient cults along with ritual dancing and the offering of sacrificial llamas.

In **central Chile**, you'll witness the influence of colonial traditions. In the days of the conquest, an important ingredient of any fiesta was the verbal sparring between itinerant bards called *payadores*, who would compose and then try to resolve each other's impromptu rhyming riddles. The custom is kept alive at many fiestas in the Central Valley, where young poets spontaneously improvise *lolismos* and *locuciones*, forms of jocular verse that are quite unintelligible to an outsider. These rural fiestas always culminate in an energetic display of *cueca* dancing, washed down with plenty of wine and *chicha* – reminiscent of the entertainment organized by indulgent hacienda-owners for their peons.

In the **south**, the solemn Mapuche festivals are closely linked to mythology, magic and faith healing, agricultural rituals, and supplications to gods and spirits. Group dances (*purrún*) are performed with gentle movements; participants either move around in a circle or advance and retreat in lines. Most ceremonies are accompanied by mounted horn players whose 4m-long bamboo instruments, *trutrucas*, require enormous lung power to produce a note. Other types of traditional wind instruments include a small pipe (*lolkiñ*), flute (*pinkulwe*), cow's horn (*kullkull*) and whistle (*pifílka*). Of all Mapuche musical instruments, the most important is the sacred drum (*kultrún*), which is only used by faith healers (*machis*).

For more on *altiplano* fiestas and ceremonies, see p.200 and box on p.202.

A FESTIVAL CALENDAR

January 20 San Sebastián. Spaniards brought the first wooden image of San Sebastián to Chile in the seventeenth century. After a Mapuche raid on Chillán, the image was buried in a nearby field, and no one was able to raise it. The saint's feast day has become an important Mapuche festival, especially in Lonquimay, where it's celebrated with horse racing, feasting and drinking.

February 1–3 La Candelaria. Celebrated throughout Chile since 1780, when a group of miners and muleteers discovered a stone image of the Virgin and Child while sheltering from an inexplicable thunderstorm in the Atacama. Typical festivities include religious processions and traditional dances.

End of February Festival Internacional de la Canción. This glitzy and wildly popular five-day festival is held in Viña del Mar's open-air amphitheatre, featuring performers from all over Latin America and broadcast to most Spanish-speaking countries.

Easter Semana Santa (Holy Week). Among the nationwide Easter celebrations, look out for Santiago's solemn procession of penitents dressed in black habits, carrying crosses through the streets, and La Ligua's parade of mounted *huasos* followed by a giant penguin.

First Sunday after Easter Fiesta del Cuasimodo. In many parts of central Chile, *huasos* (see box opposite) parade through the streets on their horses, often accompanied by a priest sitting on a float covered in white lilies.

May 3 Santa Cruz de Mayo. Throughout the *altiplano*, villages celebrate the cult of the Holy Cross, inspired in the seventeenth century by the Spaniards' obsession with crosses, which they carried everywhere, erected on hillsides and even carved in the air with their fingers. The festivities have strong pre-Christian elements, often including the sacrifice of a llama.

May 13 Procesión del Cristo de Mayo. A huge parade through the streets of Santiago bearing the *Cristo de Mayo* – a sixteenth-century carving of Christ whose crown of thorns slipped to its neck during an earthquake, and which is said to have shed tears of blood when attempts were made to put the crown back in place.

June 13 Noche de San Juan Bautista. An important feast night, celebrated by families up and down the country with a giant stew, known as the *Estofado de San Juan*. In Chiloé, an integral part of the feast are roasted potato balls called *tropones*, which burn the fingers and make people "dance the *tropón*" as they jig up and down, juggling them from hand to hand.

June 29 Fiesta de San Pedro. Along the length of Chile's coast, fishermen decorate their boats and take the image of their patron saint out to sea – often at night with candles and flares burning – to pray for good weather and large catches.

July 12–18 Virgen de la Tirana. The largest religious festival in Chile, held in La Tirana in the Far North, and attended by over 80,000 pilgrims and hundreds of costumed dancers (see p.196).

July 16 Virgen del Carmen. Military parades throughout Chile honour the patron saint of the armed forces; the largest are in Maipú, on the southern outskirts of Santiago, where San Martín and Bernardo O'Higgins defeated Spanish Royalists in 1818.

August 21–31 Jesús Nazareno de Caguach. Thousands of Chilotes flock to the archipelago's tiny island of Caguach to worship at a 2m-high figure of Christ, donated by the Jesuits in the eighteenth century.

September 18 Fiestas Patrias. Chile's Independence Day is celebrated throughout the country with street parties, music and dancing.

First Sunday of October Virgen de las Peñas. Each year, numerous dance groups and more than 10,000 pilgrims from Chile, Peru, Bolivia and Argentina make their way along a tortuous cliff path to visit a rock carving of the Virgin in the Azapa valley, near Arica. There are many smaller festivals in other parts of Chile, too.

November 1 Todos los Santos (All Saints' Day). Traditionally, this is the day when Chileans tend their family graves. In the north, where Aymara customs have become entwined with Christian ones, crosses are often removed from graves and left on the former bed of the deceased overnight. Candles are kept burning in the room, and a feast is served for family members, past and present.

November 2 Día de los Muertos (All Souls' Day). A second vigil to the dead is held in cemeteries, with offerings of food and wine sprinkled on the graves. In some far north villages, there's a tradition of reading a liturgy, always in Latin.

December 8 La Purísima. Celebrated in many parts of Chile, the festival of the Immaculate Conception is at its liveliest in San Pedro de Atacama, where it's accompanied by traditional Aymara music and dancing.

December 23–27 Fiesta Grande de la Virgen de Andacollo. More than 100,000 pilgrims from all over the north come to Andacollo, in Norte Chico, to worship its Virgin and watch the famous masked dancers (see p.131).

Spectator sports

The Chileans are not a particularly exuberant people, but passions are roused by several national enthusiasms – chiefly football and rodeo, which at their best are performed with electrifying skill and theatricality.

Football

El **fútbol** reigns supreme as Chile's favourite sport. Introduced by British immigrants in the early 1800s, football in Chile can trace its history back to the playing fields of the Mackay School, one of the first English schools in Valparaíso, and its heritage is reflected in the names of the first clubs: Santiago Wanderers, Everton, Badminton, Morning Star and Green Cross.

Everton and Wanderers are still going strong, but the sport is now dominated by the Santiago teams of Colo Colo, Universidad Católica and Universidad de Chile. Matches featuring any of these teams are guaranteed a good turn-out and a great atmosphere. There's rarely any trouble, with whole families coming along to enjoy the fun. If you can't make it to a match, you'll still see plenty of football on the huge TVs that dominate most cafés and bars, including European games shown on cable channels (you may notice, too, that widespread exposure to English football has led many young Chileans to refer to an Englishman as a *húligan* rather than a gringo).

Football hardly has a season in Chile. In addition to the league games played between March and December, there are numerous other competitions of which the Copa de Libertadores is the most important. So you'll generally be able to catch the action whatever time of year you visit.

Horse racing

There are two very different types of horse racing in Chile: conventional track racing, known as *hípica*, and the much rougher and wilder *carreras a la chilena*. Hípica is a sport for rich Santiaguinos, who don their tweeds and posh frocks to go and watch it at the capital's Club Hípico and Hipódromo Chile, which have races throughout the year. The most important of these are the St Leger at the Hipódromo Chile on December 14, and the Ensayo at the Club Hípico on the first Sunday in November.

Carreras a la chilena are held anywhere in the country where two horses can be found to race against each other. Apart from the organized events that take place at village fiestas, these races are normally a result of one *huaso* betting another that his horse is faster. Held in any suitable field, well

---

THE CHILEAN HUASO

"Of the many cowboys of the Americas, none remains as shrouded in mystery and contradiction as Chile's *huaso*," says Richard Slatta in *Cowboys of the Americas*. Certainly the *huaso* holds a special place in Chile's perception of its national identity. But the definition of the *huaso* is somewhat confused and subject to differing interpretations. The one you're most likely to come across is that of the "**gentleman rider**", the middle-class horseman who, while not a part of the landed elite, is a good few social rungs up from the landless labourer. This is the *huaso* you'll see in *cueca* performances (see p.38) and at rodeos.

These gentlemen riders are part of a romanticized image of the Chilean countryside and a far cry from the much larger and perhaps more authentic group who carried out the real horse-work on the land. More akin to the Argentine gaucho and the Mexican *vaquero*, this other type of *huaso* was a landless, badly paid and poorly dressed ranch-hand who worked on the large haciendas during the cattle round-up season. Despite the harsh reality of his lifestyle, the lower-class *huaso* is also the victim of myth-making, frequently depicted as a paragon of virtue and happiness.

All types of *huasos*, whatever their social status, were renowned for outstanding **horsemanship**, marvelled at for their practice of training their horses to stop dead in their tracks at a single command (*la sentada*). A skill mastered in the southern Central Valley was that of the *bolas* – three stones or metal balls attached to long leather straps, which were hurled at animals and wrapped around their legs, bringing them to the ground. *Huasos* also developed a host of equestrian contests including the *juego de cañas* (jousting with canes), the *tiro al gallo* (a mounted tug-of-war) and *topeadura* (a side-by-side pushing contest). Today these displays have a formal outlet in the regular **rodeos** (see p.221) in the Central Valley. As for the working *huaso*, you'll still come across him in the back roads of rural central Chile.

THE CUECA

Huasos are the chief performers of *cueca*, **Chile's national dance** – a curious cross between English morris dancing and smouldering Sevillanas. Its history can, in fact, be traced to the African slave dances, which were also the basis of the Brazilian samba and Peruvian *zamacueca*, and were introduced to Chile by a battalion of black soldiers in 1824. During the War of Independence, Chileans adopted their own forms of these dances known as la Chilena, la Marinera and el Minero, which eventually became a national victory dance known simply as the *cueca*. Although there are regional variations, the basic elements remain unchanged, consisting of couples strutting around each other in a **courtship ritual**, spurs jingling and handkerchiefs waving over their heads. The men are decked out in their finest *huaso* gear, while the women wear wide skirts and shawls. In the background, guitar-strumming musicians sing romantic ballads full of patriotic sentiments. If you are going to a fiesta and want to take part in a *cueca*, remember to take along a clean white handkerchief.

away from the prying eyes of the *carabineros*, the two-horse race can attract large crowds (who bet heavily on the outcome).

Rodeo

Rodeos evolved from the early colonial days when the cattle on the large estancias had to be rounded up and branded or slaughtered by *huasos* (see p.37). The feats of horsemanship required to do so soon took on a competitive element, which eventually found an expression in the form of rodeos. Even though ranching has long declined in Chile, organized rodeos remain wildly popular, with many free competitions taking place in local stadiums (known as *medialunas*) throughout the season, which runs from September to April. Taking in a rodeo not only allows you to watch the most dazzling equestrian skills inside the arena, but also to see the *huasos* decked out in all their traditional gear: ponchos, silver spurs and all. Added to this, the atmosphere is invariably loads of fun, with lots of whooping families and excited kids, and plenty of food and drink afterwards.

Outdoor activities

Chile offers an enormous range of outdoor activities, including volcano-climbing, skiing, surfing, white-water rafting, fly-fishing and horseriding. An increasing number of operators and outfitters have wised-up to the potential of organized adventure tourism, offering one- or multi-day guided excursions.

Many of these companies are based in Pucón, in the Lake District, with a good sprinkling of other outfitters spread throughout the south. There are fewer opportunities for outdoor activities in the harsh deserts of the north, where *altiplano* jeep trips and mountain biking are the main options. If you plan to do take part in adventurous activities, be sure to check that you're covered by your travel insurance, or take out specialist insurance where necessary.

Rafting and kayaking

Chile's many frothy rivers and streams afford incomparable rafting opportunities. Indeed, the country's top destinations, the mighty **Rio Biobío** and the **Río Futaleufú**, entice visitors from around the globe. Rafting trips generally range in length from one to eight days and, in the case of the Biobío, sometimes include the option of climbing 3160m Volcán Callaquén. In addition to these challenging rivers, gentler alternatives exist on the **Río Maipo** close to Santiago, the **Río Trancura** near Pucón, and the **Río Petrohue** near Puerto Varas. The Maipo makes a good day-trip from Santiago, while excursions on the latter two are just half-day affairs and can usually be arranged on the spot, without advance reservations. In general, all rafting trips are extremely well organized, but you should always take great care in choosing your outfitter – this activity can be very dangerous in the hands of an inexperienced guide.

Chile's white-water rapids also offer excellent **kayaking**, though this is less developed as an organized activity – your best bet is probably to contact one of the US-based outfitters that have camps on the Biobío and Futaleufú (see p.246 & p.359). **Sea kayaking** is becoming increasingly popular, generally in the calm, flat waters of Chile's southern fjords, though people have been known to kayak around Cape Horn. Note that the Chilean navy is very sensitive about any foreign vessels (even kayaks) cruising in their waters, and if you're

FIVE GREAT OUTDOOR ACTIVITIES

Paragliding over Iquique. See p.189.
Skiing at Portillo. See p.92.
Dog sledding near Villarrica. See p.272.
Dawn kayaking in the Chepu Valley, Chiloé. See p.325.
Trekking in Parque Patagonia. See p.376.

planning a trip through military waters, you'd be wise to inform the Chilean consulate or embassy in your country beforehand.

Hiking

For the most part, Chile is a very empty country with vast tracts of wilderness offering potential for fantastic hiking. Chileans, moreover, are often reluctant to stray far from their parked cars when they visit the countryside, so you'll find that most trails without vehicle access are blissfully quiet. However, the absence of a national enthusiasm for hiking also means that, compared with places of similar scenic beauty like California, British Columbia and New Zealand, Chile isn't particularly geared up to the hiking scene, with relatively few long-distance trails (given the total area) and a shortage of decent trekking maps. That said, what is on offer is superb, and ranks among the country's most rewarding attractions.

The **north** of Chile, with its harsh climate and landscape, isn't really suitable for hiking, and most walkers head for the lush native forests of Chile's **south**, peppered with waterfalls, lakes, hot springs and volcanoes. The best trails are nearly always inside **national parks** or reserves, where the *guardaparques* (rangers) are a good source of advice on finding and following the paths. They should always be informed if you plan to do an overnight hike (so that if you don't come back, they'll know where to search for you). The majority of trails are for half-day or day hikes, though some parks offer a few long-distance hikes, sometimes linking up with trails in adjoining parks. The level of path maintenance and signing varies greatly from one park to another, and many of the more remote trails are indistinct and difficult to follow.

Hardly any parks allow wild **camping**, while the few others that now allow it have a series of rustic camping areas that you're required to stick to – check with the *guardaparque*. If you do camp (the best way to experience the Chilean wilderness) note

that **forest and bush fires** are a very real hazard. Take great care when making a campfire (check before that they're allowed; don't light fires in Torres del Paine). Also, never chop down vegetation for fuel, as most of Chile's native flora is endangered.

By far the most popular destination for hiking is **Torres del Paine** in the far south, which offers magnificent scenery but fairly crowded trails, especially in January and February. Many quieter, less well-known alternatives are scattered between Santiago and Tierra del Fuego, ranging from narrow paths in the towering, snow-streaked central Andes to hikes up to glaciers off the Carretera Austral.

If you go hiking, it's essential to be well prepared – always carry plenty of water, wear a hat and sun block for protection against the sun, and carry extra layers of warm clothing to guard against the sharp drop in temperature after sundown. Even on day hikes, take enough supplies to provide for the eventuality of getting lost, and always carry a map and **compass** (*brújula*), preferably one bought in the southern hemisphere or adjusted for southern latitudes. Also, make a conscious effort to help preserve Chile's environment – where there's no toilet, bury human waste at least 20cm under the ground and 30m from the nearest river or lake; take away or burn all your **rubbish**; and use specially designed **eco-friendly detergents** for use in lakes and streams.

Climbing

The massive Andean cordillera offers a wide range of climbing possibilities. In the far north of Chile, you can trek up several volcanoes over 6000m, including Volcán Parinacota (6330m), Volcán Llullaillaco (6739m) and Volcán Ojos del Salado (6950m). Although ropes and crampons aren't always needed, these ascents are suitable only for experienced climbers, and need a fair amount of independent planning, with only a few companies offering guided excursions.

In the central Andes, exciting climbs include Volcán Marmolejo (6100m) and Volcán Tupungato (6750m), while in the south, climbers head for Volcán Villarrica (2840m) and Volcán Osorno (2652m), both of which you can tackle even with little mountaineering experience.

Throughout Chile there's a lot of tedious bureaucracy to get through before you can climb. To go up any mountain straddling an international border (which means most of the high Andean peaks), you need advance **permission** from the **Dirección de Fronteras y Límites del Estado** (DIFROL), Seventh Floor, Teatinos 180, Santiago (☎2 2827 5900,

W www.difrol.gob.cl). To get this, write to or email DIFROL with the planned dates and itinerary of the climb, listing full details (name, nationality, date of birth, occupation, passport number, address) of each member of the climbing team, and your dates of entry and exit from Chile. Authorization will then be sent to you on a piece of paper that you must present to Conaf before ascending (if the peak is not within a national park, you must take the authorization to the nearest *carabineros* station). If your plans change while you're in Chile, you can usually amend the authorization or get a new one at the *Gobernación* of each provincial capital. You can also apply through a Chilean embassy in advance of your departure, or print and send a form from their website. There's further information on climbing in Chile online at W trekkingchile.com.

Fly-fishing

Chile has a well-deserved international reputation as one of the finest fly-fishing destinations in the world. Its pristine waters teem with rainbow, brown and brook trout, and silver and Atlantic salmon. These fish are not native, but were introduced for sport in the late nineteenth century; since then, the wild population has flourished and multiplied, and is also supplemented by generous numbers of escapees from local fish farms. The fishing season varies slightly from region to region, but in general runs from November to May.

Traditionally, the best sport-fishing was considered to be in the Lake District, but while this region still offers great possibilities, attention has shifted to the more remote, pristine waters of Aisén, where a number of classy fishing lodges have sprung up, catering mainly to wealthy North American clients. Fishing in the Lake District is frequently done from riverboats, while a typical day's fishing in Aisén begins with a ride in a motor dinghy through fjords, channels and islets towards an isolated river. You'll then wade upstream to shallow waters, usually equipped with a light six or seven weight rod, dry flies and brightly coloured streamers. Catches weigh in between 1kg and 3kg – but note that many outfitters operate only on a catch and release basis.

Skiing

Chile offers the finest and most challenging **skiing** in South America. Many of the country's top slopes and resorts lie within very easy reach of Santiago, including **El Colorado**, **La Parva**, **Valle Nevado** and world-renowned **Portillo**. A bit further south,

but no less impressive, stands the popular **Termas de Chillán**.

Horse-trekking

Exploring Chile's dramatic landscapes on horseback is a memorable experience. The best possibilities are **around Santiago**, and in the **Central Valley**, where riding has been a way of life for centuries. In addition to the spectacular scenery, you can also expect to see condors and other birds of prey. Trips are usually guided by local *arrieros*, who herd cattle up to high pastures in springtime and know the mountain paths intimately. You normally spend about five or six hours in the saddle each day; a lingering *asado* (barbecue), cooked over an open fire and accompanied by plenty of Chilean wine, will be part of the pleasure. At night, you sleep in tents transported by mules, and you'll be treated to the most breathtaking display of stars.

The only disadvantage of riding treks in the central Andes is that, due to the terrain, you're unlikely to get beyond a walk, and cantering is usually out of the question. If you want a faster pace, opt for the treks offered by some companies in Patagonia, where rolling grasslands provide plenty of opportunity for gallops – though the weather can often put a dampener on your trip.

Mountain biking

For most of Chile's length, there are extremely good and little-used dirt roads perfect for **cycling** – although the numerous potholes mean it's only worth attempting them on a **mountain bike**. For a serious trip, you should bring your own bike or buy one in Santiago – **renting** a bike of the quality required can be difficult to arrange. An alternative is to go on an organized biking excursion, where all equipment, including tents, will be provided. Note that during the summer, cycling in Patagonia and Tierra del Fuego is made almost impossible by incessant and ferociously strong winds.

Surfing

Chile's beaches are pulling in an increasing number of surfers, who come to ride the year-round breaks that pound the Pacific shore. By unanimous consent, the **best breaks** – mainly long left-handers – are concentrated around Pichilemu, near Rancagua, which is the site of the annual National Surfing Championships. Further north, the warmer seas around Iquique and Arica are also increasingly popular.

Adventure tourism operators and outfitters

Below is a selection of operators and outfitters for various outdoor activities. The list is by no means comprehensive, and new companies are constantly springing up to add to it – you can get more details from the relevant regional Sernatur office.

ALL-ROUNDERS

Altue Active Travel General Salvo 159, Providencia, Santiago ☎ 2 2333 1390, ⓦ altue.com. Reliable, slick operation whose options include rafting the Río Maipo, Aconcagua and Ojos del Salado expeditions, and horse-treks.

Azimut 360 General Salvo 159, Providencia, Santiago ☎ 2 2235 1519, ⓦ azimut360.com. Franco–Chilean outfit with a dynamic team of guides and a wide range of programmes, including mountain biking, Aconcagua expeditions and climbs up Chile's highest volcanoes.

Cascada Expediciones Don Carlos 3219, Las Condes, Santiago ☎ 2 2232 9878, ⓦ cascada.travel. One of the pioneers of adventure tourism in Chile, with a particular emphasis on activities in the Andes close to Santiago, where it has a permanent base in the Cajón del Maipo. Programmes include rafting and kayaking the Río Maipo, horse-treks in the high cordillera and hiking and mountain biking.

Sportstour Av El Bosque Norte 500, 15th Floor, Santiago ☎ 2 2589 5200, ⓦ www.sportstour.cl. This well-run operation offers balloon rides and flights, among other tours.

CLIMBING

See also Azimut 360 and Altue Active Travel in "All-rounders" (see above) for details of tours up Volcán Osorno and Volcán Villarrica.

Mountain Service Paseo Las Palmas 2209, Providencia, Santiago ☎ 2 2234 3439. An experienced, specialist company, dedicated to climbing Aconcagua, the major volcanoes and Torres del Paine.

FLY-FISHING

For a list of guides and lodges on and around the Carretera Austral, see p.364.

Bahía Escocia Fly Fishing Lago Rupanco ☎ 64 2197 4731, ⓔ lodgepuntiagudo@gmail.cl. Small, beautifully located lodge with fly-fishing excursions run by a US–Chilean couple.

Cumilahue Lodge PO Box 2, Llifen ☎ 2 2196 1601, ⓦ anglingtours.com. Very expensive packages at a luxury Lake District lodge run by Adrian Dufflocq, something of a legend on the Chilean fly-fishing scene.

Off Limits Adventures Av Bernardo O'Higgins 560, Pucón ☎ 09 9949 2481, ⓦ offlimits.cl. Half-day and full-day excursions, plus fly-fishing lessons. One of the more affordable options.

HORSE-TREKKING

See also Altue Active Travel and Cascada Expediciones in "All-rounders" (see above).

Chile Nativo Casilla 42, Puerto Natales ☎ 2 2717 5961, ⓦ chilenativo.com. Dynamic young outfit specializing in five- to twelve-day horse-trekking tours of the region, visiting out-of-the-way locations in addition to the Parque Nacional Torres del Paine.

Hacienda de los Andes Río Hurtado, near Ovalle ☎ 53 269 1822, ⓦ haciendalosandes.com. Beautiful ranch in a fantastic location in the Hurtado valley, between La Serena and Ovalle, offering exciting mountain treks on some of the finest mounts in the country.

Pared Sur Juan Esteban Montero 5497, Las Condes, Santiago ☎ 2 2207 3525, ⓦ paredsur.cl. In addition to its extensive mountain-biking programme, Pared Sur offers a one-week horse-trek through the virgin landscape of Aisén, off the Carretera Austral.

Rancho de Caballos Casilla 142, Pucón ☎ 09 8346 1764, ⓦ rancho-de-caballos.com. Ranch offering a range of treks from one to six days.

Ride World Wide Staddon Farm, North Tawton, Devon, UK ☎ 01837 82544, ⓦ rideworldwide.com. UK-based company that hooks up with local riding outfitters around the world. In Chile, it offers a range of horseback treks in the central cordillera, the Lake District and Patagonia.

KAYAKING

Al Sur Expediciones Aconcagua and Imperial, Puerto Varas ☎ 65 223 2300, ⓦ alsurexpeditions.com. One of the foremost adventure tour companies in the Lake District, and the first one to introduce sea kayaking in the fjords south of Puerto Montt.

Bío Bío Expeditions PO Box 2028, Truckee, CA 96160, US ☎ 562 196 4258, ⓦ bbxrafting.com. This rafting outfitter also rents out kayaks to experienced kayakers, who accompany the rafting party down the Biobío or Futaleufú.

¡ecole! Urrutia 592, Pucón ☎ 45 244 1675, ⓦ ecole.cl. Ecologically focused tour company offering, among other activities, sea kayaking classes and day outings in the fjords south of Puerto Montt, and around Parque Pumalín, from its Puerto Montt branch.

Expediciones Chile Gabriela Mistral 296, Futaleufú ☎ 65 272 1386, ⓦ exchile.com. River kayaking outfitter, operated by former Olympic kayaker Chris Spelius, catering to all levels of experience, especially seasoned paddlers.

Onas Patagonia Blanco Encalada 211, Puerto Natales ☎ 61 261 4300. Sea kayaking excursions in the bleak, remote waters of Patagonia.

MOUNTAIN BIKING

See also Azimut 360 and Cascada Expediciones in "All-rounders" (see above).

Pared Sur Juan Esteban Montero 5497, Las Condes, Santiago ☎ 2 2207 3525, ⓦ paredsur.cl. Pared Sur has been running mountain bike trips in Chile for longer than anyone else. It offers a wide range of programmes throughout the whole country.

SKIING

For full details of the resorts near Santiago, see p.92.

Sportstour Av El Bosque Norte 500, 15th Floor, Santiago ☎ 2 2549 5260, ⓦ sportstour.cl. Among a wide-ranging national programme, including hot-air balloon rides and flights on cockpit biplanes and gliders, this travel agent offers fully-inclusive ski packages at the resorts near Santiago, and the Termas de Chillán ski centre.

TREKKING AND HIKING

See also "All-rounders" (see p.41).

Cascada Expediciones Don Carlos 3219, Las Condes, Santiago ☎ 2 2232 9878, ⓦ cascada.travel. Leading adventure operator, offering guided treks across Chile, including the Lake District, Patagonia and the Atacama Desert.

Cosmo Andino Caracoles s/n, San Pedro de Atacama ☎ 55 285 1069, ⓦ cosmoandino.cl. Focusing on the Atacama Desert, with several guided hikes and treks.

Erratic Rock Baquedano 719, Puerto Natales ☎ 61 241 4317, ⓦ erraticrock.com. Offering a wide range of standard and tailor-made treks in Patagonia and Tierra del Fuego.

WHITE-WATER RAFTING

See also Cascada Expediciones (see above).

Bío Bío Expeditions PO Box 2028, Truckee, CA 96160, US ☎ 56 2196 4258, ⓦ bbxrafting.com. Headed by Laurence Alvarez, the captain of the US World Championships rafting team, this experienced and friendly outfit offers ten-day packages on the Biobío and Futaleufú, plus one- to three-day excursions down the latter.

Trancura O'Higgins 211-C, Pucón ☎ 45 244 1189, ⓦ www .trancura.cl. Major southern operator with high standards and friendly guides, offering rafting excursions down the Río Trancura and the Biobío.

National parks and reserves

Some eighteen percent of Chile's mainland territory is protected by the state under the extensive Sistema Nacional de Areas Silvestres Protegidas (National Protected Wildlife Areas System), which is made up of thirty national parks, thirty-eight national reserves and eleven natural monuments. These inevitably include the country's most outstanding scenic attractions, but while there are provisions for tourism, the main aim is always to protect and manage native fauna and flora. Given Chile's great biodiversity, these vary tremendously, and park objectives are as varied as protecting flamingo populations and monitoring glaciers. All protected areas are managed by the Corporación Nacional Forestal, better known as Conaf (ⓦ www.conaf.cl).

Definitions and terms

National parks (*parques nacionales*) are generally large areas of unspoilt wilderness, usually featuring fragile endemic ecosystems. They include the most touristy and beautiful of the protected areas, and often offer walking trails and sometimes camping areas too. **National reserves** (*reservas nacionales*) are areas of ecological importance that have suffered some degree of natural degradation; there are fewer regulations to protect these areas, and "sustainable" commercial exploitation (such as mineral extraction) is allowed to take place. **Natural monuments** (*monumentos naturales*) tend to be important or endangered geological formations, or small areas of biological, anthropological or archeological significance.

In addition to these three main categories, there are a few **nature sanctuaries** (*santuarios de la naturaleza*) and **protected areas** (*areas de protección*), usually earmarked for their scientific or scenic interest. It is not difficult for the government to change the status of these areas, and it has been known for national parks to be downgraded so that their resources could be commercially exploited. In addition to these state-owned parks, there are several important private initiatives, including **Parque Pumalín** (see p.354).

Park administration

The administration of Chile's protected areas is highly centralized with all important decisions

---

HIKING IN CHILE'S PARKS AND RESERVES

Chile boasts some outstanding hiking trails, with plenty of options for both novice and experienced hikers. Most are found in the following national parks and reserves:

Monumento Nacional El Morado (p.90)
Parque Nacional Chiloé (p.335)
Parque Nacional Huerquehue (p.278)
Parque Nacional La Campana (p.120)
Parque Nacional Queulat (p.361)
Parque Nacional Tolhuaca (p.265)
Parque Nacional Torres del Paine (p.402)
Parque Nacional Vicente Pérez Rosales (p.303)
Parque Patagonia (p.375)
Parque Pumalín (p.354)
Parque Nacional Radal Siete Tazas (p.234)
Parque Nacional Río de los Cipreses (p.224)

coming from **Conaf's head office** in Santiago (see p.78). This is a good place to visit before heading out of the capital, as you can pick up brochures, books and basic maps. In addition, each regional capital has a Conaf headquarters, which is useful for more practical pre-visit information. The parks and reserves are staffed by **guardaparques** (park wardens), who live in ranger stations (called *guarderías*). Most parks are divided into several areas, known as "sectors" (*sectores*), and the larger ones have a small *guardería* in each sector.

Visiting the parks

No permit is needed to visit any of Chile's national parks; you simply turn up and pay your **entrance fee** (usually CH$1200–5000), though some parks are free. Alternatively, Conaf's Annual Pass (CH$10,000) allows unlimited access to all of Chile's national parks and reserves – except Torres del Paine and Easter Island – for a year; it can be purchased from Conaf offices.

Ease of **access** differs wildly from one park to the next – a few have paved highways running through them, while others are served by dirt tracks that are only passable for a few months of the year. Getting to them often involves renting a vehicle or going on an organized trip, as around two-thirds of Chile's national parks can't be reached by public transport.

Arriving at the park boundary, you'll normally pass a small hut (called the Conaf control) where you pay your entrance fee and pick up a basic map. Some of the larger parks have more than one entrance point. The main ranger station is always separate from the hut; it contains the rangers' living quarters and administrative office, and often a large map or scale model of the park. The more popular parks also have a **Centro de Información Ambiental** attached to the station, with displays on the park's flora and fauna. A few parks now have **camping** areas. These are often rustic sites with basic facilities, run by Conaf, which charge around CH$5000–10,000 per tent. In other parks, particularly in the south, Conaf gives licences to concessionaires, who operate campsites and *cabañas*, which tend to be very expensive. Some of the more remote national parks, especially in the north, have small **refugios** (see p.215) attached to the ranger stations. Some of them are in stunning locations, overlooking the Salar de Surire, for example, or with views across Lago Chungará to Volcán Parinacota. Sadly, however, they are increasingly unreliable.

Health

Chile is a fairly risk-free country to travel in as far as health problems are concerned. No inoculations are required, though you might want to consider a hepatitis A jab, as a precaution. Check, too, that your tetanus boosters are up to date. Many travellers experience the occasional stomach upset, and sunstroke is also quite common, especially at high altitudes.

Chile is well endowed with **pharmacies** (*farmacias*) – even smaller towns usually have at least a handful. If you need to see a **doctor**, make an appointment at the outpatient department of the nearest hospital, usually known as a *clínica*. The majority of *clínicas* are private, and expensive, so make sure your **travel insurance** provides good medical cover.

Rabies

Rabies, though only a remote risk, does exist in Chile. If you get bitten or scratched by a dog, you should seek medical attention *immediately*. The disease can be cured, but only through a series of stomach injections administered before the onset of symptoms, which can appear within 24 hours or lie dormant for months, and include irrational behaviour, fear of water and foaming at the mouth. There is a vaccine, but it's expensive and doesn't prevent you from contracting rabies, though it does buy you time to get to hospital.

Altitude sickness

Anyone travelling in Chile's northern *altiplano*, where altitudes commonly reach 4500m – or indeed anyone going higher than 3000m in the cordillera – needs to be aware of the risks of **altitude sickness**, locally known as *soroche* or *apunamiento*. This debilitating and sometimes dangerous condition is caused by the reduced atmospheric pressure and corresponding reduction in oxygen that occurs around 3000m above sea level. **Basic symptoms** include breathlessness, headaches, nausea and extreme tiredness, rather like a bad hangover. There's no way of predicting whether or not you'll be susceptible to the condition, which seems to strike quite randomly, affecting people differently from one ascent to another. You can, however, take steps to avoid it by ascending slowly and allowing yourself to

---

MAREA ROJA

Chile's **shellfish** should be treated with the utmost caution. Every year, a handful of people die because they inadvertently eat bivalve shellfish contaminated by red tide, or *marea roja*, algae that becomes toxic when the seawater temperature rises. The government monitors the presence of this algae with extreme diligence and bans all commercial shellfish collection when the phenomenon occurs. There is little health risk when eating in restaurants or buying shellfish in markets, as these are regularly inspected by the health authorities, but it's extremely dangerous to collect shellfish for your own consumption unless you're absolutely certain that the area is free of red tide. Note that red tide affects all shellfish, cooked or uncooked.

---

acclimatize. In particular, don't be tempted to whizz straight up to the *altiplano* from sea level, but spend a night or two acclimatizing en route. You should also avoid alcohol and salt, and drink lots of water. The bitter-tasting coca leaves chewed by most locals in the *altiplano* (where they're widely available at markets and village stores), can help ease headaches and the sense of exhaustion.

Although extremely unpleasant, the basic form of altitude sickness is essentially harmless and passes after about 24 hours (if it doesn't, descend at least 500m). However, in its more serious forms, altitude sickness can be dangerous and even life-threatening. One to two percent of people travelling to 4000m develop HAPO (high-altitude pulmonary oedema), caused by the build-up of liquid in the lungs. Symptoms include fever, an increased pulse rate, and coughing up white fluid; sufferers should descend immediately, whereupon recovery is usually quick and complete. Rarer, but more serious, is HACO (high-altitude cerebral oedema), which occurs when the brain gets waterlogged with fluid. Symptoms include loss of balance, severe lassitude, weakness or numbness on one side of the body and a confused mental state. If you or a fellow traveller display any of these symptoms, descend immediately and get to a doctor; HACO can be fatal within 24 hours.

Sunburn and dehydration

In many parts of Chile, **sunburn** and **dehydration** are threats. They are obviously more of a problem in the excessively dry climate of the north, but even in the south of the country, it's easy to underestimate the strength of the summer sun. To prevent sunburn, take a **high-factor sunscreen** and wear a wide-brimmed hat. It's also essential to drink plenty of fluids before you go out, and always carry large quantities of water with you when you're hiking in the sun. As you lose a lot of salt when you sweat, add more to your food, or take a rehydration solution.

Hypothermia

Another potential enemy, especially at high altitudes and in Chile's far southern reaches, is **hypothermia**. Because early symptoms can include an almost euphoric sense of sleepiness and disorientation, your body's core temperature can plummet to danger level before you know what has happened. Chile's northern deserts have such clear air that it can drop to -20°C (-4°F) at night, which makes you very vulnerable to hypothermia while sleeping if proper precautions aren't taken. If you get hypothermia, the best thing to do is take your clothes off and jump into a sleeping bag with someone else – sharing another person's body heat is the most effective way of restoring your own. If you're alone, or have no willing partners, then get out of the wind and the rain, remove all wet or damp clothes, get dry, and drink plenty of hot fluids.

MEDICAL RESOURCES

Canadian Society for International Health ☎ 613 241 5785, ⓦ csih.org. Extensive list of travel health centres.
CDC ☎ 1 800 232 4636, ⓦ cdc.gov/travel. Official US government travel health site.
Hospital for Tropical Diseases Travel Clinic UK ☎ 0845 155 5000, ⓦ www.thehtd.org.
International Society for Travel Medicine US ☎ 1 404 373 8282, ⓦ istm.org. Has a full list of travel health clinics.
MASTA (Medical Advisory Service for Travellers Abroad) UK ⓦ masta-travel-health.com for the nearest clinic.
Tropical Medical Bureau Ireland ☎ 1850 487 674, ⓦ tmb.ie.
The Travel Doctor – TMVC ☎ 1300 658 844, ⓦ traveldoctor.com.au. Lists travel clinics in Australia, New Zealand and South Africa.

Culture and etiquette

Chile's social mores reflect the European ancestry of the majority of its population, and travellers from the West will

have little trouble fitting in, especially if they have a good grasp of Spanish. Chileans are not especially ebullient and high-spirited – particularly when compared with their Argentine neighbours – and are often considered rather formal.

However, they are also known for their quick wit and wordplay, and considering its relatively small population, Chile has produced an impressive array of writers, poets, artists and musicians. The overwhelming majority of Chileans identify themselves as Catholic, and the church still has significant – though waning – influence in the country. Unsurprisingly, then, this is a rather conservative country: divorce was only legalised in 2004 and attitudes towards homosexuality, though improving, are generally far from enlightened (see p.47). Chileans are very family-oriented: children are popular and travelling families can expect special treatment and friendly attention. Although stereotypical Latin American machismo undoubtedly exists, it is not as strong as in some other countries in the region.

Travel essentials

Climate

As you might expect given its incredibly long, thin shape, Chile encompasses a wide range of climates (and micro climates). Its seasons are the reverse of those in Europe and North America, with, broadly speaking, winter falling in the June to September period and summer in the December to March period.

Costs

Chile is an expensive country compared with most of South America. Accommodation is comparatively expensive, but eating out is relatively good value if you avoid the flashier restaurants and take advantage of set lunch menus. Transport is, by contrast, inexpensive.

In general, per week, you'll need to allow US$250 to get by on a tight budget; around US$600 to live a little more comfortably, staying in mid-range hotels and eating in restaurants most days; and upwards of US$1000 to live in luxury.

The most widespread hidden cost in Chile is the **IVA** (Impuesto al Valor Agregado), a tax of nineteen percent added to most goods and services. Although most prices include IVA, there are many irritating exceptions. Hotel rates sometimes include IVA and sometimes don't; as a tourist, you're supposed to be exempt from IVA if you pay for your accommodation in US dollars. Car rental is almost always quoted without IVA. If in doubt, you should always clarify whether a price quoted to you includes IVA.

Once obtained, various official and quasi-official **youth/student ID cards** soon pay for themselves in savings. Full-time students are eligible for the International Student ID Card (ISIC, Ⓦ isiccard.com).

The **exchange rate** at the time of writing was: £1 = CH$940; $1 = CH$610; Euro1 = CH$740.

Crime and personal safety

Chile is one of the safest South American countries, and violent crime against tourists is rare. The kind of sophisticated tactics used by thieves in neighbouring Peru and Bolivia are extremely uncommon in Chile, and the fact that you can walk around without being gripped by paranoia is one of the country's major bonuses.

That's not to say, of course, that you don't need to be careful. Opportunistic pickpocketing and petty theft is common in Santiago and major cities such as Valparaíso, Arica and Puerto Montt, and you should take all the normal precautions to safeguard your money and valuables, paying special attention in bus terminals and markets – wear a money belt, and keep it tucked inside the waistband of your trousers or skirt, out of sight, and don't wear flashy jewellery, flaunt expensive cameras or carry a handbag. It's also a good idea to keep photocopies of your passport, tourist card, driving licence, air tickets and credit card details separate from the originals – whether it's safer to carry the originals with you or leave them in your hotel is debatable, but whatever you do, you should always have some form of ID on you, even if this is just a photocopy of your passport.

Chile's police force, the **carabineros**, has the whole country covered, with stations in even the most remote areas, particularly in border regions. If you're robbed and need a police report for an insurance claim, you should go to the nearest *retén* (police station), where details of the theft are entered in a logbook. You'll be issued a slip of paper with the record number of the entry, but in most cases a full report won't be typed out until your insurance company requests it.

Electricity

220V/50Hz is the standard throughout Chile. The sockets are two-pronged, with round pins (as

CLIMATE

	Jan	Feb	Mar	Apr	May	Jun	Jul	Aug	Sep	Oct	Nov	Dec
ARICA												
Max (°C)	26	27	25	24	22	19	18	18	19	20	22	24
Max (°F)	79	80	78	75	71	67	65	65	66	69	72	76
Min (°C)	20	20	19	17	15	14	14	14	15	15	17	18
Min (°F)	68	68	66	63	60	58	57	58	59	60	62	65
rainfall (mm)	1	0	0	0	0	0	0	3	0	0	0	2
PUNTA ARENAS												
Max (°C)	15	14	12	10	7	5	4	6	8	11	12	14
Max (°F)	59	57	54	50	45	41	39	43	46	52	54	57
Min (°C)	7	7	5	4	2	1	-1	1	2	3	4	6
Min (°F)	45	45	41	39	36	34	30	34	36	37	39	43
rainfall (mm)	38	23	33	36	33	41	28	31	23	28	18	36
SANTIAGO												
Max (°C)	29	29	27	23	18	14	15	17	19	22	26	28
Max (°F)	84	84	81	73	64	57	59	63	66	72	79	82
Min (°C)	12	11	9	7	5	3	3	4	6	7	9	11
Min (°F)	54	52	48	45	41	37	37	39	43	45	48	52
rainfall (mm)	3	3	5	13	64	84	76	56	31	15	8	5

opposed to the flat pins common in neighbouring countries).

Entry requirements

Most foreign visitors to Chile do not need a visa. The exceptions are citizens of Cuba, Russia, Middle Eastern countries (except Israel) and African counties (except South Africa). Some nationalities also have to pay an arrival tax (see p.25).

Visitors of all nationalities are issued with a ninety-day **tourist entry card** (*Tarjeta de Turismo*) on arrival in Chile, which can be extended once for an additional ninety days. It will be checked by the International Police at the airport or border post when you leave Chile – if it's expired you won't be allowed to leave the country until you've paid the appropriate fine at the nearest *Intendencia* (up to US$100, depending on the number of days past the expiry date). If this happens when you're trying to

fly out of the international airport in Santiago, you'll have to go back downtown to Moneda 1342 (Mon–Fri 9am–1pm; ☎2 2672 5320).

If you lose your tourist card, ask for a duplicate immediately, either from the Fronteras department of the Policía Internacional, General Borgoño 1052, Santiago (☎2 2698 2211) or from the Extranjero's department of the Intendencia in any provincial capital. There's no charge for replacing lost or stolen cards.

If you want to **extend** your tourist card, you can either pay US$100 at the Intendencia of Santiago or any provincial capital, or you can simply leave the country and re-enter, getting a brand-new ninety-day *Tarjeta de Turismo* for free. Note that **under-18s** travelling to Chile without parents need written parental consent authorized by the Chilean Embassy, and that minors travelling to Chile with just one parent need the written, authorized consent of the absent parent.

CHILEAN EMBASSIES ABROAD

Australia 10 Culgoa Circuit, O'Malley, Canberra ACT 2606 ☎ 02 6286 2098, ⓦ chileabroad.gov.cl/australia/.
Canada 50 O'Connor St, suite 1413, Ottawa, ON K1P 6L2 ☎ 613 235 4402, ⓦ congechiletoronto.com.
New Zealand 19 Bolton St, Wellington ☎ 04 471 6270, ⓦ chileabroad.gov.cl/nueva-zelanda/.
South Africa 169 Garsfontein Rd Ashlea, Delmondo Office Park Block C, Gardens, Pretoria ☎ 012 460 1676, ⓦ chileabroad.gov.cl /sudafrica/.

EMERGENCY NUMBERS

Air rescue 138 (for mountaineering accidents)
Ambulance 131
Carabineros 133
Coast Guard 137
Fire 132
Investigaciones 134 (for serious crimes)

UK 12 Devonshire St, London W1N 2DS ☎ 020 7580 1023,
ⓦ chileabroad.gov.cl/reino-unido/.
US 1732 Massachusetts Ave NW, Washington, DC 20036 ☎ 202 785
1746, ⓦ chileabroad.gov.cl/estados-unidos/en.

Gay and lesbian travellers

Chilean society is extremely **conservative**, and
homosexuality is still a taboo subject for many
Chileans. Outside Santiago – with the minor exceptions of some northern cities such as La Serena and
Antofagasta – there are no gay venues, and it is
advisable for same-sex couples to do as the locals
do and remain discreet, especially in public.
Machismo, while not as evident here as in other
Latin American countries, is nevertheless deeply
ingrained and mostly unchallenged by women,
despite a growing feminist movement. That said,
gay-bashing and other homophobic acts are rare
and the government has passed anti-discrimination
legislation. The International Gay and Lesbian
Association (ⓦ iglta.org) has information on gay-
and lesbian-friendly travel companies in Chile (and
around the world).

Insurance

You'd do well to take out an insurance policy before
travelling to cover against theft, loss and illness or
injury. Before paying for a new policy, however, it's
worth checking whether you are already covered:
some all-risks home insurance policies may cover
your possessions when overseas, and many private
medical schemes include cover when abroad.

After checking out these possibilities, you might
want to contact a **specialist travel insurance
company**, or consider the travel insurance deal we
offer (see box below). A typical travel insurance
policy usually provides cover for the loss of
baggage, tickets and – up to a certain limit – cash
or cheques, as well as cancellation or curtailment of
your journey. Most exclude so-called dangerous

sports unless an extra premium is paid; in Chile this
can mean scuba-diving, white-water rafting,
windsurfing and trekking, though probably not
kayaking or jeep safaris. If you take medical
coverage, ascertain whether benefits will be paid as
treatment proceeds or only after you return home,
and if there is a 24-hour medical emergency
number. When securing baggage cover, make sure
that the per-article limit will cover your most
valuable possession. If you need to make a claim,
you should keep receipts for medicines and
medical treatment, and in the event you have
anything stolen, you must obtain an official
statement from the police.

Internet

Chile is very well connected. Cybercafés are
everywhere, and broadband (*banda ancha*) access is
quite common. Most hotels, hostels, cafes, bars and
restaurants provide wi-fi access, often for free. Since
most accommodation in Chile offers free wi-fi,
reviews in the Guide only highlight places where
there is no wi-fi or where you have to pay for it.

Living and/or working in Chile

There are plenty of short-term work opportunities
for foreigners in Chile; the difficulty lies in obtaining
and maintaining a work visa.

A tourist card does not allow you to undertake
any **paid employment** in Chile – for this, you need
to get a work visa before you enter the country,
which can either be arranged by your employer in
Chile or by yourself on presentation (to your
embassy or consulate) of an employment contract
authorized by a Chilean public notary.

You can't swap a tourist card for a work visa while
you're in Chile, which means that legally you can't
just go out and find a job – though many language
schools are happy to ignore the rules when
employing teachers.

ROUGH GUIDES TRAVEL INSURANCE

Rough Guides has teamed up with WorldNomads.com to offer great travel insurance deals.
Policies are available to residents of over 150 countries, with cover for a wide range of
adventure sports, 24hr emergency assistance, high levels of medical and evacuation cover and
a stream of travel safety information. Roughguides.com users can take advantage of their
policies online 24/7, from anywhere in the world – even if you're already travelling. And since
plans often change when you're on the road, you can extend your policy and even claim
online. Roughguides.com users who buy travel insurance with WorldNomads.com can also
leave a positive footprint and donate to a community development project. For more
information go to ⓦ roughguides.com/shop.

If you're pre-planning a longer stay, consult the websites of the **Overseas Jobs Express** (Ⓦ overseasjobs.com) and the **International Career and Employment Center** (Ⓦ international jobs.org); both list internships, jobs and volunteer opportunities across the world.

Many students come to Chile taking advantage of semester or **year-abroad programmes** offered by their universities. Go to Ⓦ studyabroad.com for links and listings to study programmes worldwide.

Teaching English

Demand for native-speaking English teachers in Chilean cities is high and makes **language teaching** an obvious work option. Though it can be competitive, it's relatively easy to find work either teaching general English in private language schools or business English within companies. A lucky few get by with minimal teaching experience, but with an **EFL** (English Language Teaching), **TEFL** (Teaching English as a Foreign Language) or **CELTA** (Certificate in English Language Teaching to Adults) qualification you're in a far better position to get a job with a reputable employer. The most lucrative work is private, one-to-one lessons, which are best sought through word-of-mouth or by placing an ad in a local newspaper. The British Council website (Ⓦ britishcouncil.org) has a list of vacancies.

Volunteering

Opportunities for work need not be limited to language teaching. You can easily become a **volunteer** in Chile, but you'll often have to pay for the privilege. Many organizations target people on gap years (at whatever stage in their lives) and offer placements on both inner city and environmental projects. For free or low-cost volunteer positions have a look at the excellent Ⓦ volunteersouthamerica.net.

STUDY AND WORK PROGRAMMES

AFS Intercultural Programs Ⓦ afs.org. Intercultural exchange organization with programmes in over 50 countries.

Amerispan Ⓦ amerispan.com. Highly rated educational travel company that specializes in language courses, but also runs volunteer programmes all over Latin America.

British Council Ⓦ britishcouncil.org. Produces a free leaflet which details study opportunities abroad. The website has a list of current job vacancies for recruiting TEFL teachers for posts worldwide.

Council on International Educational Exchange (CIEE) Ⓦ ciee.org. Leading NGO offering study programmes and volunteer projects around the world.

Earthwatch Institute Ⓦ earthwatch.org. Scientific expedition project that spans over fifty countries with environmental and archeological ventures worldwide.

Rainforest Concern Ⓦ rainforestconcern.org. Volunteering opportunities protecting threatened habitats in South and Central America. The Chilean project is based in the Nasampulli Reserve in the south of the country.

Raleigh International Ⓦ raleighinternational.org. Volunteer projects across the world for young travellers.

Mail

The Chilean **postal service** is very reliable for international items, but can be surprisingly erratic for domestic items. A letter from Santiago takes about five days to reach Europe, a little less time to reach North America and usually no more than a couple of weeks to more remote destinations. Allow a few extra days for letters posted from other towns and cities in Chile. Do not send any gifts to Chile using regular post; theft is extremely common for incoming shipments. For important shipping to Chile try express services such as FedEx and DHL.

Post offices are marked by a blue Correos sign, and are usually on or near the Plaza de Armas of any town; postboxes are blue, and bear the blue Correos symbol.

Maps

No two **road maps** of Chile are identical, and none is absolutely correct. The bulk of errors lie in the representation of dirt roads: some maps mark them incorrectly as tarred roads, some leave out a random selection of dirt roads altogether, and some mark them quite clearly where nothing exists at all.

You'll find a number of reliable country maps, including the **Rough Guides'** detailed, waterproof Chile map. The comprehensive **TurisTel** map is printed in the back of its guides to Chile and also published in a separate booklet. Sernatur produces a good fold-out map of the whole of Chile, called the Gran Mapa Caminero de Chile, on sale at the main office in Santiago, and an excellent map of the north, called the Mapa Rutero Turístico Macroregión Norte, free from Sernatur offices in Santiago and the north. Other useful maps include **Auto Mapa's** Rutas de Chile series, distributed internationally. Outside Chile, also look for the **Reise Know-How Verlag** and **Nelles Verlag** maps of Chile, which combine clear road detail along with contours and colour tinting.

You can pick up free and usually adequate street plans in the tourist office of most cities, but better by far are those contained in the Turistel guidebooks, with a map for practically every town and village you're likely to want to visit. Bookshops and kiosks sell street-indexed maps of Santiago, but the most comprehensive A–Z of Santiago appears in the back of the CTC phone directory.

The best maps to use for **hiking** are the series of **JLM** maps, which cover some of the main national parks and occasionally extend into Argentina. They're produced in collaboration with Conaf and are available in bookshops and some souvenir or outdoor stores.

Money

The basic unit of currency is the peso, usually represented by the $ sign (and by CH$ in this book, for clarity). Many hotels, particularly the more expensive ones, accept US dollars cash (and will give you a discount for paying this way; see p.30). Apart from this, you'll be expected to pay for everything in local currency. You may, however, come across prices quoted in the mysterious "UF". This stands for *unidad de fomento* and is an index-linked monetary unit that is adjusted (every minute) daily to remain in line with inflation. The only time you're likely to come across it is if you rent a vehicle (your liability, in the event of an accident, will probably be quoted in UFs on the rental contract). You'll find the exchange rate of the UF against the Chilean peso in the daily newspapers, along with the rates for all the other currencies. Note that prices throughout the guide are quoted in either pesos or dollars, according to how the establishment or company in question quotes them on the ground.

Credit and debit cards can be used either in **ATM**s or over the counter. MasterCard, Visa and American Express are accepted just about everywhere, but other cards may not be recognized. Alternatively, pick up a pre-paid debit card such as Travelex's Cash Passport (℗ travelex.co.uk).

Travellers' cheques should always be in US dollars, and though most brands are accepted, it's best to be on the safe side and take one of the main brands such as American Express, Citibank or Thomas Cook. You will have to change them in a **casa de cambio** (exchange bureau), usually for a small commission.

Opening hours and public holidays

Most **shops and services** are open Monday to Friday from 9am to 1pm and 3pm to 6pm or 7pm, and on Saturday from 10am or 11am until 2pm. Supermarkets stay open at lunchtime and may close as late as 11pm on weekdays and Saturdays in big cities. Large shopping malls are often open all day on Sundays. **Banks** have more limited hours, generally Monday to Friday from 9am to 2pm, but *casas de cambio* tend to use the same opening hours as shops.

Museums are nearly always shut on Mondays, and are often free on Sundays. Many tourist offices only open Monday to Friday throughout the year, with a break for lunch, but in summer (usually between Dec 15 and March 15) some increase their weekday hours and open on Saturday and sometimes Sunday; note that their hours are subject to frequent change. Post offices don't close at lunchtime on weekdays and are open on Saturdays from 9am to 1pm.

February is the main holiday month in Chile, when there's an exodus from the big cities to the beaches or the Lake District, leaving some shops and restaurants closed. February is also an easy time to get around in Santiago, as the city appears half-abandoned.

MAJOR HOLIDAYS

January 1 New Year's Day (*Año nuevo*)
Easter Good Friday, Easter Saturday and Easter Sunday are the climax to Holy Week (*Semana Santa*)
May 1 Labour Day (*Día del Trabajo*)
May 21 *Combate Naval de Iquique*. A Remembrance Day celebrating the end of the War of the Pacific after the naval victory at Iquique
June 15 Corpus Christi
June, last Monday San Pedro and San Pablo
August 15 Assumption of the Virgin
September 18 National Independence Day (*Fiestas Patrias*), in celebration of the first provisional government of 1810
September 19 Armed Forces Day (*Día del Ejército*)
October 12 Columbus Day (*Día de la Raza*), marking the discovery of America
November 1 All Saints' Day (*Todos los Santos*)
December 8 Immaculate Conception
December 25 Christmas Day (*Navidad*)

Phones

In 2013, the government completed the roll-out of a new numbering system, adding a "2" to the start of every fixed line number. While many businesses have still not updated their details, most landline numbers now nevertheless consist of seven or eight digits, preceded by the city/area code; if dialling from the same area, drop the city or area code and dial the seven or eight digits directly. If you are making a long-distance call you need to first dial a "carrier code" (for example "188" for

CALLING HOME FROM ABROAD

To make an international call, dial the "carrier code" (see p.49), then "0", and then the destination's country code (see below) before the rest of the number. Note that the initial zero is omitted from the area code when dialling numbers in the UK, Ireland, Australia and New Zealand from abroad.

US and Canada + 1
Australia + 61
New Zealand + 64
UK + 44
Republic of Ireland + 353
South Africa + 27

Telefónica or "181" for Movistar), then an area code (for example "2" for the Santiago metropolitan region or "32" for the Valparaíso region) and finally the number itself. Mobile phone numbers have eight digits. When calling from a landline to a mobile, dial "09" and then the rest of the number (for mobile to mobile calls, the "09" is not necessary).

Using **phonecards** is a practical way to phone abroad, and it's worth stocking up on them in major cities, as you can't always buy them elsewhere. Alternatively there are dozens of call centres or **centros de llamadas** in most cities. Another convenient option is to take along an **international calling card**. The least expensive way to call home, however, is via Skype.

The cheapest way to use your mobile is to pick up a local sim card, though you may also have to get your phone unlocked to ensure it works. The main operators are Movistar, Entel and Claro, and you'll find several branches of each in the larger cities.

Shopping

While Chile's handicrafts (*artesanía*) are nowhere near as diverse or colourful as in Peru or Bolivia, you can still find a range of beautiful souvenirs, which are usually sold in *ferias artesanales* (craft markets) on or near the central squares of the main towns. As for day-to-day essentials, you'll be able to locate just about everything you need, from sun block to contact lens solution, in the main towns across the country.

The finest and arguably most beautiful goods you can buy in Chile are the items – mainly jewellery – made of **lapis lazuli**, the deep-blue semi-precious stone found only in Chile and Afghanistan. The best place to buy these is in Bellavista, Santiago: note that the deeper the colour of the stone, the better its quality. Though certainly less expensive than lapis exports sold abroad, they're still pricey.

Most *artesanía* is considerably less expensive. In the **Norte Grande**, the most common articles are alpaca sweaters, gloves and scarves, which you'll find in *altiplano* villages like Parinacota, or in Arica and Iquique. The quality is usually fairly low, but they're inexpensive and very attractive all the same. In the **Norte Chico**, you can pick up some beautiful leather goods, particularly in the crafts markets of La Serena. You might also be tempted to buy a bottle of pisco there, so that you can recreate that pisco sour experience back home – though you're probably better off getting it at a supermarket in Santiago before you leave, to save yourself carting it about. The **Central Valley**, as the agricultural heartland of Chile, is famous for its *huaso* gear, and you'll find brightly coloured ponchos and stiff straw hats in the numerous working *huaso* shops. The highlight in the **Lake District** is the traditional Mapuche silver jewellery, while the **far south** is a good place to buy chunky, colourful knitwear.

A range of these goods can also be bought in the major crafts markets in **Santiago**, notably Los Dominicos market. Also worth checking out are Santiago's little **flea markets** (see p.86).

Hard **haggling** is neither commonly practised nor expected in Chile, though a bit of bargaining is in order at many markets. It's also worth trying to bargain down the price of hotel rooms, especially outside the peak months of January and February.

Time

As of 2015, Chile remains on what used to be its Daylight Saving Time throughout the year, just three hours behind GMT, meaning the sun is generally overhead in the late afternoon and mornings are dark and cold. Easter Island is two hours behind the mainland.

Tourist information

Chile's government-run tourist board is called **Sernatur** (ⓦ sernatur.cl). There's a large office in Santiago, plus branches in every provincial capital. It produces a huge amount of material, including themed booklets on camping, skiing, national parks, beaches, thermal springs and so on. In smaller towns you're more likely to find a municipal **Oficina de Turismo**, sometimes attached to the

Municipalidad (town hall) and usually with a very limited supply of printed information to hand out. If there's no separate tourist office it's worth trying the Municipalidad itself. Another source of information is the excellent series of TurisTel guidebooks, published annually by the Chilean phone company CTC, and available at numerous pavement kiosks in Santiago, and CTC offices in Chilean cities. They come in three volumes, covering the north, the centre and the south, and give extremely detailed information on even the tiniest of places, with comprehensive street plans and road maps. The English translation, available at many kiosks, however, suffers from infrequent updating.

GOVERNMENT WEBSITES

Australian Department of Foreign Affairs Ⓦ dfat.gov.au.
British Foreign & Commonwealth Office Ⓦ fco.gov.uk.
Canadian Department of Foreign Affairs Ⓦ international.gc.ca.
Irish Department of Foreign Affairs Ⓦ foreignaffairs.gov.ie.
New Zealand Ministry of Foreign Affairs Ⓦ mfat.govt.nz.
South African Department of Foreign Affairs Ⓦ www.dfa.gov.za.
US State Department Ⓦ travel.state.gov.

OTHER USEFUL WEBSITES

Chilean Austral Ⓦ chileaustral.com. Website dedicated to tourism in Chilean Patagonia, including city guides, national parks, hotels and weather forecasts.
I Love Chile Ⓦ ilovechile.cl. Useful website with news, features, music and blogs, plus its own online radio station.
Latin America Bureau Ⓦ lab.org.uk. The website of this well-respected UK-based charity has the latest news, analysis and information from across the region, including Chile.
South American Explorers Ⓦ saexplorers.org. Useful site of the long-established travel NGO. Offers travel advisories and warnings, trip reports, a bulletin board and links with other sites.
Turismo Chile Ⓦ chiletourism.travel. Descriptions of the major attractions in each region, with some historical and cultural background.

Travellers with disabilities

Chile makes very few provisions for people with disabilities, and travellers with mobility problems will have to contend with a lack of lifts, high kerbs, dangerous potholes on pavements and worse. However, Chileans are courteous people and are likely to offer assistance when needed. Spacious, specially designed toilets are becoming more common in airports and the newer shopping malls, but restaurants and bars are progressing at a slower pace. New public buildings are legally required to provide **disabled access**, and there will usually be a full range of facilities in the more expensive hotels. It is worth employing the help of the **local tourist office** for information on the most suitable place to stay. Public transport on the other hand is far more of a challenge. Most bus companies do not have any dedicated disabled facilities so, given that reserved disabled parking is increasingly common, travelling with your **own vehicle** might be the easier option.

Travelling with children

Families are highly regarded in Latin American societies, and Chile is no exception. Chile's **restaurants** are well used to catering for children and will happily provide smaller portions for younger mouths. In hotels, you should try to negotiate cheaper rates. The main health hazards to watch out for are the heat and sun. Very high factor suncream can be difficult to come by in remote towns so it is best to stock up on **sunblock** at pharmacies in the bigger cities. Always remember that the sun in Chile is fierce, so hats and bonnets are essential; this is especially true in the south where the ozone layer is particularly thin. **High altitudes** may cause children problems and, like adults, they must acclimatize before walking too strenuously above 2000m. If you intend to travel with babies and very young children to high altitudes, consult your doctor for advice before you leave.

Long-distances buses charge for each seat so you'll only pay less if a child is sitting on your knee. On **city buses**, however, small children often travel for free but will be expected to give up their seat for paying customers without one. Airline companies generally charge a third less for passengers under 12 so look out for last-minute **discount flights** – they can make flying an affordable alternative to an arduous bus ride.

Santiago and around

56 Santiago

75 Arrival and departure

76 Getting around

78 Information

78 Accommodation

80 Eating and drinking

84 Nightlife

85 Entertainment

86 Gay and lesbian Santiago

86 Shopping

88 Directory

89 Cajón del Maipo

91 Los Andes and around

SANHATTAN WITH THE GRAN TORRE SANTIAGO

1

Santiago and around

Set on a wide plain near the foot of the Andes, Santiago boasts one of the most dazzling backdrops of any capital city on earth. The views onto the towering cordillera after a rainstorm clears the air are truly magnificent, especially in winter, when the snow-covered peaks rise behind the city like a giant white rampart against the blue sky (though smog, unfortunately, often obscures such vistas). The city itself is a rapidly expanding metropolis of around seven million people, and though long in the shadow of some other major South American cities, such as Buenos Aires and Rio de Janeiro, it has its own proud identity.

Santiago is divided into 32 autonomous *comunas*, most of them squat, flat suburbs stretching out from the heart of the city. The historic centre, in contrast, is compact, manageable, and has a pleasant atmosphere. Part of the appeal comes from the fact that it's so green: tall, luxuriant trees fill the main square, and there are numerous meticulously landscaped parks. Above all, though, it's the all-pervading sense of energy that makes the place so alluring, with crowds of Santiaguinos constantly milling through narrow streets packed with shoe-shiners, fruit barrows, news kiosks and sellers of everything from coat hangers to pirated DVDs.

Architecturally, the city is a bit of a hotchpotch, thanks to a succession of earthquakes and a spate of haphazard rebuilding in the 1960s and 1970s. Ugly office blocks and shopping arcades (*galerías*) compete for space with beautifully maintained colonial buildings, while east of the centre Santiago's economic boom is reflected in the glittering new commercial buildings, skyscrapers and luxury hotels of the *comunas* of Vitacura, Providencia and Las Condes. These different faces are part of a wider set of contrasts – between the American-style shopping malls in the *barrios altos*, for example, and the old-fashioned shops in the historic centre; between the modish lounge bars and the greasy-spoon cafes known as *fuentes de soda*; and, in particular, between the sharp-suited professionals and the scores of street sellers scrambling to make a living. It's not a place of excesses, however: homelessness is minimal compared with many other cities of its size, and Santiago is pretty safe.

Santiago is also a great base for exploring the surrounding region. With the **Andes** so close and accessible, you can be right in the mountains in an hour or two. In winter people go **skiing** for the day; in warmer months the **Cajón del Maipo** offers fantastic trekking, horseriding and rafting. The port city of Valparaíso (see p.96) and beach resorts in and around Viña del Mar (see p.112) are in day-trip territory from the capital, while nearby villages such as **Los Andes** and **Pomaire** can provide a relaxing antidote to Santiago's bustle. Still more tempting are the many **vineyards** within easy reach (see box, p.89).

The legend of the slipping crown p.63
Palacios of the alameda p.68
Treks around Santiago p.74
Café con piernas p.80
Top 5 places to eat traditional Chilean food p.81

Crossing into Argentina p.88
Wine tours near Santiago p.89
Hiking in the Monumento Nacional El Morado p.90
Pottery in Pomaire p.91
Skiing near Santiago p.92

CATEDRAL METROPOLITANA, PLAZA DE ARMAS, SANTIAGO

Highlights

❶ Plaza de Armas Gaze at the colonial
architecture surrounding Santiago's lively central
plaza – or sit on a bench and take in the hustle
and bustle. **See p.57**

❷ Museo Chileno de Arte Precolombino
This exquisite collection of artefacts from
dozens of pre-Hispanic civilizations features fine
tapestries, intricate ceramics and dazzling
jewels. **See p.61**

**❸ Museo de la Memoria y los Derechos
Humanos** This large new museum is dedicated
to remembering the victims of Chile's
dictatorship. It does not make comfortable

viewing but it is essential to understanding
those dark years. **See p.70**

❹ Mercado Central and La Vega Explore the
city's two main markets and sample a selection
of excellent fresh fish and seafood. **See p.70**

❺ Cerro San Cristóbal Ride the elevator to the
top of this steep hill where, on a clear day, you
have great views of the snowcapped Andes
towering over the city. **See p.73**

❻ Andean skiing Skiers and snowboarders will
delight in the world-class ski areas near
Santiago, including the world-famous Portillo
resort. **See p.92**

HIGHLIGHTS ARE MARKED ON THE MAP ON P.56 & PP.58–59

1

Santiago

Increasingly becoming a destination in its own right rather than simply the entry point into Chile, **SANTIAGO** is a cultural, economic and historical hub, and the best place to get a handle on the country's identity. Dipping into the city's vibrant and constantly developing cultural scene, checking out its museums, and dining at its varied restaurants will really help you make the most of your time in this kaleidoscopic country.

You can get round many of Santiago's attractions on foot in two to three days. The historic centre has the bustling **Plaza de Armas** at its core, while north of downtown, on the other side of the Río Mapocho, it's an easy funicular ride up **Cerro San Cristóbal**, whose summit provides unrivalled views. At its foot, **Barrio Bellavista** is replete with cafés, restaurants, bars and clubs. West of the centre, the once glamorous *barrios* that housed Santiago's moneyed classes at the beginning of the twentieth century make for rewarding, romantic wanders, and contain some splendid old mansions and museums. Moving east into Providencia and Las Condes, the tone is newer and flasher, with shiny malls and upmarket restaurants, as well as the crafts market at **Los Dominicos**.

Brief history

In 1540, some seven years after Francisco Pizarro conquered Cuzco in Peru, he dispatched **Pedro de Valdivia** southwards to claim and settle more territory for the

Spanish crown. After eleven months of travelling, Valdivia and his 150 men reached what he considered to be a suitable site for a new city, and, on February 12, 1541, officially founded "Santiago de la Nueva Extremadura", wedged into a triangle of land bounded by the Río Mapocho to the north, its southern branch to the south and the rocky Santa Lucía hill to the east. A native population of **Picunche** was scattered around the region, but this didn't deter Valdivia from getting down to business: with great alacrity the main square was established and the surrounding streets were marked out with a string and ruler, a fort was built in the square (thus named "Plaza de Armas") and several other buildings were erected. Six months later they were all razed in a Picunche raid.

The town was doggedly rebuilt to the same plans, and Santiago began to take on the shape of a new colonial capital. But nine years after founding it, the Spaniards, in search of gold, shifted their attention to Arauco in the south, and Santiago became something of a backwater. Following the violent Mapuche uprising in 1553, however, the Spaniards were forced to abandon their towns south of the Biobío, and many returned to Santiago. Nonetheless, growth continued to be very slow: settlers were never large in number, and what opportunities the land offered were thwarted by strict trade restrictions. Moreover, expansion was repeatedly knocked back by regular **earthquakes**.

Independence

Santiago started to look like a real capital during the course of the eighteenth century, as trade restrictions were eased, more wealth was created, and the population increased. However, it wasn't until after **independence** in 1818 that expansion really got going, as the rich clamoured to build themselves glamorous mansions and the state erected beautiful public buildings such as the Teatro Municipal.

Santiago today

As the city entered the twentieth century it began to push eastwards into the new *barrio alto* and north into Bellavista. The horizontal spread has gone well beyond these limits since then, gobbling up outlying towns and villages at great speed; Gran Santiago now stretches 40km by 40km. Its central zones have shot up vertically, too, particularly in Providencia and Las Condes, where the showy high-rise buildings reflect the country's rapid economic growth since the 1990s. Despite this dramatic transformation, however, the city's central core still sticks to the same street pattern marked out by Pedro de Valdivia in 1541, and its first public space, the Plaza de Armas, is still at the heart of its street life.

Plaza de Armas and around

The **Plaza de Armas** is the centre of Santiago and the country, both literally – all distances to the rest of Chile are measured from here – and symbolically. It was the first public space laid out by Pedro de Valdivia when he founded the city in 1541 and quickly became the nucleus of Santiago's administrative, commercial and social life. This is where the young capital's most important seats of power – the law courts, the governor's palace, and the cathedral – were built, and where its markets, bullfights (no longer allowed), festivals and other public activities took place. Four and a half centuries later, this is still where the city's pulse beats loudest, and half an hour's people-watching here is perhaps the best introduction to Santiago.

These days the open market space has been replaced by flower gardens and numerous trees; palms, poplars and eucalyptus tower over benches packed with giggling schoolchildren, gossiping old men, lovers, tourists, indulgent grandmothers and packs of uniformed shop girls on their lunch break. Thirsty dogs hang around

1

the fountain; shoe-shiners polish the feet of dour businessmen clutching *El Mercurio*; and ancient-looking chess players hold sombre tournaments inside the bandstand. Against this is a backdrop of constant noise supplied by street performers, singers and evangelical preachers. Meanwhile, a constant ebb and flow of people march in and out of the great civic and religious buildings enclosing the square.

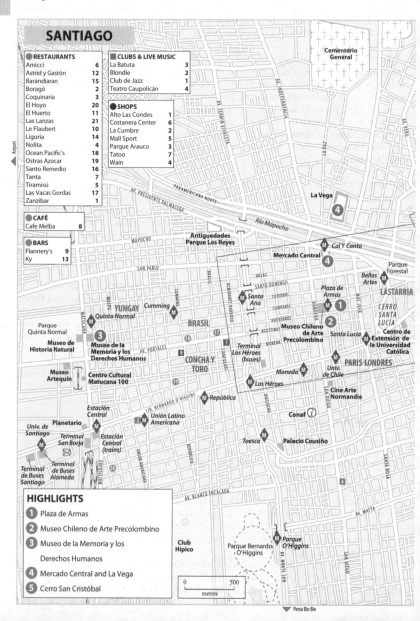

SANTIAGO

● RESTAURANTS	
Amicci	6
Astrid y Gastón	12
Barandiaran	15
Boragó	2
Coquinaria	3
El Hoyo	20
El Huerto	11
Las Lanzas	21
Le Flaubert	10
Liguria	14
Nolita	4
Ocean Pacific's	18
Ostras Azocar	19
Santo Remedio	16
Tanta	7
Tiramisú	5
Las Vacas Gordas	17
Zanzibar	1

● CAFÉ	
Cafe Melba	8

● BARS	
Flannery's	9
Ky	13

■ CLUBS & LIVE MUSIC	
La Batuta	3
Blondie	2
Club de Jazz	1
Teatro Caupolicán	4

● SHOPS	
Alto Las Condes	1
Costanera Center	6
La Cumbre	2
Mall Sport	5
Parque Arauco	3
Tatoo	7
Wain	4

HIGHLIGHTS

1 Plaza de Armas

2 Museo Chileno de Arte Precolombino

3 Museo de la Memoria y los Derechos Humanos

4 Mercado Central and La Vega

5 Cerro San Cristóbal

0 — 500 metres

Correo Central

Plaza de Armas 559 • Mon–Fri 8.30am–7pm, Sat 8.30am–1pm

On the northwest corner of the Plaza de Armas stands the **Correo Central** (central post office), whose interior, with its tiered galleries crowned by a beautiful glass roof, is every bit as impressive as its elaborate facade. It was built in 1882 on the foundations of what had been the Palacio de los Gobernadores (governors' palace)

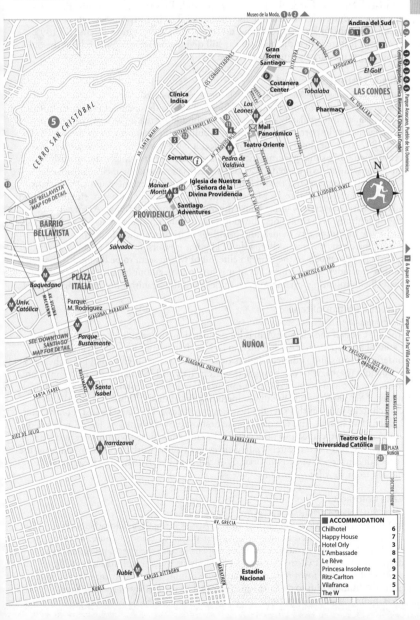

■ ACCOMMODATION	
Chilhotel	6
Happy House	7
Hotel Orly	3
L'Ambassade	8
Le Rêve	4
Princesa Insolente	9
Ritz-Carlton	2
Vilafranca	5
The W	1

during colonial times, and the Palacio de los Presidentes de Chile (presidential palace) after independence.

Municipalidad

Plaza de Armas s/n

On the northeast corner of the Plaza de Armas is the pale, Neoclassical edifice of Santiago's **Municipalidad**. The first *cabildo* (town hall) was erected on this site back in the early seventeenth century and also contained the city's prison. Several reconstructions and restorations have taken place since then, most recently in 1895. A curious feature is that the basement is still divided into the original cells of the old prison, now used by the tourist office (see p.78).

Museo Histórico Nacional

Plaza de Armas • Tues–Sun 10am–6pm • Free • ☎ 2 2411 7010, ⓦ museohistoriconacional.cl

Wedged between the Correo and the Municipalidad is the splendid **Palacio de la Real Audiencia**, an immaculately preserved colonial building that's borne witness to some of Santiago's most important turns of history. Built by the Spanish Crown between 1804 and 1807 to house the royal courts of justice, it had served this purpose for just two years when Chile's first government junta assembled here to replace the Spanish governor with its own elected leader. Eight years later it was the meeting place of Chile's first Congress, and the building was the seat of government until 1846, when President Bulnes moved to La Moneda. The Palacio's grand old rooms, situated around a large central courtyard, today house the **Museo Histórico Nacional**. Arranged chronologically over two floors, the rooms are crammed with eclectic relics of the past, including furniture, city models and paintings of historic rather than artistic value – note the classic portrait of Bernardo O'Higgins upstairs, followed by a row of paintings of members of the Chilean elite, all of whom seem to be doing their best to imitate the independence hero. All of it is fun to look at, but it's a little too chaotic to be really illuminating, even if you can understand the Spanish-only information panels.

Catedral Metropolitana

Plaza de Armas • Mon–Sat 9am–7pm, Sun 9am–noon • Free

The west side of the Plaza de Armas is dominated by the grandiose stone bulk of the **Catedral Metropolitana**. A combination of Neoclassical and Baroque styles, with its orderly columns and pediment and its ornate bell towers, the cathedral bears the mark of **Joaquín Toesca,** who was brought over from Italy in 1780 to oversee its completion. Toesca went on to become the most important architect of colonial Chile, designing many of Santiago's public buildings, including La Moneda. This is actually the fifth church to be built on this site; the first was burnt down by Picunche just months after Valdivia had it built, and the others were destroyed by earthquakes. Inside, take a look at the main altar, carved out of marble and richly embellished with bronze and lapis lazuli. Note also the intricately crafted silver frontal, the work of Bavarian Jesuits in the sixteenth century. Extensive restoration work began in 2014, and the facade may be hidden from view for some time.

Casa Colorada

Merced 860 • Closed for restoration at time of writing

Just off the southeast corner of the Plaza de Armas is the **Casa Colorada**, built in 1769 and generally considered to be Santiago's best-preserved colonial house. With its clay-tiled roof, row of balconied windows opening onto the street and distinctive, deep-red walls, the two-storey mansion certainly provides a striking example of an eighteenth-century town residence. The house is built around two large patios, and hosts the humble **Museo de Santiago**, dedicated to the history of the city from pre-Columbian to modern times.

Ex-Congreso Nacional

Morandé and Compañía • Not generally open to the public

The impressive white, classically built **Ex Congreso Nacional**, set amid lush gardens two blocks west of the Plaza de Armas, is where Congress used to meet until it was dissolved on September 11, 1973, the day of the coup d'état. In 1990, following the end of the military regime, a new congress building was erected in Valparaíso, although members of Congress still use this one for its library and meeting rooms.

Museo Chileno de Arte Precolombino

Compañía and Bandera • Tues–Sun 10am–6pm • CH$3500 • ☎ 2 2928 1500, ⓦ precolombino.cl

Just off the southwest corner of the Plaza de Armas is the beautifully restored 1807 Real Casa de la Aduana (the old royal customs house), which now houses the **Museo Chileno de Arte Precolombino**. Perhaps Chile's best museum, it was reopened in 2014 after a thorough renovation.

The museum's collection spans a period of about ten thousand years and covers an area stretching from present-day Mexico down to southern Chile, brilliantly illustrating the artistic wealth and diversity of Latin America's many cultures. The items were selected primarily on the basis of their artistic merit, rather than on their scientific or anthropological significance. As well as the permanent exhibits in the basement and upstairs, the ground floor has three rooms containing temporary exhibitions.

Chile antes de Chile

The basement houses the "Chile antes de Chile" (Chile before Chile) exhibition, which showcases items from pre-Columbian indigenous groups native to the sliver of land and islands that are now Chile. Highlights here include **Aymara** silverware, wooden **Easter Island** statues and **Inca** tunics and bags with geometric designs that would not look out of a place in an Andes village market today, although these examples are hundreds of years old. The curious exhibit that looks like a grass skirt is also a relic from the Inca, who made it all the way down to central Chile during their expansion in the fifteenth century. Known as a **quipú**, it consists of many strands of wool attached to a single cord, and was used to keep records by means of a complex system of knots tied in the strands.

América Precolombina

The upstairs rooms hold works from around Latin America, arranged geographically. Many of the best items are grouped together in room 1, **Obras Maestras** (master works), including a beautifully worked Aztec ear ornament of pure gold, one of the few **Aztec** relics to escape being melted down by the Spanish *conquistadores*, and a huge bas-relief carving of a **Mayan** armed warrior with two small figures at his feet.

One of the most startling pieces in the collection is found in the **Mesoamérica** section (corresponding to present-day Mexico and central America) – a statue of **Xipé-Totec**. This god of spring is represented as a man covered in the skin of a monkey, exposing both male and female genitalia. At the time of the Spanish conquest, the cult of Xipé-Totec was widespread through the region, and was celebrated in a bizarre ritual in which a young man would cover himself with the skin of a sacrificial victim and wear it until it rotted off, revealing his young, fresh skin and symbolizing the growth of new vegetation from the earth.

In the **Area Intermedia**, covering what is now Ecuador, Colombia, and central America, look out for wonderful **coca-leaf-chewing figures** known as *coqueros*, carved with a telltale lump in their mouth by the Capulí culture. The collection's best textiles, meanwhile, are preserved in the cool environment of the **Sala Textil**, illuminated by motion-sensitive lighting. Hanging here is a fragment of painted cloth depicting three human figures with fanged jaws. The oldest textile in the museum, it was produced by the Chavín culture almost three thousand years ago, and is still in astonishingly good condition.

DOWNTOWN SANTIAGO

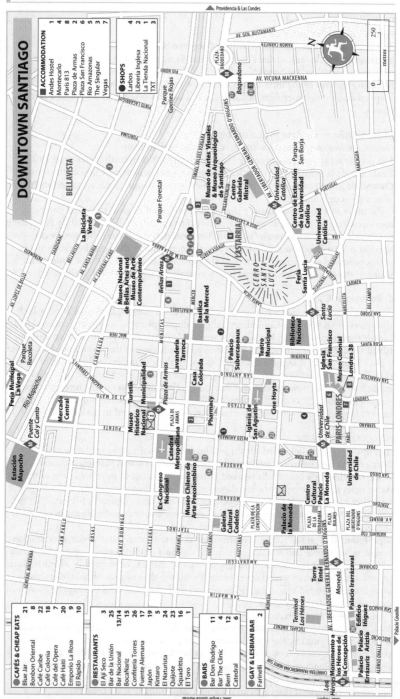

▲ Providencia & Las Condes

N

0 — 250 metres

■ ACCOMMODATION

Andes Hostel	1
Montecarlo	4
Paris 813	8
Plaza de Armas	2
Plaza San Francisco	6
Rio Amazonas	5
The Singular	3
Vegas	7

■ SHOPS

Larbos	4
Librería Inglesa	2
La Tienda Nacional	1
TXT	3

● CAFÉS & CHEAP EATS

Blue Jar	21
Bonbon Oriental	8
Café Caribe	22
Café Colonia	18
Café del Opera	7
Café Haití	20
Emporio La Rosa	9
El Rápido	10

● RESTAURANTS

El Ají Seco	3
Bar de la Unión	25
Bar Nacional	13/14
BocaNariz	15
Confitería Torres	26
Fuente Alemana	17
Japón	19
Kintaro	5
El Naturista	24
Quijote	23
Squadritto	16
El Toro	1

● BARS

Bar Don Rodrigo	11
Bar The Clinic	4
Berri	12
Catedral	6

● GAY & LESBIAN BAR

Farinelli	2

Ahumada

One of the city's busiest pedestrian thoroughfares, **Ahumada**, runs south from the west side of the Plaza de Armas to the Alameda. Walking down, you'll pass sombre doorways leading into labyrinthine shopping arcades, *confiterías* and, between Agustinas and Moneda, the famous **Café Caribe** (see p.80) and **Café Haiti** (see p.80). Take a moment to pop into the **Banco de Chile**, between Huérfanos and Agustinas; its vast hall, polished counters and beautiful old clock have barely changed since the bank opened in 1925.

Huérfanos and around

One of the city's busiest pedestrian streets, **Huérfanos** crosses Ahumada at right angles, one block south of the plaza, and is lined with numerous banks and cinemas. Several places of interest are dotted among the shops, office blocks and *galerías* of the surrounding streets.

Basílica de la Merced

Mac Iver 341 • Mon–Fri 10am–6pm • Free

The **Basílica de la Merced** is a towering, Neo-Renaissance structure just off Huérfanos, on the corner of Merced and MacIver, with a beautifully carved eighteenth-century pulpit. Attached to the church is a small **museum**, closed for restoration at time of writing, which houses a collection of Easter Island artefacts, including a wooden **rongo rongo tablet**, carved in the undeciphered Easter Island script – one of just 29 left in the world.

Teatro Municipal

Agustinas 749 • ☎ 800 471000, ⊛ municipal.cl

A splendid French-style Neoclassical building, the **Teatro Municipal** boasts a dazzling white facade of arches, columns and perfect symmetry. This has been the capital's most prestigious ballet, opera and classical music venue (see p.85) since its inauguration in 1857. It's worth asking to have a look around inside; the main auditorium is quite a sight, with its sumptuous red upholstery and crystal chandeliers.

Palacio Subercaseaux

Agustinas 741 • Not open to the public

Opposite the Teatro Municipal, and in the same French Neoclassical style, is the **Palacio Subercaseaux**, topped with a fine mansard roof. It was built at the beginning of the twentieth century for the Subercaseaux, one of the country's wealthiest families, after they had lived in Paris for twenty years, and it is said that Señora Subercaseaux would only agree to return to Santiago if her window looked out on to the Teatro Municipal. Today it is used by banks and the airforce officers' club.

Iglesia de San Agustín

Agustinas and Estado • Daily 8am–8pm • Free

The yellow church of **San Agustín** dates from 1608 but has been extensively rebuilt since then. The chief interest within its highly decorative interior is the wooden carving of Christ, just left of the main altar as you face it (see box below).

THE LEGEND OF THE SLIPPING CROWN

Known as the *Cristo de Mayo*, the wooden carving of Christ in the Iglesia de San Augustín (see above) is the subject of an intriguing local legend. The story goes that the crown of thorns around the figure's head slipped down to its neck during the 1647 earthquake, and that when someone tried to move the crown back up to its head, the carved face of Christ began to bleed. For this reason, the crown has remained untouched ever since, still hanging around the neck.

1

Galeria Cultural Codelco

Huérfanos 1270 • Mon–Fri 9am–6pm • Free

Copper is everywhere in the gleaming, appropriately burnished headquarters of the Corporacion Nacional del Cobre de Chile, usually known simply as **Codelco**. The company – by far the world's largest producer of copper – was nationalised by Allende in the 1970s. A cash cow for the Chilean government ever since, even the most pro-free market politicians have not seriously attempted to return it to private hands. The facade of the building has copper panels, the door handles are made with anti-microbial copper, and the metal lines the interior walls. Inside, a small **gallery** open to the public offers changing exhibitions, usually themed on a slightly odd mixture of community outreach and – yes – copper.

Palacio de la Moneda and around

The presidential palace **La Moneda**, which can be approached either via the Alameda or the vast **Plaza de la Constitución**, is at the heart of the *centro cívico*, Chile's political centre. Ministers and their aides hurry back and forth between the ministry buildings in the area and the palace, while on the south side of La Moneda the newly landscaped Plaza de la Ciudadanía gives access to an underground cultural centre.

Palacio de La Moneda

Plaza de la Ciudadanía 26 • Guided visits four times daily, reserve in advance at ✉ visitas@presidencia.cl; changing of the guard on alternate days, 10am on weekdays and 11am at weekends • Free, but bring your passport for identification

One of Chile's best-known buildings, the perfect symmetry and compact elegance of the **Palacio de La Moneda** is spread across the entire block. The low-lying Neoclassical presidential palace was built between 1784 and 1805 by the celebrated Italian architect Joaquín Toesca for the purpose of housing the royal mint (hence the name *La Moneda* – literally, 'the coin'). After some forty years it became the residential palace for the presidents of Chile, starting with Manuel Bulnes in 1848 and ending with Carlos Ibáñez del Campo in 1958. At this point it stopped being used as the president's home, but it continues to be the official seat of government. On September 11, 1973, President Salvador Allende committed suicide in his office in La Moneda rather than surrender to the encroaching military (see box, p.483), and photos of the airforce strafing the palace as Pinochet's coup closed in became among the most defining images of those troubled years.

Plaza de la Constitución

The **Plaza de la Constitución** is surrounded by other important institutions, including the central bank, the foreign ministry and the finance ministry. In front of the justice ministry in the southeast corner of the square is one of Chile's few monuments to Allende, with his arm outstretched.

Centro Cultural Palacio La Moneda

Plaza de la Ciudadanía 26 • Daily 9am–9pm, exhibitions 9am–6.30pm • CH$5000, half price Mon–Fri before noon • ☎ 2 2355 6500, Ⓦ ccplm.cl

The **Centro Cultural Palacio La Moneda**, on the Alameda side of the Palacio de la Moneda, opened in 2006 as an early part of Chile's 2010 bicentennial celebrations. This flagship underground art gallery and cultural space has a huge modernist concrete central hall, which houses ever-changing exhibitions. The permanent displays in the adjacent galleries feature an eclectic array of artwork, jewellery, pottery, textiles and photography from across Chile (none of the exhibits is captioned in English). There's also an art cinema, film archive, craft store, bookshop, *Confitería Torres* branch (see p.81), restaurant and café.

1 Along the Alameda

Officially the Avenida del Libertador General Bernardo O'Higgins, Santiago's most vital east–west artery is universally known as the **Alameda**, a term used to describe a poplar-lined avenue used for strolling and recreation, and found in many Latin American cities. This one began life as *La Cañada* (or "channel"), when a branch of the Mapocho was sealed off shortly before independence, and a roadway was created over the old riverbed. A few years later, when the Supreme Director Bernardo O'Higgins decided that Santiago required an *alameda*, La Cañada was deemed the best place to put it: "There is no public boulevard where people may get together for honest relief and amusement during the resting hours, since the one known as Tajamar, because of its narrowness and irregularity, far from being cheerful, inspires sadness. La Cañada, because of its condition, extension, abundance of water and other circumstances, is the most apparent place for an alameda." Three rows of poplars were promptly planted along each side, and the Alameda was born, soon to become *the* place to take the evening promenade.

Since those quieter times the boulevard has evolved into the city's biggest, busiest, noisiest and most polluted thoroughfare. Still, it's an unavoidable axis and you'll probably spend a fair bit of time on it or under it: the main metro line runs beneath it, and some of Santiago's most interesting landmarks stand along it.

Cerro Santa Lucía and around

The lushly forested **Cerro Santa Lucía** is Santiago's most imaginative and exuberant piece of landscaping. Looking at it now, it's hard to believe that for the first three centuries of the city's development this was nothing more than a barren, rocky outcrop, completely ignored despite its historical importance – it was at the foot of this hill that Santiago was officially founded by Valdivia, on February 12, 1541. It wasn't until 1872 that the city turned its attention to Santa Lucía once more, when the mayor of Santiago, Vicuña Mackenna, enlisted the labour of 150 prisoners to transform it into a grand public park.

Quasi-Gaudíesque in appearance, with swirling pathways and Baroque terraces and turrets, this is a great place to come for panoramic views across the city. If slogging up the steps doesn't appeal, use the free lift on the western side of the park, by the junction with Huérfanos (erratic opening hours). While it's busy and safe by day, muggings have been reported in the Cerro Santa Lucía after dark.

Immediately west of the hill stands the massive **Biblioteca Nacional** (Mon–Fri 9am–7pm, Sat 9am–2pm), one of Latin America's largest libraries, with temporary exhibitions of rather specialist interest and free-to-use computers with internet.

Barrio Lastarria

ⓦ barriolastarria.com

Just east of Cerro Santa Lucía, set back from the Alameda, is the quiet, arty **Barrio Lastarria** neighbourhood, centred on the small, cobbled **Plaza Mulato Gil**, at the corner of Merced and Lastarria. As well as artists' workshops, galleries, and bookshops, the neighbourhood is well known for its sparkling restaurant and bar scene (see p.82 & p.84).

Centro Gabriela Mistral

Av O'Higgins 227 • Exhibitions Tues–Sat 10am–9pm, Sun 11am–8pm • Free • ☎ 2 2566 5500, ⓦ gam.cl

Named after famous Chilean poet Gabriela Mistral, this enormous arts centre – usually referred to as **GAM** – was an exciting new addition to Santiago's burgeoning cultural scene when it was opened in 2010. Its ten large, airy halls show off the best of Chile's art, literature, music and dance, while its plazas house contemporary sculptures, many relating to Chilean themes such as copper or the Mapuche. There's also an onsite wine shop, bookshop and antiques fair (fair Wed–Sun 11am–8pm).

Museo de Artes Visuales

José Victorino Lastarria 307 • Tues–Sun 10.30am–6.30pm • CH$1000, Sun free • ☎ 2 2638 3502, ⓦ mavi.cl

The **Museo de Artes Visuales** in the centre of Lastarria features some of the best new sculptures, painting and photography by Chile's emerging artists. It also houses the small but well-stocked **Museo Arqueológico de Santiago** (same hours and entry fee), with hats, bags, jewellery, baskets and other items from all over the country.

Iglesia San Francisco

Av O'Higgins 834 • Daily 8am–8pm • Free

The red **Iglesia San Francisco** is Santiago's oldest building, erected between 1586 and 1628. Take a look inside at the **Virgen del Socorro**, a small polychrome carving (rather lost in the vast main altar) brought to Chile on the saddle of Pedro de Valdivia in 1540 and credited with guiding him on his way, as well as fending off Indian attackers by throwing sand in their eyes. For all its age and beauty, the most remarkable feature of this church is its deep, hushed silence; you're just metres from the din of the Alameda but the traffic seems a million miles away.

Museo Colonial

Londres 4 • Mon–Fri 9.30am–1.30pm & 3–6pm, Sat & Sun 10am–2pm • CH$1000 • ⓦ museosanfrancisco.com

The monastery adjacent to the Iglesia San Francisco houses the **Museo Colonial**, which has a highly evocative collection of paintings, sculpture, furniture, keys and other objects dating from the colonial period, most of it religious and a good deal of it created in Peru, the seat of colonial government. Note the immense eighteenth-century **cedar door** of the first room you come to off the cloisters; carved into hundreds of intricately designed squares, this is one of the museum's most beautiful possessions. On the other side of the cloisters, across a peaceful, palm-filled garden, the Gran Sala hosts another highlight – an astonishing 54 paintings of the life of **St Francis of Assissi**. Dating from the seventeenth century, the paintings were all done by the Cuzco school in Peru, colonial South America's foremost art movement, who combined colourful religious imagery with indigenous motifs.

Barrio París-Londres

Formed where Calle Londres intersects Calle París, **Barrio París-Londres** is tucked behind the Iglesia San Francisco on what used to be the monastery's orchards. These sinuous, cobbled streets lined with refurbished mansions, stylish hotels and busy hostels, look like a tiny piece of Paris's Latin Quarter. Created in 1923 by a team of architects, the *barrio* is undeniably attractive but feels incongruous to its surroundings. There is, however, a dark side to the area, at Londres 38.

Londres 38

Londres 38 • Tues–Fri 10am–1pm & 3–6pm, Sat 10am–2pm; guided tours Mon–Fri noon & 4pm, Sat noon • Free entry & tour • ☎ 2 2325 0374, ⓦ londres38.cl

Londres 38, the seemingly innocuous building at Calle Londres 38 was one of the four main torture and detention centres in Santiago during the Pinochet dictatorship – and the only one not subsequently destroyed. Between September 1973 and September 1974, 96 people – considered opponents of the dictatorship – were killed here by the Dirección de Inteligencia Nacional (DINA). After a long battle by survivors, victims' families and human rights groups, the building was taken over and opened to the public in an effort to highlight the grave human rights abuses of the Pinochet years and the ongoing fight for justice. As well as displays on the building's history, Londres 38 also serves as a space for exhibitions, workshops and talks.

Universidad de Chile and around

West of Barrio París-Londres, on the Alameda, is the **Universidad de Chile**, a fine French Neoclassical building dating from 1863. Opposite is the **Bolsa de Comercio**, Santiago's stock exchange, housed in a flamboyant, French Renaissance-style building that tapers to a thin wedge at the main entrance. One block further along you reach Plaza Bulnes, flanked by the **tomb** and massive **equestrian statue of Bernardo O'Higgins** to the south, and to the north by the grey stone outline of the **Palacio de la Moneda** (see p.64), sitting with its back to the Alameda. Just west of here is a 128m telecommunications tower, known as the **Torre Entel**, the focus of New Year's Eve fireworks displays.

South of the Alameda

South of downtown, along line two on the metro, there's a clutch of interesting sights, including one of the best of Santiago's nineteenth-century French-style palaces, and, in a very different vein, a park that is a popular excursion for the city's more down-at-heel classes.

Palacio Cousiño

Dieciocho 438 • Closed for renovation at time of writing

The **Palacio Cousiño** was the most magnificent of the historic palaces that lie south of the Alameda, the one that dazzled Santiago's high society by the sheer scale of its luxury and opulence. It was built between 1870 and 1878 for Doña Isidora Goyenechea, the widow of Luis Cousiño, who had amassed a fortune with his coal and silver mines. All the furnishings and decoration were shipped over from Europe, especially France, and top European craftsmen were brought here to work on the house: Italian hand-painted tiles; Bohemian crystal chandeliers; mahogany, walnut and ebony parquet floors; a mosaic marble staircase; and French brocade and silk furnishings are just a few of the splendours of the palace. Damaged in the 2010 earthquake (see p.225), it is not clear when it will reopen to visitors.

Parque Bernardo O'Higgins

Three blocks from Ⓜ Parque O'Higgins

Perhaps the best reason to come to **Parque Bernardo O'Higgins**, a few blocks southwest of Palacio Cousiño, is to soak up the Chilean family atmosphere, as it's one of the most

---

PALACIOS OF THE ALAMEDA

Walk west of Torre Entel along the Alameda and you enter what was once the preserve of Santiago's moneyed elite, with several glorious mansions built around 1900 serving as reminders. The first to look out for is the French-style **Palacio Irarrázaval**, on the south side of the Alameda between San Ignacio and Dieciocho; built in 1906 by Cruz Montt, it now houses an old-fashioned restaurant. Adjoining it at the corner of Dieciocho, the slightly later and more ornate **Edificio Iñíguez**, by the same architect in league with Larraín Bravo, houses *Confitería Torres* (see p.81), said to be where the "national" sandwich, the Barros Luco, was invented in honour of a leading politician.

Then check out the 1917 **Palacio Ariztía**, being remodelled as the future home of Chile's constitutional court, a little further on in the next block; a fine copy of an Art Nouveau French mansion, again by Cruz Montt, it is set off by an iron-and-glass door canopy. Next door, the late-nineteenth-century **Palacio Errázuriz**, is the oldest of these Alameda mansions. It's looking a little sad these days, but its owners and previous occupants the Brazilian embassy have promised restoration work and plan to move back in once they're finished. Built for Maximiano Errázuriz, mining mogul and leading socialite, it is a soberly elegant two-storey building in a Neoclassical style. You're now standing opposite the triumphant **Monumento a los Héroes de la Concepción**, an imposing statue which borders the junction of the Alameda with the Avenida Norte Sur (the Panamericana); this is where metro Lines #1 and #2 intersect at Los Héroes station.

popular green spaces in the city. It was originally the Parque Cousiño, commissioned by Luis Cousiño, the entrepreneurial millionaire, in 1869, and the place to take your carriage rides in the late nineteenth century. These days working-class families and groups of kids flock here on summer weekends to enjoy the picnic areas, outdoor pools (very crowded), roller rink, basketball court, gut-churning rides of amusement park **Fantasilandia** (ⓦ www.fantasilandia.cl), and concert venue Movistar Arena (ⓦ movistararena.cl). There is also **El Pueblito**, a collection of adobe buildings typical of the Chilean countryside and housing several cheap restaurants, some craft stalls and a handful of small museums.

The western neighbourhoods

West of Los Héroes, the Alameda continues through the once-wealthy neighbourhoods abandoned by Santiago's well-heeled residents a few decades ago, when the moneyed classes shifted to the more fashionable east side of town. After falling into serious decline, these areas are finally coming into their own again, as a younger generation has started renovating decaying mansions, opening up trendy cafés and bookshops and injecting a new vigour into the streets.

Barrios Concha y Toro, Brasil and Yungay

One of the most beautiful neighbourhoods on the northern side of the Alameda, between Avenidas Brasil and Ricardo Cumming, is **Barrio Concha y Toro**, a jumble of twisting cobbled streets leading to a tiny round plaza with a fountain in the middle. Further north you'll find **Barrio Brasil**, one of the liveliest of the newly revived neighbourhoods, centred on the large, grand Plaza Brasil, full of children playing at the amusing cement sculpture playground and among the old silk-cotton and lime trees. Bordering Barrio Brasil to the west and stretching over to Parque Quinta Normal, **Barrio Yungay** has a growing number of bohemian restaurants and bars, many housed in attractively crumbling buildings.

Estación Central

Twelve blocks west of Plaza Brasil stands one of the Alameda's great landmarks: the stately **Estación Central**, featuring a colossal metal roof that was cast in the Schneider-Creusot foundry in France in 1896. It's the only functioning train station left in the city, with regular services to the south.

Parque Quinta Normal and around

Parque Quinta Normal is perhaps the most elegant and peaceful of Santiago's parks, created in 1830 as a place to introduce and acclimatize foreign trees and plants to the city. Today the park is packed with some beautifully mature examples: Babylonian willows, Monterey pine, cypress, Douglas fir and poplars, to name just a few. Additional attractions include a pond with rowing boats for hire, and several **museums**. Often deserted during the week, the park is packed on summer weekends.

Museo de Historia Natural

Parque Quinta Normal • Tues–Sat 10am–5.30pm, Sun 11am–5.30pm • Free • ☎ 2 2680 4600, ⓦ mnhn.cl

The grand, Neoclassical building near the entrance of Parque Quinta Normal houses the **Museo de Historia Natural**. Founded in 1830 and occupying its present building since 1875, this is Latin America's oldest natural history museum and still one of the most important. It has a colossal blue whale skeleton, and an Easter Island collection that features a *moai*, an upturned topknot or hat, and the famous Santiago Staff, inscribed with the mysterious, undeciphered *rongo rongo* script.

1

Museo Artequín

Av Portales 3530 • Tues–Fri 9am–5pm, Sat & Sun 11am–6pm • CH$800, free Sun • ☎ 2 2681 8656, ⊕ artequin.cl

The wildly colourful glass and metal building standing opposite Parque Quinta Normal's Avenida Portales entrance was originally the Chilean pavilion in the Universal Exhibition in Paris, 1889. It now contains the engaging **Museo Artequín** – short for Arte en la Quinta – which aims to bring people, especially schoolchildren, closer to art by exposing them to reproductions of the world's greatest paintings in a relaxed, less intimidating environment. They're all here, from El Greco and Delacroix through to Andy Warhol and Jackson Pollock.

Museo de la Memoria y los Derechos Humanos

Matucama 501 • Tues–Sun 10am–6pm • Free • ☎ 2 2365 1165, ⊕ museodelamemoria.cl

The **Museo de la Memoria y los Derechos Humanos** (Museum of Memory and Human Rights), housed in an large, eye-catching glass building just outside Parque Quinta Normal, is dedicated to the victims of human rights abuses during the years of the Pinochet dictatorship, a period in which an estimated three thousand people were killed or "disappeared", and thousands more tortured, detained or sent into exile, including current President Michelle Bachelet. Opened in 2010 at the time of Chile's bicentennial, the museum houses a powerful combination of multimedia displays, exhibits, photos, art, poetry and literature to tell the story of the military coup and its enduring impact. Exhibits include moving eyewitness accounts, TV footage from the time, and heartbreaking letters and personal items belonging to junta victims. Although a knowledge of Spanish and recent history is useful in understanding some of the archive material, it is not essential. A sight not to be missed.

Mercado Central and around

Puente and San Pablo • Daily 7am–5/6pm • Free

The **Mercado Cental** is situated close to the southern bank of the Río Mapocho. This huge metal structure, prefabricated in England and erected in Santiago in 1868, contains a very picturesque fruit, vegetable and fish market. The highlight is the fish stalls, packed with glistening eels, sharks and salmon, buckets of oysters, mussels and clams, and unidentifiable shells out of which live things with tentacles make occasional appearances. The best time to come here is at lunchtime, when you can feast at one of the many **fish restaurants** dotted around the market; the cheapest and most authentic are on the outer edge, while those in the centre are touristy and pricier. Keep an eye on your belongings, as pickpockets are not unknown here.

Feria Municipal La Vega

Antonio López de Bello and Salas • Mon–Sat 5.30am–6pm, Sun 6am–3pm • Free

The gargantuan **Feria Municipal La Vega** is a couple of blocks back from the riverbank opposite the Mercado Central. There's no pretty architecture here, and few tourists; just serious shoppers and hundreds of stalls selling the whole gamut of Central Valley produce, from cows' innards and pigs' bellies to mountains of potatoes and onions, at a fraction of the price charged in the Mercado Central. There is also a gallery of economical **seafood restaurants**, popular with locals and rarely visited by tourists. Few have alcohol licences, but if you ask for an "iced tea" ("*te helado*") you'll be served either white wine in a Sprite bottle or red wine in a Coca-Cola bottle.

Estación Mapocho

Just west of the Mercado Central, right by the river, is the immense stone and metal **Estación Mapocho**, built in 1912 to house the terminal of the Valparaíso–Santiago railway line. With the train service long discontinued, the station is now a cultural centre, housing exhibitions, plays and concerts. Take a look inside at the great copper, glass and marble roof. One of the continent's most important book fairs is also held here in November, the **Feria Nacional del Libro**.

Parque Forestal

The **Parque Forestal**, stretching along the southern bank of the Mapocho between Puente Recoleta and Puente Pío Nono, was created at the end of the nineteenth century on land that was reclaimed from the river after it was channelled. Lined with long rows of trees and lampposts, it provides a picturesque setting for the **Palacio de Bellas Artes**, built to commemorate the centenary of Chilean independence. The funky restaurant and bar scene of Barrio Lastarria (see p.82 & p.84) backs on to this area, now sometimes referred to as Barrio Bellas Artes.

Museo Nacional de Bellas Artes and Museo de Arte Contemporáneo

Both museums: Parque Forestal s/n • Tues–Sun 10am–6.50pm • Free • ⓦ mnba.cl • Ⓜ Bellas Arte is close to the museums; on foot it is an easy walk from downtown

The **Palacio de Bellas Artes** houses the **Museo Nacional de Bellas Artes,** featuring predominantly Chilean works from the beginning of the colonial period onwards. The quality of the work is mixed, and none of the paintings equals the beauty of the building's vast white hall with its marble statues bathing in the natural light pouring in from the glass-and-iron ceiling. The works on display change frequently, but look out for the surrealist paintings of Chilean master Roberto Matta and the close-up portrait photos of Jorge Brantmayer. The **Museo de Arte Contemporáneo**, accessed from the other side of the building, hosts temporary exhibitions focused on international or Chilean contemporary artists.

Barrio Bellavista

There's no metro in Bellavista itself, but it's a short walk from Ⓜ Baquedano

Originally – and sometimes still – known as *La Chimba*, which means "the other side of the river" in Quechua (Inca language), **Barrio Bellavista** grew first into a residential area when Santiago's population started spilling across the river in the nineteenth century. Head across the Pío Nono bridge at the eastern end of the Parque Forestal and you'll find yourself on Calle Pío Nono, Bellavista's main street. Nestling between the northern bank of the Mapocho and the steep slopes of Cerro San Cristóbal, Bellavista is a warren of leafy streets and a centre for restaurants, bars and pubs. A popular night-time destination for both locals and visitors, the neighbourhood has a slightly edgy feel; it is generally safe, but it is wise to stay on your guard after dark. An evening handicraft market that spreads along the length of Pío Nono is held at weekends.

You might also be tempted by the dozens of lapis lazuli outlets running along Avenida Bellavista, between Puente Pío Nono and Puente del Arzobispo, though there are few bargains to be found. **Patio Bellavista**, Pío Nono 73, is a shopping and dining complex – and a popular gringo hangout.

La Chascona

Marquéz de la Plata 192 • Jan & Feb Tues–Sun 10am–7pm; March–Dec Tues–Sun 10am–6pm • CH$5000 • ☎ 2 2737 8712, ⓦ fundacionneruda.org

Tucked away in a tiny street at the foot of Cerro San Cristóbal is **La Chascona**, the house the poet Pablo Neruda shared with his third wife, Matilde Urrutia, from 1955 until his death in 1973. It was named *La Chascona* ("tangle-haired woman") by Neruda, as a tribute to his wife's thick red hair. Today it's the

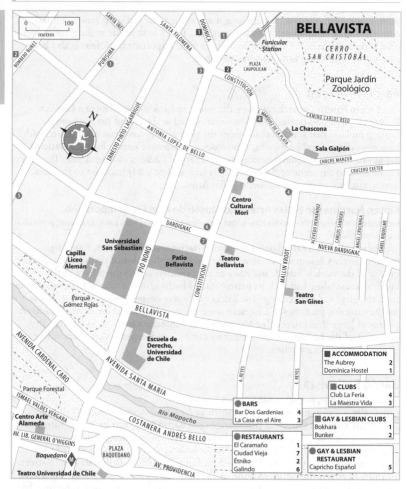

headquarters of the Fundación Neruda, which has painstakingly restored this and the poet's two other houses – La Sebastiana in Valparaíso (see p.104) and Isla Negra, about 90km down the coast (see p.111) – to their original condition, opening them to the public. The ticket price includes a worthwhile self-guided audio tour, available in English.

This house, split into three separate sections that climb up the hillside, is packed to the rafters with objects collected by Neruda, illuminating his loves, enthusiasms and obsessions. Beautiful African carvings jostle for space with Victorian dolls, music boxes, paperweights and coloured glasses; the floors are littered with old armchairs, stools, a rocking horse, exotic rugs and a sleeping toy lion. There are numerous references to Neruda's and Matilde's love for each other, such as the bars on the windows, in which their initials are entwined and lapped by breaking waves, and the portrait of Matilde by Diego Rivera, which has the profile of Neruda hidden in her hair. The third and highest level houses Neruda's library, containing more than nine thousand books, as well as the diploma he was given when awarded the Nobel Prize for Literature in 1971, and a replica of the medal.

Cerro San Cristóbal

Funicular Mon 1–7pm, Tues–Sun 10am–7pm • CH$2000 return weekday, CH$2600 return weekend

A trip to the summit of **Cerro San Cristóbal** – which includes parkland, botanical gardens, a dismal zoo and two swimming pools (see below) – is one of the city's highlights, particularly on a clear, sunny day when the views are stunning. The hill is, in fact, an Andean spur, jutting into the capital's heart and rising to a peak of 860m, a point marked by a 22m-high statue of the *Virgen de la Inmaculada*. The easiest way to get up is via the **funicular** from the station at the north end of Pío Nono in Bellavista, which takes you via the zoo up to the Terraza Bellavista, where there are a handful of food and craft stalls. From here it's a short but steep walk up to the huge white Virgin, where you'll be rewarded with fine views over Santiago's suburbs vanishing into hazy mountains. If you are fortunate enough to be in Santiago after a rain in the winter, this view includes rows of snowy mountain peaks. Trails wind through the woods to the base of the hill if you prefer a little exercise on the way up or down.

Piscina Tupahue and Piscina Antilén

Av Alberto Mackenna s/n • Mid-Nov to mid-March Tues–Sun 10am–7.30pm • CH$6000–7500 • You can walk from the Terraza Bellavista, take a taxi from the bottom of the hill, or at weekends hop on a free shuttle bus

For an afternoon picnic and **swimming** in the summer months, there is no better place in Santiago than the two **huge pools** atop the Cerro San Cristóbal. The jointly run Piscina Tupahue and Piscina Antilén offer cool, clean swimming and, at 736m above the city, wonderful views.

Los barrios altos

The *barrios* east of the city centre spreading into the foothills of the Andes are home to Santiago's moneyed elite; the farther and higher you get, the richer the people, the bigger the houses and the higher the gates. It's hard to believe that up until the beginning of the twentieth century there was virtually no one here; it was for its isolation and tranquillity that the Sisters of Providencia chose to build their convent on what is now Avenida Providencia in 1853. Later, following a slow trickle of eastbound movement, there was a great exodus of wealthy families from their traditional preserves west of the city over to the new *barrio alto* in the 1920s, where they've been entrenched ever since. The parallel street running in the other direction from Avenida Providencia was originally called Avenida Nueva Providencia but was renamed Avenida 11 de Septiembre under the dictatorship to commemorate the date of the 1973 military coup; it is in the process of being changed back to its original name.

Providencia

Northeast of the city centre, **Providencia** has little in the way of sights as such, but is home to hotels, restaurants and travel agencies. Away from the main drags, you'll find attractive tree-lined streets, stylish stores and elegant cafés. At its eastern edge, around the border with Las Condes, a cluster of skyscrapers, offices and restaurants make up the buzzing financial and dining district nicknamed 'Sanhattan', site of some of the most expensive real estate in Chile. Dominating the area, and indeed the entire Santiago skyline, is the 300m-high **Gran Torre Santiago**, Latin America's tallest skyscraper, designed by Argentine architect Cesar Pelli. With stunning views promised from the top when it is finished in 2015, it will be used mainly for offices, part of a complex that includes the equally enormous Costanera Center shopping mall (see p.86).

Las Condes

As you head east from Providencia towards **Las Condes**, the shops and office blocks gradually thin out into a more residential district, punctuated with the occasional giant shopping mall, such as **Alto Las Condes** (see p.86).

1

> ## TREKS AROUND SANTIAGO
>
> On a clear day, the mountains look so close to Santiago you feel as if you could reach out and touch them, and indeed it doesn't take long to reach at least the foothills if you want a walk that's a bit more challenging than Cerro San Cristóbal without leaving town. **Treks into the precordillera** pretty much all involve an upward climb – but will quickly reward you with fantastic views over the city and beyond (wear shoes with good grip). Within the confines of Santiago, **Cerro Manquehue** is an extinct volcano, whose woodcut-worthy cone towers over the *barrios altos*. It's a stiff but rewarding hike to the top (5hr return) – the path begins near the end of a road called Via Roja, which twists and turns up the fringes of Vitacura (nearest metro is Manquehue; from there you'll need to take a taxi). Skirting the eastern edge of the city, a chain of nature reserves (⑩asociacionparquecordillera.cl) takes you further up into the Andes proper. The pick of these parks is probably **Aguas de Ramón** (winter daily 8am–5pm, summer 8am–6.30pm; CH$1500), whose main route heads towards a river and series of small waterfalls. The park entrance is in Onofre Jarpa, in the neighbourhood of La Reina – the nearest metro is Príncipe de Gales, from where you can catch a taxi.

Pueblito de los Dominicos

Apoquindo 9085 • Daily 10am–8pm • Near Ⓜ Los Dominicos

The best collection of arts and crafts in Santiago is found at the **Pueblito de los Dominicos** market, a large, lively and expensive craft fair. Held in a mock village in Las Condes, the market sits in the shadow of the lovely white Iglesia de los Dominicos, topped with greening copper cupolas, which looks colonial but was built by Dominican monks in the nineteenth century. The market hosts a wide range of beautiful handicrafts, as well as antiques, books, fossil shark teeth, a decent restaurant, and a quiet respite from the noise and grime of the city.

Museo de la Moda

Av Vitacura 4562 • Tues–Sun 10am–6pm • CH$3000 • ☎ 2 2219 3623, ⑩ museodelamoda.cl • Bus #112, #425, #425e, #419e or #C22 from Ⓜ Escuela Militar

The **Museo de la Moda** is an essential stop-off for fashionistas, with a collection of over ten thousand exhibits, dating from the fifth century BC to the present day. Dresses worn by Princess Diana and Marilyn Monroe, Madonna's bra from her Blond Ambition tour, and Diego Maradona's football boots, are among the items held in the collection, although not all may be on display at any one time.

Parque Araucano

Presidente Riesco 5555 • Park Tues–Sun 9am–9pm • Free • 20min walk or taxi from Ⓜ Escuela Militar

Right opposite the Parque Arauco shopping mall (see p.88), this is a particularly lovely **park** to wander around, clean and well tended, with a rose garden and fountains. It's also a good place to come if you have youngsters to entertain, with a couple of attractions in the park aimed at children or the young at heart (note that they get very crowded at weekends and holiday times). **Selva Viva** (Mon–Fri 9am–6pm, Sat & Sun 10am–7pm; CH$9950; ☎ 2 2944 6300, ⑩ selvaviva.cl) is a hot and humid 'jungle' space, where butterflies and parrots fly overhead and you can stroke snakes, iguanas and toucans. **KidZania** (Tues–Fri 9am–2pm & 3–8pm, Sat & Sun 11am–7pm; adults CH$7450, children CH$11,950; ☎ 2 2964 4000, ⑩ kidzania.cl) allows children to learn about different professions in a hands-on way, operating on 'patients', making sushi or sitting in a real plane cockpit.

Peñalolén

On Santiago's outskirts, southwest of Las Condes, is **Peñalolén**. This mostly lower middle-class neighbourhood was the site of Villa Grimaldi, one of the main torture and interrogation centres during the Pinochet years.

1

Parque por la Paz Villa Grimaldi

Av José Arrieta 8401, Peñalolén • Daily 10am–6pm; guided visits Tues–Fri 10.30am, noon & 3pm • Free entry & tour • ☎ 2 2292 5229 • Bus #513 or #D09 from ⓜ Plaza Egaña

From mid-1974 to mid-1978, Villa Grimaldi – a privately owned country house that was taken over by the secret police – was used for the torture of those deemed political opponents of the Pinochet regime. Around five thousand people were detained here; at least 240 were killed. The buildings have since been knocked down, and the grounds turned into the **Parque por la Paz Villa Grimaldi** (Peace Park Villa Grimaldi), with a series of monuments that include a wall listing names of victims and a recreation of the huts prisoners were kept in. The park now serves as both a memorial to the victims and to educate future generations about the dictatorship. Bilingual audioguides are available.

ARRIVAL AND DEPARTURE   SANTIAGO

Santiago is one of the easiest and least intimidating South American capitals to arrive in. Connections from the airport and bus terminals to the city centre are frequent and straightforward, and while you should take normal precautions, you're unlikely to be hassled or feel threatened while you're finding your feet.

BY PLANE

Aeropuerto Arturo Merino Benítez International and domestic flights arrive at Arturo Merino Benítez airport in Pudahuel (the commune the airport is sometimes named after; ☎ 2 2690 1752, ⓦ aeropuertosantiago.cl), 26km northwest of Santiago. The smart international terminal has a tourist information desk, bureau de change (rates are fairly poor) and ATMs. There are flights from here throughout Chile and South America; most are operated by LAN (central office Av Providencia 2006 ☎ 600 526 2000, ⓦ lan.com).

By bus The cheapest way to get between the airport and the city centre is by bus. Centropuerto (daily 6am–11.30pm; every 10min; CH$1450) drops you off or picks you up at Los Héroes metro station, while Tur Bus (daily 5am–midnight every 20min, midnight–5am hourly; CH$1500) uses the Terminal de Buses Alameda (see below). Minibus firms such as TransVIP (☎ 2 2677 3000, ⓦ www.transvip.cl), operating from the row of desks by the airport exit, offer door-to-door services from the airport to your hotel, charging around CH$7000 per person. You have to wait around until the bus is full, and you'll probably get an unwanted city tour as other passengers are dropped off before you reach your own hotel.

By taxi By the airport exit there's a desk where you can book official airport taxis, which cost around CH$20,000 to the city centre. If you bargain with the private taxi drivers touting for business, you can usually pay less, but taking these taxis is at your own risk. Returning to the airport, the taxis charge a few thousand pesos less – it's a good idea to book a radiotaxi ahead (see p.76).

By car There are a number of car rental booths at the airport, including Avis (☎ 2 2795 3971, ⓦ avis.com), Rosselot (ⓦ rosselot.cl) and Dollar (ⓦ dollar.com).

Destinations Antofagasta (15 daily; 2hr); Arica (3 daily; 2hr 40min); Calama (10 daily; 2hr); Concepcíon (9 daily; 1hr); Copiapó (5 daily; 1hr 30min); Easter Island (1 daily; 5hr 40min); Iquique (12 daily; 2hr 30min); La Serena (7

daily; 1hr); Osorno (1 daily; 1hr 30min); Puerto Montt (12 daily; 1hr 45min); Punta Arenas (5 daily; 3hr 30min); Temuco (7 daily; 1hr 20min); Valdivia (1 daily; 1hr 30 min).

BY BUS

By far the greatest majority of transport services are provided by buses, run by a bewildering number of private companies. These operate out of four main terminals. While you can normally turn up and buy a ticket for travelling the same day, it's better to get it in advance, especially at weekends. For travel on the days around Christmas, New Year's Eve, Easter and the September 18 national holiday, you should buy your ticket at least a week ahead.

TERMINAL DE BUSES SANTIAGO

The Terminal de Buses Santiago, also known as Terminal de Estación Central (☎ 2 2376 1750, ⓦ terminaldebuses santiago.cl), just west of the Universidad de Santiago metro station, is the largest (and most chaotic) of the terminals, with more than a hundred bus companies operating out of here. Services south down the Panamericana from this terminal are provided by all the major companies, including Cóndor Bus (☎ 2 2680 6900, ⓦ condorbus.cl), Inter Sur (☎ 2 2779 6312) and Tas Choapa (☎ 2 2779 4694, ⓦ www.taschoapa.cl). Buses to the coastal resorts of the Litoral Central are run by Cóndor Bus and Pullman Bus (☎ 2 2779 2026, ⓦ www.pullman.cl).

Destinations Chillán (20 daily; 5hr); Concepción (every 30min; 6hr); Curicó (every 30min; 2hr 45min); Osorno (hourly; 10hr); Puerto Montt (every 30min; 14hr); Talca (every 15min; 3hr 30min); Valdivia (hourly; 11hr).

TERMINAL DE BUSES ALAMEDA

This terminal, just east of the Terminal de Buses Santiago, is used by Tur Bus (☎ 2 2270 7500, ⓦ www.turbus.cl) and Pullman Bus, Chile's largest and most comprehensive bus companies, going to a wide variety of destinations.

1

Destinations Valparaíso (every 15min; 1hr 30min–1hr 45min); Viña del Mar (every 15min; 1hr 30min–1hr 45min).

TERMINAL SAN BORJA

San Borja (☎ 2 2776 0645) is at the back of a shopping mall behind the Estación Central (from the metro, follow the signs carefully to exit at the terminal). This is the main departure point for buses to the north of Chile. There are several regional buses, as well, and some services to the coastal resorts. Bus companies going north include Elqui Bus (☎ 2 2778 7045), Pullman Bus and Tas Choapa. Tur Bus also runs services to the Litoral.

Destinations Antofagasta (hourly; 19hr); Arica (hourly; 30hr); Calama (hourly; 22hr); Iquique (hourly; 24hr); La Serena (hourly; 6hr 30min).

TERMINAL LOS HÉROES

Los Héroes (☎ 2 2420 0099), is located on Tucapel Jiménez, just north of the Plaza de Los Héroes, near the metro stop of the same name. It hosts a mixture of northbound, southbound and buses to destinations in Argentina. The terminal is used by companies including Buses Ahumada (☎ 2 2696 9798, ⊛ busesahumada.cl), Cruz del Sur (☎ 2 2696 9324, ⊛ www.pullmansur.cl), Libac (☎ 2 2698 5974, ⊛ buseslibac.cl), Pullman del Sur (☎ 2 2673 1967, ⊛ pdelsur.cl) and Tas Choapa.

Destinations Bariloche (several daily; 16hr), Buenos Aires (several daily; 22hr); Mendoza (several daily; 7hr).

BY TRAIN

The only train services are between Santiago and destinations in the central valley to the south, with all trains departing from the Estación Central, next to the metro stop of the same name. For train information, call ☎ 600 585 5000 or check ⊛ efe.cl.

Destinations Chillán (2 daily; 5hr 30min); Curicó (3 daily; 2hr 45min); Rancagua (10 daily; 1hr 30min); San Fernando (5 daily; 2hr); Talca (3 daily; 3hr 30min).

GETTING AROUND

You'll probably spend most time in the city centre, which is entirely walkable, but for journeys further afield public transport on the Transantiago network of metro trains and buses is inexpensive, safe and abundant. You can plan your journey via the website ⊛ transantiago.cl.

BY METRO

Santiago's spotless metro system (most lines Mon–Fri 6.30am–11pm, Sat, Sun & public holidays 8.30am–10.30pm; ⊛ www.metro.cl) is modern and efficient, though packed solid at rush hour. Many stations are decorated with huge murals, and often offer free wi-fi. Fares are the same regardless of the length of your journey, but vary according to time of day (CH$590–700). You can buy single-use tickets from the cashiers, but if you plan on making more than a couple of trips it's worth investing in a Tarjeta Bip!, a magnetic-stripcard (CH$1400), which you load up with credit at machines or ticket windows; the same card is also used on the buses.

METRO LINES

Line #1 is the most useful, running east–west under the Alameda and Av Providencia. Line #5 runs parallel to it for part of its length, stopping at the Plaza de Armas and Bellavista. A new Line #3, which was under construction at the time of writing, will cut through the centre north to south. The other lines mostly serve residential *barrios*, while large chunks of the city, including Vitacura and the airport, are off the network completely.

BY BUS

The bus network doesn't take cash; instead you have to use a Tarjeta Bip! card (see above). The fare is $620, which lasts up to 2hr with a maximum of two changes. Buses often involve a long wait but are useful for reaching destinations

off the metro, or going east or west along the Alameda – as a general rule, buses displaying Estación Central will take you west, while those displaying Providencia or Apoquindo are going east.

BY TAXI

Santiago has more taxis than New York, and in the centre you'll have no trouble flagging one down. Taxis are black with yellow roofs and have a small light in the top right-hand corner of the windscreen that's lit to show the cab is available. If you're going somewhere out of the way, don't expect the driver to know it; it's best to check where it is beforehand. Radiotaxis (such as Metropolitana on ☎ 2 2506 6595) are a bit less of a lottery and can be booked beforehand.

FARES

Fares are relatively low and displayed on the window – usually CH$280 when the meter's started and CH$120 for every 200m; you're not expected to tip. Drivers are allowed to charge more at night, so try to verbally confirm an estimate to your location. Scams such as drivers taking extra-long routes, and rip-offs on large bills, do happen. Be firm and pay with small notes.

BY COLECTIVO

Santiago's *colectivos* (shared taxis) look like ordinary taxis except they're black all over and cram in as many as four passengers at a time. They travel along fixed routes, mostly from the centre out to the suburbs; a sign on the roof indicates

1

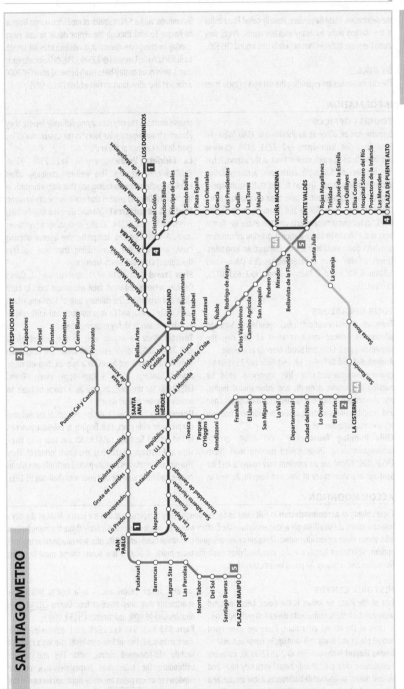

SANTIAGO METRO

LOS DOMINICOS
H. de Magallanes
Manquehue
Escuela Militar
Alcántara
El Golf
TOBALABA
Los Leones
Pedro de Valdivia
Manuel Montt
Salvador
BAQUEDANO
Parque Bustamante
Santa Isabel
Irarrázaval
Ñuble
Rodrigo de Araya
Carlos Valdovinos
Camino Agrícola
San Joaquín
Pedrero
Mirador
Bellavista de la Florida
VICUÑA MACKENNA
VICENTE VALDÉS
Rojas Magallanes
Trinidad
San José de la Estrella
Los Quillayes
Elisa Correa
Hospital Sótero del Río
Protectora de la Infancia
Las Mercedes
PLAZA DE PUENTE ALTO

Cristóbal Colón
Francisco Bilbao
Príncipe de Gales
Simón Bolívar
Plaza Egaña
Los Orientales
Grecia
Los Presidentes
Quilín
Las Torres
Macul

Santa Julia
La Granja
Santa Rosa
San Ramón
LA CISTERNA

VESPUCIO NORTE
Zapadores
Dorsal
Einstein
Cementerios
Cerro Blanco
Patronato
Bellas Artes
Universidad Católica
Santa Lucía
Universidad de Chile
La Moneda
SANTA ANA
LOS HÉROES
Puente Cal y Canto
Plaza de Armas

Franklin
El Llano
San Miguel
Lo Vial
Departamental
Ciudad del Niño
Lo Ovalle
El Parrón

Cumming
República
U.L.A.
Toesca
Parque O'Higgins
Rondizzoni
Quinta Normal
Gruta de Lourdes
Estación Central
Universidad de Santiago
San Alberto Hurtado
Las Rejas

Blanqueado
Ecuador
SAN PABLO
Neptuno
Lo Prado
San Pablo
Pudahuel
Barrancas
Laguna Star
Las Parcelas
Monte Tabor
Del Sol
Santiago Bueras
PLAZA DE MAIPÚ

1

the destination. Plaza Baquedano (usually called Plaza Italia) is the starting point for many *colectivo* routes. Prices vary along the route, but *colectivos* generally cost around CH$500.

BY BIKE

The city authorities are expanding the network of cycle lanes in Santiago, with a 5.6km stretch of road from Quinta Normal to Parque Forestal through the centre closed to cars every Sunday morning (see ⓦ munisantiago.info/bicicletas for latest). La Bicicleta Verde, Loreto 6 (☎ 2 2570 9338, ⓦ labicicletaverde .com), rents good quality bikes (with helmets) from CH$9000 a day and also offers tours on two wheels (see below).

INFORMATION

TOURIST OFFICES

Sernatur has an office at Av Providencia 1550 (Mon–Fri 9am–6pm, Sat 9am–2pm; ☎ 2 2731 8310, ⓦ www .sernatur.cl), and a much smaller kiosk at the airport. It has free booklets on Santiago's attractions, accommodation and restaurants, maps, free wi-fi, and staff usually speak English. The city authorities have their own tourist office (Mon–Fri 9am–6pm, Sat & Sun 10am–4pm; ☎ 2 2713 6745, ✉ turismo@munistgo.cl), on the Plaza de Armas next to the Museo Histórico Nacional, offering information on what's going on as well as free, bilingual walking tours. There's a Conaf office at Paseo Bulnes 285 (Mon–Thurs 9.30am–5.30pm, Fri 9.30am–4.30pm; ☎ 2 663 0125, ⓦ conaf.cl).

TOUR OPERATORS

There are several excellent travel agencies in Santiago offering an eclectic range of tours of the city, the surrounding area, Chile and South America as a whole.

Andina del Sud Av El Golf 99, 2nd floor ☎ 2 2388 0144, ⓦ www.andinadelsud.com. This agency is good for booking inexpensive domestic and international flights, and also offers holidays and guided trips throughout Chile and neighbouring countries aimed at younger travellers (ⓦ www.turismojoven.cl).

Chile Running Tours ☎ 09 9330 6804, ⓦ chile runningtours.com. These guided running tours (from CH$36,000; 10km) are an excellent way to get a feel for Santiago in a short space of time and keep fit. As well as

several routes in the city (of varying difficulty levels), they also offer "running and wine tours" in the Casablanca Valley (you do the tastings at the end).

La Bicicleta Verde Loreto 6 ☎ 2 2570 9338, ⓦ labicicletaverde.com. This well-run company offers excellent cycling trips, including one that visits vineyards in the Maipo valley and another that explores the city by night.

Santiago Adventures Dr Manuel Borros Borgoño 198, Providencia ☎ 2 2244 2750, ⓦ santiagoadventures .com. A well-respected, comprehensive agency offering cycle, wine and city tours, skiing trips and holidays throughout Chile and South America.

Slow Travel ☎ 09 9919 8471, ⓦ slowtravel.cl. Offers flexible, personalized wine, food and nature tours in both Chile and Argentina. The culinary tour of Santiago, which takes in the Central and La Vega markets, and finishes with a cookery lesson, is highly recommended.

Turistik Plaza de Armas next to the tourist office ☎ 2 2820 1000, ⓦ viajesturistik.com. The ubiquitous Turistik runs bright red buses on a hop-on, hop-off route around Santiago (daily 9.30am–6pm, every 30min, CH$20,000 for the day), as well as a range of tours to nearby wineries and ski resorts.

Uncorked ☎ 2 2981 6242, ⓦ uncorked.cl. Maria and José run premium wine tours, all in English, to boutique wineries in and around Santiago (US$195 for day tour with three visits and tastings, all transfers and lunch included). They also run cooking classes that are packed with info on Chilean cuisine, and come with the odd pisco sour (half-day US$95).

ACCOMMODATION

There's plenty of **accommodation** to suit most budgets, though really inexpensive places are scarce. Most of the city's low-cost rooms are small, simple and sparsely furnished, often without a window but usually fairly clean; the many hostels with dorms make a good alternative. There are numerous good mid-range hotels and B&Bs, plus several luxurious top-end options. Apartment hotels are also popular. Prices don't fluctuate much, though a few hotels charge more between November and February. All prices include breakfast.

HISTORIC CENTRE

East of the Plaza de Armas is the tidier, better-restored section of the historic centre, with the easiest walking access to most of the central attractions. There are some good budget places and many mid- and upper-range options.

Andes Hostel Monjitas 506 ☎ 2 2632 9990, ⓦ andes hostel.com; map p.62. Funky hostel with tidy four- and six-bed dorms, swish marble bathrooms, a roof terrace, and a bar area featuring a big-screen TV and a pool table. There

are also private rooms and – in a nearby building – apartments that sleep three or four. Dorms CH$13,000, doubles CH$48,000, apartments CH$54,000

París 813 París 813 ☎ 2 2664 0921, ⓦ hotelparis813 .com; map p.62. Decent low-cost hotel offering a range of slightly old-fashioned rooms, with TVs and private bathrooms; the older ones sometimes lack outside windows so unless pesos are really tight, opt for one in the newer annexe. CH$26,000

This gem of a hostel, on the sixth floor of a building hidden within an alleyway filled with fast-food joints, has a prime location on the Plaza de Armas. There are bright dorms, colourful if compact private rooms, ample communal space, and a terrace with fine views. Dorms CH$10,000, doubles with private bathroom CH$26,000

Plaza San Francisco Alameda 816 ☎2 2639 3832, ⓦplazasanfrancisco.cl; map p.62. This is the most luxurious downtown top-end hotel choice: the en suites are large and handsome with tubs and easy chairs; there's also an indoor pool, mini art gallery and quality restaurant. Good online deals. US$190

Vegas Londres 49 ☎2 2632 2514, ⓦhotelvegas.net; map p.62. A national monument, in the quiet París-Londres neighbourhood, this hotel is great value, with spacious en suites, friendly service, and thoughtful touches like secondhand novels to read and a collection of umbrellas for use on rainy days. Apartments with small kitchens also available. Doubles CH$45,000, apartments CH$32,000

BARRO LASTARRIA

Although this lively neighbourhood is focused more on restaurants and bars than hotels, there are a handful of choices and the location is excellent – easy walking distance from the centre and Bellavista, and a bit smarter than both.

Montecarlo Victoria Subercaseaux 209 ☎2 2633 9905, ⓦhotelmontecarlo.cl; map p.62. Location is the main selling point of this hotel: it overlooks Cerro Santa Lucia, and the Alameda is a couple of blocks away. The building has an unusual modernist shape, and the small rooms could do with a freshen-up, but overall it's a decent choice. CH$64,000

Río Amazonas Vicuña Mackenna 47 ☎2 2635 1631, ⓦhostalrioamazonas.cl; map p.62. Travellers of all ages flock to this charming hostal, next to the Argentine embassy. Each room has a private bathroom (and often a bath), colourful decor, phone, TV and plenty of space. The communal areas are attractive, and there is a good breakfast. CH$38,000

The Singular Merced 294 ☎2 2306 8821, ⓦthesingular.com; map p.62. Well located in Lastarria, this new, elegant five-star is an excellent choice. Highlights include spacious and stylish en suites, a rooftop bar and swimming pool, well-equipped spa, fine restaurant, and attentive service. It has an equally impressive sister hotel in Puerto Natales (see p.399). US$261

BARRIO BRASIL

Bohemian Barrio Brasil, to the north of the Alameda, is growing in popularity, thanks to its ever-increasing supply of cool cafés, restaurants and bars.

★**Happy House** Moneda 1829 ☎2 2688 4849, ⓦhappyhousehostel.cl; map pp.58–59. *Happy House* is a cut above most other hostels. This restored early twentieth-century town house has stylish six- to eight-bed dorms, beautiful, airy rooms (with shared or attached

bathrooms) that put many mid-range hotels to shame as well as a bar, terrace and pool table. Dorms CH$20,000, doubles with private bathroom CH$40,000

Princesa Insolente Moneda 2350 ☎2 2671 6551, ⓦprincesainsolentehostel.cl; map pp.58–59. This popular and sociable hostel has clean and economical private rooms, three- to ten-bed dorms, TV lounge and patio. The cheerful staff members host regular barbecues. Dorms CH$7500, doubles CH$35,000

BARRIO BELLAVISTA

Bellavista is within walking distance or a short cab ride from downtown on one side and Providencia on the other, and is a particularly good option if you want to be close to Santiago's nightlife.

The Aubrey Constitución 317 ☎2 2940 2800, ⓦtheaubrey.com; map p.72. Nestling beside Cerro San Cristóbal, with Bellavista's restaurants and bars just a stone's throw away, *The Aubrey* is based in two beautifully restored 1920s mansions, and boasts some of Santiago's most stylish en suites: swish bathrooms, Tom Dixon lamps, and docks for MP3 players are just a few of the features. The hotel also has a pool, piano lounge and a fine restaurant. US$250

Dominica Hostel Dominica 24 ☎2 2732 7196, ⓦdominicahostel.com; map p.72. In a restored 1920s building, cabin-style beds afford some privacy as well as large locker space in eight-bed dorms, and there's a nice terrace from where you can enjoy a beer and watch Bellavista in full flow. Popular with travellers who like to party (the hostel gives out free entry tickets to nearby discos). Dorms CH$8000, doubles with private bathroom CH$28,000

PROVIDENCIA

As the glitzy commercial heart of Santiago, Providencia has a number of pricey hotels, as well as a range of B&Bs and small mid-range hotels. It's worth considering basing yourself here if you'd rather avoid the grittier centre; metro line #1 runs along the main Av Providencia.

Chilhotel Cirujano Guzmán 103 ☎2 2264 0643, ⓦchilhotel.cl; map pp.58–59. This small hotel, located on a quiet street in central Providencia, is a good choice. The rooms are comfortable and good value, though the decor is a bit twee; all of them come with private bathrooms, TVs and fridges. CH$43,000

Hotel Orly Pedro de Valdivia 27 ☎2 2231 8947, ⓦorlyhotel.com; map pp.58–59. Welcoming and cosy hotel in the heart of Providencia. The immaculate en suites have wood fittings, colourful throws, mini fridges and TVs; they can range quite considerably in size, however, so ask to see a few. The apartments, which sleep up to four, are good value. Doubles CH$93,000, apartments CH$85,000

L'Ambassade Av Suiza 2084 ☎2 2761 9711, ⓦambassade.cl; map pp.58–59. Run by a very welcoming Franco–Chilean family, this intimate and peaceful boutique B&B has tasteful en-suite doubles, an artwork-filled lounge, a small outdoor pool and a sauna. The breakfast is excellent. CH$78,000

Le Rêve Orrego Luco 23 ☎ 2 2757 6000, ⓦ lerevehotel.cl; map pp.58–59. An excellent addition to Santiago's luxury accommodation options, *Le Rêve* is a welcoming boutique hotel with plenty of French touches in both the architecture and the furnishings. The en suites are elegant (though a bit overpriced), and service is welcoming and efficient. US$260

★ **Vilafranca** Pérez Valenzuela 1650 ☎ 2 2235 1413, ⓦ vilafranca.cl; map pp.58–59. A charming eight-room B&B in a 1940s-era home on a peaceful street: each room is unique and all are supremely tasteful, service is personalized, black and white photos of historic Santiago cover the walls and there's a sunny patio area. CH$49,000

LAS CONDES

Las Condes – and, in particular, Sanhattan – is Santiago's burgeoning luxury hotel neighbourhood, with large shopping centres and art galleries nearby. The metro goes as far as Los Dominicos and a taxi to the centre runs to about CH$5,000–10,000.

Ritz-Carlton El Alcalde 15 ☎ 2 2470 8500, ⓦ ritzcarlton .com; map pp.58–59. One of Santiago's top five-stars, Sanhattan's *Ritz-Carlton* has classically styled en suites, attentive but not overbearing service, excellent restaurants and bars, and a fifteenth-floor swimming pool, gym and spa sheltered from the elements by a glass dome. The restaurant zone of Isidora Goyenechea is a short walk away. US$300

The W Isidora Goyenechea 3000 ☎ 2 2770 0000, ⓦ starwoodhotels.com; map pp.58–59. In an eye-catching skyscraper, *The W* is a glamorous, achingly hip hotel. Highlights include the über-modern en suites with floor-to-ceiling windows, and the rooftop (21st-floor) pool and bar with superlative views. Service, however, can be inconsistent. US$430

EATING AND DRINKING

Santiago has a wide range of **places to eat**, from humble *picadas* serving traditional favourites to slick modern restaurants offering cuisines such as Japanese, Southeast Asian, Spanish, Peruvian, French and Italian. Some are modestly priced but most are fairly expensive, although at lunchtime many offer a good-value fixed-price *menú del día* or *menú ejecutivo*. In most places there's no need to **book**. There are also innumerable fast food joints and (generally) unappealing *fuentes de soda*.

CAFÉS AND CHEAP EATS

Santiago is not a café city, but a number of places cater to the great tradition of *onces* (afternoon tea). There are also some decent ice-cream parlours and innumerable joints specialising in *empanadas*.

HISTORIC CENTRE

Blue Jar Almirante Gotuzzo 102 ☎ 2 2696 1890 ⓦ bluejar.cl; map p.62. Just around the corner from La Moneda, this is where government officials from the nearby ministry buildings come to gossip about politics and sip excellent coffees and cocktails. Meals also available (set lunch CH$10,000). Mon–Fri 8am–9pm.

Café Caribe Ahumada 120 ⓦ www.cafecaribe.cl; map p.62. Traditional *café con piernas* (see box below) where male members of Chile's ageing business class stand around for what seems like hours, ogling the waitresses and talking on their mobile phones. Coffee from CH$1000. Mon–Fri 8am–9pm.

Café Colonia Mac Iver 161 ☎ 2 2639 7256, ⓦ cafecolonia.cl; map p.62. At this cute little café, which

has been going for over fifty years, matronly waitresses serve the best cakes, tarts, *küchen* and strudel (all from CH$500 per slice) in Santiago. Mon–Fri 8am–9pm, Sat & Sun 10am–8pm.

Café Haiti Ahumada 140; map p.62. Another of the timewarp *cafés con piernas* (see box below) but the coffee (from CH$1000) is not to be sniffed at. Mon–Fri 8am–9pm.

El Rápido Bandera 347 ☎ 2 2672 2375; map p.62. For decades, *El Rápido* has lived up to its name, with a brisk turnover in excellent *empanadas* (from CH$1000). Call out your order as you enter and by the time you reach the counter your food will be waiting for you. Mon–Fri 9am–9pm, Sat 9am–3.30pm.

BARRIO LASTARRIA

Bonbon Oriental Merced 355 ☎ 2 2639 1069; map p.62. Photos of regular customers cover the walls of this tiny Middle Eastern café, which serves cardamom-scented Arabic coffee (CH$1500), falafel sandwiches and sticky-sweet baklavas; there's also a sister joint a few doors down. Daily 9am–9pm.

CAFÉ CON PIERNAS

An unusual (and politically incorrect) feature of the city is the tradition of **stand-up coffee bars**, known as *cafés con piernas* (literally, coffee with legs); they're staffed by scantily dressed waitresses serving inexpensive coffee. While mainly patronized by men, there's no taboo against women entering, and plenty of people do go just for the coffee, which is often better than anywhere else. The two classic ones are *Café Caribe* (see above) and *Café Haiti* (see above).

Café del Opera Corner of Merced and Jose Miguel de la Barra ☏ 2 2664 3048, ⓦ operacatedral.cl; map p.62. This slick *heladería* (ice-cream parlour) has a great range of flavours including the wonderful *maracujá* (passion fruit), served in cones, cups or in sundaes (CH$3500–7500), as well as coffee, sandwiches and snacks. Mon–Fri 9am–9pm, Sat & Sun 10.30am–10pm.

Emporio La Rosa Merced 291, Barrio Lastarria ☏ 2 2638 0502, ⓦ emporiolarosa.com; map p.62. Popular with students, this ice-cream parlour has delicious, inventive flavours, such as green tea with mango, and banana with palm honey (from CH$1,900), as well as fine croissants and *pain au chocolat*. There are several other branches too. Mon–Thurs 8am–9pm, Fri 8am–10pm, Sat 9am–10pm, Sun 9am–9pm.

LAS CONDES

Cafe Melba Don Carlos 2898 ☏ 2 2232 4546; map pp.58–59. Next to the British embassy and run by New Zealanders, this is a favourite expat hangout. Brunch (around CH$5000), with options such as eggs Benedict or eggs and bacon, as well as fine coffee, is a Sunday ritual for many. Mon–Fri 7.30am–7pm, Sat & Sun 8am–3.30pm.

RESTAURANTS

Most of Santiago's restaurants are concentrated in the historic centre, Barrio Lastarria, Bellavista, Barrio Brasil, Providencia, and Las Condes. There are also some imaginative places springing up around Plaza Ñuñoa in the southeast part of town, and in pricey Vitacura. A memorable place for lunch is the Mercado Central (see p.70), whose central hall is lined with seafood restaurants (*marisquerías*). Alternatively follow the locals to the cheaper joints across the river in the Feria Municipal La Vega.

HISTORIC CENTRE

El Ají Seco San Antonio 530 ☏ 2 2638 8818, ⓦ elajiseco.cl; map p.62. A hectic Peruvian joint serving sizeable portions of ceviche, fried chicken, seafood and *lomo saltado* (a heaped plate of beef, onions, tomatoes, chips and rice), which you can wash down with an Inca Cola or a Cusqueña beer. Mains CH$4500–9000, set lunch CH$5000. There are several other branches. Mon–Thurs & Sun 12.30–11pm, Fri & Sat 12.30pm–1am.

Bar de la Unión Nueva York 11; map p.62. Old wooden floors, shelves of dusty wine bottles and animated, garrulous old men make this an atmospheric place to pop in for a cheap glass of wine or a leisurely meal. Set lunch CH$3500, mains around CH$7000. Mon–Fri 10am–10.30pm, Sat 10am–5pm.

Bar Nacional Paseo Huérfanos 1151 ☏ 2 2696 5986; map p.62. This unpretentious stalwart of the Santiago dining scene serves hearty Chilean staples with the

TOP 5 PLACES TO EAT TRADITIONAL CHILEAN FOOD

El Caramaño p.82
Fuente Alemana p.82
Galindo p.82
El Hoyo p.81
Liguria p.83

minimum of fuss. There's another branch at Bandera 317. Mains CH$5000–8000. Mon–Sat 8am–11pm.

Confitería Torres Alameda, at Dieciocho ☏ 2 2688 0751, ⓦ confiteriatorres.cl; map p.62. Open since 1879, this is one of Santiago's oldest restaurants. While the food is a little overpriced (mains around CH$9000), the wood-panelled walls, old mirrors and sagging chairs provide a fabulous atmosphere. The classic Chilean *barros luco* beef and cheese sandwich ($5800) was supposedly invented here. There are a couple of other branches, including one at the Centro Cultural Palacio La Moneda. Mon–Sat 10.30am–midnight.

★**Kintaro** Monjitas 460 ⓦ kintaro.cl; map p.62. A busy – particularly at lunchtime – Japanese canteen serving a delicious range of sushi, sashimi, tempura and *yakisoba* (mains around CH$4500). If you sit at the counter you can watch the chefs at work. Mon–Fri 12.30–3pm & 7.30–11pm, Sat 7.30–11.30pm.

El Naturista Moneda 846 ☏ 2 2390 5940, ⓦ elnaturista.cl; map p.62. The original pioneer of vegetarian food in Santiago, this large, inexpensive restaurant attracts a huge, frenetic crowd at lunchtime. Dishes (around CH$3000) include potato and onion soufflé and quinoa risotto. There are a couple of other branches around town. Mon–Fri 8am–9pm, Sat 9am–4pm.

Quijote Nueva York 52 ☏ 2 2243 7715, ⓦ quijoterestaurant.cl; map p.62. Another restaurant aimed at the weekday lunchtime crowd, a bit more refined than most. Despite the name, the menu is international rather than Spanish; the tuna with passion fruit sauce and Peruvian-style potatoes (CH$11,000) is absolutely delicious. Mon–Fri 8.30am–8pm.

BARRIO BRASIL AND ESTACIÓN CENTRAL

Interesting, off-beat cafés, restaurants and bars are springing up all the time in Barrio Brasil, with seafood a particular speciality. Reservations at weekends are recommended for all the establishments listed below.

★**El Hoyo** San Vicente 375, just south of Estación Central ☏ 2 2689 0339, ⓦ elhoyo.cl; map pp.58–59. Travelling gastronome Anthony Bourdain said the best food he ate in Chile was at *El Hoyo*, and the hearty, pork-focused dishes (CH$4500–9800) don't disappoint. Specialities include *pernil* (leg of pork) and *arrollado* (rolled pork). The restaurant is also the originator of the *terremoto* (earthquake), an earth-tremblingly potent mix of young white *pipeño* wine, pisco and pineapple ice cream. Mon–Fri 11am–11pm, Sat 11am–8pm.

Ocean Pacific's Ricardo Cumming 221, Barrio Brasil ☎2 2770 0300, ⓦoceanpacifics.cl; map pp.58–59. Worth going for the interior design alone, which can only be described as nautical kitsch. Every inch of wall is covered with whalebones, ships' instruments etc, the staff dress as sailors and the food is – of course – seafood orientated, with an enormous menu that is nearly as dizzying as the décor. Mains around CH$6000. There is a smaller branch in Vitacura at Padre Hurtado 1480. Daily noon–11.30pm.

Ostras Azocar General Bulnes 37, Barrio Brasil ☎2 2681 6109, ⓦostrasazocar.cl; map pp.58–59. This seafood restaurant has been serving king crab, lobster, squid and more since 1945. The house speciality is baked razor clams in a cheese sauce. Sadly the waiting staff can be a bit slack. Mains CH$8000–15,000. Mon–Wed 1.30–4.30pm & 7.30–11.30pm, Thurs–Sat 12.30–11.30pm, Sun 12.30–4.30pm.

★ **Las Vacas Gordas** Cienfuegos 280, Barrio Brasil ☎2 2697 1066; map pp.58–59. This superior steakhouse has earned a well-deserved reputation for top-quality meat (from CH$7000) – try the melt-in-the-mouth *wagyu* beef or the flavoursome *entrecôte*. Service is sharp, and the large, airy dining room has a pleasantly relaxed ambience. Mon–Sat 12.30pm–12.30am, Sun 12.30–5pm.

BARRIO LASTARRIA AND AROUND

Reservations are recommended here in the evenings, as many of the restaurants have fewer than ten tables. Parking is easy, and the *barrio* is just a 2min walk from the Universidad Católica metro stop. This neighbourhood generally is safe, but Cerro Santa Lucia park should be avoided at night.

BocaNariz Jose V. Lastarria 276 ☎2 2638 9893, ⓦbocanariz.cl; map p.62. With over three hundred wine labels in its cellar, this is a restaurant that seeks to introduce you to new tipples and the ideal food with which to pair it. Its most popular wine tasting options are the 'vuelos' of three glasses, each a different blend. Set lunch menus CH$7000. Mon–Sat noon–midnight, Sun 7pm–midnight.

Fuente Alemana Alameda 58 ☎2 2639 3231; map p.62. This fun Santiago institution feels a bit like a Germanic take on an American-style diner. Grab a seat at the counter, order a draught beer, and watch your vast *lomito* beef sandwich (CH$3300), *churrasco* or other artery-clogging meal being prepared before you. Mon–Sat 10am–10.30pm.

Japón Baron Pierre de Coubertin 39 ☎2 2222 4517; map p.62. Tucked away on a quiet side street close to the Argentine embassy is Santiago's oldest and best Japanese restaurant. The sushi, in particular, is outstanding, making

full-use of Chile's wonderful range of seafood. Mains CH$4000–14,000. Mon–Sat noon–3pm & 8–11pm.

Squadritto Rosal 332 ☎2 2632 2121, ⓦsquadritto ristorante.cl; map p.62. This long-running Genoese Italian restaurant serves superb, if rather pricey, pizzas, pastas and other traditional dishes – the risottos are a particular highlight. Staff are welcoming, though the atmosphere is somewhat formal. Mains around CH$8500, weekday set lunch CH$11,900. Mon–Sat 1–4pm & 7pm–midnight, Sun 1–4pm.

BELLAVISTA

Bellavista – particularly Calle Constitución, which runs parallel with the area's main drag, Pio Nono – is at the heart of Santiago's eating-out scene, with a wide range of excellent, and often innovative, restaurants.

El Caramaño Purísima 257 ☎2 2737 7043, ⓦelcaramaño.cl; map p.72. Graffiti-covered walls, soft live guitar music, amiable waiters, excellent, wallet-friendly Chilean food like *pastel de choclo*, and frequently a free aperitif make this restaurant a stand-out choice. Mains CH$4000–7000. Daily 2pm–midnight.

★ **Ciudad Vieja** Constitución 92 ☎2 2248 9412, ⓦcaramano.tripod.com; map p.72. This cool *sanguchería* turns sandwich-making into an art form: varieties (CH$4600–5200) include teriyaki chicken, suckling pig, fried *merluza* (hake) and the *chivito*, Uruguay's take on the steak sandwich. Deliciously salty French fries come on the side, and there's an extensive range of artisanal beers too. Mon 12.30pm–midnight, Tues 12.30pm–1am, Wed 12.30pm–1.30am, Thurs 12.30pm–2am, Fri & Sat 12.30pm–2.30am.

Étniko Constitución 172, at Lopez de Bello ☎2 2732 0119, ⓦwww.etniko.cl; map p.72. The blue neon-lit, Japanese-inspired interior attracts a cool 20s–30s crowd drawn by more than forty types of sushi and sashimi, plus numerous other Southeast Asian dishes, and excellent ceviche. It turns into a bar-club (with a focus on house/electro) later on – try the knockout sake-based cocktails. You have to ring the doorbell to enter. Mains from CH$6000. Mon–Thurs 8pm–midnight, Fri & Sat 8pm–2am.

Galindo Constitución, at Dardignac ☎2 2777 0116, ⓦgalindo.cl; map p.72 Classic Bellavista hangout, busy at all hours for hearty dishes like beef casserole and *longaniza* (spicy sausage) and chips. During the summer the tables spill out onto the street. Mains CH$4000–7000. Mon–Sat 10am–2am.

★ **El Toro** Loreto 33 ☎2 2936 6715; map p.62. An effortlessly trendy restaurant with an appealing whimsical air – pots of crayons are left on each table so that you can doodle while you wait for your food – and an array of tempting dishes such as shrimp crêpes. Mains CH$5000–9000. Mon–Sat 1–4pm & 7pm–midnight.

PROVIDENCIA AND ÑUÑOA

Conveniently located on the metro, Providencia offers many lunch and dinner options. Nearby, though less accessible, Ñuñoa has trendier eateries, often with good music thrown in.

Astrid y Gastón Antonio Bellet 201, Providencia ☎ 2 2650 9125, ⓦ astridygaston.cl; map pp.58–59. The owners' Peruvian origins show through in the menu, but you can also find European and Asian influences. Dishes (CH$10,000–CH$20,000) include a ceviche sampler, beef with red wine and pepper sauce, and chocolate soufflé. Sadly the restaurant has lost some of its sparkle in recent times and given the high prices and reputation (it's a good idea to reserve ahead), the quality can be disappointing. Mon–Fri 1–3pm & 8pm–midnight, Sat 8pm–midnight.

Barandiaran Manuel Montt 315, Providencia ☎ 2 2236 6854, ⓦ barandiaran.cl; map pp.58–59. Some of the best Peruvian food in Santiago is served here: ceviche, sea bass and the more leftfield choice of Patagonian lamb in a coriander sauce are all on offer. There are also branches in Patio Bellavista and Plaza Ñuñoa. Mains CH$8000–11,000. Tues–Thurs 1–4pm & 8pm–midnight, Fri & Sat 1–4pm & 8pm–1am, Sun 1–4pm.

El Huerto Orrego Luco 54, Providencia ☎ 2 2233 2690, ⓦ elhuerto.cl; map pp.58–59. The best vegetarian restaurant in Santiago, with a mouthwatering range of inventive, seasonal dishes (around CH$6000); asparagus and ricotta strudel, paneer tikka masala, and vegetable quesadillas all feature on the menu. The freshly squeezed juices and artisan beers are also well worth a try. Mon–Sat noon–11pm, Sun 12.30–4.30pm.

Las Lanzas Humberto Trucco 25, Plaza Ñuñoa ☎ 2 2225 5589; map pp.58–59. This traditional bar-restaurant, with tables spilling onto the pavement, is *the* classic drinking spot in Ñuñoa. It also offers a range of meat and fish dishes at amazingly low prices (mains CH$2500–5000). Mon–Thurs 10am–1am, Fri & Sat 10am–3am.

★**Le Flaubert** Orrego Luco 125, Providencia ☎ 2 2231 9424, ⓦ leflaubert.cl; map pp.58–59. This exemplary Chilean–French bistro and *salon de thé* has an ever-changing menu marked up on chalkboards. Dishes (around CH$8000) could include country pâté, coq au vin and *tarte tatin*. There are also thirty different varieties of tea, and home-made cheeses and preserves for sale too. Tea with cakes and sandwiches CH$5000. Mon 10.30am–9pm, Tues–Fri 10.30am–11pm, Sat 12.30–11pm, Sun 12.30–7pm.

Liguria Av Providencia 1373, Providencia ☎ 2 2235 7914, ⓦ liguria.cl; map pp.58–59. Portraits, film posters, flower designs and football pennants adorn the walls of this legendary Santiago restaurant-bar, which has outdoor tables, a bar area, main dining area and several back rooms, so you can normally find a seat. Dishes include pork ribs in mustard sauce, sea bass with capers, and pot roast. There are two other branches, but this one is the best. Mains from CH$5000. Mon–Sat 11am–2am.

Santo Remedio Roman Diaz 152, Providencia ☎ 2 2235 0984, ⓦ santoremedio.cl; map pp.58–59. The idiosyncratic decor has a surreal edge – including high-backed wooden chairs and a zebra print sofa – and the food is billed as "an aphrodisiacal experience", with pastas, Thai curries, steaks and seafood all featuring on the menu. It's also *the* place for a Sunday night out, as well as a good stopover for drinks any night of the week. Mains CH$6300–9400, set lunches CH$4400–6400. Mon–Fri 1–3.30pm & 6.30pm–late, Sat & Sun 9pm–late.

LAS CONDES AND VITACURA

As you'd expect in these exclusive neighbourhoods, restaurants are often more about money than taste, but those listed below are well worth the extra outlay.

Amicci Apoquindo 7741 ☎ 2 2934 3722, ⓦ amicci.cl; map pp.58–59. A short walk from Los Dominicos craft market (see p.86), this restaurant combines attentive service, a creative cocktail menu (about CH$3,500 each) and refined Italian cuisine, including a particularly memorable seafood risotto (CH$10,500). Mon–Sat 12.30–3.30pm & 7.30–11.30pm, Sun 12.30–3.30pm.

Boragó Nueva Costanera 3467 ☎ 2 2953 8893, ⓦ borago.cl; map pp.58–59. Considered one of Latin America's best restaurants, *Boragó* employs a tasting menu (CH$35,000–55,000) to present its innovative take on Chilean traditional cuisine. The dishes vary according to the season and whim of the chef, but include such delights as *machas* marinated in garlic, or parma violet icecream. Reserve ahead. Mon–Sat 8–11pm.

Coquinaria Isidora Goyenechea 3000 ☎ 2 2245 1934, ⓦ coquinaria.cl; map pp.58–59. This gourmet food store-cum-restaurant is an appealing place at any time of day. The menu features a host of breakfast, brunch, lunch and dinner options – if you're feeling decadent, try the *wagyu* beef burger with foie gras. Brunch CH$9550, set lunch CH$10,250. Mon–Tues 9am–7.30pm, Wed–Sat 9am–11pm, Sun 9am–8pm.

Nolita Isidora Goyenechea 3456 ☎ 2 2232 6114, ⓦ nolita.cl; map pp.58–59. Self-consciously aping the style of the eponymous New York district, *Nolita* produces top-quality, artfully presented Italian cuisine (mains around CH$9000), with the seafood dishes, pastas and desserts all outstanding. Mon–Thurs 1–3.30pm & 8–11pm, Fri & Sat 1–3.30pm & 8pm–midnight, Sun 1–3.30pm.

Tanta Boulevard Parque Arauco ☎ 2 2364 1368, ⓦ tantaperu.com; map pp.58–59. By far the best restaurant in the popular Parque Arauco shopping complex, this branch of a bright and breezy Peruvian chain does large portions of very tasty Peruvian fare, including *tacu tacu*,

1

lomo saltado and, of course, huge pisco sours. *Tanta* is also found in the other main malls (see p.86). Daily 11am–9pm.

Tiramisú Isidora Goyenechea 3141 ☎2 2519 4900, ⓦtiramisu.cl; map pp.58–59. Long-running Italian restaurant with a vast array of salads, thin-crust pizzas (CH$3900–6950), pastas and desserts, all at – considering the location – reasonable prices. The *calzones* are particularly good. Daily 12.45–4pm & 7pm–midnight.

Zanzibar Monseñor Escriva de Balaguer 6400, inside the Borde del Río complex, Vitacura ☎2 2218 0120, ⓦzanzibar.cl; map pp.58–59. One of Santiago's most beautiful restaurants, with a host of Moroccan-style dining rooms, including a rooftop tented lounge. The global menu has an eclectic range of dishes including lamb tagine and conger eel with a black olive crust. Mains CH$8000–15,000. Mon–Sat noon–midnight, Sun noon–6pm.

BARS

Santiago's bars range from dusty, mahogany-panelled corner bars full of ancient regulars to ultra-trendy spaces. Lastarria has a number of cool, idiosyncratic bars and there are also plenty of options in grungier Bellavista. Providencia sports a number of bar-restaurants, but the dozens of dispiriting American-style bars, particularly around the junction of Suecia and Holley, are best avoided.

BARRIO LASTARRIA

Bar Don Rodrigo Victoria Subercaseaux 353; map p.62. Officially a hotel bar, attached to the *Hotel Floresta*, this place channels the 1950s, with an old-school bar area and live piano. The drinks aren't quite at 1950s prices, but are pretty cheap nonetheless ($2500 for a cocktail); be careful, they pack a punch. Mon–Sat 7pm–2am.

Bar The Clinic Monjitas 578 ☎2 2639 9548, ⓦbartheclinic.cl; map p.62. Run by the people behind satirical magazine *The Clinic*, this restaurant-bar maintains an appealingly irreverent air, from the quote of the day chalked up on a blackboard outside to the regular stand-up shows (in Spanish). There are also inexpensive snacks and meals (CH$4000–8000). Daily 12.30pm–2am.

★ **Berri** Rosal 321; map p.62. Small bar, hidden away on

a side street east of Santa Lucía with an understated, bohemian feel. Friendly staff and a loyal local following give this place a great atmosphere, even during the week. Mon–Thurs 7pm–3am, Sat 7pm–4am.

Catedral Merced, at Jose Miguel de la Barra ☎2 2664 3048, ⓦoperacatedral.cl; map p.62. This second-floor bar is a swish, modern space with a roof terrace ideal for a summer evening. There's a good menu of drinks (from CH$3000), and a small selection of dishes such as fried *tilapia* if you get peckish. Mon–Thurs 12.30pm–3am, Fri & Sat 12.30pm–5am.

BELLAVISTA

Bar Dos Gardenias Antonia López de Bello 199 ⓦbardosgardenias.cl; map p.72. A chilled-out and welcoming Cuban bar, with a faded red and yellow exterior, the obligatory Che picture, live Latin music and refreshing drinks (a mojito will set you back CH$3500). It's always lively on Fri and Sat nights. Tues–Thurs 8pm–2am, Fri 8pm–4am, Sat 8.30pm–4am.

La Casa en el Aire Antonia López de Bello 125 ☎2 2735 6680, ⓦlacasaenelaire.cl; map p.72. Named after Neruda's poem *Voy a hacerte una casa en el aire* ('I will build you a house in the air') this bar-café is one of the nicest places in Bellavista to enjoy a drink and live folk music, with occasional poetry recitals thrown in. There's also a much less atmospheric branch in Patio Bellavista. Daily 8pm–2/3am.

Ky Av Peru 631 ☎2 2777 7245, ⓦrestobarky.cl; map pp.58–59. From the outside this old house appears to have been abandoned, but once inside you find a beautifully renovated "resto-bar" kitted out with an eclectic array of knick-knacks. It's great for a late-night drink or a Southeast Asian meal. Tues–Sat 8pm–2am.

LAS CONDES

Flannery's Encomenderos 83 ☎2 2233 6675, ⓦflannerys.cl; map pp.58–59. The inevitable Irish pub, but a good choice for a night out in the Sanhattan area – large and busy, with both a loyal local clientele and good number of expats, who come to sup Guinness and English ale, watch the football or rugby and eat Irish stew or fish and chips (CH$6000). Mon–Fri noon–2.30am, Sat 5.30pm–3am, Sun 5.30pm–12.30am.

NIGHTLIFE

Santiago is not a 24/7 party town, but Thursday, Friday and Saturday nights are lively, and the club scene is constantly evolving, while **live music** – from folk to heavy metal – is popular. Dance festival Creamfields (ⓦcreamfields.cl) and rock festival Lollapalooza (ⓦlollapalooza.cl) have run Chilean editions in recent years (in Nov and March respectively).

CLUBS AND LIVE MUSIC

You'll find venues everywhere from the historic centre to bohemian Ñuñoa, in bars, jazz clubs and concert venues. Bellavista, in particular, has many "resto-bars" with live

music, as well as a number of (generally unappealing) clubs on Pío Nono; this area can be a bit unsafe at night, so take care.

La Batuta Jorge Washington 52, Plaza Ñuñoa

☎2 2724 4037, ⓦbatuta.cl; map pp.58–59. There's a wonderful grungy atmosphere at this dark, packed club just off Plaza Ñuñoa, which hosts rock bands, hip hop groups and heavy metal outfits. Wed & Thurs 10pm–2am, Fri & Sat 10pm–4.30am.

Blondie Alameda 2879, north side, near ⓜULA ☎2 2681 7793, ⓦblondie.cl; map pp.58–59. A popular student hangout with loud – and often live – music (lots of techno, dance, electro and indie), and dancing. Generally Thurs–Sat midnight–4/5am, though it sometimes hosts events on other nights too.

Club de Jazz Av Ossa 123, Mall Plaza Egaña, La Reina, close to ⓜPlaza Egaña ⓦclubdejazz.cl; map pp.58–59. Founded in 1943 and still going strong, the *Club de Jazz* has an invariably excellent line-up of Chilean and international jazz musicians. Fri & Sat 10.30pm–late, plus occasional Sun evening shows.

Club La Feria Constitución 275, Bellavista ☎2 2735 8433, ⓦclublaferia.cl; map p.72. The best place in Santiago for electro, *Club La Feria* – which has been running since 1996 – plays host to an illustrious cast of Chilean and international DJs. Wed–Sat 10pm–4/5am.

La Maestra Vida Pío Nono 380, Bellavista ☎2 2777 5325, ⓦmaestravida.cl; map p.72. One of Santiago's oldest *salsatecas* and popular with dancers of all ages, giving it a friendly vibe – there's no need to feel shy about practising your steps here. It also runs salsa classes. Tues 10pm–3.30am, Wed & Thurs 10.30pm–3.30am, Fri 10.30pm–4.30am, Sat 11.30pm–4.30am, Sun 10pm–3.30am.

Teatro Caupolicán San Diego 850, close to ⓜParque O'Higgins, ⓦteatrocaupolican.cl; map pp.58–59. Long-running gig venue near Parque O'Higgins, used by popular international, Latin American and local musicians. Check the website to see listings ('*cartelera*').

ENTERTAINMENT

Santiago is generally the best place in Chile to enjoy the arts. The Friday newspapers include comprehensive entertainment listings, and you can also check listings for the bigger events and buy tickets at Ticketek Chile (ⓦticketek.cl). The guide website ⓦsantiagochile.com also has what's on listings.

CINEMA

There are plenty of cinemas in Santiago, though the choice of movies in the larger ones tends to be limited to the latest Hollywood blockbusters; those that have family appeal are usually dubbed. Huérfanos is the main cinema street in the historic centre. Tickets start at around CH$4000.

Centro Arte Alameda Alameda 139, historic centre ☎2 2664 8821, ⓦwww.centroartealameda.cl. Comfy cinema with a regularly changing and wide-ranging choice of foreign films.

Centro de Extensión de la Universidad Católica Alameda 390, historic centre ☎2 2354 6516, ⓦextension.uc.cl. Especially good for older films, often presented as part of themed programmes. Many free showings for students with ID.

Centro Cultural Matucana 100 Matucana 100, near Parque Quinta Normal ☎2 2682 4502, ⓦm100.cl. Runs regular film seasons, sometimes in English, plus art exhibitions and concerts.

Cine Arte Normandie Tarapacá 1181, historic centre ☎2 2697 2979, ⓦnormandie.cl. Cinema with a reputation for showing obscure contemporary European films.

Cine Hoyts Moneda 835, historic centre ☎600 500 0400, ⓦcinehoyts.cl. In a convenient location in the historic centre of Santiago, this cinema has six screens.

Cinemark Theatres Av Kennedy 9001, Mall Alto Las Condes ☎600 586 0058, ⓦwww.cinemark.cl. Modern multiplex offering Hollywood's latest flicks.

THEATRE, CLASSICAL MUSIC, DANCE AND OPERA

The best time to experience Chilean theatre is in January, when Santiago hosts Santiago a Mil (ⓦstgoamil.cl), an enormous international festival of theatre (plus dance and other arts). During the rest of the year, many theatres are only open Thursday to Saturday. Ticket prices are usually reasonable, from around CH$4000–5000.

Centro Cultural Mori Constitución 183, Bellavista ☎2 2777 6246, ⓦcentromori.cl. A cutting-edge theatre, dance and arts venue.

Centro Gabriela Mistral Bernardo O'Higgins 227, Lastarria ☎2 2566 5500, ⓦgam.cl. You can't miss Santiago's newest and most exciting cultural offering – a huge weathered steel edifice on the Alameda (see p.66). GAM has a wide-ranging programme of contemporary theatre, dance, music, art and cinema – it's always worth popping in to see what they have going on.

Teatro Bellavista Dardignac 110, Bellavista ☎2 2735 2395. This long-established and reliable theatre usually stages modern foreign plays, often comedies.

Teatro de la Universidad Católica Jorge Washington 26, Ñuñoa ☎2 2205 5652, ⓦteatrouc.uc.cl. This university-run venue offers classic shows and adaptations of international works.

Teatro Municipal Agustinas 749, historic centre ☎800 471 000, ⓦmunicipal.cl. Santiago's most prestigious performing arts venue, offering a menu of classical concerts, ballet and opera in a splendid old building (see p.63).

1

Teatro San Ginés Mallinkrodt 112, Bellavista ☎2 2738 2159, ⓦsangines.cl5. Top Chilean productions are staged here, as are fine children's shows on weekend afternoons.

GAY AND LESBIAN SANTIAGO

Santiago is the only city in Chile with anything resembling an organized gay community. The scene, such as it is, centres around **Bellavista**, and consists of a small collection of bars, restaurants, discos and saunas. Local gay rights organization Movilh (ⓦmovilh.cl) holds an annual gay pride march and cinema festival.

RESTAURANTS AND BARS

Capricho Español Purísima 65 ☎2 2777 7674; map p.72. Spanish and international cuisine (mains around CH$5000–8000) served by an all-male waiting staff in an atmospheric, neo-colonial building. Try to grab the cow-print sofa on the terrace. Free passes to *Bokhara* are often handed out. Mon–Thurs 8pm–2.30am, Fri & Sat 8pm–3am.

Farinelli Bombero Nuñez 68 ☎2 2732 8966; map p.62. Bar with shows every evening, many of them hilarious comic drag acts requiring a decent level of Spanish to be fully appreciated. Tues–Thurs 7pm–3.30am, Fri & Sat 7pm–4.30am, Sun 7pm–2am.

CLUBS

Bokhara Pío Nono 430; map p.72. A legendary, multi-storey club with a mixed gay and lesbian crowd, and shows featuring drag artists and Brazilian dance troupes. The queues to get in, however, can be long. Daily 10pm–4/5am.

Bunker Bombero Nuñez 159 ☎2 2737 1716, ⓦbunker.cl; map.72. This refurbished theatre is one of the most popular gay clubs in Santiago, thanks mainly to its dance and techno policy. There's a cavernous back room, filled with large crowds. Fri & Sat 11pm–4/5am.

SHOPPING

Chileans love to go **shopping** and the capital has a number of modern, American-style **shopping centres** packed with imported brands from the U.S. and elsewhere. The historic centre is perhaps of more interest to visitors, with its small, old-fashioned shops and a warren of arcades (*galerías*) that seem to lurk behind every other doorway.

The city's **markets** offer some great shopping: **Feria Santa Lucía** (daily 11am–9pm) sells crafts, clothes and lapis lazuli; the enormous and very lively **Persa Bío Bío** (Sat & Sun 9am–around 2pm) runs the length of Franklin and Bío Bío, and at the junction with Victor Manual has a great flea market, and lots of antiques stalls; the excellent **Pueblito de los Dominicos** (daily: summer 10.30am–8pm; winter 10am–7pm) has over two hundred stalls selling knitwear, ceramics, glass objects, books, and antiques (see p.74); **Antiguedades Parque Los Reyes** (Brasil 1157; daily 10am–around 2pm) is a great place to browse for antique furniture, musical instruments, books and bric-à-brac. Also don't miss the stalls at the **Mercado Central** and the **Feria Municipal La Vega** (see p.70), which are great places to explore and eat at. In Bellavista head to Avenida Bellavista, between Puente Pío Nono and Puente del Arzobispo, where there are a string of workshops and salesrooms selling jewellery and other objects made of lapis lazuli.

BOOKS AND CDS

Librería Inglesa Huérfanos 669, local 11, historic centre ☎2 2632 5153, ⓦlibreriainglesa.cl; map p.62. Fairly good, expensive choice of Penguin paperbacks and other English-language books. Mon–Fri 10am–7.30pm, Sat 10am–1.30pm.

La Tienda Nacional Merced 369, Lastarria ☎2 2638 4706, ⓦlatiendanacional.cl; map p.62. As the name suggests, this shop specialises in all things Chilean, with an emphasis on music and film, although it also sells all sorts of knick-knacks. A good place to find something different to take home, from a Chilean folk music CD to a rainbow-coloured anti-dictatorship NO mug. Mon–Sat noon–8pm.

TXT Ahumada 268, historic centre; map p.62. Sells a mix of independent and classic DVDs, music and books, including lots of Chilean music CDs. Mon–Fri 10am–9pm, Sat & Sun 10am–8pm.

SHOPPING CENTRES

Alto Las Condes Av Kennedy 9001, Las Condes ☎2 2299 6965, ⓦaltolascondes.cl; map pp.58–59. Huge, modern shopping centres with over two hundred shops, food court, and bowling alley. Daily 10am–10pm.

Costanera Center Andrés Bello 2425, Providencia ☎2 2916 9200, ⓦwww.costaneracenter.cl; map pp.58–59. One of Latin America's largest shopping centres at the base of one of its tallest skyscrapers (see p.73). The six floors of retailing are rather bland, even by shopping centre standards, though it does have the virtue of being close to a metro station (Tobalaba). Daily 10am–10pm.

Mall Sport Av Las Condes 13451, La Dehesa ☎2 2429 3030, ⓦmallsport.cl; map pp.58–59. On the main route up to the ski resorts at Farellones, this shopping centre is dedicated, as its name suggests, to sports. As well as a plethora of stores selling trekking, skiing and gym gear, it

has a climbing wall, artificial wave for surf lessons, and winter ice rink. Daily 10am–9pm.

Parque Arauco Av Kennedy 5413, Las Condes ☎ 2 2299 0629, ⓦ parquearauco.cl; map pp.58–59. The best mall in town, with some unexpectedly good restaurants, plus cinemas and a theatre. Take a taxi or walk from Estación Militar metro; the Turistik bus (see p.78) also stops here. Daily 11am–9pm.

FOOD AND DRINK

Larbos Estado 26, historic centre ☎ 2 2639 3434, ⓦ larbos.cl; map p.62. A lovely, old-fashioned shop selling fine wines, spirits (such as pisco) and fancy foodstuffs including chocolates. Mon–Sat 10am–8pm, Sun 10am–5pm.

Wain Nueva Costanera 3955, Vitacura ☎ 2 2953 6290, ⓦ wain.cl; map pp.58–59. Well-informed staff guide you through an extensive range of quality wine from across Chile; the shop also produces its own wine magazine. Mon–Sat 10am–6pm.

MOUNTAIN CLIMBING AND OUTDOOR EQUIPMENT

As well as the places listed below, Mall Sport (see p.86) has a wide range of stores selling outdoor clothing and equipment, although not usually at the cheapest prices.

La Cumbre Av Apoquindo 5220, Las Condes ☎ 2 2220 9907, ⓦ lacumbreonline.cl; map pp.58–59. Run by friendly staff, this shop has world-class boots, eyewear and climbing accessories as well as a small library of books about exploring the Andes. Mon–Fri 11am–8pm, Sat 11am–4pm.

Tatoo Los Leones 81, Providencia ☎ 2 2946 0008, ⓦ tatoo.ws; map pp.58–59. Hiking, climbing and camping equipment at competitive prices. Mon–Fri 10.30am–8pm, Sat 10.30am–7pm.

DIRECTORY

Embassies Argentina, Miraflores 285 ☎ 2 2582 2606; Australia, Isidora Goyenechea 3621 ☎ 2 2550 3500; Brazil, Alonso Ovalle 1665 ☎ 2 2659 1911; Canada, 12th floor, World Trade Centre, Nueva Tajamar 481 ☎ 2 2652 3800; France, Condell 65 ☎ 2 2470 8000; Germany, Las Hualtatas 5677 ☎ 2 2463 2500; Israel, San Sebastián 2812 ☎ 2 2750 0500; Netherlands, Apoquindo 3500 ☎ 2 2756 9200; New Zealand, Isidora Goyenechea 3000, 12th floor ☎ 2 2616 3000; Peru, Antonio Bellet 444 ☎ 2 2940 2900; South Africa, 4th floor, Apoquindo 2827 ☎ 2 2820 0300; UK, Av El Bosque Norte 0125 ☎ 2 2370 4100; US, Av Andrés Bello 2800 ☎ 2 2330 3000.

Emergencies Ambulance ☎ 131; fire department (*bomberos*) ☎ 132; police (*carabineros*) ☎ 133.

Hospitals Clínica Alemana, Vitacura 5951, Vitacura ☎ 2 2210 1111, ⓦ alemana.cl; Clínica Las Condes, Estoril 450, Las Condes ☎ 2 2210 4000, ⓦ www .clinicalascondes.cl; Clínica Indisa, Av Santa María 1810, Providencia ☎ 2 2362 5555, ⓦ indisa.cl.

Language courses BridgeChile, Los Leones 439 ☎ 2 2233 4356, ⓦ bridgechile.com; Centro Chileno Canadiense,

Office 601, Luis Thayer Ojeda 191 ☎ 2 2334 1090, ⓦ canadiense.cl; Natalislang, Arturo Bürhle 47, Providencia, ⓦ natalislang.com.

Laundry Most hostels and hotels offer a laundry service, and there are also numerous laundries throughout the city. Lavandería Tarroca, Mac Iver 490, is conveniently located in the historic centre.

Maps Topographical maps on all parts of Chile are available at the Instituto Geográfico Militar, Calle Dieciocho 369, near Toesca metro (☎ 2 4210 9463, ⓦ igm.cl). For tourist and walking maps, go to Sernatur (see p.78).

Money and exchange Most banks are open 9am–2pm only; almost all have 24hr ATMs – look for the maroon and white Redbanc sign. Many commercial establishments (particularly pharmacies) also have ATMs. The best place to change cash and travellers' cheques is the cluster of change houses on Agustinas between Ahumada and Bandera in the historic centre. Few Chilean banks are useful for changing dollars, but Citibank (many branches, including Huérfanos 770, Ahumada 40, Teatinos 180 and La Bolsa 64) charges no commission for changing US dollars into pesos.

CROSSING INTO ARGENTINA

The international highway that connects Santiago with Mendoza, capital of Argentina's wine-growing region, is probably the most popular overland route between the two cross-Andes neighbours. It's a spectacular journey, and one that you should certainly do by day if possible so as to see the scenery. The **border crossing** is 7km further on from the Portillo turn off; basic food and drink and money exchange is available on both sides, but be prepared for long queues at passport control and customs, especially at holiday times. On the Argentine side, the **Alta Montaña** route, with fantastic views of Aconcagua, snakes past mountain villages, sulphur springs and small ski resorts and on into Mendoza. The whole journey takes about six or seven hours, although a busy border crossing can easily pile a couple of hours onto that; buses regularly make the trip in both directions.

WINE TOURS NEAR SANTIAGO

Santiago is within easy reach of some of Chile's oldest **wineries**, several of which offer tours and tastings. Those by the Río Maipo, in particular, are beautifully located, with large swaths of emerald-green vines framed by the snowcapped cordillera and bright-blue skies. Harvesting takes place in March, and if you visit during then you'll see the grapes being sorted and pressed. If you want to visit a vineyard you should book at least a day beforehand. We've listed some relatively easily reached wineries below, which are accessible by public transport. All the tours include free tastings.

Concha y Toro Virginia Subercaseaux 210, Pirque ☎2 2476 5269, ⓦconchaytoro.com; From ⓜLas Mercedes it's a short taxi ride to the vineyard. This handsome vineyard, behind the famous Casillero del Diablo wine brand, was founded in 1883 by Don Melchor Concha y Toro. It is now the largest wine producer in Latin America and one of the world's leading brands. Tours CH$9000, or CH$19,000 for premium tasting tour. Tours regularly daily between 10am and 4pm in English, premium tours at 4pm in English.

Cousiño Macul 7100 Av Quilin ☎2 2351 4135, ⓦcousinomacul.com; From ⓜQuilin take a taxi or walk 30min east along Av Quilin. The main estate and park of Chile's oldest winery (dating from 1550) make a nice quick trip from central Santiago. Bilingual tours CH$9000 or CH$18,000 for premium tasting. Mon–Fri 11am, noon, 3pm and 4pm, Sat & Sun 11am & noon.

Santa Rita Padre Hurtado 695, Alto Jahuel ☎2 2362 2520, ⓦwww.santarita.com; train to Buin, from where you can catch a bus or taxi, or take the Turistik tour (p.78). Santa Rita and sister vineyard Carmen are the home of Carmenere, where the signature Chilean grape, thought extinct, was rediscovered in the 1990s by a visiting French oenologist. As well as tours and tastings, the site has the anthropological *Museo Andino*, an elegant restaurant and a beautifully located hotel (doubles CH$140,000) in the old family hacienda that even has its own ghost (ask the hotel manager to show you the photos). Tours from CH$10,000. Several tours daily Tues–Sun.

Undurraga Old road to Melipilla, Km 34 ☎2 2372 2900, ⓦwww.undurraga.cl; bus to Talagante from Terminal San Borja (every 15min; 30min), and ask to be dropped off at the vineyard. Still run by the Undurraga family, the vineyard was established in 1885, complete with mansion and park. It's now a large, modern winery, and you're likely to be shown around by someone who's directly involved in the wine-making process. Bilingual tours CH$9000. Mon–Fri 10.15am, noon, 2pm and 3.30pm, Sat & Sun 10.15am, noon & 3.30pm.

Newspapers There are numerous newspaper kiosks around town; those at the corner of Huérfanos and Ahumada sell a reasonable range of foreign newspapers, including *Die Welt*, the *Financial Times* and *The New York Times*, and magazines.

Pharmacies Farmacias Ahumada (☎600 222 4000, ⓦfarmaciasahumada.cl) has a number of 24hr branches, including Huérfanos 896, and El Bosque 164, Providencia; they'll deliver for a small charge.

Post offices Correo Central, Plaza de Armas 559 (Mon–Fri 8.30am–7pm, Sat 8.30am–1pm). Other branches at Moneda 1155, near Morandé; Local 17, Exposición 57 Paseo Estación; Av Nueva Providencia 2092.

Cajón del Maipo

The **CAJÓN DEL MAIPO** is a beautiful river valley carved out of the Andes by the Río Maipo. Served by a good paved road and punctuated by a string of hamlets offering tourist facilities, it's one of the most popular weekend escapes from the capital. The potential for outdoor adventures is enormous, with organized **hiking**, **rafting** and **mountain biking** trips all on offer.

Start at the mouth of the *cajón*, just 25km southeast of Santiago, at Las Vizcachas. Here the scenery is lush and gentle, and as you climb into the valley you'll pass vineyards (see box above), orchards, roadside stalls selling locally produced fruit, and signs advertising home-made *küchen* (cake), *miel* (honey), *pan amasado* (fresh oven-baked bread) and *chicha* (cider).

Note that there are no banks or ATMs in the Cajón del Maipo, so bring cash.

1

San José de Maipo

Twenty-five kilometres on from Las Vizcachas is the administrative centre of the valley, **SAN JOSÉ DE MAIPO**. It's quite attractive, with single-storey adobe houses and an old, colonial church. The town is also the last place along the road where you can fill up with petrol.

San Alfonso

Some 15km beyond San José is **SAN ALFONSO** (1100m altitude), a lovely place if you just want to unwind for a few hours in beautiful mountain scenery. Former nineteenth-century horse ranch *Cascada de las Animas* (see p.91) offers **horseriding**, **kayaking** and **whitewater rafting** as well as a good ninety-minute guided walk up to a 20m **waterfall** (the "**Cascada de las Animas**") on the other side of the river. You can also arrange similar trips through Altué Expediciones in Santiago (☎2 2333 1390, ☒altue.com).

San Gabriel and El Volcán

By the time you reach **SAN GABRIEL**, 50km from the start of the valley road at Las Vizcachas, you are entering increasingly rugged Andes scenery. This uninteresting village marks the end of the asphalt road, which continues as a very poor dirt track for another 20km to Lo Valdés. To carry on, you have to go through a *carabineros* (police) checkpoint, so make sure you've got all your driving documents and passport with you. Unless you're in a 4WD you should expect to go *very* slowly from this point onwards. The village of **El Volcán**, at Km 56, was practically wiped out by a landslide some years ago. By now the scenery is really dramatic as you snake between 4000m mountains coloured with jagged mineral-patterns of violet, cream and blue.

Baños Morales and Baños de Colina

The village of **BAÑOS MORALES**, the site of an uninviting thermal pool about 12 km from El Volcán, is the closest base to the beautiful, jagged-peaked **Monumento Nacional El Morado** (see box below). From here the road deteriorates into an even poorer track, but continues for another 11km to **Baños de Colina**, a series of natural thermal pools carved into the mountainside; for all their remoteness they can get horribly crowded in summer weekends, but otherwise are blissfully empty. This is also the embarkation point for multi-day **horse treks** into the Andes. Up to week-long excursions often leave in packed caravans that snake into the mountains. For less arduous trips, many locals rent out horses by the hour or afternoon.

HIKING IN THE MONUMENTO NACIONAL EL MORADO

A path from the bus stop in Baños Morales crosses a bridge and leads to the Conaf hut at the entrance to **Monumento Nacional El Morado** (daily: Oct–April 8.30am–6pm, May–Sept 8.30am–1pm; CH$2000), where you should get the latest hiking and climbing information as landslides, snowmelts and the glaciers change the terrain from year to year. The park's single 8km trail follows the Río Morales through a narrow valley that ends at the glacier that feeds the river. Towering above the glacier, and visible from almost all points along the trail, is the magnificent silhouette of El Mirador del Morado (4320m) and, just behind, El Morado itself (5060m).

Apart from the first half-hour, the path is fairly level and not hard going, though you may find yourself feeling breathless as you gradually climb in altitude. About 5km beyond the Conaf hut – after roughly two to three hours of hiking – you reach a small **lake**, Laguna de Morado, where there is free camping, a toilet and water pump. Once past the lake, the path is less defined, but it's easy enough to pick your way through the stones to the black, slimy-looking **glacier** 3km beyond, at an altitude of 2500m. Don't enter the tempting ice caves – they are unstable. This is a good place for day-trekkers to turn around and head back.

POTTERY IN POMAIRE

Some 50km southwest of Santiago, the dusty, quaint village of **Pomaire** was one of the *pueblos de indios* created by the Spanish in the eighteenth century in an attempt to control the native population. Its inhabitants quickly developed a reputation for their **pottery** and the village streets (particularly the main street, San Antonio) are packed with dozens of workshops selling a vast range of pots, bowls and kitchenware, many of them made from the characteristic attractive but brittle coffee-coloured *greda* clay. Simple eateries line the streets, some specializing in giant 1.5kg *empanadas*. To get to Pomaire by public transport, take a Melipilla bus from Terminal San Borja and ask to be set off at the side road to Pomaire (regular; 1hr–1hr 30min from Santiago). From here, it's a 30min walk into the village, or take a *colectivo* or taxi.

ARRIVAL AND DEPARTURE

CAJÓN DEL MAIPO

By bus Getting to Cajón del Maipo is easy from Santiago: the #72 bus to San José de Maipo (every 10–20min; 1hr 30min) runs from Av Concha y Toro, outside Las Mercedes metro station. There are less frequent services from Santiago to Baños Morales (#72 bus 7.30am from Bellavista La Florida metro station, daily Jan & Feb; weekends only mid-Sept to Dec; 2hr 30min) and El Volcán (several daily; 2hr). Shared taxis and minibuses connect San José de Maipo with San Alfonso and other places in the *cajón*.

By car For private vehicles the road from Santiago is fine until San Gabriel, where it may be filled with rocks and landslides. Weekend traffic can be horrendous, with 2–3hr backups. To avoid the traffic, make sure you enter the *cajón* well before 10am and leave before 3pm (or, if necessary, late at night).

ACCOMMODATION AND EATING

★**Cascada de las Animas** By the river, San Alfonso ☎2 2861 1303, ⒲cascada.net. Set in a park, this highly recommended lodge has a wide range of accommodation including camping spots, cosy rooms in a renovated 1930s building, and lovely wooden cabins, as well as a fabulous outdoor pool, a restaurant overlooking the steep river gorge and a good bar. An extensive range of activities are on offer including trekking, horseriding, rafting and ziplining. Camping/person **CH$10,000**, doubles **CH$36,000**, cabins **CH$78,000**

Refugio Lo Valdés About 1km beyond the fork to Baños Morales, Lo Valdés ☎09 230 5930, ⒲refugiolovaldes.com. This atmospheric Alpine-style mountain refuge, dating back to 1932, has comfortable dorm-style accommodation, plus a restaurant-bar. Numerous activities – such as horseriding, trekking and mountain biking – are on offer too. **CH$22,000**

Residencial España Camino al Volcán, San Alfonso 31443 ☎2 2861 1543. There are just five rooms at this simple B&B; all are clean, homely and share bathrooms. Rates include breakfast, and there's an excellent attached Spanish restaurant that serves – among other dishes – a very tasty paella. Restaurant open daily noon-7pm. **CH$22,000**

Los Andes and around

There's nothing wildly exciting about **LOS ANDES**, but this old colonial town, with its narrow streets and lively main square, makes a convenient base for day-trips to the ski resort of **Portillo** (see p.92). Eighty kilometres north of Santiago, on the international road to Mendoza, Argentina, it's set in the beautiful Aconcagua valley; the first ridge rises to 3500m and then soars to 6959m Aconcagua, the highest peak outside the Himalayas, just across the border in Argentina. The surrounding region is fertile, and as you approach Los Andes from Santiago you'll pass vineyards and numerous peach and lemon orchards.

Santuario de Santa Teresa de los Andes

About 10km from Los Andes • Daily 8am–6.30pm • Free • ☎ 34 240 1900, ⒲santuarioteresadelosandes.cl

The **Santuario de Santa Teresa de los Andes** is a huge, modern church built in 1987 to house the remains of **Santa Teresa**, who became Chile's first saint when she was canonized in 1993. Her shrine attracts thousands of pilgrims each year, especially on July 13, her feast day.

1

SKIING NEAR SANTIAGO

Santiago is close to some of the best **skiing** in South America. **Sunshine** is abundant and queues for lifts are practically nonexistent during weekdays. The season normally lasts from mid-June to early October, with snow virtually guaranteed from mid-July to the first week in September.

Sitting high in the Andes at the foot of Cerro Colorado, a 90min drive along a snaking road ('Camino a Farellones') from Santiago, **Farellones** is a straggling collection of hotels and apartments that serves the triple 'Tres Valles' resorts of El Colorado (4km north), La Parva (2km further on), and Valle Nevado (a winding 14km east). All three resorts are connected by pistes and can theoretically be skied in the same day if the runs are open. Alternatively, a 2hr drive from Santiago on the better-condition international road (Autopista Los Libertadores and R-57) takes you to posh **Portillo**, close to the Argentine border.

TRANSPORT AND EQUIPMENT RENTAL

The least expensive way to go skiing is to stay in Santiago and visit the slopes for the day. A number of **minibus** companies offer daily services to the resorts, including Ski Total, Apoquindo 4900 (☎2 2246 0156, ⓦskitotal.cl). Buses leave 8am–8.30am daily for El Colorado, La Parva (return ticket to either CH$13,000) and Valle Nevado (CH$15,000), and at the same times on Wednesdays and Saturdays to Portillo (CH$23,000); buses return from the resorts at 5pm. Ski/snowboard equipment rental starts at CH$21,000 for the full kit.

If you intend to drive up yourself, note traffic is only allowed up the road to Farellones until noon, and back down to Santiago from 2pm onwards; tyre chains are often required but seldom used; they can be rented on the way up.

Each resort has its own **lift ticket** costing around CH$43,000 in high season and CH$38,000 in low.

THE RESORTS

All of the resorts have ski schools, English-speaking instructors, and equipment rental outlets.

El Colorado ⓦelcolorado.cl. Linked to Farellones by ski lift (when there is enough snow), as well as by road, El Colorado has fifteen lifts and 22 runs. The busiest resort, it is particularly good for beginners, with a wide range of blue and green runs. The resort's base is known as Villa El Colorado, and includes several apart-hotels, restaurants and pubs.

La Parva ⓦlaparva.cl. La Parva has mostly red runs, huge areas of backcountry skiing and a classy feel. The skiing here is often excellent, with some very long intermediate cruising runs and a vertical drop of nearly 1000m. The resort has thirty pistes and fourteen lifts, but limited accommodation facilities.

Portillo ⓦskiportillo.com. Portillo is a sophisticated place in a beautiful lake setting, with no condominiums and just one hotel – the restored 1940s-vintage *Hotel Portillo* (see opposite). The ski-runs are world-class, and it's best known for its endless off-piste options; it's therefore well-suited to advanced level skiiers. There are twelve lifts, plus extensive snow-making equipment. Portillo is avidly kid-friendly and its ski school is routinely ranked one of the world's best.

Museo Arqueológico

Av Santa Teresa 398 • Tues–Sun 10am–6.30pm • CH$1000

The **Museo Arqueológico**, based in a lovely old house, has an impressive collection of pre-Columbian pottery, petroglyphs and skulls, and an astonishing mummy from the Atacama Desert, as well as more recent exhibits that date from the Independence period.

Cerro de la Virgen

If you're feeling energetic, climb **Cerro de la Virgen**, the hill rising behind the town. It takes about an hour to reach the top following the path from the picnic site on Independencia. The views are wonderful, especially just before sunset when the whole valley is bathed in a clear, golden light.

Valle Nevado @ vallenevado.com. On the whole, it's worth the short extra journey from Farellones to reach Valle Nevado, which often has better snow than El Colorado, a wider range of pistes among its 27 runs, and more modern lifts, including a new gondola. It also has first-class hotels and some good restaurants and is the clear favourite for snowboarders.

ACCOMMODATION

Alongside the hotels listed below, you can also rent an apartment – this is often a more economical option, particularly if you negotiate with private owners. Chilean Ski (@ www .chileanski.com) has a selection. The accommodation is aimed chiefly at foreign visitors and quoted in US dollars.

Condominio Nueva La Parva La Parva, Tres Valles @ 2 2964 2100, @ laparva.cl. The only commercial place to stay in La Parva with a range of apartments – each featuring a kitchen – sleeping six or eight. Note that you must book for at least a week. Six-person apartment per week US$6550

Hotel Posada de Farellones El Colorado, Tres Valles @ 2 2248 7672, @ skifarellones.com. The best place to stay near El Colorado, this hotel has smart en suites, a Jacuzzi and a good restaurant. Prices include half board and transport to the slopes. US$240

Hotel Valle Nevado Valle Nevado, Tres Valles @ 2 2477 7701, @ vallenevado.com. This hotel has classy en suites with panoramic mountain views, a gym and spa, and an excellent restaurant. You have direct "ski-in, ski-out" access to the slopes, and heli-skiing is also on offer. Rates include half board and ski lift pass; during high season you have to book a minimum seven nights. US$560

Lodge Andes Camino La Capilla 662, Farellones, Tres Valles @ 2 2264 9899, @ lodgeandes.cl.

A sociable lodge with simple private rooms and shared bathrooms, as well as four-, six- and eight-bed dorms (including a women-only one) with bunk beds and lockers; both rooms and dorms have central heating. There is also a decent restaurant and bar, a pool table, multilingual staff, and a lounge with a TV and a log fire. Rates include half board. Dorms CH$35,000, doubles CH$85,000

Hotel Portillo Portillo @ 2 2361 7000, @ skiportillo .com. The only hotel in Portillo, perched by the shores of the Laguna del Inca, offers the hippest ski scene in South America. There is a wide range of (very expensive) accommodation options, from simple bunks in the Inca Lodge to suites with stunning views. All rates are per person and include seven nights' accommodation, ski pass and full board; usually you must book for a Saturday to Saturday 'ski week', although they do run the occasional short-stay promotion. The hotel also opens in the summer as a base for walks around the lake or stopover on the route to/from Argentina (from US$64/ person/night). Inca Lodge US$1200, doubles US$3850

BACKCOUNTRY SKIING

There are some great backcountry options for skiers who want to escape the resorts. **Ski Arpa**, near the city of San Esteban, a 2hr drive from Santiago, offers cat skiing (off-trail skiing accessed via a snowcat vehicle, rather than a ski lift) and snowboarding in two beautiful valleys, el Arpa and la Honda, which lie to the west of Argentina's Cerro Aconcagua, the highest mountain in the Andes. Note there is no equipment hire available. A full-day here (featuring four runs with a guide) costs US$350. Santiago Adventures (@ 2 2244 2750, @ santiagoadventures.com) can organize transport and accommodation nearby; the company also offers (pricey) heli skiing trips.

ARRIVAL AND DEPARTURE

LOS ANDES AND AROUND

By bus Frequent buses (1hr 20min) depart from Terminal Los Héroes in Santiago, dropping you at the bus station on Membrillar, one block east of the main square; most of them stop at the Santuario de Santa Teresa en route.

ACCOMMODATION AND EATING

Casa Vieja Maipu 151 @ 34 246 0367. Classic *parrilla* style restaurant, with occasional live music, brisk service and plates piled high with beef. Fish dishes such as corvina in seafood sauce (CH$12,000) are also available, but most people share the two-person *parrillada*, or mixed barbecue (CH$25,000). Mon–Sat 1pm–midnight, Sun 1–6pm.

Hotel Plaza Manuel Rodriguez 368 @ 34 240 2157, @ hotelplazalosandes.cl. If you want to stay the night,

Hotel Plaza is a decent choice. The rooms – which have private bathrooms and TVs – are comfortable, if nothing to write home about. There's also a good restaurant. CH$60,000

Inca Hoteles Av Argentina Oriente 11 @ 34 234 5500, @ incahoteles.cl. Situated near the Cerro de la Virgen, this is the best place to stay in town, with pleasant rooms, good breakfast and an outdoor pool for the summer months. CH$97,000

Valparaíso, Viña and the Central Coast

96 Valparaíso

110 South of Valparaíso

112 Viña del Mar

117 North of Viña

120 Parque Nacional La Campana

Valparaíso, Viña and the Central Coast

Of Chile's 4000km-plus coastline, the brief central strip between Rocas de Santo Domingo and Los Vilos is the most visited and developed. Known as the Litoral Central, this 250km stretch boasts bay after bay lined with gorgeous, white-sand beaches, and a string of coastal resort towns. Valparaíso ("Valpo" for short) and Viña del Mar (or "Viña") sit next to each other near the middle of the strip. They are geographical neighbours, but poles apart in appearance and atmosphere.

Viña is Chile's largest beach resort and one of its ritziest. With its high-rises, casino, and seafront restaurants, as well as the beaches and clubs in nearby **Reñaca**, Viña typifies modern hedonism. Valparaíso, on the other hand, has far more personality, with ramshackle, colourful houses spilling chaotically down the hills to the sea (but no decent beaches). For stretches of sand, you'll need to head south or north.

Closest to Santiago, via the "Autopista del Sol" (Ruta 78), are the resorts **south of Valparaíso**, which are busier and more developed. Further south, there's an almost uninterrupted string of *cabañas*, villas and small, unappealing resorts. Even so, it's still possible to find places with charm and soul, especially where Pablo Neruda found them, at **Isla Negra** – though it, too, is fast being swallowed up by development.

Heading **north of Viña** you leave most of the concrete behind at **Concón**, and from **Horcón** up, the coast begins to look more rugged and feels distinctly wild and windswept by the time you reach **Maitencillo**, where sandstone cliffs tower above a huge, white beach. The stretch from here to **Papudo** is easily the most beautiful of the region. Not even the new villas and second-home complexes that have sprung up along here have managed to spoil **Zapallar**, the most architecturally graceful of the resorts, or Papudo, a small town dramatically hemmed in by steep, green hills. Two more resorts lie further north: **Los Vilos** and **Pichidangui**.

Inland and a world away from the coastal glitz, Parque Nacional la Campana offers excellent hiking.

Valparaíso

Valparaíso es un montón, un racimo de casas locas (Valparaíso is a heap, a bunch of crazy houses)

Pablo Neruda

Spread over an amphitheatre of hills encircling a wide bay, **Valparaíso** is the most intriguing and distinctive city in Chile. Its most striking feature is the array of houses – a mad, colourful tangle of them tumbling down the hills to a narrow shelf of land below. Few roads make it up these gradients and most people get up and down on the city's *ascensores* (lifts), ancient-looking funiculars that slowly haul you up to incredible viewpoints.

When to visit the central coast p.99
Valparaíso's antiquated lifts p.104
Pablo Neruda p.110

Casablanca Valley wine route p.112
Hiking in Parque Nacional La Campana p.121

CASA MUSEO ISLA NEGRA

Highlights

❶ Historic Valparaíso Chile's most remarkable city, sitting precariously on a series of undulating hills above a huge bay, is a historical treasure trove, with antique elevators, a grand but crumbling downtown, and some wonderfully restored mansions. **See p.96**

❷ Eating out in Valparaíso Valpo is home to some of Chile's most inventive chefs who have created a refreshingly diverse dining (and drinking) scene. **See p.108**

❸ Casa Museo Isla Negra Pablo Neruda set up home in the village of Isla Negra and wrote many of his Nobel Prize-winning poems while

gazing out at his favourite beach. His house is now an enchanting museum. **See p.111**

❹ Viña del Mar Away from the touristy gloss, Viña del Mar has a collection of beautiful palaces, verdant parks and gardens, and interesting museums. **See p.112**

❺ Casablanca Valley The vineyards in this area are famed for their production of quality white wines, and can be visited on a variety of tours, independently by car, or by bus. **See p.112**

❻ Zapallar Soothingly empty beaches, opulent holiday homes and excellent seafood make this eternally fashionable coastal resort one of the region's gems. **See p.118**

HIGHLIGHTS ARE MARKED ON THE MAP ON P.98

HIGHLIGHTS

1. Historic Valparaíso
2. Eating out in Valparaíso
3. Casa Museo Isla Negra
4. Viña del Mar
5. Casablanca Valley
6. Zapallar

VALPARAÍSO, VIÑA & THE CENTRAL COAST

N

ARGENTINA

PACIFIC OCEAN

Caleta Teniente

Combarbalá

Huentelauquén

Los Vilos

Pichidangui

Los Molles

Petorca

Cabildo

Papudo

La Ligua

Zapallar 6

Cachagua

Maitencillo

Horcón

Quintero

Ritoque

La Calera

San Felipe

Llaillay

Los Andes

Portillo

Río Blanco

Túnel Chacabuco

Quillota

PARQUE NACIONAL LA CAMPANA

Reñaca

Concón

Viña del Mar 4

Valparaíso 1

2

Quilpué

Limache

Olmué

Villa Alemana

Cerro El Plomo (6050m)

La Parva

El Colorado

Laguna Verde

Quintay

Tunquén

Casablanca 5

Aeropuerto Arturo Menino Benítez

Colina

Farallones

Valle Nevado

Quilicura

Algarrobo

El Quisco

Isla Negra 3

El Tabo

Las Cruces

Cartagena

San Antonio

Rocas de Santo Domingo

Curacaví

Túnel Zapata

Pudahuel

Las Condes

Maipú

SANTIAGO

San Bernado

La Obra

Pomaire

El Monte

Peñaflor

Talagante

Puente Alto

San José de Maipo

El Melocotón

San Alfonso

Melipilla

PARQUE NACIONAL RÍO CLARILLO

Isla de Maipo

Paine

San Gabriel

Río Colorado

Río Blanco

Río Tupungaro

0   40
kilometres

The eastern end of town near the bus station is of limited interest; instead head west to the **old town** which stretches along a narrow strip of land between Plaza Victoria and Plaza Wheelwright (also known as Plaza Aduana), at the city's historic core. The port district, with its British-style banks, atmospheric bars and old-fashioned shops, is the most idiosyncratic part of the city and should not be missed. Unfortunately you'll also have to contend with a certain amount of noise, general shabbiness and crime. However, just go up two or three **ascensores**, check out the enchanting **cerros Alegre** and **Concepción,** and sample the views by night, when the city's flickering lights are reflected in the ocean – and you're sure to fall under Valparaíso's spell.

2

Brief history

The bay was chosen as the site of the new colony's port as early as 1542, when Pedro de Valdivia decided it would "serve the trade of these lands and of Santiago". Growth was slow, however, owing to trading restrictions, but when Latin American trade was liberalized in the 1820s, after independence, Valparaíso started to come into its own. On the shipping route from Europe to America's Pacific Coast, it became the main port of call and resupply centre for ships after they crossed the Straits of Magellan. As Chile's own foreign trade expanded with the silver and copper booms of the 1830s, the port became ever more active, but it was the government's innovative creation of public warehouses where merchants could store goods at low prices that really launched Valparaíso into its economic ascent.

Progress and setbacks

Foreign businessmen, particularly British ones, flocked to the city where they ran trading empires built on copper, silver and nitrate. By the late nineteenth century they had turned Valparaíso into Chile's foremost financial and commercial centre. Even as it prospered, however, Valparaíso continued to be dogged by the kind of violent setbacks that had always punctuated its history, from looting pirates and buccaneers to earthquakes and fires. On March 31, 1866, following Chile's entanglement in a dispute between Spain and Peru, the Spanish admiralty bombarded Valparaíso, wreaking devastation. It took a long time to rebuild the city, but worse was to come. On August 16, 1906, a colossal **earthquake** practically razed the city to the ground, killing over two thousand people. The disaster took a heavy toll on Valparaíso's fortunes, which never really recovered. Eight years later, the opening of the Panama Canal signalled the city's inexorable decline.

Modern Valpo

Today, Valparaíso wears a rundown, moth-eaten air. Crime and poverty are worse than elsewhere in Chile, the sex trade is still rampant, and at night parts of the town are

---

WHEN TO VISIT THE CENTRAL COAST

Most Chileans take their annual holiday in February, when all the resort towns are unbearably crowded. They also get busy on December and January weekends, but outside these times are remarkably quiet. November and March are probably the **best months** to visit, as the weather is usually agreeable and the beaches virtually deserted, especially midweek. Even in summer, however, the coast is prone to **fog** or cloudy weather, and temperatures in Valpo can be considerably lower than in Santiago.

From April to October **accommodation rates** in Viña are sometimes half of those listed on p.116, and even in November, December and March you should be able to negotiate a midweek discount; rates in Valpo are pretty stable throughout the year, save at New Year when they double or triple. Some, but not all, beaches are safe for **swimming**, though you should definitely stay out of the water if a red flag is displayed; you might also be put off by the frigid **Humboldt current**, which leaves the water chilly even in the height of summer.

dangerous. That said, it's still a vital **working port**, moving thousands of containers annually, and has been the seat of Congress since the return to democracy in 1990. The port underwent a mini-economic boom in the early years of the new millennium, though the city's inhabitants, known as *Porteños*, do not seem to have benefited enormously. As the capital of Region V, it also has its share of galleries and museums, but the city's chief attractions lie in its crumbling, romantic atmosphere and stunning setting.

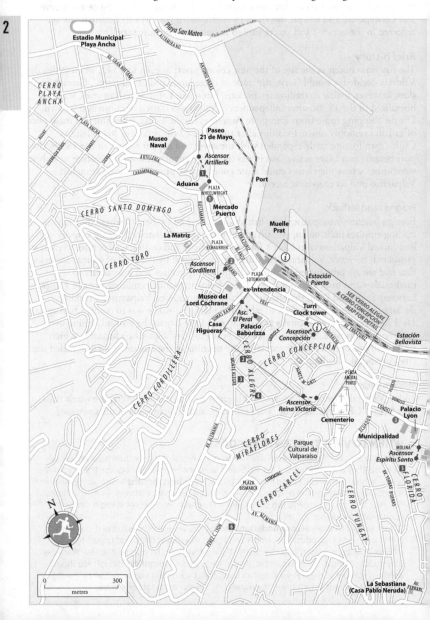

In April 2014 a devastating fire broke out in the southeastern side of the city, killing fifteen people and destroying around three thousand homes; the historical quarters were untouched. The government is currently carrying out a $500m reconstruction programme.

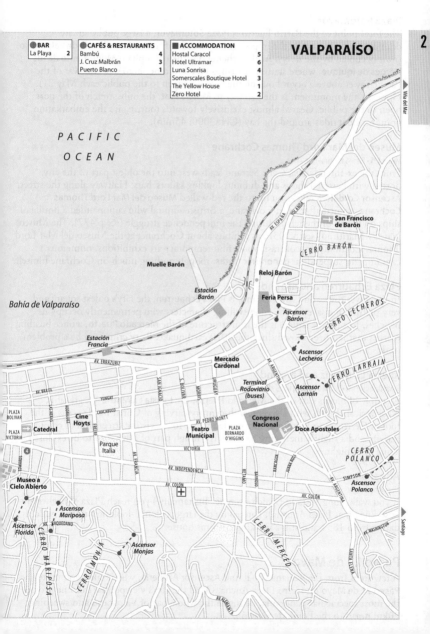

● BAR	
La Playa	2

● CAFÉS & RESTAURANTS	
Bambú	4
J. Cruz Malbrán	3
Puerto Blanco	1

■ ACCOMMODATION	
Hostal Caracol	5
Hotel Ultramar	6
Luna Sonrisa	4
Somerscales Boutique Hotel	3
The Yellow House	1
Zero Hotel	2

VALPARAÍSO

The Barrio Puerto

At the heart of Porteño history and identity, the **Barrio Puerto**, the port neighbourhood, is a good place to start exploring. However, you should keep a close eye on your belongings as pickpockets and thieves are rife during the day; at night the area is decidedly unsafe and should be avoided.

Plaza Sotomayor

The focal point of the Barrio Puerto is **Plaza Sotomayor**, a large public square dominated at one end by the imposing grey facade of the **ex-Intendencia de Valparaíso** (now occupied by the navy). At the other end is the triumphant **Monumento de los Héroes de Iquique**, where statues of Arturo Prat and other heroes of the War of the Pacific tower above a crypt housing their tombs (open to the public each May 21). Opposite the monument is the gateway to **Muelle Prat**, the only stretch of the port open to the public. Geared almost exclusively towards tourists, it's the embarkation point for **boat rides** around the bay (CH$3000; 45min).

Museo del Mar Lord Thomas Cochrane

Merlet 195 • Tues–Sat 10am–6pm • Free

From the ex-Intendencia, Calle Serrano leads west into the oldest part of the city, dotted with battered shops and dubious-looking sailors' bars. Halfway along the street, **Ascensor Cordillera** takes you up to the red-walled **Museo del Mar Lord Thomas Cochrane**, named after Lord Cochrane, a British admiral who commanded a flotilla of ships on behalf of the rebels during the independence struggle (see p.477). The Museo Naval y Marítimo (see p.103) has exhibits about Cochrane; at the Museo del Mar Lord Thomas Cochrane, by contrast, you'll find temporary art exhibitions, numerous cannon, and stupendous **panoramic vistas**, though nothing much on Cochrane himself.

Plaza Echaurren and around

In the lower town, on Calle Serrano, is **Plaza Echaurren**, the city's oldest square and very picturesque save for the wine-swilling characters who permanently occupy its benches. Just off the square is the iron structure of the **Mercado Puerto**, a once bustling market that has been closed since the 2010 earthquake. Petty crime can be a problem in this area.

Iglesia La Matriz and around

Santo Domingo s/n • No fixed opening times • Free

A couple of blocks east of the Mercado Puerto, the **Iglesia La Matriz** – a graceful, Neoclassical church with a seventeenth-century carving of Christ inside – sits at the foot of Cerro Santo Domingo surrounded by narrow, twisting streets full of colour, activity and a slightly menacing feel; this is a rough part of town, not to be explored alone or at night.

Aduana

Plaza Wheelwright

If you walk along Serrano (which becomes Bustamante) you reach Plaza Wheelwright (also known as Plaza Aduana), flanked by the large, colonial-looking **Aduana** building, dating from 1854 and still a working customs house.

Paseo 21 de Mayo

A few steps from the Aduana you'll find **Ascensor Artillería**, which takes you up to the **Paseo 21 de Mayo** on Cerro Playa Ancha. Of all the city's viewpoints, this one provides the most spectacular panorama, taking in the whole bay of Valparaíso and sweeping 20km north to the Punta de Concón.

Museo Naval y Marítimo

Paseo 21 de Mayo 45 • Tues–Sun 10am–5.30pm • CH$1000 • ☎ 32 243 7651, ⓦ museonaval.cl

The Paseo 21 de Mayo curves around the luxuriant gardens of a former naval school, an impressive whitewashed building that now houses the excellent **Museo Naval y Marítimo**. The beautifully presented displays – including paintings, photographs, weapons, uniforms, nautical instruments and personal objects – bring to life some of the central figures in Chile's history, such as Ambrosio O'Higgins, Lord Cochrane and Arturo Prat. The museum also has a display on the rescue of the 33 San José miners (see box, p.158).

2

Calle Prat and around

Valparaíso's **city centre** is formed by a narrow strip stretching from Plaza Sotomayor in the west to Plaza Victoria in the east. Almost completely devastated by the 1906 earthquake, it has evolved into a mixture of ugly, modern blocks and elegant buildings (many former banks or financial institutions) left over from the early twentieth century.

Calle Prat, which runs east from Plaza Sotomayor, has some good examples – take a look inside the **Banco Santander** opposite the Turri clocktower, originally the Banco de Londres and dripping with bronze and marble brought over from England. Next door, **Ascensor Concepción** (or Ascensor Turri) provides access to Cerro Concepción, a lovely residential area once the preserve of English businessmen. Further east, **Plaza Aníbal Pinto** is a pretty cobbled square overlooked by a couple of the city's oldest restaurants, including *El Cinzano* (see p.109).

Cerro Cárcel

From Plaza Aníbal Pinto, you can climb up Calle Cumming to **Cerro Cárcel**, where you'll find a collection of **cemeteries**; the names on the graves – Clampitt, Laussen, Van Buren, Matthews, Rivera – provide a fascinating glimpse at the diversity of the city's founders.

Palacio Lyon and the Museo de Historia Natural

Condell 1550 • Museo de Historia Natural Tues–Sat 10am–6pm, Sun 10am–2pm • Free • ☎ 32 254 4840

Southeast from Plaza Aníbal Pinto, the main drag runs along Calle Condell, where you'll find the **Palacio Lyon**, a splendid mansion dating from 1881 (one of the few to survive the 1906 earthquake) and now housing the **Museo de Historia Natural**, which has recently been renovated. The **Galería Municipal de Arte**, in the cellars of the building, occasionally stages temporary art exhibitions.

Iglesia Catedral de Valparaíso

Plaza Victoria; administrative office on Chacabuco at the north side of the building • Mon–Fri 10am–1pm & 4–6.30pm; to visit, ask at the administrative office

Calle Condell ends at **Plaza Victoria**, a large tree-filled square where most of Valparaíso seems to come to chat and sit in the sunshine. It's flanked, on its eastern side, by the gothic-looking **Iglesia Catedral de Valparaíso**, whose simply decorated interior includes a delicate ivory carving of Christ and, most intriguingly, a marble urn (in the crypt) containing the heart of famous Chilean statesman Diego Portales.

Museo a Cielo Abierto

Open access

From Plaza Victoria, calles Molina and Edwards lead up to the **Museo a Cielo Abierto**, a circuit of narrow streets and passageways painted with seventeen colourful, bold, abstract murals by students and leading local artists, the most memorable being the enormous paintings by Roberto Matta. The increased graffiti destruction of the murals is the most obvious sign, however, that it's worth keeping your wits about you.

La Sebastiana – Neruda's house

Av Ferrari 692 • Tues–Sun: Jan & Feb 10.30am–6.50pm; March–Dec 10 10am–6pm • CH$5000, including audio tour • ☎ 2 2777 8741, ⓦ fundacionneruda.org • Bus "O" (officially the #612) from Av Argentina or, if you're on cerros Alegre or Concepción and don't fancy the 25min walk, Plaza San Luis at the top of Templeman; stay on the bus for the whole route for a cheap city tour

Of the three Pablo Neruda homes open to the public – the others being La Chascona (see p.71) and Isla Negra (see p.111) – La Sebastiana offers the most informal look at the poet, who moved here in 1961 with Matilde Urrutia, his third wife. Perched high on the aptly named Bellavista hill, giving dramatic views over the bay, it was his *casa en el aire* (house in the air), and although he spent less time here than in his other homes, he imprinted his style and enthusiasms on every corner of the house. After the 1973 coup it was repeatedly vandalized by the military but has been meticulously restored by the Fundación Neruda, which opened it as a museum in 1992. Its narrow, sinuous passages and bright colours seem to mirror the spirit of Valparaíso, and the countless bizarre objects brought here by the poet are simply astonishing, from the embalmed Venezuelan Coro-Coro bird hanging from the ceiling of the dining room to the wooden horse in the living room, taken from a merry-go-round in Paris.

Cerros Alegre and Concepción

The hilltop residential quarter spread over **cerros Alegre** and **Concepción** is a rambling maze of steep streets and small alleys lined with elegant, brightly painted houses and aristocratic mansions clinging precipitously to the hillside. It grew up as the enclave of

---

VALPARAÍSO'S ANTIQUATED LIFTS

Most of Valparaíso's fifteen **ascensores**, or funicular "lifts", were built between 1883 and 1916 to provide a link between the lower town and the new residential quarters spreading up the hillsides. Today appearances would suggest that they've scarcely been modernized. However, despite their rickety frames and alarming noises they've so far proved safe and reliable. What's more, nearly all drop off passengers at a panoramic viewpoint. The municipality has now bought the *ascensores* from their private owners, and most have been reopened. They generally operate every few minutes from 7am to 11pm, and cost around CH$100–300 one-way. Here are a few of the best, from east to west:

Ascensor Polanco The most picturesque *ascensor*, and the only one that's totally vertical, Polanco is on Calle Simpson, off Avenida Argentina (opposite Independencia). It's approached through a cavernous, underground tunnel and rises 80m through a yellow wooden tower to a balcony that gives some of the best views in the city. A narrow bridge connects the tower to Cerro Polanco, with its flaking, pastel houses in varying states of repair. Cerro Polanco is known for its graffiti, but take care as the area is decidedly sketchy.

Ascensor Concepción (also known as Ascensor Turri) Hidden in a small passage opposite the Turri clock-tower, at the corner of Prat and Almirante Carreño, this was the first *ascensor* to be built, in 1883, and was originally powered by steam. It takes you up to the

beautiful residential area of Cerro Concepción, well worth a visit (see p.above).

Ascensor El Peral Next door to the Tribunales de Justicio, just off Plaza Sotomayor, this *ascensor* leads to one of the most romantic corners of the city: Paseo Yugoslavo, a little esplanade looking west onto some of Valparaíso's most beautiful houses, and backed by a flamboyant mansion housing the Museo de Bellas Artes. It's worth walking from here to Ascensor Concepción.

Ascensor Artillería Always busy with tourists, but highly recommended for the stunning vistas at the top, from the Paseo 21 de Mayo. It was built in 1893 to transport cadets to and from the naval school at the top of the hill, now the site of the Museo Naval y Marítimo (see p.103).

Valparaíso's immigrant businessmen, particularly the English, who left street names like Leighton, Templeman and Atkinson, and the Germans, whose influence can be seen in the many half-timbered, shuttered houses.

There are two points of access from the lower town; **Ascensor Concepción** (see box, p.104), near the Turri clocktower on Calle Prat, takes you up to **Paseo Gervasoni** on Cerro Concepción, while **Ascensor El Peral** (see box, p.104), next to the Tribunales de Justicia just off Plaza Sotomayor, ascends to Cerro Alegre's **Paseo Yugoslavo**, one of the most attractive and peaceful parts of the city. A good way to explore the area is to walk between the two *ascensores*: see the map below for a suggested **walking tour**, which takes you through some narrow alleys and hidden passageways.

2

Museo de Bellas Artes de Valparaíso

Paseo Yugoslavo • Tues–Sun: Jan–March 10.30am-7pm, April–Dec 10.30am–5.30pm • CH$2000 • ⓦ museobaburizza.cl

Arriving at Paseo Yugoslavo you'll see an extravagant, four-storey mansion behind the esplanade, the recently renovated **Palacio Baburizza**. Built in 1916 for a wealthy Italian family and later purchased by a Yugoslavian nitrate baron, it is now the home of the **Museo de Bellas Artes de Valparaíso**, a scarcely visited museum with a collection of nineteenth- and twentieth-century Chilean and European art. It's worth a look for the evocative paintings of an earlier Valparaíso by artists such as Juan Mauricio Rugendas, Alfred Helsby, Thomas Somerscales and, most notably, Juan Francisco González. There's a souvenir shop and a café.

■ ACCOMMODATION			● BARS		● CAFÉS & CHEAP EATS		● RESTAURANTS			
Casa Aventura	3	Pata Pata Hostel 4	El Bar Inglés	2	Amor Porteño	10	Allegretto	6	Pasta e Vino	4
Casa Higueras	5		El Cinzano	5	Café con Letras	7	Ápice	12	Vinilo	11
Hotel Da Vinci	1		Fauna	9	Café Turri	3	Le Filou de			
Palacio Astoreca	2		La Piedra Feliz	1			Montpellier	8		

Casa Mirador de Lukas

Paseo Gervasoni 448 • Tues–Sun 11am–2pm & 2.45–6pm • CH$1500 • ☎ 32 222 1344, ⓦ www.lukas.cl

The **Casa Mirador de Lukas**, near the Ascensor Concepción, pays homage to *El Mercurio*'s great satirist and cartoonist, known simply as Lukas, who possessed a sharp talent for capturing the spirit of his country in the hilarious drawings he produced for the newspaper between 1958 and 1988. There's also an appealing café.

Paseo Atkinson

As you're walking around Cerro Concepción, don't miss **Paseo Atkinson**, an esplanade affording great panoramas and lined with pretty houses whose tiny front gardens and window boxes recall their original English owners. From here you can see the tall tower of the **Lutheran church**, a distinctive, green-walled structure built in 1897; a block or so farther away you'll find the towerless **St Paul's Anglican Church** (built in 1858) whose solemn interior contains a huge organ donated by Queen Victoria in 1903.

The Congreso Nacional

If you arrive in Valparaíso by bus the first thing that hits you as you emerge from the station is the imposing **Congreso Nacional**, described by Collier and Sater in their *History of Chile* as "half neo-Babylonian, half post-modernist atrocity". It was one of Pinochet's projects, but the dictator relinquished power before it was completed. Its working life began on March 11, 1990, when Patricio Aylwin was sworn in as president and Congress resumed its activities after a sixteen-year absence – away from the capital for the first time.

Given the inconvenience of its distance from the capital, politicians have repeatedly discussed a plan to return Congress to Santiago and convert the building into a gigantic hotel, but so far no decision has been made.

Plaza Bernardo Higgins and around

One of Chile's best **antique/flea markets** is held every Saturday and Sunday at Plaza Bernardo O'Higgins, though prices are fairly high. A short walk south of the plaza takes you to **Ascensor Polanco** (see box, p.104), the most fascinating of the funiculars.

ARRIVAL AND DEPARTURE   VALPARAÍSO

By train The Metro (ⓦ metro-valparaiso.cl) departs for Viña del Mar from the centrally located Puerto and Bellavista stations (every 5–20min). Buy a plastic charge card (CH$1350) first, and then top it up with credit before travelling.

By bus The Terminal Rodoviario (☎ 32 293 9646) is on the eastern end of Pedro Montt, opposite the Congreso Nacional; it's a 20min walk to the old town centre. There are buses up and down the coast from here, mainly with Sol de Pacifico (☎ 32 228 1026), Pullman Bus (☎ 32 225

3125, ⓦ www.pullman.cl) and Mirasol (☎ 32 223 5985). To get to Viña del Mar, pick up one of the frequent *micros* on Pedro Montt; they take about 15 min, twice that time in bad traffic; the train is more convenient. Plenty of *micros* and *colectivos* also go to the centre from outside the bus station.

Destinations Isla Negra (every 15min; 1hr 30min); La Serena (hourly; 6hr); Puerto Montt (3–4 daily; 16hr); Santiago (every 15min; 1hr 30min–1hr 45min); Temuco (2–3 daily; 9hr 30min).

GETTING AROUND

By micro and colectivo Countless *micros* run through the city: those displaying "Aduana" on the window take you west through the centre, past the port, while those marked "P. Montt" take you back to the bus station. Some bus routes take you to the upper town, and you can catch *colectivos* at Plazuela Ecuador, at the

bottom of Calle Ecuador.

On foot To climb to the upper town, it's easiest to use the *ascensores*.

By taxi Taxis are numerous; there are stands at the bottom of most of the *cerros*.

INFORMATION AND TOURS

Tourist information There are several tourist information kiosks (daily 10am–2pm & 3–6pm), including one on Calle Blanco, close to Plaza Aníbal Pinto, one on Muelle Prat by the port, and one at the top of Ascensor Concepción. Note that (despite an old sign) there is no official tourist office at the bus station, which is filled with accommodation touts offering partial (at best) information.

Websites Two useful Spanish-language websites are ⓦ valparaisochile.cl and ⓦ granvalparaiso.cl.

City tours There are innumerable tours on offer in Valparaíso; two of the best operators are Ruta Valparaíso (ⓣ 32 259 2520, ⓦ rutavalparaiso.cl) and Santiago Adventures (ⓣ 32 244 2750, ⓦ santiagoadventures .com). Half-day city tours generally cost from CH$25,000 (full-day tours from CH$35,000); both agencies also offer excursions throughout the region. A good alternative for city tours is the appropriately named Tours for Tips (ⓦ tours4tips.com); they leave from Plaza Sotomayor daily at 10am and 3pm.

Wine tours Wine Tours Valparaíso (ⓦ winetoursvalparaiso .cl) organizes wine tasting trips in the Casablanca Valley (see p.112).

Cookery classes Chilean Cuisine (ⓣ 09 6621 4626, ⓦ cookingclasseschile.cl) offers enjoyable cookery classes.

ACCOMMODATION

Valparaíso has a good range of **accommodation** to suit all budgets. There are hotels in the lower sections of town, but you won't get the full Valpo experience unless you head up to one of the *cerros*: Alegre and Concepción are by far the most popular, but Bellavista, Cárcel, Artillería and several others are also developing, and provide a less touristy experience. Many places will pick you up from the bus station if you call ahead.

HOTELS AND B&BS

Casa Higueras Higuera 133, Cerro Alegre ⓣ 32 249 7900, ⓦ hotelcasahigueras.cl; map p.105. One of the best top-end hotels in the city, *Casa Higueras* has stately 1930s-style en suites, a pool and Jacuzzi with exquisite vistas, and the classy (and, considering the quality, reasonably priced) *Montealegre* restaurant. **US$320**

Hotel Da Vinci Urriola 426, Cerro Alegre ⓣ 32 317 4494, ⓦ hoteldavincivalparaiso.cl; map p.105. A cross between an art gallery and a hotel: the en suites, some split-level, are set around a central atrium, bathed with light from a towering window, while carefully placed photos and paintings provide a mellow ambience. **CH$52,000**

Hotel Ultramar Tomás Pérez 173, Cerro Cárcel ⓣ 32 221 0000, ⓦ hotelultramar.cl; map pp.100–101. Striped, spotted and checked decor – though fortunately not all together – give this thoroughly modern hotel, a refurbished 1907 Italianate town house, a unique feel. Rooms with a view are worth paying a little extra for. **CH$79,000**

Palacio Astoreca Montealegre 149, Cerro Alegre ⓣ 32 327 7700, ⓦ hotelpalacioastoreca.com; map p.105. Located just a few steps from Paseo Yugoslavo, one of the city's most picturesque spots, this gorgeously restored mansion is one of Valpo's finest luxury hotels. Chic en suites, many with stunning views, smart service, a spa and heated indoor pool, plus the excellent *Alegre* restaurant and a piano bar, make *Palacio Astoreca* a great choice. **US$318**

★**Somerscales Boutique Hotel** San Enrique 446, Cerro Alegre ⓣ 32 233 1006, ⓦ hotelsomerscales.cl; map pp.100–101. Each of the en suites at this beautifully restored home of renowned local painter Thomas Somerscales (some of whose work can be seen at the Museo de Bellas Artes, see p.105) is fitted out with period furniture and artwork, as well as modern comforts. Stunning views, a roof terrace and a large stained-glass window make this one of the most memorable hotels in town. **US$171**

The Yellow House Capitán Muñoz Gamero 91, Cerro Artillería ⓣ 32 233 9435, ⓦ theyellowhouse.cl; map pp.100–101. Even by Valpo's high standards, the views from *The Yellow House*, located in a 200-year-old building, are spectacular. Most of the rooms at this welcoming B&B are en suite, and there's also a comfortable apartment with a kitchenette. The management has changed recently, but the high standards remain the same. There's a book exchange, and tours are available. Doubles **CH$24,000**, apartments **CH$40,000**

Zero Hotel Tomás Lautaro Rosas 343, Cerro Cárcel ⓣ 32 211 3113, ⓦ zerohotel.cl; map pp.100–101. This lovely pale blue townhouse has been turned into an attractive boutique hotel with tasteful high-ceilinged en suites (the more expensive ones have sea views). There are terraces and a glass-enclosed "winter garden" to relax in, as well as nice touches such as an honesty bar. **US$233**

HOSTELS

Casa Aventura Pasaje Gálvez 11, Cerro Alegre ⓣ 32 275 5963, ⓦ casaventura.cl; map p.105. *Casa Aventura* is a friendly place, with spotless dorms and private rooms, a sunny lounge and a communal kitchen all making it rightly popular with backpackers. Dorms **CH$9000**, doubles **CH$25,000**

Hostal Caracol Hector Calvo 371, Cerro Bellavista ☏ 32 239 5817, ⊚ hostalcaracol.cl; map pp.100–101. If you find the Alegre and Concepción hills a bit too touristy, try "*Hostel Snail*", located on up-and-coming Cerro Bellavista, close to the Museo a Cielo Abierto. There are perfectly decent, though unexceptional seven-bed dorms and private rooms. Dorms C̄H̄$̄1̄0̄,̄0̄0̄0̄, doubles C̄H̄$̄3̄0̄,̄0̄0̄0̄

★**Luna Sonrisa** Templeman 833, Cerro Alegre ☏ 32 273 4117, ⊚ lunasonrisa.cl; map pp.100–101. Minimalist but comfortable rooms and dorms, pristine facilities, fine breakfast, book exchange and a sociable atmosphere make *Luna Sonrisa* an excellent choice. Staff are very friendly and knowledgeable – the hostel is owned by a travel writer, so you would expect nothing less. There are also a couple of great self-contained apartments (⊚ elnidito.cl). Dorms C̄H̄$̄9̄0̄0̄0̄, doubles C̄H̄$̄2̄5̄,̄0̄0̄0̄, apartments C̄H̄$̄6̄5̄,̄0̄0̄0̄

Pata Pata Hostel Templeman 657, Cerro Alegre ☏ 32 317 3153, ⊚ patapatahostel.cl; map p.105. If money is really tight, head to this hostel, whose four- to eight-bed dorms provide some of Valpo's cheapest accommodation. There are also cute private rooms, spacious communal areas and a great breakfast, plus a convenient location. Dorms C̄H̄$̄8̄0̄0̄0̄, doubles C̄H̄$̄2̄5̄,̄0̄0̄0̄

EATING AND DRINKING

Valparaíso has some of Chile's best and most inventive **restaurants**, and cerros Concepción and Alegre, in particular, are filled with great places to eat. Valpo has an excellent **bar** scene, especially on Thurs, Fri and Sat. The city's speciality is its old-fashioned, charming bar-restaurants serving *comida típica* to local families, who turn out in their dozens to join in the singing and dancing on weekends, when many places have live *bolero*, *tango* or *música folklórica*. There's also a range of younger, hipper bars, many with live music and dancing. Take care wherever you are after dark, especially anywhere near the port area.

CAFÉS AND CHEAP EATS

Amor Porteño Almirante Montt 418, Cerro Concepción ☏ 32 221 6253, ⊚ facebook.com /AmorPortenoValparaiso; map p.105. Excellent ice-cream parlour/coffee shop, with a cute dining area: as well as real Argentine *helado* and sundaes (CH$2950–3500 for the latter), you can tuck into *churros* and *medialunas* (sweet, doughy croissant-like pastries). Tues–Sun 9.30am–9pm.

Bambú Independencia 1790 ☏ 32 223 4216; map pp.100–101. Good-value vegetarian food such as soups, salads, omelettes, soya burgers and tofu concoctions (CH$2000 upwards)) in a city centre location. Cookery, yoga, pilates and tai chi classes are also available. Mon 10.30am–6pm, Tues 10.30am–8pm, Wed–Fri 10.30am–6pm, Sat 10.30am–5pm.

Café con Letras Almirante Montt 316, Cerro Concepción ☏ 32 223 5480; map p.105. Low-key, faintly melancholy café-cum-bookshop (mainly Spanish-language books), where aged wooden posts prop up the ceiling and black-and-white photos adorn the walls. It's a good spot for a quiet read, a coffee (CH$1200–2900) and an *alfajore* (a *dulce de leche*-filled biscuit); set lunch CH$5500. It's also known as *Café con Cuento*. Mon–Sat 11am–10pm, Sun 4–10pm.

Café Turri Paseo Gervasoni, Cerro Concepción ☏ 32 225 2091, ⊚ www.turri.cl; map p.105. Come for a coffee (CH$1500–3000) sundowner or a dessert – such as the toothsome meringue torte with *lúcuma*, an indigenous fruit with a vaguely toffee-like flavour – rather than an overpriced full meal at this touristy spot. The real star, however, is the panoramic view from the terrace. Mon–Sat 10am–11pm, Sun 10am–10pm.

Puerto Blanco Cochrane 25 ☏ 32 225 0106, ⊚ facebook.com/puertoblancocafe; map pp.100–101. The unprepossessing locale, opposite a demolished building and close to the port doesn't exactly appeal, but inside this coffee shop you'll find a slice of Brooklyn or Shoreditch: exposed brick walls, MacBooks, hip(ster) clientele and excellent coffee (CH$1100–2800). Tues–Sun 10am–8pm.

RESTAURANTS

Allegretto Pilcomayo 259, Cerro Concepción ☏ 32 296 8839, ⊚ allegretto.cl; map p.105. British–Chilean-run restaurant with colourful decor, black-and-white photos, local beer on tap and *taca taca* (table football). The menu features thin-crust pizzas (CH$5200–8400), risottos, and gnocchi, and there's a good weekday lunch special (CH$5900). The owners also run a B&B. Daily noon–4pm & 7–11pm.

Ápice Montt 462, Cerro Concepción ☏ 32 208 9737, ⊚ restaurantapice.cl; map p.105. This slick restaurant with a pared-down dining room and a chef with a "philosophy" may not be to everyone's taste, but the inventive, artfully presented food is undeniably good - think octopus with a chorizo emulsion, oysters with goat's cheese and leeks, and chocolate fondant (mains CH$9000–11,000). Book a table in advance. Mon & Thurs–Sun 8–9.30pm.

★**J. Cruz Malbrán** Condell 1466, up side alley next to the Municipalidad; map pp.100–101. An extraordinary place, more like a museum than a restaurant, packed with china, old clocks, musical instruments, crucifixes and other kitsch trinkets. It also claims to have invented the *chorrillana* (a vast plate of steak strips, onions, eggs and French fries), which is not to be missed. Mains around CH$5000. Mon–Thurs noon–2am, Fri & Sat noon–4.30am, Sun 1pm–2am.

★ **Le Filou de Montpellier** Almirante Montt 382, Cerro Concepción ☎ 32 222 4663, ⓦ lefiloude montpellier.cl; map p.105. A delightful little piece of France in Valpo: postcards of Montpellier and paintings by local artists decorate the place, while the ever-changing set lunch (CH$7200) may include quiche lorraine, boeuf bourguignon and cherry clafoutis. Tues–Thurs 1–4pm, Fri & Sat 1–4pm & 8–11.30pm, Sun 1–4pm.

Pasta e Vino Papudo 427, Cerro Concepción ☎ 32 249 6187, ⓦ pastaevinoristorante.cl; map p.105. One of Valpo's finest restaurants, now in a new location, *Pasta e Vino* provides an inventive and ambitious take on Italian cuisine – crab gnocchi with a parmesan sauce, for example. Reservations are vital at weekends. Mains CH$10,500–14,200. Tues–Sat 1–3.30pm & 8pm–midnight.

Vinilo Almirante Montt 540, Cerro Concepción ☎ 32 223 0665; map p.105. Intimate bistro with a select menu of contemporary Chilean dishes (CH$9000–12,000) such as rabbit in a red wine and strawberry sauce, a bizarre mix of abstract and children's artwork and a stack of vintage vinyl. The owners also run a pisco bar a few doors up. Mon–Thurs 9am–1am, Fri & Sat 9am–2.30am, Sun 10am–10pm.

BARS AND PUBS

★ **El Bar Inglés** Cochrane 851 (rear entrance at Blanco 870) ☎ 32 221 4625; map p.105. This wonderfully atmospheric bar dates back to the early 1900s and is a great place for a beer (from CH$1500). Check out the wall map with listings of incoming boats from all over the world, and – if you're feeling confident – take on the regulars at a game of dominoes. Mon–Fri noon–11pm.

El Cinzano Plaza Aníbal Pinto 1182 ☎ 32 221 3043, ⓦ barcinzano.cl; map p.105. Hugely popular restaurant-bar (set lunch CH$3900) with a fantastic atmosphere, especially on Thurs, Fri and Sat nights when the place fills with locals and ageing crooners singing sentimental ballads. Mon–Wed 10am–1am, Thurs 10am–2am, Fri & Sat 10.30am–4.30am.

Fauna Dimalow 166, Cerro Alegre ☎ 32 327 0719, ⓦ faunahotel.cl; map p.105. The terrace at this restaurant-bar has panoramic views of Valpo's *cerros* and bay, making it an ideal spot for a sundowner, especially given the range of craft beers (CH$2000–2500) on offer. The food's good too. Daily 1–10.30pm.

La Piedra Feliz Errázuriz 1054, near the junction with Blanco ☎ 32 225 6788, ⓦ lapiedrafeliz.cl; map p.105. Mellow place with creaky wooden floors and live music – including jazz, bolero, rock and disco – every night, as well as regular art exhibitions, salsa classes and poetry readings. Tues–Sat 9pm–late.

★ **La Playa** Serrano 567 ☎ 32 259 4262, ⓦ barlaplaya.cl; map pp.100–101. Sociable spot with a long, mahogany bar, dark wood-panelled walls and posters of Jack Nicholson, James Dean and BB King. There's live evening music at the weekend, when a downstairs dance area is opened up and the crowds don't disperse until sunrise. Mon–Wed 10am–10.30pm, Thurs–Sat 10am–late.

ENTERTAINMENT

Valpo is *the* place to go in Chile to ring in the **New Year**, with huge parties and fireworks extravaganzas; be sure to arrive by midday on the 30th or you'll get stuck in horrible traffic.

Cine Hoyts Pedro Montt 2111 ☎ 32 259 4709, ⓦ www .cinehoyts.cl; map pp.100–101. Cinema screening mainstream films; check the website for listings. You can also find art movies at various cultural centres about town; check *El Mercurio de Valparaíso* for details.

Parque Cultural de Valparaíso Castro s/n ☎ 32 225 8567, ⓦ pcdv.cl. Midway up Cerro Cárcel is Parque Cultural de Valparaíso, a former prison that has been transformed into a vibrant cultural hub. As well as hosting artist workshops, the complex stages a wide range of – generally free – cultural events including exhibitions, concerts and theatrical performances.

Teatro Municipal Corner of Pedro Montt and Plaza O'Higgins ☎ 32 225 7480; map pp.100–101. For an evening of culture, check out the programme at the city's main theatre, which plays host to regular plays, music and dance performances.

SHOPPING

Cummings1 Cummings 1, just off Plaza Aníbal Pinto ☎ 09 7527 0796, ⓦ cummings1.cl; map p.105 An excellent range of novels and non-fiction, predominantly in English and Spanish, including many hard-to-find South American titles. Mon–Sat 11am–6pm, Sun 11am–4pm.

DIRECTORY

Hospital Try public hospital Carlos Van Buren, Colón and San Ignacio (☎ 32 236 4000, ⊕ hospitalcarlosvanburen.cl), or private clinic Clínica Valparaíso, Avenida Brasil 2350 (☎ 600 411 2000, ⊕ clinicavalparaiso.cl).

Money and exchange The main financial street is Prat, with many banks, ATMs and *cambios*. Banco de Santiago is generally the best bet for currency exchange.
Post office Prat 856 (Mon–Fri 9am–6pm, Sat 10am–1pm).

South of Valparaíso

The resorts **south of Valparaíso** are among the busiest and most developed in the region. Most – including Algarrobo, El Tabo and Cartagena – sit on overcrowded beaches, are overrun with ugly apartment blocks and are jam-packed with noisy vacationers. However, a few places in the area are well worth a visit: peaceful **Quintay**, the **vineyards** of the Casablanca Valley, and – most notably – the village of **Isla Negra**, site of Pablo Neruda's extraordinary house and now a museum.

Quintay

Secluded and relatively untouched by tourism, the village of **Quintay** makes an ideal day-trip from Valparaíso. It has a scenic cove and a series of small beaches, backed by pine and eucalyptus trees, cacti and wild flowers, perfect for an idle wander. A 45min walk to the north takes you to Playa Grande, a lovely stretch of golden sand, now sadly marred by building work. There are a few fish

---

PABLO NERUDA

The tiny village of **Isla Negra** was put on the map when **Pablo Neruda** moved into a half-built house on the beach in 1939. Born **Neftalí Reyes** in 1904, this son of a local railwayman made his name in the world of poetry as a teenager under the pseudonym Pablo Neruda. He published his first collection, *Crepusculario*, in 1923 at his own expense, and success came quickly. The following year, he published a slim volume of sensual, tormented verses, *Veinte Poemas de Amor y una Canción Desesperada* (Twenty Love Poems and a Song of Despair), and suddenly found himself, aged 20, with one of the fastest-growing readerships on the continent.

RANGOON AND BEYOND

Despite this success, Neruda still needed to earn a living to fund his writing, and so, aged 24, he began his career as **Chilean consul** in Rangoon, the first of many posts. It seems ironic that this most "Chilean" of poets, whose verses are imprinted with the forests, rain, sea, lakes and volcanoes of southern Chile, should have spent so much of his adult life far from his native land. His years in Rangoon, Colombo, Jakarta and Singapore were often intensely lonely, but also coloured with vivid episodes and sexual adventures. The most dramatic of these was his love affair in Rangoon with **Josie Bliss**. Described by Neruda as his "Burmese panther… a love-smitten terrorist capable of anything", she was a jealous and possessive lover who would sometimes terrorize him with her silver dagger. When he was transferred to Ceylon (now Sri Lanka), he left without telling her, but she turned up on his doorstep several months later. Neruda's outright rejection of her was to haunt him for many years, and Bliss makes several appearances in his poems.

POLITICIZATION AND EXILE

During his time in Asia, Neruda's poetry was inward-looking, reflecting his experience of dislocation and solitude. His posts in Barcelona (1934) and Madrid (1935–36), however, marked a major turning-point in his life and work: with the outbreak of the **Spanish Civil War**, and the assassination of his friend, Federico García Lorca, Neruda became increasingly politicized. He threw himself into the task of providing Spanish refugees with a safe passage to Chile, and at the same time sought to give his poetry a meaningful "place in

restaurants, a former whaling station and a lighthouse. Keep an eye out for sea otters in the harbour.

Casa Museo Isla Negra

Poeta Neruda s/n, Isla Negra • Tues–Sun: Jan & Feb 10am–8pm; March–Dec 10am–6pm • CH$5000, including audio tour; advance reservations necessary • ☎ 2 2777 8741, ⓦ fundacionneruda.org

From 1939, poet **Pablo Neruda** (see box below) spent forty years of his life, on and off, in the village of Isla Negra, enlarging his house and filling it with the strange and beautiful objects he ceaselessly gathered from far-flung corners of the world. The Fundación Neruda, acting on the wishes of the poet's widow, Matilde Urrutia, transferred Neruda's and Matilde's graves to its garden and operates the house as the **Casa Museo Isla Negra**. Inside this museum, the winding passages and odd-shaped rooms are crammed full of fascinating exotic objects like ships' figureheads, Hindu carvings, African and Japanese masks, ships in bottles, seashells, butterflies, coloured bottles, Victorian postcards and a good deal more.

There's little else to Isla Negra save a small, pretty beach, which makes a great picnic spot.

ARRIVAL AND DEPARTURE	**SOUTH OF VALPARAÍSO**

QUINTAY
By bus Buses depart from the corner of 12 de Febrero and Rawson in Valparaíso (5 daily, fewer at weekends; 1hr); there are also frequent *colectivos* from the rank on 12 de Febrero.

---

man's struggle", with *España en el Corazón*. On returning to Chile he joined the Communist Party, and was **elected as a senator**. His politics were to land him in serious trouble, however, when newly elected president González Videla, who had previously enlisted Neruda's help, switched sides from left to right, and outlawed communism. When Neruda publicly attacked him, the president issued a warrant for his arrest, and he was forced into hiding. In 1949 the poet was smuggled across the Andes on horseback, and spent the next three years in exile, mainly in Europe.

MATILDE URRUTIA

It was during his **exile** that Neruda met the woman who was to inspire some of his most beautiful poetry: Matilde Urrutia, whom he was later to marry. Neruda had been married twice before: first, briefly, to a Dutch woman he'd met as a young consul in Rangoon; and then for eighteen years to the Argentinian painter, Delia del Carril. The poet's writings scarcely mention his first wife, nor their daughter – his only child – who died when she was 8, but Delia is described as "sweetest of consorts, thread of steel and honey… my perfect mate for 18 years". It was so as not to hurt Delia that *Los Versos del Capitán* – a book of passionate love poems written for Matilde – was published anonymously.

THE RETURN HOME

Nonetheless, when the order for his arrest was revoked in 1955, three years after his return to Santiago, Neruda divorced Delia and moved into **La Chascona**, in Santiago, and then to **Isla Negra** with Matilde. Based in Chile from then on, Neruda devoted himself to politics and poetry almost in equal measure. In 1970, Salvador Allende, whose campaign Neruda had tirelessly participated in, was elected president at the head of the socialist Unidad Popular. The following year, Neruda was awarded the Nobel Prize for Literature. His happiness was to be short-lived, however. Diagnosed with cancer, and already bedridden, the poet was unable to withstand the shock brought on by the 1973 military coup, which left his dear friend Allende dead. Less than two weeks later, on September 23, Neruda died in Santiago.

2

CASABLANCA VALLEY WINE ROUTE

The Casablanca Valley, famed for its excellent white wines, is accessed via Ruta 68, which connects Valparaíso and Viña with Santiago. **Ruta del Vino Valle de Casablanca** (☎ 32 274 3933, ⓦ casablancavalley.cl), Portales 90, in Casablanca, organizes tours (from CH$30,000) of the wineries, as do operators in Valparaíso (see p.107) and Santiago (see p.78). You can also visit the vineyards independently (a list of all those participating in the *ruta del vino* is available on the website); having your own car makes things a lot easier, but it is possible to visit some using the frequent Valparaíso/Viña–Santiago buses.

ISLA NEGRA

By bus Pullman (ⓦ pullman.cl) and Tur Bus (ⓦ turbus.cl) run buses from Santiago's Terminal Alameda (every 30min; 2hr). There are also services from Valparaíso (every 15min; 1hr 30min).

Viña del Mar

A fifteen-minute bus or train ride is all it takes to exchange the colourful *cerros* and chaotic alleys of Valparaíso for the tree-lined avenues and ostentatious high-rises of **VIÑA DEL MAR**. This is Chile's largest and best-known beach resort, drawing tens of thousands of mostly Chilean vacationers each summer. In many ways, it's indistinguishable from beach resorts elsewhere in the world, with oceanfront condos, bars, restaurants and a casino.

Lurking in the older corners of town, however, are extravagant palaces, elegant villas and sumptuous gardens. Many date from the late nineteenth century when Viña del Mar – then a large hacienda – was subdivided into plots that were sold or rented to the wealthy families of Valparaíso and Santiago who came to spend their summers by the sea.

The city also has a pair of **beautiful botanical gardens** and a museum with an important collection of Easter Island art.

Plaza Vergara

Viña's centre is marked by the large, green **Plaza Vergara**, full of tall, stately trees and surrounded by some fine, early twentieth-century buildings including the Neoclassical **Teatro Municipal**, the stately **Hotel O'Higgins** and the Italian Renaissance-style **Club de Viña**, a gentlemen's dining club.

Avenida Valparaíso

Avenida Valparaíso, Viña's main commercial street, borders the south side of Plaza Vergara. Much of the shopping activity occurs in the five blocks between the plaza and Calle Ecuador. There's also a good **feria artesanal** in Pasaje Cousiño, a narrow passage off the south side of the avenue, just west of Plaza Vergara.

Quinta Vergara

Off Errázuriz • Daily: summer 7am–7pm; winter 7am–6pm • Free

The exceptionally beautiful **Quinta Vergara** park, filled with exotic, subtropical trees and surrounded by wooded hills, sits two blocks south of Plaza Vergara, across the railway tracks. The amphitheatre hosts regular concerts, including the hugely hyped, kitsch **Festival Internacional de la Canción** (International Music Festival) every February. During this time, the traffic and the crowds are out of hand, and booking accommodation ahead is essential.

ACCOMMODATION
Casa del Sol	5
Hotel Agora	1
Hotel del Mar	2
Hotel Monterilla	3
Kalagen Hostel	4
My Father's House	6

RESTAURANTS
Delicias del Mar	2
Divino Pecado	4
La Flor de Chile	1
Panzoni	6

CAFÉS & CHEAP EATS
Cevasco	5
Entre Masas	3
Jerusalem	7

BAR
Café Journal	8

CLUBS
Ovo	2
Scratch	1

Museo de Bellas Artes

Quinta Vergara

In the centre of Quinta Vergara sits **Palacio Vergara**, a dazzling, whitewashed Venetian-style palace built in 1906. The palace is now home to the **Museo de Bellas Artes**, which has a decent collection of Chilean and European paintings, including works by **Rubens**, **Poussin** and **Tintoretto**; it was closed for restoration at the time of research.

Palacio Rioja

Quillota 214

Closed for restoration at the time of research, the **Palacio Rioja**, built in the style of an eighteenth-century French chateau and surrounded by a sumptuous park, is all that remains of the once extensive vineyards that gave the town its name. Situated just north of the Marga Marga, it was built in 1906 for Don Fernando Rioja Medel, a Spanish millionaire who owned the Banco Español. His family lived here until 1956, when the building was acquired by the Municipalidad which turned it into a reception centre and **museum**. The ground floor is perfectly preserved and provides a fascinating close-up view of early twentieth-century luxury, with its *belle-époque* furniture and glittering ballroom. In the summer, the **Conservatorio de Música** in the basement gives concerts.

Palacio Carrasco

Libertad 250

Near the Palacio Rioja is the **Palacio Carrasco**, an elegant, three-storey building designed in a French Neoclassical style. It now functions as the city's cultural centre, hosting regular exhibitions of work by both Chilean and international artists. The palacio was closed at the time of research for restoration work.

Museo Francisco Fonck

4 Norte 784 • Mon 10am–2pm & 3–6pm, Tues–Sat 10am–6pm, Sun 10am–2pm • CH$2500 • ☎ 32 268 6753, ⓦ museofonck.cl

The excellent **Museo Francisco Fonck** has one of Chile's most important **Easter Island collections**, plus some fascinating pre-Hispanic exhibits. It is named after Prussian medic Franz Fonck (1830–1912), who studied botanical and archeological sites in central Chile and left his collections to the state. One of the museum's best pieces stands by the entrance in the garden: a giant stone *moai*, one of just six that exist outside Easter Island. Inside, the three ground-floor rooms dedicated to Easter Island include wooden and stone carvings of those long, stylized faces (some around five hundred years old), as well as jewellery, weapons, household and fishing utensils, and ceremonial objects.

Castillo Wulff

Av Marina 37 • Tues–Sat 10am–1.30pm & 3–5.30pm • Free

In a prime waterfront location, the neo-Gothic **Castillo Wulff** was built in 1906 for a local nitrate and coal baron. Formerly a museum, it is now an exhibition space, and is well worth a quick look around: check out the glass-floored passage through which you can gaze at the waves breaking below.

The beaches

Take any of the Reñaca or Concón buses from Puente Libertad (the bridge just north of Plaza Vergara), and get off at 10 or 12 Norte for Playas Acapulco and El Sol, or ask the driver to let you off on the coast road for the beaches further north

Viña's most central beach, and the only one south of the Marga Marga, is the sheltered, sandy **Playa Caleta Abarca** at the eastern end of Calle Viana. Just off the beach, at the foot of Cerro Castillo, is the **Reloj de Flores**, a large clock composed of colourful plants and mechanical dials.

Just beyond Castillo Wulff is the **Estero Marga Marga** – follow it inland a couple of blocks to reach the bridge that crosses it. On the other side is the **Casino Municipal** and the coast road, **Avenida Perú**. A pedestrian promenade runs alongside the ocean but there's no sand here, just a stretch of rocks.

A few blocks north, Avenida Perú swerves inland to make way for the long unbroken strip of sand stretching for over 3km towards Reñaca (see p.117). Though effectively a single beach, the different sections each have their own name: just north of Avenida Perú is the 200m-long **Playa Acapulco**, which is very popular but a bit hemmed in by high-rises, followed by **Playa El Sol** and **Playa Los Marineros**, where it's often too rough for swimming. Finally there is **Playa Larga**, which has restaurants and showers – it's very crowded in the summer.

Jardín Botánico Nacional

6km outside Viña • **Jardín Botánico** Daily: May–Aug 10am–6pm; Sept–April 10am–7pm • CH$2000 **Zipline** March–Nov Sat & Sun 10.30am–6pm; Dec–Feb daily 10.30am–7pm • CH$8000–12,000 • ⓦ jardin-botanico.cl • Bus #20, eastbound, from Calle Bohn (10min)

Set in a sheltered valley 6km from central Viña and surrounded by sun-baked hills, the **Jardín Botánico Nacional** contains three thousand plant species from Latin America, Europe and Asia. The gardens are a great place to unwind, but if you fancy a bit of action, it is also possible to go ziplining here. There are five different routes, some suitable for children.

ARRIVAL AND DEPARTURE   **VIÑA DEL MAR**

By train The Metro (ⓦ metro-valparaiso.cl) departs for Valparaíso from the centrally located Miramar and Viña del Mar stations (every 5–20min). Buy a plastic charge card (CH$1350) first, and then top it up with credit before travelling.

By bus The bus terminal is at the eastern end of Av

Valparaíso. To go down the coast, your best bet is to catch a bus from Valparaíso (see p.106), reached by any *micro* (every 10min) marked "Puerto" or "Aduana" from Plaza Vergara or Arlegui; alternatively take the Metro (see p.106). Buses/*micros* up the coast don't stop at the bus terminal, but at Libertad (just north of Puente Libertad), with frequent services to Reñaca and Concón, and several daily to Horcón, Maitencillo, Zapallar and Papudo.

Destinations Cachagua (hourly; 1hr 30min); Concón (every 15min; 15min); Horcón (hourly; 1hr); La Ligua (hourly; 2hr); Maitencillo (hourly; 1hr 20min); Papudo (2–3 daily; 1hr 45min); Reñaca (every 15min; 25min); Santiago (every 15min; 1hr 30min–1hr 45min); Zapallar (hourly; 1hr 30min).

INFORMATION

Tourist office Off the northeast corner of Plaza Vergara, next to *Hotel O'Higgins* (Mon–Fri 9am–2pm & 3–7pm, Sat & Sun 10am–2pm & 3–7pm; ☎800 800830, ⓦ visitevinadelmar.cl).

Sernatur Valparaíso 507, on the third floor (office #305) of an office block set back from the main street, next to an amusement arcade (Mon–Thurs 8.30am–2pm & 3–5.30pm, Fri 8.30am–2pm & 3–4.30pm; ☎32 269 0082).

ACCOMMODATION

Viña has all manner of **places to stay**, but most are overpriced and only a few offer sea views, as the oceanfront is taken up by residential condominiums. Book well in advance during the high season or national holidays; at other times prices drop.

Casa del Sol Romero 375 ☎32 296 7243. This friendly B&B in the Recreo neighbourhood has a collection of simple but clean and comfortable en suites. There's a kitchen for guests, wi-fi access, and board games, books and DVDs to keep you entertained. CH$46,000

★**Hotel Agora** 5 1/2 Poniente 253 ☎32 269 4669, ⓦ hotelagora.cl. Appealing Art Deco-style hotel that wouldn't look out of place in Miami. Located on a quiet side street, it has impeccable pastel-shaded en suites with fridges and flatscreen TVs, and a stylish yellow-and-white tiled lobby. CH$59,000

Hotel del Mar San Martin 199 ☎32 250 0700, ⓦ enjoy. cl. Viña's flagship 5-star hotel, a cylindrical building right on the seafront, has a grand Romanesque feel. The exquisite en suites have balconies, and there's a casino and several restaurants, including the outstanding *Savinya*. US$276

Hotel Monterilla 2 Norte 65 ☎32 297 6950, ⓦ monterilla.cl. The en suites at this intimate family-run boutique hotel have been decorated with considerable flair, while the service is personalized and the location convenient for Viña del Mar's bars and restaurants. CH$51,000

Kalagen Hostel Av Valparaiso 618 ☎32 299 1669, ⓦ kalagenhostel.com. Smart, large and lively hostel on Vina's main shopping drag, with dorms (8 to 12-bed), private rooms, spacious communal areas, daily activities and free/discounted entry to clubs in town. Expect parties. Dorms CH$10,000, doubles CH$25,000

My Father's House Gregorio Marañón 1210 ☎32 261 6136, ⓦ myfathershouse.cl. Spacious, quiet single, double and triple rooms (with shared or private bathrooms), swimming pool and gracious owners. The only drawback is that it's about 2km from the centre of town; catch *colectivo* #31, #82 or #131. CH$40,000

EATING AND DRINKING

Café Journal Agua Santa and Alvarez ☎32 266 6654. Proximity to Viña's university ensures a healthy crowd of student drinkers, with pitchers of beer setting them up for a night dancing and carousing. It's busy throughout the week (Wed is a big night). Drinks from CH$1500. Daily 10am–3am.

Cevasco Av Valparaiso 688–700 ☎32 271 4256, ⓦ cevasco.cl. Bustling *fuente de soda*, split between two locations, either side of an arcade, serving up tasty – if decidedly unhealthy – *completos*, burgers and *barros lucos* (CH$1350–5000) to a steady stream of locals. Mon–Sat 8am–11.30pm.

Delicias del Mar San Martín 459 ☎32 290 1837, ⓦ deliciasdelmar.com. Smart Basque-influenced *marisquería* with a loyal clientele, relaxed atmosphere, and great wine to accompany the crab lasagne, paella or the "Corvina DiCaprio", which was created to honour the visit of the Hollywood star. Mains around CH$10,000–15,000. Daily noon–4pm & 7pm–midnight.

★**Divino Pecado** San Martín 180 ☎32 297 5790. Classy Italian offering mouthwatering fish and seafood dishes (most mains CH$10,000–16,000) like tuna carpaccio and *scallops au gratin*. Reservations are necessary at the weekend. Mon–Thurs 12.30–3pm, & 8–11pm, Fri & Sat 12.30–3pm & 8pm–midnight, Sun 12.30–2pm & 8–11pm.

Entre Masas 5 Norte 235 ☎32 297 9919. Excellent little bakery, specializing in *empanadas* (CH$1500–2200): there are dozens of varieties including crab and cheese, spinach and ricotta, and chorizo and goat's cheese. There's another branch in Reñaca (Av Central 75). Daily 10am–10pm.

La Flor de Chile 8 Norte 601 ☎ 32 268 9554, ⓦ laflorde chile.cl. Atmospheric restaurant with a Spanish-influenced menu – try the rabbit stew or share one of the *tablas* (platters of cheeses, cured meats and olives) – and a good-value set lunch (CH$48,000). Mon–Sat 10am–midnight.

Jerusalem Quinta and Alvarez ☎ 32 247 4704. Popular with students, this no-frills Middle Eastern place serves a steady stream of inexpensive juices, falafel wraps and kebabs (from CH$2000). There are plenty of vegetarian options, and you can eat at the plastic tables outside or get a takeaway. Mon–Sat 11.30am–9.30pm.

Panzoni Paseo Cousiño 12B ☎ 32 271 4134. This charming Italian joint has a handful of tables, great service and inexpensive pastas and salads (set lunch CH$3800). You may have to queue at lunchtime, but it's worth the wait. Mon–Sat noon–4pm & 8pm–midnight.

NIGHTLIFE AND ENTERTAINMENT

Nightlife tends to be seasonal, reaching a heady peak in Jan and Feb when everyone flocks to the **bars and clubs of Reñaca**, a suburb further up the coast (see below). During the summer months, *micros* run to and from Reñaca right through the night. In winter, the partying dies out, and the focus shifts back to Viña.

Cine Arte Plaza Vergara (through passage off west side of square) ☎ 32 288 2798, ⓦ cinearte.cl. Excellent little arts cinema – check the website to see what's on. Especially worth a visit during the Festival Internacional de Cine Viña del Mar (ⓦ cinevina.cl) in Nov/Dec.

Ovo Casino Municipal ☎ 32 284 6100, ⓦ enjoy.cl. *The* place to be seen sipping a pisco sour and striking a pose; without a doubt, Viña del Mar's flashiest nightclub, with a dress code, attitude and clientele to match. Thurs–Sat 12.30am–4/5am.

Scratch Quillota 830 ☎ 32 238 1381, ⓦ scratch.cl. For more than twenty years this club – which has recently moved a few buildings down the road – has been pulling in the crowds and on weekends is packed to capacity (1200 people) until sunrise. DJs play a mix of reggaeton, dance, electronica and pop. Thurs, Fri & Sat 10pm–5/6am.

Teatro Municipal Plaza Vergara ☎ 32 268 1739. The grand Neoclassical Teatro Municipal, which dates back to the 1920s, puts on theatrical performances, classical music concerts and dance shows.

DIRECTORY

Money and exchange Most banks and *cambios* are on Arlegui and Libertad, and there are innumerable ATMs scattered about town.

Post office Between Plaza Vergara and Puente Libertad (Mon–Fri 9am–7pm, Sat 10am–1pm).

North of Viña

North of Viña, **Reñaca** and neighbouring **Concón** are easy to get to, though **Cachagua** and **Zapallar** are the most exclusive resorts. Beyond here, the coast road meanders to the small fishing village of **Papudo**, about 75km from Viña, and beyond to the farming town of **La Ligua** from where you can reach the family resort of **Los Vilos**. Hugging the oceanside in some stretches, darting inland in others, the northern coast road is far quieter than its southern counterpart, and very beautiful in parts.

GETTING AROUND

By bus Services to resorts further north are less frequent, though most can also be reached from Valparaíso and Santiago. Unless you have your own vehicle, the best option is to pick one or two places and head for these, rather than resort-hopping on public transport.

Reñaca

Lively, developed **REÑACA**, 6km north of central Viña, is a 1.5km stretch of coast swamped by bars, restaurants and apartment blocks. The beaches here are among the cleanest in the country, and the resort is particularly popular with Chile and Argentina's beautiful young things. Reñaca's **clubs** are pretty pricey but remain resolutely popular throughout the summer season. Every summer a host of new clubs appears, and others disappear, so ask around for the latest. Accommodation is generally overpriced and you're better off staying in Viña.

Concón

CONCÓN, 10km north of Reñaca, is a strange sort of place: part concrete terraced apartment blocks, part elegant villas with flower-filled gardens, and part rundown, working-class fishing village, with six beaches spread out along the bay. When the wind is blowing south, nasty fumes drift over from the nearby oil refinery.

The most interesting bit of town is **La Boca**, the ramshackle commercial centre at the mouth of the Río Aconcagua. The *caleta* here was used to export the produce of the haciendas of the Aconcagua valley in the nineteenth century and is now a bustling fish quay, lined with modest **marisquerías**.

The most popular beaches are the rapidly developing **Playa Amarilla** and **Playa Negra**, south of La Boca, both good for bodyboarding. More attractive, and quieter, is **Playa Ritoque**, a long stretch of sand a few kilometres north of town.

Horcón

The charming and picturesque – if slightly tatty – fishing village of **HORCÓN**, about 30km north of Concón, is a chaotic tumble of houses straggling down the hill to a rocky bay. (En route, you'll pass Quintero, a scruffy, forbidding town with filthy beaches, to be avoided at all costs.) In the summer, Horcón is taken over by artisans on the beach selling jewellery made from seashells and unfeasible numbers of young Chileans who come to chill out for the weekend; this is the hippy alternative to Reñaca.

The **beach** in front of the village is crowded and uninviting, but a short walk up the main street and then along Avenida Cau-Cau takes you down a steep, rickety staircase to the remote **Playa Cau-Cau**, a pleasantly sheltered beach surrounded by wooded hills, though a hideous condo mars the beauty of the area. An hour's walk along the beach north towards Maitencillo takes you to Playa Luna, a nudist beach.

Maitencillo

Stretching 4km along one main street, **MAITENCILLO** is little more than a long, narrow strip of holiday homes, *cabañas* and hotels along the shoreline. The chief reason for coming here is **Playa Aguas Blancas**, a superb white-sand beach sweeping 5km south of the village, backed by steep sandstone cliffs and good for surfing. Maitencillo is also a popular spot for paragliding and there are several locally based instructors.

Cachagua

CACHAGUA, a short way north of Maitencillo, has a stunning beach, with a wide expanse of pale sand curling round the bay, backed by gentle hills, and is synonymous with Chile's upper crust. It is blessed by a relative lack of holiday homes on the land off the beach, which instead is home to a golf course. Ask for directions to the long staircase from Avenida del Mar down to **Playa Las Cujas**, a tiny, spectacular and often empty beach. Just off the coast, the Isla de los Pingüinos is a **penguin sanctuary** to which local fishermen sometimes offer boat rides; canoe tours are also available. Visit the island at your peril: the smell of hundreds of Humboldt penguins can be nauseating.

Zapallar

The classiest and most attractive of the Litoral resorts, **ZAPALLAR** is a sheltered, horseshoe bay backed by lushly wooded hills where luxurious holiday homes and handsome old mansions nestle between the pine trees. Apart from the beach, you can also stroll along the coastal path around the bay, or walk up Avenida Zapallar, admiring the early twentieth-century townhouses, manicured gardens, and a pretty stone church.

More strenuous possibilities include hiring a sea-kayak, climbing the 692m **Cerro Higuera** or following the coastal path back to Maitencillo.

Papudo

The development in **PAPUDO**, just 10km around the headland, hasn't been as graceful as in Zapallar, and several ugly buildings mar the seafront. However, the steep hills looming dramatically behind the town are undeniably beautiful, and the place has a friendly, local atmosphere. The best beach in the area is the dully named **Playa Grande**.

La Ligua

The chief appeal of **LA LIGUA**, a bustling agricultural town, is its setting, enfolded by undulating hills that take on a rich honey glow in the early evening sunlight. It is also known for its confectionery: *dulces de La Ligua* – sweet, sugary cakes famous throughout Chile. There's also a small museum and an artisans' market in the main square. La Ligua was once notorious as the home of one of Chile's darkest figures: Catalina de los Ríos y Lisperguer. Born in 1604, La Quintrala, as she was known, murdered over forty people in a brutal lifetime, including her father, a Knight of the Order of St John (after first seducing him), and numerous slaves. She evaded justice, dying before she could be put on trial.

Pichidangui

North of the Papudo–La Ligua crossroads, the Panamericana follows the coast for some 200km before dipping inland again, towards Ovalle (see p.127). This stretch of highway takes you past a succession of gorgeous, white-sand **beaches** dotted with fishing villages and small resorts. Set 4km back from the Panamericana, 50km beyond the Papudo–La Ligua interchange, is **PICHIDANGUI**, with a lovely beach: 7km of white, powdery sand fringed by eucalyptus trees, with little beachfront development.

Los Vilos

Local legend has it that **LOS VILOS**, 30km north of Pichidangui, takes its name from the Hispanic corruption of "Lord Willow", a British pirate who was shipwrecked on the coast and decided to stay. The town later became notorious for highway robberies. Today it is a great place to spend a couple of days by the sea without paying over the odds. However, it gets incredibly packed in January and February. The town's chief attraction is its long golden **beach**, but there's also a **fish market** and **Isla de los Lobos**, a seal colony 5km south of the bay.

ARRIVAL AND DEPARTURE

NORTH OF VIÑA

By bus Cachagua, Concón, Horcón, La Ligua, Maitencillo, Reñaca and Zapallar are all served by regular bus to and from Viña del Mar, while Papudo has a twice-daily service. From Santiago there are also buses to La Ligua and hourly buses (twice hourly; 3hr 15min) to Los Vilos from the Terminal de Buses Santiago and the Terminal San Borja.

Daily buses likewise head to Pichidangui from the capital's Terminal de Buses Santiago (Condor Bus; ☏ 2 2779 3721, ⓦ www.condorbus.cl) and also from Valparaíso (Buses La Porteña, which leave from the company's office at Molina 366; ☏ 32 221 6568). Journey time (2hr 30min) is the same from either city.

ACCOMMODATION AND EATING

CONCÓN

Mantagua 3km north of town ☏ 32 215 5900, ⓦ mantagua.cl. Concón is an easy day-trip from Viña, but if you want to stay try *Mantagua*, a smart, modern and very

pricey hotel with minimalist en suites and cosy *cabañas* suitable for families. There's a pool, good restaurant and plenty of activities on offer. Doubles US$190, *cabañas* US$310

2

MAITENCILLO

Cabañas Hermansen Avenida del Mar 0592 ☎ 32 277 1028, ⓦ hermansen.cl. A 5min drive north of Aguas Blancas, this lodge has great views of the beach, rustic *cabañas* with cute wooden picnic tables, bike rental and switched-on staff. The attached *La Canasta* is the only decent restaurant-bar in the area. **CH$77,000**

ZAPALLAR

★ **El Chiringuito** At the southern tip of the bay ☎ 33 274 1024. Down by the *caleta*, this restaurant serves up legendary seafood (around CH$10,000–15,000) – the scallops, in particular, are absolutely divine. Summer Mon–Thurs 12.30–6pm, Fri & Sat 12.30pm–midnight; autumn and winter often weekend only.

★ **Hotel Isla Seca** At the northern end of the bay ☎ 33 274 1224, ⓦ hotelislaseca.cl. If you feel like splashing out, this swanky hotel offers classically styled rooms with balconies; note that those with sea views cost significantly more than those without. There's also an excellent restaurant. **US$163**

PAPUDO

Hotel Carande Chorrillos 89 ☎ 33 279 1105, ⓦ hotelcarande.cl. The best of Papudo's nondescript hotels, Carande has rather drab if clean en-suite rooms; those at the top of the building have sea views. There's also a reasonable restaurant. **CH$42,000**

PICHIDANGUI

La Rosa Náutica El Dorado 120 ☎ 53 253 1133, ⓦ rosanautica.cl. There are a mixture of standard hotel rooms and more atmospheric wooden *cabañas* at *La Rosa Náutica*; both types are simple but comfortable. There's also a pool and a good restaurant. Doubles **CH$43,900**, *cabañas* **CH$47,900**

LOS VILOS

Hotel Lord Willow Calle Hostería 1444 ☎ 53 254 8854, ⓦ hotellordwillow.cl. Overlooking the beach, this whitewashed, palm-tree-shaded hotel has a range of clean if dated and slightly cramped rooms with TVs and private bathrooms. There's a pool and a restaurant. **CH$28,000**

Parque Nacional La Campana

Cordillera de la Costa • Daily 9am–5.30pm • CH$2000 • ⓦ www.conaf.cl/parques/parque-nacional-la-campana

Set in the dry, dusty mountains of the coastal range, **PARQUE NACIONAL LA CAMPANA** is a wonderful place to go hiking and offers some of the best views in Chile. From the 1880m-high summit of Cerro La Campana you can see the Andes on one side and the Pacific Ocean on the other – in the words of Charles Darwin, who climbed the mountain in 1834, Chile is seen "as in a map". Another draw is the chance to see a profusion of **Chilean palms** in their natural habitat; this native tree was all but wiped out in the nineteenth century, and the Palmar de Ocoa, a grove in the northern section of the park, is one of just two remaining places in the country where you can find wild palms. You can also expect to see eagles and giant hummingbirds and, if you're lucky, mountain cats and foxes.

The park is located about 60km east of Valparaíso and 110km northwest of Santiago. It's divided into three "sectors" – Granizo, Cajón Grande and Ocoa – each with its own entrance. **Sector Granizo** and **Sector Cajón Grande** are both in the south of the park, close to the village of **Olmué**; this is the part to head for if you want to follow Darwin's footsteps and climb **Cerro La Campana**. These sectors could be done as a day-trip from Valparaíso or Santiago, although if you have the time it is better to spend a night or two in Olmué. The less-accessible and less-visited **Sector Ocoa**, on the northern side of the Park, is where you'll find the palm trees – literally thousands of them. This part of the park can be reached as a day-trip from Valparaíso, Viña, or, at a push, Santiago; if you want to stay the night, you'll need to camp.

ARRIVAL AND DEPARTURE   PARQUE NACIONAL LA CAMPANA

SECTOR GRANIZO AND SECTOR CAJÓN GRANDE

By bus For these sectors, aim for the gateway village of Olmué: Ciferal Express runs buses (every 2hr; 1hr) from Playa Ancha in Valparaíso; Pullman runs buses (hourly; 1hr 30min–2hr) from Santiago's San Borja and Alameda terminals. From Olmué it's a further 9km to the park;

regular buses (every 15min) run from the main square to Granizo; the last bus stop is a 15min walk from the Conaf hut in Sector Granizo, and a 40min walk from Sector Cajón Grande.

By car If you're driving from Valparaíso, the best route is via Viña del Mar, Quilpué, Villa Alemana and Limache. If you're coming from Santiago, take the RN-5 north, then

HIKING IN PARQUE NACIONAL LA CAMPANA

There are about a dozen very scenic **walks** in the park, most of them along good, well-maintained trails and many of them interconnected. The maps given away at the Conaf hut are very useful. If you plan to do some serious walking, try to get hold of a more detailed **map** from Sernatur before you come. If you're on a day-hike you may be allowed in before 9am if you want to make an early start, but you must get back to the Conaf control before it closes (5.30pm); if you want to camp in the park, talk to the *guardaparque* when you sign in. Finally, there aren't many water sources along the trails so bring plenty with you.

SECTOR GRANIZO

The well-marked 9km **Sendero Andinista**, up Cerro La Campana, is the most popular and rewarding trek in the park. It's quite hard going, especially the last ninety minutes, when it's more a climb than a hike, but the views from the top are breathtaking – and this is where Darwin climbed. Allow at least four and a half hours to get up and three to get down.

Sendero Los Peumos is a pretty, 4km walk (about 3hr) up to the Portezuelo Ocoa, through gentle woodland for the first half, followed by a fairly steep climb. Three paths converge at the Portezuelo; you can either go back the way you came; take the right-hand path (Sendero Portezuelo Ocoa) down through the Cajón Grande to that sector's Conaf hut (about 3hr); or follow the left-hand path (Sendero El Amasijo) through Sector Ocoa to the northernmost park entrance (another 4hr; best if you're camping as there's no accommodation at the other end).

SECTOR CAJÓN GRANDE

The **Sendero Portezuelo Ocoa**, also known as **Sendero Los Robles**, is a 7km trail (about 3hr) through beautiful woods with natural *miradores* giving views down to the Cuesta La Dormida. From the Portezuelo Ocoa, at the end of the path, you can link up with other paths as described above.

SECTOR OCOA

Sendero La Cascada makes a lovely day-hike through lush palm groves to a 35m-high waterfall, most impressive in early spring. The 8km path is mainly flat; allow about seven hours there and back. It has eight well-marked *estaciones* that describe local flora. **Sendero El Amasijo** is a 7km trail (3hr) following the Estero Rabuco (a stream) through a scenic canyon before climbing steeply to the Portezuelo Ocoa. Most walkers make this a cross-park trek, continuing to Granizo or Cajón Grande (see opposite). Fast, fit walkers should be able to do it in a day, but it's more relaxing if you camp overnight.

follow the signs for Tiltil, from where the road takes the zigzagging and very scenic route from Cuesta La Dormida to Olmué.

SECTOR OCOA

By bus Sector Ocoa is approached on a gravel road branching south from the Panamericana about halfway between Llay-Llay and Hijuelas; coming from Llay-Llay, it's the left turn just before the bridge across the Río Aconcagua. Any northbound bus along the Panamericana will drop you at the turn-off, but from here it's a 12km hike to the park entrance, with minimal hitchhiking opportunities.

ACCOMMODATION

A lovely village in a fertile valley, **Olmué** has a good choice of **places to stay**. It is also possible to camp in the park itself – ask at the Conaf hut at the park entrance for more information.

Centro Turístico La Campana Blanca Encalada 4651 ☎ 33 244 1722, ⓦ campana.cl. The friendly *La Campana* has the feel of a motel: pink buildings house clean, slightly gaudy but good-value en suites with TVs, and there's a garden, pool and a children's play area. Rates include breakfast. <u>**CH$43,000**</u>

Hostería El Copihué Portales 2203 ☎ 33 244 1544, ⓦ copihue.cl. The top place in town, with comfortable en suites, a nice pool, spa, beautiful gardens full of vines and flowers, and a good restaurant. Rates include breakfast. <u>**CH$88,000**</u>

El Norte Chico

127 Ovalle

129 Around Ovalle

131 Andacollo and around

134 Coquimbo and the coast

136 La Serena

143 The Elqui Valley

151 Vallenar and around

154 Copiapó

158 Around Copiapó

164 Parque Nacional Pan de Azúcar

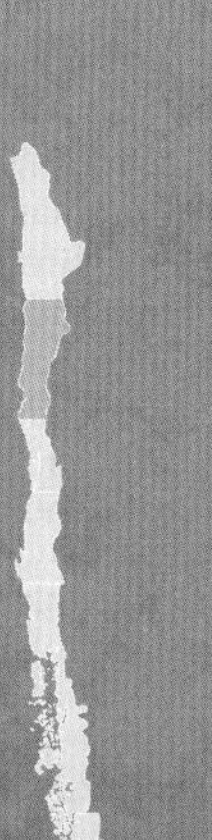

DESIERTO FLORIDO

El Norte Chico

A land of rolling, sun-baked hills streaked with sudden river valleys that cut across the earth in a flash of green, the Norte Chico, or "Little North", of Chile is what geographers call a "transitional zone". Its semi-arid scrubland and sparse vegetation mark the transformation from the country's fertile heartland to the barren deserts bordering Peru and Bolivia. Starting around the Río Aconcagua, just north of Santiago, it stretches all the way to Taltal, and the southernmost reaches of the Atacama, more than 800km further north.

3

A series of **rivers** flow through the Norte Chico region from the Andes to the coast, allowing the surrounding land to be irrigated and cultivated. The result is spectacular: lush, vibrant green terraces laden with olives, apricots and vines snake between the brown, parched walls of the valleys, forming a sensational visual contrast. The most famous product of these valleys is **pisco**, the pale, aromatic brandy distilled from sun-dried grapes and treasured by Chileans as their national drink.

The largest population centre – and one of the country's most fashionable seaside resorts – is **La Serena**, its pleasing, colonial-style architecture and lively atmosphere making it one of the few northern cities worth visiting for its own sake. It's also an ideal base for exploring the beautiful **Elqui Valley**, immortalized in the verses of the Nobel laureate Gabriela Mistral, and home to luxuriant vines and idyllic riverside hamlets. Just down the coast from La Serena lies the **Parque Nacional Fray Jorge**, with a microclimate that supports a small, damp cloudforest. Another botanical wonder is the famous *desierto florido* or **flowering desert**. Occasionally, after heavy winter rains, the normally dry earth sprouts vast expanses of vibrantly coloured flowers. This rare, unpredictable phenomenon is centred on **Vallenar**.

Skies that are guaranteed cloudless almost year-round and very little air pollution have made the region the obvious choice for some of the world's major **astronomical observatories**. They range from the state-of-the art facility at dazzling-white **Tololo** to the modest municipal installation at **Mamalluca**, near the picturesque village of **Vicuña**, where you don't have to be an expert reserving months in advance to look through the telescope.

The Norte Chico also boasts a string of superb **beaches**, some totally deserted and many of them tantalizingly visible from the Panamericana as you enter the region, just north of Santiago. **Bahía Inglesa** is famous for its turquoise waters, though increasingly prolific algae is turning the bay greener.

Copiapó, the region's northernmost major city, serves as a useful springboard for excursions into the nearby **desert** or, further afield, up into the high cordillera. Here the **Parque Nacional Nevado de Tres Cruces**, the **Volcán Ojos del Salado** and **Laguna Verde** present some of Chile's most magnificent yet least-visited landscapes: snow-topped volcanoes, bleached-white salt flats and azure lakes. A couple of hours to the north, near the towering cliffs and empty beaches of **Parque Nacional Pan de Azúcar**, a

La Serena's churches p.138
Observatories around La Serena p.140
Pisco p.148
Into Argentina on ruta 41 p.149
Gabriela Mistral p.150

The price of gold p.153
The flowering desert p.155
The rescue of Los 33 p.158
Climbing Volcán Ojos del Salado p.160

FERIA MODELO DE OVALLE

Highlights

❶ Feria Modelo de Ovalle Wander this food market and fill your bags with plump olives, giant pumpkins, ripe tomatoes and very smelly cheeses. **See p.127**

❷ La Serena Chile's second-oldest city offers long beaches, beautiful churches and a lively ambience. **See pp.136–143**

❸ Horseriding in the Elqui Valley Pretend you're in the Wild West as you trek through Chile's untrammelled northern plains. **See p.143**

❹ Planta Capel Sample the fiery, fruity brandy that is Chile's national drink, straight from the

barrel at the Elqui Valley's largest distillery. **See p.145**

❺ Stargazing Observe the unbelievably limpid night skies at impressive observatories, from Del Pangue to Mamalluca. **See p.146**

❻ Desierto florido If you're lucky to be in the right place at the right time, see the desert around Vallenar burst into bloom. **See p.155**

❼ Nevado de Tres Cruces One of the country's least-known national parks, with emerald-green lakes, snowcapped volcanoes and plentiful wildlife. **See p.159**

HIGHLIGHTS ARE MARKED ON THE MAP ON P.126

HIGHLIGHTS

1. Feria Modelo de Ovalle
2. La Serena
3. Horseriding in the Elqui Valley
4. Planta Capel
5. Stargazing
6. Desierto florido
7. Nevado de Tres Cruces

N

PACIFIC
OCEAN

Taital

PARQUE NACIONAL
PAN DE AZÚCAR

Caleta Pan de Azúcar
Chañaral

El Salvador

Diego de
Almagro

Portrerillos

Paso de
San Francisco

SALAR DE
MARICUNGA
Laguna
Santa Rosa

Laguna
Verde

Caldera

Bahía Inglesa

Volcán Copiapó
(6080m)

Mina Marte

Tres
Cruces

Ojos del
Salado

Puerto Viejo

Copiapó

Bahía Salada

Nantoco

PARQUE NACIONAL
NEVADO DE TRES CRUCES

7

Laguna del
Negro
Francisco

Carrizal Bajo

Juntas

RESERVA NACIONAL
LLANOS DE CHALLE

6

Huasco

Vallenar

Alto del Carmen
El Tránsito

Domeyko

San Félix

Isla Chañaral

RESERVA
NACIONAL
PINGUINO DE
HUMBOLDT

Isla Choros

Cerro las Campanas

Cerro la Silla

Pinto

ARGENTINA

La Higuera

Mamalluca
Observatory

La Serena
Coquimbo

2

5

Vicuña

4

Montegrande

Pisco Elqui

Guanaquero

Cerro
Tololo

Del Pangue
Observatory

3

Tongoy

Andacollo

Pichasca

PARQUE
NACIONAL
FRAY JORGE

Ovalle

1

Monte Patria

Termas
de Socas

Valle del
Encanto

Caleta Teniente

EL NORTE CHICO

small island is home to colonies of seals, countless pelicans and thousands of penguins.

Note that whereas the Norte Grande, Chile's northernmost region, can be visited year-round, the Norte Chico is at its best in the **summer months** (Oct–March) when the valleys are at their greenest, the coast is likelier to be free of fog and the ocean and sky are pure blue. On the downside, the beach resorts can be horribly overcrowded and overpriced in the high season, especially January.

Brief history

Mining has shaped the region's growth, giving birth to towns, ports, railways and roads, and drawing large numbers of settlers to seek their fortune here. **Gold** was mined first by the Incas for ritual offerings, and then intensively, to exhaustion, by the Spaniards until the end of the eighteenth century. Next came the great nineteenth-century **silver** bonanza, when a series of dramatic silver strikes – some of them accidental – set a frenzy of mining and prospecting in motion, propelling the region into its heyday. Further riches and glory came when the discovery of huge **copper** deposits turned it into the world's largest copper producer from the 1840s to 1870s. Mining is still the most important industry here, its presence most visible up in the cordillera, where huge mining trucks hurtle around the mountain roads, enveloped in dust clouds.

3

Ovalle

Almost 380km north of Santiago – some 140km beyond Los Vilos – a lone sign points to the little-visited market town of **OVALLE**. The town's main claim to fame is as the birthplace of one of the country's outstanding contemporary writers, Luis Sepúlveda. It's also a good base for exploring the dramatic **Hurtado Valley** or the deeply rural **Limarí Valley**, home to a few low-key attractions, including the Monumento Natural Pichasca, the Termas de Socos hot springs and the petroglyphs at the Valle del Encanto.

The Plaza de Armas

The **Plaza de Armas**, with expansive lawns, nineteenth-century Phoenix palms and rows of jacaranda, marks Ovalle's centre. Dominating the east side of the square is the white-and-mustard **Iglesia San Vicente Ferrer**, a large, colonial-style church dating to 1849, with thick adobe walls and a diminutive tower. From the plaza, a pedestrian mall leads three blocks east along Vicuña Mackenna.

Museo del Limarí

Covarrubias and Antofagasta • Tues–Fri 10am–6pm, Sat & Sun 10am–2pm • CH$600

Ovalle's excellent **Museo del Limarí** stands on the northeast edge of town in the grand old building that once housed the train station. The museum's collection of **Diaguita pottery** is beautifully restored and shown to great effect in modern cases. Famed for its exquisite geometric designs painted in black, white and red onto terracotta surfaces, the pottery was produced by the Diaguita people who inhabited this part of Chile from 1000 AD until the Inca invasions in the sixteenth century.

Feria Modelo de Ovalle

Av la Feria and Benavente • Mon, Wed, Fri & Sat 6am–7pm, Sun 6am–2.30pm

About ten blocks east of the plaza, you'll find a huge, ramshackle iron hangar that houses the colourful **Feria Modelo de Ovalle**, the largest fresh-produce market in the north of Chile and definitely worth a visit; you can pick up fantastic home-made cheeses (including some alarmingly pungent goat cheeses) as well as delicious dried figs and a range of fruit and vegetables.

ARRIVAL AND INFORMATION   OVALLE

By bus The bus terminal, known as Medialuna, is at Ariztía Oriente 769 (☎53 262 6612). Rural buses leave from the Feria Modelo and outside the Mercado Municipal at Victoria and Independencia.

Destinations Antofagasta (25 daily; 14hr); Arica (6 daily; 24hr); Calama (15 daily; 17hr); Chañaral (10 daily; 9hr);

Copiapó (10 daily; 7hr); La Serena (every 15min; 1hr 20min); Los Vilos (10 daily; 2.5hr); Santiago (18 daily; 6hr); Vallenar (20 daily; 4hr 30min).

Information The website O! Valle Limari (ⓦovallelimari .cl) is a useful source of information on the town and surrounding area.

ACCOMMODATION

Gran Hotel Ovalle Vicuña Mackenna 210 ☎53 262 1084, ⓦgranhotelovalle.cl. Operating for over 60 years, this solid mid-range option offers serviceable doubles – some are nicer and pricier than others, so ask to see a few – with artwork on the walls, as well as breakfast. CH$41,500

Hotel Plaza Turismo Victoria 295 ☎53 266 2500, ⓦplazaturismo.cl. This hotel occupies a handsome old building in a prime location in front of the Plaza de Armas.

Inside things aren't quite so impressive, but the rooms are spacious and well-kept, and there's a restaurant. CH$64,000

Hotel Roxy Libertad 155 ☎53 262 0080, ⓔhotelroxy @hotmail.com. For an economical option, try the *Hotel Roxy*, which has comfortable if rather dated rooms arranged around a large, brightly painted patio filled with flowers and chairs. CH$25,000

EATING AND DRINKING

Ovalle's **restaurants** tend to limit themselves to the standard dishes you find everywhere else in Chile – which is frustrating, considering this is the fresh-produce capital of the North. However, you will find a few worthwhile spots.

Los Braseros Vicuña Mackenna 595 ☎53 262 4917. Serves delicious if unoriginal fare, including juicy *parrillas* (around CH$15,000 for two) and river prawns in pleasant surroundings marred only by the giant TV screen. Mon–Sat 10am–4pm & 7.30pm–midnight, Sun10am–4pm.

Café Pub Real Vicuña Mackenna 419 ☎53 262 3926 . If you're in need of real coffee (around CH$1500–2000), head

to this appropriately named café which morphs into a pub five nights a week. Café Mon–Sat 9am–8.30pm; pub Tues–Sat 9pm–late.

El Quijote Arauco 294 ☎53 262 0501. An intimate, bohemian sort of restaurant-bar, with political graffiti and poetry on the walls, and an inexpensive menu (dishes CH$2000–5000) featuring simple staples like *cazuela* and *lomo*. Mon–Sat 11am–5pm & 7pm–2am.

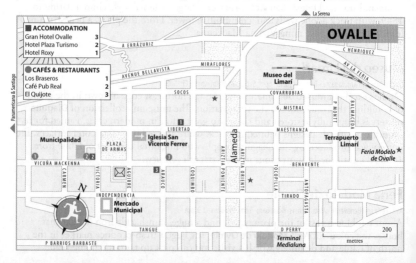

Around Ovalle

If you have your own car, you can take the scenic road northeast of Ovalle – an alternative route to Vicuña and the Elqui Valley (see p.143) – which winds slowly up into the mountains, passing ancient petrified wood stumps at **Pichasca** and the delightful oasis village of **Hurtado**, the main settlement along the dramatic but seldom visited **Hurtado Valley**. If you head west, you'll find a concentration of rock carvings in the **Valle del Encanto**, a hot springs resort at the **Termas de Socos** and the impressive cloudforest reserve of **Parque Nacional Fray Jorge**.

Monumento Natural Pichasca

About 30km southwest of Hurtado • April–Nov Wed–Sun 9am–5.30pm; Dec–March daily 9am–5.30pm • CH$2500 • ☎ 53 262 0058, ⓦ www.conaf.cl • On market days (Mon, Wed, Fri, Sat & Sun) it's possible to get to the turn-off to San Pedro de Pichasca on a rickety bus from Ovalle's Feria Modelo (see p.128), but this involves walking 3km from the main road to the site entrance, and then a further 2km to the cave and fossil remains

Northeast of Ovalle, a first-rate paved road climbs through the fertile Hurtado Valley, skirting – 12km out of town – the deep-blue expanse of water formed by the Recoleta Dam, one of three that irrigate the Limarí Valley. About 50km up the road, past a string of tiny villages, a side road to San Pedro Norte dips down across the river leading, just beyond the village, to the Conaf-run **Monumento Natural Pichasca**, the site of a seventy-million-year-old petrified wood. As you arrive at the parking area, two paths diverge: the right-hand path leads north to a hillside scattered with stumps of **fossilized tree trunks**, some of them imprinted with the shape of leaves; the left-hand, or southern, path leads down to an enormous **cave** formed by an 80m gash in the hillside topped by a massive overhanging rock. Archeological discoveries inside the cave point to human habitation some ten thousand years ago.

Hurtado

Around 30km northeast of Pichasca, set amid dramatic mountain scenery, is the traditional oasis village of **HURTADO**. Set at an altitude of around 1200m, with just four hundred inhabitants, the main draw, a few kilometres outside the village, is a Mexican-style ranch, the *Hacienda Los Andes* (see p.131).

Valle del Encanto

19km west of Ovalle • Daily 8am–4.30pm • CH$500 • Take any westbound bus and asked to be dropped off at the highway turn-off and then walk the heavily potholed dirt road that leads 5km south of Ruta 45 into the ravine

The dry, dusty **Valle del Encanto** boasts one of Chile's densest collections of **petroglyphs** – images engraved on the surface of rocks – carved mainly by people of the El Molle culture (see p.469) between 100 and 600 AD. Most of the images are geometric motifs or stylized human outlines, including faces with large, wide eyes and elaborate headdresses. A few of the images are very striking, while others are faint and difficult to make out; the best time to visit is between 2 and 3pm, when the outlines are at their sharpest, unobscured by shadows. You're allowed to camp in the park for free, but the toilets are in poor condition.

Termas de Socos

Panamericana Norte km 370, 35km southwest of Ovalle • Baths CH$4500 (or free for hotel guests); pool reserved for guests of the hotel (see p.131) • ☎ 53 198 2505, Santiago ☎ 2 2236 3336, ⓦ termasocos.cl • Twice daily bus services from Ovalle (30min) and La Serena (1.5hr)

The thermal baths complex of **Termas de Socos** lies 2km down a track just south of the turn-off to Ovalle. It is notable for its 22°C (72°F) outdoor pool, surrounded by

3

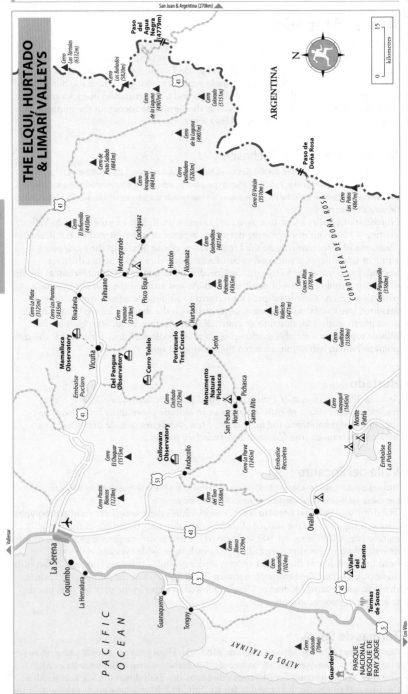

THE ELQUI, HURTADO & LIMARÍ VALLEYS

San Juan & Argentina (270km)

Paso del Agua Negra (4779m)

ARGENTINA

Cerro Los Tórtolos (6332m)

Cerro Los Bañados (5820m)

Cerro de la Laguna (4907m)

Cerro Colorado (5151m)

Cerro de la Laguna (4907m)

Paso de Doña Rosa

Cerro El Infiernillo (4450m)

Cerro de Pasto Salado (4843m)

Cerro Incaguasi (4843m)

Cerro Deshiladero (5263m)

Cerro El Volcán (3570m)

Cerro Los Patos (4867m)

Cochiguaz

Cerro Quebraditas (4815m)

CORDILLERA DE DOÑA ROSA

Montegrande

Horcón

Alcohuaz

Cerro Cruces Altos (3780m)

Cerro Pampecillo (3160m)

Pisco Elqui

Cerro Potreras (4365m)

Paihuano

Hurtado

Cerro Vallecito (3471m)

Cerro La Plata (3125m)

Cerro Los Poratos (3435m)

Rivadavia

Cerro Paranao (3120m)

Portezuelo Tres Cruces

Setón

Cerro Guaitatas (3558m)

Mamalluca Observatory

Embalse Puclaro

Vicuña

Del Pangue Observatory

Cerro Tololo

Monumento Natural Pichasca

Pichasca

Cerro Cinchado (2129m)

San Pedro Norte

Samo Alto

Cerro Guayaquil (1645m)

Monte Patria

Colowara Observatory

Cerro El Chaguar (1515m)

Andacollo

Cerro La Parva (1245m)

Embalse Recoleta

Embalse La Paloma

Cerro Pastos Blancos (1228m)

Cerro del Toro (1566m)

Ovalle

La Serena

Coquimbo

La Herradura

Cerro Blanco (1329m)

Cerro Manantial (1024m)

Valle del Encanto

Termas de Socos

Guanaqueros

Tongoy

Cerro Quiscudo (704m)

ALTOS DE TALINAY

Guardia

PARQUE NACIONAL BOSQUE DE FRAY JORGE

PACIFIC OCEAN

Valenar

Los Vilos

N

0   15
kilometres

palm and eucalyptus trees, wicker armchairs and huge potted ferns, as well as the cubicles containing private bathtubs where you can soak in warm spring water, supposedly rich in medicinal properties.

Parque Nacional Bosque de Fray Jorge

Panamericana Ruta CH 5, Autopista del Elqui • April–Nov Thurs–Sun 9am–4pm; Dec–March daily 9am–4pm • CH$2500 • ☎ 09 9346 2706, ⓦ www.conaf.cl • No public transport to the park; for taxis try Tacso in Ovalle (☎ 53 263 0989), or El Faro in La Serena (☎ 51 222 5060) or take a tour from La Serena (see p.141); if driving, allow about 1.5hr from Ovalle, and 2hr from La Serena – the park is reached by a dirt road that branches west from the Panamericana 14km north of the junction with Ruta 45 to Ovalle; from the turn-off, it's 27km to the park entrance, where you pay your fee and register

A UNESCO world biosphere reserve since 1977, **Parque Nacional Bosque de Fray Jorge** sits on the Altos de Talinay, a range of steep coastal hills plunging into the Pacific some 80km west of Ovalle and 110km south of La Serena. It extends over 100 square kilometres, but its focal point, and what visitors come to see, is the small **cloudforest** perched on the highest part of the sierra, about 600m above sea level.

The extraordinary thing about this forest is how sharply it contrasts with its surroundings, indeed with everywhere else in the area. Its existence is the result of **camanchaca**, the thick coastal fog that rises from the ocean and condenses as it meets the land, supporting a cover of dense vegetation – fern, bracken and myrtle trees – normally found only in southern Chile. Close to the parking area, a 1km path dotted with information panels guides you through a poorly labelled range of plants and trees, and leads to the **forest** proper, where a slippery, wooden boardwalk takes you through tall trees dripping with moisture. The whole trail takes less than half an hour to walk. Three kilometres beyond the Conaf control there's a **picnic** area, but note that camping is not allowed anywhere in the park.

ARRIVAL AND DEPARTURE   **AROUND OVALLE**

By bus Hurtado-bound buses leave from Ovalle's Feria Modelo (3–4 daily; 3hr).

ACCOMMODATION

Hacienda Los Andes Casilla 98, Río Hurtado ☎ 53 269 1822, ⓦ haciendalosandes.com. A Mexican-style ranch run by German expats, with spacious rooms enjoying mesmerizing views across the verdant valley. Excellent meals are served and they have their own private observatory. The main focus here is equestrian, and they also offer horseback adventures (from CH$51,000/person), with all meals and transfers to and from Vicuña or Ovalle included. Camping/person CH$4500, doubles CH$49,000

Camping Termas de Socos ☎ 53 263 1490, ⓦ campingtermassocos.cl. Right next to the hotel and thermal baths is this campsite with its own outdoor pool and a handful of *cabañas* that sleep up to four people. Nov–March. Camping/person CH$6000, *cabañas* CH$18,000

Hotel Termas Socos Panamericana Norte km 370, 35km southwest of Ovalle ☎ 53 198 2505, Santiago ☎ 2 2236 3336, ⓦ termasocos.cl. This studiously rustic hotel offers comfortable rooms and easy access to the hot springs. In addition to the B&B rates listed here, there are also excellent package deals that include three meals in the restaurant. CH$57,600

Andacollo and around

Enfolded by rolling, sun-bleached hills midway between Ovalle and La Serena, **ANDACOLLO** is a tidy little town of small adobe houses grouped around a long main street. It lies along a side road which branches northeast from the Ruta 43, the most direct, scenic route between Ovalle and La Serena. Andacollo has been an important gold- and copper-mining centre ever since the Inca mined its hills in the sixteenth century, but is best known as the home of the **Virgen de Andacollo**, a small wooden carving that draws over one hundred thousand pilgrims to the town each year between December 23 and 26 for the Fiesta Grande de la Virgen, four days of music and riotous dancing performed by costumed groups from all over Chile. The town is also home to one of the country's newest observatories.

The Basílica

Plaza Pedro Nolasco Videla · Daily 9am–6.30pm · Free, but donation expected

Andacolla is home to two temples erected in honour of the Virgin. Larger and grander is the **Basílica**, which towers over Plaza Pedro Nolasco Videla, the main square, in breathtaking contrast to the small, simple scale of the rest of the town. Built from 1873 to 1893, almost entirely of wood in a Roman–Byzantine style, its pale, cream-coloured walls are topped by two colossal 50m towers and a stunning 45m dome. Inside, sunlight floods through the dome, falling onto huge wooden pillars painted to look like marble.

Templo Antiguo

Plaza Pedro Nolasco Videla **Templo** Daily 9am–9pm · Free **Museo del Pelegrino** Mon–Fri 10am–1pm & 3–7pm, Sat & Sun 10am–7pm · Free, but donation expected

On the other side of the square stands the smaller, stone-built **Templo Antiguo**, dating from 1789. This is where the image of the Virgin stands for most of the year, perched on the main altar, awaiting the great festival when it's transported to the Basílica to receive the petitions and prayers of the pilgrims. Devotees of the Virgin de Andacollo have left an astonishing quantity of gifts here over the years, all displayed in the crypt of the Templo Antiguo as part of the **Museo del Pelegrino**.

Collowara Observatory

Ticket office Urmeneta 599 · Daily 9am–1pm & 2.30–8pm; tours summer 9pm, 10.30pm & midnight, winter 7pm, 8.30pm & 10pm · CH$3500 · ☎ 51 243 2964, ⓦ collowara.cl · No organized transport to the observatory but a return taxi costs around CH$10,000; ask the driver to pick you up when the tour ends

For a celestial experience, the **Collowara Observatory** (named after the Aymara term for "land of the stars") lies some 15km northeast of Andacollo, atop the 1300m Cerro Churqui. Built specifically for public use, like that run by the Municipalidad of Vicuña (see p.146), this observatory also features a top-quality Smith-Cassegrain telescope. The two-hour **evening tours** start with a high-tech audiovisual talk (in Spanish and English) about the galaxy and other astronomical matters, followed by the opportunity to observe the heavens through one of the telescopes – unless, of course, you're unlucky enough to be here on a cloudy night. Reserve in advance.

ARRIVAL AND INFORMATION   ANDACOLLO

By bus/colectivo You can reach Andacollo by bus (every 2hr) or *colectivo* from La Serena (1hr) or Coquimbo (1hr 20min).

Tourist information Urmeneta 599 (Mon–Fri 9am–1.30pm & 2.30–5.30pm; ☎ 51 254 6494, ⓦ andacollochile.cl).

ACCOMMODATION AND EATING

Hostal Arcón de Oro Alfonso 652 ☎ 09 8950 8226, ⓦ hostalarcondeoro.cl. This family-run hotel has spick and span rooms with TVs and private bathrooms. There's even a special deal for wedding night guests, should the urge strike to tie the knot. **CH$42,000**

Sol de Andacollo Chepiquilla 90 ☎ 09 8815 8723. Come to *Sol de Andacollo* to feast on typical Chilean dishes cooked in solar-powered ovens (mains around CH$5,000). It's worth the 10min walk out of town. Daily noon–5pm.

Coquimbo and the coast

West of Ovalle, the Panamericana turns towards the ocean and skirts a string of small resorts that provide a calmer and more attractive beach setting than the built-up coast at La Serena. Spread over a rocky peninsula studded with colourful houses, the busy port of **COQUIMBO** was established during colonial times to serve neighbouring La Serena and became Chile's main copper exporter during the nineteenth century. Despite its impressive setting, the town has a slightly rough-edged, down-at-heel air, but is useful as an inexpensive base from which to enjoy La Serena's beaches, or visiting the nearby resorts of Guanaqueros – a fishing village 37km south with a sweeping beach – and Tongoy, 13km further south. A couple of blocks north of Coquimbo's main street, Avenida Costanera runs along the shore, past the large **port**, the **terminal pesquero**, and along to the lively **fish market**. This area makes for a pleasant stroll along the ocean, provided you don't mind the strong whiff of fish.

3

Cruz del Tercer Milenio

Juan Pablo II s/n • Daily 9.30am–6pm • CH$2000 • ☎ 51 232 0125 • ⓦ cruzdeltercermilenio.cl

From Coquimbo's main street, Aldunate, several stairways lead up to lookout points with sweeping views down to the port and across the bay; if you can't face the climb, take any *micro* marked "**Parte Alta**". The peak is crowned with a hideous, concrete 93m-high Cruz del Tercer Milenio ("Third Millennium Cross"), ablaze at night, and claims to be the only major spiritual monument in the world built at the turn of the millennium (which is just as well if they all looked like this one). The only conceivably redeeming feature is that you can enjoy superb panoramic views of the coast from up here. There is a religious museum here and an elevator which whisks visitors up to the arms of the cross.

Mezquito Centro Mohammed VI

Los Granados 500, Cerro Dominante • April–Nov Mon–Fri 9am–12.30pm & 2.30–5pm; Dec–March daily 9am–12.30pm & 2.30–6.30pm • ☎ 51 231 0440

A gift from the king of Morocco, this hilltop mosque provides a curious religious counterbalance, competing for attention (and panoramic vistas) with the Cruz del Tercer Milenio. It's a replica of the Mezquita Kutubia in Marrakech and construction was completed in 2007. As well as a mosque, it also functions as a cultural centre and library. Visitors can marvel at the ornate tile work inside.

Barrio Inglés

North of the central **Plaza de Armas**, and mostly on Aldunate, you'll find the **Barrio Inglés**, a district with the city's finest houses, many of them carved in wood by English craftsmen during the prosperous mining era. The restored buildings are beautifully lit at night and often double as bars, restaurants or music venues. Halfway along Aldunate is the pretty **Plaza Gabriela Mistral**, with its colourful artisan markets (Mon–Fri 11am–8pm).

Domo Cultura Ánimas

Plaza Gabriela Mistral • Mon–Fri 9am–5pm • ☎ 51 231 7006 • Free

In the middle of Plaza Gabriela Mistral is the **Domo Cultura Ánimas**, a small archeological museum exhibiting a pre-Columbian sacrificial graveyard dating from between 900 and 1100AD, with the skeletal remains of humans and llamas.

Guayacán

The southern shore of the peninsula, known as **Guayacán**, has a sandy beach, dominated at one end by a huge mechanized port used for exporting iron. While you're here, take a look at the tall steeple of the nearby **Iglesia de Guayacán**, a prefabricated steel church designed and built in 1888 by Alexandre Gustave Eiffel, of the tower fame, and the **British cemetery**, built in 1860 at the behest of the British Admiralty and full of the graves of young sailors etched with heart-rending inscriptions like "died falling from aloft" (if the gates are locked, ask in the caretaker's house).

La Herradura

Guayacán's beach curves south to that of **La Herradura**, which although long, golden and sandy is marred by its proximity to the Panamericana. That said, the night-time views across the bay to the tip of Coquimbo are superb, and if you want to spend a night or two at the seaside, La Herradura makes a convenient, cheaper alternative to La Serena's Avenida del Mar.

3

Tongoy

Some 30km south of Coquimbo and 5km west of the Panamericana along a toll-paying side road lies **TONGOY**, a popular family resort spread over a hilly peninsula. It has two attractive sandy **beaches**, the Playa Socos, north of the peninsula, and the enormous Playa Grande, stretching 14km south. While there are plenty of hotels, *cabañas* and restaurants, development has been low-key, and the place remains relatively unspoiled.

ARRIVAL AND DEPARTURE
COQUIMBO AND THE COAST

By bus Coquimbo's busy bus terminal is on the main road into town, at Varela and Garriga. Nearly all the main north–south inter-city buses stop here, as do local buses to coastal resorts like Tongoy (every 30min; 40min) and Guanaqueros (every 30min; 30min). Buses to La Serena (every 10min; 25min) can be picked up from the corner of Melgarejo and Alcalde. Tongoy can also be accessed from La Serena (hourly; 1hr) via Buses Serenamar (☎ 51 223 9144) and Sol de Elqui (☎ 51 221 5946).

By colectivo You can also get to the resorts, and to Guayacán and La Herradura, by *colectivo* – they pick up behind the bus terminal and throughout the centre of town.

ACCOMMODATION

COQUIMBO

Hostal Nomade Regimiento Coquimbo 5 ☎ 51 231 5665. There's a haunted mansion feel to this rambling old Hostelling International-affiliated hostel in the building that once housed the French Consulate. Spacious, if austere, dorms are complemented by superb views over the bay, kitchen and large common area. Dorms CH$13,000, doubles CH$26,000

Hotel Iberia Lastra 400 ☎ 51 231 2141. Located just off Aldunate in Barrio Inglés, *Hotel Iberia* offers reasonable, well-sized rooms – with either shared or private bathrooms – in an attractive old building. Aim for a room with a balcony. CH$17,900

Hotel Lig Aldunate 1577 ☎ 51 231 1171, ✉ hotellig @gmail.com. A satisfactory option just two blocks from the bus terminal with 24 bright and comfortable rooms with TVs and private parking. Breakfast costs extra. CH$26,000

LA HERRADURA

Cabañas Bucanero Av La Marina 201 ☎ 51 265 5153. There are terrific views of the bay from these eleven fully equipped *cabañas* set around an inviting pool. Each cabin has two bathrooms, a kitchen and TV. CH$40,000

Hotel La Herradura Av La Marina 200 ☎ 51 265 1647. Just off the beach, this family-friendly hotel offers decent rooms at reasonable prices. Rates include breakfast and cable TV. No credit cards. CH$30,000

TONGOY

Cabañas Tongoy Urmeneta Norte 237 ☎ 09 9956 2401, ⊛ cabanastongoy.cl. These rustic, wooden A-framed huts, located close to the water's edge, come with kitchenettes and small gardens. There are also play areas for children and private parking is available. CH$35,000

Camping Ripipal Av Playa Grande ☎ 51 239 1192. On

the beach 2km from the centre of town, this quiet, year-round campsite has good facilities: showers, drinking water, washing machines, a shop, a children's play area and games room. Camping/person CH$5000

Hotel Panorámico Av Mirador 745 ☎ 51 239 1944, ⓦ hotelpanoramico.cl. Set right on the water, this small, mid-range hotel has decent rooms and is crammed with 1950s items including a great TV set and a stand-up hairdryer. Marine spa treatments are also on offer (CH$20,000). CH$40,000

EATING AND DRINKING

COQUIMBO

For simple, cheap seafood lunches, go to the little *marisquerías* by the fish market; some have lovely water views. There are a number of lively bars clustered around Barrio Inglés.

Dolce Gelato Aldunate 862 ☎ 51 231 4300. If the ice-cream stand out front doesn't tempt you in, then live music wafting from the terrace will. Filling and reasonably priced Italian fare includes seafood lasagne. Ice cream from CH$1500. Mon–Fri 10am–11pm, Sat 1–11pm, Sun 1–8pm.

Pub Aduana Argandoña 360 ☎ 51 231 3932. Cold beer, Pisco-based cocktails and people-watching are the orders of the night at this popular bar with street-side tables and live music. Drinks from CH$2000. Thurs–Sat 10pm–5am.

LA HERRADURA

Bucanero Av La Marina 201 ☎ 51 265 5153. Perched on a jetty projecting into the ocean, this is one of La Herradura's poshest restaurants, offering good but overpriced seafood (mains around CH$8000–10,000) and great views across to Coquimbo (best at night). Daily midday–7pm.

Club de Yates Av Costanera ☎ 51 256 4698. This sea-facing restaurant does decent steak as well as seafood and pasta mains (around CH$7000–11,000) and a popular Sun buffet lunch. Tues–Thurs noon–8pm, Fri & Sat noon–midnight, Sun 1–5pm.

TONGOY

La Picá del Veguita Av Playa Grande ☎ 51 239 1475. A seaside restaurant with amicable service, a well-positioned terrace and giant portions of simple yet honest fare. Grilled fish and chips are CH$6500. Daily 9am–10pm.

La Serena

Sitting by the mouth of the Río Elqui, 11km north of Coquimbo and 88km north of Ovalle, **LA SERENA** is for many visitors their first taste of northern Chile, after whizzing straight up from Santiago by road or air. Situated 2km inland from the northern sweep of the Bahía de Coquimbo, the **city centre** is an attractive mix of pale colonial-style houses, carefully restored churches and bustling crowds. Aside from the noteworthy **Museo Arqueológico**, the city's main appeal lies in just strolling the streets and squares, admiring the grand old houses, browsing through the numerous craft markets, wandering in and out of its many stone churches and hanging out in the leafy, central Plaza de Armas.

In the warmer months, hordes of Chilean tourists head for the 6km **beach**, just 3km away along the Avenida del Mar – a rather charmless esplanade lined with oceanfront aparthotels and *cabañas* that are gloomily empty out of season. La Serena is also surrounded by some rewarding places to visit: the fine beaches at Tongoy (see p.135) and, above all, the glorious **Elqui Valley** (see p.143).

Brief history

La Serena is Chile's second-oldest city, with a history chequered by violence and drama. Founded by Pedro de Valdivia in 1544 as a staging post on the way to Peru, it got off to an unpromising start when it was completely destroyed in an **Indian attack** four years later. Undeterred, Valdivia refounded the city in a new location the following year, but La Serena continued to lead a precarious existence, subjected to frequent and often violent raids by pirates, many of them British.

The nineteenth century

Happier times arrived in the nineteenth century, when the discovery of large silver deposits at Arqueros, just north of La Serena, marked the beginning of the region's great **silver boom**. These heady days saw the erection of some of the city's finest mansions and churches, as the mining magnates competed in their efforts to dazzle with their wealth.

The twentieth century

In the 1940s, **Gabriel González Videla**, president of Chile and a local Serenense, instituted his "**Plan Serena**", through which the city developed its signature architectural style. One of the key elements of Videla's urban remodelling scheme was the vigorous promotion of the Spanish colonial style, with facades restored or rebuilt on existing structures and strict stylistic controls imposed on new ones. Unimaginative and inflexible though some claimed these measures to be, the results are undeniably pleasing, and La Serena boasts an architectural harmony and beauty noticeably lacking in most Chilean cities.

Iglesia Catedral

East side of the Plaza de Armas • Mon–Fri 9.30am–1pm & 3.30–7pm • Free

Grand and dominating, the pale walls of the **Iglesia Catedral** date from 1844, when the previous church on the site was finally pulled down because of the damage wrought by

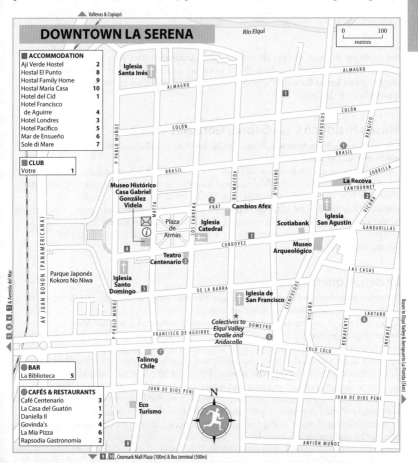

DOWNTOWN LA SERENA

Vallenas & Copiapó

Río Elqui

0 — 100 metres

ACCOMMODATION	
Aji Verde Hostel	2
Hostal El Punto	8
Hostal Family Home	9
Hostal Maria Casa	10
Hotel del Cid	1
Hotel Francisco de Aguirre	4
Hotel Londres	3
Hotel Pacífico	5
Mar de Ensueño	6
Sole di Mare	7

CLUB	
Votre	1

BAR	
La Biblioteca	5

CAFÉS & RESTAURANTS	
Café Centenario	3
La Casa del Guatón	1
Daniella II	7
Govinda's	4
La Mia Pizza	6
Rapsodia Gastronomía	2

Iglesia Santa Inés

ALMAGRO

ALMAGRO

COLÓN

COLÓN

CIENFUEGOS

RENGIFO

P. PABLO MUÑOZ

BRASIL

ZORRILLA

BRASIL

La Recova

CANTOURNET

Museo Histórico Casa Gabriel González Videla

MATTA

BALMACEDA

O'HIGGINS

PRAT

Cambios Afex

LOS CARRERA

VICUÑA

Iglesia San Agustín

GANDARILLAS

Plaza de Armas

Iglesia Catedral

Scotiabank

CORDOVEZ

Museo Arqueológico

Teatro Centenario

AV JUAN BOHON (PANAMERICANA)

Parque Japonés Kokoro No Niwa

Iglesia Santo Domingo

DE LA BARRA

LAS CASAS

Buses to Elqui Valley & Aeropuerto La Florida (5km)

CIENFUEGOS

VICUÑA

LAUTARO

BENAVENTE

INFANTE

Iglesia de San Francisco

P. PABLO MUÑOZ

FRANCISCO DE AGUIRRE

Colectivos to Elqui Valley Ovalle and Andacollo

DOMEYKO

COLO COLO

Talinng Chile

Av Avenida del Mar

JUAN DE DIOS PENI

Eco Turismo

JUAN DE DIOS PENI

N

ANFIÓN MUÑOZ

Cinemark Mall Plaza (100m) & Bus terminal (500m)

LA SERENA'S CHURCHES

Including Iglesia Catedral and Iglesia Santo Domingo on the Plaza de Armas, a remarkable 29 **churches** dot La Serena, lending an almost fairy-tale look to the city. This proliferation of places of worship dates from the earliest days of the city, when all the religious orders established bases to provide shelter for their clergy's frequent journeys between Santiago and Lima (the viceregal capital). Nearly all the churches are built of stone, which is unusual for Chile, and all are in mint condition.

Standing at the corner of Balmaceda and de la Barra, the **Iglesia San Francisco** is one of La Serena's oldest churches, though the date of its construction is unknown, as the city archives were burnt in the pirate Sharp's raid of 1680. Its huge walls are 1m thick, covered in a stone facade carved in fanciful Baroque designs. Inside, the **Museo de Arte Religioso** (Tues & Thurs 10am–1pm & 4–7pm; donation welcome) contains a small but impressive collection of religious sculpture and paintings from the colonial period.

Beautiful for its very plainness, the 1755 **Iglesia San Agustín**, on the corner of Cienfuegos and Cantournet, was originally the Jesuit church but was taken over by the Augustinians after the Jesuits were expelled from Chile in 1767. Its honey-toned stone walls were badly damaged in the 1975 earthquake, but have been skilfully restored. On the northern edge of town, overlooking the banks of the Río Elqui, the recently restored seventeenth-century **Iglesia Santa Inés** was constructed on the site of a rudimentary chapel erected by the first colonists and its thick white adobe walls recall the Andean churches of the northern *altiplano*.

the 1796 earthquake. Inside, among its more curious features are the wooden pillars, disguised to look like stone. Just off the opposite side of the square, on Cordovez, the pretty **Iglesia Santo Domingo** was first built in 1673 and then again in 1755, after it was sacked by the pirate Sharp.

Museo Histórico Casa Gabriel González Videla

Southwest corner of the Plaza de Armas • Mon–Fri 10am–6pm, Sat 10am–1pm • ☏ 51 220 6797, ⓦ museohistoricolaserena.cl • CH$600 (includes admission to the Museo Arqueológico)

This two-storey adobe house was, from 1927 to 1977, home to Chile's erstwhile president, Gabriel González Videla, best known for outlawing the Communist party after using its support to gain power in 1946. Inside, a small and rather dull **museum** has an eclectic display of photos, objects, documents and paintings relating to the president's life and works, along with a section on regional history; the temporary art exhibitions, occasionally held here, are often better than the permanent display.

Museo Arqueológico

Corner of Cordovez and Cienfuegos • Tues–Fri 9.30am–5.50pm, Sat 10am–1pm & 4–7pm, Sun 10am–1pm • ☏ 51 222 4492 • CH$600 (includes admission to the Museo Histórico Casa Gabriel González Videla)

Entered through an imposing nineteenth-century portico, La Serena's **Museo Arqueológico** boasts two outstanding treasures, though most of the displays could do with improving. The first of these is its large collection of **Diaguita pottery**, considered by many to be among the most beautiful pre-Columbian ceramics in South America. The terracotta pieces, dating from around 1000 to 1500 AD, are covered in intricate geometric designs painted in black and white and, in the later phases, red. Starting with simple bowls and dishes made for domestic use, the Diaguita went on to produce elaborately shaped ceremonial pots and jars, often in the form of humans or animals, or sometimes both, such as the famous *jarros patos*, or "duck jars", moulded in the form of a duck's body with a human head.

OPPOSITE PLAZA DE ARMAS, LA SERENA (P.136) >

The moai

The museum's other gem is the giant stone statue, or **moai**, from Easter Island, "donated" to La Serena at the behest of President González Videla in 1952. Until the mid 1990s, it stood in a park on Avenida Colo Colo, covered in graffiti and urinated on by drunks. Then, as part of an exhibition of Easter Island art in 1996, it travelled to Barcelona, where it was accidentally decapitated. Tragedy turned to good fortune, however, when the insurance money from the accident paid for a brand-new *sala* to be built for the statue in the archeological museum. This is where you'll find it today, standing on a raised platform against a flattering azure backdrop, the joins at the neck hardly showing.

La Recova

Corner of Cienfuegos and Cantournet • Daily 10am–7pm

Of La Serena's numerous **craft markets**, the biggest and best is the bustling **La Recova**, occupying two large patios inside an arcaded building opposite the Iglesia San Agustín. The quality of the merchandise is generally high, and goods include finely worked objects in *combabalita* (a locally mined marble), lapis lazuli jewellery, alpaca sweaters and candied papaya.

Parque Japonés Kokoro No Niwa

Pedro Pablo Muñoz and Eduardo de la Barra • Tues–Sun 10am–6pm • CH$1000

Backing onto the Panamericana, two blocks west of the Plaza de Armas, the **Parque Japonés Kokoro No Niwa**, whose Japanese name means "Garden of the Heart", is an

---

OBSERVATORIES AROUND LA SERENA

Thanks to the exceptional transparency of its skies, northern Chile is home to the largest concentration of astronomical **observatories** in the world. The region around La Serena, in particular, has been chosen by a number of international astronomical research institutions as the site of their telescopes, housed in white, futuristic domes that loom over the valleys from their hilltop locations. Among the research organizations that own the observatories are North American and European groups that need a base in the southern hemisphere (about a third of the sky seen here is never visible in the northern hemisphere).

Some of the observatories offer guided tours, including the impressive **Cerro Tololo Inter-American Observatory**, whose 4m telescope was the strongest in the southern hemisphere until it was overtaken by Cerro Paranal's Very Large Telescope, the most powerful in the world, located near Antofagasta (see p.171). All the tours listed below take place during the day and are free of charge but are strictly no-touching; a more hands-on night-time experience is provided by the small but user-friendly observatory on **Cerro Mamalluca** (see p.146), 9km north of Vicuña, the newer Del Pangue observatory 17km south of Vicuña (see p.146) and the **Collowara** observatory outside Andacollo (see p.132).

Las Campanas 155km northeast of La Serena ☎ 51 220 7301, ⓦ lco.cl. The Carnegie Institute's observatory contains four telescopes, with two 6.5m telescopes under construction as part of its Magellan Project. Contact the observatory's offices in La Serena to make reservations; they're located next to Cerro Tololo's offices on Colina El Pino. Sat 2.30–5.30pm.

Cerro Tololo 88km east of La Serena, reached by a side road branching south of the Elqui Valley road ☎ 51 220 5200, ⓦ www.ctio.noao.edu. Tours need to be booked several days in advance; you'll need to collect your visitor's permit from the observatory's offices in La Serena (up the hill behind the university, at Colina El Pino) the day before the tour. Sat 9.15am–noon & 1.15–4pm.

La Silla 150km northeast of La Serena, reached by a side road branching east from the Panamericana ☎ 51 227 2601, ⓦ eso.org. The site of the European Southern Observatory's fourteen telescopes, including two 3.6m optical reflectors. Book tours in advance through the observatory's Santiago offices or the La Serena office near the airport at Panorámica 4461. Aug–May Sat 2–4pm.

oasis of perfectly manicured lawns, ponds awash with water lilies, ice-white geese and little Japanese bridges and pagodas. Unfortunately, the sense of peace and tranquillity it creates is undermined by the din of the highway.

Avenida del Mar

No bus or colectivo service along Av del Mar; take a micro headed for Coquimbo from almost any street corner (if in doubt, go to Av Francisco de Aguirre) and get off on the Panamericana at Cuatro Esquinas or Peñuelas (6km from the city), both a short walk from the beach

Stretching 6km round the rim of a wide, horseshoe bay 2km west of the city, the **Avenida del Mar** is a staid collection of glitzy hotels, tourist complexes and *cabañas* that bulge with visitors for two months of the year and are otherwise empty. In January and February hundreds of cars inch their way up and down the avenue, bumper to bumper, and mostly Chilean tourists pile onto the sandy beaches, which are clean but spoiled by the horrific high-rise backdrop.

ARRIVAL AND DEPARTURE

LA SERENA

By plane The Aeropuerto La Florida (☎51 227 0191) is 5km east of the city and served by taxis (CH$6000) and shared transfers (CH$2500), as well as *micros*.

Airlines LAN, Balmaceda 406 (☎51 222 9069 or ☎600 526 2000, ⓦlan.com); Sky Airline, Eduardo de la Barra 495 (☎51 221 8372, ⓦwww.skyairline.cl).

Destinations Antofagasta (2 daily; 1hr 25min); Santiago (6 daily; 1hr).

By bus Inter-city buses operate from La Serena's large bus terminal on El Santo, a 15min walk southwest of the central plaza. There's no direct bus from the terminal into town, but there are plenty of taxis, charging about CH$3000. Buses for the Elqui Valley depart every 30min and also stop southeast of the centre at the Plaza de Abastos, on Calle Esmeralda (just south of Colo Colo). To get to Tongoy, take a Serenamar or Sol de Elqui bus from the terminal.

Destinations Andacollo (every 2hr; 1hr); Antofagasta (20 daily; 12hr); Arica (5 daily; 24hr); Calama (11 daily; 15hr); Chañaral (11 daily; 7hr); Copiapó (every 30min–1hr; 5hr); Horcón (3 daily; 2hr 45min); Iquique (8 daily; 18hr); Montegrande (every 30min–1hr; 1hr 50min); Ovalle (every 15min; 1hr 20min); Pisco Elqui (every 30min–1hr; 2hr); Santiago (every 30min; 7hr); Vallenar (every 30min–1hr; 2hr 45min); Tongoy (hourly; 1hr); Valparaíso (6 daily; 5hr); Vicuña (every 30min–1hr; 1hr).

By micro The coastal resorts of Tongoy and La Herradura are more easily reached from Coquimbo – to get there, take a *micro* (marked "Coquimbo Directo 1") from Av Francisco de Aguirre or calles Brasil, Infante or Matta. Alternatively, you can flag down a *micro* from the Panamericana, a 5min walk west.

By colectivo Two *colectivo* services (look for the yellow taxis) from La Serena operate from Calle Domeyko one block south of Iglesia San Francisco: Anserco, at no. 530 (☎51 221 7567), goes to Andacollo, Vicuña and Ovalle; Tasco, at no. 575 (☎51 222 4517), goes to Vicuña, Montegrande and Pisco Elqui. The service is slightly more expensive than the bus.

GETTING AROUND

Car rental In addition to the airport, there are many outlets on Av Francisco de Aguirre, including Avis at no. 063 (☎51 254 5300, ⓦavis.cl); Budget at no. 015 (☎51 221 8272, ⓦbudget.cl); Econorent at no. 0135 (☎51 222 0113, ⓦeconorent.cl); and Hertz at no. 0225 (☎51 222 6171, ⓦhertz.cl).

INFORMATION AND TOURS

Sernatur There is a helpful and friendly Sernatur office on the west side of the Plaza de Armas at Matta 461 (Dec–Feb daily 9am–9pm; March–Nov Mon–Fri 9am–6pm, Sat 10am–4pm; ☎51 225199.

Tours The two most popular day tours from La Serena are to the Elqui Valley (also easily reached on public transport) and to the cloudforest reserve at Parque Nacional Fray Jorge (see p.129), about 2hr south of the city and not served by public transport. Other favourite destinations include night tours to the Cerro Mamalluca observatory near Vicuña; the ancient petroglyph site of the Valle del Encanto, near Ovalle (see p.129); Monumento Natural Pichasca, where you'll find the remains of a "fossilized wood" (see p.129); and the Reserva Nacional Pinguino de Humboldt, a penguin and dolphin sanctuary 120km north of La Serena that is not served by public transport. Most tours cost from CH$20,000–30,000 per person. Try Eco Turismo, Andres Bello 937 (☎51 221 8970, ⓦecoturismolaserena.cl) or Talinay Chile, Av Francisco de Aguirre (☎09 9836 06464, ⓦtalinaychile.com). This agency also offers mountaineering trips in the Andes.

ACCOMMODATION

You'll find a large choice of budget **accommodation** and mid- to upscale options in the centre, while Av del Mar, 3km from town, is lined with overpriced beachside *cabañas* and hotels.

HOTELS

Hostal Family Home Av El Santo 1056 ☎ 51 221 2099, ⓦfamilyhome.cl. Good-value hostal that lives up to its name and is conveniently located close to the bus terminal (albeit on a busy road), with singles, doubles and triples (some en suite), plus use of a kitchen. CH$25,000

Hotel del Cid O'Higgins 138 ☎ 51 221 2692, ⓦhoteldelcid.cl. Beyond the drab exterior is a charming hotel run by a welcoming Scottish–Chilean couple, with a selection of spotless and comfortable rooms set around a flower-filled terrace. Secure parking is offered. CH$50,000

Hotel Francisco de Aguirre Cordovez 210 ☎ 51 222 2991, ⓦhotelfranciscodeaguirre.com. One of La Serena's smartest hotels, a few steps away from the plaza, *Francisco de Aguirre* has somewhat overpriced but spacious rooms in a handsome old three-storey building, as well as a poolside restaurant with toothsome food. US$177

Hotel Londres Cordovez 550 ☎ 51 221 9066, ⓦhotellondres.cl. The centrally located *Hotel Londres* has clean and tidy rooms, some with private bathrooms and others with just a washbasin; all have TV and wi-fi. If you have your own vehicle, parking costs CH$2000 extra. CH$40,000

Hotel Pacífico Av de la Barra 252 ☎ 51 222 5674, ⓦhotelpacifico.cl. Located three blocks from the Plaza de Armas, this long-standing, rambling hotel offers basic but clean and comfortable rooms (with either shared or private bathrooms) and a friendly welcome. Good-value singles too. CH$46,000

Mar de Ensueño Av del Mar 900 ☎ 51 222 2381, ⓦhotelmarensueno.com. If you're in La Serena in summer with the kids in tow, this beachside complex with ocean-facing rooms and fully equipped *cabañas* is a good bet. Facilities include a swimming pool, gym, bicycles for guest use, and a games room. Doubles US$167, *cabañas* US$350

HOSTELS

Ají Verde Hostel Vicuña 415 ☎ 51 248 9016, ⓦajiverdehostel.cl. A fun atmosphere pervades this central, HI-affiliated hostel with young staff, a roof terrace, kitchen and plenty of common areas for connecting with fellow travellers. A good fall-back if *Hostal El Punto* (see below) is full. Dorms CH$8,500, doubles CH$22,000

★ **Hostal El Punto** Andres Bello 979 ☎ 51 222 8474, ⓦhostalelpunto.cl. Charming, German-run hostel with spacious, impeccably clean rooms (some with private bath) and one dorm. Mosaic-tiled courtyards, a restaurant and big breakfasts with home-made jam and goat's cheese ensure this place books up fast. There's also parking and a kitchen. Dorms CH$9,000, doubles CH$21,000

Hostal Maria Casa Las Rojas 18 ☎ 51 222 9282, ⓦhostalmariacasa.cl. This friendly, family-run option is situated a block from the bus terminal with dorms and basic rooms off a lovely garden. There's a communal kitchen, book exchange and bikes to rent. Dorms CH$10,000, doubles CH$20,000

CAMPSITE

Sole di Mare Parcela 66, Peñuelas ☎ 51 231 2531. Lovely, grassy campsite down at the quieter end of the beach, halfway between La Serena and Coquimbo. Good facilities and lots of shade. Buses between La Serena and Coquimbo stop nearby. Camping/person CH$5000

EATING AND DRINKING

The **restaurants** on Av del Mar are overpriced but have fine sea views, while those downtown are better value yet unexceptional. The La Recova **market** has dozens of good-value *marisquerías* (seafood restaurants) on the upper gallery of the handicrafts market, making it a perfect place for lunch. For the freshest seafood around, head to the Sector de Pescadores at Playa Peñuelas, 6km along the coast between La Serena and Coquimbo.

La Biblioteca O'Higgins and Av Francisco de Aguirre ☎ 09 8139 0449. "The Library" is anything but: students congregate around small wooden tables, feeding the jukebox while downing *terremoto* cocktails (sweet white wine, pineapple ice cream and Amaretto). Drinks from CH$1500. Daily 2.30pm–4am.

Café Centenario Cordovez 391. Lavazza coffee (CH$1500–3000), regional wines and local beer are served in this chic corner spot on the southeast corner of Plaza de Armas. Try the house speciality, *café camanchaca* – a mix of pisco, espresso and milk. Mon–Fri 8am–8pm.

La Casa del Guatón Brasil 750 ☎ 51 221 1519. Lively, friendly and intimate, this colonial-style restaurant serves the best *parrilladas* (from CH$15,000) in La Serena, as well as some more unusual dishes like fried conger eel and Chiloé-style shellfish (mains CH$6000–11,000). There's often live music to keep you entertained. Mon–Sat 12.30pm–12.30am, Sun 12.30–6pm.

Daniella II Av Francisco de Aguirre 335 ☎ 51 222 7537. Typical Chilean restaurant with friendly service and a traditional menu (mains from CH$3000–4000) of local fish and meat dishes like *pastel de jaiba* (a crab and corn pie) and *lomo a lo pobre* (steak with chips, onions and fried egg). Mon–Fri & Sun 10am–9pm, Sat 10am–6pm.

Govinda's Lautaro 841 ☎51 222 4289. A lunchtime vegetarian spot run by Hare Krishnas, serving wholegrain bread, fresh and healthy Italian and Indian-inspired fare (around CH$2000–4000) as well as fragrant teas. Yoga and cookery classes are available. Mon–Fri 1–3pm.

La Mia Pizza Av del Mar 2100 ☎51 221 2232. Locals pile into this beachside restaurant for its crisp, thin-crust pizzas loaded with fresh toppings (from CH$5000). The pastas,

steaks and fish dishes are also recommendable. Mon–Sat 12.30pm–midnight, Sun 12.30–4.30pm.

Rapsodia Gastronomía Prat 470 ☎51 221 2695. A good bet for a tasty lunch or dinner (dishes are in the CH$3000–9000 range and include the usual grilled meats and sandwiches, plus more creative options like Mediterranean salad with salmon carpaccio), or just a decent coffee or cold beer. Tables are dotted around a little patio shaded by a huge palm tree. Mon–Wed 9am–9pm, Thurs & Fri 9am–11pm, Sat 10.30am–4.30pm.

NIGHTLIFE AND ENTERTAINMENT

Nightlife is concentrated on O'Higgins between Av Francisco de Aguirre and de la Barra, where there are many student bars. The pubs and discos by the beach are more seasonal, reaching their heady zenith in Jan and Feb.

Cinemark Mall Plaza Av Albert Solari 1400 ☎51 247 0310, ⓦcinemark.cl. This six-screen cinema near the bus terminal shows blockbuster films and also hosts themed festivals – check the website to see what's on.

Teatro Centenario Cordoves 391 ☎51 221 2659, ⓦteatrocentenario.blogspot.com. One of the best jazz venues in Chile, located in a remodelled theatre in the city's old cinema. Local and international acts perform to a head-

nodding, wine-sipping crowd. March–Nov every second Sat 7/8pm–late; Dec–Feb every Sat 7/8pm–late.

Votre Av del Mar 5685 ☎09 5699 3297, ⓦfacebook .com/ClubVotre. If you're looking for some nocturnal action, this three-level beachside disco, bar and sushi lounge pulls in all ages – all year round. March–Nov Wed–Sat 11.30pm–5am; Dec–Feb Mon–Thurs & Sun 11pm–4am, Fri & Sat 11.30pm–5am.

DIRECTORY

Money and exchange There are plenty of ATMs on or near the Plaza de Armas and at Cordovez and Cienfuegos. For currency exchange, try Cambios Afex, Balmaceda 413.

Post office On the west side of Plaza de Armas, on the corner of Prat and Matta (Mon–Fri 9am–7pm, Sat 10am–1pm).

Taxis 24hr radio taxis (☎51 221 2122).

The Elqui Valley

Quiet, rural and extremely beautiful, the **ELQUI VALLEY** unfolds east from La Serena and into the Andes. Irrigated by canals fed by the Puclara and La Laguna dams, the valley floor is given over entirely to cultivation – of papayas, custard apples (*chirimoyas*), oranges, avocados and, most famously, the vast expanses of grape vines grown to produce **pisco**. It's the fluorescent green of these vines that makes the valley so stunning, forming a spectacular contrast with the charred, brown hills that rise on either side.

Some 60km east of La Serena, appealing little **Vicuña** is the main town and transport hub of the Elqui Valley. Moving east from here, the valley gets higher and narrower and is dotted with tiny villages like **Montegrande** and the odd pisco distillery. **Pisco Elqui**, 105km east of La Serena, is a very pretty village that makes a great place to unwind for a couple of days. If you really want to get away from it all, head for one of the rustic *cabañas* dotted along the banks of the **Río Cochiguaz**, which forks east of the main valley at Montegrande, or delve beyond Pisco Elqui into the farthest reaches of the Elqui Valley itself. Buses and a paved road will get you all the way to Horcón but not to the farthest village of all, **Alcohuaz**.

GETTING AROUND	THE ELQUI VALLEY

By bus Many tour companies in La Serena offer day-trips to the Elqui Valley, but it's hardly worth taking a tour, as public transport up and down the valley is so frequent and cheap. If you're here in Jan or Feb, it might be worth investing in a

24hr day pass (available at the bus station), so that you can hop on and off any bus plying the valley as many times as you choose. The two main bus companies are Sol de Elqui (☎51 221 5946) and Via Elqui (☎51 221 1707).

Vicuña

An hour by bus inland from La Serena, **VICUÑA** is a neat and tidy agricultural town ringed by mountains and laid out around a large, luxuriantly landscaped square. It's a pleasant, easy-going place with a few low-key attractions, a good choice of places to stay and eat, a couple of pisco distilleries just out of town and two visitor-friendly observatories on its doorstep. If you're looking to stretch your legs, there are panoramic views of the town and entire Elqui Valley from the top of Cerro de la Virgen, northeast of the centre.

Plaza de Armas

Life revolves firmly around the central **Plaza de Armas**, which has at its centre a huge stone replica of the **death mask** of Nobel Prize-winning poet **Gabriela Mistral**, the Elqui Valley's most famous daughter. On the square's northwest corner stands the **Iglesia de la Inmaculada Concepción**, topped by an impressive wooden tower built in 1909 – take a look inside at its vaulted polychrome ceiling, painted with delicate religious images and supported by immense wooden columns. Right next door, the eccentric **Torre Bauer** is a bright-red, mock-medieval tower prefabricated in Germany in 1905 and brought to Vicuña on the instructions of the town's German-born mayor, Adolfo Bauer.

Museo Entomológico

Chacabuco 334, on the south side of the Plaza de Armas • Jan–March daily 10am–8pm; April–Dec Mon–Fri 10.30am–1.30pm & 3.30–7pm, Sat & Sun 10.30am–7pm • CH$600

The **Museo Entomológico** hoards a fascinating collection of horror-movie creepy-crawlies hailing from Chile, the Amazon, Africa and Asia, including hairy spiders and vicious-looking millipedes, plus exotic butterflies and shells. Hopefully this is the closest you'll get to two of Chile's deadliest critters: the *araña del rincón* (recluse spider) and the blood-sucking *vinchuca*, which spreads Chagas disease.

Museo Gabriela Mistral

Calle Gabriela Mistral 759 • Museum Jan & Feb Mon–Sat 10am–7pm, Sun 10am–6pm; March–Dec Mon–Fri 10am–5.45pm, Sat 10.30am–6pm, Sun 10am–1pm; Children's Library Mon–Fri 10am–5.45pm • CH$600 • ☎ 51 241 1233

Four blocks east of the square, the **Museo Gabriela Mistral** displays photos, prizes,

articles and personal objects bequeathed to the city by the poet, along with panels giving an account of her life and works. The museum itself is a striking building, taking its inspiration from the natural elements of Mistral's beloved Elqui Valley – stone, light, water and mountains. Also on the grounds is a children's library housing a four-thousand-strong collection of books. Next door is the modest house where Mistral was born in 1889.

El Solar de los Madariaga

Calle Gabriela Mistral 683 • Daily 10am–7pm • CH$600 • ☎ 51 241 1220

Just a few steps away from the Museo Gabriela Mistral is the **Solar de los Madariaga**, an old, colonial-style house that has been preserved and turned into a museum, displaying a modest collection of nineteenth-century furniture and clothes.

Pisco Capel distillery

Camino Peralillo, 2km southeast of Vicuña • Daily 10am–5pm • CH$2500–15,000 • ☎ 51 255 4337, ⓦ piscocapel.cl

Just out of town, across the bridge by the filling station, you'll find the **Planta Capel**, the largest pisco distillery in the Elqui Valley. It offers a range of guided tours in English and Spanish every half hour or so, with tastings, visits to the small onsite museum and (of course) the chance to buy bottles and souvenirs at the end.

Pisco ABA distillery

Ruta 41 Km 63, 8km east of Vicuña • Spring & summer daily 10am–7pm, though sometimes closes early • Free • ☎ 51 241 1039, ⓦ piscoaba.cl

ABA is a family-owned boutique distillery in the village of El Arenal, a short drive from Vicuña. It produces around sixty thousand bottles a year, including the ABA and Fuegos piscos as well as a creamy mango sour cocktail. Tours include tastings, a glimpse of its bucolic 148-acre farm where Muscat grapes are hand-picked, and a visit to its production facilities, where distillation takes place in huge copper stills. Call ahead for a tour in English (also free).

ARRIVAL AND INFORMATION

VICUÑA

By bus Buses drop passengers off at the terminal on the corner of O'Higgins and Prat, one block south of the Plaza de Armas. Santiago services are operated by Expreso Norte (☎ 51 241 1348) and Pullman Buses (☎ 51 241 1466).
Destinations La Serena (every 30min–1hr; 1hr); Montegrande (every 30min–1hr; 50min), Pisco Elqui (every 30min–1hr; 1hr); Santiago (4 daily; 7hr).

Colectivos Taxi *colectivos* leave from the bus terminal for La Serena and while their set fares are marginally more than the bus, the journey takes less time. They also service the immediate area, and for local journeys you'll need to negotiate a price with the driver.
Tourist office Northwest corner of the plaza, beneath the Torre Bauer (Mon–Fri 8.30am–6pm, Sat 9am–6pm, Sun 9am–2pm; ☎ 51 220 9125).

ACCOMMODATION

Hostal La Elquina O'Higgins 65 ☎ 51 241 1317. Dowdy rooms with and without private bathrooms are set around a breezy, central flower-filled patio; the garden is perfect for camping. Kitchen access and breakfast are included. Doubles CH$25,000, camping/person CH$3000
★**Hostal Valle Hermoso** Gabriela Mistral 706 ☎ 51 241 1206, ⓦ hostalvallehermoso.com. Motherly Lucia presides over this restored century-old abode house with a bright central patio. Minimalist but sweet rooms have comfortable beds and private bathrooms complete with piping-hot showers. Some English spoken. CH$25,000

Hostería Vicuña Sargento Aldea 101 ☎ 51 241 1301, ⓦ hosteriavicuna.cl. *Hostería Vicuña* has slightly overpriced rooms – all en suite, with TVs – but comes with a fabulous pool and one of the town's better restaurants, which serves unadventurous if good-quality meat and fish dishes. CH$54,000
Hotel Halley Gabriela Mistral 542 ☎ 51 241 2070, ⓦ turismohalley.cl. This central hotel comes recommended, offering large albeit somewhat dark, impeccably decorated rooms in a colonial-style building. There are pleasant communal areas, a restaurant, and a swimming pool in the garden. CH$34,000

EATING AND DRINKING

Keep an eye out for beers from the award-winning Elqui Valley brewery, Guayacán.

Chaski O'Higgins 159 ☏ 09 9793 7237, ✉ chaski gastronomia@gmail.com. This restaurant's rustic outdoor setting belies its sophisticated cuisine: think salmon curry, beef with chutney and quinoa, as well as pizza, pasta and salads (CH$3000–9000). The owners also offer cycling and horseriding tours. Mon & Wed–Sat 10am–4pm & 6–9.30pm, Sun midday–6pm.

Club Social Gabriel Mistral 445 ☏ 51 241 1853. The atmosphere is always convivial inside this grand, sprawling colonial building which is popular for its typical Chilean dishes (mains CH$5500–10,000), seafood pancakes and gut-busting *parrilladas* to share between two (or more). Daily 10am–midnight.

Yo y Soledad Carrera 320 ☏ 51 241 9002. If you're returning from an observatory tour and have the late-night munchies, you'll find this lively bar-restaurant (drinks from around CH$1500) at your service - look out for the red Pisco Capel sign out front. Mon–Thurs 11am–1am, Fri–Sun 11am–3am.

3 Cerro Mamalluca observatory

Office Gabriela Mistral 260, Vicuña • Office Mon–Fri 8.30am–8.30pm, Sat & Sun 10am–2pm & 4–8pm; tours Oct–April 8.30pm, 10.30pm & 12.30am; May–Sept 6.30pm & 8.30pm • CH$4500 • ☏ 51 241 1352 • Assemble 30min before your slot at the office, from where transport is provided (CH$1500 return); reservations essential; if you have your own transport you must still report to the office, to confirm and pay, and to follow the minibus in a convoy

Nine kilometres northeast of Vicuña, the **Cerro Mamalluca observatory**, built specifically for public use, is run by the Municipalidad de Vicuña and features a 30cm Smith-Cassegrain telescope donated by the Cerro Tololo team. The two-hour **evening tours** start with a high-tech audiovisual talk on the history of the universe, and end with the chance to look through the telescope. If you're lucky, you might see a dazzling display of stars, planets, galaxies, nebulas and clusters, including Jupiter, Saturn's rings, the Orion nebula, the Andromeda galaxy and Sirius. These tours are aimed at complete beginners, but serious astronomers can arrange in-depth, small-group sessions with at least a few weeks' notice.

Del Pangue Observatory

Office San Martin 233, Vicuña • Office daily 10am–7pm; tours Jan & Feb 9pm & 11pm; June–Aug 6pm; rest of year 8pm; no tours five days around the full moon; tour times often change depending on planet positions; group tours are limited to ten people • CH$18,000 • ☏ 51 241 2584, ⊛ observatoriodelpangue.blogspot.com • Assemble 30min before the tour at the Vicuña office, from where you must take the transport provided (free); private vehicles are not allowed

With a spectacular mountaintop setting 17km south of Vicuña and not far from the Tololo scientific observatory, **Del Pangue** offers an intimate and personalized star-gazing experience specifically designed for amateur astronomers. Two-hour tours are conducted by bona fide astronomers, and Del Pangue's new, state-of-the-art 63cm Obsession telescope is light years ahead of other public observatories. Two telescopes and a variety of adjustable eyepieces ensure you get up close and personal with the moon's craters, distant galaxies and blazing stars.

English, Spanish and French-speaking astronomers deliver sophisticated yet down-to-earth celestial commentary and can also answer questions on life, the universe and everything in between. Wear warm clothes as it gets cold.

Montegrande

The picturesque village of **MONTEGRANDE**, 34km east of Vicuña (if you're driving, take the right turn for Paihuano at Rivadavia), features a pretty church whose late-nineteenth-century wooden belfry looms over a surprisingly large square. The childhood home of Gabriela Mistral, Montegrande assiduously devotes itself to preserving her memory: her profile has been outlined in white stones on the valley wall opposite the plaza, and the school where she lived with, and was taught by, her sister, has been turned into a **museum** (Tues–Sun 10am–1pm & 3–6pm; CH$600), displaying some of her furniture and belongings. Just south of the village, her **tomb** rests on a hillside, opposite the turn-off for Cochiguaz.

One kilometre before the village is the Cavas del Valle organic winery, run by a retired couple who offer free tours and tastings (daily: summer 10am–8pm; winter 10am–7pm; ☎09 6842 5592, ⓦcavasdelvalle.cl).

ARRIVAL AND DEPARTURE

MONTEGRANDE

By bus Buses stop in the village and pass by half-hourly. Three buses weekly (Mon, Wed & Fri) go along the Río Cochiguaz.

Destinations Pisco Elqui (every 30min–1hr; 10min); Vicuña (every 30min–1hr; 50min).

ACCOMMODATION AND EATING

El Galpón La Jarilla ☎51 198 2587, ⓦelgalpon -elqui.cl. Halfway between Montegrande and Pisco Elqui, in a wonderful quiet location with mountain views, is one of the area's best places to stay. Stylishly built, it is owned by a friendly Chilean who lived for many years in the US. Each of the rooms has a huge bathroom, TV and a minibar; two- and five-person *cabañas* are also available. The well-kept grounds have an eye-catching swimming pool. Doubles CH$55,000, *cabañas* CH$60,000

El Mesón del Fraile ☎51 245 1232. Beckoning opposite the museum, this restaurant has tables on a wide, breezy balcony and serves delectable stone-oven pizzas and the regional goat speciality, *cabrito al jugo* (mains around CH$7000–9000). Tues–Sun midday–9pm.

Las Pléyades Montegrande ☎51 245 1107. The only hotel located in Montegrande itself, set in an old mansion. Its five rustic, chic rooms have artistic touches and come with private bathroom, swimming pool and access to a river beach. CH$40,000

Pisco Elqui and around

PISCO ELQUI was known as La Unión until 1939, when Gabriel González Videla – later President of Chile – cunningly renamed it to thwart Peru's efforts to gain exclusive rights to the name "Pisco". An idyllic village, increasingly popular with backpackers and independent travellers, it boasts a beautiful square filled with lush palm trees and flowers, overlooked by a colourful church with a tall, wooden tower. Locals sell home-made jam and jewellery in the square, and its abundant shade provides a welcome relief from the sun.

Pisco distilleries

Pisco Mistral O'Higgins s/n • Guided tours daily Jan & Feb 11.30am–9pm; rest of year Tues–Sun 10am–6pm • CH$6000 • ☎51 245 1358, ⓦpiscomistral.cl **Los Nichos** 4km outside Pisco Elqui on road to Horcón • Guided tours daily April–Nov 10am–6pm; Dec–March 11am–7pm • CH$1000 •☎51 245 1085, ⓦfundolosnichos.cl

On the south side of the Plaza de Armas, the **Pisco Mistral** is Chile's oldest pisco distillery, which today (and now considerably modernized) produces the famous Tres Erres brand. There are **guided tours** around the old part of the plant, with tastings and a pisco sour at the end. You can also visit the 144-year-old private distillery at **Los Nichos**, 4km on from Pisco Elqui.

Pueblo Artesanal de Horcón

Horcón • Tues–Sun noon–6.30pm

Beyond Pisco Elqui, the narrow road leads through increasingly unspoiled countryside and ever deeper into the valley. After 8km you'll pass by a large craft market known as the *Pueblo Artesanal de Horcón*, which lies just before the sleepy village of the same name (the end of the road for two buses daily from La Serena). Here you can browse among the many craft and food stalls, or just enjoy a fresh juice and a massage by the river.

3

PISCO

Pisco has been enjoyed by Chileans for more than four centuries, but it wasn't until the 1930s that it was organized into an effective commercial industry, starting with the official creation of a pisco *denominación de origen*. Shortly afterwards, a large number of growers, who'd always been at the mercy of the private distilleries for the price they got for their grapes, joined together to form cooperatives to produce their own pisco. The largest were the tongue-twisting *Sociedad Cooperativa Control Pisquero de Elqui y Vitivinículo de Norte Ltda* (known as "Pisco Control") and the *Cooperativa Agrícola y Pisquera del Elqui Ltda* (known as "Pisco Capel"), today the two most important producers in Chile, accounting for over ninety percent of all pisco to hit the shops.

The basic **distillation technique** is the same one that's been used since colonial times: in short, the fermented wine is boiled in copper stills at 90°C, releasing vapours that are condensed, then kept in oak vats for three to six months. The alcohol – of 55° to 65° – is then diluted with water, according to the type of pisco it's being sold as: 30° or 32° for *Selección*; 35° for *Reservado*; 40° for *Especial*; and 43°, 46° and 50° for *Gran Pisco*. It's most commonly consumed as a tangy, refreshing aperitif known as **Pisco Sour**, an ice-cold mix of pisco, lemon juice and sugar – sometimes with whisked egg-white for a frothy head and angostura bitters for an extra zing.

Note that the Peruvians also produce pisco and consider their own to be the only authentic sort, maintaining that the Chilean stuff is nothing short of counterfeit. The Chileans, of course, pass this off as jealousy, insisting that their pisco is far superior (it is certainly grapier) and proudly claiming that pisco is a Chilean, not Peruvian, drink. Whoever produced it first, there's no denying that the pisco lovingly distilled in the Elqui Valley is absolutely delicious, drunk neat or in a cocktail. A visit to one of the distilleries in the region is not to be missed – if only for the free tasting at the end.

ARRIVAL AND INFORMATION

By bus Buses stop by the plaza and also go up into the village. Three buses weekly (Mon, Wed & Fri) go along the Río Cochiguaz.

Destinations Montegrande (every 30min–1hr; 10min); Vicuña (every 30min–1hr; 50min).

By jeep Jeep Tours La Serena (☎09 9454 6000, ⓦ jeeptour-laserena.cl) offers day-long tours and transfers (Nov–April; CH$95,000/person) to San Juan in Argentina.

PISCO ELQUI AND AROUND

Tourist information ⓦ piscoelqui.com is a useful source of local information.

Tours Elqui Expediciones (☎09 7421 0488) and Turismo Migrantes (☎51 245 1917, ⓦ turismomigrantes .cl), both on O'Higgins, offer horseriding, trekking, cycling and observatory excursions, as well as day-trips to remote thermal springs near the Argentinian border.

ACCOMMODATION

Elquimista Aurora de Chile s/n ☎51 245 1185, ⓦ elquimista.cl. Enjoy the silence and dazzling views from your own *cabaña* perched on a hillside about 1km from town. *Cabañas* are kitted out with antique Asian furniture and quality mattresses. English spoken. CH$65,000

Hostal Triskel Baquedano ☎09 9419 8680, ⓦ hostaltriskel.cl. Genial owner Yayo is a wealth of local information and offers simple yet cosy rooms with shared bathrooms in a stylishly rustic setting with a peaceful, labyrinthine garden. Dorms CH$15,000, doubles CH$30,000

★**Misterios de Elqui** Prat s/n ☎51 245 1126, ⓦ misteriosdeelqui.cl. For a real treat, stay 800m out of town on the road to Alcohuaz. Design magazine *cabañas* with fabulous views are spaced comfortably apart among landscaped gardens leading down to a stunning swimming pool. Golfers can practise on the putting green. CH$75,000

Refugio del Angel El Condor s/n ☎51 245 1292, ⓦ campingrefugiodelangel.cl. Less than 1km southeast of the plaza, this pretty riverside campground feels a world away from the village. Rustic wooden bridges lead to shady camping spots, with picnic tables and hot showers. The cute "teahouse" provides breakfast, drinks and snacks. Camping/person CH$7000

★**El Tesoro de Elqui** Prat s/n ☎51 245 1069, ⓦ tesoro-elqui.cl. The friendly German owners offer attractive, spotless abode-style *cabañas* with hammocks slung on the verandas, amid fragrant gardens, vine-covered terraces and a gorgeous pool. There is one dorm and the restaurant is one of the best in town. Dorms CH$11,000, *cabañas* CH$35,000

INTO ARGENTINA ON RUTA 41

After Rivadavia – where the right fork leads to Pisco Elqui – **Ruta 41** from La Serena follows first the Río Turbio and then the Río de la Laguna all the way to the Paso del Agua Negra (4779m) and the **Argentine border**, nearly 170km away. Only partly tarmacked, often narrow and hemmed in by imposing mountains, many of them over 4000m high, this **road (Oct/Nov–April only)** is one of the most dramatic linking the two countries. Seventy-five kilometres on from Rivadavia you'll come to the Complejo Aduanero Junta del Toro, the Chilean customs post (Nov–April daily 8am–6pm; ☎ 51 265 1184). The Argentine border lies some 95km from the customs post. On the other side of the frontier, the RN 150 winds down to the easygoing market town of Rodeo and hits the adobe-built town of Jachal, from where the RN 40 strikes south to the laid-back provincial capital of San Juan, nearly 270km on from the border post. For more details on these places consult the *Rough Guide to Argentina*.

EATING AND DRINKING

El Durmiente Elquino Las Carreras s/n ☎ 09 8906 2754. Pebble floors, local artwork and mellow music set the scene for dining on Chilean staples (CH$5000 upwards) as well as chicken and corn pancakes, and nutritious quinoa salads. Local wines and pisco cocktails fuel the late-night revelry. Daily noon–1am.

★ **Miraflores** Road to Horcón ☎ 51 228 5901, ⊕ hacienda miraflores.cl. Not to be missed, this wonderful restaurant is a family-run place a couple of kilometres along the road that goes out of town towards Alcohuaz. Here you can feast on excellent roast meats (CH$8000–11,000) like suckling pig and *bife de chorizo* cooked up on the *parrillada* while savouring

mesmerizing views down the valley. Tues–Sun 1–6pm.

Misterios de Elqui Prat s/n ☎ 51 245 1126, ⊕ misteriosdeelqui.cl. This tastefully decorated restaurant offers the most romantic setting in town: a wide wooden balcony with sweeping views down the valley. A gourmet chef prepares delicious food (dishes around CH$8000–10,000), such as prawn crêpes. Wed–Sun 1–3pm & 8–10pm.

El Tesoro de Elqui Prat s/n ☎ 51 245 1069, ⊕ tesoro-elqui.cl. An eclectic menu (mains CH$8000–12,000) mixes international and Chilean influences, ranging from goulash and grilled fish to home-made muesli, waffles, real coffee and to-die-for papaya ice cream. Daily 11am–10pm.

Alcohuaz

Some 15km beyond Pisco Elqui is the tiny community of **ALCOHUAZ**. Apart from a handsome terracotta-hued church (in sharp contrast to Horcón's, which is sky blue), this remote settlement has little to offer in the way of standard attractions.

Colmenares Alcohuaz

No fixed opening hours, so phone or email ahead of your visit • ☎ 09 9003 5297, ✉ nelsoncorreacl@yahoo.com

Alcohuaz is home to a popular curiosity, the **bee-cure centre** known as Colmenares Alcohuaz, or "Alcohuaz Hives". People come from throughout the country to treat all kinds of ills by means of apitherapy (bee stings) – after being tested for allergies, of course. You can also buy a variety of excellent bee products such as honey, royal jelly, propolis and creams to treat skin ailments.

ARRIVAL AND DEPARTURE   ALCOHUAZ

By bus Though there are two buses daily to Horcón, 8km beyond Pisco Elqui (and not to be confused with its more popular coastal namesake), there is no public transport along the final 7km rough stretch to Alcohuaz. Hitchhiking

is common or tour companies in Pisco Elqui offer half-day bicycle excursions, dropping you off in Alcohuaz by minibus and letting you ride back.

ACCOMMODATION

La Casona Distante ☎ 09 9226 5440, ⊕ casonadistante .cl. "The secluded ranch" is a seventy-year-old adobe house offering verdant grounds, stunning valley views from the charming rooms, and a swimming pool. Meals, massage, bike hire and horseriding trips can all be arranged. **CH$50,000**

Refugios La Frontera ☎ 09 9279 8109, ⊕ refugiosla frontera.cl. These seven *cabañas* (sleeping two to eight people) boast a magical setting by the river willows. Onsite is a swimming pool, a restaurant where you can sample the region's tasty river prawns, and an observatory. **CH$60,000**

Along the Río Cochiguaz

Back in Montegrande, a rough, unpaved road branches off the main route, dips down the valley and follows the northern bank of the **RÍO COCHIGUAZ**, a tributary of the Elqui. Rustic *cabañas* dot the riverbank; many offer holistic therapies and meditation classes. The small community of **Cochiguaz**, 11km along the valley, was founded in the 1960s by a group of hippies in the belief that the Age of Aquarius had shifted the earth's magnetic centre from the Himalayas to the Elqui Valley. But don't let this put you off – the multicoloured highland scenery is fabulous and the remoteness and tranquillity of the valley irresistible.

Cancana

11km outside Montegrande • Summer 10pm & midnight; winter 7pm & 9pm • CH$7,500 • ☎ 09 9047 3859, ⓦ cancana.cl

In keeping with the valley's reputation for UFO sightings and celestial activity, the new Cancana observatory at Cochiguaz offers nightly bouts of stargazing through two 35cm Meade telescopes; most people visit on a tour from Pisco Elqui.

3

> #### GABRIELA MISTRAL
>
> Possibly even more than its pisco, the Elqui Valley's greatest source of pride is **Gabriela Mistral**, born in Vicuña in 1889 and, in 1945, the first Latin American to be awarded the **Nobel Prize for Literature**. A schoolmistress, a confirmed spinster and a deeply religious woman, Mistral wrote poetry with an aching sensitivity and passion, and her much romanticized life was punctuated with tragedy and grief.
>
> Lucila Godoy de Alcayaga, as she was christened, was just three when her father abandoned the family, the first of several experiences of loss in her life. It was left to her older sister, Emiliana, to support her and her mother, and for the next eight years the three of them lived in the schoolhouse in the village of **Montegrande**, where Emiliana worked as a teacher. At the age of 14, she started work herself as an assistant schoolteacher, in a village close to La Serena. It was here, also, that she took her first steps into the world of literature, publishing several pieces in the local newspaper under the pseudonyms "Alguien" ("Someone"), "Soledad" ("Solitude") and "Alma" ("Soul"). When she was 20 years old, a railway worker, Romelio Ureta, who for three years had been asking her to marry him, committed suicide; in his pocket, a card was found bearing her name.
>
> Although it would seem that his love for her was unrequited, the intense grief caused by Ureta's suicide was to inform much of Mistral's intensely morbid poetry, to which she devoted her time with increasing dedication while supporting herself with a series of teaching posts. In 1914 she won first prize in an important national poetry competition with *Los Sonetos de la Muerte* (Sonnets of Death), and in 1922 her first collection of verse was published under the title *Desolación* (Desolation), followed a couple of years later by a second collection, *Ternura* (Tenderness). Her work received international acclaim, and in recognition the Chilean Government offered Gabriela Mistral a position in the consular service, allowing her to concentrate almost exclusively on her poetry; here the parallel with Pablo Neruda is at its strongest. As consul, she spent many years abroad, particularly in the US, but her poems continued to look back to Chile, particularly her beloved **Elqui Valley**, which she described as "a cry of nature rising amidst the opaque mountains and intense blue sky". Her most frequently recurring themes, however, were her love of children and her perceived sorrow at her childlessness.
>
> Gabriela Mistral did however serve as a surrogate mother for her adored nephew, **Juan Miguel** or "Yin Yin", who had been placed in her care when he was just 9 months old. Once again, though, tragedy struck: at the age of 17, Yin Yin committed suicide in Brazil, where she was serving as consul. It was a loss from which she never recovered, and for which her Nobel Prize, awarded two years later, could do little to console her. Gabriela Mistral outlived her nephew by twelve years, and in 1957, at the age of 67, she died in New York of cancer of the pancreas, leaving the proceeds of all her works published in South America to the children of Montegrande.

ARRIVAL AND DEPARTURE

By bus Public transport between Montegrande and Cochiguaz is limited to three weekly bus services (Mon, Wed & Fri; 30min), leaving Pisco Elqui early in the morning,

ALONG THE RÍO COCHIGUAZ

before following the Río Cochiguaz and then turning back and heading on to La Serena. Hitchhiking is common along this route.

ACCOMMODATION

El Alma Zen 11km from Montegrande 🕿 09 9047 3861. Spa therapies and river swimming meet poolside posing at this hotel across from the Cancana observatory. The two-storey *cabañas* by the pool are nice but uninspiring; for something more back-to-nature, try the riverside domes with shared bathroom. Domes CH$25,000, *cabañas* CH$45,000

Camping Cochiguaz 17km from Montegrande 🕿 51 245 1154, 🖥 campingcochiguaz.blogspot.com. At the end of the road from Montegrande, this riverside campground is as far as you can get from civilization

without forfeiting hot showers or picnic tables. Staff can arrange horseriding trips. Camping/person CH$6000

Spa Cochiguaz Parcela 8B, El Pangue, 11.5km from Montegrande 🕿 09 8501 2680, 🖥 spacochiguaz.cl. This wellness complex offers rudimentary rooms as well as much nicer cabins with indigenous wallhangings. If you're not into meditation or spa therapies, there's a fine pool to splash about in. The vegetarian restaurant is open to the public and serves three top-notch meals a day. CH$42,000

Vallenar and around

North of La Serena, the Panamericana turns inland and heads via a couple of winding passes towards the busy but somewhat run-down little town of **VALLENAR**, 190km up the road. The town, a service centre for local mining and agricultural industries, was founded in 1789 by Governor Ambrosio O'Higgins, who named the city after his native Ballinagh in Ireland. It makes a convenient base for an excursion east into the fertile **upper Huasco Valley** or northwest towards the coast and, in the spring, the wild flowers of the **Parque Nacional Llanos de Challe**.

The self-appointed "*capital del desierto florido*", Vallenar is indeed the best base for forays into the **flowering desert** (see box, p.155), if you're here at the right time. The **Museo del Huasco** at Ramírez 1001 (Mon–Fri 9am–1pm & 3–6pm; CH$600) has some moderately diverting displays on indigenous cultures and photos of the nearby flowering desert.

ARRIVAL AND INFORMATION

By bus Vallenar's main bus terminal is on the corner of Prat and Av Guillermo Matta, some six blocks west of the main square.
Destinations Antofagasta (10 daily; 9hr); Calama (10 daily; 11hr); Caldera (10 daily; 3hr); Chañaral (10 daily; 4hr); Copiapó (every 30min–1hr; 2hr); Iquique (2 daily; 14hr); La Serena (every 30min–1hr; 2hr 45min);

VALLENAR

Santiago (26 daily; 9hr 30min).
Tourist office Staff at the small tourist office on the 2nd floor of the building on the corner of calles Colchagua and Prat (Mon–Fri 8.30am–6pm; 🕿 51 611501, 🖥 turimovallenar@gmail.com) can advise on tour guides and car rentals.

ACCOMMODATION

Hotel Garra de León Serrano 1052 🕿 51 261 3753, 🖥 reservas@hotelgarradeleon.cl. A 5min stroll from the Plaza de Armas, the solid, mid-range *Hotel Garra de León* has comfortable and spacious rooms (with a/c, TVs and pristine attached bathrooms), as well as friendly service. CH$60,000

Hotel Puerto de Vega Ramírez 201 🕿 51 261 3870, 🖥 puertodevega.cl. A boutique-style hotel near the bus terminal, with beautifully decorated rooms and suites, covered parking, a small swimming

pool in a tidy garden, afternoon tea and huge, delicious breakfasts. Doubles CH$70,000, suites CH$93,000

Residencial Oriental Serrano 720 🕿 51 261 3889, 🖥 laoriental_chang@hotmail.com. If pesos are tight, *Residencial Oriental* is okay for a night. Slightly shabby rooms, some with private bathrooms, are set around a quiet patio. The hot water is erratic and breakfast costs extra. CH$20,000

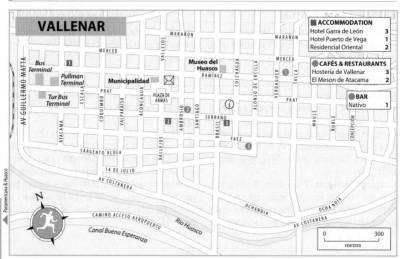

EATING AND DRINKING

Hostería de Vallenar Alonso de Ercilla 848 ☎ 51 261 4379, ⦿ hotelesatacama.cl. This surprisingly good restaurant attached to a *hostería* offers well-cooked Chilean cuisine with imaginative sauces. Seafood mains cost around CH\$7000. Daily 12.30–3pm & 7.30–11pm.

El Mesón de Atacama Serrano 802 ☎ 09 7466 1706. A second-storey restaurant where, as well as Chilean meat and fish staples, you'll also find more adventurous offerings like soy and vodka salmon, stuffed eggplants, and paella (mains around CH\$6000–8000). Mon–Sat 12.30–4pm & 8pm–late, Sun 12.30–4pm.

Nativo Ramirez 1387 ☎ 51 261 8308. With its loud music and rock art-inspired walls, this is a good spot to sink a beer over a plate of *picadillos*. Pizzas and seafood mains (including ceviche) are made to be shared – and portions are generous (mains from CH\$7000). There are also plenty of salad options. Mon–Sat 1pm–3am.

Reserva Nacional Pinguino de Humboldt

129km northwest of La Serena and 126km southwest of Vallenar • April–Nov Wed–Sun 9am–5.30pm; Dec–March daily 9am–5.30pm • CH\$2500 • ☎ 51 261 1555 or ☎ 09 9544 3052, ⦿ www.conaf.cl

Bottle-nosed dolphins, colonies of Humboldt penguins, sea lions and otters frolic in the two-thousand-acre-plus **Reserva Nacional Pinguino de Humboldt**. The reserve comprises three main islands: Choros, Damas and Chañaral, the first two best visited from La Serena. Travelling 87km north of La Serena, a dirt road heads 42km west to Punta de Choros, from where you can sail along the east coast of Isla Choros and go ashore on Isla Damas, the only island where it's possible to disembark. A rough 22km coastal road links Punta de Choros with Caleta Chañaral, the jumping-off point for the furthest and most wildlife-rich island, Isla Chañaral. It's more common, however, to visit Isla Chañaral from Vallenar: 50km south of town is a turn-off opposite Domeyko and the 76km dirt track leads to Caleta Chañaral. Plenty of tour operators in La Serena and Vallenar offer day-trips.

ARRIVAL AND DEPARTURE   RESERVA NACIONAL PINGUINO DE HUMBOLDT

By boat Boats can be hired (CH\$8,000/person) at Punta de Chorros. The tour company ExploraSub (☎ 09 9402 4947, ⦿ explorasub.cl) runs diving, kayaking and boat trips to Isla Chañaral

By bus and boat From Vallenar, buses leave for Caleta Chañaral every Friday at 3pm (also Wed Jan–March) and return Sunday at 5pm with Buses Alvarez (☎ 09 7618 4389). From Caleta Chañaral you can take boat trips (around CH\$80,000/boat; Aurora Campusano is a reliable local guide ☎ 09 9349 3192) that circumnavigate the island.

THE PRICE OF GOLD

A massive threat currently hangs over the Upper Huasco valley: locals fear water shortages and contamination of the pristine Río Huasco from a massive **gold-mining project** by Canadian giant Barrick Gold. The company is currently exploring the Pascua Lama deposits straddling the Argentinian border, believed to be the world's largest untapped gold deposit, and environmental groups claim the company's activities have already had a detrimental effect on glaciers. In 2013 the project was "temporarily suspended", and Barrick Gold is currently embroiled in a legal battle with Chile's environmental agencies.

ACCOMMODATION

Several people on Isla Chañaral rent out simple rooms in their homes (around CH$20,000 a double), including Aurora Campusano (see p.152). Camping is not permitted on Isla Damas.

The upper Huasco Valley

From Vallenar, a paved road follows the Río Huasco through a deep, attractive valley that climbs towards the mountains. The road weaves back and forth across the river, taking you through dry, mauve-coloured hills and green orchards and vineyards. About 20km from Vallenar, you pass the enormous **Santa Juana dam**, which after a season of heavy rainfall overflows into a magnificent waterfall that can be viewed close-up from an observation deck.

Alto del Carmen

Thirty-eight kilometres from Vallenar, the valley forks at the confluence of the El Carmen and El Tránsito rivers. The right-hand road takes you up the **El Carmen Valley** where, just beyond the fork, you'll find **Alto del Carmen**, a pretty village that produces one of the best-known brands of pisco in Chile; you can visit the Planta Pisquera Alto del Carmen for a free tour and tastings (Mon–Fri 9am–noon & 2–6pm, Sat 9am–noon; ☎51 261 6035).

San Félix

A further 26km up the road, **San Félix** has a beautiful setting and a hundred-year-old **pisco plant** that produces high-quality, traditionally made pisco called Horcón Quemado. You can try – and buy – the pisco in their shop (daily 8am–5pm; ☎51 261 0985).

ARRIVAL AND DEPARTURE — UPPER HUASCO VALLEY

By bus Buses Pallauta (☎51 261 2117) leave from the corner of Marañon and Alonso de Ercilla in Vallenar.

Destinations Alto del Carmen (5 daily; 1hr); San Félix (5 daily; 1hr 30min).

ACCOMMODATION

Complejo Turístico y Deportivo Portezuelo Sector La Falda s/n, Alto del Carmen ☎09 9548 3571. A relaxed and leafy spot by the river, with fifty camping sites, twenty *cabañas*, and natural swimming pools (open to non-guests for a small fee). Horseriding and other activities can be arranged. Camping/person **CH$10,000**, *cabañas* **CH$20,000**

Hospedaje y Restaurante El Churcal Hijuela 75 ☎09 7684 4222, ⓦelchurcal.cl. Just 1km outside San Félix, you'll find a range of rooms (all with private bathrooms and TVs; breakfast costs extra) at this eco-minded place with solar-powered showers and plenty of fruit trees. The restaurant offers a lunch menu. **CH$20,000**

Parque Nacional Llanos de Challe

Jan & Feb 8.30am–8pm; March–Dec 8.30am–5.30pm • CH$4000 • ☎52 261 1555, ⓦwww.conaf.cl

If you have the good luck to be around while the desert's in bloom, head for the **PARQUE NACIONAL LLANOS DE CHALLE**, northwest of Vallenar, for the full impact. This

450-square-kilometre swath of coastal plain has been singled out for national park status because of the abundance of **garra de león** – an exquisite, deep-red flower in danger of extinction – that grows here during the years of the *desierto florido*. The park is crossed by an 82km dirt road branching west from the Panamericana, 17km north of Vallenar, and terminating at **Carrizal Bajo**, a once-important mining port now home to a tiny fishing community.

ARRIVAL AND INFORMATION

PARK NACIONAL LLANOS DE CHALLE

By bus Buses leave from Vallenar's bus terminal for Carrizal Bajo with Buses Carmelita (☎ 51 261 3037).

Destinations Carrizal Bajo (3 weekly; around 2hr).

By 4WD If you have a 4WD, a tent and a taste for wilderness, follow the very rough track north of Carrizal Bajo up to Puerto Viejo, near Caldera and Copiapó. The deserted beaches along

this stretch, particularly the northern half, are breathtaking, with white sands and clear, turquoise waters.

Conaf The Conaf information office is 11km north of Carrizal Bajo at the pretty, white-sand Playa Blanca (Jan & Feb 8.30am–8pm; March–Dec 8.30am–5.30pm; ☎ 52 261 1555).

ACCOMMODATION

Camping Playa Blanca There is a beachside campsite near the Conaf office with solar-powered hot showers (for

which there is a small extra charge), barbecues, picnic tables and drinking water. Camping/person $\overline{\text{CH\$5000}}$

Copiapó

Overlooked by arid, rippling mountains, the prosperous city of **COPIAPÓ** sits in the flat basin of the **Río Copiapó**, some 60km from the coast and 145km north of Vallenar. To the east is the most northerly of Chile's "transverse valleys" and beyond it the transformation from semi-desert to serious desert is complete, and the bare, barren Atacama stretches a staggering 1000km north towards the Peruvian border. Just to the north of the city, Arabian-style dunes await exploration. There isn't a great deal to do here, however, and Copiapó's main use to travellers is as a springboard for excursions into the surrounding region (see p.157).

■ ACCOMMODATION	
Hotel La Casona	4
Hotel Chagall	3
Hotel Montecatini	1
Hotel Palace	5
Residencial Benbow	2

● CAFÉS & RESTAURANTS	
Café Colombia	3
Don Elías	2
Flor de la Canela	1
Il Giardino	5
Legado	4

■ CLUB	
Orum Discoteque	1

COPIAPÓ

THE FLOWERING DESERT

For most of the year, as you travel up the Panamericana between Vallenar and Copiapó you'll cross a seemingly endless, semi-desert plain, stretching for nearly 100km, sparsely covered with low shrubs and *copao* cacti. But take the same journey in spring, and in place of the parched, brown earth, you'll find green grass dotted with beautiful flowers. If you're really lucky and you know where to go after a particularly wet winter, you'll happen upon fluorescent carpets of multicoloured flowers, stretching into the horizon.

This extraordinarily dramatic transformation is known as the **desierto florido**, or "flowering desert"; it occurs when unusually heavy rainfall (normally very light in this region) causes dormant bulbs and seeds, hidden beneath the earth, to sprout into sudden bloom, mostly from early September to late October. In the central strip, crossed by the highway, the flowers tend to appear in huge single blocks of colour (*praderas*), formed chiefly by the purple *pata de guanaco* ("guanaco's hoof"), the yellow *corona de fraile* ("monk's halo") and the blue *suspiro de campo* ("field's sigh"). The tiny forget-me-not-like *azulillo* also creates delicate blankets of baby blue.

On the banks of the *quebradas*, or ravines, that snake across the land from the cordillera to the ocean, many different varieties of flowers are mixed together, producing a kaleidoscope of contrasting colours known as *jardines*. These may include the yellow or orange lily-like *añañuca* and the speckled white, pink, red or yellow *alstroemeria*, a popular plant with florists also known as the "Peruvian lily". West, towards the coast, you'll also find large crimson swaths of the endangered *garra de león* ("lion's claw"), particularly in the Parque Nacional Llanos de Challe (see p.153), near Carrizal Bajo, created especially to protect them. Of course, removing any plant, whole or in part, is strictly forbidden by law.

There's no predicting the *desierto florido*, which is relatively rare – the frequency and intensity varies enormously, but the general phenomenon seems to occur every four to five years, although this has been more frequent in recent years. The best **guide** in Vallenar, and a veritable gold-mine of information about the dozens of flower varieties, is Roberto Alegría (☎51 261 3908, ✉desiertoflorido2010@hotmail.cl).

Brief history

When Diego de Almagro made his long trek south from Cuzco in 1536, following the Inca Royal Road down the spine of the Andes, it was into this valley that he descended, recuperating from the gruelling journey at the *tambo*, or resting place, where Copiapó now stands. The valley had been occupied and cultivated by the Diaguita people starting around 1000 AD and was then inhabited, beginning around 1470, by the Inca, who mined gold and copper here. Although Spanish *encomenderos* (see p.473) occupied the valley from the beginning of the conquest, it wasn't until 1744 that the city of Copiapó was founded, initially as "San Francisco de la Selva". A series of random silver strikes in the nineteenth century, most notably at Chañarcillo, threw the region into a frenzied boom.

Copiapó today

Following a period of decline at the beginning of the twentieth century, Copiapó is once more at the centre of a rich mining industry, revolving around copper, iron and gold. The city shot to international notoriety in October 2010, when 33 workers from the nearby San José mine were rescued after 69 days trapped underground (see box, p.158).

Plaza Prat

A lively, busy city, Copiapó has a fairly compact downtown composed of typical adobe houses, some churches and the odd mansion, with the large, tree-filled **Plaza Prat** at its centre. The square is lined with 84 towering old pepper trees planted in 1880. On its southwest corner stands the mid-nineteenth-century **Iglesia Catedral**, designed by the

English architect William Rogers, sporting a Neoclassical three-door portico and topped by an unusual, tiered wooden steeple.

Museo Mineralógico

Corner of Colipí and Rodriguez • Mon–Fri 10am–1pm & 3.30–7pm, Sat 10am–1pm • CH$600

Just off the northeast corner of Plaza Prat, the University of Atacama's **Museo Mineralógico** displays a glittering collection of over two thousand mineral samples from around the world, including huge chunks of malachite, amethyst, quartz, marble and onyx; it's a pity that the museum is so poorly presented, with virtually no explanations or guides of any kind.

Museo Regional de Atacama

Corner of Atacama and Rancagua • Tues–Fri 9am–5.45pm, Sat 10am–12.45pm & 3–5.45pm, Sun 10am–12.45pm • CH$600, free on Sun • ☎ 52 221 2313, ⓦ museodeatacama.cl

The **Museo Regional** repays a visit, not least for its display on the trapped miners of the San José mine (see p.158), which includes their fateful hand-written note: "We are fine in the shelter – the 33." The handsome mansion that houses the museum, the **Casa Matta**, was built in the 1840s for one of Copiapó's wealthy mining barons. The other well-presented displays cover the exploration of the desert, the development of mining, the War of the Pacific, pre-Columbian peoples of the region and the Inca road system.

Plazoleta Juan Godoy

Towering over a tiny square that is the site of a busy Friday market selling fresh produce and household items, the imposing, red-walled 1872 **Iglesia San Francisco** sits one block south and west of the museum. The square's centre is marked by a statue of a rough-clad miner, tools in hand – none other than **Juan Godoy**, the goatherd who accidentally discovered the enormous silver deposits of nearby Chañarcillo in 1832, now honoured in Copiapó as a local legend.

ARRIVAL AND DEPARTURE
COPIAPÓ

BY PLANE

The Desierto de Atacama international airport (☎ 52 252 5104) is just over 50km northwest of the city, at Chamomate, not far from Caldera. Both the Manuel Flores Salinas minibus and Casther bus meet arriving planes and travel into town; a taxi costs around CH$25,000.

Airlines LAN, Colipí and Los Carrera (☎ 52 221 3512); Sky Airlines, O'Higgins 460 (☎ 52 221 4640).

Destinations Note that some of these routes require stopovers, which the travel times listed here take into account: Calama (1–2 daily; 1hr 10min–4hr); Santiago (5–7 daily; 1hr 20min).

BY BUS

Copiapó's main bus terminal is at Chañarcillo 655, two blocks south of Plaza Prat. Across the road, also on Chañarcillo, is the Tur Bus terminal, while one block south, at Freire and Colipí,

sits the Pullman Bus terminal. Inter-city services are offered by all the main companies, including Flota Barrios (☎ 52 221 3645), Pullman Bus (☎ 52 221 2977), Expreso Norte (☎ 52 223 1176) and Tur Bus (☎ 52 223 8612). For Caldera and Bahía Inglesa, Casther (☎ 52 221 8889), Expreso Caldera (☎ 09 6155 8048) and Trans Puma (☎ 52 223 5841) run a frequent service from the small bus station on the corner of Esperanza and Chacabuco, opposite the Líder Hypermarket (you can also catch a Casther transfer to the airport here). Alternately you can catch one of the yellow *colectivos* that wait on the same corner opposite Líder.

Destinations Antofagasta (15 daily; 7hr); Arica (11 daily; 17hr); Calama (15 daily; 10hr); Caldera (every 30min; 1hr); Chañaral (10 daily; 2hr); Iquique (12 daily; 13hr); La Serena (every 30min–1hr; 5hr); Ovalle (6 daily; 7hr); Santiago (22 daily; 12hr); Vallenar (every 30min–1hr; 2hr); Valparaíso (6 daily; 12hr).

INFORMATION AND TOURS

Sernatur Los Carrera 691 on Plaza Prat (Mon–Fri 8.30am–7pm; ☎ 52 221 2838).

Conaf Juan Martínez 56 (Mon–Thurs 8.30am–5.30pm & Fri 8.30am–4pm; ☎ 52 221 3404). Provides information on protected areas in the region, including Pan de Azúcar and Nevado de Tres Cruces national parks; it's also a good source of information on road conditions in the *altiplano*.

TOUR OPERATORS

The main full-day destinations are located east into the cordillera, taking in Parque Nacional Nevado de Tres Cruces and sometimes Laguna Verde and Ojos del Salado (see p.159 & p.160); and north to Parque Nacional Pan de Azúcar (see p.164). Half-day trips go north into the Atacama dunes, west to the beaches around Bahía Inglesa (see p.162), or east up the Copiapó River Valley (see p.159). Ask at Sernatur (see p.156) for a list of guides.

Atacama Chile ☎56 221 1191, ⓦatacamachile.cl. This agency runs a range of trips, including to Parque Nacional Nevado de Tres Cruces, Pan de Azúcar and Llanos de Challe.

Aventurismo Vallejo 577 ☎09 9599 2184, ⓦaventurismo.cl. Maximiliano Martínez has been taking tourists up to Ojos del Salado (eight-day trips from US$1800/person), Laguna Verde and around for longer than anyone else in the business.

GETTING AROUND

Car Rental Rodaggio, Colipí 127 (☎52 221 2153, ⓦrodaggio.cl), rents out good-value 4x4 jeeps. Most other firms are situated on Ramón Freire, including Europcar at no. 50 (☎52 221 6272, ⓦeuropcar.cl) and Salfa Rent at no. 330 (☎52 220 0400, ⓦsalfa.cl). Hertz is on the opposite side of the highway at Copayapú 173 (☎52 221 3522, ⓦhertz.cl).

ACCOMMODATION

★**Hotel La Casona** O'Higgins 150 ☎52 221 7277, ⓦlacasonahotel.cl. This small, charming and impeccably decorated hotel provides attractive en suites, pleasant garden, and an English-speaking owner, as well as excellent breakfasts (which are included in the rates). **CH$65,000**

Hotel Chagall O'Higgins 760 ☎52 221 3775, ⓦchagall.cl. The large, upscale *Hotel Chagall* has comfortable, fully-fitted en suites (though they are a little short on character), a good restaurant and bar, outdoor pool, gym and private parking. **CH$79,000**

Hotel Montecatini Infante 766 ☎52 221 1363, ⓦhotelmontecatini.cl. Bright, spacious rooms which fall into two classes: smart, newer *ejecutivo* and older but cheaper *turista*, both with private bathrooms. There's also a tiny pool, and parking facilities. **CH$41,000**

Hotel Palace Atacama 741 ☎52 221 2852, ⓦpalace hotel.cl. Copious wood-panelling gives *Hotel Palace* a vaguely 70s feel. The carpeted rooms are comfortable enough, though overpriced (try bargaining the price down): all have private bathrooms and TVs. **CH$38,000**

Residencial Benbow Rodriguez 541 ☎52 221 7634. If you're on a tight budget, this is an acceptable option. Rooms are cramped, but perfectly fine; most have shared bathrooms but you can pay CH$6000 more for an en suite. Breakfast costs extra. **CH$18,000**

EATING AND DRINKING

Café Colombia Colipi 484 ☎52 223 7288. Located right on the plaza, with a shady open-air seating area, *Café Colombia* is a good place for a coffee (CH$1000–2100), snack or treat: the menu ranges from sandwiches and pizzas to cakes and ice-cream sundaes. Mon–Sat 9am–9pm.

Don Elías Los Carrera 421 ☎52 236 4146. For a cheap and cheerful meal, the least insalubrious option in town is this great-value diner with bargain set lunches, fish and meat dishes (from CH$2000) that keep the locals piling in. Mon–Sat 10am–10.30pm, Sun 10am–5.30pm.

Flor de la Canela Chacabuco 710 ☎52 221 9570. This cheerful Peruvian joint offers a change from the Copiapó norm, with tasty dishes like ceviche and *lomo saltado* (stir-fried strips of beef with tomatoes, onions, chips and rice), as well as a killer (Peruvian-style) pisco sour. Prices are a little steep (mains CH$8300–14,900). Daily 1–3pm & 8–11pm.

Il Giardino Rancagua 341 ☎52 223 2246, ⓦilgiardino .cl. Pretty, colourful restaurant (the exterior is lime green) with a romantic ambience, sun-dappled courtyard and a young chef who prepares tasty fish, salads and pastas. Most mains around CH$8000–10,000. Tues–Sat 1–4pm & 8pm–midnight, Sun 1–4.30pm.

Legado O'Higgins 12 ☎52 252 3895. One of Copiapó's top restaurants, the intimate and friendly *Legado* offers pricey yet good-quality meat and fish dinners (most mains around CH$10,000). The star dish is the Wagyu beef steak. Mon–Sat 7pm–midnight.

NIGHTLIFE

Orum Discoteque Los Carrera 2440 ☎52 223 4100, ⓦantaycasinohotel.cl. This sleek club inside the *Antay Casino & Hotel* is one of the hottest spots in town. Weekends are all about retro and pop standards, while week nights mix things up with salsa and karaoke. Wed & Thurs 9pm–2am, Fri & Sat 9pm–late.

DIRECTORY

Camping gear *Bencina blanca* (white gas) and butane gas are available at Ferretería El Herrerito, Atacama 699. Dolomiti, 469 Atacama (☎ 56 253 5451, ⊛dolomiti.cl), has a range of Camping Gaz appliances and other outdoor stuff.

Money and exchange There are several ATMs on the main square. Intercambios Limitada is the only *casa de cambio* in town, located on the first floor of the Mall Plaza Real off the main square at Colipí 484.

Post office North side of Plaza Prat at Los Carrera 691 (Mon–Fri 9am–6pm, Sat 10am–1pm).

Around Copiapó

The region around Copiapó features some of Chile's most striking and varied landscapes. To the east, the **Río Copiapó Valley** offers the extraordinary spectacle of emerald-green vines growing in desert-dry hills, while high up in the Andes, you'll ascend a world of salt flats, volcanoes and lakes, encompassed by the **Parque Nacional Nevado de Tres Cruces**, the **Volcán Ojos del Salado** and the blue-green **Laguna Verde**. To the west, **Bahía Inglesa**, near the port of **Caldera**, could be a little chunk of the Mediterranean, with its pristine sands and odd-shaped rocks rising out of the sea. Further south, reached only in a 4WD, the coast is lined with wild, deserted **beaches** lapped by turquoise waters.

THE RESCUE OF LOS 33

On August 5, 2010, a boulder collapsed inside the San José copper and gold mine, 32km northeast of Copiapó, trapping 33 workers some 700m below the desert. That may well have been the end of the story – the miners consigned to statistics in Chile's notoriously dangerous mining industry – but for a fortuitous combination of determined families, a captivated media and a president in dire need of a ratings boost. In the aftermath of the accident, relatives of the trapped miners set up camp outside the pithead and refused to budge, urging the company to continue their search effort.

LIMELIGHT IN THE DARKNESS

The families kept up the pressure via the national media, compelling the then new right-wing president Sebastián Piñera – perceived to be out of touch with the working class and reeling from a ratings blow following his handling of February's earthquake and tsunami – to get involved. On day 17 of the search operation, just as hope was fading, rescue workers struck media gold – a handwritten note attached to their drillhead which read: "We are fine in the shelter – the 33." The miners' relatives were euphoric, the president triumphant and the international media dispatched to "Camp Hope" to cover the miracle (and soap opera) unfolding in the Chilean desert.

Food, medicine, pornography and video cameras were sent down a narrow communications shaft to the desperate men. What happened next was beamed around the world: one miner proposed a church marriage to his partner; a two-timer was exposed when his wife *and* mistress turned up at Camp Hope to lend support; a musical miner kept his colleagues entertained with Elvis impersonations; and another lay in the hot, dark tunnel while above ground his wife gave birth to his daughter, named, appropriately, "Esperanza" (hope).

SAVED

Just after midnight on October 13, 69 days after the miners were buried alive (the longest underground entrapment in history), state-of-the-art rescue capsules hauled the first of "Los 33" to freedom, to an estimated global TV audience of 1.5 billion people. In the aftermath of the rescue, the miners enjoyed a flurry of media attention and were flown around the world and paraded as heroes. Most, however, chose to remain tight-lipped about what really went on in that subterranean hell, and as well as struggling with post-traumatic stress, the majority now live quiet, unassuming lives in Copiapó.

Río Copiapó Valley

Despite an acute shortage of rainfall, the **RÍO COPIAPÓ VALLEY** is one of the most important grape-growing areas of Chile. This is thanks mainly to new irrigation techniques that have been developed over the past fifteen years, tapping into the valley's abundance of underground flowing water. While the Copiapó Valley is not quite as pastoral or picturesque as the Elqui Valley, its cultivated areas provide, more than anywhere else in the north, the most stunning contrast between deep-green produce and parched, dry earth – from September to May, in particular, it really is a sight to behold.

Museo Minero

16km southeast of Copiapó • Mon–Fri 8am–5pm, Sat & Sun 9am–1pm • Free • ☎ 52 232 9136, ⓦ museominerodetierraamarilla.cl

Aside from the Río Copiapó Valley's scenery, you'll find the excellent new Museo Minero in the town of Tierra Amarilla, 16km southeast of Copiapó; it is set inside a restored nineteenth-century house and provides an overview of mining in the Atacama region.

GETTING AROUND   RIO COPIAPÓ VALLEY

By bus From Copiapó, Casther, Expreso Caldera and Trans Puma have several daily services up the Copiapó River Valley. Buses go as far as Manflas, 150km southeast (the last 12km of the journey is along an unpaved road).

Parque Nacional Nevado de Tres Cruces

Around 95km east of Copiapó • 8.30am–6pm • CH$4000 • ☎ 52 221 3404, ⓦ www.conaf.cl

East of Copiapó, the Andes divide into two separate ranges – the Cordillera de Domeyko and the Cordillera de Claudio Gay – joined by a high basin, or plateau, that stretches all the way north to Bolivia. The waters trapped in this basin form vast salt flats and lakes towered over by enormous, snowcapped volcanoes, and wild vicuña and guanaco roam the sparsely vegetated hills. This is a truly awe-inspiring landscape, conveying an acute sense of wilderness and space. It's easier to fully appreciate it here than around San Pedro de Atacama, for instance, thanks to the general absence of tourists. The number of visitors has started to increase, however, following the creation in 1994 of the **PARQUE NACIONAL NEVADO DE TRES CRUCES**, which takes in a dazzling white salt flat, the **Salar de Maricunga**; two beautiful lakes, the **Laguna Santa Rosa** and **Laguna del Negro Francisco**; and the 6753m volcano **Tres Cruces**.

The bumpy road up to Parque Nacional Nevado de Tres Cruces takes you through a brief stretch of desert before twisting up narrow canyons flanked by mineral-stained rocks. As you climb higher, the colours of the scoured, bare mountains become increasingly vibrant, ranging from oranges and golds to greens and violets. Some 165km from Copiapó, at an altitude of around 3700m, the road (following the signs to Mina Marta) reaches the first sector of the park, skirting the pale-blue **Laguna Santa Rosa**, home to dozens of pink flamingos.

Immediately adjacent, the gleaming white **Salar de Maricunga** is Chile's most southerly salt flat, covering an area of over eighty square kilometres. A two- to three-hour drive south from here, past Mina Marta, the park's second sector is based around the large, deep-blue **Laguna del Negro Francisco**, some 4200m above sea level and home to abundant birdlife, including wild ducks and flamingos. Towering over the lake, the 6080m **Volcán Copiapó** was the site of an Inca sacrificial altar.

Laguna Verde

Close to but not part of the park, by the border with Argentina, the stunning, blue-green **Laguna Verde** lies at the foot of the highest active volcano in the world, the 6893m **Volcán Ojos del Salado**. The first, sudden sight of **Laguna Verde** is stupendous. The intense colour of its waters – green or turquoise, depending on the

---

CLIMBING VOLCÁN OJOS DEL SALADO

As the volcano sits on the border with Argentina, climbers need to present written permission from the Dirección de Fronteras y Límites (DIFROL; ✉ infodifrol@minrel.gov.cl) plus a *permiso regional*, obtained from the tourist office, to the *carabineros* before climbing up. If you need to arrange transport to the base, or a guide for the ascent, contact Aventurismo or Sernatur in Copiapó (see p.156).

---

time of day – almost leaps out at you from the muted browns and ochres of the surrounding landscape. The lake lies at an altitude of 4500m, about 250km from Copiapó on the international road to Argentina (follow the signs to Paso San Francisco or Tinogasta). At the western end of the lake, a small shack contains a fabulous **hot-spring bath**, where you can soak and take blissful refuge from the biting wind outdoors. The best place to camp is just outside the bath, where a stone wall offers some protection from the wind, and hot streams provide useful washing-up water. At the lake's eastern end there's a *carabineros* checkpoint, where you should make yourself known if you plan to camp.

Volcán Ojos del Salado

Laguna Verde is surrounded by huge volcanoes: Mulas Muertas, Incahuasi and the monumental **Ojos del Salado**. At 6893m, this is the highest peak in Chile and the highest active volcano in the world; its last two eruptions were in 1937 and 1956. A popular climb (Oct–March), it takes up to twelve days and is not technically difficult, apart from the last 50m that border the crater. The base of the volcano is a 12km walk from the abandoned *carabineros* checkpoint on the main road, and there are two *refugios* on the way up, one at 5100m (four beds, with latrines) and another at 5750m (twelve beds with kitchen and lounge). Temperatures are low at all times of year, so take plenty of warm gear.

ARRIVAL AND INFORMATION   PARQUE NACIONAL NEVADO DE TRES CRUCES

By car From Copiapó, it's about a 3hr drive to Laguna Santa Rosa, and a 6hr drive to Laguna Verde. There's no public transport to this area – for information on tours, see p.157.

Conaf In summer (Dec–March), Conaf has its two park headquarters at Laguna Santa Rosa and about 4km from Laguna del Negro Francisco (both 8.30am–6pm; ☎ 52 221

3404); the *guardaparques* are very friendly and take visitors on educational excursions to the lake and around, but if you want to stay over check with Conaf in Copiapó first. Park fees are not enforced through the rest of the year but there are *guardaparques* at the Chilean immigration post at Complejo Fronterizo Maricunga, 100km west of the Argentinian border.

ACCOMMODATION

Refugio Laguna del Negro Francisco 4km from the lake ☎ 52 221 3404. This large, comfortable *refugio* sleeps up to fifteen people and has bunk beds, electricity, hot showers and a kitchen. It is necessary to bring your own food and drinking water. Dorms **CH$10,000**

Refugio Laguna Santa Rosa Western shore of the lake ☎ 52 221 3404. A tiny wooden *refugio* maintained by Conaf, this is a basic but convenient place to sleep (no bunk beds, floor space only), with great views of the lake backed by the snowcapped Volcán Tres Cruces. Note that there is no water here. **Free**

Caldera

Just over 70km northwest of Copiapó, **CALDERA** is a small, easygoing seaside town with a smattering of nineteenth-century buildings, a beach, a pier and a few good fish restaurants. Chosen as the terminus of Chile's first railway by mining and railway pioneer William Wheelwright, it became the country's second-largest port in the last decades of the nineteenth century, when it exported all the silver extracted in the region's dramatic silver boom.

Caldera's two ports are still busy – one exporting table grapes, the other exporting copper – but they don't totally dominate the bay, which remains fairly attractive. The town's principal landmarks are the Gothic-towered **Iglesia de San Vicente** on the main square, built by English carpenters in 1862, and the former **train station** at the pier, dating from 1850.

Centro Cultural Estación

Wheelwright s/n • Museo Paleontológico Tues–Sun 10am–2pm & 4–7pm • CH$600 • ☎ 52 231 6891

The former train station has been converted into the Centro Cultural Estación Caldera, which hosts community events and houses the fascinating little Museo Paleontológico, with its collection of fossils, rocks and locally unearthed artefacts.

Museo Casa Tornini

Gana 210 • Guided tours daily: Jan & Feb 11am, noon, 1pm, 6.30pm, 7.30pm & 8.30pm; March–Dec 11.30am & 3.40pm • CH$2000 • ☎ 52 231 7930, ⊚ casatornini.cl

This handsome, ochre-coloured house, which dates back to 1890, was the residence of a wealthy Italian family, the Torninis. The fifty-minute guided tours of the well-preserved house provide a snapshot of Caldera's nineteenth-century heyday. There are also temporary art exhibitions, and the owners run the nearby *Caffè Museo* (see p.162).

The pier and beaches

The **pier**, down by the beach, makes for a pleasant stroll and is the starting point for **boat rides** around the bay in summer. Caldera's main **beach** is the sheltered, mid-sized and rather dirty Copiapina, while to the west of the pier, the large, windswept Playa Brava stretches towards the desert sands of the Norte Grande.

CALDERA

● CAFÉS & RESTAURANTS	
Caffè Museo	2
Il Pirón de Oro	3
Nuevo Miramar	1

■ ACCOMMODATION	
Costa Fósil	1
Hotel Montecarlo	3
Residencial Millaray	2

3

The cemetery

Av Diego de Almeyda s/n • Daily 8am–7pm • Free

The cemetery 1km east of town is also worth a wander; dating from 1876, it was the first non-denominational cemetery in Chile, and harbours the weathered graves and mausoleums of English, Welsh, Scottish, German, French, Chinese and Japanese immigrants.

ARRIVAL AND INFORMATION   CALDERA

By plane Caldera lies 20km northwest of the Desierto de Atacama international airport (see p.156). There are minibus transfers into town, or you can take a taxi (around CH$15,000).

By bus Buses to Copiapó leave from a small terminal at the corner of Cifuentes and Ossa Varas. Long-distance services to Chañaral and further north are provided by Pullman Bus and Tur-Bus, from Caldera's main terminal at Gallo and Vallejos.

Destinations Chañaral (12 daily; 1hr); Copiapó (every 30min; 1hr).

By micro and colectivo *Micros* for Bahía Inglesa leave from the Plaza de Armas (Jan & Feb every 15min). The rest of the year, black taxi *colectivos* leave from the plaza.

Tourist office Plaza de Armas (daily: Jan & Feb 10am–1am; March–Dec 9am–2pm & 4–7pm; ☎ 52 231 6076).

ACCOMMODATION

Costa Fósil Gallo 560 ☎ 52 231 6451, ⓦ jandy.cl. Three levels of bright and spotless rooms, some with (partial) ocean views, sit around a tranquil, flower-filled patio. An information board, a massive map of the region and friendly staff ensure guests feel right at home. Breakfast included. **CH$39,000**

Hotel Montecarlo Carvallo 627 ☎ 52 231 5388, ⓦ hotel-montecarlo.cl. Reasonable, though overpriced mid-range hotel, with a faded yellow exterior, a lush

courtyard garden, straightforward rooms with colourful bedspreads, clean attached bathrooms, TVs and safes. Breakfast costs extra. **CH$36,000**

Residencial Millaray Cousiño 331 ☎ 52 231 5528, ⓔ rubenhmarre@yahoo.es. Right on the central plaza, this is probably the nicest budget choice in town (not a contested title it must be said), with simple, airy rooms (with shared or private bathrooms) looking onto a leafy patio. Breakfast costs extra. **CH$20,000**

EATING

Fresh seafood is sold at Caldera's *muelle pesquera* (fishing jetty) where a handful of outdoor **restaurants** hustle up fish dishes, paella and piping hot octopus *empanadas*.

Caffé Museo Edwards 479 ☎ 52 231 5790. Under the same management as Museo Casa Tornini, this cute café is good spot for breakfast or *onces*, with a concise menu featuring coffees (CH$1000–2600), sandwiches and cakes. While you're waiting, check out the old newspaper front pages on the walls. Mon–Fri 9am–1.30pm & 4.30–8.30pm, Sat & Sun 10.30am–2pm & 5–9pm.

Il Pirón de Oro Cousiño 218 ☎ 52 231 5790. In a town that prides itself on its fish and shellfish, this no-frills restaurant with lime-green tablecloths is arguably the

best, serving imaginatively prepared dishes (around CH$4000–7000), including exquisite crab pie. Daily 11am–4pm & 7–10pm.

Nuevo Miramar Gana 090 ☎ 52 231 5381. The location of this seafood restaurant couldn't be better, right on the beach, with wonderful views of the bay. For a romantic evening, order a plate of oysters, prawn omelette or crab gratin (mains CH$4100–8500) and watch the lights flicker on the water. Daily noon–4pm & 7pm–midnight.

Bahía Inglesa and around

The **beaches** of **Bahía Inglesa** are probably the most photographed in Chile, adorning wall calendars up and down the country. More than their white, powdery sands – which, after all, you can find the length of Chile's coast – it's the exquisite clarity of the turquoise sea and the curious rock formations that rise out of it which set these beaches apart.

Northern beaches

Several beaches are strung along the bay to the north of Caldera, separated by rocky outcrops: the long Playa Machas is the southernmost beach, followed by Playa La

Piscina, then by Playa El Chuncho and finally Playa Blanca. Surprisingly, this resort area has not been swamped by the kind of ugly, large-scale construction that mars Viña del Mar and La Serena, and Bahía Inglesa remains a fairly compact collection of *cabañas* and a few hotels. While the place gets hideously crowded in the height of summer, at most other times it's peaceful and relaxing.

Southern beaches

South of Bahía Inglesa, beyond the little fishing village of Puerto Viejo that marks the end of the paved road, the coast is studded with a string of **superb beaches** lapped with crystal-clear water and backed by immense sand dunes. The scenery is particularly striking around **Bahía Salada**, a deserted bay indented with tiny coves some 130km south of Bahía Inglesa. You might be able to find a tour operator that arranges excursions to these beaches, but if you really want to appreciate the solitude and wilderness of this stretch of coast, you're better off renting a jeep and doing it yourself.

3

ARRIVAL AND DEPARTURE   BAHÍA INGLESA

By colectivo You can visit Bahía Inglesa for the day from Caldera, just 6km away; plenty of taxi *colectivos* leaving from Caldera's plaza connect the two resorts, and also Copiapó. The best place to catch a *colectivo* back to Caldera is on the corner by *Rocas de Bahía*.

ACCOMMODATION

The problem with staying here is that **accommodation** tends to be ridiculously overpriced, but you should be able to bargain the rates down outside summer.

Camping Bahía Inglesa Playa Las Machas ☎52 231 5424. A large, expensive campsite just off Playa Las Machas and overlooking Bahía Inglesa, with hot showers, picnic tables and a swimming pool. There are also *cabañas* which sleep up to four people, the cheapest with shared bathroom. Camping/person CH$26,000, *cabañas* CH$40,000

Coral de Bahía El Morro 564 ☎52 231 9160, ⓦcoraldebahia.cl. Long-standing, popular hotel with an extensive selection of rooms, from simple en-suite doubles (the cheapest ones don't have sea views) to big apartments sleeping up to eight people. There's also a good restaurant. Doubles US$80,000, apartments US$252

Domo Bahía Inglesa El Morro 610 ☎09 8162 8642, ⓦfacebook.com/domobahia. At the end of the promenade, these three futuristic mini-dome *cabañas*, with huge beds and private bathrooms, are quite the novelty. Staff can also arrange tours to remote beaches as well as the Parque Nacional Pan de Azúcar. CH$50,000

Los Jardines de Bahía Inglesa Copiapó 100 ☎52 231 5359, ⓦjardinesbahia.cl. Located a few blocks back from the beachfront, these smart *cabañas* sleep up to eleven people (the rate below is for two people sharing). There's a good-sized pool, a table tennis table and a decent Italian restaurant. CH$41,000

EATING AND DRINKING

El Domo El Morro 610 ☎09 8162 8642. Sitting in front of its namesake hotel (see above) this tent-like cupola is the place to try satiating dishes like mixed seafood ceviche. It's also a great spot to just linger over a real coffee (CH$1500–2500) or nurse a drink while taking in the ocean vistas. Tues–Sun 12.30–11.30pm.

El Plateado El Morro 756 ☎09 9826 0007. The most sophisticated restaurant in town with deck chairs on a terrace opposite the seafront. *El Plateado* serves international cuisine including flavoursome Thai and Indian curries (most mains around CH$8000–10,000). Daily 1–3pm & 5pm–midnight.

Chañaral

Sitting by a wide, white bay and the Panamericana, **CHAÑARAL**, 167km north of Copiapó, is a rather sorry-looking town of houses staggered up a hillside, with more than its fair share of stray dogs. Originally a small *caleta* used for shipping out the produce of an inland desert oasis, it still serves chiefly as an export centre, these days for the giant El Salvador copper mine, 130km east in the cordillera. Despite efforts to clean it up, Chañaral's huge beach remains contaminated by the toxic wastes deposited by the mine. You can visit the **Parque Nacional Pan de Azúcar** from Chañaral, which sits 30km up the coast, although it is preferable to visit as a day-trip from Copiapó.

ARRIVAL AND DEPARTURE   CHAÑARAL

By bus Many north–south buses make a stop in the town; those that don't will drop you off if you ask.
Destinations Antofagasta (11 daily; 5hr); Arica (6 daily; 15hr); Calama (11 daily; 8hr); Copiapó (12 daily; 1hr); Iquique (9 daily; 11hr); La Serena (12 daily; 7hr); Mejillones (4 daily; 6hr); Ovalle (11 daily; 9hr); Santiago (11 daily; 14hr); Taltal (2 daily; 2hr 30min); Tocopilla (7 daily; 8hr); Vallenar (12 daily; 4hr).

ACCOMMODATION AND EATING

Alicanto Panamericana Norte 49 ☎ 52 248 1168. Take in ocean views as you make your way through fresh seafood hauled in by local fisherman at the adjacent cove. Mains around CH$6000. Daily 9.30am–5pm.
Hotel Aqualuna Merino Jarpa 521 ☎ 52 252 3868, ⓦ aqualunahotel.cl. For a central option, this simple, ten-room hotel pulls out all the stops: comfy mattresses, TVs, breakfast and private parking. It also has a few apartments. Doubles CH$42,000, apartments CH$56,000
Hotel Jiménez Merino Jarpa 551 ☎ 52 248 0328, ⓦ hoteljimenez.cl. A budget choice with a prime position on the main street close to the Pullman Bus stop, with basic but clean and bright rooms, some with private bath, and all with cable TV. Breakfast costs extra. CH$24,000

Parque Nacional Pan de Azúcar

8.30am–12.30pm & 2–6pm • CH$4000 • ☎ 52 221 3404, ⓦ www.conaf.cl

Home to two dozen varieties of cactus, guanacos and foxes, and countless birds, **PARQUE NACIONAL PAN DE AZÚCAR** is a 40km strip of desert containing the most stunning coastal scenery in the north of Chile. Steep hills and cliffs rise abruptly from the shore, which is lined with a series of pristine white-sand beaches. Though bare and stark, these hills make an unforgettable sight as they catch the late afternoon sun, when the whole coastline is bathed in rich shades of gold, pink and yellow. The only inhabited part of the park is **Caleta Pan de Azúcar**, 30km north of Chañaral, where you'll find a cluster of twenty or so fishermen's shacks as well as the Conaf information centre and a campsite (see p.165).

Isla Pan de Azúcar

Opposite the village, 2km off the shore, the **Isla Pan de Azúcar** is a small island sheltering a huge collection of marine wildlife, including seals, sea otters, plovers, cormorants, pelicans and more than three thousand Humboldt penguins; you can (and should) take a boat trip out to get a close look at the wildlife. The island's distinctive conical silhouette gives the park its name "sugarloaf".

Mirador Pan de Azúcar

For fabulous panoramic views up and down the coast, head to **Mirador Pan de Azúcar**, a well-signposted lookout point 10km north of the village; the different varieties of cactus are fascinating and you may have the place all to yourself – unless you're joined by a curious grey fox or guanaco.

Las Lomitas

More difficult to reach, and less rewarding, **Las Lomitas** is a 700m-high clifftop about 30km north of the village; it's almost permanently shrouded in mist and is the site of a large black net, or "fog catcher", that condenses fog into water and collects it below.

ARRIVAL AND INFORMATION

By car There are two access roads to the park, both branching off the Panamericana: approaching from the south, the turn-off is at the north end of Chañaral, just past the cemetery; approaching from the north, take the turn-off at Las Bombas, 45km north of Chañaral. Both roads are bumpy but passable in a car.

By taxi There are no public buses to the park. Taxis from Chañaral cost around CH$20,000 each way – worth it for a group. Alternatively, take a day-trip tour from Copiapó.

Conaf Near the village (daily 8.30am–12.30pm &

PARQUE NACIONAL PAN DE AZÚCAR

2–6pm). Offers maps, leaflets and souvenirs. This is where you pay your park fee.

Tours Several tour operators in Copiapó (see p.157) offer day-trips to the park. Boat trips to the Isla Pan de Azúcar depart from the *caleta* and cost around CH$5000/person (minimum 15 people). It takes about 90min to do the circuit; the best times are around 7–8am and 6pm, when the penguins come out to eat. Ask in the village for Segundo Lizana, Manuel Carasco or Alex Guerra who all offer the same trip at the standard price.

ACCOMMODATION AND EATING

Rough camping is not allowed in the park, but there are a number of authorized **camping** areas.

Camping Los Pingüinos Just north of the Caleta Pan de Azúcar ☎ 52 248 1209. If you've got your own camping gear, this campsite has decent facilities, including bathrooms, drinking water, picnic tables, rubbish collection and first-aid supplies. Camping/person **CH$5000**

Pan de Azúcar Lodge Playa Piqueros, south of Caleta

Pan de Azúcar ☎ 52 221 9271, ⓦ pandeazucarlodge.cl. *Pan de Azúcar Lodge* has the national park's best camping facilities, with barbecues and picnic tables, as well as a handful of fully equipped solar-powered *cabañas* sleeping up to eight people. Camping/person **CH$7000**, *cabañas* **CH$60,000**

3

El Norte Grande

171 Antofagasta

174 Around Antofagasta

176 Calama and around

178 San Pedro de Atacama

183 Around San Pedro

186 Iquique

193 Inland from Iquique

198 Parque Nacional Volcán Isluga

201 Pisagua

201 Hacienda de Tiliviche

203 Arica

209 The Azapa Valley

210 Putre

211 Parque Nacional Lauca

214 Reserva Nacional las Vicuñas

215 Salar de Surire

VOLCÁN PARINACOTA, PARQUE NACIONAL LAUCA

El Norte Grande

"El Norte Grande" occupies almost a quarter of Chile's mainland territory but contains barely five percent of its population. Its most outstanding feature is the Atacama Desert; the driest desert in the world, it contains areas where no rainfall has been recorded – ever. Its landscape is typically made up of rock and gravel spread over a wide plain, alleviated only by crinkly mountains. To the west, the plain is lined by a range of coastal hills that drop abruptly to a shelf of land where most of the region's towns and cities are scattered. To the east, the desert climbs towards the altiplano: a high, windswept plateau composed of lakes and salt flats ringed with snowcapped volcanoes.

Formidable and desolate as it is, the region contains a wealth of superb attractions, and, for many visitors, constitutes the highlight of a trip to Chile – particularly for European travellers, who will find nothing remotely like it back home. The Pacific seaboard is lined by vast tracts of stunning **coastal scenery**, while inland the **desert pampa** itself impresses not only with its otherworldly geography, but also with fascinating testimonies left by man. One of these is the trail of decaying nitrate **ghost towns**, including **Humberstone** and **Santa Laura**, easily reached from Iquique. Another is the immense images known as **geoglyphs** left by indigenous peoples on the hillsides and ravines of the desert – you'll find impressive examples at **Cerro Pintados**, south of Iquique, **Cerro Unitas**, east of Huara, and **Tiliviche**, between Huara and Arica.

As you journey towards and up into the cordillera, you'll come across attractive **oasis villages**, some – such as **Pica** and **Mamiña** – with **hot springs**. Up in the Andes, the altiplano is undoubtedly one of the country's highlights, with its dazzling **lakes**, **salt flats and volcanoes**, its abundance of **wildlife** and its tiny, whitewashed villages inhabited by native Aymara. The main altiplano touring base – and, indeed, one of the most popular destinations in the whole country, for Chileans and foreigners alike – is **San Pedro de Atacama**, a pleasant oasis 315km northeast of Antofagasta, where numerous operators offer excursions to the famous **El Tatio geysers** and the haunting moonscapes of the **Valle de la Luna**.

Further north, the stretch of altiplano within reach of Iquique and Arica boasts wild vicuña and spectacular scenery, preserved in **Parque Nacional Lauca** and several adjoining parks and reserves. Some towns and cities of the Far North, mainly Antofagasta and Calama, tend to be dreary and uninviting, but serve as unavoidable departure points for excursions into the hinterland. Bear in mind also, the **Bolivian Winter**, when sporadic heavy rains between December and February in the altiplano can wash roads away and seriously disrupt communications and access.

ALMA observatory p.175
Tours from San Pedro p.181
Paragliding paradise p.189
The nitrate boom p.194
The Legend of La Tirana p.197
Crossing the Altiplano p.200
Pinochet's legacy in Pisagua p.201

The Aymara of Chile p.202
Tours from Arica p.207
Chinchorro mummies p.209
Parinacota's wandering table p.213
Walks and climbs in Parque Nacional Lauca p.214
Conaf refugios p.215

THE SALAR DE ATACAMA, ATACAMA DESERT

Highlights

❶ Valle de la Luna Watch the setting sun heighten the textures and deepen the colours of the valley's sweeping dunes and undulating rock formations. **See p.185**

❷ The Salar de Atacama Explore the vast salt flats of the Atacama Desert, the driest place on Earth – parts of it never, ever see rain. **See p.185**

❸ El Tatio geysers At 4300m, pools of boiling water send clouds of steam into the air at the crack of dawn. **See p.186**

❹ Iquique's beaches and mountains The city has made a name for itself as a surfers' haven

and is also one of the best places to paraglide in the world. **See p.186**

❺ Cerro Pintados geoglyphs Discover these mysterious, indigenous images, the largest collection of geoglyphs in South America. **See p.195**

❻ Lauca and Isluga parks Trek through a landscape of mineral baths, cobalt lakes, sparkling salt flats and spongy bogs at dizzying altitudes. **See p.211 & p.198**

❼ Altiplano wildlife Thousands of llamas and alpacas, vicuñas and vizcachas, flamingos and condors – a photographer's dream. **See p.211**

HIGHLIGHTS ARE MARKED ON THE MAP ON P.170

HIGHLIGHTS

1. Valle de la Luna
2. The Salar de Atacama
3. El Tatio geysers
4. Iquique's beaches and mountains
5. Cerro Pintados geoglyphs
6. Lauca and Isluga parks
7. Altiplano wildlife

EL NORTE GRANDE

PERU

Tacna

Visviri **7**

PARQUE
NACIONAL
LAUCA

Putre

Socoroma **6** Parinacota

Tambo Quemado

Arica

San Miguel
de Azapa

RESERVA
NATURAL
LAS VICUÑAS

SALAR DE
SURIRE

Enquelga

Islunga Colchane

BOLIVIA

PARQUE
NACIONAL
VOLCAN ISLUGA

6

SALAR DE
COLPASA

Pisagua

Tiliviche

Chusmisa

Huara

Cerro Unitas

Mamiña

SALAR DE UYUNI

Humberstone

4 Pozo Almonte

Iquique

La Tirana

Pica

5 Matilla

Cerro
Pintados

RESERVA
NACIONAL
PAMPA DEL
TAMARUGAL

Ollagüe

PACIFIC
OCEAN

Tocopilla

Chug Chug
Geoglyphs

Chiu
Chiu

Caspana

RESERVA
NACIONAL
EDUARDO
AVARDA

Maria Elena

Chuquicamata

Ayquina

Gatico

Pedro de
Valdivia

Calama

El Tatio **3**

Cobija

San Pedro
de Atacama

Chacabuco

Valle de la Luna

1 Toconao

Mejillones

Baquedano

SALAR DE
ATACAMA

2 Camar

Socaire

Peine

Antofagasta

Cerro Paranal

ARGENTINA

N

PACIFIC
OCEAN

0   80
kilometres

Taital

Brief history

It seems almost inconceivable that such a hostile land can support life, but for thousands of years El Norte Grande has been home to indigenous peoples who've wrested a living either from the sea or from the fertile oases that nestle in the Andean foothills. The excessive dryness of the climate has left countless relics of these people almost perfectly intact – most remarkably the **Chinchorro mummies** (see box, p.209), buried on the desert coast near Arica some seven thousand years ago. It wasn't until the nineteenth century that Chile's more recent inhabitants – along with British and German businesses – turned their attention to the Atacama, when it became apparent that the desert was rich in **nitrates** that could be exported at great commercial value. So lucrative was this burgeoning industry that Chile was prepared to go to war over it, for most of the region at that time in fact belonged to Bolivia and Peru. The **War of the Pacific**, waged against Bolivia and Peru between 1878 and 1883, acquired for Chile the desired prize, and the desert pampas went on to yield enormous revenues for the next three decades.

With the German invention of synthetic nitrates at the end of World War I, Chile's industry entered a rapid decline, but a financial crisis was averted when new mining techniques enabled low-grade **copper**, of which there are huge quantities in the region, to be profitably extracted. Today, this mineral continues to play the most important role in the country's economy, making Chile the world's leading copper supplier.

GETTING AROUND   **EL NORTE GRANDE**

Many of the region's attractions can be reached by public transport, though in order to explore the region in depth you'll need to book some tours or, better still, rent a 4WD vehicle. Whatever your mode of transport, don't underestimate the distances involved in getting to most points of interest, particularly in the altiplano. It makes sense to isolate a few chosen highlights rather than try to see everything, which would be interminably time-consuming.

Antofagasta

A Bolivian town until 1879, when it was annexed by Chile in the War of the Pacific, Antofagasta is one of Chile's largest and most rapidly growing cities. Many tourists bypass this decidedly lacklustre desert city altogether, and with good reason. Overpriced and unattractive, the regional capital holds little of cultural or aesthetic interest, but is a major transport hub and one of Chile's most prosperous cities, serving as an export centre for the region's great mines, most notably Chuquicamata (see p.178). Sitting on a flat shelf between the ocean and the hills, Antofagasta has a compact downtown core, made up of dingy, traffic-choked streets that sport a few handsome but run-down old public buildings, and a modern stretch along the coastal avenue. The area around Latorre and Condell, between Bolivar and Riquelme streets, is best avoided after 9.30pm – Antofagasta has a prostitution problem.

A couple of blocks northeast of the central square, along Bolívar, you'll find the magnificently restored nineteenth-century **offices and railway terminus** of the former Antofagasta and Bolivia Railway Company, complete with polished wooden verandas and dark-green stucco walls (albeit with no public access). Further north still, and an easy stop-off if you're heading out to the airport, is **La Portada**, an iconic natural arch of rock looming out of the sea.

South of the city centre the busy coastal avenue runs past a couple of tiny, coarse-sand **beaches**, first at the Balneario Municipal, then, much further south, at the Playa Huascar, the latter only suitable for sunbathing – take *micro* #103 from Washington, near the square. In this direction lies one of the city's most curious sights, the **Ruinas de Huanchaca**, vestiges of a disused silver refinery, as well as the **Museo Desierto de Atacama**, which shares the same site.

Plaza Colón

In Antofagasta's centre sprawls the large, green **Plaza Colón**, dominated by a tall clock tower whose face is supposedly a replica of London's Big Ben – one of many tangible signs of the role played by the British in Antofagasta's commercial development. The city's administrative and public buildings, including the Neo-Gothic Iglesia Catedral, built between 1906 and 1917, surround the square.

Museo Regional

Bolívar 188 • Tues–Fri 9am–5pm, Sat & Sun 11am–2pm • Free • ☏ 55 222 7016, ⓦ museodeantofagasta.cl

The 1866 customs house (or Ex-aduana as it is now called) is the oldest building in the city, and within it sits the Museo Regional. The museum houses an impressive mineral display downstairs and, upstairs, a collection of clothes, furniture and toys.

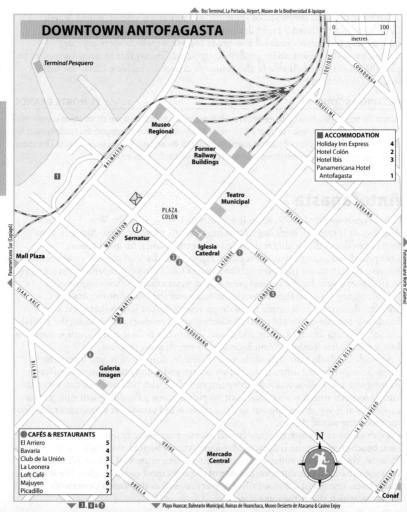

DOWNTOWN ANTOFAGASTA

Bus Terminal, La Portada, Airport, Museo de la Biodiversidad & Iquique

0 — 100
metres

Terminal Pesquero

Museo Regional

Former Railway Buildings

ACCOMMODATION
Holiday Inn Express	4
Hotel Colón	2
Hotel Ibis	3
Panamericana Hotel Antofagasta	1

Teatro Municipal

PLAZA COLÓN

Sernatur

Iglesia Catedral

Mall Plaza

Galeria Imagen

Mercado Central

N

CAFÉS & RESTAURANTS
El Arriero	5
Bavaria	4
Club de la Unión	3
La Leonera	1
Loft Café	2
Majuyen	6
Picadillo	7

Panamericana Sur (Copiapó)

Panamericana Norte (Calama)

Playa Huascar, Balneario Municipal, Ruinas de Huanchaca, Museo Desierto de Atacama & Casino Enjoy

Conaf

Ruinas de Huanchaca and the Museo Desierto de Atacama

Av Angamos 01606 • **Ruinas de Huanchaca** No fixed opening hours • Free **Museo Desierto de Atacama** Tues–Sun 10am–1pm & 2.30–7pm • CH$2000 • ☎ 55 241 7862, ⍵ ruinasdehuanchaca.cl • Bus #303 from Plaza Colón; several southbound micros also make the journey

These remains of an old Bolivian silver refinery sit on a hilltop a short distance inland, 3km south of the centre by the Universidad del Norte, yet still within the city. The **Ruinas de Huanchaca** were built to process the silver brought down from the Potosí mine (at that time the most important silver mine in South America), before being shipped out of Antofagasta. Looking at the square and circular walls of the complex from below, you'd be forgiven for thinking they were ruins of a pre-Columbian fortress.

On the same site is the impressive **Museo Desierto de Atacama**. A must for aspiring geographers and geologists, this modern museum is divided into several parts. These include a "rock garden", exhibiting rocks and minerals indigenous to northern Chile; rooms named "the creation of space" dedicated to explaining how the desert and altiplano were formed; an exhibition on "the miner", looking at the history of mining in this part of Chile; and a room financed by the European Southern Observatory exploring astrology in the Atacama desert. There's also a space dedicated to temporary exhibitions. Audio tours (included in the entry fee) are available in Spanish and English.

ARRIVAL AND GETTING AROUND   ANTOFAGASTA

By plane Aeropuerto Cerro Moreno is 25km north of the city, right on the Tropic of Capricorn. Regular *colectivos* and infrequent *micros* head to the centre or you can take a minibus directly to your accommodation (they await every arrival).

Airlines LAN, Prat 445 (☎ 55 226 5151); Sky Airlines, Washington 2548 (☎ 55 245 9090).

Destinations Iquique (4–6 daily; 55min); La Serena (2 daily; 1hr 25min); Santiago (9–20 daily; 1hr 50min–3hr).

By bus The main Terminal Carlos Oviedo Cavada is located on Pedro A. Cerda 5750, about a 15min drive from the centre – a cab will set you back approximately CH$6000.

A much cheaper option is to take *colectivo* (shared taxi) #111 – also from right outside the terminal – which will drop you off in the centre.

Destinations Arica (every 1–3hr; 10hr); Calama (every 1–2hr; 3hr); Caldera (hourly; 6hr); Chañaral (16 daily; 5hr); Chuquicamata (5 daily; 3hr); Copiapó (15 daily; 7hr); La Serena (20 daily; 12hr); Mejillones (every 30min; 40min); Santiago (hourly; 20hr).

Car rental Avis, Baquedano 364 (☎ 55 256 3140, ⍵ avis .cl); Budget, Aeropuerto (☎ 55 256 3143, ⍵ budget.cl); Econorent, Pedro Aguirre Cerda 6100 (☎ 55 259 4177, ⍵ econorent.cl).

INFORMATION AND TOURS

Sernatur Prat 384 (Mon–Thurs 8.30am–5.30pm, Fri 8.30am–4.30pm; ☎ 55 245 1820, ✉ infoantofagasta @sernatur.cl). For tourist information on the city of Antofagasta, head to the ground floor of the Intendencia at the corner of the central plaza.

Conaf Av Argentina 2510 (Mon–Fri 9am–1pm & 2.30–5.30pm; ☎ 55 238 3320). This is the place to come for

details on the protected areas around San Pedro de Atacama, which lies within this region.

Travel agencies You'll find many travel agencies downtown, including Desertica Expediciones (Antonio Poupin 978; ☎ 09 9792 6791, ⍵ deserticaexpediciones .com), which offers a range of tours in the surrounding region.

ACCOMMODATION

You'll find an abundance of **accommodation** in Antofagasta, but the range tends to jump from cheap and basic to expensive (and not necessarily good quality), with very few mid-priced options in between. Most places are in the downtown core, with the mostly expensive hotels, catering primarily to business travellers, on the coastal avenue.

Holiday Inn Express Av Grecia 1490, ☎ 800 808080 or ☎ 55 222 8888, ⍵ hilatam.com/cl/. Modern, super-clean US chain hotel around 2km southwest of the main plaza (plenty of *micros* run into the centre), with pool and parking – a good place to pamper yourself if the desert is getting to you. CH$81,000

Hotel Colón San Martín 2434 ☎ 55 226 1851,

✉ colonantofagasta@gmail.com. Decent option with clean, fairly comfortable and light en-suite rooms with TVs. Those facing the road can be rather noisy though. There's a restaurant next door owned by the same people, serving good-value home-cooked meals. CH$35,000

Hotel Ibis Av Jose Miguel Carrera 1627 ☎ 55 245 8200, ⍵ ibis.com. This mid-range hotel around 1.5km southwest of the main plaza (the route is served by plenty of *micros*), is a reassuring choice: staff are professional, the en suites are comfortable and well equipped (some even have sea views), there's a good restaurant, and the rates represent good value. CH$34,000

Panamericana Hotel Antofagasta Balmaceda 2575 ☎55 222 8811, ⓦpanamericanahoteles.cl /antofagasta.html. Large, venerable chain hotel overlooking the ocean, with well-furnished but overpriced rooms. The onsite restaurant's outdoor terrace, however, is one of the most pleasant lunch spots in the city. CH$67,000

EATING

Antofagasta's **restaurants** tend to be busy and lively, with a couple of classy establishments standing out among the grill houses and pizzerias. On the coast just west of the town centre is the **Mall Plaza**, Balmaceda 2355, home to several newer eating establishments. Among these are the usual American fast-food outlets, but also a few more sophisticated options. At the corner of Ossa and Maipú, the huge, pink-and-cream Mercado Central sells fresh food and *artesanía*.

★ **El Arriero** Condell 2644 ☎55 226 4371, ⓦarrieroafta .cl. Two brothers play old jazz tunes on the piano every night at this inviting spot. Try the excellent *parrilladas* (CH$10,500 for one person, CH$17,400 for two) or go for the good-value lunch menu (CH$4500). Mon–Sat 11.30am–4pm & 7.30pm–midnight, Sun 11.30am–4pm.

Bavaria Latorre 2624 ☎55 228 3821, ⓦwww.bavaria .cl. The same pine decor, the same grilled meat, the same indifferent service you find in every other branch of the *Bavaria* chain in the country. At least you know what you're getting – and the German-style food's not bad, after all, nor is it particularly expensive (a hearty *parrillada* for two costs CH$15,500). Daily noon–midnight.

Club de la Unión Prat 474, ☎55 226 8371. This attractive restaurant, housed in a 1904 building, offers old school charm, efficient service and international fare. The ground floor is for members only, while the first floor is open to the public. There's a daily lunch menu (CH$5900), as well as à la carte options (mains CH$4500–8000). Mon–Sat 1–4pm & 8–11pm, Sun 1–4pm.

La Leonera Latorre 2670 ☎55 225 1436. Perhaps the best cheap eat in town, no-frills *La Leonera* has been a locals' favourite for years, offering brisk service and a good-value lunch menu (CH$3300). Expect the likes of fried fish, *empanadas* and stews. Mon–Sat 9am–1am.

Loft Café Prat 470 ☎09 8838 6514. Just a few steps from Plaza Colón, *Loft Cafe* serves up salads, baguettes and coffee (CH$1200–2500) to businessmen and students alike. Multicoloured lamps and modern paintings make this café stand out among the other dreary central options. Mon–Sat 8.30am–9.30pm.

Majuyen San Martín 2326 ☎55 282 8318. Set back from the road in the Patio Alcántara, this tiny Japanese-Peruvian joint has a handful of tables and a delivery service. Tasty sushi, sashimi and ceviche (CH$1800–6500) are the order of the day here. Daily 1–4pm & 7–11pm.

★ **Picadillo** Av Grecia 1000 ☎55 224 7503. Popular restaurant offering the likes of beef carpaccio marinated in ginger for starters and delicious, unusual sushi, plus inventive desserts (most mains CH$6000–10,000); both music and service are faultless. Reservations recommended at weekends. Mon–Fri 12.30–3.30pm & 7.30pm–1am, Sat 8pm–2am.

NIGHTLIFE

The nightlife scene, thanks mainly to the number of university students around town, is surprisingly vibrant, with a few decent **bars** to choose from outside the city centre and a choice of **dance spots** all located down at Playa Huáscar, way south of town (take a taxi).

DIRECTORY

Money and exchange There are several ATMs on the central square and the main commercial streets, including Prat, Washington and San Martín. You can change the major foreign currencies at Ancla, Baquedano 524.

Post office On the central square, at Washington 2613 (Mon–Fri 9am–6pm, Sat 10am–1pm).

Around Antofagasta

If you have time to kill or if deserted nitrate-era ghost towns and different types of rock formations are your thing, you may want to dedicate a day or afternoon to exploring the area surrounding the city of Antofagasta. Highlights include the cliff formations of La Portada (a natural arch, now a symbol of the region), a couple of observatories and the Chug Chug geolyphs.

La Portada

16km north of Antofagasta along the coast road • **La Portada** Open access • Free **Museo de la Bioversidad** Tues–Sun 10am–6pm • Free • *Micro* #15 from the Terminal Pesquero; if you're driving, follow the coast road north and take the turn-off to Juan López, from where La Portada is well signed

A huge eroded arch looming out of the ocean, **La Portada** was declared a national monument in 1990, and has become something of a regional symbol, with its picture gracing postcards and wall calendars all over Chile. Makeshift signs quite rightly warn you not to approach the crumbling cliffs or descend the rickety steps to the unsafe beach, while the nearby bar-restaurant and shops are often closed, even in high season, lending the place a sadly abandoned air. Upkeep of La Portada has improved, however, since the opening of the **Museo de la Biodiversidad** located on the site and dedicated to the flora and fauna of northern Chile's coastal region.

The Cerro Paranal Observatory

Cerro Paranal • Tours Jan–Nov last two weekends of the month, Sat & Sun 2pm; you'll need to book months in advance • Free • ☎ 55 243 5000, ⓦ eso.org/paranal • Head south from Antofagasta on the Panamericana (Ruta 5); the unpaved turn-off 24km south of the Mina Escondida crossroads leads due south over a mountain pass to the observatory; If you do not have your own transport, you can join an organized tour from Antofagasta with Desertica Expediciones (see p.173)

A little under two hours south of Antofagasta, perched on **Cerro Paranal** at 2644m above sea level, is the **CERRO PARANAL OBSERVATORY,** run by the ESO. While you have to be a recognized researcher to stand any chance of looking through its **Very Large Telescope** (VLT), one of the world's strongest, on certain weekends you can visit the dazzling site, set among suitably lunar, and even Mars-like, landscapes of reddish rock. In fact, NASA tested the Mars Pathfinder rover in the nearby Atacama Desert (a more glamorous claim to fame is that parts of the James Bond movie *Quantum of Solace* were filmed here).

The VLT – strictly speaking a set of four 8.2m telescopes, each weighing 430 tonnes, whose combined might enables observers to see objects as small as humans on the Moon – has been fully operational since 2001. It's housed in a futuristic-looking set of four trapezoidal cylinders dramatically located on the barren Cerro Paranal, which averages 330 clear nights a year. A luxurious 120-room residence (for scientists only), complete with a cafeteria and an indoor garden (both open to the public), stands nearby. Remember to take warm clothing, as it is very cold inside the observatory.

The nitrate pampa

Northeast of Antofagasta, the vast *pampa salitrera*, or **NITRATE PAMPA**, pans across the desert towards the cordillera – it's not the prettiest landscape in the world, a mass of

---

ALMA OBSERVATORY

The **Atacama Large Millimeter Array** (ALMA; ⓦ almaobservatory.org), a joint North American, East Asian, European and Chilean venture, started scientific observations in 2011 and is the largest, most powerful astronomical project in existence. Positioned at a staggering 5000m above sea level at a site east of San Pedro de Atacama called the Chajnantor plateau, this is the highest astronomical observatory of its kind on the planet. The ALMA uses state of the art technology, initially comprising 66 giant high-precision antennae working together at millimetre and submillimetre wavelengths. These can be moved up to 16km across the desert, but act as a single giant telescope. ALMA's slogan – "in search of our cosmic origins" – gives an exciting sense of what this project is really about.

For the first time in history, astronomers will be able to study new stars being born, watch planetary systems and galaxies with unprecedented clarity, and, with time, be able to answer big questions about the origins of life itself.

scruffy plains that look as though they have been ploughed, fertilized and then left for fallow. Between 1890 and 1925 there were over eighty *oficinas* here, extracting the nitrate ore and sending it down to the ports by railroad. Some of them are still standing, abandoned and in ruins, including Chacabuco, crumbling in the desert heat.

Two highways cross the pampa: the Panamericana, heading due north to Iquique, and Ruta 25, branching off northeast to the mining city of Calama. The former skirts **María Elena**, home to the last remaining nitrate *oficina* (or plant), and a place that can be reached on public transport. Although you can find basic accommodation if you look hard enough (there are two hotels), you may as well forge on if you can; it's a desperately soulless place to spend the night.

The Chug Chug geoglyphs

The Panamericana is crossed by a lateral road, Ruta 24, 107km north of the Carmen Alto junction. This is connected to Tocopilla, 60km west, and Chuquicamata, 66km east. Just short of 50km along the road for Chuquicamata, a sign points north to the **CHUG CHUG GEOGLYPHS**, reached by a 13km dirt road that's just about passable in a car. These consist of some three hundred images spread over several hills, many of them clearly visible from below, including circles, zoomorphic figures, human faces and geometric designs. It's an impressive site, and certainly deserves a visit if you're driving in the area.

Calama and around

Sitting on the banks of the Río Loa, at an altitude of 2250m, **CALAMA** is an ugly, bland town, whose chief role is as a service centre and residential base for

Chuquicamata, the massive copper mine 16km north (see p.178). It's best avoided if possible, but many visitors end up spending a night here on their way to or from San Pedro de Atacama, the famous oasis village and tourist centre 100km east.

Brief history

Calama began life as a *tambo*, or resting place, at the intersection of two Inca roads – one running down the Andes, the other connecting the altiplano with the Pacific – and both Diego de Almagro and Pedro de Valdivia visited on their journeys into Chile. It was never heavily populated by pre-Hispanic peoples, who preferred nearby Chiu Chiu, with its less saline water supply. The town took on a new prominence, however, as an important stop on the Oruro–Antofagasta railway in the late nineteenth century, and its future was sealed with the creation of the Chuquicamata copper mine in 1911. Today its busy streets are built around a surprisingly small and laid-back central core.

Parque El Loa

Av O'Higgins s/n • **Park** Daily 10am–8pm; **museum** daily 10am–noon & 3–6.30pm • Free

About 2km from the centre of town is the Parque El Loa, a good spot for a picnic. One of the park's star attractions, the archeological museum, which holds displays on pre-Columbian history, reopened in 2013 after being damaged during the 2007 earthquake. The other famous landmark, a mini-reconstruction of the famous Chiu Chiu church, is still there.

ARRIVAL AND INFORMATION

By plane Aeropuerto El Loa is 5km south of the centre – the only way into town from here is by taxi (around CH$6000).
Destinations Copiapo (1–2 daily; 1hr 10min–4hr); Santiago (4–12 daily; 2hr).
By bus Arriving by bus you'll be dropped at your bus company's office, generally near the city centre; there's no single terminal, and the Tur Bus terminal is inconveniently situated more than 1km north of town. Hail down *colectivo* (shared taxi) #5 or #11 right outside the latter to get to the centre, or take a taxi (around CH$3500).

CALAMA AND AROUND

Destinations Antofagasta (every 1–2hr; 3hr); Arica (5–6 daily; 10hr); Chañaral (10 daily; 8hr); Chuquicamata (every 30min; 30min); Copiapó (15 daily; 10hr); Iquique (3–4 daily; 6–7hr); La Serena (11 daily; 12hr 30min–15hr); San Pedro de Atacama (every 2–3hr; 1hr 30min); Santiago (hourly; 22hr 30min).
Tourist office Latorre 1689, on the corner of Vicuña Mackenna (Mon–Fri 8am–1pm & 2–6pm; ☎55 253 1707). Offers maps and other basic information, but not much else.

ACCOMMODATION

Calama has a wide range of **accommodation**, but many places are overpriced owing to the mining clientele, and many can get fully booked during the San Pedro tourist seasons. Beware of overbooking and always call or send an email to confirm if possible.

Hostal Nativo Sotomayor 2215 ☎55 231 0377, ⓦ nativo.cl. This centrally located, family-run hotel offers friendly service and plain, immaculately clean rooms with TV; ones with private bathrooms cost CH$10,000 more. They also offer inexpensive car rental. CH$30,000
Hostal Toño Vivar 1970 ☎55 234 1185, ⓔ david6013 @live.com. Located a short walk from Plaza 23 de Mayo, this *residencial* is a decent, pretty quiet budget choice which has been going for years, offering very simple rooms, some with private bathrooms. CH$18,000
Hotel El Mirador Sotomayor 2064 ☎55 234 0329,

ⓦ hotelmirador.cl. A smart, small hotel with spacious rooms – including one with a Victorian cast-iron bath – and attractive furnishings, set in a colonial-style house that dates from the nineteenth century. CH$55,000
Park Hotel Camino al Aeropuerto 1392 ☎55 271 5800, ⓦ www.parkplaza.cl. Popular with business travellers, the *Park Hotel* boasts elegant decor, a good restaurant (try the all-you-can-eat Sunday brunch; CH$19,000) and an attractive swimming pool – a godsend in the sweltering summer months. CH$60,000

EATING

Bavaria Sotomayor 2093 ☎55 234 1496, ⓦ www .bavaria.cl. *Bavaria*, on the plaza, is part of a well-known nationwide chain offering decent if very predictable mid-price meat dishes (CH$4500–11,000) and sandwiches from its downstairs café and upstairs restaurant. Café daily 8am–midnight; restaurant daily noon–4.30pm & 7.30pm–midnight.
JP Felix Hoyos 2127 ☎55 231 2559. Another good choice is the friendly and unpretentious *JP* – just a short walk from the plaza – that serves tasty, if

rather pricey, fish and seafood dishes (CH$5000–12,000) such as *sopa de mariscos* and *pescado frito*. Tues–Sat noon–3.30pm & 8–11.30pm, Sun noon–3.30pm.
Paladar Vivar 1797 ☎55 292 6554. The swish *Paladar* has an imaginative menu compared with other Calama eating options (mains CH$5000–15,000), comprising sharing platters and international cuisine with a French twist, plus a great Chilean wine list. Mon–Sat 12.30pm–1.30am.

DIRECTORY

Car rental Avis, Aeropuerto (☎55 279 3968, ⓦ avis.cl); and Hertz, Aeropuerto (☎55 231 5762, ⓦ hertz.cl).

Money and exchange You'll find plenty of ATMs on Sotomayor, as well as a *cambio* around the corner at Vivar 1818.

Chuquicamata

Official guided tours (by minibus, departing Mon–Fri 1.30pm; tours also leave at 3.30pm Jan & Feb; 1hr 30min) must be booked in advance from Codelco's Calama office on Av. Granadero and Av. Central (☎ 55 232 2122, ⓦ codelco.cl), or through Calama's tourist information office (see p.177) • Free, but donations to a children's charity supported by the mine are welcomed

One of the world's largest open-pit copper mines, **CHUQUICAMATA** (16km north of Calama) produces six hundred thousand tonnes per year – outstripped only by Mina Escondida, 200km southeast of Antofagasta, whose capacity exceeds eight hundred thousand tonnes. Carved out of the ground like a giant, sunken amphitheatre, the massive mine dwarfs everything within it, making the huge trucks carrying the ore up from the crater floor – whose wheels alone are an incredible 4m high – look like tiny, crawling ants. Its size is the result of some ninety years of excavation, and its reserves are predicted to last at least until the middle of the twenty-first century.

Along with all of Chile's large-scale copper mines, or *"grandes minerías"* as they're called, Chuquicamata belongs to Codelco, the government-owned copper corporation. Codelco also used to maintain an adjacent company town, complete with its own school, hospital, cinema and football stadium, but the nine thousand workers and their families who lived there have now been moved to Calama, making way for further excavation.

The **tours** (see above) take place almost entirely on a bus, though you're allowed to get out at the viewpoint looking down to the pit – wear sensible shoes and clothing that covers most of your body. The rest of the tour takes you round the machinery yards and buildings of the plant, which you see from the outside only.

San Pedro de Atacama

The little oasis village of **SAN PEDRO DE ATACAMA** (100km southeast of Calama), with its narrow dirt streets and attractive adobe houses, has transformed itself, since the 1990s, into *the* tourism centre of Chile. Sitting at an altitude of 2400m between the desert and the altiplano, or *puna* (the high basin connecting the two branches of the cordillera), this has been an important settlement since pre-Hispanic times, originally as a major stop on the trading route connecting the llama herders of these highlands with the fishing communities of the Pacific. Later, during the nitrate era, it was the main rest stop on the cattle trail from Salta in Argentina to the nitrate *oficinas*, where the cattle were driven to supply the workers with fresh meat.

The large numbers of Chilean tourists and hordes of gringos here can come as quite a shock if you have just arrived from more remote parts of northern Chile, and San Pedro has recently begun to lose some of its charm. Its main street is **Caracoles**, which is where you'll find the biggest concentration of accommodation, eating places and services. Early in the new millennium, Calle Antofagasta was renamed Gustavo Le Paige and all houses in the village were given a number, but, with some establishments, you might find that the changes have still not sunk in. Fortunately, as San Pedro is a very small place, you should always be able to find your destination without difficulty. The village celebrates its saint's day on June 29 with exuberant dancing and feasting.

There's a swimming pool (permanently open) at Pozo Tres, a 3km walk east of the archeological museum along the Paso de Jama. In the winter of 2013, San Pedro witnessed a rare and spectacular **snowfall** – the heaviest in the region in three decades.

SAN PEDRO DE ATACAMA

ACCOMMODATION
Alto Atacama	2
Awasi	11
Camping Los Perales	10
Casa de Don Tomás	12
Doña Matilde Hostal	5
Hostal Mama Tierra	3
Hostal Sonchek	6
Hostal Takha-Takha	8
Hotel Altiplánico	1
Hotel Cumbres San Pedro de Atacama	13
Hotel Kimal	9
Hotel Terrantai	7
Vilacoyo Residencial	4

BARS
Chela Cabur	5
Grado 6	2

CAFÉS
Babalu	4/6
Peregrino	1
Salon de Té O2	12

RESTAURANTS
Adobe	9
Blanco	8
La Casona	7
Las Delicias de Carmen	10
Pizzeria El Charrúa	3
Tierra Todo Natural	11

0   100
metres

Iglesia de San Pedro

The focus of San Pedro is the little **plaza** at its centre, dotted with pepper trees and wooden benches. On its western side stands the squat white **Iglesia de San Pedro**, one of the largest Andean churches in the region and closed for renovation at the time of research. It's actually San Pedro's second church, built in 1744, just over one hundred years after the original church was erected near the present site of the archeological museum. The bell tower was added towards the end of the nineteenth century, and the thick adobe walls surrounding the church rebuilt in 1978.

The interior

Inside, religious icons look down from the brightly painted altar, among them a stern-looking Saint Peter, the village's patron saint. Overhead, the sloping roof is made of rough-hewn planks of cactus wood and gnarled rafters of reddish algarrobo timber, bound together with leather straps.

Casa Incaica

Opposite the Iglesia de San Pedro, on the other side of the square at Toconao 421b, sits San Pedro's oldest building, the lopsided **Casa Incaica**, now a souvenir store. The house dates from the earliest days of the colony (a plaque outside claims it is the former home of Spanish conquistador Pedro de Valdivia), though its roof seems to be in imminent danger of collapse. A narrow alley full of **artesanía** stalls, where you can buy alpaca knitwear and other souvenirs, leads off the northern side of the square.

Museo Arqueológico Gustavo Le Paige

Gustavo Le Paige 380 • Mon–Fri 9am–6pm, Sat & Sun 10am–6pm; guided tours in various languages nine times daily Tues–Sun; with 24hr notice, you can organize a private tour on Mon • CH$2500; tours CH$1800 extra

Don't miss the excellent **Museo Arqueológico Gustavo Le Paige**, just off the northeast corner of the square. Named after the Belgian missionary-cum-archeologist who founded it in 1957, the museum houses more than 380,000 artefacts gathered from the region around San Pedro, of which the best examples are displayed in eight "naves" arranged around a central hall. Charting the development, step by step, of local pre-Columbian peoples, the displays range from Neolithic tools to sophisticated ceramics, taking in delicately carved wooden tablets and tubes used for inhaling hallucinogenic substances, and a number of gold cups with engraved faces used by village elders during religious ceremonies.

ARRIVAL AND INFORMATION   SAN PEDRO DE ATACAMA

By bus Several bus companies have regular services from Calama to San Pedro; they all arrive at, and depart from, the new bus terminal on Tumiza, a 10min walk southeast from the plaza. You have to change at Calama (often with a delay) for major destinations, including Iquique, Arica and Santiago.

Destinations Antofagasta (3 daily; 5hr 30min–6hr), Arica (1–2 daily; 14hr), Calama (every 2–3hr; 1hr 30min), Salta and Jujuy (Argentina; 4–8 weekly; 14–16hr).

Tourist office Toconao, corner of Gustavo Le Paige (Mon, Tues, Thurs & Fri 9.15am–8.15pm, Wed 9.15am–6pm, Sat & Sun 10am–8.15pm; ☎ 55 285 1420, ✉ sanpedrode atacama@gmail.com, ✆ sernatur.cl). The helpful tourist office on the main plaza hands out regional maps and lists of tour companies. Check ✆ sanpedroatacama.com for more information and links.

GETTING AROUND

By bike There are many places that rent bikes in San Pedro, notably along Caracoles: most charge around CH$4000 per half-day or CH$6000 per day; try to get an emergency bike-repair kit too.

By taxi The taxi situation in San Pedro is complicated – you must call ahead so ask your hotel to arrange this for you.

Car rental Europcar, Calama 479 (☎ 09 7388 9848, ✆ europcar.cl).

ACCOMMODATION

There are loads of places offering **rooms** in San Pedro, including a number of comfortable *residenciales* plus some classy places for those on a far more generous budget; prices tend to be higher across the range than elsewhere in the region. Recently, more high-end places have sprung up, often with a now hackneyed pseudo-native architectural style – lots of adobe, stone walls and thatched roofs – but mercifully, there have been no high-rises (it's against the law to construct anything higher than two storeys). A wonderful alternative for those on a smaller budget is provided by a scheme of *albergues turísticos*, rural guesthouses in the nearby villages of Peine and Socaire. For details and bookings contact the tourist office. You'll also find a few **campsites** within easy reach of the village centre; the best is listed below. If you're travelling alone and at a busy time, some *residenciales* may ask you to share with another traveller.

HOTELS

Alto Atacama Camino Pukará s/n, Suchor, Ayllú de Quitor, 3.5km northwest of San Pedro 4 ☎ 2 2912 3910, ✆ altoatacama.com. This tranquil top-end hotel has super-stylish en suites (all with private terraces), plus no fewer than six pools, well-equipped spa, and highly rated restaurant. Rates include full board, daily excursions and transfers. US$1200

★**Awasi** Tocopilla 4 ☎ 55 285 1460, ✆ awasi.cl. This special place is exclusive, without being stuffy. Eight rooms each come with a guide and vehicle for guests to tailor the shape of their stay. The staff are young and friendly, the food outstanding and comfort paramount. Relax and be spoiled. Rates are for two nights and include full-board, activities and transfers. US$3300

Casa de Don Tomás Tocopilla s/n ☎ 55 285 1055, ✆ dontomas.cl. Located away from the buzz of central San Pedro, 300m south of the crossroads with Caracoles, this rustic, well-established hotel has spacious rooms, a pool, good breakfasts, a friendly welcome, and subsequent to all of the above, consistently good reviews. US$150

Doña Matilde Hostal Domingo Atienza 404 ☎ 55 285 1017, ✆ hostaldonamatilda.cl. Simple but rather uninspiring rooms (with shared or private bathrooms) kept very clean by the friendly owner. There is also a

TOURS FROM SAN PEDRO

San Pedro has a high concentration of **tour operators** offering excursions into the surrounding altiplano, all broadly similar and all at pretty much the same price. This can, of course, be a curse as well as a blessing, for it increases tourist traffic in the region to the point where it can be difficult to visit the awe-inspiring landscape of the *puna* in the kind of silence and isolation in which it really ought to be experienced. Some of the tours are responsibly managed but many are not; the astounding environmental damage of late has finally, if belatedly, forced local communities (but not the national authorities) to take action; they now charge entrance fees to each site and do their best to clean up after visits. The **tourist office** (see p.180) keeps volumes of complaints registered by tourists (usually concerning reliability of vehicles or lack of professionalism) and they are worth consulting to find out which operators to avoid.

Tours usually take place in minibuses, though smaller groups may travel in jeeps. Competition keeps prices relatively low – you can expect to pay from around CH\$10,000 to visit the Valle de la Luna, CH\$22,000 for a tour to the Tatio geysers, and around CH\$30,000 for a full-day tour of the local lakes and oases (excluding entrance fees); three- to four-day tours (around US\$185–220) that finish in Bolivia and take in the spectacular Salar de Uyuni are also popular. Don't necessarily choose the cheapest tour, as some companies cram passengers in and offer below-par services, so it is often worth paying a bit more. Talk to other travellers and visit several companies – or their websites, where available – to get a feel for how they operate and to work out which one you prefer. If you don't speak Spanish, check that they can offer guides who speak your language (French, German and English are the most common languages on offer).

TOUR OPERATORS

★**Cosmo Andino** Caracoles s/n ☎ 55 285 1069, ⓦ cosmoandino.cl. Well-established and respected company offering interesting variations on the most popular tours, as well as off-the-beaten track expeditions. Choose to explore the countryside on foot, or go on a 4x4 tour across the mountains. Both day and overnight tours are highly recommended.

Rancho Cactus Tocanao 568 ☎ 55 285 1506, ⓦ rancho-cactus.cl. For an alternative San Pedro experience, try the horse treks (from CH\$15,000) run by Rancho Cactus. Treks last from a few hours to three days and are led by guides passionate about both the region and the horses. English and French spoken.

★**Space Obs** Caracoles 166 ☎ 55 256 6278, ⓦ spaceobs.com. Excellent, highly memorable tours (in English, French, Spanish and German; CH\$18,000/2hr 30min) of Northern Chile's night sky led by enthusiastic and personable astronomers. Book in advance.

Vulcano Expediciones Caracoles 317 ☎ 55 285 1023, ⓦ vulcanochile.com. This is the best operator for mountain and volcano ascents, trekking, sandboarding (CH\$15,000) and bike tours. They also offer fun horseriding tours around San Pedro and even adventurous four-day treks into Bolivia.

restaurant serving a good-value *menú del día*. CH\$30,000

Hostal Sonchek Gustavo Le Paige 198 ☎ 55 285 1112, ⓦ hostalsonchek.cl. Great-value hotel run by a personable and eco-conscious Slovenian–Chilean couple (recycling system and solar panel in place) and their cats. Rooms are cosy (those with private bathrooms are particularly attractive) and there's a small communal kitchen and garden. CH\$20,000

Hostal Takha-Takha Caracoles 101a ☎ 55 285 1038, ⓦ takhatakha.cl. Small but tidy and quiet rooms giving onto a pleasant garden. There's a lovely new (but small) pool and you can also camp here. Also some good-value, though basic singles. Doubles CH\$53,000, camping/person CH\$10,000

Hotel Altiplánico Domingo Atienza 282 ☎ 55 285 1212, ⓦ altiplanico.cl. Located in a calm spot 250m from the centre, on the way to the Pukará de Quitor, this gorgeous hotel complex is built in typical San Pedro adobe style, with fantastic views, tasteful decor, comfortable en-suite rooms, a swimming pool, a café-bar and bicycle rental. US\$240

★**Hotel Cumbres San Pedro de Atacama** Av las Chilcas s/n, ☎ 55 285 2136, ⓦ cumbressanpedro .com. Located outside the village, and formerly known as *Hotel Kunza*, this mega-stylish boutique hotel is decorated in gorgeous Atacama chic. Panoramic views of the snowcapped Andes from each private adobe-style hut are a highlight, as is the spa and wonderful restaurant. The staff are exceptionally professional and friendly, and the hotel organizes regional excursions. US\$269

Hotel Kimal Domingo Atienza ☎ 55 285 1030,

W kimal.cl. Spacious, light and very attractive rooms, combining contemporary, spartan architecture with plants and warm rugs. A better deal is to be had in the new section of the hotel directly opposite, called *Poblado Kimal*, where you can stay in lovely private *cabañas* for slightly less. Both sections have pools. *Hotel Kimal* US$210, *Poblado Kimal* US$182

Hotel Terrantai Tocopilla 411 ☏ 55 285 1045, W terrantai.com. Modern, stylish but slightly snobbish B&B with bare stone walls and minimalist wooden furniture, conveniently located near the plaza. There's a little orchard out back and a small pool with sun-loungers. US$240

HOSTELS

Hostal Mama Tierra Pachamama 615 ☏ 55 285 1418, W hostalmamatierra.cl. Popular with backpackers and a 10min walk from the centre, this tidy hostel offers dorms, singles and doubles with private or shared bathrooms. Extras include laundry service, and the congenial hostess can help organize volcano climbs in the area. Dorms CH$16,000, doubles CH$42,000

Vilacoyo Residencial Tocopilla 387 ☏ 55 285 1006, e vilacoyo@sanpedroatacama.com. Very friendly, homely hostel with private and shared rooms set around a relaxing hammock-strewn courtyard. The kitchen and shared bathrooms are spotless. Twelve hours of hot water per day. Dorms CH$8000, doubles CH$16,000

CAMPSITE

Camping Los Perales Tocopilla 481 ☏ 55 285 1114. The best campsite in San Pedro, located a short distance south of the plaza, with lots of trees, hot water, a climbing wall and an outdoor kitchen. Camping/person CH$5000

EATING AND DRINKING

Thanks to the steady flow of young travellers passing through town, San Pedro boasts a lively **restaurant scene**. Just about every restaurant offers a fixed-price evening meal, usually including a vegetarian option; despite fierce competition, though, prices are notably higher than in other parts of the country. For cheaper, filling set meals, try one of the handful of restaurants at the top end of Licancabur or near the bus station. As with the accommodation, you'll see a definite "San Pedro look" among local restaurants, with a predilection for "native-style" adobe walls, wooden tables with benches, faux rock-paintings and other wacky decorations, and trendy staff who, more often than not, are working migrants from cities in the south. While most restaurants double up as **bars**, party animals should note that **nightlife** in San Pedro is very tame: bar-restaurants close at 1–2am and there are no nightclubs to speak of.

CAFÉS

Babalu Caracoles 160 & 419. The two branches of this tiny *heladería* offer home-made ice creams (from CH$1500) that quench the thirst. Daily-changing flavours include pisco sour, chirimoya and lip-smackingly good fruits of the forest. Both branches daily 10am–8pm.

Peregrino Le Paige 348 ☏ 09 8885 8197. Occupying a prime spot overlooking the plaza, this café is a good option for coffees and teas (CH$1300–3000), as well as reasonably-priced (for San Pedro at least) snacks and light meals – think pancakes, quesadillas, omelettes, salads and sandwiches (all around CH$2500–5000). Daily 8am–8pm.

Salon de Té 02 Caracoles 295B. This unpretentious café, right in the centre of town, serves up good-value, hearty breakfasts (from CH$2500), tasty quiches (often available as part of a meal deal) and home-made cakes, as well as the usual range of snacks and hot drinks. Daily 8am–8pm.

RESTAURANTS

Adobe Caracoles 211 ☏ 55 285 1132, W cafeadobe.cl. Bustling outdoor restaurant with a roaring fire lit every night, serving the usual Chilean fare (mains CH$6600–11,000). Try the *carne a lo pobre* (beef with chips, fried egg and fried onion). Uncomfortable benches and perhaps not the best value in town but a warm atmosphere nevertheless. Live music every night from 9pm. Daily 11am–1am.

★ **Blanco** Caracoles s/n ☏ 55 285 1164. Conceived in white minimalist-chic adobe, this stylish joint certainly stands out from the crowd and is arguably the best restaurant in town. The select, sophisticated menu – try the caramelised salmon or the Thai chicken soup (mains CH$7900–9400) – and great beers, wines and cocktails (from CH$2800) will not disappoint. Daily 6pm–12.30am.

La Casona Caracoles 195a ☏ 55 285 1337. Busy, informal restaurant with an elegant dining room (mains CH$6700–9500; *menú del día* CH$8000) inside a large, colonial-style house. The fire-lit bar out back, complete with a mini Virgin Mary shrine, is a great spot for after-dinner drinks (beer CH$2800–3500). Daily 9am–midnight.

Las Delicias de Carmen Caracoles 259B ☏ 09 9089 5673. Popular spot dishing up enormous portions of hearty, home-cooked food (mains CH$6000–10,000), served by the charismatic owner Carmen. Try the freshly baked *empanadas* and sweeter treats such as the lemon meringue pie. Grab a spot on the lovely patio behind the main building if you can. Daily 8am–10.30pm.

Pizzeria El Charrúa Tocopilla 442 ☎ 55 285 1443. The wonderful aroma wafting out of this intimate pizzeria entices hungry punters inside. It may only have four tables but it serves the best thin crust pizza (from CH$4500) in town, plus exciting salads. Note that there's no alcohol on sale – opt for a fresh fruit juice instead. Daily 11am–11pm.

Tierra Todo Natural Caracoles 271 ☎ 55 285 1585. Friendly restaurant specializing in wholesome home-made food (mains CH$5000–11,000; set menu CH$8000), including wholemeal bread, pizzas, *empanadas*, fish,

fantastic salads and pancakes – a good choice for vegetarians. There are also delicious but expensive fruit juices. Daily 8.30am–12.30am.

BARS

Chela Cabur Caracoles 211 ☎ 55 285 1576. The name says it all: *Chela Cabur* translates as "mountain of beer" in Kunza-Chilean. Owned by a Finnish beer aficionado, this laid-back bar (beer CH$2500–3500) – kitted out with wooden benches and music posters on the walls – is extremely popular with the local youth. Mon–Thurs & Sun noon–1am, Fri & Sat noon–2am.

Grado 6 Le Paige 456 ☎ 09 8155 5619. This pocket-sized, low-ceilinged cave-like bar does very good cocktails. An imaginative lunch and dinner set menu for CH$6000 also pulls in the punters. Tues–Sun noon–3pm & 7pm–1.30am.

DIRECTORY

Money and exchange BCI bank on Caracoles and four ATMS dotted around the small centre. Several *casas de cambio*, on Toconao and Caracoles.

Post office Just off the main plaza on Toconao s/n, opposite the archeological museum (Mon–Fri 9am–6pm, Sat 10am–1pm).

4

Around San Pedro

The spectacular landscape around San Pedro includes vast, desolate plains cradling numerous **volcanoes** of the most delicate colours imaginable, and beautiful **lakes** speckled pink with flamingos. You'll also find the largest **salt flat** in Chile, the **Salar de Atacama**, a whole field full of fuming **geysers** at El Tatio, a scattering of fertile **oasis villages**, and several fascinating **pre-Columbian ruins**.

The otherworldliness of this region is reflected in the poetic names of its geographical features – Valle de la Luna (Valley of the Moon), Llano de la Paciencia (Plain of Patience), Garganta del Diablo (Devil's Throat) and Valle de la Muerte (Valley of Death), to mention but a few. You might prefer to explore these marvels by yourself (there's no public transport, so you'd have to rent a 4WD), but several companies in San Pedro trip over themselves to take you on guided tours, often a more convenient option (see p.181). There is a fee to pay at each of the park entrances, though with the exception of the Puritama thermal baths (controversially owned by the luxury *Hotel Explora*), these go straight back to the local community and help maintain the parks.

Pukará de Quitor

3km north of San Pedro • Daily 9am–6pm • CH$3000

Just 3km north of San Pedro (head up Calle Tocopilla then follow the river), the **PUKARÁ DE QUITOR** is a ruined twelfth-century fortress built into a steep hillside on the west bank of the Río San Pedro. It has been partially restored and you can make out the defence wall encircling a group of stone buildings huddled inside. According to Spanish chronicles, this *pukará* was stormed and taken by Francisco de Aguirre and thirty men as part of Pedro de Valdivia's conquest in 1540. Another 4km up the road you'll find the ruins of what used to be an Inca administrative centre at **Catarpe**, but there's little to see in comparison with the ruins of Quitor.

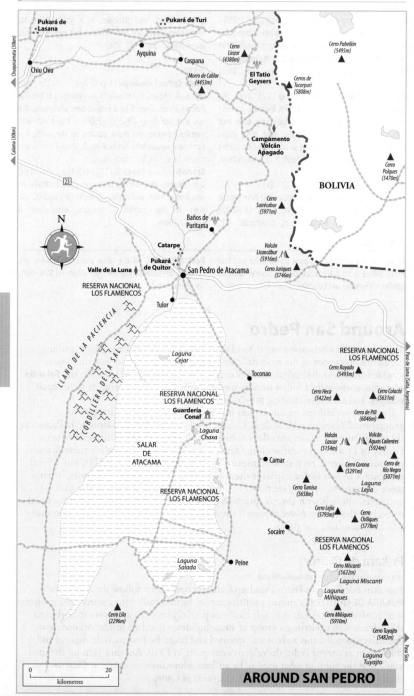

Chuquicamata (30km)

Calama (30km)

Pukará de Turi

Pukará de Lasana

Chiu Chiu

Ayquina

Caspana

Cerro Linzor (4380m)

Cerro Pabellón (5495m)

Morro de Cablor (4453m)

El Tatio Geysers

Cerros de Tocorpuri (5808m)

23

Campamento Volcán Apagado

Cerro Polques (5470m)

BOLIVIA

Cerro Sairécabur (5971m)

N

Baños de Puritama

Volcán Licancábur (5916m)

Catarpe

Pukará de Quitor

San Pedro de Atacama

Cerro Juriques (5746m)

Valle de la Luna

RESERVA NACIONAL LOS FLAMENCOS

Tulor

LLANO DE LA PACIENCIA

CORDILLERA DE LA SAL

Laguna Cejar

Toconao

Paso de Jama (Salta, Argentina)

RESERVA NACIONAL LOS FLAMENCOS

Cerro Rayado (5493m)

Cerro Heca (5422m)

Cerro Colachi (5631m)

Cerro de Pili (6046m)

RESERVA NACIONAL LOS FLAMENCOS

Guardería Conaf

Laguna Chaxa

SALAR DE ATACAMA

Volcán Lascar (5154m)

Volcán Aguas Calientes (5924m)

Cerro Corona (5291m)

Cerro de Río Negro (5071m)

Camar

Cerro Tumisa (5658m)

Laguna Lejía

RESERVA NACIONAL LOS FLAMENCOS

Cerro Lejía (5793m)

Cerro Chiliques (5778m)

Socaire

RESERVA NACIONAL LOS FLAMENCOS

Laguna Salada

Peine

Cerro Miscanti (5622m)

Laguna Miscanti

Laguna Miñiques

Cerro Miñiques (5910m)

Cerro Lila (2296m)

Cerro Tuyajto (5482m)

Laguna Tuyajto

Paso Sico

0   20
kilometres

AROUND SAN PEDRO

Valle de la Luna

16km west of San Pedro on the old road to Calama • Summer 8.30am–7.30pm; winter 8.30am–5.30pm • CH$2000

The **VALLE DE LA LUNA**, or Valley of the Moon, really lives up to its name, presenting a dramatic lunar landscape of wind-eroded hills surrounding a crust-like valley floor, once the bottom of a lake. An immense sand dune sweeps across the valley, easy enough to climb and a great place to sit and survey the scenery.

The valley is at its best at sunset, when it's transformed into a spellbinding palette of golds and reds, but you'll have to share this view with a multitude of fellow visitors, as all San Pedro tour operators offer daily sunset trips here. A more memorable (but more demanding) experience would be to get up before daybreak and cycle to the valley, arriving at sunrise; for bike rental info see p.180. Note that the valley is part of the Conaf-run Reserva Nacional Los Flamencos, and camping is not permitted.

Tulor

9km southwest of San Pedro • Summer 8.30am–7.30pm; winter 8.30am–5.30pm • CH$3000

The site of the earliest example of settled habitation in the region, **TULOR** dates from around 800 BC. It was discovered only in the mid-twentieth century by Padre Le Paige, founder of the Museo Arqueológico in San Pedro. Today, the uppermost parts of the walls are exposed, protruding from the earth, while the rest remains buried under the sand. Two reconstructions of these igloo-like houses stand alongside the site.

Salar de Atacama

10km south of San Pedro • Summer 9am–7pm; winter 8am–6pm • CH$2500

The northern edge of this 3000-square-kilometre basin covered by a vast crust of saline minerals lies some 10km south of San Pedro. The largest salt flat in Chile, **SALAR DE ATACAMA** is formed by waters flowing down from the Andes which, unable to escape from the basin, are forced to evaporate, leaving salt deposits on the earth. It's not a dazzling white like the Salar de Surire (see p.215), or Bolivia's Salar de Uyuni, but it's fascinating all the same – especially when you get out and take a close look at the crust, which looks like coffee-coloured coral reef, or ice shards, and clanks when you walk on it. The *salar* contains several small lakes, including **Laguna Chaxa**, home to dozens of flamingos, and the beautiful **Laguna Salada**, whose waters are covered with floating plates of salt.

Many tour companies also take you for a float in the saline waters of **Laguna Cejar**, 19km from San Pedro. This emerald green lagoon contains even more salt than the Dead Sea. Your guide will warn you to wear shoes when walking on the banks, as very sharp salt crests can cut your feet. Remember to bring bottles of water to wash the salt off afterwards.

The southern oases

Heading south from San Pedro, on the eastern side of the Salar de Atacama, you enter a region of beautiful lakes and tiny oasis villages. The first oasis, 38km south, is **Toconao**, whose softwater stream enters the village through the **Quebrada de Jérez** (CH$2000), a steep, narrow gorge with figs and quinces growing on its southern banks. Though not as pretty as some of the other villages, Toconao does possess a handsome whitewashed bell tower dating to 1750 and set apart from the main church.

Some 35km further south you reach **Camar**, a tiny hamlet with just sixty inhabitants, set amid lush green terraces. **Socaire**, 15km beyond, is less picturesque, save for its little church set by a field of sunflowers. **Peine**, off a track branching west from the "main road" between Camar and Socaire, has a mid-eighteenth-century church and a large swimming pool, invariably full of squealing children. It is possible **to stay** in Peine and Socaire under the rural guesthouse scheme run from San Pedro, for details of which consult the San Pedro tourist office (see p.180).

The lakes

One of the most stunning lakes in the region, **Laguna Miscanti** (near Socaire, 4350m above sea level; CH$2500), boasts brilliant blue waters. Adjacent lies the much smaller **Laguna Miñeques**, whose waters are a deep, dark blue; both lakes are protected areas, part of the Reserva Nacional Los Flamencos. Further south, pastel-coloured **Laguna Tuyajto** is home to dozens of flamingos and is set against a fabulous backdrop of mineral-streaked mountains, while **Laguna Lejía**, further north, is filled with emerald-green waters tinged white with salt deposits floating on the surface; it, too, is home to large numbers of flamingos.

El Tatio geysers and Baños de Puritama

El Tatio geysers 95km north of San Pedro • CH$5000 **Baños de Puritama** 35km north of San Pedro • CH$15,000

A trip to the **EL TATIO GEYSERS** is quite an ordeal: first, you drag yourself out of bed in the dead of night with no electric lights to see by; then you stand shivering in the street while you wait for your tour company to come and pick you up at around 4am; and finally, you embark on a three-hour journey on a rough, bumpy road. Added to this is the somewhat surreal experience of finding yourself in a pre-dawn rush hour, part of a caravan of minibuses following each other's lights across the desert.

But hardly anyone who makes the trip regrets it. At 4300m above sea level, these geysers form the highest **geothermal** field in the world. It's essentially a large, flat field containing countless blowholes full of bubbling water that, between around 6am and 8am, send billowing clouds of steam high into the air (strictly speaking, though, geysers spurt water, not steam). At the same time, the spray forms pools of water on the ground, streaked with silver reflections as they catch the first rays of the sun. It's a magnificent spectacle. Take great care, however, when walking around the field; the crust of earth is very thin in some parts, and serious accidents can happen.

You should also remember that it will be freezing cold when you arrive, though once the sun's out the place warms up quite quickly. There's also a swimming pool near the geysers, visited by most tour companies, so remember to take your swimming gear. It's worth noting, however, that tour guides will refuse to take you if you're visibly hungover when they come to pick you up at 4am, so it's best to have a quiet one the evening before.

On the way back from trips to the El Tatio geysers, some tour companies also pay a visit to the **Baños de Puritama**, a rocky pool filled with warm thermal water, 60km south of the geysers and run by a local community but owned and maintained by San Pedro's *Hotel Explora*.

Iquique

Dramatically situated at the foot of the 800m coastal cordillera, with an enormous sand dune looming precariously above one of its barrios, **IQUIQUE**, 390km north of Calama, is a sprawling, busy and surprisingly cosmopolitan city. The town is also fast gaining a reputation as one of the world's finest spots for paragliding (see box, p.189). Predictably cloudless skies and winds that come in off the Pacific and rise up the dunes create near-perfect conditions; you'll see many enthusiasts swooping down to the

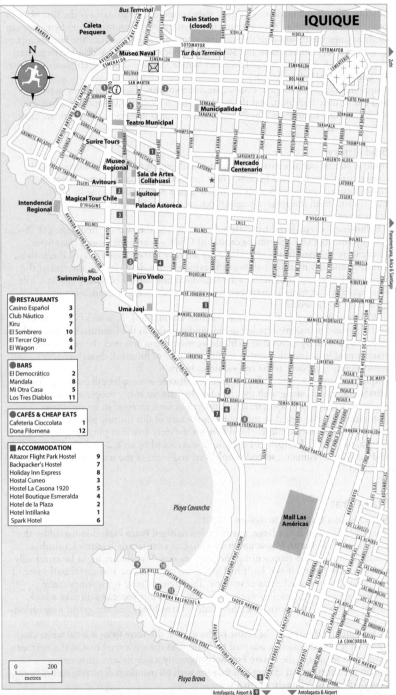

IQUIQUE

RESTAURANTS
Casino Español	3
Club Náutico	9
Kiru	7
El Sombrero	10
El Tercer Ojito	6
El Wagon	4

BARS
El Democrático	2
Mandala	8
Mi Otra Casa	5
Los Tres Diablos	11

CAFÉS & CHEAP EATS
Cafeteria Cioccolata	1
Dona Filomena	12

ACCOMMODATION
Altazor Flight Park Hostel	9
Backpacker's Hostel	7
Holiday Inn Express	8
Hostal Cuneo	3
Hostel La Casona 1920	5
Hotel Boutique Esmeralda	4
Hotel de la Plaza	2
Hotel Intillanka	1
Spark Hotel	6

0   200
metres

Antofagasta, Airport & 9 ▼   ▼ Antofagasta & Airport

beaches, silhouetted by dawn or dusky sunsets. Iquique rivals Arica as the best place to base yourself for a tour of the extreme northern tip of the country. From here, you can easily arrange excursions into the interior, whose attractions include the famous nitrate ghost towns of **Humberstone** and **Santa Laura** (both UNESCO World Heritage sites) , the beautiful hot-spring oases of **Pica** and **Matilla**, and the stunning altiplano scenery of **Parque Nacional Volcán Isluga**.

Iquique falls into two quite distinct areas: **downtown**, lined with shops, services and old historic buildings, and the modern stretch along the **oceanfront**, given over almost entirely to tourism. The **Zofri** duty-free zone is just north of the centre, in an industrial area.

Brief history

Iquique started out as a small settlement of indigenous fishing communities, and during the colonial period became a base for extracting guano deposits from the coast. It continued to grow with the opening of a nearby silver mine in 1730, but it wasn't until the great nineteenth-century nitrate boom that it really took off as a city.

Following its transferral to Chilean hands during the War of the Pacific (1878–83), Iquique became the **nitrate capital** of Chile – where the largest quantities of ore were shipped from, and where the wealthy nitrate barons based themselves, building opulent mansions all over the rapidly expanding city. By the end of the nineteenth century, Iquique was the wealthiest and most hedonistic city in Chile – it was said that more champagne was consumed here, per head, than in any other city in the world.

With the abrupt end of the nitrate era after World War I, Iquique's boom was over, and the grand mansions were left to fade and crumble as the industrialists headed back to Santiago. Fishing stepped in to fill the economic gap and over the years Iquique transformed itself into the world's leading exporter of fishmeal, though copper subsequently took over as the city's main industry.

Iquique's central square and main avenue conserve some splendid buildings from the **nitrate era**, which, along with the city's beaches, are for many people a good enough reason to visit. Seizing upon this, the authorities have invested in an ambitious restoration scheme aimed at enhancing the beauty of this historic part of the city. Still more people, mainly Chileans, head here for the duty-free shopping at Iquique's **Zona Franca**, or "Zofri". In April 2014, Iquique was rocked by an 8.2-magnitude earthquake and subsequent tsunami; several people died and some of the main highways were damaged.

Plaza Prat

Teatro Municipal Mon–Fri 10am–6pm, Sat 10am–2pm • CH$1500

The focus of town is the large, partly pedestrianized **Plaza Prat**, dominated by the gleaming white **Teatro Municipal**, whose magnificent facade features Corinthian columns and statues representing the four seasons – spoiled at night by criminally hideous fairy lights. It was built in 1889 as an opera house and showcased some of the most distinguished divas of its time. Productions have been temporarily suspended while restoration works are carried out, but you can still take a look inside to admire the lavish, if slightly faded, furnishings and the grand proportions of the auditorium.

Opposite the theatre, in the centre of the square, the **Torre Reloj** is a tall white clock tower with Moorish arches, adopted by Iquique as the city's symbol. On the northeast corner of the square, the **Casino Español** – formerly a gentlemen's club, now a restaurant – features an extravagant interior with oil paintings depicting scenes from *Don Quijote*; it's definitely worth a visit.

Calle Baquedano

Leading south, **Calle Baquedano** is lined with an extraordinary collection of late nineteenth-century timber houses, all with porches, balconies and fine wooden balustrades, and many undergoing loving restoration. This is the showcase of Iquique's nitrate architecture and has been designated a national monument. The street is pedestrianized from the plaza all the way down to the seafront, using noble materials such as fine stone for the paving and polished timber for the sidewalks. There are often bric-a-brac stalls at the Plaza Prat end, and an old tram sometimes trundles up and down the road.

Three buildings are open to the public: the **Sala de Artes Collahuasi** at no. 930 (Mon–Fri 10am–2pm & 3.30–7pm, Sat 10am–2pm; free), an impeccably restored building used for temporary art exhibitions, usually of outstanding quality; the **Museo Regional** at no. 951 (Tues–Sat 9am–5.30pm; CH$1500), which houses an eclectic collection of pre-Columbian and natural history artefacts, including deformed skulls and a pickled two-headed shark; and the **Palacio Astoreca** (entrance on O'Higgins; Mon–Fri 10am–1pm & 4–7pm, Sat 11am–2pm; free), a glorious, though deteriorating, mansion featuring a massive wood-panelled entrance hall with a painted glass Art Nouveau ceiling.

The harbour

A short walk north from Plaza Prat at Esmeralda 250 is the **Museo Naval** (Mon & Sat 10am–1pm, Tues–Fri 10am–1pm & 4–7pm; free), which displays letters, maps and photos relating to Arturo Prat, hero of the War of the Pacific (see p.478). If this whets your appetite, head to the **Museo Corbeta Esmeralda**, Prat s/n (obligatory guided tours Tues–Sun 10am–12.15pm & 2–5pm; CH$3000; ☎57 253 0812, ⊛museoesmeralda .cl), a full-scale model of the *Esmeralda*, a corvette captained by Prat during the war. From the **Caleta Pesquera**, or fishermen's wharfs, the huge, yawning pelicans strutting around the pier make compelling viewing. You can take **boat tours** around the harbour which leave from Muelle Pasajero (CH$3000), worth it for the views onto the steep desert mountains, rising like huge slabs of chocolate cake behind the city.

The beaches

Two beaches lie within striking distance of the city centre: **Playa Cavancha**, the nearest, most popular, and more sheltered; and **Playa Brava**, larger, less crowded and more windswept, which is only suitable for sunbathing due to a strong current and crashing

---

PARAGLIDING PARADISE

Iquique is one of the best places on Earth to **paraglide**, thanks to the unique geography of the city; the mountain range and air current that comes all the way from the Antarctic create the perfect conditions for flying. Plus, you'll regularly hear paragliding instructors proudly boast about the fact you can fly 365 days a year in Iquique – it hardly ever rains and temperatures hover between 16 and 25 degree Celsius all year round. Tandem flights lasting approximately 45 minutes usually leave from Alto Hospicio and land on either Playa Cavancha or Playa Brava (equipment, pick-up and drop-off are included). If you've time to spare and you're really serious about flying, you might consider enrolling on a two-week course, at the end of which you'll receive a licence which allows you to brave the Iquique skies on your own, without an instructor. Be sure to book in advance.

The pros at **Puro Vuelo** (☎57 231 1127, ⊛purovuelo.cl) come highly recommended. A tandem flight will set you back CH$40,000 and includes a set of photos of you flying, which you can download from their website afterwards. Altazor (☎09 9886 2362, ⊛altazor.cl) also has a good reputation.

waves rendering it dangerous for swimming (although you do see adrenaline junkies surfing at either end of the beach). You can walk to Playa Cavancha, which begins at the southern end of Amunategui, but it's very cheap to take one of the numerous taxis constantly travelling between the plaza and the beach; many continue to Playa Brava, as well, for a slightly higher fare. Further south, between Playa Brava and the airport, there's a series of attractive sandy beaches including **Playa Blanca**, 13km south of the centre, **Playa Lobito**, at Km 22, and the fishing cove of **Los Verdes**, at Km 24. You can get to these on the airport bus or *colectivo* (see below).

The Zofri

About 3km north of the centre • Mon–Sat 11am–9pm

located in a large industrial compound, the duty-free shopping complex known as the **Zofri** is widely touted as one of the great attractions of the north. Thousands of Chileans flock here from up and down the country to spend their money at what turns out, at close quarters, to be a big, ugly mall crammed full of small shops selling mainly electronic items like cameras, watches and domestic gadgets, but also perfumes and food. There's a curious mixture of the upmarket and the tacky, with the latter tending to dominate.

The building itself is shabby and old-fashioned, and the bargains aren't really good enough to deserve a special trip. If you do want to check it out, take any *colectivo* marked "Zofri" heading north out of town – the east side of the Plaza or Calle Amunategui are both good bets for catching one.

ARRIVAL AND DEPARTURE
IQUIQUE

BY PLANE
Diego Aracena airport is a whacking 40km south of the city. You can get to the centre by transfer (☎57 231 0800; CH$5000), regular taxi (CH$8000 shared, or CH$16,000 private) or *colectivo*.

Airlines LAN, Tarapacá 465 (☎57 242 7600); Sky Airlines, Tarapacá 530 (☎57 241 5013 or 57 242 4139 at airport).

Destinations Antofagasta (4–6 daily; 55min); Arica (4 daily; 45min); Santiago (6–11 daily; 2hr 15min–3hr 15min).

BY BUS
Iquique's main bus terminal is in a rather run-down quarter at the northern end of Patricio Lynch, several blocks from the centre – best take a taxi to the centre, or wait for a

colectivo. Tur Bus, however, has its own terminal (also known as Terminal Esmeralda) in a beautifully converted town house, proudly sporting a dazzling 1917 vintage black Ford, in a more agreeable area at the corner of Ramírez and Esmeralda. To save yourself from trekking to the terminals to buy a ticket in advance, you can purchase (and compare prices) at the bus company stands opposite the Mercado Centenario on Barros Arana. A taxi into the centre from either costs CH$2000–3000.

Destinations Antofagasta (17 daily; 7hr); Arica (every 30min; 4hr 30min); Calama (3–4 daily; 6–7hr); Caldera (12 daily; 12hr); Chañaral (12 daily; 11hr); Copiapó (12 daily; 13hr); La Serena (8 daily; 18hr); La Tirana (7 daily; 1hr 40min); Mamiña (2 daily; 2hr 30min); Mejillones (3 daily; 5hr); Pica (7 daily; 2hr); Santiago (hourly; 25hr).

GETTING AROUND

Car rental Autos Procar, Serrano 796 (☎57 247 0668); Budget, Bulnes 542 (☎57 241 6332, ⓦbudget .cl); or Hertz, Aníbal Pinto 1303 (☎57 251 0432, ⓦhertz.cl).

By taxi Except for fares from the bus terminal and airport, nearly all Iquique's taxis function like *colectivos*, with fixed, low prices but flexible routes. This is very

handy for shuttling to and from the beach, or even going from your hotel to a restaurant. Find out from Sernatur (see below) or your hotel what the going rate is, and confirm this with the taxi driver before you get in. Recommended companies include Taxi Aeropuerto Plaza Prat (☎57 241 3368) and Playa Brava Radio Taxi (☎57 244 3460).

INFORMATION AND TOURS

TOURIST INFORMATION
Sernatur Aníbal Pinto 436 (Mon–Fri 9am–5pm, Sat & Sun 10am–2pm; ☎57 241 9241, ✉infoiquique@sernatur.cl).

TOURS
A number of Iquique tour companies (see p.181) offer one-day circular tours – from around CH$25,000 per

person – taking in the nitrate ghost towns of Humberstone and Santa Laura (see p.193); the geoglyphs of Pintados (see p.195); the oases villages of Matilla and Pica, with a plunge in Pica's hot springs (see p.195); and the basilica and nitrate museum of La Tirana (see p.196). Another standard tour offered by some companies is the highly memorable route up into the cordillera, continuing north across the altiplano and descending in Arica; these excursions take in Parque Nacional Volcán Isluga (see p.198), the Salar de Surire (see p.215) and Parque Nacional Lauca (see p.211). The tour entails three overnight stays, with prices starting around CH$220,000 per person (see box, p.207).

TOUR OPERATORS AND TRAVEL AGENTS

Avitours Baquedano 997 ☎ 57 241 3334, ⊛ avitours.cl. Avitours offers an extensive range of trips across northern Chile, including a three-day excursion to Arica via Lauca and Isluga national parks, and a day-trip to the hot springs of Mamiña (see p.196).

Iquitour Patricio Lynch 563 ☎ 57 242 8772, ⊛ iquitour .cl. This travel agency is useful for flight and hotel bookings, as well as multi-day tours throughout Chile (and South America).

Magical Tour Chile Baquedano 1035 ☎ 57 221 7290, ⊛ magicaltour.cl. A good all-rounder, Magical Tour Chile offers city and cycling tours, day-trips to the ghost towns of Humberstone and Santa Laura (see p.194), and multi-day tours to destinations like Parque Nacional Volcán Isluga (see p.198).

Surire Tours Baquedano 170 ☎ 57 244 5440 ⊛ suriretours.cl. Specialises in multi-day, group tours in northern Chile (and beyond), including to Humberstone and Santa Laura, Pica and Matilla (see p.196), and the Atacama Desert.

Uma Jaqi Obispo Labbé 1591 ☎ 09 8771 5768, ⊜ umajaqi@gmail.com. Based in the hostel of the same name, Uma Jaqi offers private and group surfing lessons, organises surf-themed trips in northern Chile and Peru, and hires out boards.

ACCOMMODATION

Iquique is a popular holiday resort and offers an abundance of **accommodation**. Both in the centre and by the beaches, always ask what the "best price" is, as many places will give discounts when pushed. One thing to bear in mind is that, owing to the region's severe water shortage, supplies are occasionally cut in the busy summer months, sometimes without warning.

DOWNTOWN IQUIQUE

Hostal Cuneo Baquedano 1175 ☎ 57 242 8654, ⊜ hostalcuneo@hotmail.com. With a good location in an old timber building (painted a striking turquoise) on the historic stretch of Calle Baquedano, this hospitable, homely and good-value *hostal* has small and neat if slightly dark rooms off a leafy patio. CH$25,000

★**Hostel La Casona 1920** Barros Arana 1585 ☎ 57 241 3000, ⊛ casonahostel.com. Once the family residence of the very personable owner Isabel, *La Casona 1920* is an original nitrate-era building. A home away from home, this hostel has a lovely outdoor patio (films shown on projector every Sun), an attractive, well-equipped kitchen and, best of all, a very pleasant, friendly atmosphere. Ask Isabel to take you salsa dancing – she's a pro. French, English and Portuguese spoken. Dorms CH$8000, doubles CH$15,000

Hotel Boutique Esmeralda Obispo Labbé 1386 ☎ 57 221 6996, ⊛ esmeraldahotel.cl. Solid, mid-range hotel in a modern building a 10–15min walk from the plaza. All of the spotless rooms are en suite and have TVs and phones, and staff are friendly and helpful. CH$42,000

Hotel de la Plaza Paseo Baquedano 1025 ☎ 57 241 7172, ⊜ contacto@kilantur.cl. An airy and light Georgian building on the main stretch with pictures of old Iquique adorning the walls and some

racially-dubious statues in the lobby. A leafy staircase leads up to pleasant, clean rooms, and there's a restaurant and bar. CH$30,000

Hotel Intillanka Obispo Labbé 825 ☎ 57 231 1105, ⊛ inti-llanka.cl. Friendly and efficiently run hotel offering spacious, light rooms with fans rather than a/c, and private bathrooms. The place could do with a revamp, but it's very clean. CH$45,500

THE BEACHES AND AROUND

Altazor Flight Park Hostel Via 6, Manzana Am Sitio 3, Bajo Molle, about a 15min bus ride from town ☎ 57 238 0110, ☎ 09 9886 2362, ⊛ altazor.cl. Built almost entirely of ship containers, the rooms at this international paragliding centre are surprisingly inviting, with shared kitchen and chilled-out communal areas. There are also smarter apartments, and camping spots. Check their website for directions. Doubles CH$14,000, apartments CH$25,000, camping/person CH$5000

Backpacker's Hostel Amunategui 2075 ☎ 57 232 0223, ⊛ hosteliquique.cl. Solid HI-affiliated hostel (discount for HI members) offering weekly barbecues, surfboard and wetsuit rental, and clean dorms, rooms and facilities. The huge kitchen is a big plus point, as is the leafy outdoor space and location right next to the beach. Dorms CH$7500, doubles CH$22,000

4

Holiday Inn Express 11 de Septiembre 1690 ☎ 57 243 3300, ⓦ ihg.com. You know what you're getting at this impersonal but immaculate US chain hotel, with a pool, a/c and spacious rooms with ocean views (though only from those at the front of the hotel). Discounts available Fri–Sun. CH$64,000

Spark Hotel Amunategui 2034 ☎ 600 641 0100, ⓦ sparkhoteles.cl. This super-slick hotel has a rather formal feel to it, and is popular with business guests and couples on a romantic break. There's a lovely outdoor pool on the ground floor as well as what is probably the best sushi restaurant in town. Top-floor rooms have amazing views of the beach and city. CH$67,000

EATING AND DRINKING

While there's a reasonable choice of **restaurants** in the centre, it's worth coming out to have at least one evening meal by the beach, to see the ocean lit up with coloured lights projected from the promenade. Almost all restaurants serve a good value *menú del día* at lunchtime. For a quick, cheap eat, the lively **Mercado Centenario** on Barros Arana between Latorre and Sargento Aldea is popular for fish lunch specials, though hygiene standards are dubious. Most bars in Iquique double up as restaurants, so it's perfectly fine to go to a restaurant just for drinks, and vice versa.

CAFÉS AND CHEAP EATS

Cafeteria Cioccolata Av Aníbal Pinto 487 ☎ 57 253 2290. This sweet, old-fashioned tearoom opposite the tourist office serves up good coffee (CH$1400–3100) and obscenely huge slices of cake, waffles and pancakes. The lemon yellow interior is filled with businessmen and ladies who lunch (*menú del día* CH$4500). There are other branches on Arturo Prat and the Zofri. Mon–Fri 8.45am–10pm, Sat 11am–10pm.

Dona Filomena Filomena Valenzuela 298 ☎ 57 231 1235. Very reliable *empanada*, beer and pizza joint, popular with a young-ish crowd (dishes from CH$3000). Simple wooden decor and attractive outside seating. Also does delivery. Mon–Sat 12.30pm–12.30am.

RESTAURANTS

DOWNTOWN IQUIQUE

Casino Español Plaza Prat 584 ☎ 57 233 3911. Huge, fabulous dining room decorated like a mock Moorish palace, complete with beautiful tiles and suits of armour. The Spanish food is unexceptional, and a little overpriced (mains CH$7000–12,000), but this is a must-visit. Mon, Sat & Sun noon–3.30pm, Tues–Fri noon–3.30pm & 8–10.30pm.

★ **El Tercer Ojito** Patricio Lynch 1420a ☎ 57 242 6517, ⓦ eltercerojito.cl. This peaceful garden oasis is the mellowest place to spend a shady afternoon or candle-lit evening. A healthy menu (mains CH$4900–11,000) darts from Chilean seafood to Thai curries, via salads, pasta and various veggie options, showcasing the best ingredients the region has to offer. Service is impeccable. Be sure to leave room for pudding; the home-made *kulfi* (Indian ice cream) is superb. Tues–Sat 12.30–5pm & 7.30pm–1am, Sun 12.30–5pm.

El Wagon Thompson 85 ☎ 57 234 1428. Nitrate-era paraphernalia lines the walls of this warm and friendly restaurant. Take your pick from an extensive menu of imaginative fish and seafood dishes (CH$6000–12,000): the spicy *pescado a la Huara-Huara* is particularly good. There's also a great choice of wines and live music at weekends. Mon–Sat 1–4pm & 8pm–2am, Sun 1–4pm.

THE BEACHES

Club Náutico Los Rieles 110 ☎ 57 243 2951. *Club Náutico* is a first-rate, reasonably priced restaurant that's been going strong for years, with great views from its outdoor terrace, especially at night (mains CH$7000–12,000). Daily noon–3pm & 7pm–midnight.

★ **Kiru** Amunategui 1912 ☎ 57 276 0795, ⓦ kiru.cl. Peruvian restaurant that feels sophisticated and exclusive – there's no sign at the door; just follow the palm-fringed corridor and chill-out music. The chef rustles up fantastic fusion dishes and memorable ceviche, and there are plenty of wines and cocktails at the trendy, well-stocked bar. Expect to pay around CH$15,000–20,000/person. Mon–Sat 1–3.30pm & 8pm–12.30am, Sun 1–4pm.

El Sombrero Los Rieles 704 ☎ 57 236 3900, ⓦ terrado.cl. Part of the *Hotel Terrado Suites*, this rather formal, expensive restaurant specializes in seafood – invariably served in rich, roux-based sauces (mains CH$9000–15,000). It's right by the sea, with floor-to-ceiling windows giving great views. Daily 1–3.30pm & 8–11.30pm.

BARS

El Democrático Obispo Labbé 466 ☎ 57 276 6875, ⓦ bardemocratico.cl. If it's the true essence of Chile you're after, this scruffy 80-year-old local, with huge dried fish hanging from the walls, fits the bill. On weekdays it's filled with drunk fishermen, but come the weekend, young locals and live bands join the party. Don't come to eat, unless it's a boiled egg you're after, but do try the Chilean beers (from CH$1500) and, if you're brave, an old-school Chilean cocktail, "El Terremoto", made from pineapple ice cream, sweet white wine, whisky and grenadine. Don't dress up! Daily 11.30am–late.

Mandala Hernan Fuenzalida 1028 ☎ 57 241 2449. This stylish hangout has benefited from the creative flair of its architect-cum-artist-cum-chef and owner, Rodrigo. Attractive recycled lampshades and other bits and bobs adorn the place, and there's an airy patio with sofas – perfect on a balmy summer's night. There are also great cocktails (around CH$7000–10,000) and a sushi bar on the roof terrace. DJs on weekends. Mon–Thurs noon–4pm & 7pm–1am, Fri & Sat noon–4pm & 7pm–3am.

Mi Otra Casa Baquedano 1334 ☎ 09 8733 9167. Lovely "bar cultural" set in an attractive building that dates back to the 1700s, when Iquique was a Peruvian city. This artist hang-out holds poetry and gallery nights and serves an Argentine-inspired menu and unusual cocktails such as "palmito sour" (palm hearts, pisco, lemon and sugar). Reggae music adds to the chilled-out vibe and there are a handful of tables outside. Mon–Thurs 12.30–4pm & 7pm–2am, Fri & Sat 12.30–4pm & 8pm–4am.

Los Tres Diablos Filomena Valenzuela 784 ☎ 57 248 0530. This smart resto-bar is one of Iquique's places to be seen. Come here for a pisco cocktail and snack on fusion food with a Mexican slant. The ceviche is to die for, as is the Chinese red decor and terrace, complete with night lanterns, hibiscus and pool (the latter just for show). Mon–Wed 1–4pm & 8pm–1am, Thurs–Sat 1–4pm & 8pm–2am.

NIGHTLIFE AND ENTERTAINMENT

You'll find several **nightclubs** that get very crowded in summer and maintain a gentle buzz during low season. They are nearly all down on the Costanera Sur. Much of Iquique's nightlife is concentrated around Playa Brava.

DIRECTORY

Money and exchange Iquique has numerous ATMs, including those at Banco Santander, Plaza Prat; BCI, Tarapacá 404; Corp-Banca, Serrano 343; Scotiabank, Uribe 530. There are a few *casas de cambio* on Patricio Lynch.

Post office The main office is at Bolívar 485, a few blocks northeast of Plaza Prat (Mon–Fri 9am–6pm, Sat 10am–1pm).

4

Inland from Iquique

Iquique lies within easy reach of many inland sights. Just half an hour away, **Humberstone** and **Santa Laura** are perhaps the most haunting of all the nitrate ghost towns. South of here, close to the Panamericana, **Cerro Pintados** features a dense collection of geoglyphs, among the most impressive in Chile. East of Pintados sits the pretty oasis village of **Pica**, with a lovely thermal pool, while **Mamiña**, further north, is the Norte Grande's hot-springs town *par excellence*. You can also visit **La Tirana**, an important pilgrimage centre, famous for its colourful festival in July. Public transport around this area is sporadic but manageable.

Humberstone

45km inland from Iquique • Daily: Jan–March 9am–7pm; April–Dec 9am–6pm • CH$3000 (includes entry to Santa Laura)

The best-preserved ghost town in Chile, **HUMBERSTONE** is a nitrate *oficina* that was abandoned in 1960 and today appeals especially to lovers of industrial architecture. It sits some 45km inland from Iquique, by Ruta 16 just before it meets the Panamericana. The town began life in 1862 as Oficina La Palma, but was renamed in 1925 in honour of James "Santiago" Humberstone, an important nitrate entrepreneur famous for introducing the "Shanks" ore-refining system to the industry. In its time it was one of the busiest *oficinas* on the pampas; today it is an eerie, empty ghost town, slowly crumbling beneath the desert sun.

What sets Humberstone apart from the other ghost towns is that just about all of it is still standing – from the white, terraced workers' houses (now in total disrepair) and the plaza with its bandstand, to the theatre, church and company store. The **theatre**, in particular, is highly evocative, with its rows of dusty seats staring at the stage. You should also seek out the **hotel**, and walk through to the back where you'll find a huge, empty **swimming pool** with a diving board – curiously the pool is made from the sections of a ship's iron hull. Located a short distance from the town are the sheds and workshops, with old tools and bits of machinery lying around, and invoices and order forms littering the floors.

In recent years there has been significant restoration work, and many of the homes have been revamped to show what life was like in the 1930s – the room with old toys is particularly evocative.

Santa Laura

At **SANTA LAURA**, about 2km down the road and clearly visible from Humberstone, you'll see only a couple of remaining houses (one of which has been turned into a small museum), but the processing plant is amazing, seeming to loom into the air like a rusty old dinosaur. As you walk around the site, listening to the endless clanging of machinery banging in the wind, the sense of abandonment is nigh-on overwhelming.

THE NITRATE BOOM

Looking around the desert pampa, it's hard to believe that this scorched, lifeless wasteland was once so highly prized that a war was fought over it – and still more difficult to imagine it alive with smoking chimneys, grinding machinery, offices, houses and a massive workforce. But less than a century ago, the Far North of Chile was the scene of a thriving industry built on its vast **nitrate deposits**, heavily in demand in Europe and North America as a fertilizer. Nitrates were first exploited in the Atacama Desert in the 1860s, when the region belonged to Bolivia (around Antofagasta) and Peru (around Iquique and Arica). From the early stages, however, the Chilean presence was very strong, both in terms of capital and labour.

THE WAR OF THE PACIFIC

When in 1878 the Bolivian government violated an official agreement by raising export taxes on nitrate (hitting Chilean shareholders, including several prominent politicians), Chile protested by sending troops into Antofagasta. Two weeks later, Chile and Bolivia were at war, with Peru joining in (on the Bolivian side) within a couple of months. **The War of the Pacific** (see p.478) went on for five years, and resulted in Chile taking over all of the nitrate grounds.

THE BOOM YEARS

With the return of political stability after the war, the nitrate industry began to boom in earnest, bringing in enormous export revenues for Chile, and a trail of processing plants, known as **oficinas**, sprang up all over the pampa. Each *oficina* sat in the centre of its prescribed land, from where the raw nitrate ore was blasted using gunpowder. The chunks of ore, known as *caliche*, were then boiled in large copper vats, releasing a nitrate solution which was crystallized in the sun before being sent down to the ports to be shipped abroad. The plants themselves were grimy, noisy places. It was a hard life for the labourers, who worked long hours in dangerous conditions, and were housed in squalid shacks, often without running water and sewerage. The (mostly British) managers, meanwhile, lived in grand residences, dined on imported delicacies and enjoyed a whirl of elegant social activities. Nitrate provided more than half of the Chilean government's revenues until 1920, by which time the boom was over and the industry in decline.

THE BEGINNING OF THE END

It was **World War I** that dealt the first serious blow to the nitrate companies, when the suspension of sales to Germany – Chile's major European buyer – forced almost half the *oficinas* to close down. The final death knell was sounded when Germany, forced to seek alternative fertilizers, developed cheap synthetic nitrates which quickly displaced Chile's natural nitrates from their dominant role in the world market. Most of what was left of the industry was killed off by the **World Depression** in the 1930s, and today just one *oficina* – **María Elena** – remains in operation.

Reserva Nacional Pampa del Tamarugal

About 20km south of the junction between Ruta 16 and the Panamericana, the latter passes through the **RESERVA NACIONAL PAMPA DEL TAMARUGAL**, an extensive plantation of wispy, bush-like *tamarugo* trees. These are native to the region and are especially adapted to saline soils, with roots that are long enough to tap underground water supplies. There's a Conaf-run **campsite** here, exactly 24km south of Pozo Almonte, on the west side of the Panamericana. While the *tamarugos* aren't really interesting enough to merit a special trip, you can take a look at them on your way to the far more impressive **Cerro Pintados**, with the largest collection of **geoglyphs** in South America, situated within the reserve's boundaries.

Cerro Pintados geoglyphs

45km south of Pozo Almonte, 5km west of the Panamericana on a gravel road that branches off the highway, almost opposite the turn-off to Pica • Daily 9.30am–6.30pm • CH$2000 (payable at the Conaf control point 2km along the access road) • ☎ 57 275 1055, Ⓦ www.conaf.cl • You should be able to arrange a lift there and back with a *colectivo* from the stand outside Iquique's Mercado Centenario

Extending 4km along a hillside, the **Cerro Pintados** site features approximately four hundred images (not all of them visible from the ground) of animals, birds, humans and geometric patterns, etched on the surface or formed by a mosaic of little stones around the year 1000 AD. The felines, birds, snakes and flocks of llamas and vicuñas scratched into the rock are thought to have been indicators for livestock farmers. The circles, squares, dotted lines and human figures are more enigmatic, however, and may have had something to do with rituals, perhaps even sacrifices. Note that it's probably not a good idea to hitch and then try walking to the site from the Panamericana, owing to the relentless heat and lack of shade.

Pica

As you cross the vast, desert pampa, the neighbouring oases of Pica and Matilla first appear as an improbable green smudge on the hazy horizon. As you get nearer, it becomes apparent that this is not a mirage and you are, indeed, approaching cultivated fields and trees. It's a remarkable sight, and anyone who has not seen a desert oasis should make a special effort to visit. By far the larger of the two oases, **PICA** is a sleepy little town overflowing with lemon and lime trees, bougainvilleas and jasmine.

It's the largest supplier of fruits to Iquique – *limas de Pica* are famous throughout the country – and one of the treats of visiting is drinking the delicious *jugos naturales* – orange, mango, pear, guava and grapefruit juices – freshly squeezed in front of you in the little streetside kiosks. The tidy plaza, by the entrance to town, is overlooked by a beautiful, pale-coloured **church** dedicated to St Andrew. It has a grand Neoclassical facade and was built in 1880.

Cocha Resbaladero

General Ibáñez s/n • Daily 9am–9pm • CH$1000

Pica's real selling point is the **Cocha Resbaladero**, a gorgeous **hot-springs pool** carved into a rocky hollow with two caves at one end. It's quite a walk from the main part of town, but there are several places to stay up here if you want to be close to the waters. To enjoy the waters in peace, arrive early before the buses of day-trippers start arriving at midday.

ARRIVAL AND INFORMATION   **PICA**

By bus Seven daily buses depart Iquique for Pica (2hr).
Tourist office Balmaceda 299 (Mon–Fri 8.30am–1.30pm & 3–6pm, Sat & Sun 10.30am–1.30pm & 3–6.30pm;

☎ 57 274 1310). The town's friendly Oficina de Turismo sits opposite the Municipalidad building just past the main square on the way to the hot springs.

ACCOMMODATION AND EATING

Hotel Los Emilios Lord Cochrane 213 ☎ 57 274 1126. The nicest place to stay in the centre, *Hotel Los Emilios* offers comfortable rooms with private bathrooms and TVs in a handsome old house with a plunge pool in the back garden. CH$20,000

Los Naranjos Barbosa 200. For something a bit different, this homely little place has a hearty menu of tasty Andean specialities (CH$4000–8000) like llama stew with quinoa. Mon–Sat 12.30–3pm & 8.30–11pm, Sun 12.30–3pm.

Refugio Sombra Verde La Banda ☎ 09 8403 2348. A 10min walk from the centre, signposted off Balmaceda, is this excellent campsite, offering great facilities and plenty of trees for shade. Bring your own camping equipment. Camping/person CH$5000

Matilla

The tiny, pretty village of **MATILLA**, about 5km southwest of Pica, has a beautiful church, albeit more humble than Pica's. You'll also see an eighteenth-century wine press, just off the plaza, originally used by the Spaniards; the roots of grapevines were brought over by the conquistadors.

Santuario de la Tirana

Around 20km northwest of Pica • All buses between Iquique and Pica make a stop in La Tirana

Driving back to the Panamericana from Pica, if you take the right-hand (northbound) road, rather than the left-hand one, you'll pass through the little town of La Tirana, 10km before you get back to the highway. It's a rather cheerless place, made up of dusty streets and neglected adobe houses, which makes it all the more surprising when you come upon the immense, paved square stretching out before the imposing **SANTUARIO DE LA TIRANA**. This curious church, at once grand and shabby, is made of wood covered in cream-coloured corrugated iron. It's the home of the Virgen del Carmen, a polychrome carving that is the object of a fervent cult of devotion.

The fiesta

Every year, from July 12 to 18, up to eighty thousand pilgrims come to honour the Virgin and take part in the riotous fiesta in which dozens of masked, costumed dancers perform *bailes religiosos*. These dances have their roots in pre-Spanish, pre-Christian times, with an exuberant, carnival feel wholly out of keeping with traditional Catholic celebrations. If you're not around to see them in action, you should at least visit the small museum in a wing of the church where many of the costumes and masks are displayed (no fixed hours; try asking the caretaker to let you in if it's shut).

Mamiña

A paved road branches east from the Panamericana at Pozo Almonte and climbs gently through the desert to **MAMIÑA**, 125km – a two-and-a-half-hour drive – northeast of Iquique. First impressions are not encouraging; huddled on a hillside overlooking a valley, its narrow streets and crumbling stone houses seem to belong to a forgotten town, left to the mercy of the heat and dust. Continue down the valley, however, and its charms become more apparent as you come upon the fertile terraces emerald with alfalfa, and the little stream running through the gorge (*quebrada*).

The hot springs

The real lure of Mamiña, though, is the **hot springs** for which the town is famous throughout Chile; the delicious bottled mineral water from here is on sale in the region only, as production is small. Unlike Pica, Mamiña doesn't have just one hot spring, but many, and their waters are piped to every house in the village.

THE LEGEND OF LA TIRANA

La Tirana is named after an Inca princess whose story is vividly recorded in twelve large panels inside the town's church. It all began in 1535 when **Diego de Almagro** marched south from Cuzco to conquer Chile. He took with him some five hundred Spaniards and ten thousand locals, including Huillac Huma, high priest of the cult of the Sun God, who was accompanied by his beautiful 23-year-old daughter, **la ñusta** (the princess). Unknown to Almagro, the party also included a number of **Wilkas**, or high-ranking warriors from the Inca Royal Army. When the party reached Atacama la Grande, the high priest slipped away from the group and fled to Charcas, where he planned to stir up rebellion against the Spaniards.

Later, the princess followed her father's lead and she too escaped – with a hundred Wilkas and followers – and fled to the *tamarugo* forests of the pampa. She organized her followers into a fierce army that, for the next four years, waged a relentless war against their oppressors. Her mission was clear: death to all Spaniards, and to all Indians who had been baptized by them. Before long, this indomitable woman became known far and wide as La Tirana del Tamarugal – the **Tyrant of the Tamarugal**.

STAR-CROSSED LOVERS

One day, in 1544, La Tirana's army returned to their leader with a prisoner – a certain **Don Vasco de Almeyda**, one of the Portuguese miners established in Huantajaya. According to the legend, "*Mirarle y enamorarse fue una sola cosa*", simply to look at him was to fall in love with him. La Tirana, hitherto immovable, fell passionately in love with the foreigner. But according to everything she stood and fought for, he must be sentenced to death. In desperation, she consulted the stars and her tribe's gods, and claimed that they had ordered her to keep him alive until four moons had passed.

For the next four months, a tender love grew between La Tirana and her prisoner. The princess neglected her people and her duties, arousing the suspicion of the Wilkas. As the fourth month was coming to an end, La Tirana asked her loved one if they would be reunited for eternity in heaven if she too were a Christian. On his affirmative reply, she begged him to baptize her. Almeyda began to do so, but before he could finish, the couple were showered with arrows from the bows of the betrayed Wilkas. As she lay dying in the wood, the princess cried, "I am dying happy, sure as I am that my immortal soul will ascend to God's throne. All I ask is that after my death, you will bury me next to my lover and place a cross over our grave."

A TOWN IS BORN

Ten years later, when Padre Antonio Rondon arrived in these parts to evangelize the Indians, it was with astonishment and joy that he discovered a simple cross in a clearing of the wood. The priest erected a humble chapel on the site, later replaced by a larger building that became, in time, the centre of worship in a town that took its name from the beautiful princess who had died there.

Furthermore, these waters are not merely hot, but are reputed to cure all manner of afflictions, from eczema and psoriasis to respiratory problems and anxiety. Indeed, the town is named in honour of an Inca princess whose blindness was reputedly cured here. Whatever their medicinal value, there's no doubt that the waters are supremely relaxing to bathe in. This you can do in any of the village's hotels or *residenciales*, usually in your own private *tina*, or bathtub.

Baños Ipla

Daily 8am–1.30pm & 3–9pm • CH$1500

There are also a number of public springs, including the **Baños Ipla**, down in the valley, whose four unattractive *tinas* are filled with hot sulphurous water (45°C/115°F) bubbling up from underground. Nearby, the **Vertiente del Radium** is a little fountain whose radioactive waters are supposed to cure eye infections and, according to legend, once restored the sight of an Inca princess.

Barros Chino

Daily 9am–4pm • CH$1500

A short walk from the Vertiente del Radium, behind the water-bottling plant, you'll find the mud baths of **Barros Chino** where you can plaster yourself in mud (don't let the caretaker do it for you), lie on a wooden rack while it dries, then wash it off in a small thermal pool.

ARRIVAL AND DEPARTURE   MAMIÑA

By bus Buses leave from outside the market in Iquique twice daily (2hr 30min).

ACCOMMODATION

Accommodation is centred in two quite separate areas, one on the ridge overlooking the valley, and the other down in the valley, by the Baños Ipla. Many are run on a **full-board basis**. You can **camp** for free by the pool on the track out to Cerro del Inca, about a 30min walk from the Ipla baths.

Hotel Kusitambu Sulumpa s/n ☏57 257 4644, ⓦhotelkusitambu.cl. Meaning 'place of rest' in Aymara, the recently refurbished *Hotel Kusitambu* has basic rooms, all with private bathrooms, and two *cabañas* with thermal water in the bathrooms, but sadly no pool. Breakfast costs extra. Popular with miners. CH$25,000

Hotel Termas la Coruña Santa Rosa 687 ☏57 257 3664, ⓦtermaslacoruña.cl. With unbeatable views of the Mamiña valley, and just 100m from the plaza, this strategically located hotel has an outdoor hot spring pool, tennis court and games room. Rooms are simple but clean; there are also smarter *cabañas* sleeping up to four people. Doubles CH$20,000, *cabañas* CH$40,000

Parque Nacional Volcán Isluga

At the one-horse town of **Huara**, 33km up the Panamericana from the turn-off to Iquique, a good road branches east into the desert, then climbs high into the mountains, continuing all the way to Oruro in Bolivia. It's paved as far as **Colchane**, on the Chilean side of the border, but the main appeal lies in getting off the tarmac once you're up into the cordillera and heading for the deserted wilderness in and around **Parque Nacional Volcán Isluga.** Here you'll find a remote, isolated landscape of wide plains, dramatic, snowcapped volcanoes (one of which is the park's namesake) and semi-abandoned villages, home to indigenous Aymara herding communities that have been a part of this windswept land for thousands of years.

Unlike Parque Nacional Lauca, further north, this region hasn't yet been "discovered", and it's unlikely you'll come across many other tourists. There are a number of attractions on the way up, as well, in particular the weird desert geoglyph known as the **Gigante de Atacama**, in the pampa, and the frozen geysers of **Puchuldiza**, on the lower slopes of the Andes.

Enquelga

Parque Nacional Volcán Isluga's administrative centre is in **Enquelga**, a dusty, tumbledown hamlet – 3850m above sea level – home to a small Aymara community. Many of its inhabitants, particularly the women, still dress in traditional, brightly coloured clothes, and live from tending llamas and cultivating potatoes and barley.

Aguas Calientes

Two kilometres on from Enquelga, **Aguas Calientes** is a long, spring-fed pool containing warm (but not hot) waters, set in an idyllic location with terrific views of

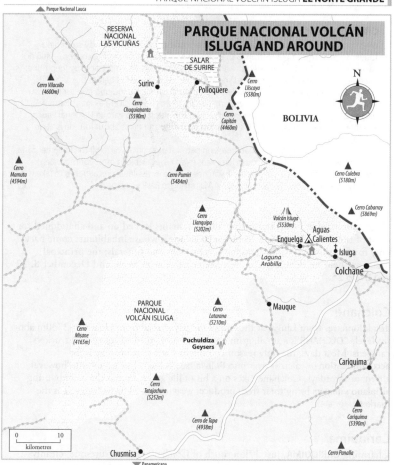

PARQUE NACIONAL VOLCÁN ISLUGA AND AROUND

Volcán Isluga. The pool is surrounded by pea-green *bofedal* – a spongy grass, typical of the altiplano – and drains into a little stream, crossed every morning and evening by herds of llamas driven to and from the sierra by Aymara shepherdesses. There's a stone changing-hut next to it, and a few **camping** spaces and picnic areas, protected from the evening wind by thick stone walls.

Isluga

Six kilometres east of Enquelga, still within the park's boundaries, **Isluga** is composed of a hundred or so stone and adobe houses huddled around one of the most beautiful churches on the altiplano. Built in the seventeenth century (it's not known when, exactly), it's a humble little construction of thick, whitewashed adobe that flashes like snow in the constant glare of the sun. The main building, containing a single nave, is enclosed by a low wall trimmed with delicate arches; just outside the wall sits the two-tier bell tower with steps leading up to the top, where you can sit and survey the scenery or watch the hummingbirds that fly in and out.

CROSSING THE ALTIPLANO

With the proposed **Ruta Altiplánica de Integración** – a paved highway stretching 1500km across the altiplano, from San Pedro de Atacama in Chile to Cusco, Peru – still not having come to fruition, crossing the altiplano's pothole-riddled dirt tracks by jeep remains the road adventure of a lifetime and should be enjoyed to the full before the arrival of tarmac and increased traffic. Probably the best starting point is Iquique (the ascent in altitude is more gradual in this direction), heading into the cordillera as far as Parque Nacional Volcán Isluga, continuing north across the altiplano to Parque Nacional Lauca, and finally descending in Arica. It's a **700km journey**, and takes about four days at an easy pace.

If you do the trip, remember that there's no petrol station once you're off the Panamericana, which means taking it all with you in jerry cans (*bidones*, available in most ironmongers). Always take far, far more than you think you need. Another essential precaution is to take two spare tyres, not just one. There's more on 4WD driving in Basics (see p.28).

The church, along with the entire village, remains locked up and abandoned for most of the year – Isluga is a "**ceremonial village**", whose inhabitants come back only for festivals, important religious ceremonies and funerals; the principal fiestas are held on February 2 and 3, March 10, Easter week, and December 8, 12 and 21 to 25.

Colchane

Ten kilometres from Isluga, at the end of the paved road from Huara, at 3730m above sea level, **COLCHANE** is a small, grim border town of grid-laid streets and truckers' canteens. Most days, the only reason you might want to come here is for **accommodation** or to cross over into **Bolivia** (see below). Twice a month, however, on alternate Saturdays, Colchane takes on a bit of life and colour as the neighbouring altiplano villagers bring their fresh produce, weavings and knitwear to sell at the **market**.

Cariquima

Charming **CARIQUIMA**, just 17km south of Colchane, has picturesque, cleanly swept streets and an old altiplano-style church with a painted interior. Seek out the **crafts cooperative**, housed in a beautifully decorated building along one of the village's few streets, and where you'll find high-quality woollens for sale. Cariquima sits in the lee of the dramatic Nevado Cariquima, while, 5km to the north is the minute hamlet of **Ancovinto**. There you'll see a forest of giant cacti that sway in the breeze and enjoy fantastic views across the altiplano to Bolivia and the Salar de Coipasa.

ARRIVAL AND DEPARTURE

By organized tour There's no public transport around this region, so you must take an organized tour from Iquique (see p.191) or rent a 4WD.

ACCOMMODATION

Camino del Inca Teniente Gonzalez s/n, Colchane ⊕ 09 8446 3586. Given the lack of other accommodation options, it's fortunate that this family-run budget hotel is a solid option. It has very basic but clean rooms with shared bathrooms and hot water. **CH$16,000**

PARQUE NACIONAL VOLCÁN ISLUGA

CROSSING THE BOLIVIAN BORDER
Via Colchane Note that border control (daily 8am–7pm) is sometimes closed at lunch time.

Conaf refugio Enquelga. This Conaf-run *refugio* can provide accommodation for up to five people; it's supposed to be open year-round, but sometimes isn't. Call Arica's Conaf office (see p.207) to reserve a bed in advance. Dorms **CH$5500**

> ### PINOCHET'S LEGACY IN PISAGUA
> At the far end of town, next to the carabineros station, Pisagua's more recent history is the subject of a haunting **mural** dedicated to the memory of those executed here during the military dictatorship, when the village was used as a concentration camp. A couple of kilometres north, on the edge of the cemetery, the former site of the mass graves is marked by an open pit bearing a simple cross, a scattering of wreaths and a block of stone inscribed with a single line by Pablo Neruda: "Even though a thousand years shall pass, this site will never be cleansed of the blood of those who fell here."

Pisagua

Most people whizz up the Panamericana between Iquique and Arica in about four hours without stopping, but some 80km north of the turn-off to Iquique, a poorly paved side road (no public transport) leads 52km west down to **Pisagua** – a crumbling, evocative nitrate port that makes an interesting option for a night's stopover. The final stretch down to the port is very steep, giving dramatic views down to the little toy town cowering by the ocean, the only sign of life on this barren desert coast.

Pisagua is a funny sort of place, part scruffy, ramshackle fishing town, part fascinating relic of the past. It was one of the busiest and wealthiest ports of the nitrate era, and is still dotted with many grand nineteenth-century buildings, some of them restored and repainted, others decaying at the same slow pace as the rest of the town (which has only about 150 inhabitants today). Most striking of all is the handsome, white-and-blue timber **clock tower**, built in 1887 and still standing watch from the hillside.

The old theatre
In front of the main square

This fine wooden building erected in 1892, with a typical nineteenth-century facade featuring tall wooden pillars, a balcony and a balustrade, is Pisagua's main monument to the nitrate era. You can borrow the key from the *carabineros* station at the far end of town, and wander inside to take a look at the large, empty stage, the rows of polished wooden seats, and the high ceiling, lavishly painted with cherubs dancing on clouds. The ghostliness of the place is made all the more intense by the monotonous sound of the waves crashing against the building's rear wall, which plunges directly down to the sea.

ACCOMMODATION   PISAGUA

Hostal La Roca Manuel Rodriguez 20 ☎ 57 273 1502. Lovely modern-rustic, family-run hotel with big clean rooms, all boasting private bathrooms with hot water. Ask for a room with sea view. Friendly owner Sra Catherine will make you feel right at home. CH$24,000

Hacienda de Tiliviche

Ten kilometres north of the turn-off for Pisagua, just before the bridge across the Quebrada de Tiliviche, a short track branches left (west) to the **HACIENDA DE TILIVICHE**. At the end of the track you'll find the old *casa patronal*, a charmingly dilapidated house overlooking a yard full of clucking chickens and lethargic dogs. It was built in 1855 for a British nitrate family and remained in British hands until very recently; the current owners have vague plans to renovate it and turn it into a hotel.

THE AYMARA OF CHILE

The **Aymara** people are the second-largest indigenous linguistic group of South America (after the Quechua). The culture flourished around **Lake Titicaca** and spread throughout the high-plain region, known as the altiplano, of what is now Bolivia, Peru and Chile. Today there are around three million Aymara scattered through these three countries, with the Chilean Aymara forming the smallest group, totalling some forty thousand people. Following the big migrations from the highlands to the coast that took place in the 1960s, most of the Aymara people of Chile now live and work in the coastal cities of **Arica** and **Iquique**. At least thirteen thousand Aymara, however, remain in the altiplano of northern Chile, where their lifestyle is still firmly rooted in the traditions of the past thousand years. The main economic activities are llama and sheep herding and the cultivation of crops such as potatoes and barley.

Traditionally, the Aymara live in **small communities**, called *ayllu*, based on extended family kinship. Their houses are made of stone and mud with rough thatched roofs, and most villages have a square and a small whitewashed church with a separate bell tower – often dating from the seventeenth century when **Spanish missionaries** evangelized the region.

RELIGIOUS BELIEFS

Nowadays many of the smaller villages, such as Isluga (see p.199), are left abandoned for most of the year, the houses securely locked up while their owners make their living down in the city or in the larger cordillera towns like **Putre**. Known as "ceremonial villages" they're shaken from their slumber and burst into life when people return for important religious festivals or funerals. Andean **fiestas** are based on a fascinating blend of Catholic and indigenous rites. At the centre of Aymara culture is respect for the life-giving **Mother Earth**, known as *pachamama*, and traditional ceremonies – involving singing and dancing – are still carried out in some communities at sowing and harvest time.

The Aymara also believe that the tallest mountains looming over their villages contain spirits, or *mallku*, that guard over them, protecting their animals and crops. Once a year, on **May 3** – Cruz de Mayo – the most traditional communities climb up the sacred mountains, where a village elder speaks to the *mallku*, which appears in the form of a condor. Today's young Aymara go to local state schools and speak Spanish as their main language, and while traditional lifestyles continue in the altiplano, it's with increasingly closer links with mainstream Chilean life.

The British Cemetery

Set within the grounds of Hacienda de Tiliviche, on the other side of the stream, stands a nostalgic testimony to the nitrate era: the old **British Cemetery**, enclosed by tall iron railings and a huge, rusty gate – you can borrow the key from the hacienda caretaker. Inside, about a hundred lonely graves stand in the shade of a few *tamarugo* trees at the foot of the desolate mountain that rises over the *quebrada*. This stark desert setting is strikingly at odds with the very English inscriptions on the tombstones ("Thy will be done" and the like). The graves read like a who's who of the erstwhile British business community, including people like Herbert Harrison, the manager of the Tarapacá Waterworks Company and, most famously, **James Humberstone**, the manager of several nitrate *oficinas*.

The geoglyphs

The southern wall of Tiliviche's *quebrada* also features some of the most impressive **geoglyphs** in Chile. They're best viewed from the lay-by just off the Panamericana, a few hundred metres up from the bridge on the northern side of the *quebrada*. From this vantage point, you can see the images in all their splendour – a large crowd of llamas covering the hillside. All of the llamas are moving in the same direction, towards the sea, and it's thought that the drawings were designed to guide caravans descending from the mountains on their journey towards the coast.

Arica

ARICA likes to call itself "*la ciudad de la eterna primavera*" – "city of everlasting spring". Chile's northernmost city, only 19km south of the Peruvian border, is certainly blessed with a mild climate, which, along with its sandy beaches, makes it a popular holiday resort for Chileans and Bolivians. Although a lingering sea fog can dampen spirits, in the winter especially, just head a few kilometres inland and you'll usually find blue skies.

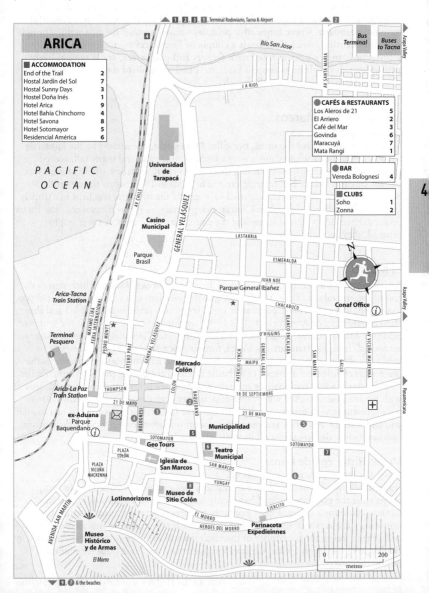

ARICA

ACCOMMODATION

End of the Trail	2
Hostal Jardín del Sol	7
Hostal Sunny Days	3
Hostel Doña Inés	1
Hotel Arica	9
Hotel Bahía Chinchorro	4
Hotel Savona	8
Hotel Sotomayor	5
Residencial América	6

CAFÉS & RESTAURANTS

Los Aleros de 21	5
El Arriero	2
Café del Mar	3
Govinda	6
Maracuyá	7
Mata Rangi	1

BAR

Vereda Bolognesi	4

CLUBS

Soho	1
Zonna	2

Terminal Rodoviario, Tacna & Airport

Bus Terminal

Buses to Tacna

Azapa Valley

Río San Jose

AV SANTA MARIA

J A RIOS

PACIFIC OCEAN

Universidad de Tarapacá

AV CHILE

GENERAL VELASQUEZ

Casino Municipal

Parque Brasil

LASTARRIA

ESMERALDA

JUAN NOE

Parque General Ibañez

CHACABUCO

Conaf Office

Arica-Tacna Train Station

MAXIMO LIRA

FERIA INTERNACIONAL

PEDRO MONTT

Terminal Pesquero

O'HIGGINS

BLANCO ENCALADA

GENERAL LAGOS

SAN MARTIN

GALLO

AV VICUÑA MACKENNA

ARTURO PRAT

GENERAL VELASQUEZ

Mercado Colón

MAIPU

PATRICIO LYNCH

Arica-La Paz Train Station

THOMPSON

21 DE MAYO

COLÓN

BAQUEDANO

18 DE SEPTIEMBRE

ex-Aduana

BOLOGNESI

21 DE MAYO

Parque Baquedano

Municipalidad

SOTOMAYOR

Geo Tours

PLAZA COLÓN

Teatro Municipal

SOTOMAYOR

PLAZA VICUÑA MACKENNA

Iglesia de San Marcos

SAN MARCOS

Lotinnorizons

YUNGAY

Museo de Sitio Colón

AVENIDA SAN MARTIN

EL MORRO

EJERCITO

HEROES DEL MORRO

Parinacota Expedieinnes

Museo Histórico y de Armas

El Morro

0   200
metres

Panamericana

Azapa Valley

The city's compact, tidy centre sits proudly at the foot of the Morro cliff, the site of a major Chilean victory in the War of the Pacific (and cherished as a symbol of national glory). It was this war that delivered Arica, formerly Peruvian, into Chilean hands, in 1883, and while the city is emphatically Chilean today, there's no denying the strong presence of *mestizo* and Quechua-speaking Peruvians on the streets, trading their fresh produce and *artesanía*. This, added to its role as Bolivia's main export centre, makes Arica more colourful, ethnically diverse and vibrant than most northern Chilean cities, even if parts of it look somewhat impoverished.

The liveliest streets are pedestrianized Calles 21 de Mayo and Bolognesi, the latter clogged with **artesanía stalls**, while by the port you'll see the smelly but colourful **terminal pesquero**, where inquisitive pelicans wander around the fish stalls. Though far from beautiful, Arica does boast a couple of fine pieces of nineteenth-century architecture, pretty squares filled with flowers and palm trees, and a young, lively atmosphere. It's a pleasant enough place to spend a couple of days – or longer, if you feel like kicking back on the beach.

Iglesia de San Marcos

Plaza Colón • Daily 9am–2pm & 6–8pm • Free

In the centre you'll find the small, tree-filled **Plaza Colón**, dominated by the **Iglesia de San Marcos**, a pretty white church with a high, Gothic spire and many tall, arched windows. Designed by Gustave Eiffel, this curious church, made entirely of iron, was prefabricated in France before being erected in Arica in 1876, when the city still belonged to Peru. The riveting key used to assemble the structure was kept in a display case inside the church, but when Chilean troops attacked, it was thrown into the sea to prevent the invaders from dismantling the church and stealing it as a war trophy (instead, they took the whole city).

El Morro

Arica's most visible feature is the 110m-high cliff known as **El Morro**, which signals the end of the coastal cordillera. Steps starting at the southern end of Calle Colón lead you to the top, where sweeping, panoramic views (especially impressive at night) and the **Museo Histórico y de Armas** await. This 130m cappuccino-coloured cliff is *the* source of pride for Arica's citizens, heightened by a big sign saying "*Arica siempre Arica, mayor es mi lealtad*" (roughly translated as "Arica, forever Arica, my loyalty will always be to you"). It's also an important national landmark, given its historical significance as the place where Chile won a crucial 1880 battle against Peru during the War of the Pacific.

At the top is a very nationalistic military museum (see below) and a statue of Christ with his arms outstretched – a symbol of peace between the two once-enemy nations. It's a pleasant ten- to fifteen-minute hike up Calle Colón, but you can get a taxi to take you and wait for you while you explore and admire the wonderful view of the city and beaches, before dropping you off in town afterwards.

Museo Histórico y de Armas

El Morro • Mon–Fri 8am–6pm, Sat & Sun 8am–8pm • CH$800

Built on top of a former Peruvian fortification, this museum is owned by the army, rather than the government, and has clearly had more money spent on it than most Chilean museums. The exhibits – primarily nineteenth-century guns and military uniforms – are very well displayed, but the theme is rather chauvinistic in tone, the main thrust being the superiority of the Chileans and the inferiority of the Peruvians in the Battle of the Morro, when Chilean forces stormed and took possession of the hilltop defence post.

Museo de sitio Colón

Colón 10 • Tues–Sun 10am–6pm • CH$2000

This museum has a rather curious history: while carrying out construction work for a new hotel back in 2004, the builders came across some very old human remains. Plans for the new hotel stopped and the University of Tarapacá was called in and it soon became apparent that the site was a four thousand-year-old funerary space for the Chinchorro people. Because of the extremely fragile nature of these age-old human remains, transportation was out of the question and a museum on the site was opened to exhibit the 48 Chinchorro mummies found.

Ex-aduana

Parque Baquedano • Mon–Fri 8.30am–8pm • Free

The 1874 **Ex-aduana** (customs house) is another Eiffel-designed building with an attractive stone facade of pink and white horizontal stripes. These days it's used as a cultural centre (it's also known as the "*casa de la cultura*") and puts on regular photographic and art exhibitions. Its pleasant location on a little square full of palm trees and shady benches, flanked to the south by the coastal avenue, adds to its charm.

The beaches

Arica is a major destination for serious surfers, who travel far and wide to test out the famous waves. The city holds a couple of important international surfing competitions every year, though sunbathers and swimmers will also appreciate Arica's beaches; although not as attractive as Iquique's sandy shores, the water is noticeably warmer. The closest beach to the centre is the popular **Playa El Laucho**, a curved, sandy cove about a twenty-minute walk down Avenida San Martín, south of El Morro. You can also get *micros* down the avenue, which continue to several other beaches, including **Playa La Lisera** and **Playa Brava**, both attractive, and the usually deserted **Playa Arenillas Negras**, a wide expanse of dark sand backed by low sand dunes, with a fish-processing factory at its southern end.

Northern beaches

Two kilometres north of the centre, **Playa Chinchorro** is a large, clean beach where you can rent jet skis in high season (Dec–March; CH$12,000 for 30min). To get there, take bus #12 or #14; both will drop you off one block from the beach. Further north, **Playa Las Machas** is quieter but more exposed to the wind, and popular with surfers. The only beaches suitable for swimmers are Playa Lisera, Playa Laucho and Playa Chinchorro – these all have lifeguards during the summer months.

ARRIVAL AND DEPARTURE	**ARICA**

BY PLANE

Arica's Chacalluta airport lies 18km north of the city and is connected to the centre by reasonably priced airport taxis (around CH$6000–7000) or minibus transfers.

Airlines LAN, Arturo Prat 391 (☎ 58 225 2650); Sky Airlines, 21 de Mayo 356 (☎ 58 225 1816 or 229 0768 at airport).

Destinations Iquique (4 daily; 45min); Santiago (4–7 daily; 2hr 30min–3hr 35min).

BY BUS

Coming in by bus, you'll arrive at Arica's Terminal Rodoviario, which uniquely charges a CH$200 platform fee for all departures; make sure to pay this fee at your bus company desk, even if you already have a bus ticket. The terminal is quite a distance from town on Av Diego Portales, but you can easily catch a *colectivo* or *micro* into the centre.

Destinations Antofagasta (every 1–3hr; 10hr); Calama (5–6 daily; 10hr); Chañaral (7 daily; 15hr); Copiapó (11 daily; 17hr); Iquique (every 30min; 4hr 30min); Putre (1 daily; 3hr); San Pedro de Atacama (1–2 daily; 14hr); Santiago (10 daily; 29hr); Vallenar (10 daily; 20hr).

TOURS FROM ARICA

Three or four companies in Arica regularly offer **tours** up to **Parque Nacional Lauca** (see p.211). The problem is that the most commonly available tour takes place in a single day, which means rushing from sea level to up to 4500m and down again in a short space of time – really not a good idea, and very likely to cause some ill effects, ranging from tiredness and mild headaches to acute dizziness and nausea. In very rare cases the effects can be more serious, and you should always check that the company carries a supply of oxygen and has a staff member trained to deal with emergencies.

Altitude aside, the amount of time you spend inside a minibus is very tiring, which can spoil your experience of what is one of the most beautiful parts of Chile. Therefore it's really worth paying extra and taking a tour that includes at least one overnight stop in the town of Putre (see p.210); better still is one continuing south to the Salar de Surire (see p.215) and Parque Nacional Isluga (see p.198). However, it's worth noting that the availability of these longer tours can be frustratingly scarce during the quieter low season months. One-day trips usually cost from around CH$25,000–30,000 per person while you can expect to pay around CH$55,000–100,000 for a one- or two-night tour, overnighting in Putre, and from around CH$200,000 for a three-night tour, sleeping in Putre and Colchane. See below for a list of tour operators.

TOUR OPERATORS

Geotour Bolognesi 421 ☎ 58 225 3927, ⓦgeotour .cl. Slick, professional but fairly impersonal company offering mostly one-day tours around Arica, as well as trips further afield to Lauca, Matilla and Pica. There are two other branches in San Pedro de Atacama and Iquique.

★**Latinorizons** Colón 7 ☎ 58 225 0007, ⓦlatinorizons.com. Friendly and extremely reliable Belgian-run company offering a wide range of altiplano tours, including overnight, with a more adventurous feel than most of the others on offer. French and English spoken. Charlie, the very knowledgeable owner, also offers nice, clean rooms to rent in his home near El Morro.

Parinacota Expediciones Héroes del Morro 632 ☎ 58 223 3305, ⓦparinacotaexpediciones.cl. Well-established company offering several options for visiting Parque Nacional Lauca and around, including the usual day-trip, an overnight stop in Putre and a two-night tour taking in the Salar de Surire.

GETTING AROUND

By colectivo The colour and number on top of the taxi *colectivo* denotes which direction it´s heading. To avoid confusion, it´s best to take a private taxi from the bus station when you first arrive, until you figure out the number system.

Private taxis Radiotaxi Chacalluta, Patricio Lynch 371 ☎ 58 225 4812; Radio Taxi ☎ 58 225 7000.
Car rental Europcar, Colón 996 (☎ 58 225 8911); Cactus, General Lagos 666 (☎ 58 225 8353); or Hertz, Baquedano 999 (☎ 58 223 1487).

INFORMATION

Sernatur San Marcos 101 (Jan & Feb Mon–Fri 9am–9pm; March–Dec Mon–Thurs 9am–6pm, Fri 9am–5pm; ☎ 58 225 4506 or 225 2054, ⓦwww.sernatur.cl).
Conaf Vicuña Mackenna 820 (Mon–Fri 8.30am–5.30pm; ☎ 58 220 1200, ⓦwww.conaf.cl). The regional Conaf office

has basic maps and information on Parque Nacional Lauca and adjoining protected areas. You can also reserve beds at the Conaf *refugios* in these areas, if you know exactly when you'll be arriving (see box, p.215).

ACCOMMODATION

Unlike Iquique, Arica has very little seafront **accommodation** and most places to stay are situated in and around the town's centre. Here, there's no shortage of *residenciales*, ranging from the dirt-cheap to the polished and comfortable. Typically for these parts, however, there's a lack of decent mid-range accommodation.

HOTELS

Hostal Jardín del Sol Sotomayor 848 ☎ 58 223 2795, ⓦhostaljardindelsol.cl. Small, tidy rooms with private bathrooms off a flower-filled courtyard with tables, chairs

and loungers. Good value for money and very friendly too, a great place to mix with like-minded travellers. All in, the best budget option in town. CH$33,000
Hotel Arica Av San Martín 599 ☎ 58 225 4540,

@ panamericanahoteles.cl. High-end but rather dated and overpriced hotel overlooking the ocean, with pleasant rooms and *cabañas*, plus a pool, tennis courts and mini golf, as well as a mediocre restaurant. Doubles US$139, *cabañas* US$170

Hotel Bahía Chinchorro Av Luis Beretta Porcel 2031 ☎ 58 226 0676, @ bahia_arica @latinmail.com. A 15min walk from the centre, this place has direct access to Chinchorro beach. The simple rooms – with attached bathrooms, a/c and TVs – are all glass-fronted, giving them superb ocean views. CH$50,000

Hotel Savona Yungay 380 ☎ 58 223 1000, @ hotel savona.cl. Low-rise, 1970s-style hotel built around a bright patio garden with a swimming pool. Rather tasteless yet comfortable rooms have small private bathrooms and TVs. Bikes are available for hire. CH$49,000

Hotel Sotomayor Sotomayor 367 ☎ 58 258 5761, @ hotelsotomayor.cl. Formerly the *Hotel San Marcos*, this terracotta-coloured building features clean, airy yet somewhat dated rooms (disappointing after the beautiful old Spanish tiles in the lobby) with private bath and parking. CH$40,000

Residencial América Sotomayor 430 ☎ 58 225 4148, @ residencialamerica.com. Right in the heart of the city, opposite the town hall, this *residencial* offers good-value budget rooms with an encouraging odour of furniture polish. Some rooms have private bathrooms. CH$25,000

HOSTELS

End of the Trail Esteban Alvarado 117 ☎ 58 231 4316, @ endofthetrail-arica.cl. A congenial American owner runs this hostel, which has comfortable, quiet rooms around an indoor courtyard, amazing showers and a specially designed roof that keeps the house cool. To get here from the bus station, walk two blocks west on Diego Portales, then four blocks south on Pedro de Valdivia. Dorms CH$9000, doubles CH$22,000

Hostal Sunny Days Tomas Aravena 161 ☎ 58 224 1038, @ sunny-days-arica.cl. Extremely friendly and knowledgeable Kiwi-Chilean hosts preside over travellers of all ages in this custom-built hostel. An excellent breakfast, kitchen and lounge facilities and a relaxed communal atmosphere all add to its appeal. Dorms CH$9000, doubles CH$22,000

Hostel Doña Inés Manuel Rojas 2864 ☎ 58 224 8108, @ hiarica@hostelling.cl. Situated a 15min drive outside the centre (but easily accessible by *colectivo*), this HI hostel, owned by the very hyper, very sociable Roberto, is the place to come if you want to mix with other travellers and are up for a party. Do stay for one of Roberto's weekly *asados*. Dorms CH$9500, doubles CH$25,000

EATING AND DRINKING

Los Aleros de 21 21 de Mayo 736 ☎ 58 225 4641. Traditional Chilean restaurant serving pricey yet excellent steaks, seafood and other meat dishes (mains around CH$8000–12,000). Great quality and service – it's a favourite among locals, and deservedly so. Mon–Sat noon–4pm & 8pm–midnight, Sun noon–4pm.

El Arriero 21 de Mayo 385 ☎ 58 223 2636, @ restaurantelarriero.cl. Recommended grill house serving tasty fillet steaks and other meat dishes (from CH$7000); often has live folk music at the weekends. Book ahead as it gets busy. Mon–Sat noon–4pm & 7–11pm.

Café del Mar 21 de Mayo 260 ☎ 58 223 1936, @ cafedelmararica.cl. This café on the main pedestrian strip is popular with Arica's residents, both young and old, thanks to its colourful decor, outside seating and tasty menu, which includes big salads, sandwiches, pizzas and, best of all, delicious crêpes (from CH$2000). There are more sophisticated dishes served in the evenings. Mon–Sat 9.30am–midnight.

Govinda Blanco Encalada 200 ☎ 09 8928 8642. Zen-like place a short walk from the centre, with tasty, vegetarian set menu lunches (from around CH$2500) that include soup, salad and a main dish. Great for a healthy meal on a small budget. Mon–Sat 1–3.30pm & 8–10.30pm.

★**Maracuyá** Av San Martín 0321, Playa La Lisera ☎ 58 222 7600, @ restaurantmaracuya.cl. Dramatically sited as it is, right over the ocean's edge, this smart restaurant (one of Arica's best) offers boldly prepared fish and seafood (dishes around CH$6000–12,000) amid a spectacle of breaking waves. Daily noon–4pm & 8.30pm–midnight.

Mata Rangi Terminal pesquero ☎ 58 223 3404. Tucked inside the fishermen's harbour, a rustic inexpensive place serving unfussy fish and seafood lunches (around CH$5000) – sit by the window and watch the pelicans eat theirs as you eat yours. Picnic trips to a nearby penguin colony on the owner's boat can also be arranged. Daily noon–3.30pm.

Vereda Bolognesi Bolognesi 340 ☎ 58 223 1273, @ veredabolognesi.cl. By night, from about 8pm, this smart little shopping gallery in town turns into a buzzing patio bar zone – several resto-bars compete with their happy hours so it´s easy to get a good cocktail at a decent price. Mon–Sat 10am–10pm.

NIGHTLIFE

Soho Buenos Aires 209, Playa Chinchorro ☎ 09 8905 1806, @ discosoho.com. A stone's throw from Chinchorro beach, this nightclub is attached to *Pub Capitán Drake* and often has live music acts and several DJs. Entry is often free before 1.30am. Daily midnight till late.

Zonna Av Argentina 2787 ☎ 58 222 1509, ⓦ zonna.cl. Zonna, the biggest, best-known and most popular nightclub in Arica, has multiple rooms each playing different types of music ranging from salsa to 1980s hits. Ask about the weekly drink promotion. Thurs–Sun midnight till late.

DIRECTORY

Money and exchange Arica has many ATMs – mostly on 21 de Mayo – and *casas de cambio* on Calle Colón.

Post office Arturo Prat 305 (Mon–Fri 9am–6pm, Sat 10am–1pm).

The Azapa Valley

Avenida Diego Portales extends out of Arica's city centre into the green **AZAPA VALLEY**. The far western end of the valley is, to all intents and purposes, a suburb of Arica, crammed as it is with condos and villas, some of which have been converted into trendy discos, along with a couple of good restaurants. The highlight of a trip to the Azapa Valley is the Museo Archeológico, which houses a collection of the world's most ancient mummies. This museum is among Chile's best and is definitely worth the trip

CHINCHORRO MUMMIES

In 1983, while laying a new pipeline near the foot of El Morro, the Arica water company came across a hoard of withered corpses buried a couple of metres beneath the sand. Work immediately ceased and archeologists from the University of Tarapacá were rushed in to assess the scene, which turned out to be a seven-thousand-year-old burial site containing 96 bodies – the largest and best-preserved find, to date, of **Chinchorro mummies**.

The ancient practice of mummification in this region – the oldest known in the world – was first identified in 1917 when a series of highly unusual human remains were discovered. Further excavations revealed similar findings spread along the coast, concentrated between Arica and Camerones, 65km south, and it became apparent that they were relics of an ancient society that archeologists have named the Chinchorro culture. Modern radiocarbon dating has established that the practice was well under way by 5000 BC – more than two millennia before the Egyptians began practising mummification.

ORIGINS OF THE CHINCHORRO

No one knows exactly where the Chinchorro people came from; some archeologists speculate that they moved down from the north, others that they came from the Andean highlands. What's clear, however, is that by 7000 BC scattered groups of people – possibly extended families – were spread along the coast of Chile's Far North, where they lived on the abundant crabs, clams, mussels, seaweed, pelicans, sea lions and other marine life of the region, supplementing their diet with guanaco and wild berries.

THE MUMMIFICATION PROCESS

The great simplicity of their hunter-gatherer lifestyle makes the sophisticated techniques they developed to **preserve the dead** all the more extraordinary. The practice involved removing the brain through a hole at the base of the skull, and removing all internal organs, which were probably discarded. After this, the cavities were dried with hot stones or fire and then refilled with straw and ashes. The bones of the arms and legs were replaced with sticks bound into place with reeds, and the skeleton was given extra padding before the body was stitched up. The face was then coated in paste, which dried into a hard mask with a sculpted nose and incisions marking the eyes and mouth. The finishing touch was provided by a wig made of human hair, which was attached to the skull.

The Chinchorro culture performed this elaborate process for over three thousand years until, for unknown reasons, the practice died out around 1500 BC, and the era of the oldest known form of artificial mummification came to an end.

out here. If you're booked on a multi-day tour of the Altiplano, it's very likely this will be a stop-off.

Poblado Artesanal

On your way out towards the Azapa Valley, on Calle Hualles, just south of the river, the **Poblado Artesanal** is a replica of an altiplano village, where twelve white houses serve as workshops for artisans selling handicrafts ranging from ceramics and glass to knitwear and leather items; its hours of operation are erratic.

Museo Arqueológico

Km12, Azapa Valley • Daily: Jan & Feb 10am–7pm; March–Dec 10am–6pm • CH$2000 • ☎ 58 220 5551, ⊛ www.uta.cl/masma/

Twelve kilometres along the road from the Poblado Artesanal, the outstanding **Museo Arqueológico**, part of the University of Tarapacá, houses an excellent collection of regional pre-Columbian artefacts, including a collection of extraordinary Chinchorro mummies (see box, p.209) buried over four thousand years ago. Other exhibits include finely decorated Tiwanaku ceramics, ancient Andean musical instruments and snuff trays, and many beautifully embroidered tapestries – look out for the one in Case 11, decorated with images of smiling women – and displays on contemporary Aymara culture.

All the pieces are extremely well presented, and there are unusually explanatory leaflets available in several languages, including English, French and German.

San Miguel de Azapa

In the nearby village of **San Miguel de Azapa**, the only place of interest is the fabulously multicoloured desert **cemetery**, which climbs like a mini-Valparaíso for the deceased towards a dune-like cliff. The colour comes from the artificial flowers laid on the graves. By the entrance sits the morbidly named **restaurant** *La Picá del Muertito* (the "Little Dead Man's Snack-Bar"), famous for miles around for its first-rate *pastel de choclo*, a sugar-glazed corn-bake containing meat, egg and olives.

Alto Ramírez

The Azapa Valley is also the site of several **geoglyphs**. The most impressive example is **Alto Ramírez**, a large, stylized human figure surrounded by geometric shapes; you can see it, at a distance, from the main road on the way to the museum (ask your *colectivo* driver to point it out to you) or take a detour to get a closer look.

ARRIVAL AND DEPARTURE
THE AZAPA VALLEY

By colectivo *Colectivos* for the Azapa Valley, including the Museo Arqueológico and the nearby geoglyphs, leave from the corner of Lynch and Chacabuco in Arica's centre.

Putre

The busy little mountain town of **PUTRE**, surrounded by a patchwork of green fields and Inca terraces, lies 150km on from Arica at a height of 3500m. It's a popular overnight stop en route to the higher altitudes of **Parque Nacional Lauca** – climbers, in particular, like to spend a few days walking in the hills here before attempting the volcanoes in the park. Putre's rustic houses are clustered around a large, green square, overlooked by the Municipalidad.

The church

Off the northeast corner of the square you'll find the **church**, built in 1670 after an earthquake destroyed the original one, which, according to old Spanish chronicles, was clad in gold and silver. The current building, heavily restored in 1871, is considerably more modest, consisting of a small stone chapel and a whitewashed, straw-roofed bell tower.

The village observes the Feast of the Assumption, August 15, with a week-long celebration that features much singing and dancing; accommodation is hard to find during this time.

ARRIVAL AND INFORMATION   PUTRE

By bus Buses La Paloma, Germán Riesco 2071 (☎ 58 222 2710), has a daily bus to Putre from Arica (3hr).

Tourist information Arturo Prat s/n (Mon–Fri 9am–6pm; ☎ 58 225 2803).

TOURS

Alto Andino Nature Tours Baquedano 299 ☎ 58 230 0013, ✉ altoandino@yahoo.com. Run by an Alaskan naturalist who offers wildlife-viewing excursions, specializing in ornithology and marine mammals in Parque Nacional Lauca and coastal areas; phone or email for more details. She also has a few simple, inexpensive rooms to rent.

Alvaro Mamani ☎ 09 9763 9318 ✉ amamaniguia @gmail.com. For informative trips into the altiplano, Alvaro Mamani is a very personable Aymara guide.

Terrace Lodge ☎ 58 258 4275, ⓦ terracelodge.com. Offers a wide range of tours (maximum five people) throughout the region.

ACCOMMODATION

Hotel Kukuli Baquedano 301 ☎ 09 9161 4709. Run by the very friendly Libertad, this hotel has comfortable en-suite rooms in a modern-ish building. An onsite restaurant, hearty breakfasts (included in the room rates) and parking are plus points. CH$30,000

Hotel Qantati Hijuela 208 ☎ 58 232 8763, ⓦ hotelqantati.blogspot.co.uk. On the western edges of town, about a 10min walk from the plaza, *Qantati* is the smartest, and most expensive, place to stay in Putre,

offering modern heated bedrooms with views out to the valley. CH$57,000

Terrace Lodge 5km outside Putre ☎ 58 258 4275, ⓦ terracelodge.com. This charming guesthouse is the best place to stay in and around Putre, boasting a tranquil location outside town, comfortable en suites, helpful staff and a range of tour options. It's a popular choice so book ahead. CH$34,000

EATING

★**Kuchu Marka** Baquedano s/n ☎ 09 9011 4007. At this cosy place, you can get alpaca stew and other hearty mountain dishes like *picante de conejo* (a sort of rabbit curry), llama steaks and trout in a butter sauce (mains around CH$8000). Mon–Sat noon–11.30pm.

Rosamel Cochrane s/n ☎ 56 258 7202. Simple restaurant on the square serving good set menus made up of local dishes such as stews and spicy meat dishes at affordable prices (CH$5000–8000). Mon–Sat noon–3pm & 8–11pm, Sun noon–3pm.

Parque Nacional Lauca

A few hours east of Putre, up in the cordillera, **Parque Nacional Lauca** has become one of the most popular attractions in the north of Chile. A few of Arica's tour operators (see p.207) will get you there if you don't relish the idea of driving yourself.

Las Cuevas

A 4400m-high mountain pass signals the boundary of Parque Nacional Lauca. Up here the air is thin and cold, and the road is flanked by light-green *bofedal* (highland pasture) where herds of wild vicuña come to feed in the mornings. Ten

PARQUE NACIONAL LAUCA AND AROUND

Putre

Socoroma

Guardería Las Cuevas

Termas de Jurasí

Chucullo

Cerro Guane Guane (5096m)

PARQUE

NACIONAL

LAUCA

Parinacota

Lagunas de Cotacotani

Cerro Choquelimpie (5288m)

Volcán Pomerape (6240m)

Volcán Parinacota (6330m)

Lago Chungara

Tambo Quemado

BOLIVIA

Arica

N

RESERVA

NACIONAL

LAS VICUÑAS

Volcán Guallatiri (6060m)

Guallatire

SALAR DE SURIRE

0   25

kilometres

Polloquere & Parque Nacional Volcán Isluga

kilometres into the park, you reach the Conaf hut (erratic opening hours) at **Las Cuevas**, a good place to stop to check on weather and road conditions and observe the comical antics of vizcachas, cuddly chinchilla-like rodents with curly tails and a spring-like leap.

Parinacota

From Las Cuevas the road continues through a wide, green plain filled with grazing llamas and alpacas. Some 19km on from the Conaf hut, it passes the turn-off for **PARINACOTA** (the name means "flamingo lake" in Aymara), site of the park's headquarters and an idyllic *pueblo altiplánico* in its own right, composed of fifty or so crumbling, whitewashed houses huddled around a beautiful little **church**. Opposite the church, in the plaza, local women sell alpaca knitwear and other **artesanía**. Many of the village houses are under lock and key for much of the year, their owners returning only for important fiestas and funerals.

The church

Built in 1789, this is one of Chile's most assiduously maintained Andean churches, sporting brilliant white walls and a bright-blue wooden door, trimmed with yellow and green. Like most churches of the altiplano, it has thick stone and adobe walls and a sloping straw roof, and is enclosed within a little white wall incorporating the bell

---

PARINACOTA'S WANDERING TABLE

Among the oddities of Parinacota's venerable church (see p.212) is a **magical "walking" table** that's kept chained to the wall, for fear it will wander off in the night. According to local legend, the table can predict death and, if left unchained, stops outside the home of the next villager to die.

---

tower into one of its corners. It's usually open in the morning (if not, you can borrow the key from the caretaker – ask at the *artesanía* stalls). Inside, you'll find a series of faded, centuries-old friezes depicting the Stations of the Cross and vivid scenes of sinners suffering in hell. There's also an unusual collection of skulls belonging to former priests.

ACCOMMODATION   PARINACOTA

Hostal y Restorant Uta Kala de Don Leo Parinacota s/n ❶ 58 226 1526, ✉ leonel_parinacota@hotmail .com. This is the first and only hostel in Parinacota – and thankfully it's a good one, with several comfy beds, hot water, heating, meals and splendid views onto fields of grazing llama. Meals available. Dorms CH$10,000

Lagunas de Cotacotani

A collection of small, interconnected lakes lying in a dark lava field, filled with exquisite jade-green water, the **LAGUNAS DE COTACOTANI** lie about 8km east of Parinacota, clearly visible from the paved highway to Bolivia. The lakes were formed by volcanic eruptions and are surrounded by fine dust and cinder cones, further adding to their lunar appearance. The waters are filtered down from Lago Chungará and then continue to the *bofedal de Parinacota*, which is the source of the Río Lauca. On closer inspection the lakes aren't as lifeless as they first appear; many wild Andean geese flock here, while plentiful herds of alpaca graze the soggy marshland. This area is definitely worth exploring as a day hike from Parinacota, but if you are pressed for time take a good look from the *mirador* on the highway, marked by a giant multicoloured *zampoña* (Andean panpipes).

Lago Chungará

Eighteen kilometres on from Parinacota, at an altitude of 4515m, you'll see **LAGO CHUNGARÁ**, a wide blue lake spectacularly positioned at the foot of a snowcapped volcano that rises over its rim like a giant Christmas pudding covered in cream. This is 6330m-high **Volcán Parinacota**, one of the highest peaks in Chile and the park's most challenging climb (see box, p.214). When the lake is mill-pond calm, in other words when there is no wind, the reflection of the volcano is the most memorable view in the entire region. On the southern shore, right by the highway, you'll find a small stone **Conaf refugio** (see p.215). This is unquestionably the best place to stay in the park, allowing you to observe the changing colours of the lake and volcano at different times of day, from the transparent pinks of early morning to the deep blues and gleaming whites of the afternoon.

ARRIVAL AND INFORMATION   PARQUE NACIONAL LAUCA

By bus You can reach Parinacota, where the park's headquarters are located, by bus from Arica with Buses La Paloma, Germán Riesco 2071 (Tues & Fri 11.30am; 3hr; ❶ 58 222 2710, ⓦ translapaloma.cl).
By car Take the CH-11 motorway from Arica for approximately 145km.
Conaf The Conaf administration centre (❶ 58 258 5704), housed in a large, chalet-style building at Parinacota, makes a valiant attempt at informing the public about the park and its wildlife, though opening times are erratic.

WALKS AND CLIMBS IN PARQUE NACIONAL LAUCA

Parque Nacional Lauca doesn't offer a great many hiking possibilities, and most people are content to just admire the scenery and the wildlife. There are, however, at least three half-day or day **walks** you can do, and many more possibilities for **climbing**. Remember to respect the altitude, and to allow yourself more time to cover distances that you could walk quite easily at lower elevations. You must get authorization from DIFROL (governmental borders organization) if you are planning on climbing any of the mountains or volcanoes in the region. Fill in the authorization form on their website (ⓦdifrol.cl) at least two days before climbing, or else ask Putre's municipalidad to do it for you.

Cerro Choquelimpie No technical experience or equipment is necessary to climb this 5288m peak, reached in about four hours from the refugio at Lago Chungará. From the top, you get views down to the gold mine behind the mountain, and on to Lago Chungará and Volcán Parinacota.

Cerro Guane Guane A slow but straightforward climb up this 5096m peak is rewarded by panoramic views over the park. It's suitable for any fit person used to hill-climbing and takes around four hours to the top from the Conaf centre at Parinacota, and two to three hours back down.

Lago Chungará to Parinacota (or reverse) This 18km walk from the refugio at Lago Chungará to Parinacota takes about six hours. Follow the paved highway as far as the *mirador de Lagunas Cotacotani*, then climb down to the lakes, from where a jeep track continues to Parinacota.

Parinacota to Lagunas de Cotacotani A rewarding, not-too-difficult walk, taking about three hours (one way) from Parinacota; ask the Conaf *guardaparque* to point you in the direction of the jeep track you need to follow.

Sendero de excursión de Parinacota An easy, 6km circular walk, marked by blue stones starting behind the Conaf centre, taking you past the *bofedal de Parinacota*, where you can observe numerous grazing alpaca. Good views onto surrounding mountains. Allow two to three hours.

Volcán Parinacota Suitable only for experienced climbers carrying crampons and ropes (though it's not always necessary to use them). Allow two days to get up and down from the base camp (a day's hike from Parinacota), including one night camping on the volcano. Avoid this climb between mid-December and February, because of the weather conditions. Volcan Parincota's brother volcano, Pomerape, is just across the border and makes an equally interesting climb.

ACCOMMODATION

The **Conaf** administration centre (see p.213) sometimes offers **camping** space out the back. Alternatively, some villagers offer very basic rooms (without hot water); ask around.

Conaf refugio On the southern shore of Lago Chungará, right by the highway, ☎58 220 1200, ⓦwww.conaf.cl. Run by Conaf, this small, stone *refugio* has just four beds, a kitchen and unbeatable views across Lago Chungará. Dorms CH$5000

Reserva Nacional las Vicuñas

Directly south of Parque Nacional Lauca, the **RESERVA NACIONAL LAS VICUÑAS** stretches over 100km south across spectacular altiplano wilderness filled with wild vicuña, green *bofedales*, abandoned Aymara villages, groves of *queñoa* – spindly, rickety-looking trees belonging to a species that miraculously defies the treeline – and sweeping vistas of volcanoes. The reserve's administrative centre is about a ninety-minute drive from Putre, in **Guallatire** (4428m altitude), a pretty hamlet with a traditional seventeenth-century Andean church. There's also an obligatory *carabineros* checkpoint here, and a Conaf *refugio* that is seldom in

> **CONAF REFUGIOS**
>
> If you are travelling under your own steam but do not fancy camping in the open wilds of the cold, high altiplano, the various **Conaf refugios** (ⓦwww.conaf.cl) dotted around the Parque Nacional Lauca, Parque Nacional Isluga and in between make for excellent places to stay. They have proper beds, some have decent facilities, and they are nearly all located in amazing spots, with views to linger over. The only problem is that in recent years their upkeep has been shoddy and they are sometimes left in a pitiful state by previous visitors. Worst of all, even if you book ahead through the Conaf offices in Arica (see p.207) or Iquique, reservations are not always respected and you might turn up to find it shut or no room at the inn.

service. Looming over the village, snowcapped **Volcán Guallatire** puffs wispy plumes of smoke from its 6060m peak, while a grassy-banked stream snakes at its foot.

ARRIVAL AND DEPARTURE

By organized tour and 4WD There's no public transport, so you need to hire a high-clearance 4WD vehicle or take an organized tour; try one of the travel agencies in Putre (see p.211). Note that the drive

RESERVA NACIONAL LAS VICUÑAS

into the reserve involves fording several streams, which are usually very low but can swell dangerously with heavy summer rains – check with Conaf in Arica before setting out.

Salar de Surire

4

Following the road south of Guallatire, you'll be rewarded, about 40km on, with sudden, dramatic views of the **SALAR DE SURIRE**, a dazzling white salt flat containing several lakes with nesting colonies of three species of flamingo. Originally part of Parque Nacional Lauca, its status was changed to that of national monument in 1983 to allow borax to be mined from its surface. The mining is still going on today, and you can see the mine's enormous trucks driving over the *salar*, dwarfed by its massive dimensions but a nuisance nonetheless.

Polloquere

Sixteen kilometres on from the Salar de Surire, skirting the southern edge of the salt flat, **Polloquere** (also known as Aguas Calientes) is the site of several pale-blue pools filled with hot thermal water and with a muddy bottom reminiscent of the Dead Sea, an absolutely stunning place to take a bath, despite the lack of facilities – though be sure to get here in the morning, before the bone-chilling afternoon wind picks up. There are a couple of picnic areas and **camping** spaces here, too, but it's a treacherously exposed site.

ARRIVAL AND DEPARTURE

By 4WD There is no public transport, and although it is sometimes possible to get a ride from the trucks that carry

SALAR DE SURIRE

minerals to and fro, it's best to hire your own 4WD vehicle.

ACCOMMODATION

Conaf refugio On the west shore of the Salar, ☎58 220 1200, ⓦwww.conaf.cl. In a wonderful location with terrific views onto the salt flat, this *refugio* has four beds, hot water and a kitchen, though is often closed and bookings are not always respected so do not rely on staying here. Dorms CH$5500

The Central Valley

221 The Rapel Valley

225 The Colchagua Valley

232 The Mataquito Valley

235 The Maule Valley

242 The Itata Valley

245 Nevados de Chillán

246 The Biobío Valley

SALTO DEL LAJA

5

The Central Valley

Extending south from Santiago as far as the Río Biobío, Chile's Central Valley is a long, narrow plain hemmed in by the Andes to the east and the coastal range to the west, with lateral river valleys running between the two. This is the most fertile land in Chile, and the immense orchards, vineyards and pastures that cover the valley floor form a dazzling patchwork of greenery. Even in urban zones, country ways hold sway, and the Central Valley is perhaps the only part of Chile where it is not uncommon to see horse-drawn carts plodding down the Panamericana Highway.

While the main artery of the Panamericana – Ruta 5 – runs all the way south from Santiago, through Rancagua to Los Angeles and beyond, the kernel of the Central Valley lies between the capital and the city of **Chillán**, some 400km south – a region where, during the colonial era, the vast private estates known as **estancias**, or haciendas, were established. The people have held on to many of their rural traditions and the cult of the *huaso*, or cowboy, is as strong as ever, as can be witnessed at the frequent **rodeos** held in stadiums known as *medialunas*.

Further south again, the busy city of **Concepción** guards the mouth of the **Biobío**, the mighty river that for over three hundred years was the boundary between conquered, colonial Chile and unconquered **Mapuche territory**, whose occupants withstood domination until 1883. Traces of the frontier still linger, visible in the ruins of colonial Spanish forts, the proliferation of Mapuche place names and the tin-roof pioneer architecture. Beyond the Bío Bío, towards the Lake District, the gently sloping plains give way to verdant native forests and remote Andean lakes.

Many visitors bypass the Central Valley altogether, whizzing south towards the more dramatic landscapes of the Lake District and beyond. Certainly the agricultural towns dotted along the highway – **Rancagua**, **San Fernando**, **Curicó**, **Talca** and **Los Angeles** – are, on the whole, rather dull, although they make useful stopovers on the long hike between Patagonia and the capital. Stray a few kilometres off the Panamericana and you'll catch a glimpse of an older Chile abounding with pastoral charms. Chief among these are the region's small, **colonial villages**, with their colourful adobe houses topped by overhanging clay-tiled roofs. Among the prettiest examples are **Vichuquén**, west of Curicó, and **Villa Alegre**, south of Talca in the Maule Valley, where you can also visit a trail of lush, emerald **vineyards**. Wine is also the main draw in attractive **Santa Cruz**, a popular weekend destination from Santiago from where you can gaze out over vineyards as you sip vintages on your hotel veranda.

Away from the valley floor, you'll find attractions of a very different nature. To the west, up in the coastal hills, a couple of lakes offer great **watersports** facilities, notably **Lago Rapel**, while further west a number of inviting **beaches** and cheerful seaside towns are scattered down the coast, among them the popular surfer hangout of **Pichilemu**. East of the valley, the dry, dusty slopes of the Andes offer excellent **horseriding** and

Rodeos p.221
Aftershocks p.225
Ruta del Vino Valle de Colchagua p.229
Surfing in Pichilemu p.230
Wine tours around Curicó p.232

Ruta del Vino Valle del Maule p.237
Lights in the sky p.239
Treks in Parque Nacional Nahuelbuta p.257

RUTA DEL VINO

Highlights

❶ Santa Cruz Visit the exceptional museum in this pretty wine valley town, then taste your way through some of the world's best red wines on the "Ruta del Vino". **See p.228**

❷ Pichilemu Relax or hit the waves at this inexpensive haven for surfing and other watersports. **See p.230**

❸ Parque Nacional Radal Siete Tazas This stunning park features lush forests, abundant waterfalls and natural swimming pools. **See p.234**

❹ Reserva Nacional Altos del Lircay Hiking trails, spectacular views and relatively easy access make this one of Chile's few Andean parks perfect for camping trips. **See p.238**

❺ Nevados de Chillán Legendary hot springs on the side of a volcano; in the winter, the skiing is excellent, while the rest of the year you can hike, bike and embark on horse treks. **See p.245**

❻ Salto del Laja Marvel at these thundering waterfalls, an ideal journey break just a stone's throw from the main highway. **See p.254**

HIGHLIGHTS ARE MARKED ON THE MAP ON P.220

THE CENTRAL VALLEY

N

PACIFIC OCEAN

SANTIAGO

Rocas de Santo Domingo

Melipilla

Navidad

Río Rapel

Chapa Verde ski centre

Sewell

El Teniente Mine

Rancagua

Machali

Termas de Cauquenes

Lago Rapel

El Manzano

Rengo

Río Tinguiririca

RESERVA NACIONAL RÍO LOS CIPRESES

Pichilemu **②**

San José del Carmen del Huique Museum

RESERVA NACIONAL LAGUNA TORCA

Llico

Santa Cruz **①**

San Fernando

Lago Vichuquén

Vichuquén

Termas del Flaco

Hualañe

Río Mataquito

Curicó

Constitución

Río Maule

San Rafael

Talca

PARQUE NACIONAL RADAL SIETE TAZAS **③**

Villa Cultural Huilquilemu

San Javier

San Clemente

④

RESERVA NACIONAL ALTOS DEL LIRCAY

RESERVA NACIONAL FEDERICO ALBERT

Chanco

Villa Alegre

Colbún

Lago Colbún

TRICAHÚE PARQUE

Peluhue

Curanipe

Linares

Caverna de Brujas

Cauquenes

Buchupureo

Iglesia de Piedra

Cobquecura

Playa Rinconada

Parral

Santuario Cuna de Prat

Ninhue

Dichato

Río Itata

Talcahuano

Tomé

Chillán

Concepción

⑤ Nevados de Chillán

ARGENTINA

Isla Santa María

Lota

Río Bío Bío

⑥

Salto del Laja

PARQUE NACIONAL LAGUNA DEL LAJA

Laguna de la Laja

El Álamo

Antuco

Los Angeles

Lebu

Cañete

PARQUE NACIONAL NAHUELBUTA

Angol

Mulchén

Río Bíobío

Lago Lanalhue

Contulmo

Ercilla

Victoria

Termas de Tolhuaca

Curacautín

Longuimay

CORDILLERA DE NAHUELBUTA

0 — 40 kilometres

HIGHLIGHTS

① Santa Cruz

② Pichilemu

③ Parque Nacional Radal Siete Tazas

④ Parque Nacional Altos del Lircay

⑤ Nevados de Chillán

⑥ Salto del Laja

hiking opportunities, particularly along the trails of protected areas such as **Reserva Nacional Altos del Lircay**, near Talca. After a strenuous day in the mountains, relax in one of the many **hot springs** in the area, including the **Nevados de Chillán** at the base of a booming ski resort.

The amount of annual **rainfall** picks up steadily as you head south; by the time you reach the Biobío there is a significant amount of rain every month. While winter is never too cold, most visitors come here between October and March.

GETTING AROUND   **THE CENTRAL VALLEY**

By bus Getting down the Central Valley by public transport is easy, with hundreds of buses ploughing down the Panamericana. Branching off into the cordillera and to the coast normally requires catching a "rural bus" from one of the cities dotted down the highway, though some of the more remote places can only be reached with your own transport.

By train A more leisurely and scenic option is the train from Santiago, which stops at Rancagua, San Fernando, Curicó, Talca and Chillán.

The Rapel Valley

Zipping down the Panamericana from Santiago, you can be in the **RAPEL VALLEY**, centred around the agricultural town of **Rancagua**, in about an hour. With a little more time and your own transport, however, the old road from Santiago (via Alto Jahuel, running east along the highway) is more appealing, winding its way past estates of vines, fruit trees and old haciendas, half-hidden behind their great adobe walls. The best place in the country to see Chile's traditional rodeo, the Rapel Valley is also home to the 40km-long **Lago Rapel**, the largest artificial lake in Chile, the copper mining town of **Sewell**, close to a small **ski centre**, and the rarely visited **Reserva Nacional Río los Cipreses**.

RODEOS

The Central Valley is the birthplace and heartland of Chilean **rodeo**, whose season kicks off on Independence Day, September 18. Over the following six months, regional competitions eliminate all but the finest horses and *huasos* in the country, who go on to take part in the national championships in Rancagua (Chile's rodeo capital) on the first weekend in April. Rodeos are performed in *medialunas* ("half moons"), circular arenas divided by a curved wall, forming a crescent-shaped stadium and a smaller oval pen called an *apiñadero*. In Rancagua it is on the northern edge of town (on the corner of Av España and Germán Ibarra). The participants are **huasos** – cowboys, or horsemen – who cut a dashing figure with their bright, finely woven ponchos, broad-rimmed hats, carved wooden stirrups and shining silver spurs. The horses they ride in the rodeo are specially bred and trained *corraleros* that are far too valuable for day-to-day work.

A rodeo begins with an inspection of the horses and their riders by the judges, who award points for appearance. This is followed by individual displays of horsemanship that make ordinary dressage look tame. In the main part of a rodeo, pairs of *huasos* have to drive a young cow, or *novillo*, around the edge of the arena and pin it up against a padded section of the wall. This isn't a popular sport with everyone – local animal rights groups campaign against it, arguing that it leads to injuries to both horses and cows. The rodeos are in any case as much about eating and drinking as anything else, and the canteen and foodstalls by a *medialuna* are a good place to sample **regional food**, gourmet wine and the sweet fruity alcohol known as *chicha*. Rodeo events are spread over the course of a weekend and end with music and dancing. This is where you can see the **cueca** (see p.38) being danced at its flirtatious best. For the dates of official rodeos, contact the **Federación del Rodeo Chileno** in Santiago (☏ 2 2481 0990) or visit ⓦ huasosyrodeo.cl.

5

Rancagua

RANCAGUA presents a picture that is to repeat itself in most of the Central Valley towns – a large, well-tended central plaza; single-storey adobe houses; a few colonial buildings, which were damaged in the 2010 earthquake but to a greater or lesser extent are being restored; sprawling, faceless outskirts. Once in town, you'll find little to hold your interest for more than a few hours – unless your arrival coincides with a **rodeo** (see box, p.221) – but Rancagua makes a useful jumping-off point for attractions in the adjacent Rapel Valley. The town has also begun work on a chapel that is set to be the only structure designed by famed Barcelona architect Antoni Gaudí to be built outside of his Spanish homeland; it is due to be completed by 2017.

Plaza de los Héroes and around

Unusually, Rancagua's square is known not as the Plaza de Armas, but as the **Plaza de los Héroes**. The name honours the patriot soldiers, headed by Bernardo O'Higgins, who defended the city against Royalist forces in 1814, only to be crushed in what has gone down in Chilean history as the "Disaster of Rancagua" (see box, p.476). In the centre of the square, a rearing equestrian statue celebrates O'Higgins' triumphant return to the city, four years after he had left it in ruins, to present it with a coat of arms depicting a phoenix rising from the ashes. The square's other major monument is the towering, pink-walled **Iglesia Catedral**. One block north of the square, at the corner of Cuevas and Estado, the **Iglesia de la Merced** was used as O'Higgins' headquarters; you can still see where the 2010 earthquake split it nearly in two, and the congregation now uses a marquee erected next door.

Museo Regional Rancagua and around

Paseo Estado 685 & 682 • Tues–Fri 10am–6pm • Free • ☎ 72 222 1524, ⓦ museorancagua.cl

Most of Rancagua's historic buildings are found along **Paseo Estado**, a pedestrianized street that runs from the Plaza de los Héroes to Avenida Millán. Along it you'll find two splendid eighteenth-century houses opposite each other that host the **Museo Regional Rancagua**, recently reopened after restoration, with exhibits on local history, crafts and mining. Just across the Avenida Millán, another eighteenth-century building, now the municipally-owned **Casa de Cultura** (Mon–Fri 8.30am–1.30pm & 3–5pm) hosts local art exhibitions and is a fine example of rural colonial architecture, including thick foundations made of river boulders mortared with mud.

ARRIVAL AND DEPARTURE   RANCAGUA

By bus The main terminal for long-distance services, known as Terminal O'Higgins, is at O'Higgins 0480 (☎ 72 222 5425, ⓦ terminalohiggins.cl). The regional bus terminal, called Rodoviario, is at Salinas 1165 (☎ 72 223 6938, ⓦ terminalrodoviario.cl).

Destinations Chillán (8 daily; 4hr); Concepción (16 daily; 5hr); Curicó (every 30min; 1hr 45min); Lago Rapel–El Manzano (every 20min; 2hr); Los Angeles (5 daily; 5hr); Pichilemu (every 30min; 3hr 30min); Puerto Montt (8 daily; 11hr); San Fernando (every 15min; 50min); Santa Cruz (every 15min; 2hr); Santiago (every 10min; 1hr–1hr 30min); Talca (every 30min; 2hr); Temuco (10 daily; 7hr).

By train The train station is at the corner of Estación and Carrera Pinto (☎ 72 223 8530).

Destinations Chillán (2 daily; 3hr 40min); Curicó (2 daily; 1hr 5min); San Fernando (6 daily; 30min); Santiago (9 daily; 1hr 30 min); Talca (2 daily; 1hr 50min).

INFORMATION AND TOURS

Conaf Cuevas 480 (Mon–Fri 8.30am–5.30pm; ☎ 72 220 4610, ⓔ rancagua.oirs@conaf.cl).

Tourist information Sernatur, Germán Riesco 277 (Mon–Thurs 8.30am–5.30pm, Fri 8.30am–4.30pm; ☎ 72 223 0413, ⓔ inforancagua@sernatur.cl).

Tours Turismo Dakota at Mujica 605 (☎ 72 222 8166, ⓦ turismodakota.cl) can arrange local tours, treks and horseriding.

ACCOMMODATION

Hotel Rancagua Av San Martín 85 ☎ 72 223 2663, ⓦ hotelrancagua.cl. One of the nicer places to stay in town; there are twenty rooms in total, but aim to get one of the more modern en suites in the extension out the back. CH$41,800

Hotel Turismo Santiago Brasil 1036 ☎ 72 223 0860. Squarely aimed at the business traveller with comfortable but antiseptic en suites, this 64-room hotel nevertheless boasts an outdoor pool and a restaurant. CH$56,500

EATING AND DRINKING

Reina Victoria Paseo Independencia 667 ☎ 72 223 9867. For something sweet, join the steady stream of shoppers and schoolchildren at this bustling café for coffee, cakes, biscuits and huge tubs of ice cream. Savoury offerings include the ubiquitous *completo* (hot dog with all the trimmings; CH$1500). Daily 7.30am–10pm.

El Viejo Rancagua Estado 607 ☎ 72 222 7715. Crammed with historic photos and memorabilia, this ramshackle restaurant does a cheap lunch menu (CH$2000) and on Fri and Sat nights transforms into an atmospheric bar, with live tango, bolero and folkloric music. Mon–Thurs 12.30–3pm, Fri 12.30–3pm & 8pm–4am, Sat 8pm–4am.

Sewell

60km east of Rancagua • Tours with VTS Sat & Sun leaving from Rancagua or Santiago • From CH$35,000 per person • ☎ 72 295 2692, ⓦ vts.cl or ⓦ www.sewell.cl

Sewell is an abandoned company mining town, staggered in dramatic tiers up the mountainside by **El Teniente**, the largest underground copper mine in the world. Local legend has it that the name of the mine – "the lieutenant" – refers to a disgraced Spanish officer who, while heading to Argentina to escape his creditors, discovered enormous copper deposits, thus making a fortune and saving himself from bankruptcy. Today the mine, not currently open to visitors, belongs to Codelco, the government-owned copper corporation (see p.64), which also

5

owns the famous Chuquicamata mine in northern Chile. You aren't allowed to just turn up and visit the town, but tour agency VTS offers excursions, which include the photogenic brightly coloured housing, the old church and theatre and a copper-mining museum.

Chapa Verde ski centre

Ticket office Miguel Ramírez 655, Rancagua • July–Sept • Lift tickets CH$27,000; equipment rental CH$22,000 • ☎ 72 221 7651, Ⓦ chapaverde.cl

A few kilometres north of the El Teniente mine, and ranging from 2300m to 3100m, is the Codelco-owned **Chapa Verde ski centre**, initially built for the company's miners but now open to the public between July and September. There are no hotels or other accommodation, but check with ski area administration for information on private homes for rent.

Reserva Nacional Río de Los Cipreses

Machalí, Cachapoal province • Daily 8.30am–5pm • CH$2200 • ☎ 72 229 7505

A little-visited gem, the **Reserva Nacional Río de Los Cipreses**, 20km beyond El Teniente, encompasses 36 square kilometres of protected land stretched along the narrow canyon of the Río de los Cipreses, with altitudes ranging from 900m to 4900m. It's a great spot for multi-day **hiking** or **horseriding**, and you may spot rare burrowing parrots, foxes, eagles and condors.

Sector El Ranchillo

At the entrance of Reserva Nacional Río de Los Cipreses, a Conaf office provides maps and a diorama of the park. Ask about the trails that offer a look at the parakeets nesting in the cliffs. From the office, a jeep track leads 6km to **Sector El Ranchillo**, a camping and picnic area with a swimming pool. This is the end of the track, and vehicles must be parked.

Sector Maitenes

From the camping and picnic area, take the left fork just before El Ranchillo, continue past a second gate (locked) and after another 6km you'll reach **Sector Maitenes**, with a few camping spots and running water. Beyond, a trail follows the river along the canyon, passing through forests and with occasional views of high Andean peaks like Cerro El Indio and Cerro El Cotón. Lateral ravines regularly branch out from the river, leading to waterfalls, lakes and "hanging" valleys carved out of the hills by glaciers. These aren't signed, however, so unless you're with an *arriero* (horseman), stick to the main path.

Sector Urriola

Twenty kilometres on from Sector Maitenes, you reach **Sector Urriola**, where there's a rustic *refugio* (1500m) and a few camping areas; count on taking around six or seven hours to get here on foot from Maitenes, and about four or five hours on horseback. Beyond Urriola, the path continues for a further ten or so kilometres, giving great views onto the 4900m-high Volcán Palomo. To hire a horse, ask around at the community of Chacayes at the park's entrance.

Lago Rapel

The forty-kilometre-long artificial **Lago Rapel** nestles in the low coastal hills southwest of Rancagua. Most of the action is centred around the main town of El Manzano, on the lake's eastern shore. The lake's main attractions are its excellent

watersports facilities, with speedboats, windsurfers and jet skis available for rent from several hotels and campsites.

ARRIVAL AND DEPARTURE   CHAPA VERDE, RIO DE LOS CIPRESES AND LAGO RAPEL

CHAPA VERDE SKI CENTRE

By bus Codelco's own bus service, Buses El Teniente, runs from Av Miguel Ramírez 665, Rancagua, next to the Lider Vecino supermarket (departures daily between 8.30am & 9.30am, return trip daily 4.30pm; CH$12,000; times are prone to change so it is worth confirming with the ski centre).

By car You can drive up in your own vehicle (4WD is advisable) as long as you call for a permit beforehand.

RESERVA NACIONAL RÍO DE LOS CIPRESES

By bus and taxi There's no direct public transport to the park, but you can take a bus from Rancagua to Coya (1hr) from where taxis can drive you the 12km to the park entrance (CH$7000).

LAGO RAPEL

By bus Gal Bus (☎72 223 0640) runs buses to El Manzano from Rancagua's regional terminal (every 20min; 2hr 30min) as does Sextur (☎72 223 1342; 4 daily; 2hr 30min).

ACCOMMODATION

Camping Náutico Rapel Lago Rapel ☎2 2862 6300, ⓦcampingnauticorapel.cl. Campers have access to a pool and volleyball court as well as a wharf that's ideal for a spot of lake fishing. Camping/site CH$30,000

Club Alemán Along the lakeshore 8km west of El Manzano, Lago Rapel ☎09 9883 3397, ⓦclubaleman lagorapel.cl. Fully equipped cabins sleep up to five or eight people, and 'glamping' domed tents that sleep up to four

are also offered. Facilities include a swimming pool and children's playground. Glamping tents CH$45,000, five-person cabin CH$60,000

Jardín del Lago 10km north of El Manzano, Lago Rapel ☎09 9743 4420, ⓦjardindellago.cl. Smart, self-contained, apartment-style cabin accommodation sleeping up to nine people. There are also jet skis, canoes and row boats for hire. Cabins from CH$48,000

The Colchagua Valley

The 120-kilometre-long valley of the Río Tinguiririca is known locally as the **COLCHAGUA VALLEY** after the province through which it runs. This is serious fruit-production territory, as signalled by the numerous fruit stalls and large Del Monte factories that line the highway on the approach to San Fernando. Forty-one kilometres west of San Fernando is **Santa Cruz**, one of the best places to stay in the region, and a starting point for the **Ruta del Vino del Valle de Colchagua**. Further east, high in the cordillera, the **Termas del Flaco** is an inexpensive option for soaking in hot springs, while if you continue to the coast,

AFTERSHOCKS

Central Chile was devastated by one of the most powerful **earthquakes** in recorded history when an 8.8-magnitude earthquake struck off its coast on February 27, 2010, triggering a powerful Pacific-wide **tsunami**. The earthquake cost 521 lives, injured twelve thousand people and left more than 800,000 people homeless. Concepción, 115km southeast of the epicentre, was hardest hit, with looting and violence bringing further chaos to the city. The cities of Curicó, Talca and Chillán also suffered severe damage, while the tsunami washed away parts of the coastal towns of Constitución, Talcahuano, Pichilemu and Iloca. The cities of Valparaíso and Santiago sustained some, albeit comparatively small, damage.

Roads and bridges were repaired soon after the earthquake, and in the ensuing months and years the region has picked itself up and rebuilt with heroic determination. Note however that many of the region's century-old adobe homes and haciendas, particularly those in the Colchagua Valley, were lost forever or still have expensive and lengthy renovations ahead of them.

5

you'll get to the hip, budget seaside town of **Pichilemu**, which is popular with surfers. Note that the main highway connecting San Fernando and Pichilemu, the Ruta 90, is still often referred to by its old name the I-50, and also sometimes denominated the 'Carretera del Vino'.

San Fernando

Surrounded by low, rippling hills that are washed golden in the sunlight, **SAN FERNANDO**, some 55km south of Rancagua, is a busy little agricultural town that makes a useful stop-off as the area's hub. Though it is less beguiling than the smaller Santa Cruz (see p.228), once you get out of town and into the vineyards there are some appealing places to stay or eat. The main commercial artery is Manuel Rodríguez, which, on the corner with Valdivia, has the huge nineteenth-century **Iglesia de San Francisco**, a Neo-Gothic church with a 32m-high tower, which took quite a blow in the 2010 earthquake. The verdant Plaza de Armas is surrounded by handsome colonial buildings, with the cavernous nineteenth-century **Parroquia San Fernando Rey** church on its southeastern corner.

Casa Patronal de Lircunlauta

Manso de Velasco and Jiménez • Closed at the time of writing

The **Casa Patronal de Lircunlauta** is the oldest building in San Fernando. It was originally the homestead of the eighteenth-century Hacienda Lircunlauta, whose owner donated 450 "blocks" of land to San Fernando when the town was founded in 1742. Previously it housed a museum containing an exhibit on the Uruguayan rugby team whose plane crashed into the Andes some 55km east of San Fernando in October 1972, their plight made famous by the book and film *Alive*. However, the museum has been closed since the building was damaged in the 2010 earthquake and it is not clear if or when it will reopen.

ARRIVAL AND TOURS
SAN FERNANDO

By bus The main bus terminal (☏ 72 271 3912) is on Av Manso de Velasco and Rancagua.

Destinations Angol (1 daily; 7hr); Chillán (6 daily; 3hr); Concepción (4 daily; 4hr 30min); Curicó (every 30min; 50min); Los Angeles (9 daily; 4hr 30min); Pichilemu (every 30min; 2hr 50min); Puerto Montt (5 daily; 12hr); Rancagua (every 15min; 50min); Santa Cruz (every 15min; 50min); Santiago (every 15min; 2hr); Talca (9 daily; 1hr 30min); Temuco (11 daily; 7hr); Termas del Flaco (Dec–Easter 2 daily; 2hr 30min); Valdivia (4 daily; 9hr).

By train The train station is three blocks south of the bus terminal at Quechereguas s/n (☏ 600 585 5000).

Destinations Chillán (2 daily; 3hr 10min); Curicó (2 daily; 30min); Rancagua (2 daily; 30min); Santiago (5 daily; 1hr 30min); Talca (2 daily; 1hr 20min).

Tours Andes Adventures (☏ 09 9630 1152, ⓦ andesadventures.cl) offers fishing, trekking and horseriding trips in the Colchagua Valley as well as overnight excursions into the high Andes.

ACCOMMODATION

While hotel options are uninspiring in San Fernando itself, for those with their own transport, the Colchagua Valley's verdant charms can be soaked up at one of the rustic guesthouses that lie right on its doorstep.

★**Mapuyampay Hostal Gastronómico** Parcela 2, Huemul, 45km southeast of San Fernando ☏ 09 9327 2589, ⓦ mapuyampay.cl. The rural retreat and cooking school of Ruth Van Waerebeek, the Belgian-born executive chef of Concha y Toro winery, is a real foodie find. Spacious guest rooms are set within landscaped gardens and tastefully accented with tribal furnishings. Gourmet meals are prepared by Ruth and her husband Vicente, using ingredients plucked straight from the garden. Meals and

cooking classes cost extra. Open Oct–April, over-14s only. **CH$78,000**

Posada Curali Curali 130 ☏ 72 271 3445, ⓦ posadacurali.cl. A decent budget option in town, whose eight musty, canary-yellow rooms have immense en suites and are set around a pretty, vine-covered patio. Staff are warm and welcoming. **CH$49,000**

★**Tumunan Lodge** Las Peñas, 27km southeast of San Fernando ☏ 09 9630 1152, ⓦ tumunanlodge.com.

5

A destination in itself, this British-Chilean-run lodge in the foothills of the Andes is surrounded by dazzling scenery, with a series of trails leading into the mountains. There are just four luxurious en-suite rooms, and guests can socialise wine-in-hand by the cosy fireplace. There's also attentive service, an inviting pool, a wood-fired hot tub, sumptuous home-cooked meals and the opportunity to go on guided fly-fishing, horseriding and hiking trips. CH$75,000

EATING AND DRINKING

Arenpastycaf Chillán 557 ☎72 271 5314, Ⓦ arenpastycaf.cl. An international menu and good buffet lunches (CH$3500) keep punters pouring into this bright and breezy café-bar-restaurant. One glimpse of the drinks menu, and you'll want to make a night of it. Mon–Sat 10am–11.30pm.

Café Roma Manuel Rodríguez 815 ☎72 274 9100. With its welcoming red-brick interior and a TV tuned to *telenovelas*, this café is a good spot for a light meal, icecream, cake or coffee. Lunches (from CH$4000) are more substantial, with meat, fish and pasta dishes. Daily 8am–10.30pm.

★ **Casa Silva** Polo Club House, Casa Lotel A Angostura, 7km north of San Fernando ☎72 271 6519 or ☎09 6847 5786, Ⓦ casasilva.cl. This winery restaurant is one of the Central Valley's top dining experiences: feast on imaginative tapas and top-quality beef (mains around CH$10,000) while overlooking lush vineyards and manicured polo fields. Daily 12.30–3.30pm & 7.30–11.30pm.

Termas del Flaco

78km east of San Fernando • Dec–Easter daily 6am–11pm • CH$2000 • Buses Amistad (☎72 238 4188) provides transport to the *termas*, with two daily afternoon departures from San Fernando and one daily from Santiago

Sitting high in the cordillera 1700m above sea level, the **Termas del Flaco** are among the cheapest and consequently most-visited thermal baths in the Central Valley. They're reached by a serpentine dirt road that follows the Río Tinguiririca through a beautiful gorge, so narrow in parts that traffic may go in only one direction at a time. Bizarrely, traffic is only allowed up late in the day, after 4pm (Mon–Sat), while traffic travels down in the morning until 2pm (Mon–Sat); Sunday is the opposite way round (up until noon, down from 2pm). Given the awkwardness of these hours, you'll need to stay at the baths overnight if you visit during the week.

The baths

The wild beauty of the cordillera and the feeling of remoteness and solitude are, upon arriving, suddenly interrupted with the appearance of numerous shack-like, tin-roofed houses – almost all of them *residenciales*, with little to distinguish one place from the next, and most operating on a full-board basis – crowded around the thermal baths. Nor are the actual baths themselves particularly attractive, consisting of several rectangular concrete, open-air pools. The waters, however – which reach up to 57°C (135°F) in some pools – are bliss. If you manage to get here midweek, when there are no crowds (except during high season, Jan & Feb), you can lie back, close your eyes and just relax, without another soul around.

Around the termas

You'll find several short treks around the *termas*, including one that leads to a set of dinosaur footprints preserved in the rock. Many local guides offer horseriding trips in the summer, including Eugenio Mancilla (☎09 8987 4453).

ACCOMMODATION | TERMAS DEL FLACO

Hotel Cabaña Las Vegas Ruta I-45, 1 km west of baths ☎72 222 2478, Ⓦ vegasdelflaco.cl. Guests at these comfortable and roomy wooden *cabañas* have access to a large dining room with floor-to-ceiling windows looking down to the valley and the hotel's own small thermal pool. The price is per person and includes all meals; minibus transfer from Santiago or Rancagua is CH$15,000. CH$55,000

Posada Amistad Camino Las Pozas s/n ☎72 281 7227, Ⓔ turismo.willy@hotmail.com. Roll straight off the bus and into these small, basic rooms set around a garden patio. The *posada* enjoys a prime position overlooking the baths. Open Nov/Dec–Feb, prices are full-board/person. CH$25,000

5

Santa Cruz and around

The paved Ruta 90 running through the Colchagua Valley to the coast takes you past a trail of **wineries** (see box, p.229). The small, well-preserved town of **SANTA CRUZ**, 40km from San Fernando, sits in the heart of this renowned wine-making district and boasts the **Museo de Colchagua**, one of the best museums in the country, as well as a clutch of fantastic places to stay, eat and imbibe the local produce.

Museo de Colchagua

Errázuriz 145 • Daily: Sept–Feb 10am–7pm; March–Aug 10am–6pm • CH$7000 • ☎ 72 282 1050, ⓦ museocolchagua.cl

The private **Museo de Colchagua** is housed in a splendid, plum-coloured colonial hacienda. Owned by international arms dealer Carlos Cardoen (the so-called "king of cluster bombs"), it has a well-designed, extensive and eclectic collection, which includes fossils, a huge amount of amber, pre-Columbian pottery and jewellery, relics from the War of the Pacific and memorabilia from the Chilean Independence movement. Among the most evocative exhibits are the beautiful old saddles, carved wooden stirrups and silver spurs in the *huaso* display, as well as the multimedia exhibit on the 2010 rescue of "Los 33" (see box, p.158), complete with a reconstruction of their "refugio".

San José del Carmen del Huique Museum

Ruta 90 Km56 • Tues–Sun 10–11.30am & 2.30–4.30pm by reservation only • Free • ☎ 09 7331105, ⓦ www.museoelhuique.cl • Yellow taxi *colectivos* depart from in front of Santa Cruz's bus terminal for the 30min journey to the museum

Twenty-four kilometres beyond Santa Cruz, along the road towards the coast, and 6km past the Los Errázuriz bridge, sits the superb **San José del Carmen del Huique Museum**. One of the Central Valley's loveliest haciendas, its history dates from the seventeenth-century colonial period, but the current *casa patronal* was built in the early years of independence, in 1829. Standing alongside, and entered through a huge doorway, is the **chapel**, sporting a 23m-high bell tower.

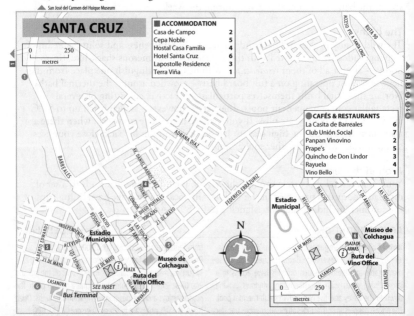

▲ San José del Carmen del Huique Museum

SANTA CRUZ

0 — 250 metres

ACCOMMODATION	
Casa de Campo	2
Cepa Noble	5
Hostal Casa Familia	4
Hotel Santa Cruz	6
Lapostolle Residence	3
Terra Viña	1

CAFÉS & RESTAURANTS	
La Casita de Barreales	6
Club Unión Social	7
Panpan Vinovino	2
Prape's	5
Quincho de Don Lindor	3
Rayuela	4
Vino Bello	1

ACCESO PTE A SANTA CRUZ

RUTA 90

ADRANA DÍAZ

AV. DANIEL BARROS GREL

BARRELES

PILÓ

CONDELL

AV. DIEGO PORTALES

TOSCAS

INDEPENDENCIA

PALACIOS

BERLÍN

ACEVEDO

ALBERTO EDWARDS

LOS ESPINOS

3 DE MAYO

21 DE MAYO

CASANOVA

Estadio Municipal

Museo de Colchagua

FEDERICO ERRÁZURIZ

Estadio Municipal

PLAZA DE ARMAS

ⓘ **Ruta del Vino Office**

27 DE MAYO

BEGONIA

PALACIOS

5 DE ABRIL

LAS TOSCAS

CASANOVA

ORLANDO

CARVACHO

0 — 250 metres

SEE INSET

Bus Terminal

Museo de Colchagua

ⓘ PLAZA **Ruta del Vino Office**

N

RUTA DEL VINO VALLE DE COLCHAGUA

5

The Valle de Colchagua lies in the middle of one of Chile's finest wine-making districts and eight wineries in the area have formed an itinerary called the **Ruta del Vino**. Tours (half-day/two wineries CH$50,000, full-day/three wineries CH$70,000) run daily and include multilingual guides and the chance to sample wines at each winery. Reservations must be made at least 24 hours in advance via Ruta del Vino (Plaza de Armas 298, Santa Cruz; ☎ 72 282 3199, ✉ reservas@rutadelvino.cl, ⊕ rutadelvino.cl). The agency can also arrange accommodation and transfers from Santiago. Tours run year round but the best time to go is in late March, during harvest. The following are some of the best wineries to visit, either as part of a tour or independently:

Viña Casa Silva Casa Lotel A Angostura, 7km north of San Fernando ☎ 72 291 3117, ⊕ casasilva.cl. Founded in 1892, this picturesque vineyard has classic wine-tasting facilities and a top-notch restaurant (see p.227). Hour-long tours cost around CH$20,000. Tours are offered five times daily.

Viña Clos Apalta Ruta 90 Km36, Cunaquito ☎ 72 295 3350, ⊕ lapostolle.com. The titular tipple produced at Lapostolle's gravity-fed winery is organic and biodynamic. There are standard 1hr tasting tours of the 445-acre estate (CH$20,000) as well as visits with horseriding (CH$50,000). Accommodation at *Lapostolle Residence* is also available (see p.230). Standard tasting tours are offered twice daily.

Viña Laura Hartwig Camino Barreales s/n ☎ 72 282 3179, ⊕ laurahartwig.cl. On the outskirts of Santa Cruz, this compact winery has 198 acres of vines dating from 1979. As well as tasting tours (CH$10,000–15,000), the winery has the excellent *Hotel Terra Viña* (see p.230) and restaurant *Vino Bello* (p.230). Tasting tours run daily 9.30am–7pm; book ahead.

Viña Montes Parcela 15, Millahue de Apalta ☎ 72 281 7815, ⊕ monteswines.com. A tractor ride through the picturesque 23-year-old vineyard is included in the tours of Monte's Apalta estate 43km northeast of Santa Cruz. As well as standard 1hr tours (daily 10.30am, noon, 3pm & 5pm; CH$12,000–30,000), they offer guided nature hikes and a lunch option (CH$27,000).

Viña MontGras Camino Isla de Yáquil s/n, Palmilla ☎ 72 282 2845, ⊕ www.montgras.cl. This 494-acre *bodega* 12km west of Santa Cruz produces, among others, the once rare and now classic Chilean Carmenère wine. The vineyard tours (from CH$12,000) are packed with interesting information about Chilean wine, and include a tasting. Tours run three or four times daily.

Viña Viu Manent Ruta 90 Km37, Santa Cruz ☎ 72 285 8751, ⊕ viumanent.cl. Just 7km east of Santa Cruz, this is one of the most visited vineyards in the area. A trip to the third-generation, family-owned winery includes a vintage carriage ride through the 370-acre estate and a comprehensive tasting (CH$16,000). There's also a nice on-site wine and crafts store and gourmet restaurant *Rayuela* (see p.230). Tours run four times daily.

ARRIVAL AND INFORMATION

By bus The bus terminal is at Casanova 478 (☎ 72 282 2191).
Destinations Pichilemu (every 30min; 1hr 50min); Rancagua (every 15min; 2hr); San Fernando (every 15min; 50min); Santiago (every 15min; 3hr).

Tourist information The tourist office is in the municipal building at Plaza de Armas 242 (Mon–Fri 8.30am–4pm; ☎ 72 297 8890).

SANTA CRUZ AND AROUND

ACCOMMODATION

★ **Casa de Campo** Los Pidenes Km40 Ruta 90 ☎ 72 282 3540, ⊕ hotelcasadecampo.cl. Wonderful family-run hotel just outside of town, with comfortable rural-chic rooms and cosy shared living spaces. The best rooms are those in the main house with balconies or verandas overlooking the extensive gardens, vineyards and open-air pool. CH$89,000

Cepa Noble Alberto Edwards 205 ☎ 72 282 1644, ⊕ hostalcepanoble.cl. The eleven modern rooms at this welcoming B&B in the town centre all have incredibly comfy beds; there's also a small pool, a good breakfast, and bicycles for rent. CH$60,000

Hostal Casa Familia Los Pidenes 421 ☎ 72 282 5766, ⊕ hostalcasafamilia.cl. This hostel is located on a quiet residential street northeast of the plaza, with neat but unremarkable rooms. The friendly owners serve a good breakfast with fruit and eggs. CH$48,000

Hotel Santa Cruz Plaza de Armas 286 ☎ 72 220 9600, ⊕ www.hotelsantacruzplaza.cl. On the edge of the Plaza de Armas sits this impressive hotel owned by Carlos Cardoen (see p.228) with a large and somewhat incongruous casino attached to it. There are two swimming pools, a spa and a good restaurant. US$400

Lapostolle Residence Ruta 90 Km36 ☎72 295 3360, ⓦlapostolle.com. Four enchanting, luxurious cabins nestled into the forested hillside above the Clos Apalta vineyards (see box, p.229); price is per person and

includes all meals and activities. US$750

Terra Viña Camino Los Boldos s/n ☎72 282 1284, ⓦterravina.cl. Part of the Laura Hartwig winery (see box, p.229), each oak-floored room here has a balcony overlooking the vineyards, and there's a pool for use in summer. US$160

EATING AND DRINKING

You're spoiled for dining options both in Santa Cruz and in the surrounding area, where many of the vineyards have their own restaurants.

La Casita de Barreales Rafael Casanova 570 ☎72 282 4468, ⓦlacasitadebarreales.cl. If you're looking for spice in your life, head to this popular Peruvian restaurant. Seafood-centric dishes like *ceviche mixto* (CH$6500) are balanced by carb-and-carne classics like *lomo saltado* (beef strips with fries, rice and vegetables) for CH$8000. Tues–Sun 1–3.30pm & 8–11.30pm.

Club Unión Social Plaza de Armas 178 ☎72 282 2529. Chilean staples (around CH$7000) and more adventurous dishes like eel omelette are served beneath a relaxing vine-covered terrace. Mon–Sat noon–11pm, Sun noon–6pm.

★**Panpan Vinovino** Km 31 Ruta 90 ☎09 9519 3823, ⓦpanpanvinovino.cl. Dine among antique cartwheels and furniture (some of which is for sale) in this cute restaurant housed in an old hacienda bakery. Dishes include steak with red wine sauce and pork marinated in chardonnay and rosemary. Mains around CH$7500. Mon–Thurs & Sun 1–3pm, Fri & Sat 1–3pm & 8–11pm.

Prape's Errázuriz 319 ☎72 282 1158. This Japanese restaurant has pretty authentic food, including California

rolls (from CH$3500), teriyaki salmon and tempura ice cream. It's also a fine spot for an evening cocktail. Mon–Sat noon–3pm & 6pm–midnight.

Quincho de Don Lindor Km25 Ruta 90 ☎72 285 8409. Near Santa Cruz's next-door village of Nancagua, this picturesque country *parrilla* (barbecue restaurant) has outdoor tables and attentive but not formal service. The pisco sours and empanadas are especially tasty. Mains around CH$5000. Mon & Sun 11am–5pm, Tues–Sat 10am–midnight.

Rayuela Ruta 90 Km37 ☎2 2840 3180. Dine among the vines at the Viu Manent wineyard (see box, p.229), just outside of Santa Cruz. The wines are matched to the food – try oysters (CH$8000) with the sauvignon blanc, or lamb cutlets (CH$11,000) with the malbec. Daily noon–4.30pm.

★**Vino Bello** Camino Los Boldos s/n ☎72 282 2755. Attached to the Laura Hartwig winery (see box, p.229), this is one of the most atmospheric places to eat in the area, serving Italian dishes like gnocchi and *ossobuco cannelloni* (CHS8000) on a candelit terrace looking out over the vines. Mon–Sat 11.30am–11.30pm, Sun 11.30am–3.30pm.

Pichilemu

The bustling surfer town of **PICHILEMU** lies 87km west of Santa Cruz. Built around a wide, sandy bay at the foot of a steep hill, the town dates from the second half of the nineteenth century, when Agustín Ross Edwards set out to create a European-style

---

SURFING IN PICHILEMU

The most challenging surf is at Punta de Lobos, 6km south of Pichilemu town, where the **national surfing championships** are held. Look out for the sea lions in the beach's peculiar escarpments. Closer to town, surfers wade into the chilly sea (the ocean temperature rarely rises above 14°C) at La Puntilla, which juts out at the western end of the calmer main beach, Playa Las Terrazas. Just south of here lies Playa Infiernillo, with a faster wave for more experienced surfers. Surf schools abound in Pichilemu, including:

Lobos del Pacifico Av Costanera 720 ⓦlobosdelpacifico.cl. Has 2hr classes for CH$12,000 and full-day surfboard and wetsuit hire for CH$8000.

Manzana 54 Av Costanera s/n ☎09 9574 5984, ⓦmanzana54.cl. Classes of surfing (from CH$10,000) and paddle boarding (CH$20,000) are on offer, as well as occasional day-trips to beaches down the coast.

seaside resort. Today Pichilemu wears the charming, melancholy air of a faded Victorian seaside town. From the seafront, a broad flight of steps sweep up the hillside to the splendid **Parque Ross**, planted with century-old Phoenix palms and extravagant topiary.

On the edge of the park, jutting out over the hillside, the grand old **casino** – Chile's first but now functioning as a cultural centre – is perhaps the most evocative of Ross's legacies. In contrast, Pichilemu's central streets are crammed with snack bars and *schoperías* (cafés serving beers) catering to the crowds of young surfers who come to ride the waves – among the best in all of Chile.

ARRIVAL AND INFORMATION
PICHILEMU

By bus Arriving in town by bus, you'll be dropped a couple of blocks north of the main street, Ortúzar, or at the terminal at the corner of Millaco and Los Alerces. Services are provided by Pullman del Sur and Buses Nilahue.

Destinations Rancagua (every 30min; 3hr 30min); San Fernando (every 30min; 2hr 50min); Santiago (12 daily; 3hr 30min).

Tourist information The tourist office is at Costanera 170 (Mon–Fri 8am–5pm; ☎72 276 6530).

ACCOMMODATION

Pichilemu has a good selection of budget and mid-price accommodation. Most of the town's accommodation caters to surfers, much of which spreads out of town along the beachfront Costanera. Book ahead at busy times as many of the places to stay have a two-night minimum or more at weekends and during holidays.

Cabañas Buena Vista Cerro La Cruz ☎72 284 2488, ⓦcabanasbuenavista.com. This eco-friendly resort has fully equipped cabins and the English-speaking staff can help organize a range of activities including Spanish, surf and kayak classes. CH$35,000

Camping La Caletilla Doctor Eugenio Suárez 905 ☎72 284 1010, ⓦcampingpichilemu.cl. The delightful owner lavishes campers with every modern comfort: electricity, hot showers, barbecues and bike rental. And wait till you see the ocean views. Camping/person CH$5000

DunaMar Km3 Camino a Cahuil ☎09 9138 5708, ⓦdunamar.cl. Located 3km south of town, this modern beach resort boasts rooms with kitsch seaside paintings and balconies with great views. The breakfasts are fit for a surfer's appetite. CH$72,000

Natural Surf Lodge Comercio 2980 ☎09 9001 0179 ⓦnaturalsurflodge.cl. This beautifully designed lodge at Punta del Lobos is a favourite with interior design magazines, incorporating lots of natural materials such as wood and stone. Also the staff can help organize surf lessons and excursions to find the best waves. CH$40,000

★**Pichilemu Surf Hostal** Eugenia Diaz Lira 167 ☎09 9270 9555, ⓦsurfhostal.cl. Stylish private rooms with ocean views and heaters? Check. Chic restaurant right on the beach? You bet. Free bike rental? They've got it. Surf school? Of course. Beachfront hot tubs? Absolutely. What this Dutch-owned boutique hostel-cum-B&B doesn't have is not worth mentioning. Dorms CH$13,000, doubles CH$45,000

EATING AND DRINKING

La Casa de la Empanadas Anibal Pinto 268. Even the street dogs drooling out front know *empanadas* don't come better than this: here they are huge, deep-fried and prepared while you wait. Plus with 36 varieties to choose from, at CH$1500 each, you know you are on to a winner.. Daily 11am–11pm.

Costa Luna Costanera 870, Infiernillo ☎72 284 2905. A swish setting for a sunset cocktail, this oceanfront restaurant has live music most nights and boasts a hip

decor. Seafood mains (CH$9000) are satisfying, but the main draw here is the view. Daily 1–5pm & 8pm–midnight.

La Gloria JJ Prieto 980 ☎72 284 1052. Located ten blocks south of the seafront, this popular restaurant is worth the walk for its excellent and inexpensive seafood, which includes tasty *machas a la parmesana* (cheese gratinated clams) (CH$7000) and dressed crab. Daily 10am–10pm.

NIGHTLIFE

Waitara Av Costanera 1039 ☎72 284 3004. The party starts late at this massive beachside club, where reggaeton and drum'n'bass dominate the dance floor. The terrace,

meanwhile, is a breezy place to sink a beer. Entry CH$3500; free before 1am. Fri & Sat 10pm–5am.

5

The Mataquito Valley

The Teno and Lontué rivers converge to form the broad Río Mataquito, which meanders west through Chilean wine country towards the Pacific. The town of **Curicó** (54km south of San Fernando) sits in the Mataquito Valley and makes a convenient place to break your journey or to visit the main attractions of the **MATAQUITO VALLEY** – wineries (see box below), Lago Vichuquén, near the coast, and the Siete Tazas waterfalls, southeast towards the mountains.

Curicó

Bustling little **CURICÓ**, founded in 1743, is the only town of any significance in the Mataquito Valley. An agro-industrial centre servicing the surrounding vineyards (see box below), it has little to hold your interest for more than a few hours, but is the gateway for excursions in the surrounding area.

Plaza de Armas

Curicó is built around one of the most beautiful central **plazas** in Chile, luxuriantly planted with sixty giant Canary Island palms. Standing in their shade, on the northern side of the square, is a highly ornate, dark-green wrought-iron **bandstand**, constructed in a New Orleans style in 1904, while close by an elaborate fountain features a cast-iron replica of *The Three Graces*. In contrast to these rather fanciful civic commissions, the memorial to **Toqui Lautaro** – the Mapuche chief at whose hands Spanish conquistador Pedro de Valdivia came to a grisly end – is a raw and powerful work, carved out of an ancient tree trunk.

Standing on the northwest corner of the square, the **Iglesia La Matriz** makes for a curious sight, its grand Neoclassical facade giving way to a spacious and modern brick interior.

Cerro Carlos Condell

You can climb **Cerro Carlos Condell**, the little hill on the eastern edge of town, and survey the scene from its 99m-high summit or take a dip in its public swimming pool (Dec–Feb daily 10am–8pm; CH$2000).

ARRIVAL AND DEPARTURE — CURICÓ

By bus Curicó's main bus terminal (T 75 255 8118) is at Maipú and Prat, about four blocks west and one block north of the Plaza de Armas. Tur Bus (T 75 231 2115) has long-distance services and is inconveniently located a good 20min walk southeast of the Plaza at Manso de Velasco and Castellón, while Linea Azul (T 75 222 7017)

WINE TOURS AROUND CURICÓ

While you're in Curicó, it's worth making the easy excursion 5km south to the **winery** of Miguel Torres (daily 10am–5pm; T 75 256 4121, W migueltorres.cl; 45min tours CH$4000 without tasting, from CH$6000 with tastings), the innovative Spanish vintner who revolutionized Chile's wine industry in the 1980s. The superb *Restaurant Miguel Torres* (Mon–Thurs, Sat & Sun 12.30–4pm, Fri 12.30–4pm & 8–11pm) serves gourmet dishes (CH$33,000 for tour with lunch and wine), and there is a guesthouse with a pool overlooking the vineyards (CH$72,000). To get here, take a bus heading to Molina (every 10min) and ask to be let off outside the *bodega*, which is right next to the Panamericana.

Other wine tours are arranged by **Ruta del Vino Valles de Curicó**, Prat 301-A, Curicó (Mon–Fri 9am–2pm & 3.30–7.30pm; T 75 232 8972, W rutadelvinocurico.cl). Prices start from CH$72,500, including lunch and transport and a visit to two wineries. Over the third weekend in March, a **wine festival** takes place in **Curicó's Plaza de Armas**, a celebration of the grape harvest, complete with dances and beauty pageants.

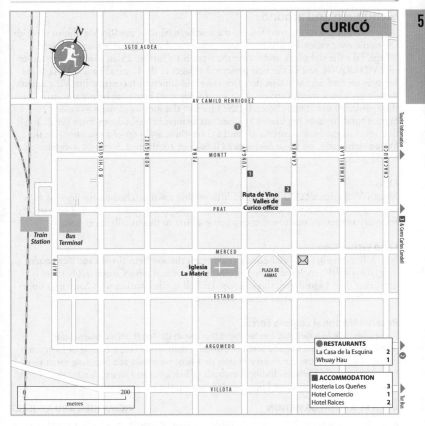

is half a block north of Tur Bus on Manso de Velasco.

Destinations Chillán (16 daily; 2hr 50min); Puerto Montt (2 daily; 11hr 30min); San Fernando (every 30min; 50min); Santiago (every 30min; 2hr 30min); Talca (every 15min; 1hr 15min); Vichuquén (2 daily; 2hr 30min).

By train The station (☎ 600 585 5000) is at Maipú 697, opposite the bus terminal.

Destinations Chillán (2 daily; 2hr 35min); Rancagua (2 daily; 1hr 5min); San Fernando (2 daily; 30min); Santiago (3 daily; 2hr); Talca (2 daily; 50min).

ACCOMMODATION AND EATING

La Casa de la Esquina Isabel la Católica 392 ☎ 75 231 0767. Spanish bullfighting posters adorn the walls, but the menu is a journey through the entire Mediterranean, from Greek salad to pasta to seafood paella (mains around CH$6000). Mon–Sat 1–3pm & 8–11pm.

Hosteria Los Queñes Km36 Camino Los Queñes, 40km east of Curicó ☎ 09 8447 5186, ⓦ hosterialosquenes.cl; direct buses from Curicó (5–8 daily; 1hr) leave from the bus station with Buses San Cristobal (☎ 75 232 1512). This American-Chilean-run lodge offers a comfortable way to experience the great outdoors, with a restaurant, bar, pool and hot tub. Rafting, kayaking and other outdoor activities organized. **CH$40,000**

Hotel Comercio Yungay 730 ☎ 75 257 6300,

ⓦ hotelescurico.cl. The attractive "superior class" rooms with flat-screen TVs are the main draw at this classic mid-range town hotel, although the standard en suites are also decent. **CH$62,000**

Hotel Raices Carmen 727 ☎ 75 254 3440, ⓦ hotelraices.cl. The best place to stay and eat in town is this slick modern hotel with cream and white en suites, as well as a large lounge area complete with palm-fringed garden, giant fireplace, bar, café and restaurant. **CH$70,000**

Whuay Hau Yungay 853 ☎ 75 232 6526. This restaurant serves reliable Cantonese dishes – fried rice, noodles and stir fries (CH$3000) – in a formal dining room with mini chandeliers. Daily noon–midnight.

5

Vichuquén and around

West of Curicó, a scenic road follows the northern bank of the Río Mataquito through the fertile river valley. Eighty-five kilometres along the road, just beyond Hualañé village, take the right fork and follow the signs for a further 25km along a dirt road to tiny **VICHUQUÉN**, one of the best-preserved villages in the Central Valley. Most of the brightly painted adobe houses date from the mid-nineteenth century, but Vichuquén's history goes back much further: there was a settlement here long before the arrival of the Spaniards, and it was chosen by the Inca as a site for one of their *mitimaes* (agricultural colonies populated by Quechua farmers brought down from Peru). You'll find relics of the Inca occupation – and a three-thousand-year-old mummy – in the **Museo Vichuquén**, on Calle Rodríguez (Tues–Sun 10.30am–1.30pm & 4–6pm; CH$1500).

Llico

Nearby Vichuquén, **LLICO** is a rugged little seaside town perched on the edge of an exposed sandy beach whose turbulent waves attract many surfers – during January and February numerous surf tournaments bring a buzz to this usually quiet beach.

Lago Vichuquén

Four kilometres beyond Vichuquén you'll reach the southern tip of **Lago Vichuquén**, a long, narrow lake enclosed by deep-green, pine-covered hills. Considerably more upmarket than Lago Rapel, this is a popular holiday destination with Santiago's upper crust, whose beautiful villas line the lakeshore.

Reserva Nacional Laguna Torca

Llico, Vichuquén • Daily: April–Nov 8.30am–6pm; Dec–March 8.30am–8pm • CH$3500 • ☎ 75 240 0269, ⓦ lagunatorca.cl

The **Reserva Nacional Laguna Torca** is a marshy man-made lake a couple of kilometres outside of Llico across the rickety Puente de Llico, preserved as a breeding sanctuary for 106 species of birds, including hundreds of black-necked swans. Conaf runs a small campsite near the Puente de Llico, nestled in a eucalyptus grove.

By bus There are daily buses to Vichuquén from Curicó (2hr 30min), and several daily to Llico (2hr 30min), with Buses Diaz (☎ 75 231 1905) and Buses Bravo (☎ 75 231 2193); the Llico services pass by the Conaf office at Laguna Torca.

Tourist information There's a Conaf office just beyond the Puente de Llico bridge, hiding behind the large house with the veranda.

ACCOMMODATION AND EATING

Camping Vichuquén Camino El Mirador s/n, Bahia El Durazno, Lago Vichuquén ☎ 75 240 0062, ⓦ camping vichuquen.cl. This family-friendly campground rents out boats and kayaks and also organizes biking and hiking excursions, and night-time activities. It has a laundry, bakery and mini-market. Open Nov–March, with prices much lower outside Jan & Feb. Camping/person CH$13,000

Marina Vichuquén On the southern shore of Lago Vichuquén, in the village of Aquelarre ☎ 75 240 0265, ⓦ marinavichuquen.cl. You'll find good food and accommodation at this hotel, with smart, spacious rooms with lots of natural light, as well as excellent watersports facilities and horseriding (all available for non-guests, too). CH$73,000

Parque Nacional Radal Siete Tazas

55km east of Molina • April–Nov 8.30am–5.30pm; Dec–March 8.30am–8pm • CH$4000 • ☎ 71 222 4461

Of all the natural phenomena in Chile, the **Siete Tazas**, 71km southeast of Curicó, must be one of the most extraordinary. In the depths of the native forest, a crystal-clear mountain river drops down a series of seven waterfalls, each of which has carved a sparkling *taza* ("teacup") out of the rock. The falls are inside **PARQUE**

NACIONAL RADAL SIETE TAZAS, reached by a poor dirt road from the village of Molina, 18km south of Curicó and 55km from the park – be sure to fill up with petrol there. Popular with locals on summer weekends but mostly ignored by foreign visitors, this park is almost empty much of the time. Also within the reserve are forests, several hiking trails and the **Velo de Novia** ("Bride's Veil"), a 50m waterfall spilling out of a narrow gorge. For keen hikers, it's also possible to trek from Siete Tazas to Reserva Nacional Altos del Lircay (see p.238), but you'll need to hire a local guide.

ARRIVAL AND INFORMATION

PARQUE NACIONAL RADAL SIETE TAZAS

By bus You can get to Siete Tazas on public transport during summer only from Molina (8 daily; 2hr 30min) or Curicó (1 daily; 3hr).

Tourist information and tours Conaf has a small hut on the road towards the Siete Tazas, but for more information you need to go to the administrative office at the Parque

Inglés sector of the park, 9km further east (daily: Dec–Feb 8.30am–8pm; March–Nov 8.30am–5.30pm). Local agencies can be reluctant to run tours to the park because of the bad road, but you may be able to pick up a tour from Talca (see p.236).

ACCOMMODATION

Camping Rocas Basálticas Parque Inglés ☎71 222 8029. Conaf runs this popular camprgound, without electricity but with hot showers. Camping/person CH$2000

Hostería Flor de Canela Parque Inglés ☎75 249 1613. This guesthouse near the administrative office offers adequate but small and draughty rooms with either private

or shared facilities, as well as a simple restaurant. CH$25,000

Valle de Las Catas Halfway between Parque Inglés and the Siete Tazas, close to the Puente de Frutillar ☎09 9168 7820, ⓦwww.sietetazas.cl. For swimming, horse rides and accommodation ranging from camping to cabins (for up to six people), try this private ranch inside the park. Camping/person CH$6000, cabins CH$45,000

The Maule Valley

The **MAULE VALLEY**, some 70km south of the Mataquito, is formed by the **Río Maule**, which flows into the sea almost 75km west of its principal town of Talca at the industrial port of **Constitución**. South of here a coast road leads to a string of seaside villages, which include the surfer hangout **Buchupureo**. To the east of Talca, meanwhile, the river has been dammed, resulting in Lago Colbún. Further east, high in the cordillera, the **Reserva Nacional Altos del Lircay** provides some of the region's best hiking trails, through dramatic mountain scenery. The area is sprinkled with hot springs and a proliferation of **vineyards**, many of them conveniently located between the town of **Villa Alegre** and village of **San Javier** on a route served by plenty of local buses from Talca.

Talca

TALCA is mainly used as a jumping-off point for several rewarding excursions spread along the Maule Valley. The city boasts its fair share of services and commercial activity, mostly centred on the main shopping street, **1 Sur**, with a pedestrianized section between 3 Oriente and 6 Oriente. Away from the frantic bustle of this thoroughfare, however, the rest of Talca seems to move at a snail's pace, not least the tranquil **Plaza de Armas**, shaded by graceful bougainvilleas, jacarandas and magnolias. Half-hidden beneath their foliage is a handsome 1904 iron bandstand.

Catedral de Talca

Northwest corner of Plaza de Armas • Daily 10am–12.30pm & 5–7pm • Free

The Neo-Gothic **Cathedral**, built in 1954, and restored in 2011 following earthquake damage, is pale grey with a long, thin spire and series of turrets running along each

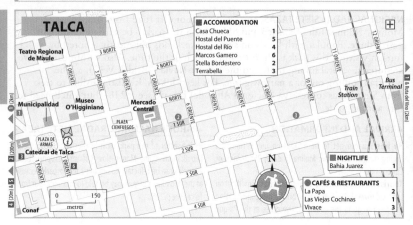

side. It's worth popping inside to look at the delicately coloured stained-glass Belgian windows and the sombre main altar.

Museo O'Higginiano

1 Norte and 2 Oriente • Closed for repairs at time of writing • ⓦ museodetalca.cl

The **Museo O'Higginiano** occupies a handsome colonial house that hosted some of the most important developments of Chile's independence movement. It was here that Bernardo O'Higgins, future "Liberator" of Chile, lived as a child; where the Carrera brothers established the first Junta de Gobierno in 1813; and where in 1818, O'Higgins signed the country's declaration of independence.

ARRIVAL AND DEPARTURE   TALCA

By bus Most buses pull in at the terminal (☏ 71 220 3992) on 2 Sur and 12 Oriente, ten blocks east of the Plaza de Armas. To get into the centre, take any *colectivo* or *micro* along 2 Sur (and to get back, along 1 Norte).
Destinations Chanco (3 daily; 3hr); Chillán (8 daily; 2hr 30min); Concepción (every hour; 3hr 30min); Constitución (summer every 30min; winter 7 daily; 2hr 20min); Curanipe (summer 8 daily; winter 4 daily; 2hr 45min); Los Angeles (10 daily; 3hr 45min); Pelluhue (summer 8 daily; winter 4 daily; 2hr 30min); Puerto Montt (8 daily; 8hr 30min); Rancagua (every 30min;

2hr); San Fernando (every 30min; 1hr 30min); San Javier (every 20min; 30min); Santiago (every 20min; 3hr 30min); Temuco (12 daily; 5hr 30min); Vilches Alto (summer: 9 daily; winter 4 daily; 2hr); Villa Alegre (every 30min; 1hr).
By train The train station (☏ 600 585 5000) is at 11 Oriente 1150.
Destinations Chillán (2 daily; 1hr 45min); Constitución (2 daily, 3hr 30 min); Curicó (2 daily; 45min); Rancagua (2 daily; 1hr 50min); San Fernando (2 daily; 1hr 20min); Santiago (4 daily; 2hr 45min).

INFORMATION AND TOURS

TOURIST INFORMATION
Conaf 2 Poniente and 3 Sur (☏ 71 222 8029).
Sernatur 1 Oriente 1150 (Mon–Thurs 8.30am–5.30pm, Fri 8.30am–4.30pm, Sat 10am–1pm; ☏ 71 223 3669, ⊜ infomaule@sernatur.cl). The extremely helpful Sernatur office is on the Plaza.

TOUR OPERATORS
Costa y Cumbre Tours ☏ 09 9943 5766, ⓦ costay cumbretours.cl. This operator offers both coastal and mountain tours, including multi-day trekking trips

and day excursions to Radal Tazas.
Maule Sorprendente ☏ 09 6668 8640, ⓦ maule sorprendente.cl. This company runs day-trips to the coast, including tours to the Sahara-like Dunas de Putú sand dunes.
Turismo El Caminante ☏ 71 197 0097, ⓦ trekking chile.com. A great general adventure tour operator, offering treks, snowshoeing, horseriding and kayaking. The company is run by the owners of *Casa Chueca* (see p.237).

5

RUTA DEL VINO VALLE DEL MAULE

The **Ruta del Vino Valle del Maule** includes nine wineries which are open to the public, and visits can be arranged independently or through the Ruta agency (*Corral Victoria*, Camino a San Clemente km10; ⓦvalledelmaule.cl). All these wineries are easy to visit on day-trips from Talca, either by taxi or by using public transport down the Panamericana, into Villa Alegre, up to San Javier and back to Talca; they do not have set opening hours but run according to demand and should be reserved in advance unless otherwise indicated.

Viña Balduzzi Balmaceda 1189 in San Javier ☎73 232 2138, ⓦbalduzziwines.cl. One of the best wineries to visit on your own, as you can drop in without a reservation for a 45min guided tour (CH$7000) of its *bodegas*. With 200 acres of vineyards and beautiful grounds featuring an old *casa patronal*, a chapel and a *parque centenario* full of 100-year-old trees, this is a very picturesque example of a Central Valley winery. Mon–Sat 9am–6pm.

Viña Gillmore Camino Constitución Km 20 in San Javier ☎73 197 5539, ⓦtabonko.cl. This family-run winery is one of the oldest vineyards in Chile. Also known as Tabontinaja or Tabonko, it has a good set-up for tourists, with tours (45min; CH$6000) examining the ecology of its vineyards.

Viña Via Wines Fundo La Esperanza s/n in San Rafael ☎2 2355 9900, ⓦviawines.com. North of Talca, covering 1300 acres, this is the flagship vineyard for the Oveja Negra (Black Sheep) brand. Two-hour tours start from CH$12,500.

ACCOMMODATION

★**Casa Chueca** 4km down the road to Las Rastras ☎71 197 0096 or ☎09 9419 0625, ⓦtrekkingchile .com. This German-Austrian guesthouse/hostel is well worth the detour. Surrounded by banana and palm trees, the "Crooked House" offers an abundance of services, amenities and tours, including a pool and intensive Spanish lessons. To get here, phone ahead and then catch the Taxutal "A" bus on 13 Oriente to the *El Toro Bayo* restaurant, an old colonial building at the end of the route, where you'll be picked up. The knowledgeable owners, who also run the tour company Turismo El Caminante (see p.236) and sell maps of the local area they have drawn up themselves, also have a refuge in the beautiful Melado Valley. Closed June–Aug. Dorms CH$12,500, doubles CH$49,000

Hostal del Puente 1 Sur 407 ☎71 2220930. In a quiet spot next to the river, this welcoming place has en-suite rooms set around a patio and attractive gardens. Bike rental available. CH$28,000

Hostal del Río 1 Sur 411 ☎71 251 0218, ⓦhostaldelrio .cl. Next door to the *Hostal del Puente*, this is a reasonable budget choice. The small rooms are set around a large car park and have modern private baths and cable TV. CH$26,500

Marcos Gamero 1 Oriente 1070 ☎71 222 3388, ⓦmarcosgamero.cl. While the en suites are fairly standard for this price range, the eclectic collection of aged record players, etchings and old irons strewn about the place give it a certain charm. CH$54,000

Stella Bordestero 4 Poniente 1183 ☎71 223 6545, ⓦturismostella.cl. This excellent-value, tranquil complex has eight timber cabins set in landscaped gardens with a jellybean-shaped pool. CH$38,000

Terrabella 1 Sur 641 ☎71 222 6555, ⓔterrabella @hotel.tie.cl. Just half a block from the plaza, the best rooms at this hotel overlook a serene leafy garden with a sparkling swimming pool. There's also a restaurant, computers for guest use and friendly staff. CH$60,000

EATING AND DRINKING

The cheapest lunchtime menus are at the small restaurants inside the Mercado Municipal (enter via 1 Norte).

La Papa 1 Sur 1271 ☎71 261 3784. Ladies who *once* (do afternoon tea) and a few men who do too, catch up over cinnamon rolls (CH$700) and coffee at this popular café. Daily 10am–7pm.

Las Viejas Cochinas Rivera Poniente s/n, 2km west of the plaza ☎71 222 1749, ⓦlasviejascochinas.cl. This barnyard-sized restaurant by the River Claro has become a Talca institution on the strength of one dish: *pollo mariscal* (chicken in a seafood and brandy sauce, CH$4000). Be prepared for long waits at weekends. Daily noon–1am.

Vivace 2 Sur 1659 ☎71 223 2350. Delicious home-made pastas (around CH$7000) and grilled meats go down a treat with something off the classy, Maule Valley-centric wine list. Mon–Sat 11.30am–3.30pm & 7pm–midnight, Sun 11.30am–3.30pm.

NIGHTLIFE AND ENTERTAINMENT

Bahia Juarez 1 Poniente 1240 📞71 268 6373, ⓦbahiajuarez.cl. You'll find plenty of nocturnal action at this restaurant, pub, karaoke bar, nightclub and lounge complex. There's food and drink discounts before 10pm (go for the fajitas and tequila cocktails). Mon–Fri 6.30pm–late, Sat 7.30pm–late.

Teatro Regional de Maule 1 Oriente 1484 📞71 234 0591, ⓦteatroregional.cl. A meeting point for Talquino culture vultures, this modern theatre boasts a steady and varied programme of live music, theatre, dance and children's shows.

DIRECTORY

Money and exchange You can change money at Casa de Cambio Marcelo Cancino at 1 Sur 898, Oficina 15, and there are several ATMs on 1 Sur, just east of the plaza.

Post office 1 Oriente 1150 (Mon–Fri 9am–6pm, Sat 9am–noon).

Villa Cultural Huilquilemu

Camino San Clemente Km 7 • Closed at the time of writing

Ten kilometres along the paved San Clemente Highway, also known as Ruta 115, that heads east out of Talca towards the Argentine border, is **Villa Cultural Huilquilemu**. A *casa patronal* (homestead) built in 1850, it formerly functioned as a museum dedicated to religious art, but was damaged in the 2010 earthquake and it is not clear if or when it will reopen.

Reserva Nacional Altos del Lircay

Vilches Alto • Daily: March–Nov 8.30am–5pm; Dec–Feb 8.30am–7pm • CH$4000

The paved Ruta 115 winds up and east through the mountains, eventually leading to the Argentine border crossing Paso Pehuenche (daily 8am–6pm, sometimes closed in winter due to snow). Some 30km on from Villa Huilquilemu a left fork onto a poor dirt road (it should be paved in 2015) leads 27km to the mountain village of **Vilches Alto** and from here to the entrance of the **RESERVA NACIONAL ALTOS DEL LIRCAY**, 2km beyond. This is an extremely beautiful part of the central cordillera, with a covering of ancient native forests and fantastic views onto surrounding mountain peaks and volcanoes streaked with snow. The road is difficult to pass in winter months, so the best time to visit is between October and May. Close to the entrance, an **information centre** has displays on the park's flora and fauna and the area's indigenous inhabitants, whose traces survive in the **piedras tacitas** (bowls used for grinding corn) carved out of a flat rock face a few hundred metres away along a signed path. As well as the shorter treks listed below, there is a popular five- to eight-day "condor circuit" that begins in Vilches and takes in several hot springs and waterfalls, as well as awesome mountain landscapes; contact Franz at the *Casa Chueca* (see p.237) for more information.

The trail to Enladrillado

Of the various **trails** inside the reserve, the most-trodden is to a hilltop platform at 2300m known as **Enladrillado**. From the reserve entrance follow the steep track up the hillside for about 2.5km, then follow the signed turn-off, from where it's a stiff uphill walk of about five hours; count on an eight-hour round-trip. The views from the top are exhilarating, down to the canopy of native *coigües* and *lenga* forests covering the valley beneath, and across to the towering **Volcán Descabezado** and surrounding peaks. Up here you'll also find areas of exposed volcanic rock resembling giant crazy paving, giving the spot its name, which translates roughly as "brick paving".

The trail to Laguna del Alto

The hike from *Camping Antahuara* (see p.239) to **Laguna del Alto**, a lagoon inside a volcanic crater, is an eight-hour round trip, with great lookout spots along the way. If you want to explore further, try it on **horseback**: in Vilches Alto, contact don Eladio (☎09 9341 8064).

By bus Buses Vilches (☎71 220 3992, ⓦvilchesalto.com) runs regular daily buses to Vilches Alto from Talca.

Tourist information The staff at *Refugio Don Galo*

(see below) can help organize trips, including overnight stays, and have lots of information on hikes and excursions.

There is one official campground in the park. Note that because of wildfire dangers, no campfires are permitted. In Vilches Alto, 2km west of the park, you will find several places to stay and eat.

Camping Antahuara 500m from Conaf office inside the park ☎71 222 8029. Hot showers, well-maintained toilets and electricity ensure campers live it up at this Conaf-run campsite in the forest. Camping/person CH$2500

Refugio Don Galo Hijuela R, Vilches Alto ☎2 2196 0619. Here you'll find basic but decent digs, a restaurant and owners who are a good source of local information. They can organize guided horseriding, trekking and rappelling excursions. CH$35,000

Lago Colbún and around

Chile's largest artificial reservoir, **LAGO COLBÚN**, was created between 1980 and 1985 when the Río Maule was dammed as part of a huge hydroelectricity project, and it wasn't long before its shores, framed by undulating hills, were dotted with holiday chalets, wooden cabins and mini-markets. The town of Colbún is not actually on the lake, but just west of it. The lake's southern shore, where there are several campsites, can be a pain to get to – though two bridges span the lake, access to them is often barred by the hydroelectricity company, which means going back to the Panamericana and driving instead along the southern bank of the Río Maule. This route provides access to Colbún Alto, a small village on the southwest shore of the lake.

Tricahue Parque

Around 25km east of Lago Colbún, at the confluence of the Maule and Armerillo rivers, is the village of Armerillo, close to the little-visited and remote **Tricahue Parque**, filled with tree-covered mountains, lakes and the 2000m Picudo Peak. A great way to explore the area is by staying at *Refugio Tricahue* (see p.240).

LAGO COLBÚN

By bus From Talca there are services with Interbus (☎71 261 3140) from the main terminal (10 daily; 1hr 10min).

By car There are various approaches to Lago Colbún, stretching 40km from east to west. From Talca, drive east

and carefully follow signs to stay on the Ruta 115, which skirts the northern shore of the lake.

TRICAHUE PARQUE

By bus Interbus runs six daily buses from Talca (1hr 30min).

LIGHTS IN THE SKY

The area around San Clemente and the reserve has garnered a reputation in recent years as a focus of **UFOs**, with a high number of sightings of various kinds of lights in the sky and international film crews shooting documentaries. Some even believe that the Enladrillado platform in Altos del Lircay (see p.238) is a landing-pad for extraterrestrial craft. Whether aliens travel billions of miles across interstellar space to visit Colbún, or whether the lights have a more prosaic explanation linked to the hydroelectric project or seismic activity, or indeed whether it is all a figment of the tourist board's imagination, is for you to decide.

5

ACCOMMODATION

COLBÚN

Termas de Panamávida Catedral s/n, Colbún, 5km south of the town ☎73 221 1743, ⓦtermas depanimavida.cl. A thermal bath complex popular with elderly visitors, in a nineteenth-century hacienda-style building built around numerous courtyards and patios. The gardens are immaculate but the rambling old building has rather gone to seed. It is, however, full of character, especially the distinctly Victorian-looking wing housing the long row of cubicles where guests soak in the thermal waters (not especially hot at 33°C/91°F), mud baths and steam rooms. Non-guests can visit for the day (CH$20,000). Full-board US$250

LAGO COLBÚN

Cabañas Lago Colbún Ribera Norte ☎09 9895 6401, ⓦcabanaslagocolbun.cl. Set on the lake with head-on views of the Andes, these sheltered, fully equipped cabins in the woods sleep up to six people. There's a swimming pool and kayaks for rent. CH$50,000

Chez L'Habitant Camino Colbún Alto Km 10.5 ☎09 9132 4064, ⓦecoturismolagocolbun.cl. There are

stunning lake views from the cabins, glamping tents and rooms at this eco-friendly lodge. The owner whips up home-cooked meals, and horseriding, kayaking and trekking excursions are offered should you want to work them off. Or you can simply chill out at the private beach or stargaze while melting in the wood-fired hot tub. Glamping tents CH$49,000, cabins or doubles from CH$75,000

Complejo Turístico Valshi Paso Pehuenche Km 58 ☎09 9221 8793, ⓦvalshi.cl. A relaxing complex with swimming pool, ping-pong tables and cabins that sleep up to ten people. Reiki and reflexology treatments offered. Campers are also accommodated. Camping/person CH$4000, cabins CH$30,000

TRICAHUE PARQUE

Refugio Tricahue 1km from Armerillo ⓦrefugio -tricahue.cl. This peaceful twelve-bed hostel has a Finnish sauna and pool, and the welcoming Belgian owner organizes fishing trips, walks, bike tours, swimming in thermal pools and, in the winter, snowshoe hikes. The best rooms have private bathrooms and a glass roof. Dorms CH$7500, doubles CH$22,000

San Javier and Villa Alegre

Twenty kilometres south of Talca is a massive iron bridge over the Río Maule, followed by the turn-off to **SAN JAVIER**, a bustling little town sitting in the heart of the Maule Valley's wine country. Its main interest lies in its proximity to two dozen local **vineyards** (see box, p.237) spread between and around San Javier and the nearby village of **VILLA ALEGRE**.

Nine kilometres further south from San Javier, you approach **Villa Alegre** through a stunning avenue of trees whose branches meet overhead to form a dense green canopy. A stroll down the village's main street, lined with fragrant orange trees, takes you past grand *casas patronales* in luxuriant grounds.

ACCOMMODATION

SAN JAVIER AND VILLA ALEGRE

Hotel Colonial Maule Cancha de Carreras s/n, Villa Alegre ☎73 238 1214, ⓦhotelcolonialmaule.cl. For a peaceful place to stay in Villa Alegre, try this attractive old house with landscaped gardens, a swimming pool and restaurant. CH$41,000

Residencial Narvaez Cancha de Carreras 2365, San Javier ☎73 232 1203, ⓦresidencialnarvaez.cl. A good budget option in San Javier, this central hotel includes parking, cable TV, and a restaurant. The cheapest rooms have shared bathroom. CH$13,000

Constitución and the coastal road

At the mouth of the Río Maule is the busy port of **CONSTITUCIÓN**. While it's now a popular holiday resort, the occasional foul stench of the local cellulose plant makes it unlikely you'll want to stay too long. Apart from the weird rock formations on the town's grey sand beaches, the main reason for coming here is to move on to the 60km stretch of quiet beaches and small fishing towns to the south.

Chanco

From Constitución, a paved road follows the coast to the little seaside resort of **Curanipe**, 80km south. You pass extensive pine plantations bordered by grey, empty beaches and sand dunes before reaching **CHANCO**, a tiny village populated by ageing farmers who transport their wheat, beans and potatoes to market on creaky, ox-drawn carts. Much of the village's colonial architecture was destroyed in the 2010 earthquake and tsunami.

Reserva Nacional Federico Albert
Chanco, Maule • Daily: March–Dec 8.30am–5.30pm; Jan & Feb 8.30am–7.30pm • CH$3500 • ☎ 73 255 1004

On the northern edge of Chanco, the **Reserva Nacional Federico Albert** is a dense pine and eucalyptus forest planted in the late nineteenth century in an attempt to hold back the advance of the coastal sand dunes – which by then had already usurped much valuable farmland. A 3km **path** skirts the edge of the reserve, leading to an enormous sandy **beach** with small kiosks, picnic tables and running water.

Pelluhue and Curanipe
The summer seaside resort and popular surfing destination of **PELLUHUE** (11km south of Chanco) is a haphazard collection of houses strung around a long, curving black-sand beach. Though it's popular with backpackers and has cheap accommodation, the town has an untidy, slightly ramshackle feel to it that doesn't encourage you to stay long; unless you're here to surf, you'd be better off 7km south in the prettier village of **CURANIPE**. With a backdrop of rolling hills, wheat fields and meadows, Curanipe's dark-sand **beach**, with colourful wooden fishing boats, is a lovely place to hang out, though that's just about all there is do here. Bring enough cash with you as there are no ATMs in these parts. A further 35km south of Curanipe, the mostly paved road arrives at the isolated surfer hangout of Buchupureo (see p.244).

ARRIVAL AND DEPARTURE

CONSTITUCIÓN
By bus From Talca, Constitución is served by several buses daily with Buses Contimar and Pullman. Buses pull in opposite the train station on the riverside, a few blocks northeast of the plaza.
By train Two daily trains run here from Talca (going to Talca, the right side of the train has the best views).

RERSERVA NACIONAL FEDERICO ALBERT
By bus Pullman del Sur goes to Chanco from Talca (3 daily;

CONSTITUCIÓN AND THE COASTAL ROAD
3hr); Buses Amigo runs here from Constitución (6 daily; 1hr 30min).

PELLUHUE AND CURANIPE
By bus Interbus (☎ 71 261 3140) runs regular services from Talca to Pelluhue and Curanipe. Pullman del Sur has four daily services from Santiago to Curanipe via Talca. If you're coming from Constitución, change buses in Chanco.

ACCOMMODATION

CONSTITUCIÓN
Alonso de Ercilla Colo Colo 334 ☎ 41 222 7984, ⊛ hotelalonsodeercilla.cl. This modern hotel with warm wooden touches and friendly staff is a good mid-range choice. It's just one block from the main plaza. CH$52,000

RERSERVA NACIONAL FEDERICO ALBERT
Camping Reserva Nacional Federico Albert 300 metres from park entrance ☎ 73 255 1004. This attractive camping area inside the wooded reserve has hot showers, drinking water and electricity. Camping/site CH$10,000
Hostal Mohor Av Fuentealba 135 ☎ 09 9782 6956, ✉ hostal.mohor@gmail.com. A rudimentary but clean hotel; all rooms have cable TV but only some have private

bathroom. Breakfast is included. CH$20,000

PELLUHUE AND CURANIPE
Cabañas Campomar Camino Pelluhue, Curanipe Km3 ☎ 73 254 1000, ⊛ cabanascampomar.cl. About 3km south of Curanipe, near the top of a steep hill, these log cabins sleep between two and eight people and have great ocean views. Includes a pool, children's playground and parking. CH$32,000
Hostal de Piedra Condell 1606, Pelluhue ☎ 73 254 1115, ⊛ hostaldepiedra.cl. Set on the seafront between Pelluhue and Curanipe, this eighteenth-century stone house has comfortable rooms, a salt-water pool and a restaurant. Prices are per person for half-board. CH$39,000

5

The Itata Valley

Lush and very beautiful, the broad **ITATA VALLEY** begins at the small city of **Chillán** just off the main RN5, and stretches northwest to a string of tranquil coastal towns, including the idyllic surfing village of **Buchupureo**. En route is the **naval museum** in the village of Ninhue.

Chillán

Lively **CHILLÁN** is famous as the birthplace of Bernardo O'Higgins, the founding father of the republic. It's a useful stopover on the Panamericana, with a **market** and fascinating **Mexican murals** to while away an hour or two. As a result of periodic earthquakes and regular Mapuche attacks, Chillán has repeatedly been rebuilt since being founded in 1550. Most of Chillán's present architecture dates from just after the 1939 earthquake.

Plaza Bernardo O'Higgins

Chillán's main square **Plaza Bernardo O'Higgins** is dominated by a giant, 36m concrete cross commemorating the thirty thousand inhabitants who died in the 1939 earthquake, and the futuristic, earthquake-resistant **cathedral**, built between 1941 and 1961 in the form of nine tall arches.

Escuela México

O'Higgins 250 • Mon–Fri 10am–1pm & 3–6.30pm • Donation requested

The **Escuela México**, a school built with money donated by the Mexican government following the 1939 disaster, looks out over leafy **Plaza de los Héroes de Iquique**. On

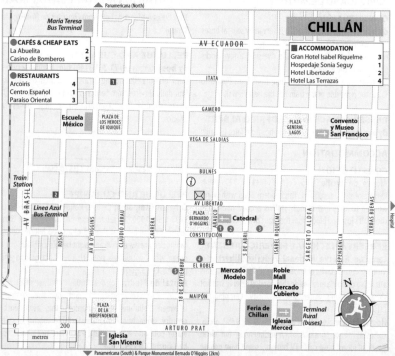

CHILLÁN

Panamericana (North)

María Teresa Bus Terminal

CAFÉS & CHEAP EATS
La Abuelita 2
Casino de Bomberos 5

RESTAURANTS
Arcoiris 4
Centro Español 1
Paraíso Oriental 3

ACCOMMODATION
Gran Hotel Isabel Riquelme 3
Hospedaje Sonia Seguy 1
Hotel Libertador 2
Hotel Las Terrazas 4

AV ECUADOR

ITATA

GAMERO

Escuela México

PLAZA DE LOS HÉROES DE IQUIQUE

PLAZA GENERAL LAGOS

Convento y Museo San Francisco

VEGA DE SALDIAS

BULNES

Train Station

AV LIBERTAD

Línea Azul Bus Terminal

PLAZA BERNARDO O'HIGGINS

Catedral

CONSTITUCIÓN

EL ROBLE

Mercado Modelo

Roble Mall

Mercado Cubierto

MAIPÓN

PLAZA DE LA INDEPENDENCIA

Feria de Chillán

Iglesia Merced

Terminal Rural (buses)

ARTURO PRAT

Iglesia San Vicente

AV BRASIL · ROSAS · AV B'O'HIGGINS · CLAUDIO ARRAU · CARRERA · 18 DE SEPTIEMBRE · ARAUCO · 5 DE ABRIL · ISABEL RIQUELME · SARGENTO ALDEA · INDEPENDENCIA · YERBAS BUENAS

Hospital

0 200 metres

Panamericana (South) & Parque Monumental Bernado O'Higgins (2km)

Pablo Neruda's initiative, two renowned Mexican artists, David Alfaro Siqueiros and Xavier Guerrero, decorated the school's main staircase and library with fabulous murals depicting pivotal figures in Mexican and Chilean history. The Mexican images, entitled *Muerte al Invasor*, feature lots of barely clothed native heroes and evil-looking, heavily armed Europeans engaged in various acts of cruelty. The Chilean tableau is even more gruesome, dominated by the lacerated, bleeding body of the Mapuche leader Galvarino, and his bloodthirsty Spanish captors. The school allows visitors access to the murals in return for a small donation.

Feria de Chillán

Maipón and 5 de Abril • Mon–Sat 8am–8pm, Sun 8am–2pm

Filling Plaza de la Merced, the **Feria de Chillán** is an exuberant open-air market that sells fresh produce and *artesanía*, ranging from knitwear and leather items to jewellery, paintings and secondhand books. The market is especially lively on Saturdays, when it bulges out of the square and spreads into the surrounding streets.

Parque Monumental Bernardo O'Higgins

O'Higgins and Parra • Daily 8.30am–8pm • Free

The **Parque Monumental Bernardo O'Higgins**, a short bus ride south along Avenida O'Higgins, is a handsomely landscaped park featuring a 60m wall covered with a badly faded mosaic depicting the life of the city's most famous son. In a small chapel nearby, O'Higgins' mother, Isabel Riquelme, and his sister, Rosita, are both buried, not far from the site where Bernardo was born.

ARRIVAL AND INFORMATION   CHILLÁN

By bus Most long-distance buses use the Terminal María Teresa at O'Higgins 010 (☎42 227 2149), on the northern edge of town. Linea Azul has its own terminal at Constitución 01, four blocks west of Plaza Bernardo O'Higgins (☎42 222 1014). Local and regional buses operate out of the Terminal Rural, Maipón 890, a few blocks southeast of the Plaza (☎42 222 3606).

Destinations Concepción (every 30min; 1hr 30min); Curicó (8 daily; 2hr 30min); Los Angeles (every half hour; 1hr 30min); Puerto Montt (8 daily; 9hr); Rancagua (8 daily; 4hr); San Fernando (5 daily; 3hr); Santiago (every 30min; 5hr); Talca (every hour; 2hr); Temuco (13 daily; 4hr).

By train The station is at Av Brasil and Av Libertad (☎600 585 5000), five blocks west of the Plaza.

Destinations Curicó (2 daily; 2hr 30min); Rancagua (2 daily; 3hr 35min); San Fernando (2 daily; 3hr); Santiago (2 daily; 4hr 30min); Talca (2 daily; 1hr 45min).

Tourist information Sernatur is at 18 de Septiembre 455 (Mon–Fri 8.30am–5.30pm; ☎42 222 3272, ✉infochillan@sernatur.cl).

ACCOMMODATION

Gran Hotel Isabel Riquelme Constitución 576 ☎42 243 4400, ⊕hotelisabelriquelme.cl. This salmon-coloured hotel gazes proudly over Plaza O'Higgins. While it is undoubtedly the grandest place in town, the en suites are a little unexciting and overpriced. Its excellent restaurant serves innovative Chilean food and is a popular local haunt. CH$81,000

Hospedaje Sonia Seguy Itata 288 ☎42 221 4879, ⊕hospedajesonia.cl. Slightly ramshackle and chaotic but very friendly digs at rock-bottom prices. Most rooms have TVs, shared facilities are clean and home-cooked meals are on offer. Solo travellers may have to share rooms at busy times. CH$10,000

Hotel Libertador Libertad 85 ☎42 222 3255, ⊕hlbo.cl. Located half a block from the train station, the rooms on the second floor are the best, but all have big bathrooms, cable TV and paintings of European cities. CH$43,000

Hotel Las Terrazas Constitución 664 ☎42 243 7000, ⊕lasterrazas.cl. Excellent hotel split between two buildings that face each other across the street. The airy whitewashed rooms have swish facilities and modern art on the walls, while a relaxed ambience permeates the whole place. CH$60,000

EATING AND DRINKING

La Abuelita Constitución 635 ☎42 223 1450. The best place in Chillán for cakes (around CH$1500) and coffee, served in an attractive *pastelería* with wood furnishings. Daily 9am–9pm.

5

Arcoiris El Roble 525 ☎ 42 222 7549. A rainbow sign guides diners into this bohemian vegetarian restaurant, which has a lunchtime buffet (CH$3500) and fresh juices. A small selection of meat dishes kindly caters to carnivores. Mon–Sat 8.30am–4pm.

Casino de Bomberos El Roble and 18 de Septiembre, 2nd floor ☎ 42 222 2233. Cheap Chilean cuisine and plenty of local colour can be found at this no-frills, bustling fire station canteen. Set lunches are CH$1800. Mon–Fri 9am–10pm.

Centro Español Arauco 555 ☎ 42 232 1061. Penguin-suited waiters at this Spanish–Chilean restaurant serve paella with prawns, mussels, scallops, salmon, chorizo, pork ribs and chicken; the huge one-person portion (CH$6000) is easily enough for two. Mon–Sat noon–4pm & 7–11.30pm, Sun noon–3.30pm.

Paraíso Oriental Constitución 715 ☎ 42 221 2296. This popular Chinese restaurant is good for generous portions of fried rice and noodles (around CH$5000), either eat in or take away. Daily 11.30am–midnight.

DIRECTORY

Car rental Larrañaga, 18 de Septiembre 870 (☎ 42 221 0112, ⊕ larranaga.cl).

Hospital Herminda Martín Argentina and Francisco Ramírez (☎ 42 221 2345).

Money and exchange There are several ATMs on Arauco and Constitución.

Post office The main *correo* is at Libertad 505 (Mon–Fri 8.30am–6.30pm, Sat 9am–12.45pm).

Santuario Cuna de Prat

Hacienda San Agustín de Puñal • Tues–Sun 10am–6pm • CH$1000

Naval enthusiasts will not be let down by the colonial **Hacienda San Agustín de Puñal** just outside the village of **Ninhue**, 50km northwest of Chillán. Arturo Prat was born here in 1848, and the area is now a shrine to the naval hero, who died in 1879 in the Battle of Iquique while trying to capture the Peruvian ironclad gunship *Huáscar* (see p.478), armed only with a sword.

Inside the hacienda is a museum devoted to the hero, the **Santuario Cuna de Prat**. While the national obsession with the young officer – a thousand Chilean plazas and streets are named after him – continues to mystify outsiders, the museum's collection of polished, lovingly cared-for naval memorabilia and colonial furniture are worth a visit in their own right, and the building they're housed in, with its large interior patio and elegant verandas, is a beautiful example of colonial rural architecture, recently reopened to visitors following restoration work after damage from the 2010 quake.

Buchupureo

The pristine surfer's paradise of **BUCHUPUREO** lies 120km northwest of Chillán and 132km north of Concepción. Word has spread in recent years, and a clutch of hotels and restaurants have been added to the sleepy fisherman's village on the sweeping, dark-sand Playa La Boca, with a verdant backdrop of thick pine forests and a stable microclimate ideal for growing papaya. At dawn and dusk, crab fishermen use oxen to haul in their colourful boats, while surfers hit the left point break to ride long, fast, tubular waves that reach up to 6m. Surf lessons can be arranged with Nanosurf (☎ 09 8941 1579).

While only hardy types in wetsuits brave the chilly sea, a slow-flowing fresh-water river runs parallel to Buchupureo's Playa La Boca, with temperatures that, in summer, are ideal for splashing about in. Horseriding is also popular along the beach, and hotels in the area can arrange excursions with local guides.

Around Buchupureo

If the surf's not up in Buchupureo explore the string of beaches up and down the coast, such as Playa Rinconada, which lies 16km south of Buchupureo. Some 13km south of Buchupureo is the livelier, but far less pretty town of Cobquecura, home to an offshore colony of sea lions. Five kilometres north of Cobquecura is the awe-inspiring Iglesia de Piedra, a series of lofty caves with passages leading down to the ocean.

By bus From Chillán, Buses Petoch leaves from the Terminal Rural (7 daily; 2hr 45min). From Concepción, Magabus (☎41 221 5147) leaves from Serrano and Las Heras (4 daily; 3hr 30min). In summer, at least one bus daily plies the coastal route south of Curanipe to Buchupureo and Cobquecura.

ACCOMMODATION AND EATING

★**La Joya del Mar** Playa La Boca ☎42 197 1733, ⓦlajoyadelmar.com. Luxurious villas perched on the hillside have wide picture windows, immense bathtubs and balconies with breathtaking ocean views. There's also an infinity pool, Jacuzzi and top-notch restaurant run by the Californian owners (mains around $8000). Surfing lessons, mountain biking and wine tours can be arranged. Restaurant open daily lunch and dinner. US$225

Los Maquis Camino Buchupureo Km 9.7 ☎09 8900 1815, ⓦlosmaquishotel.com. A stylish bed and breakfast with riverside hot tubs, run by a friendly Chilean-Australian couple. Breakfast is served in bed, guests can use the kitchen and transfers from Concepción airport are offered. CH$45,000

El Puerto Playa La Boca ☎42 197 1608. Check the surf without leaving bed at these excellent-value timber cabins, some with kitchenettes. The owner has two friendly dogs and takes good care of guests. The restaurant, which serves flavourful, simple seafood dishes (mains CH$3000–5000) is a popular local haunt. Two nights minimum stay at weekends. CH$30,000

Nevados de Chillán

Ski season runs June–Oct • Ski pass CH$37,000 per day • ⓦ nevadosdechillan.com

The most famous and developed mountain resort south of Santiago is the **NEVADOS DE CHILLÁN**, an all-season tourist complex which includes one of the largest ski resorts in Chile, 80km east of Chillán, nestled at the foot of the 3122m **Volcán Chillán**. Formerly known as the Termas de Chillán, it possesses a clutch of year-round open-air **thermal pool complexes** surrounded by glorious alpine scenery. The resort's **skiing** facilities include eleven lifts and 29 runs, one of which at almost 13km is the longest in South America. Though primarily set up as a winter destination, the resort and facilities in the surrounding area stay open during the summer, when possible activities include hiking, horseriding and mountain biking. Note that there is no ATM in the valley; withdraw cash beforehand in Chillán.

Valle de Aguas Calientes

An ideal one-day hike or horseriding trip from Nevados de Chillán is to the Valle de Aguas Calientes, where natural hot springs flow at the confluence of three rivers. The resort lies 8km uphill from the sprawling village of Valle Las Trancas.

Parque de Aguas Nevados and around

Base of Nevados de Chillán ski resort • Parque de Aguas Nevados pools daily 9am–10pm; Valle Hermoso pools daily 8.30am–5pm • Parque de Aguas Nevados pools CH$8000; Valle Hermoso pools CH$5000

At the base of the ski resort is the delightful, well-maintained **Parque de Aguas Nevados**, with four hot sulphur pools of varying temperatures, a swim-up bar and water slide. Trails also lead from the complex to a Turkish steamroom (CH$6000) and natural mud bath. Some 2km downhill the more rustic Valle Hermoso has three outdoor pools, while the two resort hotels *Hotel Nevados* and *Gran Hotel Termas de Chillán* allow visitors access to their spas with a day pass (see p.246).

By car The vast majority of people who visit do so by private transport; a 4WD is recommended in winter. If you book a tour make sure it includes transfers.

By bus Buses Nilahue has one service a day from Santiago to Valle Las Trancas (7hr). Alternatively, Rem Bus (☎42 222 9377) goes from Chillán to Valle Las Trancas (7 daily; 1hr 50min). Buses do not usually ply the 8km stretch to the ski resort from Valle Las Trancas. Private transfers cost from

5

CH\$15,000 one-way and can be organized by your hotel; hitchhiking is also common and easy in the winter.
Tours Good treks, snowshoe walks, and year-round volcano hikes can be organized with Tierra Verde (☎09 8500 2514, ⓦ verdetour.com).

ACCOMMODATION

There are three large, expensive resort hotels near the slopes. As you move downhill towards the village of Valle Las Trancas, where most people stay, a glut of cheaper cabins, lodges, hostels and restaurants lines the road. Rates vary dramatically throughout the year, with July being the most expensive month.

Alto Nevados Nevados de Chillán resort ☎42 220 6105, ⓦ nevadosdechillan.com. Owned by the same company that controls the ski centre, this large new hotel is right by the slopes, allowing for ski in/ski out, with its own spa and restaurant (winter only). Its older sister hotel *Hotel Nevados* a little further down the valley is open year round but badly in need of sprucing up. Day pass to *Hotel Nevados* spa with lunch CH\$40,000. US\$400

Cabañas Los Andes Camino Termas de Chillán Km 70.4 ☎09 9951 5238, ⓦ cabanaslosandes.com. British–Brazilian-run cabins set in undulating, forested surrounds. In winter, the large café and bar is a good après-ski hangout and in summer, the owners offer guided hiking excursions. CH\$70,000

Chil'In Hostal Camino Termas de Chillán Km 72.5 ☎42 224 7075, ⓦ chil-in.com. A large French-run hostel with clean dorms and doubles, all with shared bathrooms. A crackling fireplace warms up the living room in winter. Sound insulation is poor, however, so earplugs are essential. Dorms CH\$18,000, doubles CH\$45,000

★**Ecobox Andino** Camino Shangri-La Km 0.2, Valle Las Trancas ☎42 242 3134, ⓦ ecoboxandino.cl. Four impeccably styled cabins made from recycled shipping containers are linked by raised wooden platforms and set within a magical *ñirres* forest. Plenty of natural light streams through the picture windows, which look onto snowcapped mountains, and the pool and hot tub are pure Zen. CH\$70,000

Gran Hotel Termas de Chillán Nevados de Chillán resort ☎2 2233 1313 in Santiago, ☎42 243 4200 in Chillan, ⓦ termaschillan.cl. This imposing, five-star hotel is starting to show its age a little but has spacious en suites in soothing colours, heated pools, a restaurant, a bar and a casino. The state-of-the-art spa centre offers hot mud baths, facials, hydro-massages and a range of other treatments. A day pass with lunch and pool access is CH\$37,000. Prices are per person, full-board. US\$400

M.I. Lodge Camino a Shangri-La s/n ☎09 9321 7997, ⓦ milodge.com. With its own observatory, swimming pool, spa and exquisite French restaurant, the "Mission Impossible" lodge brings everything but the mountain right to your doorstep. Rooms are comfortable if small with head-on volcano views, and the lodge's zip-line canopy adventure park is a 30min walk away. Rates are per person and include dinner and breakfast. CH\$59,000

Riding Chile Camino Termas de Chillán Km 73 ☎09 7779 1973, ⓦ ridingchile.com. A cozy little hostel run by an affable young Argentine-Chilean couple with a handful of rooms, two lounge areas and a restaurant with delicious fajitas and chocolate fondue. Dorms CH\$14,500, doubles CH\$29,000

EATING AND DRINKING

Chil'In Restaurant Camino Termas de Chillán Km 72.5 ☎42 224 7075, ⓦ chil-in.com. On the same site as *Chil'In Hostal* (see above), this restaurant can get you through the day, with hearty breakfasts, good-value set lunches with a French touch (CH\$10,000), and the best pizzas in the valley. Daily 8am–late.

Parador, Jamón, Pan y Vino Camino Termas de Chillán Km 74 ☎42 243 2100. The longest-running restaurant in the valley serves typical food in a setting that oozes old-world charm. Quell your hunger with the *Olla Parador* (CH\$17,000), a hearty, meaty stew which feeds two or three people. Daily 12.30–9.30pm.

Snow Pub Camino Termas de Chillán Km 71.5 ☎42 221 3910. For après-ski action, look no further than this popular pub where the music is loud, the beer is cheap (CH\$1500), and by 2am, the dance floor is packed. Jan & Feb Mon–Wed & Sun 11.30am–11.30pm, Thurs–Sat 11.30am–4.30am; June–Oct daily 11.30am–late.

The Biobío Valley

South of Chillán and the Itata Valley, Chile is intersected by the great **Río Biobío** , generally considered the southern limit of the Central Valley. One of Chile's longest rivers, it cuts a 380km diagonal slash across the country, emptying into the ocean by the coastal city of **Concepción**, over 200km north of its source in the Andean mountains. For more than three hundred years the Biobío was simply "La Frontera", forming the border beyond which Spanish colonization was unable to spread, fiercely repulsed by the native **Mapuche** population.

Today, the **Biobío Valley** still feels like a border zone between the tranquil pastures and meadows of central Chile, and the lakes and volcanoes of the south. While the valley floor is still covered in the characteristic blanket of cultivation, dotted with typical Central Valley towns such as **Los Angeles** and **Angol**, the landscape on either side is clearly different. To the west, the **coastal range** – little more than gentle hills further north – takes on the abrupt outlines of real mountains, densely covered with the commercial pine forests' neat rows of trees and, further south, there are hints of the dramatic scenery to come in the Lake District, with native araucaria trees in their hundreds within **Parque Nacional Nahuelbuta**.

Cut off by these mountains, the towns strung down the coast road south of Concepción – such as **Lota**, **Arauco**, **Lebu** and **Cañete** – feel like isolated outposts. To the east, the Andes take on a different appearance, too: wetter and greener, with beautiful wilderness areas like **Parque Nacional Laguna del Laja**.

Concepción

CONCEPCIÓN is the region's administrative capital and economic powerhouse, sitting at the mouth of the Biobío. Chile's second-largest city, it nonetheless has a much more provincial feel than Santiago, and with a population of around a quarter of a million it hardly seems more than a large town. Surrounded by some of Chile's ugliest industrial suburbs, Concepción's centre is a spread of dreary, anonymous buildings. This lack of civic splendour reflects the long series of catastrophes that have punctuated Concepción's growth – from the incessant Mapuche raids during the city's days as a Spanish garrison, guarding La Frontera, to the devastating earthquakes that have razed it to the ground dozens of times since its founding in 1551. It does, however, have the energy and buzz of a thriving commercial centre, and the large number of university students here gives the place a young, lively feel and excellent nightlife.

5

Plaza de la Independencia

Concepión's focal point is the busy **Plaza de la Independencia**, where Bernardo O'Higgins read the Chilean declaration of independence in January 1818. In the centre, a classical column rises above the main fountain, atop which stands a gold-painted statue of the Greek goddess Ceres symbolizing the region's agricultural wealth. On the western side of the plaza rises the Romanesque–Byzantine **Catedral de la Santísima Concepción**, built between 1940 and 1950 and adorned with faded mosaics.

Adjacent to the cathedral at Caupolicán 441 is the **Museo de Arte Sagrado** (Mon–Fri 10am–1pm & 2–6pm, Sat 10am–2pm; free), featuring colonial artwork, marble statues, gold-embroidered vestments and a replica of the Turin Shroud.

Galería de la Historia

Parque Ecuador • Mon 3–6.30pm, Tues–Fri 10am–1.30pm & 3–6.30pm, Sat & Sun 10am–2pm & 3–7pm • Free • ☎ 41 285 3756, ⓦ www.ghconcepcion.cl

For an in-depth introduction to Concepión, the **Galería de la Historia** at the southern end of Lincoyán has a series of impressive dioramas, from pre-Columbian times through the Conquest and to the modern day; most come with sound effects and narration in Spanish.

Casa del Arte

Larenas and Chacabuco • Tues–Fri 10am–6pm, Sat 10am–5pm, Sun 11am–2pm • Free • ☎ 41 220 3835

The **Universidad de Concepción**, set in splendid, landscaped gardens surrounded by thickly wooded hills, is one of Chile's most renowned universities and houses one of the country's largest national art collections in the **Casa del Arte**. The bulk of the collection consists of nineteenth-century landscapes and portraits by Chilean artists, but the showpiece is the magnificent mural in the entrance hall, *Presencia de América Latina*, painted by the Mexican artist Jorge González Camarena in 1964. Dominating the mural is the giant visage of an *indígena*, representing all the indigenous peoples of the continent, while the many faces of different nationalities superimposed on it indicate the intrusion of outside cultures and fusion of races that characterize Latin America.

Edificio Gobierno Regional

Arturo Prat 525 • Daily 9am–6pm • Free

The **Edificio Gobierno Regional** (local government building) was formerly a railway station and houses a massive mural, though not as impressive as the one in the Casa de Arte (see above). Over 6m long and 4m tall, the *Historia de Concepción*, painted by Chilean artist Gregorio de la Fuente, was installed in 1964.

Museo Hualpén

Western end of the Biobío estuary • Tues–Sun 9am–6pm • Free; CH$2000 for parking • ☎ 41 242 6399 • A 15min taxi ride from Concepción's centre

A large park with several kilometres of footpaths and an extensive collection of native and exotic trees surrounds the **Museo Hualpén**. A traditional single-storey hacienda houses an eclectic collection of souvenirs from every corner of the globe, picked up by the millionaire industrialist Pedro del Río over three world trips in the nineteenth century.

Huáscar

Talcahuano, 16km northeast of Concepción • Tues–Sun 9.30am–noon & 2–5.30pm • CH$1000 • ☎ 41 274 5715, ⓦ huascar.cl • White buses marked "Base Naval" go from along O'Higgins right to the entrance of the base

The industrial city and naval base of Talcahuano is where the historic ironclad gunship **Huáscar** is moored. You need to ask the guard for permission to visit the ship at the

5

entrance of the base. The *Huáscar* was built for the Peruvian navy at Birkenhead in 1866 and controlled the naval engagements during the War of the Pacific until 1879, when it was trapped off Cape Angamos, near Antofagasta, and forced to surrender. Kept in an immaculate state of preservation, the *Huáscar* is one of only two vessels of its type still afloat today.

ARRIVAL AND DEPARTURE

By plane Aeropuerto Carriel Sur (☎41 273 2000, ⊛carrielsur.cl) is 5km northwest of the city. Several minibus companies offer inexpensive door-to-door transfers to the airport, including Transfer Service (☎09 8267 7607); a taxi into town will set you back around CH$8000. LAN has an office at O'Higgins 648 (☎600 526 2000); Sky Airlines is at O'Higgins 537 (☎600 600 2828).

Destinations Puerto Montt (1 weekly; 1hr 10min); Santiago (8–12 daily; 1hr 10 min); Temuco (1 weekly; 45min).

By bus Most buses arrive at Terminal Collao, northeast of the centre at Tegualda 860, just off the Autopista General Bonilla (☎41 274 9000); plenty of mini-buses and taxis will take you into town. If you arrive with Tur Bus or Linea Azul, you may be dropped at the smaller

CONCEPCIÓN

Terminal Chillancito, also called Terminal Henríquez, at Henríquez 2565. There are direct buses to most towns and cities between Santiago and Puerto Montt, most leaving from Terminal Collao. Tur Bus, whose downtown office is Tucapel 530 (☎41 223 3924), leaves from both Terminal Collao and Terminal Chillancito. If you're heading up the coast to Tomé, take a taxi *colectivo* from Chacabuco. The coastal route south of Concepción to Cañete, Arauco, Lebu and Contulmo is served by Buses Jota Ewert (☎41 285 1618).

Destinations Cañete (hourly; 3hr); Chillán (every 30min; 1hr 30min); Contulmo (4 daily; 4hr); Lebu (hourly; 3hr); Los Angeles (every 30min; 2hr); Puerto Montt (20 daily; 10hr); Santiago (every 30min; 6hr); Talca (hourly; 3hr 30min); Temuco (hourly; 4hr); Tomé (every 15min; 40min); Valdivia (11 daily; 6hr 40min).

INFORMATION AND TOURS

Conaf Barros Arana 215 (Mon–Thurs 8.30am–5.30pm, Fri 8.30am–4.30pm; ☎41 262 4000).

Tourist information Sernatur is located on the plaza at Aníbal Pinto 460 (Mon–Fri 10am–6pm; ☎41 274 1337, ✉infobiobio@sernatur.cl). The staff here are charming and helpful.

Tours Concepción is not a tourist destination and there is little in the way of organized tours, but if you can get a group together then Esquerre at Barros Arana 185 (☎41 274 9990) can organize city tours and visits to the nearby area.

ACCOMMODATION

Hostal Bianca Salas 643-C ☎41 225 2103, ⊛hostalbianca.cl. While service can be dour, this is a solid budget option, with small but bright rooms and a useful common area where you can prepare your own food. CH$30,000

Hotel Alborada Barros Arana 457 ☎41 291 1121, ⊛hotelalborada.cl. Modern hotel with a reflective glass exterior, plant-filled walkway and smart if rather bland rooms. CH$50,000

Hotel El Araucano Caupolicán 521 ☎41 274 0600, ⊛hotelaraucano.cl. A stellar – and reasonably priced – hotel boasting en suites with flat-screen TVs and tubs.

There also an indoor pool, a sauna and a good restaurant with a terrace overlooking the plaza. CH$50,000

Hotel Maquehue Barros Arana 786 ☎41 221 0261, ⊛hotelmaquehue.cl. This place offers very good value, with fresh, modern, brightly patterned rooms, some of which command fine city views. CH$30,000

Hotel San Sebastián Rengo 463 ☎41 295 6719, ⊛hotelsansebastian.cl. Rooms at this small, amiable budget hotel are a little old-fashioned if spotless and have cable TV; some have private bathrooms. Parking offered. CH$25,000

EATING AND DRINKING

Concepción has a good range of **restaurants** and boasts the liveliest nightlife in the Central Valley, fuelled by the large student population. The Barrio Estación is buzzing at night, particularly on Calle Prat and Plaza España, revolving mainly around a string of small restaurants that double up as bars on the weekend evenings. You can also enjoy inexpensive meals at one of the dozens of little *picadas* in the Mercado Central, on the corner of Freire and Caupolicán, or at the student haunts close to the university campus.

Café Rometsch Barros Arana 685 ☎41 274 7040, ⊛portalrometsch.cl. Cavity-inducing ice-cream sundaes, cakes and crêpes (around CH$3500) are available at this long-standing café, which is decorated with city sketches. Mon–Fri 8.30am–8.30pm, Sat 9am–7pm.

Cantabria Caupolicán 415 ☎41 252 2693. Prices are a little steep here on account of the prime people-watching location, but the good coffee and decadent cakes (CH$2500) make it eminently worthwhile. Mon–Sat 8am–10pm.

Cheng Nan Freire 877 ☎41 252 0202. An inexpensive self-service vegetarian joint with wholesome, mainly Chinese, dishes, a few pastas and salads (menu CH$2500). The food is much fresher at lunchtime. Mon–Sat 9.30am–6pm.

Fina Estampa Angol 298 ☎41 222 1708.

Waiters in red shirts and large white kerchiefs around their necks serve delicious Peruvian food (CH$6000–9000) like ceviche and *lomo saltado* (a popular dish of stir-fried steak strips with tomato, onion, chips and rice). Mon–Sat 1–4pm & 8pm–midnight, Sun 1–4pm.

La Fontana di Trevi Colo-Colo 336 ☎41 279 0300. Chequered tablecloths and a display of dozens of wine bottles form the backdrop for a tasty but standard Italian meal of pizza and pasta (CH$4000–10,000). Mon–Sat noon–4pm & 6.30–10.30pm, Sun 12.30–4.30pm.

DIRECTORY

Car rental For car rental head to Avis (☎41 288 7420) or Budget (☎600 441 0000). Both have booths at the airport and an office downtown at Prat 750.

Hospital San Martín and Lautaro (☎41 272 2500).

Money and exchange There are many banks with ATMs, mainly on O'Higgins, by the central plaza. To change money, try AFEX at Barros Arana 565.

Post office O'Higgins and Colo-Colo (Mon–Fri 8.30am–7pm, Sat 8.30am–1pm).

The beaches north of Concepción

North of Concepción, a series of small towns and golden, sandy bays stretches up the coastline as far as the mouth of the Río Itata, 60km beyond. Heading up the road, 12km out of the city centre, you pass through the suburb of **Penco**, where the remains of a Spanish fort, **Fuerte La Planchada**, recall the area's turbulent history.

A couple of gentle hills separate Penco from **Lirquén**, a small industrial harbour used for exporting timber. Its beach is nothing special, but the nearby tangle of narrow streets known as the **Barrio Chino** is full of first-class, excellent-value seafood restaurants, famous throughout the region for their clam dishes and *paila marina* (seafood stew). Beyond Lirquén, the road runs inland for 30km, and the only access to the ocean along here is controlled by *Punta de Parra* (see p.252).

Tomé and around

Some 28km out of Concepción, the thriving timber centre, textile town and port of **TOMÉ** is squeezed into a small flat-bottomed valley, its suburbs pushed up the slopes of surrounding hills. Hidden from the drab town by a rocky point is the long, white-sand **Playa El Morro**. The beach, while very attractive, gets dreadfully crowded on summer weekends; a quieter alternative is **Playa Cocholgue**, a fine white beach studded with rocky outcrops, reached by taking the 4km side road off the main coast road as you head out of Tomé.

Dichato and around

Eight kilometres north of Tomé, **DICHATO** is the most popular beach resort along this part of the coast, with a handful of **accommodation** options spread along the crescent-shaped, coastal avenue, Pedro Aguirre Cerda. About 4km north, the road turns to dirt and passes through dense forests with tracks leading off to a series of isolated, yellow-sand **beaches**, pounded by strong waves. Among the most beautiful of these are **Playa Purda**, 8km north of Dichato, and tiny **Playa Merquiche**, a further 2km north.

ARRIVAL AND DEPARTURE

By bus Regular buses ply the coast road, heading up from Chacabuco street in Concepción, passing through Tomé (40min) and on to Dichato.

ACCOMMODATION

Cabañas Broadway Av Werner 1210, Playa El Morro, Tomé ☎ 41 265 8475. For your own private beach pad, you could do worse than move into one of these ten fully equipped cabins, which sleep up to four people. **CH$25,000**

El Encanto 4km north of Dichato, towards the Río Itata ☎ 09 9440 0578. This restful campsite with electricity and hot showers also has a handful of cabins with kitchens that sleep up to six people. Camping/ person **CH$7000**, cabins **CH$50,000**

Hotel Althome Sotomayor 669, Playa El Morro, Tomé

THE BEACHES NORTH OF CONCEPCIÓN

☎41 265 0807, ✉ althome.hotel@gmail.com. This serviceable hotel has no-frills rooms, some with ocean views, and all with private bathrooms. Parking is included. **CH$30,000**

Punta de Parra Camino a Tomé Km 19, Tomé ☎ 09 7669 1019, ⊕ puntadeparra.com. Situated between Lirquén and Tomé, the company controlling this stretch of coast offers cabins and charges non-guests for admittance to the powdery white sands. There's a restaurant, infinity pool and a beautiful coastal walk along the old rail tracks to several even more secluded beaches. **CH$70,000**

The southern coast road and beyond

South of Concepción, a road skirts the ocean, passing through the towns of Coronel, **Lota** and Arauco. This area was deserted until the mid-nineteenth century, when the enormous submarine coal seam – the **Costa del Carbón** – was discovered running off the coast. About 150km south of Concepción, **Lebu** has great beaches, while nearby **Cañete**'s Mapuche museum is worth a visit en route to pretty **Lago Lanalhue**, 51km from Lebu.

Lota

Squeezed into a small valley on the edge of the sea, the soot-streaked town of **LOTA**, 43km south of Concepción along the R-160, was the site of Chile's first and largest coal mine, opened by industrialist Matías Cousiño in 1849. Production finally ceased in 1997, and today the ex-colliery is turning its attention to tourism, with hotels, swimming pools and a casino. The town centre, in the lower part of town known as Lota Bajo, does not inspire enthusiasm. Spread up the hillside west of the centre is Lota Alto, containing the former miners' residences, as well as the impressive **Iglesia San Matías**, where the coal baron lies buried.

Mina Chiflón del Diablo

La Conchilla • Daily 9.30am–6pm; hourly tours • CH$5700 • ☎ 41 287 0934, ⊕ lotasorprendente.cl

You can visit the **coal mine** on hourly **tours** guided by ex-miners, which take you down the 820m shaft. By the mine entrance is the Pueblito Minero (CH$800), a recreation of miners' houses that were constructed for the film set of the Chilean movie *Sub Terra*.

Parque Isidora Cousiño

El Parque • Daily 9.30am–6pm • Park CH$2300; museum CH$900 • ☎ 41 287 0934, ⊕ lotasorprendente.cl

On a headland to the west of town lies **Parque Isidora Cousiño**, a formal garden laid out by an English landscape gardener in 1862 under the direction of Cousiño's wife, *doña* Isidora Goyenechea. The park also has colonial homes, a museum containing a motley collection of photographs and colonial possessions, and actors who dress and speak like characters from the nineteenth century.

Isla Santa María

From Lota's pier you can take a two-hour boat ride to **Isla Santa María**, a small, lush island with steep cliffs, rolling hills and a population of about three thousand farmers and fishermen. The island's mild climate and fertile soil have supported small Mapuche communities for hundreds of years. There are secluded bays scattered around the island, with good beaches, sea lion colonies and excellent fishing opportunities.

Lebu

Seventy-six kilometres south of Lota, a 31km side road shoots off the highway to the small coastal town of **LEBU**, one of the few places still mining coal in this region. It has huge, unspoiled **beaches**, including **Playa Millaneco**, 3km north, where you'll find several massive caves overgrown with ferns and lichen. Lebu's only other attraction is its pair of bronze cannons on display in the plaza, which were cast in Lima in 1772 and bear the Spanish coat of arms.

Cañete

CAÑETE is a busy agricultural town perched on a small rise above a bend in the Río Tucapel, 16km south of the Lebu turn-off. Just off the northern end of the main street, commanding fine views over the river valley, the historic **Fort Tucapel** was founded by Spanish conquistador Pedro de Valdivia in 1552 and is the site of his gruesome death at the hands of the Mapuche chief Lautaro two years later.

Mapuche Museum

Camino Contulmo s/n • Jan & Feb Mon–Fri 9.30am–7pm, Sat & Sun 11am–7pm; March–Dec Tues–Fri 9.30am–5.30pm, Sat 11am–5.30pm, Sun 1–5.30pm • Free • ☎ 41 261 1093, ⓦ www.museomapuchecanete.cl

Just south of Cañete, 1km down the highway, the **Mapuche Museum** houses a fine collection of indigenous artefacts, including textiles, silver jewellery, musical instruments and weapons. Perhaps the most striking exhibit is the *ruca* in the museum's garden – a traditional Mapuche dwelling made of wood and straw.

Lago Lanalhue

Ten kilometres out of Cañete, the road reaches the northern shore of **Lago Lanalhue**, nestled among dense pine forests on the western slopes of the coastal range. Its waters are crystal clear and warmer than the Pacific, and its heavily indented shores form numerous peninsulas and bays, some of them containing fine white sand. You can buy basic provisions in the village of **Contulmo**, about 5km along the highway; while you're there, carry on a couple of kilometres around the south shore of the lake to visit the **Molino Grollmus** (officially Jan–April Mon–Sat 10–11am & 6–7pm, but in reality opening hours are more sporadic; CH$500), an early twentieth-century wooden mill whose gardens contain an impressive collection of *copihues* (Chile's national flower). Some 44km east of Contulmo, the highway forks, with one branch heading to the town of Angol (see p.256), and the other continuing south to the Panamericana.

ARRIVAL AND DEPARTURE	THE SOUTHERN COAST ROAD AND BEYOND

CAÑETE

By bus Buses J. Ewert operates numerous services from Concepción to Cañete (hourly; 3hr).

By car From Cañete, a dirt road climbs 46km to Parque Nacional Nahuelbuta (see p.256), while the highway curves south through a lower pass in the Cordillera de Nahuelbuta.

ISLA SANTA MARÍA

By boat Boats depart Sun noon, Tues 10am, and Wed and Fri at 11am (CH$5000 return; ☎ 41 288 9175, ⓦ navierasantamaria.cl). Boats return to Lota on Mon 8am, Tues 3pm, Thurs 8am and Fri 3pm.

LAGO LANALHUE

By bus Buses J. Ewert has services that run to Contulmo (4 daily; 4hr).

LEBU

By bus Regular services with Buses J. Ewert and Linea Azul go from Concepción to Lebu (hourly; 3hr).

LOTA

By bus Buses J. Ewert, Expresos del Carbón and Los Alces go from Concepción to Lota (every 15min; 1 hr 30min). Ask to be let off in Lota Alto.

5

ACCOMMODATION AND EATING

CAÑETE

Club Social de Cañete Condel 283 ☎41 261 1653. The best place to eat in town is this plaza-side restaurant in an unprepossessing building. It specializes in well-cooked meat and fish dishes, including wild boar and sea bass (mains CH$5000–8000) and desserts include the exotic potato and hazelnut ice cream. Mon–Sat noon–midnight.

Nahuelbuta Villagrán 644 ☎41 261 1593, ⓦhotelnahuelbuta.cl. The pleasant rooms have cable TV and a private bath while the adjacent café offers a wide selection of meals from sandwiches to lasagne (CH$4000). Café open until 11.30pm. CH$28,000

ISLA SANTA MARÍA

The boat schedule (see p.253) leaves you with the options of a half-day trip on Tuesday or Friday or else spending the night on the island. There are no hotels as such, but some of the fishermen rent out spare rooms in their homes; Sergio Monsalves (☎09 9950 6699) has rooms for CH$15,000/night/person, with meals included.

LAGO LANALHUE

Terrazas del Lanalhue Camino Cañete Km9.5 ☎09 9499 5330, ⓦterrazasdelanalhue.cl. On the northern side of the lake, 2km from Peleco, this range of cosy, fully equipped cabins have TV, space for up to five people and direct wharf access. For two people CH$35,000

LEBU

Plaza Lebu Saavedra 691 ☎41 251 2227, ⓦhotelboutiqueplazalebu.cl. A well-maintained hotel on the plaza with ten comfortable rooms with a private bath and cable TV. The hotel's restaurant often serves the local speciality – king crab. CH$38,000

Salto del Laja

From Concepción, the southern coastal route makes an appealing diversion but if you're in a hurry, take the direct 85km trunk road back to the Panamericana. Some 50km south from there, the first major town you reach is Los Angeles; halfway along this route, the Panamericana crosses the Río Laja. Just off the highway is the **Salto del Laja**, which ranks among the most impressive waterfalls in Chile, cascading almost 50m from two crescent-shaped cliffs down to a rocky canyon. It's a popular stop-off for Chileans, who come here to take a dip and picnic during the summer. You'll need to pick your way through a veritable village of stalls selling cheap snacks, toys and so on to get to the falls.

ARRIVAL AND DEPARTURE SALTO DEL LAJA

By bus If you are relying on public transport then your best bet is to visit the Salto del Laja on a short trip from Los Angeles – take one of the frequent Jota Be bus services – they run in both directions (hourly; 30min).

By car The Salto del Laja makes a good break spot on the long drive from Santiago, but beware of old maps that show the highway cruising by the falls. To actually get to the Salto del Laja, you'll need to follow the turn-off signs for the "Salto". From the parking areas there are short paths that can lead you to a closer viewpoint.

ACCOMMODATION

Los Manantiales Panamericana Sur Km 480 ☎43 231 4275, ⓦlosmanantiales.saltosdellaja.com. This large 1970s-style complex includes hotel rooms, fully serviced cabins (for up to six people) and a campground. There are three natural pools and the restaurant (CH$4800 set lunch) has views over the waterfalls. Restaurant open daily 12.30–3pm. Camping/site CH$20,000, doubles CH$37,000, cabins CH$60,000

El Rincón Panamericana Sur Km 494, El Olivo ☎09 9441 5019, ⓦelrinconchile.cl. This German-run guesthouse has average doubles (some with private bathrooms) in lovely surroundings. It also offers home-cooked meals and hearty breakfasts with muesli, fruit and yoghurt. CH$45,000

Salto del Laja Panamericana Sur Km 485 ☎43 232 1706, ⓦsaltodellaja.cl. This hotel is located on an island with sixty acres of parkland. It boasts swish suites, waterfall views, a restaurant and access to delightful swimming holes. CH$71,000

Los Angeles

LOS ANGELES is an easy-going agricultural town, pleasant enough but without any great attractions. At the north end of Colón, eight blocks from the orderly Plaza de Armas, is the colonial **Parroquia Perpetuo Socorro**, a church whose handsome colonnaded cloisters enclose a flower-filled garden. Otherwise, the town is really just a stop-off on the Panamericana or jumping-off point for the **Parque Nacional Laguna del Laja** (see below).

ARRIVAL AND DEPARTURE

LOS ANGELES

By bus The long-distance bus terminal is on Av Sor Vicenta 2051 (☎43 236 3035, ⓦrodoviariolosangeles.cl), on the outskirts of town. The local terminal is at Villagrán 501 (☎43 231 3232).
Destinations Angol (every 30min; 1hr); Chillán (every 30min; 1hr 30min); Concepción (every 30min; 2hr); El Abanico (every 30 min; 1hr 30min); Puerto Montt (hourly; 8hr); Rancagua (5 daily; 6hr 15min); Talca (6 daily; 3hr 45 min); Temuco (every 45min; 2hr 30min).

INFORMATION AND TOURS

Conaf Manso de Velasco 275 (Mon–Fri 8.30am–2.30pm; ☎43 232 1086). Conaf also mans a hut at the Laguna del Laja park entrance.
Tourist information The tourist office is at Colón 185 (Mon–Sat 10am–7pm; ☎43 240 9447).
Tours Harold Wicki (☎09 6326 6463) offers guided tours to Parque Nacional Laguna del Laja (English spoken). Turismo Curalemu (ⓦcuralemu.cl) owns some *cabañas* near Antuco, close to the entrance of the Parque Nacional Laguna del Laja, and can also organize guided treks in the park.

ACCOMMODATION AND EATING

Gran Hotel Muso Valdivia 222 ☎43 231 3183, ⓦhotelmuso.cl. Even if you're not a fan of 1980s architecture and decor, then you'll at least appreciate the plaza-side location of this five-storey hotel. Rooms are bright and clean but try to get one with plaza views. CH$46,000

Hotel Oceano Colo Colo 327 ☎43 234 2432, ⓦhoteloceano.cl. A good central budget option, with helpful staff and eleven neat, sunny rooms with a/c and clean private bathrooms. Breakfast and parking included. CH$41,000

Four Points by Sheraton Colo Colo 565 ☎43 240 6400, ⓦstarwoodhotels.com. The new *Four Points by Sheraton* tower is the smartest hotel in town, with the usual comfortable rooms, as well as a great pool and Jacuzzi complex and decent restaurant. CH$57,000

Puerto Maddero Alemania 393 ☎43 231 4177. Bar-restaurant which does good-value all-you-can-eat buffets with barbecue (CH$8000) as well as a standard menu. Daily 8pm–2am.

Parque Nacional Laguna del Laja

93km from Los Angeles • Daily: May–Nov 8.30am–6.30pm; Dec–April 8.30am–8pm • CH$1000 • ☎43 232 1086

Set in an otherworldly volcanic landscape of lava flows and honeycombed rock, the **Parque Nacional Laguna del Laja** takes its name from the great green lake formed by the 1752 eruption of **Volcán Antuco** (2985m). The road from Los Angeles, 93km away, is paved most of the way; the last 6km is gravel but in decent condition. The park boundary is 4km east of the village of **El Abanico**. You pay your fee and can pick up advice and maps at an information hut a further 4km east.

Salto Las Chilcas and Salto del Torbellino

From the Conaf hut, an easy path leads a couple of kilometres to a pair of large, thundering waterfalls, **Salto Las Chilcas** and **Salto del Torbellino**, fed by underground channels from the lake, which emerge here to form the source of the Río Laja. Hikes to the summit are not particularly difficult, but allow four to five hours for the trip up and three hours for the hike down. Wear strong boots as the volcanic rocks will shred light footwear.

5

The road east

The road through the park continues east from the information centre towards the lake, passing the mini single-lift **ski centre**, **Centro de Esquí Volcán Antuco** (5km along the road; July–August/September; CH$20,000; ☎42 232 2651, ⓦskiantuco.cl), which has a small restaurant. The road then skirts along the southern shore of the lake for 22km, continuing to the Argentine border at Paso Pichachén. Few vehicles make it along here, so the road serves as an excellent walking trail through the sterile landscape, with changing views of the lake and of the mountains of **Sierra Velluda** in the southwest, which are studded with hanging glaciers. Around 4km east of the ski resort you'll come to a haunting memorial to 45 young soldiers who were killed in the May 2005 'Tragedy of Antuco'; the ill-equipped conscripts died of hypothermia and exposure after being sent on a march around the volcano in a snowstorm.

ARRIVAL AND DEPARTURE — PARQUE NACIONAL LAGUNA DEL LAJA

By bus From Los Angeles' Terminal Rural, Buses Elper (☎43 236 2785) and Expresos Volcán run services to El Abanico (every 30min; 1hr 30min).

ACCOMMODATION

Cabañas y Camping Lagunillas 2km from park entrance ☎43 232 1086. A secluded camping area and four spacious cabins by the banks of the Río Laja. There is also a restaurant. Open year-round. Camping/site CH$10,000, cabins CH$30,000

Angol

Sixty-four kilometres southwest of Los Angeles, **ANGOL** is the final major town before Temuco, the gateway to the Lake District, and serves as a useful base for visiting the nearby **Parque Nacional Nahuelbuta**. In the centre of the town's attractive Plaza de Armas a large, rectangular pool is guarded by four finely carved – and comically stereotypical – marble statues of women representing the continents of Asia, Africa, Europe and America.

Museo Dillman Bullock

Camino Angol Km 5 • Daily 9.30am–6.30pm • CH$450 • ☎45 271 1142 • Regular *colectivos* from the Plaza de Armas

Located within an agricultural college in the suburbs, **Museo Dillman Bullock** has beautifully landscaped gardens and a strange assortment of archaeology including pre-Columbian funeral urns, a moth-eaten mummy, Mapuche artefacts and malformed foetuses.

ARRIVAL AND INFORMATION — ANGOL

By bus Angol's long-distance bus terminal is at Oscar Bonilla 428, seven blocks from the Plaza. **Conaf** Prat 191 (☎45 271 1870).

Tourist information Plaza de Armas (Jan & Feb Mon–Fri 8.30am–8pm, Sat & Sun 10am–1pm & 4–8pm; March–Dec Mon–Fri 8.30am–5.30pm; ☎45 2990840).

ACCOMMODATION

Duhatao Prat 420 ☎45 2714320, ⓦhotelduhatao.cl. This sleek boutique hotel has stylish rooms decorated with ethnic and recycled furnishings, and a restaurant and bar which serves international cuisine. CH$48,000

Parque Nacional Nahuelbuta

35km west of Angol • Daily: 8.30am–6pm • CH$4000 • ⓦparquenahuelbuta.cl

From Angol, a hard-going stony road (difficult to pass after rain) climbs 35km west to the entrance of **PARQUE NACIONAL NAHUELBUTA**, spread over the highest part of the Cordillera de Nahuelbuta. The park was created in 1939 to protect the last remaining **araucaria** (monkey puzzle) trees in the coastal mountains, after the surrounding native forest had been wiped out and replaced with thousands of radiata pines for the pulp and paper industry. Today it's a 68-square-kilometre enclave of mixed evergreen and deciduous forest, providing the coastal cordillera's only major refuge for wildlife such as foxes, pumas and *pudús* (pygmy deer).

You're unlikely to catch sight of any of these shy animals, although if you look up among the tree trunks you may well see large black woodpeckers hammering away. Of the park's trees, star billing goes to the towering araucarias, with their thick umbrellas of curved, overlapping branches covered in stiff pine needles. Some of these trees are over 40m high, and the most mature ones in the park are more than a thousand years old.

PARQUE NACIONAL NAHUELBUTA

ARRIVAL AND INFORMATION

By bus In the summer Buses Angol and Buses Nahuelbuta come from Angol's rural terminal and stop at El Cruce, a 1hr walk from the entrance. The park is open all year but expect snow and 4WD conditions in winter (June–Sept).

PARQUE NACIONAL NAHUELBUTA

Tourist information Centro de Informaciones, 5km west along the road from the entrance (daily 8am–1pm & 2–8pm). Here you can find out more about the park's flora and fauna.

ACCOMMODATION

Camping Pehuenco 5km from the entrance on the Angol side, ☏ 2 2196 0245. Beside the information centre and park headquarters, *Camping Pehuenco* has eleven sites with picnic tables and cold showers. Camping/site C͟H͟$͟1͟2͟,͟0͟0͟0͟

TREKS IN PARQUE NACIONAL NAHUELBUTA

From the Centro de Informaciones there are main two treks: an interesting, 700m interpretative loop through the forest and an easy one-hour, 4km hike (look out for the giant araucaria about a 5min walk along the path, estimated to be 1800 years old) up to the **Piedra del Aguila**. This craggy rock, 1450m above sea level, offers superb views that on clear days take in the whole width of Chile, from the Andes to the Pacific. At a slightly lower, flatter rock a few metres west, you can enjoy even better views onto the smoking volcanoes of the northern Lake District.

To get here by car, take the road through the park to the signed car park, from where it's a twenty-minute walk up to the viewpoint past a series of information panels on the trees. There's another rewarding trek up the gentle slopes of **Cerro Anay**, 4km north of the information centre, reached by a jeep track followed by a short path. Its 1400m peak is the best place to take in the whole of the park.

The Lake District

260 Temuco

265 Parque Nacional Tolhuaca

266 Parque Nacional Conguillío

270 Lago Villarrica and around

283 The Siete Lagos

286 Valdivia and around

292 Osorno

293 Parque Nacional Puyehue and around

296 Lago Llanquihue and around

303 Parque Nacional Vicente Pérez Rosales and around

306 Estuario de Reloncaví

310 Puerto Montt

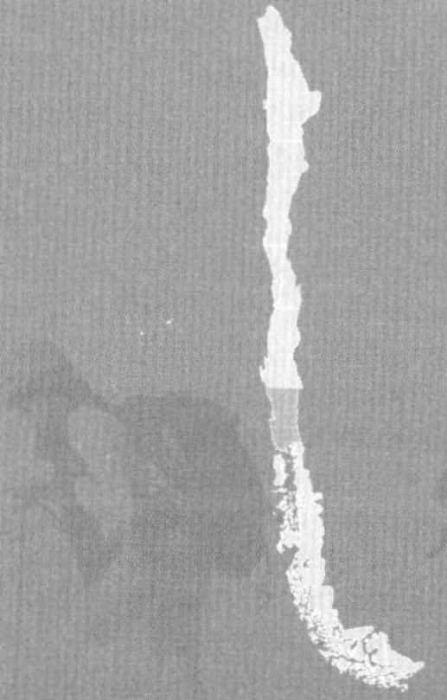

CLIMBING VOLCÁN VILLARRICA

6

The Lake District

The Lake District, which stretches 339km from Temuco in the north to Puerto Montt in the south, is a region of lush farmland, dense forest, snowcapped volcanoes and deep, clear lakes, hidden for the most part in the mountains. Until the 1880s, when small farm settlements arrived, the entire region was blanketed in thick forests: to the north, the high, spindly araucaria; on the coast, dense *selva valdiviana*; and to the very south, two-thousand-year-old *alerces* – "Chile's Yosemite". These forests were inhabited by the Mapuche (literally "people of the land"), who fought off the Inca and resisted Spanish attempts at colonization for 350 years before finally falling to the Chilean Army in the 1880s.

In the century since the subjugation of the Mapuche, German, Austrian and Swiss settlers have transformed this region into some of the finest **dairy farmland** in Chile, and the extent of German influence is evident in architectural and culinary form, particularly in Valdivia, Puerto Varas and Frutillar. Indigenous culture survives as well: the Mapuche heritage is a badge of honour in today's Chile, and at least half a million of the region's population claim this ancestry, many of whom reside on the extensive indigenous *reducciones* (reservations) throughout the Lake District.

The efforts of the European settlers also opened the area up to travellers, and visitors have been coming here for over a hundred years. The real action lies in the region's many national parks and around the adventure sports capitals of **Pucón** and **Puerto Varas**, where the options abound for hiking, volcano-climbing, rafting, kayaking, horseriding and soaking in the many thermal springs. In the winter, skiing down volcanoes draws an adventurous crowd.

Temuco

Once a Mapuche stronghold, **TEMUCO**, 677km south of Santiago, is a busy working city with a rich **Mapuche heritage**, particularly evident in and around the colourful **markets**, among the best places in the country to hear Mapudungun (the Mapuche language) spoken. An atmosphere of tension prevails between the large Mapuche population and the police and you may bear witness to student protests and clashes between the two, over land rights and other injustices.

Founded in 1881, Temuco began to prosper when the railway from Santiago arrived in 1893, followed by European immigrants from seven different countries who formed

Skiing and hiking in parque Nacional Conguillío p.267
Musher for a day p.272
Recent volcanic eruptions p.273
Hot springs around Pucón p.277
Exploring Parque Nacional Huerquehue p.278
Villarrica's demonic peaks p.279

Villarrica activities p.282
The land-and-Lake crossing into Argentina p.299
Trekking in the Río Cochamó Valley p.307
Ferries from Puerto Montt p.312

PARQUE NACIONAL CONGUILLÍO

Highlights

❶ Parque Nacional Conguillío Hiking is spectacular in this Andean park, where old lava flows mix with ancient araucaria forests. **See p.266**

❷ Villarrica Become a musher for a day with Chile's only husky dog operator, or join a week-long dog-sledding expedition across the Andes. **See p.270**

❸ Pucón The Lake District's adventure tourism capital, where you can climb smoking Volcán Villarrica, raft the rapids of the Trancura or hike in the nearby nature reserves. **See p.273**

❹ Valdivia Visit old Spanish forts, drink some of Chile's best beer and go sea lion-spotting at the lively waterfront market. **See p.286**

❺ Lago Llanquihue Spectacular waterfalls, one of the region's more challenging volcano climbs, whitewater rafting and some of the best food in the region. **See p.296**

❻ Cochamó Valley A top spot for hiking or horse-trekking into the oldest forests of the Americas, known as "Chile's Yosemite", and for rock climbing at La Junta. **See p.307**

❼ Mapuche Museums View the most impressive collections of Mapuche silver jewellery and other artefacts at the excellent Museo de Volcanes (see p.285) and Museo Regional de La Araucanía (see p.263).

HIGHLIGHTS ARE MARKED ON THE MAP ON P.262

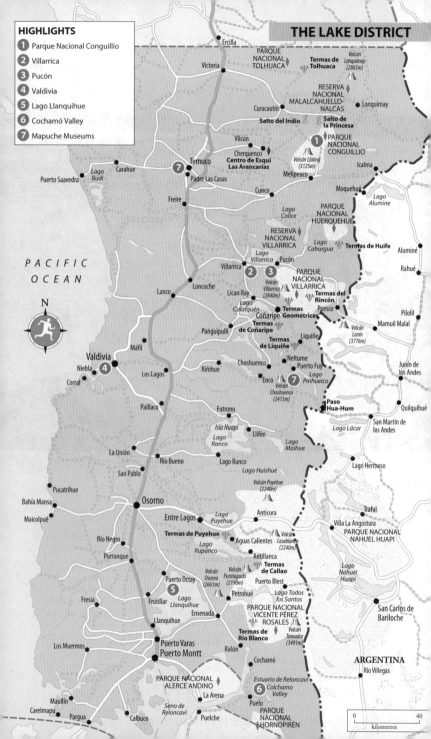

THE LAKE DISTRICT

HIGHLIGHTS

1. Parque Nacional Conguillío
2. Villarrica
3. Pucón
4. Valdivia
5. Lago Llanquihue
6. Cochamó Valley
7. Mapuche Museums

PACIFIC OCEAN

N

ARGENTINA

Ercilla

Victoria

PARQUE NACIONAL TOLHUACA

Termas de Tolhuaca

Volcán Lonquimay (2865m)

RESERVA NACIONAL MALALCAHUELLO-NALCAS

Lonquimay

Curacautín

Salto del Indio

Salto de la Princesa

Vilcún

PARQUE NACIONAL CONGUILLÍO

Cherquenco

Centro de Esquí Las Arancarias

Volcán Llaima (3125m)

Icalma

Temuco

Melipeuco

Moquehué

Lago Budi

Carahue

Padre Las Casas

Cunco

Lago Alumine

Puerto Saavedra

Freire

Lago Colico

PARQUE NACIONAL HUERQUEHUE

RESERVA NACIONAL VILLARRICA

Lago Caburgua

Termas de Huife

Aluminé

Lago Villarrica

Villarrica

Pucón

Rahué

Lanco

Loncoche

Lican Ray

Volcán Villarrica (2840m)

PARQUE NACIONAL VILLARRICA

Termas del Rincón

Pilolil

Lago Calafquén

Coñaripe

Termas Geométricas

Puesco

Mamuil Malal

Máfil

Panguipulli

Termas de Coñaripe

Termas de Liquiñe

Liquiñe

Volcán Lanín (3776m)

Valdivia

Niebla

Riñihue

Choshuenco

Neltume

Puerto Fuy

Junín de los Andes

Corral

Los Lagos

Enco

Volcán Choshuenco (2415m)

Lago Pirihueico

Quilquihué

Paillaco

Futrono

Paso Hua-Hum

San Martín de los Andes

Isla Huapi

Llifén

Lago Maihue

Lago Lácar

Lago Ranco

La Unión

Río Bueno

Lago Ranco

Lago Huishué

Lago Hermoso

San Pablo

Volcán Puyehue (2240m)

Pucatrihue

Bahía Mansa

Osorno

Anticura

Traful

Maicolpué

Entre Lagos

Lago Puyehue

Villa La Angostura

PARQUE NACIONAL NAHUEL HUAPI

Termas de Puyehue

Aguas Calientes

Volcán Casablanca (2240m)

Río Negro

Lago Rupanco

Antillanca

Termas de Callao

Lago Nahuel Huapi

Purranque

Volcán Puntiagudo (2190m)

Puerto Blest

Volcán Osorno (2661m)

Puerto Octay

Petrohué

Lago Todos los Santos

San Carlos de Bariloche

Fresia

Frutillar

Lago Llanquihue

Ensenada

PARQUE NACIONAL VICENTE PÉREZ ROSALES

Volcán Tronador (3491m)

Llanquihue

Los Muermos

Puerto Varas

Puerto Montt

Ralún

Termas de Río Blanco

Cochamó

ARGENTINA

Río Villegas

PARQUE NACIONAL ALERCE ANDINO

La Arena

Estuario de Reloncaví

Colchamo Valley

Maullín

Seno de Reloncaví

Puelo

Carelmapu

Pargua

Calbuco

Puelche

PARQUE NACIONAL HORNOPIRÉN

0 — 40 kilometres

the farming and commercial nucleus. Today, many visitors use Temuco as a transport hub or as a base for exploring nearby Parque Nacional Conguillío.

Museo Regional de la Araucanía

Av Alemania 84 • Mon–Fri 9.30am–5.30pm, Sat 11am–5pm, Sun 11am–2pm • CH$600, Sun free • Bus #1, #7 or #9 along Av Alemania

Temuco's biggest attraction is the **Museo Regional de la Araucanía**. Housed in a fine 1920s-vintage building, it charts the history and migration of the Araucanían people and the Spanish conquest and subsequent European settlement of the Lake District through beautifully presented exhibits. Spotlights in the large basement subtly illuminate displays of asymmetric *metawe* pottery, funerary urns, sceptre-like half-moon-shaped sacred stones of power, household objects and Spanish weaponry. Standout exhibits include an enormous 17th-century *wuampo* (hollow log canoe), traditional weavings, *kollong kollong* (crude wooden ceremonial masks) and *kultrung* (ceremonial drums), but the star of the show is the **Mapuche jewellery**; the Mapuche learned silverwork from the Spanish and fine examples of the craft, including heavy silver *collares*, passed on from mother to daughter, are on display here. Temporary exhibits present other aspects of Mapuche culture, most recently focusing on the celebrated Mapuche weaving and the meaning of the embroidery on women's belts. The museum is a ten-minute walk along Av Alemania.

The markets

Mercado Modelo Portales between Bulnes and Aldunate • Summer Mon–Sat 8am–8pm, Sun 8am–3pm; winter Mon–Sat 8am–5pm
Feria Libre Two blocks of Av Pinto between Lautaro and Av Balmaceda • Daily: summer 8.30am–6pm; winter 8.30am–5pm

The heart of the centrally-located, covered **Mercado Modelo** consists of countless craft stalls selling silver Mapuche jewellery, baskets, belts, handbags, musical instruments, woven ponchos and more, and some lunch stalls.

Near the old railway station is Chile's liveliest and most colourful fruit and vegetable market, the **Feria Libre**, pungent with fish and spices from the *merkén* (smoked chilli powder) stalls. This is a good place to savour typical local dishes, such as *cazuela* in one of the numerous hole-in-the-wall eateries, and one of the few places you'll see *piñones* (araucaria tree nuts traditionally boiled and eaten by the Mapuche) for sale.

ARRIVAL AND DEPARTURE

TEMUCO

BY PLANE

The new Temuco airport is located 17km away from the city, served by LAN and Sky Airline flights to Santiago and Concepción, and connected to it by minibus transfers (CH$5000). In peak season, there are direct transfers to Pucón.

Airlines LAN, Bulnes 687 (☎600 526 2000, ⌨lan.com); Sky Airline, Bulnes 677 (☎600 600 2828, ⌨skyairline.cl).

Destinations Puerto Montt (1–2 daily; 45min); Santiago via Concepción (6 daily; 2hr).

BY BUS

If you're coming from a nearby town by bus, it's best to use Buses JAC, as you'll be dropped off at their own central terminal at Aldunate and Balmaceda (☎45 223 1340). Most long-haul buses have ticket offices in the centre but depart from the main long-distance bus terminal, Terminal Rodoviario Araucario (☎45 222 5005), inconveniently

located out of the centre at Vicente Pérez Rosales 1609, and served by *colectivos* and bus #7 from the city centre. The Terminal de Buses Rurales on Pinto and Balmaceda (☎45 221 0494) runs services to more local destinations.

Companies Buses JAC has frequent departures to all major destinations in the Lake District; Igi Llaima and Nar Bus, Miraflores 1535 (☎45 240 7777), serve Argentine destinations; Tur Bus, General Lagos 576 (☎45 227 0458), and Pullman, Claro Solar 561 (☎45 221 2137), serve Santiago and all major destinations north of the Lake District; Cruz del Sur, Lagos at Claro Solar (☎45 273 0320), covers the Lake District and Chiloé.

Destinations Concepción (4 daily; 5hr); Melipeuco (6 daily; 2hr 30min); Osorno (every 30min; 4hr); Pucón (every 30min; 1hr 45min); Puerto Varas (hourly; 5hr); San Martín de Los Andes, Argentina (1 daily; 7hr); Santiago (every 30min; 9hr); Valdivia (every 30min; 2hr 30min); Villarrica (every 30min; 1hr 15min).

6

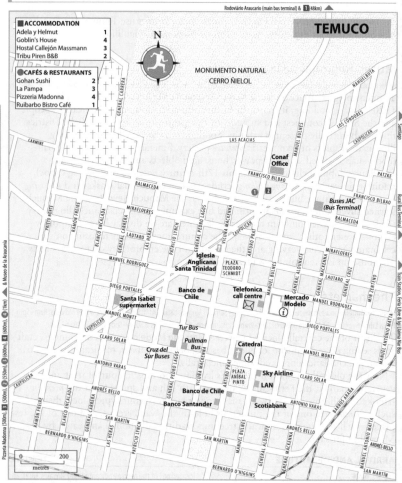

INFORMATION

Conaf Bilbao 931, second floor (Mon–Fri 8.30am–2pm; ☎45 229 8100). Offers information on the region's national parks, including Parque Nacional Conguillío.

Sernatur Bulnes 590 (Mon–Fri 9am–6pm, Sat 10am–4pm; ☎45 240 6213, ✉infoaraucania @sernatur.cl).

ACCOMMODATION

Adela y Helmut Km 5 N ☎09 8258 2230, ⍾adelay helmut.cl. This small German–Chilean-run farm comes warmly recommended by travellers. Stay either in a dorm or a fully equipped mini-apartment inside a large *cabaña*, feast on home-cooked *asado*, smoked trout or the ample breakfast (CH$4000) which includes eggs and honey from the property, or take part in one of the many tours of the Lake District organized by the helpful owners. To get here, take the frequent Nar Bus service from Temuco towards Cunco but alight at the Faja 16000 stop (call the owners before you leave Temuco). Dorms CH$12,000, apartments CH$31,000

Goblin's House Pirineos 841 ☎45 232 0044, ⍾hotel goblin.cl. A block away from trendy Av Alemania, the snug doubles and twins at this hotel-cum-Irish-pub are all smart slate-grey linen, bold contemporary prints and powerful rain showers, each named after an Irish county (or symbol). Yet while the bar décor waxes nostalgic about Dublin, the only truly Irish thing on the menu is Guinness. CH$45,000

Hostal Callejón Massmann Callejón Massmann 350 ☎45 248 5955, ⓦhostalcm.cl. Down a quiet side street but within easy walking distance of Av Alemania's charms, this brand-new guesthouse has just ten rooms, the austere black-and-white décor contrasting sharply with the bright modern art prints. The showers are on the poky side but each room has a terrace and continental breakfast is included. CH$50,000

EATING AND DRINKING

Gohan Sushi España 390 ☎45 274 1110, ⓦgohan.cl. This branch of the trendy sushi chain, just off Av Alemania, specialises in two things: prawns done sixteen different ways and imaginative sushi rolls, with fresh crab, tempura rice, scallops and razor clams featuring on the long list of options. Mon–Sat 12.30–3.30pm & 7–11pm.

La Pampa Caupolicán 155 ☎45 232 9999 ⓦlapampa.cl. The menu at this bustling Argentinian restaurant is the discerning carnivore's dream: aged rump steak, prime rib, bacon-wrapped sirloin medallion, sweetbreads, kidneys, slow-cooked ribs, bulls' testicles...Sure, you could come here for the salads, but why would you want to? Mon–Sat noon–4pm & 7pm–midnight, Sun noon–4pm.

Pizzeria Madonna Av Alemania 660 ☎45 232 9393,

Tribu Piren B&B Prat 69 ☎45 298 5711, ⓦtribupiren. cl. The helpful English-speaking owner at this small, spotless, centrally located B&B runs winter tours of the area. The compact rooms are equipped with cable TV and it's one of the few places where a single costs half the price of a double. Popular with international travellers. CH$24,000

ⓦmadonnapizza.com. This Italian *trattoria* with chequered tablecloths really delivers when it comes to some of the best pizza in the Lake District and home-made pasta dishes; the house special is *Tricotta* (meat or vegetable-filled ravioli done three different ways). The service is brisk, but would it kill them to provide pepper grinders? Daily 12.30–3.30pm & 7–11.30pm.

Ruibarbo Bistro Café Prat 20 ☎45 225 7115. This cute little café serves good coffee and features a limited lunchtime menu of a starter, two mains and a dessert. One of the mains is invariably vegetarian and you can expect the likes of spinach-stuffed crepes, quiche, sushi, couscous and salad or whatever else takes the chef's global fancy on any given day. Mon–Fri 8.30am–4.30pm.

Parque Nacional Tolhuaca

120km northeast of Temuco • Daily 8.30am–6pm • CH$3500

A pristine, forested landscape offering some very decent hiking, **PARQUE NACIONAL TOLHUACA** covers a long and relatively narrow strip of land stretching through the valley of the Río Malleco, hemmed in by steep, thickly wooded hills. Dominating the bottom of the valley is the wide and shallow **Laguna Malleco**, bordered by tall reeds rich in birdlife, while other attractions include waterfalls, small lakes and hundreds of araucaria trees.

There are two **approaches** to the park: one is along the 57km gravel road (via the village of Inspector Fernández) branching east from the Panamericana, 2km north of **Victoria**. This leads directly to the Conaf administration on the southeastern shore of Laguna Malleco, where you'll also find **camping** and picnic areas. From here, a footpath follows the northern shore of the lake for about 3km, through lush evergreen forest to the **Salto Malleco**, where the lake's waters spill down into the Río Malleco, forming a spectacular 50m waterfall. The other approach is from **Curacautín** via a 33km gravel road, which leads you straight to the Termas Malleco (see p.266).

Sendero Prados de Mesacura and Sendero Lagunillas

About halfway along the lake path, another trail branches north, climbing steeply up the hillside before forking in two. The left fork follows the 12km **Sendero Prados de Mesacura** across a gentle plain before climbing steeply again through dense forest. The right fork follows the **Sendero Lagunillas** (also 12km), climbing moderately to a group of small lakes near the summit of Cerro Amarillo, from where you get fabulous panoramic views onto the surrounding peaks, including the 2800m Volcán Tolhuaca. Both of these are full-day hikes, requiring an early start.

6

6

Sendero Laguna Verde

Following the flat path along the northern bank of the Río Malleco eastwards, after about 5km you'll reach the trailhead of the 8km **Sendero Laguna Verde**, which climbs up and around a steep hill to the small, emerald-green Laguna Verde, 1300m above sea level and surrounded by soaring peaks.

Termas Malleco

Daily 9am–6pm • CH$10,000 • ☎ 45 241 1111, ⓦ termasmalleco.cl

Nine kilometres east of the Conaf office (see p.264) or 33km north of Curacautín, the revamped **TERMAS MALLECO** (formerly the Termas de Tolhuaca) sit just outside the park's boundaries. The source of the *termas* is at the bottom of a narrow, rocky canyon, inside a large cave, where bubbling, sulphurous water seeps out of the rocks, and steam vents fill the cave with fumaroles, forming a kind of Stone-Age sauna. The small pools around the cave are too hot to paddle in, but a little further down the canyon, where the thermal water has mixed with cold stream water, there's a gorgeous natural pool that you can bathe in.

The administration operates two **guesthouses** (see below), and you can also visit the *termas* for the day. It can get very busy in January and February, especially at weekends, but outside these months the place is blissfully quiet.

ACCOMMODATION **PARQUE NACIONAL TOLHUACA**

Camping Laguna Malleco Next to the Conaf administration by the lake. Basic campsite with picnic areas, hot showers and a firepit by each site for cooking purposes. Camping/person **CH$14,000**

Refugio Araucaria & Refugio Notro Near the thermal pools ☎ 45 224 1111, ⓦ termasmalleco.cl. The two lodge-like guesthouses have the same amenities – en suite rooms

with central heating generated by thermal water (no TV or wi-fi to maximise complete relaxation), though *Refugio Araucaria* is the larger of the two and some of its rooms come with balconies. Guests have unlimited access to pool no. 2. Camping is permitted on the property, with fire pits, showers, and pool access. Full board available. Breakfast included. Doubles **CH$146**, camping/person **CH$12,000**

Parque Nacional Conguillío

120km east of Temuco • Oct–March • CH$4500 • ⓦ parquenacionalconguillio.cl

The grey peak of Volcán Llaima (3125m) looms over the horizon about 80km east of Temuco. Wrapped around its neck is **PARQUE NACIONAL CONGUILLÍO**, a park the volcano has been doing its best to destroy with belch after belch of black lava. The northern sector is lush, high forest, with steep cliffs covered in spindly-armed araucaria trees often draped in furry lime-green moss. In the south, however, the volcano has wreaked havoc. The road from Temuco passes over a wide lava flow, consisting of either rolling plains of thin dust or walls of spiked, recently congealed rock.

Volcán Llaima is actually one of the three active volcanoes on the continent; its last serious eruption was in 1957, though as recently as 1994 a lake, Laguna Arco Iris, was formed by a fresh lava flow that blocked a river.

The northern route into the park is through the village of **Curacautín** (97km from Temuco), entering the park at sector Laguna Captrén, while the paved southern road enters at sector Truful-Truful, via the compact village of **Melipeuco**. The latter makes a convenient base for visiting the park, with a few good accommodation options and shuttles into the park run by a local tour operator. From the west, a little-used dirt road runs from the village of Cherquenco past the Centro de Esquí Las Araucarias.

6

ARRIVAL AND INFORMATION

By bus Nar Bus (☎45 240 7778) runs a service from Temuco to Melipeuco (Mon–Sat 7 daily, Sun 3 daily; 1hr 45min) – the southern gateway to the eastern section of the park, 91km east of Temuco and 30km south of the park administration; from here, you'll have to take a taxi. There are frequent Buses Erbuc (☎45 223 3958) services daily from Temuco to Curacautín, the northern gateway to the park, 75km from Temuco and 30km from the administration. From Curacautín there are two shuttles to the park's Laguna Captrén (Mon and Fri); otherwise you can

PARQUE NACIONAL CONGUILLÍO

get a taxi. In winter, buses go the 106km from Temuco to the western ski slopes.

By car The bumpy road that bisects the park is just about passable in a regular car (though only in Dec–Feb when there's little snow); a high-clearance vehicle is more comfortable.

Conaf Conaf's excellent Centro de Información Ambiental (Oct–March daily 9am–1pm & 3–6.30pm) sits near the wide Lago Conguillío, with displays on the park's geology, fauna and flora.

SKIING AND HIKING IN PARQUE NACIONAL CONGUILLÍO

The park splits neatly into two main sectors. The **western slopes** (Sector Los Paraguas) come into their own in winter, boasting a small ski centre, the Centro de Esquí Las Araucarias (☎45 227 4141, ⓦ skiaraucarias.cl), with breathtaking views, three drag lifts, a chairlift, and three runs (day pass CH$24,000). In summer the focus shifts to the hiking action on the **eastern slopes**, which form the bulk of the park.

DAY HIKES

Those with sufficient experience, an ice axe and crampons can make the difficult seven-hour **ascent of Volcán Llaima**, but you need permission from Conaf. Be prepared to deal with crevasses and fumaroles, and beware of sulphur fumes at the summit. The park also offers a good selection of hikes for all abilities. For incredible views of the Sierra Nevada range through araucaria forest, take the 7km (2.5hr) trail from Playa Linda, at the east end of Lago Conguillío, to the base of the Sierra Nevada. The challenging **Travesía Río Blanco** (5km; 5hr), which crosses a small glacier before continuing into the Sierra Nevada proper, is recommended for very experienced trekkers only.

From the western shores of Laguna Verde, the 11km (5hr) **Sendero Pastos Blancos** runs to the Laguna Captrén, traversing spectacular scenery and rewarding you with panoramic views of Sierra Nevada, Lago Conguillío and the Truful-Truful valley. From the Truful-Truful Conaf ranger station, you can take the **Sendero Subtramo Arpehue**, part of the Sendero de Chile, to Laguna Captrén, passing the Andrés Huenupi Mapuche community along the way.

SHORT TRAILS

The Truful-Truful ranger station is also the starting point for two **short nature trails**: the Cañadón Truful-Truful (900m; 30min) passes by colourful strata, exposed by the Río Truful-Truful's flow, while the Las Vertientes trail (800m; 45min) is characterized by the subterranean springs that rush out of the ground. The Laguna Captrén ranger station is the starting point for the **Sendero Los Carpinteros**, also part of the Sendero de Chile, a fairly easy 8km (5hr) round-trip that starts from Lago Captrén, and loops around the lagoon before continuing to the administration centre and joining the El Contrabandista trail; the highlight is an araucaria that's estimated to be 1500 years old.

ACCOMMODATION

La Baita Conguillío 2.5km away from Laguna Verde, on the edge of a dense wood ☎45 258 1073, ⓦlabaitaconguillio.cl. A complex consisting of an attractive lodge (with hot tub) and six fully equipped, four- to six-person *cabañas*. It's also an activity centre, coordinating trekking and eco-tourism in the summer, and skiing and snow-walking in the winter. Doubles CH$58,000, *cabañas* CH$50,000

Camping ☎45 229 8100. There are five campsites in all: two by the ranger stations inside the park, one along the south shore of Lago Conguillío and two along the El Contrabandista trail in the eastern section of the park, all run by concessionaires, and accordingly expensive. Wild camping is not allowed. Nov–April. Camping/person CH$4000

Centro de Ski Las Araucarias ☎45 227 4141, ⓦskiaraucarias.cl. The revamped ski centre accommodates skiers in four buildings: *Edificio Araucaria* and *Edificio Llaima* both offer fully equipped apartments (holding 4-5 people), while comparably priced *refugios Las Paraguas* and *El Pehuén* offer large dorms (bring own sleeping bag) and a scattering of private doubles and triples. Dorms CH$12,000, doubles CH$24,000, apartments CH$70,000

Hospedaje Icalma Cerda 729, Melipeuco ☎09 9280 8210, ⓦmelipeucohospedaje.cl. Run by a larger-than-life hostess who'll mother you to bits, this simple guesthouse has seven en-suite rooms with plenty of woollen blankets and a kitchen for guest use. She can also put you in touch with the local tour company that gives hikers a lift into the park. CH$24,000

Hostal Sendero Andes Cerda 384, Melipeuco ☎45 258 1306, ⓦsenderoaventurasandes.cl. The rooms upstairs – some with bathroom, some without – of this cheerful wooden lodge are clean and sparsely decorated, while the downstairs restaurant serves enormous, immensely satisfying home-made burgers topped with avocado, as well as other Chilean comfort food. CH$36,000

The road to Lonquimay

At **Lautaro**, 30km north of Temuco, a paved road branches east from the Panamericana to the small agricultural town of **Lonquimay**, 115km away, passing the entrance to the **Reserva Nacional Malalcahuello-Nalcas** en route and traversing **Curacautín**, the northern gateway to Parque Nacional Conguillío (see p.266). There's nothing especially appealing about Lonquimay itself, but the road there – running through a narrow valley overlooked by towering volcanoes – is spectacular, particularly the stretch across the **Paso de las Raíces**.

Curacautín and around

Fifty-four kilometres out of Lautaro, the road passes through the logging town of **Curacautín**, from where a 40km dirt road branches south to Lago Conguillío in **Parque Nacional Conguillío** (see p.266). As the northern gateway to the park, Curacautín has its fair share of guesthouses, and there's dramatic scenery further along the road, including the 60m waterfall, **Salto del Indio**, just off the road, 14km out of Curacautín, and, 7km beyond, the 50m **Saltos de la Princesa**.

Reserva Nacional Malalcahuello-Nalcas

30km west of Curacautín • CH$1000

Some 30km east of Curacautín, you'll pass the entrance to the **RESERVA NACIONAL MALALCAHUELLO-NALCAS**, with the administrative office just a few hundred metres from the road. The main attractions here are hiking and, from June to October, skiing at the Corralco ski resort (day pass CH$34,000; ⓦcorralco.com), which has 28.5km of pistes on the side of the Lonquimay Volcano, four drag lifts and two chairlifts.

Hiking in the reserve

Hiking trips on the Lonquimay Volcano take about four hours up, one down, and an ice axe and crampons are required. Ask for information at Conaf or the hostel, *Suizandina Lodge* (see p.270). Another popular walk is the 7.5km (5hr) **Sendero Piedra Santa**, a trail through different types of vegetation that illustrate the techniques used by Conaf to protect and manage native forest. The trail starts at the

Conaf ranger station just off the main road in Malalcahuello and passes through quite separate areas of evergreen *tepa*, *raulí*, *coigüe*, *lenga* and the famous araucaria. Parts of the path give excellent views onto 3125m **Volcán Llaima** and 2890m **Volcán Lonquimay**. The trail joins up with the two-hour (3.5km) **Sendero El Raleo**. The longest hikes in the park, and ones for which a guide is recommended as the two trails are not always easy to follow, are the 40km (two days one way) **Sendero Laguna Blanca** that skirts the western side of the volcano, and the **Sendero Tolhuaca** (also 40km) trail that branches off from the former and follows the rivers Tolhuaca and Villucura, skirting the Cordón de la Mora, and arrives at the hot springs inside Parque Nacional Tolhuaca (p.265).

6

Paso de Las Raíces

A couple of kilometres further along the main road from the administration of the Reserva Nacional Malalcahuello-Nalcas, a paved road (signed Volcán Lonquimay) branches north, and then forks in two. The right fork leads 26km to the village of Lonquimay, across the **PASO DE LAS RAÍCES**, part of the volcanic chain that forms the highest peaks in this section of the Andes. This is a beautiful drive that switchbacks through lush araucaria forests, with birds of prey, such as buzzards, swooping around the tree branches.

From the pass at the top, you get an extraordinary view down over the araucarias, spread out below like a vast green carpet. The left fork leads 4km to the **Corralco ski centre** (see opposite). Near the ski lodge, an unpaved but easy-to-drive track skirts the desolate old lava slope up to a lookout point over **Cráter Navidad**, the gaping hole produced when the volcano last erupted, on Christmas Day 1988 (also doable as a hike from the lodge; 1.5km; 2hr return).

Túnel de Las Raíces

Open 24hr • CH$500 each way

An alternative route to Lonquimay is through the **Túnel de Las Raíces**. Built in 1930 as a railway tunnel, in an abortive attempt to connect the Pacific and Atlantic by railroad, this 4.5km tunnel was once the longest in South America, but is only wide enough for traffic to pass through in one direction at a time.

ARRIVAL AND DEPARTURE	THE ROAD TO LONQUIMAY

CURACAUTÍN

By bus Curacautín is serviced by buses from Concepción (2 daily; 5hr); Los Angeles (2 daily; 3hr); and Temuco (every 30min; 2hr). From the bus terminal, a shuttle runs to the *guardería* (ranger station) at Laguna Captrén in Parque Nacional Conguillío (Dec–Feb Mon & Fri at 6am, 9am, 2pm & 6pm, returning on Tues, Wed & Thu at 6am & 6pm; CH$500).

RESERVA NACIONAL MALALCAHUELLO-NALCAS

By bus Buses Bío Bío and Erbuc run between Lonquimay and Curacautín (at least 1 hourly; fewer on weekends; 45min) passing via the Reserva Nacional Malalcahuello-Nalcas.

ACCOMMODATION AND EATING	

CURACAUTÍN

Hostal Epu Pewen Rodríguez 705 ☎ 45 288 1793. Appealing guesthouse run by a half-Mapuche couple, with an inviting common area complete with guitar for guest use. The owners run trekking ventures into the park and can arrange other outdoor activities. Dorms CH$9,000, doubles CH$26,000

RESERVA NACIONAL MALALCAHUELLO-NALCAS AND AROUND

You can camp wild along the longer, remote trails;

otherwise there are several great lodging options along the road to Lonquimay.

Andenrose Camino Internacional Km 68.5 ☎ 09 9869 1700, ⓦ andenrose.com. Run by exuberant German, Hans, and his family, this Bavarian-style guesthouse is tucked away among the trees on the banks of the Cautín river. Recently revamped and now featuring guest *cabañas* as well as rooms, it's an ideal base for exploring the surrounding area, and the owner offers volcano ascents, mountain biking outings, kayaking and trips to the nearby hot springs. Doubles CH$52,000, *cabañas* CH$65,000

Nalcas de Malalcahuello Malalcahuello Km 88 ☎ 09 6842 1327, ⓦhotelnalcas.cl. Across the road from Malalcahuello, this boutique lodge with just seven rooms has an abundance of appealing touches – from colourful wool hangings and Mapuche artefacts to sumptuous beds, rain showers and arty stone sinks in the bathrooms. There's a good restaurant attached, and several fully-equipped four-person *cabañas* for those travelling with friends or family. Doubles CH$69,500, *cabañas* CH$40,000

Suizandina Lodge Camino Internacional Km 83 ☎ 45 197 3725, ⓦsuizandina.com. This, gorgeous, popular Swiss-Chilean-owned guesthouse lies 30km east of Curacautín and offers guests a mix of private rooms and dorms located in the main house and the adjoining (slightly cheaper) guesthouse with guest kitchen. The restaurant features Swiss dishes such as raclette, there are home-made *kuchen* (cakes) and the owners organise all manner of outdoor adventures, from horseriding to mountainboarding. Dorms CH$15,000, doubles CH$47,000

Lago Villarrica and around

LAGO VILLARRICA, tucked in the mountains some 86km to the southeast of Temuco, is Chile's most visited lake. The reason for its popularity is **Pucón**, a prime outdoor adventure centre. At the other end of the lake from Pucón is **Villarrica**, its more sedate counterpart.

The area around Lago Villarrica was first settled by the Spanish in the late sixteenth century, but they didn't have much time to enjoy their new territory: their towns were sacked by the Mapuche in 1602. Recolonization didn't take place until the Mapuche were subjugated 250 years later. With the arrival of the railroad from Santiago in 1933, the area became one of Chile's prime holiday destinations.

Villarrica

Sitting on the southwestern edge of the lake with a beautiful view of the volcano, **VILLARRICA** is one of Chile's oldest towns, although it may not feel like it – it has been destroyed several times by volcanic eruptions and skirmishes with the Mapuche. Villarrica's waterfront has been transformed with an attractive promenade, a park and a couple of small, dark sand beaches, with killer views of Volcán Villarrica on clear days across the water. Mapuche culture is strong in this town, which attracts those visitors who find it to be a more low-key destination than the ultra-touristy Pucón. The best time to immerse yourself in Mapuche culture is during the annual **Muestra Cultural Mapuche**, a festival featuring traditional crafts, food, music and dance, held in the second week of January.

Museo Histórico y Arqueológico
Pedro de Valdivia 1050 • Mon–Fri 9am–1pm & 2.30-6.30pm • Free; donations welcome

The municipal **Museo Histórico y Arqueológico**, on the main drag, offers a crash course in Mapuche culture. You can acquaint yourself with *ñillawaka* (food storage bags made from cow's udders), musical instruments such as the *trutruca* (bamboo-and-horn pipe), displays of silver jewellery, passed on from mother to daughter, and traditional weaving: you can tell a Mapuche woman's marital and social status just by looking at her embroidered belt. In the garden next door sits a thatched *ruca* (traditional dwelling). Inside you'll find carved wooden kitchen utensils, drums and a crudely carved *yuku* (similar to totem pole).

Feria Artesanal
Pedro de Valdivia 1050 • Mon–Fri 10am–6.30pm • Free

The **Feria Artesanal** is a year-round Mapuche crafts market where you can also try Mapuche cooking and pick up traditional medicines made from local plants. Amidst touristy kitsch there are some quality weavings, woollen goodies and attractive kitchen utensils carved from the native *raulí* wood.

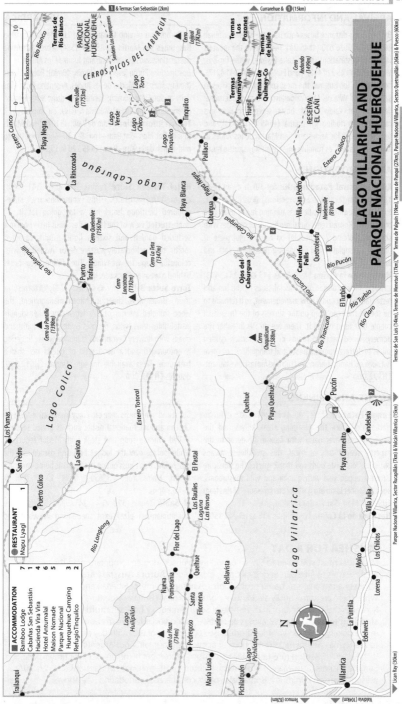

LAGO VILLARICA AND
PARQUE NACIONAL HUERQUEHUE

ACCOMMODATION
Bamboo Lodge   7
Cabañas San Sebastián   1
Hacienda Vira Vira   4
Hotel Antumalal   6
Maison Nomade   5
Parque Nacional   3
Huerquehue Camping
Refugio Tinquilco   2

● **RESTAURANT**
Mapu Lyaql   1

6

ARRIVAL AND INFORMATION

By bus Long-distance buses each have their own terminal: Buses JAC, Bilbao 610 (☎ 45 241 1447) serve the greatest variety of destinations in the Lake District, while Tur-Bus, Muñoz 657 (☎ 45 220 4102); and Pullman (☎ 45 241 4217), next door to Tur-Bus, run the most comfortable services to Santiago and Viña del Mar/Valparaíso. The central Terminal de Buses at Valdivia 621 hosts several smaller bus companies, including Igi Llaima (☎ 45 241 2733), and serves Junín de los Andes and San Martín de los Andes in Argentina, as well as running small Vipu-Ray shuttle buses

VILLARRICA

to Pucón, and serving Coñaripe and Liquiñe via Coñaripe Bus. Buses San Martín (☎ 45 241 1584) serves Argentine destinations such as Bariloche and Junín de los Andes.
Destinations Pucón (every 10–20min; 40min); Puerto Montt (hourly; 5hr); San Martín de los Andes, Argentina (Mon–Sat daily at 9am; 4hr 20min); Santiago (6 daily; 9hr); Temuco (every 30min; 1hr 20min); Valdivia (7 daily; 2hr 15min).
Tourist information Pedro de Valdivia 1070 (mid-March to mid-Dec Mon–Sat 9am–1pm & 2.30–6pm; mid-Dec to mid-March daily 9am–9pm; ☎ 45 220 6619).

ACCOMMODATION

Aurora Austral Patagonia Husky 10km away from Villarrica (contact for exact directions) ☎ 09 8901 4518, ⓦ novena-region.com. Besides running husky tours (see box below), Konrad rents out three beautiful cottages with skylights (holding 2–6 people) on his peaceful piece of property, complete with wandering pet sheep, cats and dogs. CH$40,000
Hostería de la Colina Las Colinas 115 ☎ 45 241 1503, ⓦ hosteriadelacolina.com. This fabulous hilltop inn and restaurant is now under new management, so it remains to be seen if they can keep up the success of the Oregonian couple that used to run it. There are no TVs in either the homely, wood-panelled rooms or the detached garden suites to detract from the peace and tranquillity, but there is a book exchange, library, hot tub and fantastic restaurant. CH$72,000

Hotel Terraza Suite Zegers 351 ☎ 45 241 4508, ⓦ hotelterrazasuite.cl. This contemporary, slate-coloured boutique hotel has a lot going for it: an unobstructed view of the lake, a gorgeous little pool in a secluded garden and sixteen light, bright, carpeted rooms, their deliberately austere décor livened up with colourful Mapuche weavings. The dining area hides behind a wooden stockade. US$155
Torre Suiza Bilbao 969 ☎ 45 241 1213, ⓦ torresuiza .com. Under new, cheerful Chilean management, the wood-shingled interior of this legendary, biker-friendly hostel hides snug twins, doubles (with private bath) and quads with flowery bedspreads, a lounge where lingering is encouraged and a good ratio of guests per shared bathroom. Bikes available for hire. Dorms CH$12,000, doubles CH$25,000

EATING AND DRINKNG

Fuego Patagón Montt 40 ☎ 45 241 2207 ⓦ fuego patagon.cl. From the gleaming steak knives and the lovely, glassed-over patio with faux-rustic décor to the expertly seared cuts of meat, this steakhouse means business. Your taste buds will thank you for the signature bacon-wrapped veal with quinoa and wild mushrooms, and the tender lamb in a garlicky *merkén* sauce. Mains from CH$9000. Mon–Sat 7.30pm–midnight.
Hostería de la Colina Las Colinas 115 ☎ 65 241 1503.

Guest and non-guests alike can enjoy imaginative takes on Chilean and international dishes such as grilled seabass, chilled avocado soup and steak with Merlot reduction, while looking over the lodge's beautiful garden and the lake below. Don't miss out on the fantastic home-made ice cream. Mains from CH$6500. Daily 12.30–3pm & 7–10.30pm.
El Sabio Zegers 393 ☎ 45 241 9918, ⓦ elsabio.cl. Argentinian-run pizza joint specialising in wood-fired

---

MUSHER FOR A DAY

No longer must you travel to Siberia or endure minus 35 degree temperatures in the frozen Arctic wastes to take part in dog-sledding expeditions. **Aurora Austral Patagonia Husky** (ⓦ novena-region.com), based near Villarrica, is home to a mix of Siberian and Alaskan huskies. While there are some husky-sledding opportunities near Ushuaia, Argentina (see p.439), Konrad is the only operator in the whole of South America who leads **multi-day husky-sledding expeditions** that allow you to drive your own sled. You can choose either a day-trip in the vicinity of Volcán Villarrica (from CH$65,000) or one of the multi-day expeditions – either to the Termas Geométricas hot springs or across the mountains into Argentina.

The sledding season runs from May to October, September being an excellent time to visit. Summer visitors (Dec–March) can test the half-tricycle, half-chariot contraptions (CH$33,000/ person; 2 person minimum). Konrad also offers cottage accommodation (see above).

6

RECENT VOLCANIC ERUPTIONS

On March 3, 2015 **Volcán Villarrica** had its largest eruption in over twenty years. People living within 10km of the volcano were evacuated and the volcano was closed to climbers at the time of writing. A month later, **Volcán Calbuco** erupted having lain dormant for over forty years, forcing the evacuation of inhabitants within a 20km radius; at the time of writing guesthouses in and near Ensenada were a no-go.

pizzas; their *cuatro quesos* and pepperoni pizzas are difficult to fault and portions are ample. Thurs–Sun 12.30–4pm & 6–10.30pm.

Travellers Pub Letelier 753 ⓦ thetravellers.cl. This aptly named watering hole attracts global wanderers with its diverse culinary range that spans India, China, Thailand and Mexico. The zestier offerings are an antidote to the general blandness of Chilean dishes elsewhere and the cocktails are amongst the best in the Lake District. Mains from CH$6500. Daily 9.30am–midnight.

Pucón

On a clear day, you'll be greeted by the awe-inspiring sight of **Volcán Villarrica** smouldering in the distance long before the bus pulls into **PUCÓN**, 25km from Villarrica. This small mountain town has, over the last decade, firmly established itself as a top backpacker destination. Each November to April season brings scores of hikers, climbers, whitewater rafting enthusiasts and mountain bikers looking to climb Volcán Villarrica, brave the Río Trancura rapids or hike in the remote forested corners of the nearby Parque Nacional Huerquehue.

A day outdoors is usually followed by eating, drinking and partying in the town's restaurants and bars, or by a soak in one of the many surrounding thermal springs. The place gets particularly busy in January and February when the international travellers are joined by Chilean holidaymakers.

ARRIVAL AND DEPARTURE
PUCÓN

By plane While there are summer-only flights (several weekly Dec–Feb; 1hr 40min) to Pucón's tiny aerodrome from Santiago with LAN and Sky Airline, the majority of visitors fly into Temuco's considerably larger airport (see p.263) and arrange transfers from there.

By bus JAC, Tur-Bus and Pullman each have their own purpose-built terminals. Buses JAC serves destinations within the Lake District; Tur-Bus and Pullman have overnight departures to Santiago. Buses Caburgua leave for Parque Nacional Huerquehue from their own little terminal opposite Buses JAC and Buses Currarrehue run to Curarrehue from the side of the Pullman bus station. At Palguín and Uruguay, the Agencia de Buses sells advance tickets for Igi

Llaima departures to Argentina's Junín de los Andes and San Martín de los Andes; buses stop in front of the ticket office.

Companies Igi Llaima & Nar Bus, Palguín 595 (☎45 244 4762); JAC, Palguín 605 (☎45 244 3331); Pullman, Palguín 555 (☎45 244 3498); Tur-Bus, O'Higgins 910 (☎45 244 3963).

Destinations Curarrehue (every 30min; 45min); Parque Nacional Huerquehue (3 daily; 45min); Puerto Montt (hourly; 6hr); Puerto Varas (hourly; 5hr 30min); San Martín de Los Andes, Argentina (Mon–Sat I daily at 9.20am; 5hr); Santiago (2 daily; 10hr); Temuco (every 30min; 1hr 45min); Valdivia (7 daily; 3hr); Villarrica (every 30min; 45min).

GETTING AROUND

Bicycle rental Sierra Nevada, O'Higgins at Palguín (☎09 9979 9681) rents out decent mountain bikes (CH$6000/8000/half/whole day).

Car rental Pucón Rent a Car, Pedro de Valdivia at Arauco (☎45 244 3052 ⓦ puconrentacar.cl) has the best rates.

INFORMATION AND TOURS

TOURIST INFORMATION

Tourist office O'Higgins 447 (daily: March–Nov 8.30am–7pm; Dec–Feb 8.30am–10pm; ☎45 229 3001, ⓦ informacionespucon.com).

Conaf Lincoyán 336 (Mon–Fri 8.30am–noon & 2–5pm;

☎45 244 3781). Rangers can advise as regards national park trail conditions.

Travelaid Ansorena 425, Local 4 (Mon–Fri 10am–1.30pm & 3.30–7pm, Sat 10am–2pm; ⓦ travelaid.cl). Can help book things like Navimag and offers info on the region's

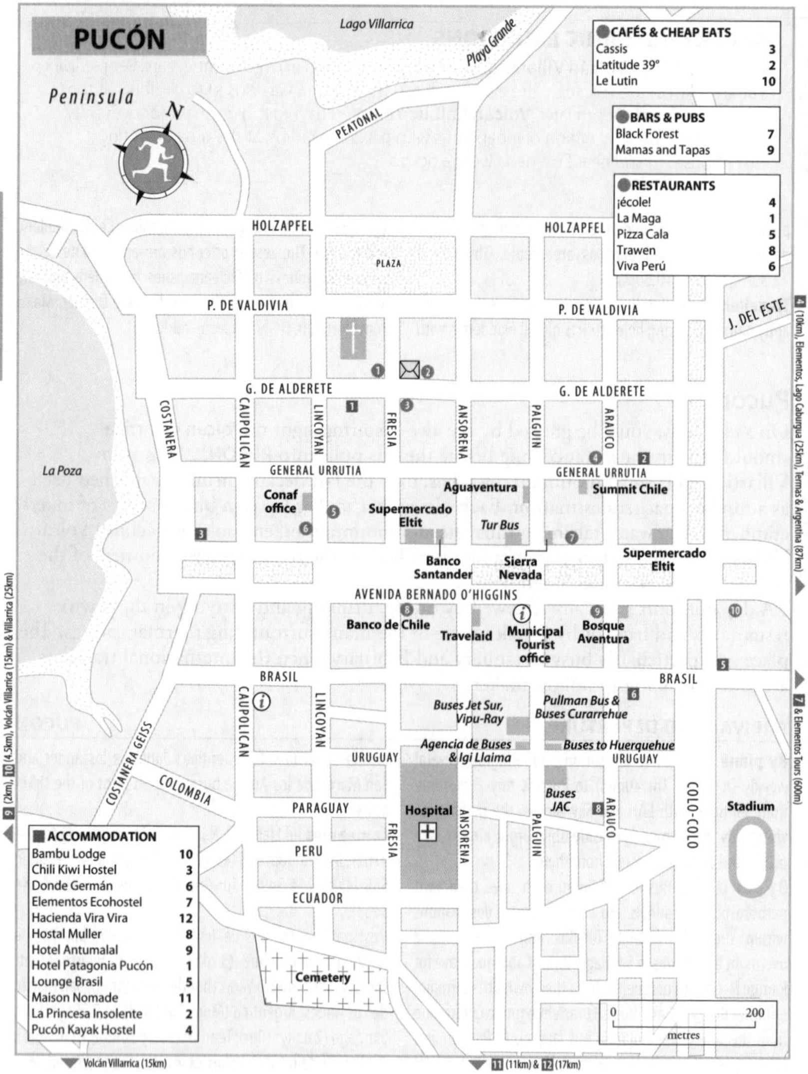
PUCÓN
Lago Villarrica
Playa Grande
Peninsula
N
PEATONAL
CAFÉS & CHEAP EATS
Cassis 3
Latitude 39° 2
Le Lutin 10
BARS & PUBS
Black Forest 7
Mamas and Tapas 9
RESTAURANTS
¡école! 4
La Maga 1
Pizza Cala 5
Trawen 8
Viva Perú 6
HOLZAPFEL
PLAZA
P. DE VALDIVIA
J. DEL ESTE
G. DE ALDERETE
COSTANERA
CAUPOLICAN
LINCOYAN
FRESIA
ANSORENA
PALGUIN
ARAUCO
La Poza
GENERAL URRUTIA
Conaf office
Supermercado Eltit
Aguaventura
Summit Chile
Tur Bus
Banco Santander
Sierra Nevada
Supermercado Eltit
AVENIDA BERNADO O'HIGGINS
Banco de Chile
Travelaid
Municipal Tourist office
Bosque Aventura
BRASIL
Buses Jet Sur, Vipu-Ray
Pullman Bus & Buses Curarrehue
Agencia de Buses & Igi Llaima
Buses to Huerquehue
URUGUAY
COSTANERA GEISS
COLOMBIA
PARAGUAY
Hospital
Buses JAC
COLO-COLO
Stadium
PERU
ECUADOR
Cemetery
ACCOMMODATION
Bambu Lodge 10
Chili Kiwi Hostel 3
Donde Germán 6
Elementos Ecohostel 7
Hacienda Vira Vira 12
Hostal Muller 8
Hotel Antumalal 9
Hotel Patagonia Pucón 1
Lounge Brasil 5
Maison Nomade 11
La Princesa Insolente 2
Pucón Kayak Hostel 4
0 200 metres
4 (10km), Elementos, Lago Caburgua (25km), Termas & Argentina (87km)
7 & Elementos Tours (600m)
9 (2km), 10 (4.5km), Volcán Villarrica (15km) & Villarrica (25km)
Volcán Villarrica (15km)
11 (11km) & 12 (17km)

attractions. Also stocks detailed trekking maps and road maps of Chile, and rents GPS systems for trekking around Pucón. English and German spoken.

TOURS

There are a multitude of tour companies in Pucón, mostly offering the same trips for similar prices. Most companies run tours of the area, which take in the Ojos de Caburgua waterfalls and any of the thermal springs at Huife, Palguín, Menetúe and Pozones (CH$16,000–20,000), as well as night-time visits to Termas Los Pozones and pricier outings to Termas Geométricas. We've picked out a selection of the more established operators, and arranged them according to the activity at which they are best.

Canopy The most reliable operator for ziplining is Bosque Aventura, Arauca at O'Higgins (T 45 244 4030, W bosqueaventura.cl). Outings typically cost from CH$18,000 and they also specialise in bungee jumping.

Dog sledding (see box, p.272).

Horseback riding You can go for a full-day or half-day ride in the mountain wilderness of the Parque Nacional Villarrica, or even on a multi-day horseback expedition across the Andes into Argentina. Prices start at about CH$25,000 for a half day, CH$45,000 for a full day. Antilco, 15km east of Pucón (☎ 09 9713 9758, ⓦ antilco.com), is an experienced and highly recommended operator organizing anything from half-day trips to a nine-day glacier and hot springs ride. English and German spoken.

Mapuche cultural tours Elementos, Pasaje Las Rosas 640 (☎ 45 244 1750, ⓦ elementos-chile.com) is a friendly German operator that offers plenty of tours focusing on Mapuche culture – from cooking with the Mapuche to homestays and multi-day, multi-activity options.

Mountaineering/rock climbing Established, highly recommended outfit, Summit Chile Tours, at General Urrutia 585 (☎ 45 244 3259, ⓦ summitchile.org) is headed by bilingual, internationally qualified mountain guide Claudio, who leads small group treks (six maximum per group) in Villarrica National Park – from the standard ascent of Volcán Villarrica (CH$45,000) to the more technical two-day ascent of Volcán Lanín (CH$180,000) on the border with Argentina. Also on offer are half-/full-day (CH$24,000/30,000) rock climbing ventures in the area, suitable both for beginners and advanced climbers, and ski touring excursions.

Rafting The nearby Río Trancura offers a popular class II–III run on the lower part of the river, with the more challenging class VI, upper Trancura, run made up almost entirely of drop pools. Both of these trips are half-day excursions; some operators allow you to combine the two. Highly professional, French-run Aguaventura at Palguín 336 (☎ 45 244 4246, ⓦ aguaventura.com) is your best bet. Prices for two to three hours rafting range from CH$15,000 for the lower Trancura to CH$20,000 for the upper Trancura.

Skydiving Aguaventura (see above) charges CH$150,000 for a 1hr tandem jump.

Volcán Villarrica This is a full-day excursion, usually leaving at around 7am, and prices are around CH$46,000–52,000. Climbing is not possible when the weather is bad, though some operators will still take customers up when it's cloudy, only to turn back halfway. There are several companies authorized by Conaf to climb the volcano, the best of which are: Paredón Andes Expeditions (☎ 45 244 4663), which takes groups no larger than eight people, and Elementos at Pasaje Las Rosas 640 (☎ 45 244 1750, ⓦ elementos-chile.com). In winter, companies such as Aguaventura (see above) rent out skis and snowboards.

Water sports The exciting sport of hydrospeeding involves bodyboarding down the Río Liucura rapids (no greater than class III); the half-day excursion, including an hour in the river, costs CH$25,000 with Aguaventura (see above). They also offer river kayaking instruction (CH$20,000) and ducky (mini-rafting) outings (CH$25,000).

ACCOMMODATION

HOTELS AND B&BS

Bambu Lodge Km 4.2, Camino al Volcán ☎ 09 6802 9145, ⓦ bambulodge.com; map p.274. The four exquisite rooms at this guesthouse on the road to the volcano offer tranquillity, a break from wi-fi, and a fantastic view of the forest and the lake beyond. All rooms come with big double beds, superior linens and bathtubs, and the white of the walls contrasts with the colourful Moroccan rugs and other exotic touches. There's a good breakfast, a guest kitchen and the friendly French-Chilean owners are a treasure trove of local advice. CH$55,000

Donde Germán Brasil 640 ☎ 45 244 2444, ⓦ dondegerman.cl; map p.274. In its new incarnation, *Donde Germán* is a beautiful, wood-shingled building with portholes, spacious rooms with rustic decor, a garden to lounge around in and even a pool with a sun deck. CH$30,000

Hacienda Vira Vira Parcela 22a, Quetroleufu ☎ 45 237 4000, ⓦ hotelviravira.com; map p.274. This secluded, Swiss-owned property, off a side road en route to Caburgua, is Pucón's most luxurious new getaway. Choose from the rooms in the main, beautifully-designed building or the more intimate villas, all with enormous windows, free-standing tubs and high-quality beds. All-inclusive stays include hiking and horseriding excursions and the excellent restaurant can be visited by non-guests. A river bisects the tranquil grounds, there's a little beach used for barbecues and the hacienda grows its own vegetables and produces its own cheese and other dairy products. Half-board obligatory. US$221

Hostal Muller Arauco 560 ☎ 45 244 3506, ⓦ hostalmuller.cl; map p.274. In this homely, family-run guesthouse there are just six beautiful, wood-panelled rooms with sumptuous beds (and one with a twin bunk). The owners are helpful and hospitable, you can relax by the volcanic stone fireplace in the lounge and there's kitchen access as a bonus to self-caterers. CH$35,000

★**Hotel Antumalal** 2km outside Pucón ☎ 45 244 1011, ⓦ antumalal.com; map p.274. Built into the slope behind it, this architectural gem was designed by a student of Frank Lloyd Wright and is the most atmospheric hotel in town (as testified to by Queen Elizabeth II, Buzz Aldrin and other famous guests). The warm decor, fireplaces and large panoramic windows drinking in views of Lago Villarrica add to the comfort of the rooms, while the newly-built spa features waterfalls, and the organic cuisine at the on-site restaurant is superb, as is the service. Doubles US$251, chalets US$500

Hotel Patagonia Pucón Alderete 275 ☎ 45 244 2293, ⓦ hotelpatagoniapucon.cl; map p.274. With its

6

super-central location (opposite Pucón's best steakhouse), this appealing, wooden-beamed hotel with a cosy ski lodge vibe, sports an enclosed patio with fireplace, upholstered in cow hide and decorated with gaucho artefacts. The rooms are stylish and spacious, post-ski/hike massages are available and prices include one trip to the Menetue hot springs. CH$79,000

★**Maison Nomade** Km15 Camino a Caburgua ☎ 09 8293 6388, ⌨ chile-nomade.com; map p.274. On this tranquil plot of land with fantastic volcano views you'll find an attractive, eco-friendly guesthouse, located next door to the house where the owners and their children live with their two friendly dogs. There are just five beautifully designed rooms with colourful woollen hangings and state-of-the-art bathrooms, a fantastic breakfast with home-made bread and jams, a playground for the kids and even hammocks in the tranquil grounds. It's signposted en route to Caburgua. CH$65,000

HOSTELS

Chili Kiwi Hostel O'Higgins 20 ☎ 45 244 9540, ⌨ hostelworld.com; map p.274. Right on the lakefront, this place features Tiki the dog and is great for meeting fellow backpackers without being a party hostel; barbecues and group outings encourage guest camaraderie. Homely dorms come with comfortable bunks and lockers; you can also bed down in a converted van or in a lofty treehouse double. Dorms CH$10,000, doubles CH$26,000

Elementos Ecohostel Las Rosas 640 ☎ 45 244 1750, ⌨ elementos-chile.com; map p.274. This rambling house, south of the centre and with a friendly menagerie of dogs, cats and sheep, has just four spacious, spartan rooms named after the elements, as well as a budget bunkhouse

(bring own bedding) for shoestringers (who are welcome to use the guest kitchen and showers). Owner Sarina's tour agency has strong links with the Mapuche community and can organise cultural immersions as well as outdoor adventures. Dorms CH$5000, doubles CH$25,000

Lounge Brasil Colo-Colo 281 ☎ 45 244 4035, ⌨ cafeloungebrasil.com; map p.274. Not only is there an adorable wood-fire-heated café on the premises, but prices at this intimate, super central guesthouse, run by a friendly Brasilian proprietress, are an absolute steal for the six snug singles and doubles (all en suite). CH$25,000

La Princesa Insolente Urrutia 660 ☎ 45 244 1492, ⌨ tpihostels.cl; map p.274. Part of a five-hostel empire and run by energetic staff, this place ticks all the boxes and more: two cosy, fireplace-warmed common rooms, a restaurant on the way, hot tub in the hammock-festooned garden, guest kitchen and free breakfast, plus plenty of info on local attractions and occasional barbecues. Snug doubles and dorms come with brand-new beds and most have own bathroom. Dorms CH$7000, doubles CH$25,000

Pucón Kayak Hostel Km 10, Camino a Caburgua ☎ 09 7545 9510, ⌨ puconkayakhostel.com; map p.274. Ideally located on the bank of Río Trancura, this is a particularly good spot for water lovers. Choose between sleeping in a comfortable room in the main house, a gypsy wagon, glamping in a geodome or roughing it in a basic bunkhouse. Kayaks are available for rent, drying facilities are provided and meals are served in the *quincho* (thatched barbecue area), which encourages socializing. Dorms CH$10,000, doubles/gypsy wagon CH$30,000, dome CH$40,000

EATING AND DRINKING

CAFÉS AND CHEAP EATS

Cassis Fresia Alderete 223 ☎ 45 244 4715. This trendy café is often full; the clientele comes for the filling multigrain sandwiches and impressive array of desserts. Try the *crêpe cassis* – a pancake you'll have to excavate from under a caramel brownie piled high with chocolate and *dulce de leche* ice cream. Desserts from CH$3500. Daily 8.30am–midnight.

★**Latitude 39°** Alderete 324 ☎ 09 7430 0016. Run by friendly Californians, this is your (newly expanded) home away from home for fish tacos, heaped breakfast burritos, imaginative burgers (the Buddha Burger with Asian slaw is a winner), and other Tex-Mexicana, accompanied by generous lemonades and regional Chilean beers. Mains from CH$4100. Daily 9.30am–11.30pm.

Le Lutin Colo-Colo at O'Higgins. Located at the strip mall on the corner, this bakery is the place to come in Pucón for proper bread and humongous *pain au chocolat* (CH$1000). Mon–Sat noon–4pm & 7.30pm–midnight.

RESTAURANTS

★**¡école!** Urrutia 592 ☎ 45 244 1675. Tasty, inexpensive and imaginative vegetarian dishes served in peace and quiet in a vine-covered courtyard or an attractive dining room. The vegetable lasagne has long been superb, as has the vegetable yellow curry with chutney and the home-made bread. Mains from CH$4500. Daily 8am–11pm.

La Maga Gerónimo de Alderete 264 ☎ 45 244 4277. Sate all your carnivorous cravings at Pucón's best (Uruguayan) *parrilla*. The meat arrives cooked to perfection; you can't go wrong with the thick slabs of *bife de chorizo* (sirloin steak). There's an extensive wine selection and if you have room for dessert, try the flan. Steaks from CH$9500. Daily noon–4pm & 7.30pm–midnight.

Pizza Cala Lincoyán 361 ☎ 45 246 3024. Pucón's best pizzeria (now in expanded premises) serves excellent thin-crust pizza with some exotic and welcome toppings, baked in a brick oven in front of you. The place really fills up when American football or baseball is on TV. Mains from CH$6000. Daily 12.30pm–midnight.

★**Trawen** O'Higgins 311 ☏45 244 2024. One of the friendliest places in town, this offbeat restaurant tantalizes your tastebuds with imaginative, organic and internationally inspired dishes, such as goat's cheese gnocchi, bacon-wrapped venison with polenta, quinoa salad and ample fresh fruit juices. Great spot for granola-rich breakfasts, too. Mains from CH$7000. Daily 8am–11.30pm.

Viva Perú Lincoyán 372 ☏45 244 2025. Peruvian restaurant popular with locals, offering classic dishes from the land of the Inca, such as ceviche and *ají de gallina*. The lunchtime specials are good value and you can join the debate as to whether the Peruvian pisco sour is better than the Chilean. Mains from CH$7000. Daily noon–1am.

BARS AND PUBS

Black Forest Av O'Higgins 526 ☏45 244 3410. Trendy, dimly lit watering hole with a large horseshoe-shaped bar, a list of cocktails as long as your arm and surprisingly palatable sushi. Daily 7pm–2am.

Mamas and Tapas O'Higgins 587 ☏45 244 9002. A well-established watering hole that consistently entices a large clientele nightly with their excellent selection of beers (from CH$1800), and two-for-one cocktail specials; after a few, the 'Mexican' food will seem less mediocre. Mon–Thurs & Sun noon–1am, Fri & Sat noon–2am.

DIRECTORY

Hospital Hospital San Francisco, Uruguay 325 (☏45 244 1177).

Money and exchange There are ATMs in banks along O'Higgins, as well as several *casas de cambio* that offer comparable rates.

Post office Fresia 183 (Mon–Sat 9am–noon & 2–7pm).

Ojos de Caburgua

20km east of Pucón • Oct–March • CH$3000 entry payable by motorists • Take the international road to Argentina, then follow signposted road for 17km or take a Caburgua-bound bus and ask to be dropped off by the entrance

If you want to escape the bustle of Pucón for a while, head for the waterfalls near the tranquil **LAGO CABURGUA**. Thousands of years ago, an eruption blocked this southern end of the valley, drowning it, and the water from the lake now flows out through subterranean streams and porous rock until it reappears as the **Ojos de**

HOT SPRINGS AROUND PUCÓN

Ample amounts of volcanic activity mean that there are more commercialized **hot springs** around Pucón than in any other town in Chile. Getting to some of the *termas* without your own car is difficult, though various companies in Pucón run **tours** (see p.274) to several of the hot springs below. The *termas* are mainly divided into two river valleys, the Río Liucura and the Río Trancura. Here are three of the best, arranged in order of proximity to Pucón; some also offer accommodation.

Termas Peumayen Km28, Camino Pucón-Huife ☏45 197 0060, ⓦtermaspeumayen.cl. This newcomer on the *termas* scene has established itself as much for its beautiful riverside pools (CH$10,000) as for its appealing lodge with luxurious rooms and also for its superb French-Mapuche fusion restaurant, serving the likes of red quinoa tabuleh and honey-glazed veal. Restaurant Tues–Sat 1.30–4pm & 7.30–9pm; termas daily 10am–8pm. CH$65,000

Termas Los Pozones Camino Km 34, Pucón-Huife ☏45 244 3059, ⓦtermas.cl/pozones.html. The most rustic and natural of the hot springs in the area, these are simple, shallow pools dug out beside the river and dammed up with stones, with basic wooden changing huts above them. These *termas* (CH$7500) are extremely popular with backpackers, and most tours from Pucón come here at night. There is a 3hr limit on visits. Daily 11am–3am.

Termas de Menetúe Camino Internacional Pucón-Curarrehue Km 30 ☏45 244 1877, ⓦmenetue.com. Set in beautiful gardens near the river, with naturally heated rock pools, spa, sauna and Jacuzzi, a small restaurant and *cabañas*. The swimming pools are seasonal, while the *termas* (CH$18,000; CH$23,000 with transfer from Pucón) operate year-round. To get here, head out of Pucón towards Argentina on the international road for 27km then turn left across the Puente (bridge) San Luis and continue west for 5km. Swimming pools Dec–April; termas daily 9am–9pm. *Cabañas* CH$158,000

6

> **EXPLORING PARQUE NACIONAL HUERQUEHUE**
>
> From the park entrance, the short and pleasant Sendero Ñirrico leads down to Lago Tinquilco through dense bamboo groves before rejoining the main trail. From Lago Tinquilco, there's a worthwhile two-hour hike up **Cerro Quinchol**, rewarding you with excellent views of Lago Caburgua beyond. A steep and more challenging hike continues up Cerro San Sebastián where you'll find snow on the summit even in summer; allow five hours for the climb. The most popular hike is the Sendero Los Lagos (9km), which climbs to a height of 1300m through dense forest to the beautiful Chico, Toro and Verde lakes from the *Refugio Tinquilco*; allow three hours one-way, as the trail is steep in sections and can be muddy. About halfway up there's a picturesque detour to the thundering **Salto Nido del Aguila**, and several scenic viewpoints along the way.
>
> Past Lago Chico, the trail splits, the left fork leading to Lago Verde and the right to Lago Toro; the two join further up. If you wander off the main trail along the shores of Lago Verde or Lago Toro, you can often have the spot completely to yourself. You can take in the tiny Lago de los Patos and Lago Huerquehue (2hr) before rejoining the Los Lagos loop, or you can continue along the **Sendero Los Huerquenes** to **Termas de San Sebastián** (see below), a hot spring outside the park's northeastern boundaries, via the stunning Renahue viewpoint overlooking the lakes below. It's possible to hike to the *termas* in one day (23km from the park entrance; 8–9hr), since much of the Sendero Los Huerquenes is downhill, and you can either stay at the comfortable *Cabañas San Sebastián* (see below) before retracing your steps, or make advance arrangements for a ride out to the nearest town, also called Renahue, and from where you can catch a bus back to Pucón. You'll find the free Conaf map of the park useful; it's readily available at the Pucón tourist office (see p.273) and Conaf office (see p.273).

Caburgua (Eyes of Caburgua): three extremely photogenic waterfalls in the forest plunging into a deep pool of crystal-clear water. The best time to visit is in the morning, before the crowds gather.

Parque Nacional Huerquehue

30km from Pucón • Officially open Jan–March but accessible at other times of year • CH$6000 • ⓦ parquehuerquehue.cl

Rising up almost 2000m from the eastern shore of Lago Caburgua are the forest-clad hills and peaks that form the 125-square-kilometre **PARQUE NACIONAL HUERQUEHUE**. Crowned by araucaria forests, the horseshoe-shaped **Cerros Picos de Caburgua** (Caburgua Mountains) enclose a dozen breathtakingly beautiful lakes of which the largest four – Tinquilco, Chico, Toro and Verde – are the most visited. At lower altitudes there are mixed forests of *coigüe* (southern beech) and the conifer *mañío*. The park is also home to over eighty **bird** species, including the Magellanic woodpecker, the delightful white-crested *fío-fío* and the red-chested *chucao*, as well as the little Darwin's frog. For details on hiking trails, see box above.

ARRIVAL AND DEPARTURE
PARQUE NACIONAL HUERQUEHUE

By bus Buses Caburgua (☏ 09 9641 5761) runs services from Pucón to the Conaf *guardería* at the park entrance during peak season (5 daily, 7am–5.30pm, last bus returning at 6.30pm; 45min).

ACCOMMODATION AND EATING

Cabañas San Sebastián Termas San Sebastián ☏ 45 238 1272, ⓦ termassansebastian.cl. Serene campsite and *cabañas* at the end of the Sendero Los Huerquenes; the rustic wood *cabañas* can accommodate two or five people, and are all equipped with bathrooms and showers supplied by the hot springs (day use CH$5000). *Cabañas* CH$35,000, camping/person CH$8000

Parque Nacional Huerquehue Camping Lago Tinquilco ☏ 09 6157 4089. Basic but pretty Conaf-run campsite near the park entrance (toilets and hot showers included); pay Conaf at the park entrance. Camping/person CH$12,000

Refugio Tinquilco Lago Tinquilco ⊙09 9278 9831, ⊛tinquilco.cl. Excellent, airy wooden guesthouse in a beautiful stream-side location a 2km hike from the park entrance, with home-cooked meals (breakfast included), sauna, book exchange and an owner you'd want to split a bottle of wine with. Dorms CH$11,500, doubles CH$27,900

Santuario El Cañi

Nov–March • CH$5000 • All buses from Pucón bound for Parque Huerquehue pass by the entrance

Twenty-one kilometres east of Pucón, this near 990-acre sanctuary, comprising mixed araucaria forest, was created in 1991 when the small Fundación Lahuen, made up of concerned locals, fought off logging interests to preserve this beautiful piece of land. The main **hiking trail** (9km; allow 3hr one-way) runs steeply up through the forest from the park entrance, ascending to the attractive Laguna Negra, from which you get an all-encompassing view of the surrounding volcanoes on a clear day.

Curarrehue

Those interested in Mapuche culture will want to stop in the frontier town of **CURARREHUE**, 40km east of Pucón, where you'll find an appealing museum and a celebrated restaurant (see below). The Aldea Intercultural Trawupeyüm (daily 10am–8pm; CH$2000) is located on the plaza behind the bright green Municipalidad buildings and housed inside a traditional Mapuche **ruca**. An enthusiastic guide is on hand to talk you through the exhibits, which include traditional musical instruments.

ARRIVAL AND DEPARTURE

By bus Buses Curarrehue runs from Pucón (every 30min; 45min).

EATING

Mapu Lyagl Camino Internacional s/n, on the right-hand side around 500m before the entrance to town ⊙09 8788 7188. An easy bus ride from Pucón, the highlight of the Mapuche town of Curarrehue is a meal with celebrated Mapuche chef Anita Epulef at the helm. You may taste roasted *piñónes* (fruit of the araucaria tree), roasted cornbread, quinoa creations and more. Mains from CH$6500. Dec–Feb daily noon–3pm (call ahead to confirm).

Parque Nacional Villarrica

15km south of Pucón • Day entry CH$1000; volcano ascent CH$4000; Villarrica traverse CH$8000

The centrepiece of the **PARQUE NACIONAL VILLARRICA** is, of course, **Volcán Villarrica**, in all its smoking, snowcapped glory (see box, p.273). Located just south of Pucón, the vast park divides into three sectors: **Rucapillán**, **Quetrupillán** and **Puesco**, and stretches 40km to the Argentine border (74km by road). It also contains two other volcanoes and is one of the few national parks in the Lake District in which you can camp wild and hike for long distances. If you plan on doing lengthy hikes, take the useful TrekkingChile (⊛trekking chile.com) combined map of Pucón and the national park, available in the town.

Sector Rucapillán

SECTOR RUCAPILLÁN, home to the magnificent **Volcán Villarrica** (2840m), presents a visual contradiction: below the tree line it's a lush forest; above, it's a black waste of

---

VILLARRICA'S DEMONIC PEAKS

The area covered by **Parque Nacional Villarrica** was inhabited long before the arrival of the Spanish, and the names of the peaks reflect this: Volcán Villarrica's original Mapuche name, Rucapillán, means "house of the devil", because of its frequent eruptions, while Quetrupillán, the dormant volcano next door, means "mute devil". Another peak towards the border with Argentina is called Quinquili, or "devil's fang".

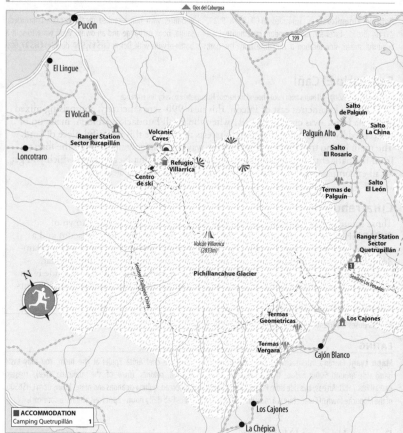

lava, dotted with snow and encrusted with an icecap. The volcano forms the obvious focal point, standing sentinel over the park, and it's very active – there were sixteen recorded eruptions in the last hundred years, the most recent in 2015 (see box, p.273). There's a good 4km trail that starts by the ski centre (see below), Los Cráteres, that runs to a lookout point (around 3hr return).

Centro de Ski Pucón

12km from Pucón • Late June to mid-Oct 9am–5pm • Day ski pass CH$30,000 • ⓦ www.skipucon.cl

A good road branches off the Pucón–Villarrica road, running up the northern slopes of the volcano. After 7km you reach the **park entrance**, and almost halfway up is the **ski centre**. Skiing here is an experience, though the snow quality is not as consistent as at the resorts around Santiago or in Valle Nevado. While on good days, the views are amazing, temperamental weather means that the seven ski lifts are affected whenever it's too windy; when smoke blows from the top of the crater, they shut down.

The twenty runs are geared mostly towards beginners and intermediate skiers, though experienced boarders and skiers can have some fun off-piste. Boarders in particular can make use of the natural half-pipes created by the lava chutes. You can hire cheaper skis and snowboards from the agencies in Pucón; most agencies run transport to the slopes in season.

6

Catripulli

Puelo Bajo

Curarruehue

0   5
kilometres

Río Trancura

Co Lepe
(1477m)

Saltos
de Carén

Garén

Las Peinetas

SIERRA MILLALIFEN

ARGENTINA

PARQUE NACIONAL
VILLARRICA

Cerro Quinquili
(2012m)

Ranger Station
Sector Puesco

Paso
Mamuil
Malal
(1270m)

Laguna
Blanca

Laguna
Quilleihue

Volcán Quetrupillán
(2350m)

Sendero La Natardas

Laguna
Plato

Laguna
Escondida

Laguna
Huinfiuca

Laguna
Azul

Sendero Mongilruca

Sendero
Lagos Andinos

Laguna
Avutardas

Laguna
Verde

Volcán Lanín
(3776m)

PARQUE NACIONAL VILLARRICA

Cuevas Volcánicas

Camino al Volcán Km 14.5 • Daily: Jan & Feb 10am–8.30pm; March–Dec 10am–6pm • Bilingual tour CH$6000 • ⓦ cuevasvolcanicas.cl

Just under 1km after the Park Nacional Villarrica entrance at Rucapillán, a
signpost points you to the **Volcanic Caves**, reachable by a seriously rough stretch of
road. A large lava tube, the main cave is dank and wet, but there's a dry path for
400m, and you can see the multicoloured minerals on the walls. Check out the
museum exhibits on volcanology and seismology before embarking on the
tour. Bring warm clothing, as the temperature inside the caves stays cool
year-round.

Sector Quetrupillán

SECTOR QUETRUPILLÁN, the middle section of the park, is dominated by the rarely
visited majesty of Volcán Quetrupillán (2350m). It's a remote area of wilderness,
tucked between two volcanoes and accessible only on foot or down a 35km dirt
road that turns south from the Camino International 18km out of Pucón,
climbing through native *coigüe* and araucaria forest. Here you can find the
contemporary hotel at **Termas de Palguín**, with its all-curing waters, and also four
splendid **waterfalls** – Palguín, La China, El León and Turbina, a little way off the
main track.

6

VILLARRICA ACTIVITIES

CLIMBING VOLCÁN VILLARRICA

Pretty much as soon as you arrive in Pucón, you'll realize that that town's main attraction is **Volcán Villarrica**, just begging to be climbed. The path leaves from the ski centre (see p.280), and it's four hours up to a crater in which, if you're lucky and the gas clears, you'll see bubbling pits of molten rock. If it's not too windy, the chairlift (CH\$9000) trims an hour off the climb. While it doesn't demand technical climbing skills, you do need a hard hat, ice-axe, sturdy boots, gaiters, waterproof overtrousers and crampons – all provided by the tour agency you go with. The view from the top on a clear day is stupendous (though you won't linger for long because of the noxious fumes), followed by a rollicking tobogganing down the side of a volcano along snow slides, using your ice-axe as a brake.

THE VILLARRICA TRAVERSE

Park Nacional Villarrica's best long-distance hike, the **Villarrica traverse** (72km; 5 days), starts at the ski centre and consists of three trails joined together, the first half being the moderately difficult **Sendero Challupen-Chinay** (28.5km; 14hr), which skirts around the southern side of Volcán Villarrica and ends at the Quetrupillán Conaf ranger post and the basic Chinay campsite, connected to the main road by a very rough 10km-long dirt track. From the ranger post, this dirt road continues on to Coñaripe; you'll need a sturdy 4WD vehicle, even in the summer. For the Sendero Challupen-Chinay section, you'll need to carry all your water with you as there are no streams to be relied on.

   Sendero Los Venados heads southeast from the same ranger post, along the south side of Volcán Quetrupillán, passing the tranquil Laguna Azul – a haven for birds – before merging with the Sendero Las Avutardas (43.4km; 3 days), which finishes at the Argentina-bound road in the Puesco sector, around 2km south of the Conaf ranger post at Puesco. From here, you can hitch a lift to Curarrehue with the Chile-bound traffic. This section is crossed by numerous streams from which drinking water can be collected.

   Many hikers choose to do the Chinay-Puesco section only, as it's more picturesque. Before you start out, you must pay the park entry fee at the Conaf office in Pucón (see p.273) and inform them of your intended route/dates.

GUIDES AND PRICES

Conaf keeps a list of companies **authorized to guide** climbers up the volcano. A maximum of nine climbers are allowed with one guide. Though the tour agencies may tell you otherwise, there is nothing to stop you from tackling the mountain without a guide, as long as you have proper equipment. Unless you're an experienced mountaineer, however, it's not advisable. Competition keeps prices down to a reasonable CH\$45,000 or so, which includes transport and all necessary equipment. Most agencies start off at around 6.30am, though a couple leave at 4.30am to beat the crowds. Do not be tempted to go for the cheapest trip – cost is commensurate with safety, and companies offering much cheaper deals can sometimes do so by using inferior equipment and hiring inexperienced guides. We do not recommend Trancura or Politur due to their record of fatalities on the mountain. For recommended operators, see p.274.

Sector Puesco

East of Quetrupillán, close by the border with Argentina, the third part of the park, **SECTOR PUESCO**, is rather like the Canadian Rockies, with pine forests and craggy mountainsides. The Conaf station is at the Puesco frontier post. South of here, the tough **Sendero Momolluco** (22km; approx 8hr) leads southeast from the main road towards Volcán Lanín, before finishing at the remote Laguna Verde. From here, the **Sendero Lagos Andinos** (11km; 4.5hr) loops back to the main road via Lagunas Huinfiuca, Plato and Escondida, ending at the east end of Lago Quilleihue, just across the main road. You can make an easy day-walk of it by taking the Sendero Lagos Andinos partway from Lago Quilleihue.

ARRIVAL AND INFORMATION

SECTOR RUCAPILLÁN

By organized tour There's no public transport to Sector Rucapillán, though there are dozens of tour buses. In the winter, most tour agencies will take you to the park for CH$9000 per person, leaving Pucón at 9.30am and returning at 4.30pm.

SECTORS QUETRUPILLÁN AND PUESCO

By bus For Sector Quetrupillán you can take a Curarrehue-bound bus from Pucón (hourly) along the international road, though the nearest you'll get will be the hamlet of

PARQUE NACIONAL VILLARRICA

Palguín Bajo, 10km away down a dirt track. For Sector Puesco, you need to get on an international bus heading to Junín de los Andes in Argentina (several weekly) and ask to be dropped off; you should be able to get off at the Puesco customs post and Conaf station.

INFORMATION

Conaf Lincoyán 336, Pucón (Mon–Fri 8.30am–noon & 2–5pm; ☎45 244 3781). Rangers can advise on trail conditions and dish out rudimentary trail maps.

ACCOMMODATION

Wild **camping** is not allowed east of the Puesco border post. There are serviced campsites near the entrance to Rucapillán but the only campsite actually in the park is near the Quetrupillán Conaf station.

Camping Quetrupillán Near the Quetrupillán Conaf station. Remote campsite that consists of simple pitches with fire pits and cold water showers. Camping/person **CH$7000**

The Siete Lagos

Overshadowed by the popular resort of Pucón, the region known as **SIETE LAGOS** – Seven Lakes – is the next one south of Villarrica. Six of the lakes are in Chile, one (Lago Lácar) in Argentina; most can all be easily reached as part of a day-trip from Pucón or Villarrica.

The busiest lakes are the largest ones, the relatively warm **Lago Calafquén**, 30km south of Villarrica, and **Lago Panguipulli**, 17km further on. The next valley down contains the slightly smaller **Lago Riñihue**, hardly visited and perfect for nature lovers and fishermen. To the east of Lagos Panguipulli and Riñihue, nestling deep in the pre-cordillera and surrounded by 2000m peaks, are the most remote of the Siete Lagos, **Lago Neltume** and **Lago Pirehueico**, near which you'll find some spectacular waterfalls, the region's best museum and its wackiest hotels.

Lago Calafquén and around

The most developed of the seven lakes, **Lago Calafquén** features a paved road for the 30km along its northern shore between the settlements of **Lican Ray** and **Coñaripe**, and a mostly paved road around the rest. To the east is tiny **Lago Pellaifa**, created by a 1960 earthquake that altered the region's water flow. It's bordered by an international road to Argentina that passes a clutch of thermal springs around the mountain hamlet of **Liquiñe**.

Lican Ray

LICAN RAY, a small holiday town, lies 30km south of Villarrica, and boasts two pleasant black-sand **beaches**: Playa Chica, with a small forested promontory crisscrossed by several short hiking trails, and Playa Grande, a long strip of dark sand framed by the surrounding hills.

During the first weekend of January, the whole length of the main street, General Urrutia, is transformed into Chile's **largest outdoor barbecue** (*asado*) in which some three hundred lambs meet their spicy ends.

Coñaripe

Laid-back **COÑARIPE**, a 21km drive along the northern shore of Lago Calafquén, has just a couple of good black-sand beaches and a sleepy air. The small image of Christ on

6

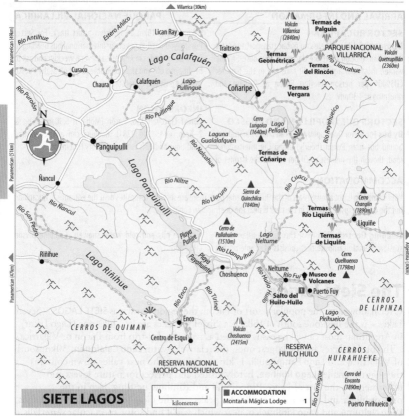

SIETE LAGOS

| | 0 | 5 | | ■ ACCOMMODATION |
| kilometres | | | | Montaña Mágica Lodge | 1 |

the lakeshore by the entrance to town is a memorial to two lava-engulfed victims and a testament to the uncertainty of living in this volcanically unstable area.

Termas Geométricas

12km northeast of Coñaripe • CH$20,000–24,000 • Late Dec to Feb daily 10am–11pm; shorter hours rest of the year • ☎ 09 7477 1708, ⓦ termasgeometricas.cl

Although the land around Coñaripe bubbles with numerous thermal springs, the most exclusive set of springs in the region is **Termas Geométricas**, with seventeen smart, slate-covered pools, linked by a series of wooden walkways strung along a half-mile of lush mountain stream. Note that there is no overnight accommodation.

| **ARRIVAL AND DEPARTURE** | **LAGO CALAFQUÉN** |

By bus Lican Ray is connected to Villarrica by hourly Buses JAC services, as is Coñaripe. There are also less-frequent Buses Pirehueico services (3 daily) from both Coñaripe and Liquiñe to Panguipulli.

Lago Panguipulli

Ten kilometres south of Lago Calafquén is the northern snout of long, thin **Lago Panguipulli**, a lake that stretches 26km southeast into the cordillera. On the lake's northwesternmost tip is the neat little town of **Panguipulli**, while a newly paved road skirts the eastern shore to the remote Lagos **Neltume** and **Pirehueico**.

Panguipulli

The attractive village of **PANGUIPULLI**, bright with colourful roses, dark copper beech trees and manicured lawns, was founded in 1885 as a trading post for Pehuenche and Mapuche Indians driven off the Argentine pampas. It grew beyond these humble origins in 1903 when a Capuchin mission was established here, and its church, the **Iglesia de San Sebastián,** is an impressive twin-towered latticed confection of yellow, red, brown and white. Panguipulli is best known today as the **town of roses**, with an estimated fourteen thousand closely pruned rose bushes lining the streets, and a crowd-pulling folk festival, **Semana de las Rosas**, during the last week of January, when the city hosts art exhibits and concerts.

6

ARRIVAL AND INFORMATION   PANGUIPULLI

By bus The bus terminal is at Gabriela Mistral 1000. Buses Pirehueico (☎ 63 231 1497) serves Valdivia and Puerto Montt, while Buses Lafit (☎ 63 231 1647) has services to Puerto Fuy via Neltume.
Destinations Puerto Fuy via Neltume (Mon–Sat at 10.40am, 5pm & 6.45pm, Sun at 6.30pm & 7.30pm; 1hr 45min); Puerto Montt (several daily; 3hr 30min); Valdivia (several daily; 2hr 30min).

Tourist information Near the church, on Plaza Arturo Prat (Jan & Feb daily 9am–8pm; March–Dec Mon–Sat 9am–5pm; ☎ 63 231 0435, ⓦ sietelagos.cl).

EATING

Restaurante People Help People Martínez de Rozas 777 ☎ 63 231 0925. A good place to stop for a break during your exploration is this cheerful restaurant with smart service and local ingredients transformed into imaginative dishes. Try the trout ceviche or the pork loin cooked in beer. Mains from CH$6700. Daily noon–3pm & 7–11pm.

Lago Neltume and around

The 38km road that skirts the eastern shore of Lago Panguipulli terminates at a t-junction. The western branch leads to the village of Choshuenco, while a good 16km gravel road heads east to the smallish **LAGO NELTUME,** passing through the village of Neltume and the Reserva Huilo Huilo en route to Lago Pirehueico. Before reaching Neltume, you pass a turnoff for the minor road that skirts the eastern shore of Lago Neltume before joining the Coñaripe-Liquiñe road; this eastern shore road is a narrow, gorgeous drive through the forest, do-able in a regular car.

Salto del Huilo-Huilo
Daily 9am–8pm • CH$2500 • ⓦ huilohuilo.cl

Between Lago Neltume and the village of Neltume is the turnoff for the 37m waterfall, **Salto del Huilo-Huilo**, a powerful torrent forced through a 10m-wide green cleft in the rock, cascading into the swirling aquamarine pool below to deafening effect. It's a ten-minute walk through the woods to reach the viewpoint, and a further ten to reach the even more spectacular **Salto de Puma.**

Museo de Volcanes
Mon–Fri 8am–6pm, Sat & Sun 10am–6pm • CH$2000 • ⓦ huilohuilo.cl

A turnoff from the Lago Neltume to Neltume village road, just before the *Montaña Mágica Lodge* hotel trio (see p.286), leads to the architecturally striking **Museo de Volcanes**, undoubtedly the best museum in the region. At research time it was only possible to visit two of the five floors (the top floors will be dedicated to exhibits on volcanoes), but they showcase the most complete collection of Mapuche items in Chile, from the crescent stones of power to the matchless collection of silver adornments – collars, pendants, necklaces, spurs. Another exhibit focuses on pre-Columbian pottery found near Arica and San Pedro.

Lago Pirehueico

Six kilometres on from Lago Neltume lies **LAGO PIREHUEICO**. Pirehueico means "worm of water" in the local Mapuche language, and there couldn't be a better name for this curving, twisting, snake-like lake, bordered by forest-clad mountains. It's crossed by a **ferry** from Puerto Fuy in the north to Puerto Pirehueico in the south. The crossing is beautiful and extremely worthwhile, not to mention far cheaper than the Puerto Varas–Bariloche crossing (see p.299).

ARRIVAL AND DEPARTURE **LAGO PIREHUEICO**

By bus In summer there are up to seven daily buses running between Panguipulli and Puerto Fuy.

By ferry Ferry Hua-Hum (w barcazas.cl) crosses the lake from Puerto Fuy in the north to Puerto Pirehueico in the south (March–Dec 1 daily at 1pm, returning at 4pm; Jan & Feb 3 daily at 8am, 1pm & 6pm, returning at 10am, 3pm & 8pm; 1hr 30min; CH$870/3275/16,390/passenger /bike/car).

CROSSING THE ARGENTINE BORDER
Via Puerto Pirehueico From Puerto Pirehueico, it's 11km to the border, where there's a café and a customs post (8am–8pm year-round). There's no public transport from the border to San Martín de los Andes but in peak season, TravelAid in Pucón (see p.273) offer a transfer-and-boat border crossing from Pucón to San Martín that takes in five Lake District lakes en route and culminates with the crossing of Lago Pirehueico.

ACCOMMODATION AND EATING

Montaña Mágica Lodge Camino Internacional Panguipulli-Puerto Fuy, Km 60 ☏ 63 267 2020, w huilohuilo.cl. This Tolkienesque creation, shaped like a grass-covered volcano with windows, encases uniquely shaped wood-panelled rooms and an entry hall with a stream running through it; if you are tall, get a room on one of the lower floors. Wooden walkways connect the volcano to the beehive-meets-treehouse that is *Nothofagus Hotel* and the organic-spaceship-like *Reino Fungi* (all doubles cost the same). Part of the Huilo Huilo reserve, this trio of hotels offers a bewildering array of tours and outdoor activities. <u>US$275</u>

Valdivia and around

Fifty kilometres to the west of the Panamericana lies the attractive city of **VALDIVIA**, one of Chile's oldest settlements, founded by Pedro de Valdivia as a supply halt on the route to Lima, six days' sail from the Magellan Strait.

Brief history

Pedro de Valdivia chose the confluence of the rivers Calle Calle and Cruces as a suitable location for the city because it was defensible and had access to both the sea and the inland plains. Yet in 1599 it had to be abandoned after the Mapuche uprisings, and was almost immediately pounced on by the Dutch. To counter this threat, and that of pirates, the Viceroy in Peru ordered a string of forts to be built. These were strengthened when Britain threatened in 1770, and, by the time of the wars of Chilean independence, Valdivia was a formidable redoubt. Post-independence there was a great influx of German settlers who founded shipyards, breweries and mills, leaving a lasting legacy.

Today Valdivia is a vibrant, cosmopolitan university town, a mixture of the colonial and the contemporary, even though many of its old buildings are gone – lost to earthquakes, fires and floods throughout the last century.

On February 9 each year, the city celebrates the founding of Valdivia, and between the second and third Saturday in February all of Valdivia comes out to celebrate "Valdivia Week": the river lights up with a **parade of boats**, and a memorable fireworks show. **Bierfest Kunstmann**, at the end of January, celebrates the joys of locally-produced German-style beer.

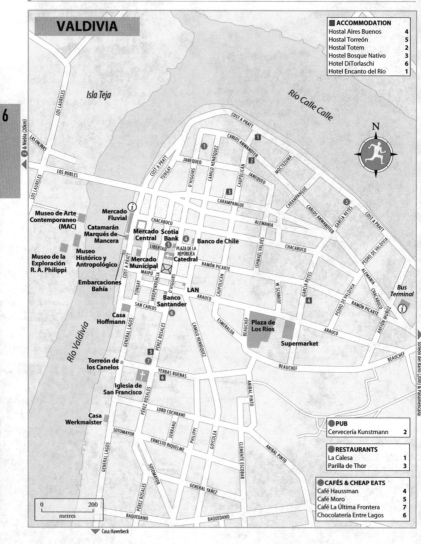

VALDIVIA

■ **ACCOMMODATION**

Hostal Aires Buenos	4
Hostal Torreón	5
Hostal Totem	2
Hostel Bosque Nativo	3
Hotel DiTorlaschi	6
Hotel Encanto del Río	1

● **PUB**

Cervecería Kunstmann	2

● **RESTAURANTS**

La Calesa	1
Parilla de Thor	3

● **CAFÉS & CHEAP EATS**

Café Haussman	4
Café Moro	5
Café La Última Frontera	7
Chocolatería Entre Lagos	6

The waterfront

Unlike most Chilean towns, Valdivia's social centre is not its plaza but its **waterfront**, where the Río Calle Calle and the Río Cau Cau meet the Río Valdivia. Just to the south of the Mercado Fluvial, touts offer ferry tours (see p.290).

Mercado Fluvial

Valdivia's lively produce market, the **Mercado Fluvial**, sits on the riverfront, with fishermen expertly gutting the day's catch and throwing scraps to the clamouring seagulls, cormorants, pelicans and the gargantuan sea lions who wait right behind the fishmongers and treat the market as their local takeaway. Opposite, on the other side of the path, vendors sell all types of fruit, vegetables, strings of smoked shellfish and smoked salmon. Across the road, on the corner of Chacabuco and Pratt, the Mercado Central hosts inexpensive *marisquerías* (seafood restaurants).

Isla Teja

Opposite the town centre, across the Pedro de Valdivia bridge, the island is home to a trio of good museums and has beautiful views back across the river to the Mercado Fluvial.

6

Museo Histórico y Antropológico Maurice van de Maele

Jan & Feb daily 10am–8pm; March–Dec Tues–Sun 10am–1pm & 2–6pm • CH$1500 or CH$2500 for combined ticket with Museo de la Exploración R.A. Philippi • Ⓦ museosaustral.cl

Isla Teja's main attraction is the splendidly sited **Museo Histórico y Antropológico Maurice van de Maele**, in an old colonial house surrounded by a veranda. Once owned by Karl Anwandter, founder of Chile's first brewery, it's still furnished with the trappings of nineteenth-century European society, including a double piano, an ornate red-marble fireplace and a magic lantern. Also on display is an absorbing collection of old sepia prints and household objects of the first German settlers, as well as the Anwandter family tree. The highlights are the collection of **Mapuche artefacts**, mainly splendid silverwork and cloth, and a room of memorabilia pertaining to British-born Lord Cochrane, who played a decisive role in securing independence for Chile.

Museo de la Exploración R.A. Philippi

Jan & Feb daily 10am–8pm; March–Dec Tues–Sun 10am–6pm • CH$1500 or CH$2500 for combined ticket with Museo Histórico y Antropológico Maurice Van de Maele • Ⓦ museosaustral.cl

Dedicated to the groundbreaking German-born naturalist, **Rudolph Philippi**, this museum is housed next door to the Museo Histórico y Antropológico Maurice van de Maele, in a Jugendstil building that was originally dismantled and then put back together at its current location. Upstairs you'll find Philippi's study, complete with period furniture, numerous pickled denizens of the sea and a superb collection of photos of local wildlife, while the ground floor is occupied by larger fauna and colourful beetle and butterfly collections.

Museo de Arte Contemporáneo

Jan & Feb daily 10am–2pm & 4–8pm; March–Dec Tues–Sun 10am–1pm & 3–7pm • Jan & Feb CH$1200; March–Dec free

Down by the water, housed in Valdivia's old Kunstmann brewery, is the **Museo de Arte Contemporáneo**, or "MAC". MAC's changing exhibitions focus on contemporary art, installations, photography and graphic design by Chilean and international artists.

Calle General Lagos and around

Inland from the rivers, to the east, lies the modern concrete town centre. You can see a couple of squat defensive towers that date from 1774 – **Torreón del Barro** on Avenida Picarte and **Torreón de los Canelos** on the corner of Yerbas Buenas and General Lagos, while north–south **Calle General Lagos** is filled with Valdivia's gems, a series of nobly proportioned nineteenth-century buildings. Take a stroll down the road and peek through the railings at the austere, double-staircased **Casa Werkmaister** (between Cochrane and Riquelme) and at the crinkly-gabled **Casa Haverbeck** on the way out of town, or else stop by **Casa Hoffman** (1870), an attractive merchant house, at Yungay 733.

ARRIVAL AND DEPARTURE   **VALDIVIA**

BY PLANE

Valdivia's Aeropuerto Pichoy (Ⓣ 63 227 2294 Ⓦ aeropuerto

valdivia.com) is 32km northeast of town and is served by LAN, Maipú 271 (Ⓦ lan.com) and Sky Airline, Schmidt 303

6

(ⓦskyairline.cl). Transfer Aeropuerto Valdivia (ⓣ63 222 5533; CH$3000/person) runs a door-to-door minibus service; a taxi should cost around CH$7,000.

Destinations Concepción (1 daily; 1hr); Puerto Montt (1 weekly, 1hr); Santiago (2 daily; 2hr).

BY BUS

Most long-distance buses travelling north–south along the Panamericana service the highly efficient bus terminal (ⓣ63 222 0498), on the corner of Anwandter and Muñoz, five blocks from the city centre; you'll also find most bus company offices here. Route taxis to Niebla operate from the corner of Yungay and Chacabuco, and you can catch bus #20 along Independencia.

Companies Buses JAC (ⓣ63 221 2925, ⓦwww.jac.cl) has frequent departures to all major Lake District destinations; Pullman (ⓣ63 227 8576, ⓦwww.pullman.cl) and Tur Bus (ⓣ63 221 3840, ⓦturbus.cl) serve the Lake District and all major destinations in central and northern Chile, while Cruz del Sur (ⓣ63 221 3840, ⓦbuscruzdelsur.cl) heads to the island of Chiloé and Igi Llaima (ⓣ63 221 3542) and Tas Choapa (ⓣ63 221 3124, ⓦwww.taschoapa.cl) crosses the border to Argentina.

Destinations Ancud (4 daily; 5hr); Bariloche, Argentina (1 daily at 8.45am; 7hr); Castro (4 daily; 7hr); Osorno (every 30min; 1hr 30min); Pucón (6 daily; 3hr); Puerto Montt (every 30min; 3hr 30min); Puerto Varas (every 30min; 3hr); Santiago (every hour; 11hr); San Martín de Los Andes, Argentina (3 weekly on Wed, Fri & Sun at 7.30am; 8hr).

INFORMATION AND TOURS

INFORMATION

Sernatur Av Arturo Prat s/n (Mon–Fri 9am–6pm, Sat & Sun 10am–4pm; ⓣ63 223 9060, ⓦturismolosrios.cl). Very helpful Sernatur office on the waterfront, with plenty of information on the region and map of the city.

TOUR OPERATORS

Catamarán Marqués de Mancera By the Mercado Fluvial ⓣ63 224 9191, ⓦmarquesdemancera.cl. This catamaran runs a large loop behind Isla del Rey, with 35min stops at the Corral and Mancera forts (5hr; bilingual guide, lunch and *onces* included); tours cost from CH$19,000 and CH$38,000, depending on your location on the boat, and depart at 1.30pm.

Embarcaciones Bahía Mercado Fluvial ⓣ63 237 8727, ⓦwww.embarcacionesbahia.cl. With its fleet of four boats, Bahía specializes in 3hr tours of the Santuario de la Naturaleza Carlos Anwandter, as well as cruises either to Isla Teja or Corral and Isla Mancera.

ACCOMMODATION

Hostal Aires Buenos García Reyes 550 ⓣ63 222 2202, ⓦairesbuenos.cl. Central, eco-aware American-owned hostel that engages its guests in its burgeoning permaculture project. Colourful, secure dorms and spartan private rooms are a popular rest stop for international backpackers, the communal spaces include a guest kitchen (they'll even let you use herbs from their garden) and breakfast includes proper coffee and good bread. Dorms CH$10,000, doubles CH$28,000

Hostal Torreón Pérez Rosales 783 ⓣ63 221 3069, ⓦhostaltorreon@gmail.com. One of the few buildings in Valdivia to have survived the 1960 earthquake, this beautiful 90-year-old guesthouse with lots of antique touches, uneven wooden floors and a pet tabby is run by a friendly family. Opt for the rooms at the top of the grand staircase rather than the basement if you like daylight. Breakfast not included. CH$30,000

Hostal Totem Carlos Anwandter 425 ⓣ63 229 2849, ⓦturismototem.cl. Quiet, welcoming guesthouse with squeaky wooden floors and spacious, en-suite doubles, triples and quads (some lacking in natural light) with cable TV. Breakfast includes home-made preserves and the helpful management speaks English and French. CH$30,000

Hostel Bosque Nativo Fresia 29 ⓣ63 243 3782, ⓦhostelnativo.cl. This beautifully restored 1920s house offers cosy wood-panelled rooms, kitchen, lounge and rooftop terrace to its guests; there's only one dorm; the rest are private rooms, with solo travellers, couples and groups of friends well-catered for. Profits go towards the preservation of native Chilean forest and continental breakfast is included. The staff don't speak English but couldn't be lovelier. Dorm CH$10,000, doubles CH$26,000

Hotel DiTorlaschi Yerbas Buenas 283 ⓣ63 222 4103, ⓦhotelditorlaschi.cl. Founded by a family from Antofagasta, this compact, wood-panelled business hotel provides homely touches such as embroidered pillowcases, as well as modern ones (cable TV, wi-fi on all floors). The fully-equipped self-catering apartments for up to four people are arranged around an attractive garden. Doubles CH$53,000, apartments CH$58,000

Hotel Encanto del Río Prat 415 ⓣ63 222 4744, ⓦhotelencantodelrio.cl. This cube-like hotel sits right on the water's edge and there's a nice contrast between the facilities of its thoroughly modern rooms and the décor, which incorporates Mapuche weavings. Rooms overlooking the river have their own little terraces and the superior rooms come with Jacuzzis. CH$65,000

EATING AND DRINKING

Café Haussman O'Higgins 394 ☎63 222 2100. Compact eatery with four small booths, founded by Don Ricardo Haussmann in 1959 and harking back to Valdivia's German roots with its specialities of *crudos* (steak tartare) on toast (CH$1900 each), Kunstmann beers and excellent cakes (*kuchen*) from CH$1600. Mon–Sat 8am–9pm.

Café Moro Paseo Libertad 174 ☎63 223 9084. Bustling, two-tiered café serving sandwiches, strong coffee, cakes and inexpensive Chilean comfort food lunch specials to a healthy mix of locals and visitors. Lunch menu CH$3000. Mon–Fri 9.30am–10pm, Sat 11.30am–10pm.

Café La Última Frontera Pérez Rosales 787 ☎63 223 5264. Everything about this café screams 'bohemian', from the reggae on the stereo, mismatched colour scheme and photos of cats and tattoos gracing the walls to the grungy staff who serve you real coffee, sandwiches named after Etta James and Chairman Mao, and a selection of local microbrews. Mon–Sat 10am–11pm.

La Calesa O'Higgins 160 ☎63 222 5467. Peruvian restaurant in a quiet neighbourhood putting some spice in your life with its *ají de gallina* (spicy garlic chicken stew), excellent ceviche and *suspiro limeño*. Mains CH$7000–9000. Tues–Sat 1–4pm & 7–11.30pm, Sun 1–4pm.

★**Cervecería Kunstmann** 950 Ruta T350 ☎63 229 2969, ⊛lacerveceria.cl. German-style beerhall serving monster portions of smoked meat, sauerkraut and potatoes to accompany its ten celebrated beers (from CH$2300). Tours of this celebrated brewery available daily in peak season. To get here, take bus #20 bound for Niebla. Daily noon–midnight.

Chocolatería Entre Lagos Pérez Rosales 622 ☎63 221 2039. Lauded chocolatier and bakery selling all sorts of delectable cakes, pastries, chocolates and *gelato* (CH$1200/ scoop). Next door is the sit-down "salon de té" which serves the cakes but also full meals and tea sets. Mon–Fri 9am–9pm, Sat 9am–10pm, Sun 11am–9pm.

Parrilla de Thor Prat 653 ☎63 227 0767. This Argentinian steakhouse overlooking the river has a ski-lodge-y feel and leisurely service, but serves satisfying slabs of grilled meats (sides extra). Mains from CH$8000. Daily 12.30–11pm.

DIRECTORY

Car rental Austral Rent a Car, Anwandter 288 (☎63 221 2770, ⊛rentacaraustral.cl) or Hertz, Picarte 640 (☎63 221 8316).

Hospital Clinica Alemana, Beaucheff 765 (☎63 224 6201).

Money and exchange There are various banks with ATMs around the Plaza de la República, including Banco Santander.

Fuerte de Niebla

18km west from Valdivia • March–Nov Tues–Sun 10am–5.30pm; Dec–Feb daily 10am–7pm • CH$1500, free on Wed • Colectivos run regularly from Yungay near the Mercado Fluvial and cost CH$1000

At the mouth of the Río Valdivia, in the village of Niebla, the **Fuerte de Niebla** (or Castillo de la Pura y Limpia Concepción de Montfort de Lemus) was originally built by the Spanish from 1667 to 1672 as part of an extensive line of defences of this key position in their empire. Today it's been restored and houses a newly revamped museum dedicated to the fortification of the Valdivia area, but more interesting are the old features: the powder room, double-walled and well below ground level, the crenellated curtain wall hacked out of the bare rock, and the twelve slightly rusting cannons.

Half the cannons are missing their cascabels (round metal knobs at the back); these are the original fort cannons which were defaced by the forces of Lord Thomas Cochrane (see p.477) when they overwhelmed the fort. Two of the original cannons now grace Santiago's Plaza de Armas.

Corral and around

On the other side of the estuary from Niebla lies the little village of **CORRAL**; it used to be a thriving port until it was flattened by the 1960 tidal wave. Another Spanish fort, the somewhat dilapidated **Castillo de San Sebastián de la Cruz**, with its 21 cannon – originally the most powerful of all the Spanish forts in the vicinity – was constructed in 1645 and is a short walk from the pier (daily 8.30am–7.30pm; CH$1500). Though the ferry journey over here is often obscured with the *niebla* (rolling fog) that lends the village its name, quite often you'll catch sight of sea lions and black-necked swans along the way.

Castillo de San Pedro de Alcántara

Isla Mancera • Tues–Sun: Jan & Feb 10am–8pm; March–Dec 10am–1pm & 2–6pm • Fort CH$700 • Regular boats from Niebla

Between Niebla and Corral sits the pretty Isla Mancera, with the most intact of the forts, **Castillo de San Pedro de Alcántara**, visible a little way up its forested side. The fort was built in 1645 and reinforced first in 1680 and later in 1762; its grounds house the atmospheric ruins of the San Francisco Convent and you can also descend into the dungeons. When the boat from Niebla drops you off, don't forget to ask to be picked up again.

ARRIVAL AND DEPARTURE	CORRAL AND AROUND
By boat The only way across the river from Niebla to Corral is by a 30min ferry ride (daily 9am–5.40pm; CH$1200). Frequent boats leave from the pier at the entrance to	Niebla, with some stopping at the small and pleasant Isla Mancera.

Santuario de la Naturaleza Carlos Anwandter

Boat tours from Valdivia (see p.292)

After the 1960 earthquake, the 50km of low-lying land around the Río Cruces north of Valdivia was flooded, forming an extensive delta which has been protected as the UNESCO-listed **Santuario de la Naturaleza Carlos Anwandter**. This marsh now forms an important breeding ground and resting place for 119 species of birds, including the black-necked swan, black skimmer and the white-faced ibis.

Osorno

Despite being founded in one of the best defensive positions of all the Spaniards' frontier forts, Osorno was regularly sacked by the Mapuche from 1553 until 1796, at which point Chile's governor, Ambrosio O'Higgins, ordered it to be resettled. From tentative beginnings, it has grown into a thriving agricultural city mainly as a result of the industry of European settlers who felled the forests and began to develop the great dairy herds that form the backbone of the local economy today. The German heritage is evident in the row of **wooden houses** along Calle Mackenna, built between 1876 and 1923.

The transport hub for the southern Lake District and starting point for the region's main road into Argentina, Osorno is also the gateway for **Parque Nacional Puyehue**, and the town's most distinguishing feature are its two contemporary **churches**: the **Catedral San Mateo** on the Plaza de Armas, and **Iglesia San Francisco** on Prat, three blocks east – controversial creations of concrete and lattice that divide opinion still.

ARRIVAL AND DEPARTURE	OSORNO
By plane Seven kilometres east of Osorno, Aeropuerto Carlos Hott Siebert is served by daily LAN flights from Santiago. Taxis to town cost around CH$5000. The LAN office is at Ramírez 802 (⌨lan.com).	Buses Rurales (being rebuilt at research time), a block away at Mercado Municipal, Errázuriz 1300, serves local destinations including Aguas Calientes, with Expreso
Destinations Santiago (2 daily; 2hr); Temuco (daily; 40min).	Lago Puyehue. Bariloche, Argentina, is served by Igi Llaima and Cruz del Sur. There are also departures for
By bus from Osorno serve all major destinations along the Carretera Austral from the central Terminal de Buses at Errázuriz 1400 (☎64 221 1120), while the Terminal de	Coyhaique (see p.365) with Queilen Bus and Buses Transaustral via Argentina.
	Companies Cruz del Sur (☎64 223 2777); Expreso Lago Puyehue (☎64 224 3919); Igi Llaima (☎64 223 4371); Tas

Choapa (☎ 64 223 3933, ⓦ www.taschoapa.cl); Tur Bus (☎ 64 223 4170, ⓦ turbus.cl); JAC (☎ 64 264 3114, ⓦ jac.cl). **Destinations** Aguas Calientes, Puyehue (6 daily; 1hr); Bariloche, Argentina (5 daily; 5hr); Coyhaique (1 weekly; 20hr); Puerto Montt (every 30min; 1hr 30min); Puerto Octay (5 daily; 1hr); Puerto Varas (every 30min; 1hr); Santiago (hourly; 10hr); Temuco (every 30min; 3hr); Valdivia (every 30min; 1hr 30min).

INFORMATION

Sernatur O'Higgins 667 (Mon–Fri 8.30am–5pm; ☎ 64 223 4164). Sernatur's helpful information office in the Gobernación building on the west side of the Plaza de Armas has good city maps and accommodation lists.

ACCOMMODATION AND EATING

Entre Sabores Rodríguez 1602 ☎ 64 231 1110. 'Between flavours' aptly describes this cheerful fusion spot that's worth the short taxi ride out of the centre. You can expect anything from beef and spinach lasagne, Cuban-style *ropa vieja* (pulled beef with rice), spiced-up *pastel de choclo* and *feijoada* (Brazilian-style stew). *Menú del día* is a good-value CH$6000. Mon–Sat 10.30am–9.30pm.

Hostal Vermont Toribio Medina 2020 ☎ 64 224 7030, ⓦ hostalvermont.cl. A proper backpacker hostel, run by a bilingual Chilean, with a set of simple rooms and a great upstairs outdoor terrace for socialising on. Unfortunately, however, with the disappearance of its many furred and feathered pets the hostel has lost a lot of its character. To get here, head south for two blocks to MacKenna from the bus station, then go five blocks east to Buenos Aires and one and a half blocks south and turn right. Dorms CH$12,000, doubles CH$30,000.

Hotel Rucaitue Freire 546 ☎ 64 223 9922, ⓦ hotelrucaitue.cl. With its warm reds and polished wooden floors, crisp linens and breakfast brought to your room on a little tray, this is a decent enough, central mid-range option. CH$45,000

Mercado Municipal Errázuriz and Prat. By far the best place to find a cheap and filling meal is the market by the rural bus terminal; the many *comedores* (eateries) serve *empanadas* and large portions of fish and the likes of *chupe de mariscos* (shellfish soup). Mains from CH$3000. Mon–Sat noon–5pm.

El Rincón de Wufehr Rodríguez 1015. The black-and-white photos and period objects conjure up images of ye olde Osorno, the menu is meat-heavy with a German influence and the portions abundant. If you've never had *crudos* (German-style carpaccio) before, this is the place to try it. Mains from CH$5500. Mon–Fri 12.30–3.30pm & 6.30–11.30pm, Sat 6.30–11.30pm.

Parque Nacional Puyehue and around

81km east of Osorno · CH$1000, payable only in the Anticura section of the park · ⓦ parquepuyehue.cl

PARQUE NACIONAL PUYEHUE is one of Chile's busiest national parks, largely because of the traffic on the international road that runs through its centre. It's part of a massive, 15,000-square-kilometre area of protected wilderness, bordering the Parque Nacional Vicente Pérez Rosales to the south, and some Argentine parks that stretch all the way to Parque Nacional Villarrica in the north. The land is high temperate rainforest spread over two volcanoes, Volcán Puyehue (2240m) to the north, and Volcán Casablanca (1990m), on the west slope of which is the Antillanca ski resort. The park is divided into three sectors: **Aguas Calientes** where the *termas* are, **Antillanca** and **Anticura**, straddling the international road near the Argentine border.

The 47km road that shoots east from Osorno to **LAGO PUYEHUE** passes through the nondescript village of Entre Lagos. Around 30km after Entre Lagos, the road forks: the left-hand road heads on to the Anticura section of the Parque Nacional Puyehue and the Argentine border, while the right-hand one leads to the Aguas Calientes section and the Antillanca ski resort.

Note that wild camping is permitted in the national park.

Aguas Calientes

At **AGUAS CALIENTES** you'll find a Conaf Centro de Información Ambiental (see p.296) where there's a large, detailed **map of the park**, along with basic park maps that you can take with you. Aguas Calientes is also home to the most accessible of the Puyehue area's

6

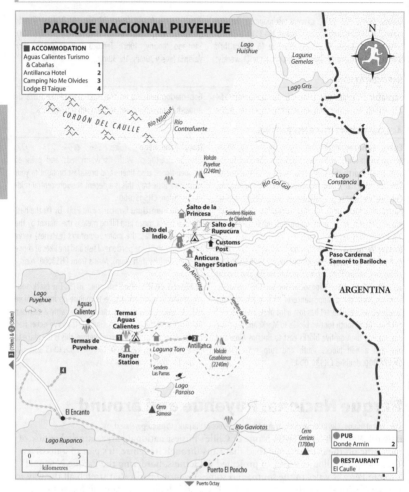

PARQUE NACIONAL PUYEHUE

ACCOMMODATION
Aguas Calientes Turismo & Cabañas	1
Antillanca Hotel	2
Camping No Me Olvides	3
Lodge El Taique	4

Lago Huishue

Laguna Gemelas

Lago Gris

CORDÓN DEL CAULLE Río Nilahue

Río Contrafuerte

Lago Constancia

Volcán Puyehue (2240m)

Río Gol Gol

Salto de la Princesa Sendero Rápidos de Chanleufú

Salto del Indio Salto de Rupucura

Customs Post

Anticura Ranger Station

Paso Cardernal Samoré to Bariloche

Río Anticura

ARGENTINA

Sendero de Ode

Lago Puyehue

Aguas Calientes

Termas Aguas Calientes

Termas de Puyehue

Ranger Station

Laguna Toro Antillanca Volcán Casablanca (2240m)

Sendero Las Parras

Lago Paraiso

El Encanto

Cerro Samoso

Lago Rupanco

Río Gaviotas

Cerro Cerrizas (1700m)

PUB
Donde Armin   2

RESTAURANT
El Caulle   1

0 ___ 5 kilometres

Puerto El Poncho

Puerto Octay

RN (190m) & RN (356m)

hot springs (ⓦtermasaguascalientes.cl), right at the park's entrance. There's a hot outdoor pool and a very hot indoor pool (daily 9am–7pm; day pass CH$23,000/25,000 for outdoor pool only/both pools – if you pay to use indoor pool you automatically get access to outdoor pool also; cheaper passes on weekdays and for those staying at the resort).

Walks in the area consist mainly of short, self-guided **nature trails**, such as the Sendero Rápidos del Chanleufú, a 1250m track alongside the river rapids. There are also a couple of **longer trails** (see p.296).

Antillanca

Ski season July & Aug · ☎ 64 261 2070, ⓦ skiantillanca.cl · Ski day-passes around CH$22,000

The **ski centre** at **ANTILLANCA** lies 18km from Aguas Calientes by rather rough road, at the foot of the Volcán Casablanca (also known as Antillanca). The centre has three T-bar lifts, one chairlift and ski slopes that are more for beginner and intermediate skiers. In summer the ski runs turn into a mountain-biking park, plus you can drive (CH$5000) or hike (see below) to the crater outlook.

Trails from Antillanca

Two trails begin at Antillanca: the 4km Cerro Miradór trail that ascends the volcano to the Raihuén crater; and the challenging 50km Anticura-Antillanca traverse that finishes at Anticura (see below). Halfway between Aguas Calientes and Antillanca, the little-trodden Lago Paraíso trail branches off from the main road towards the pretty namesake lake (3hr one-way).

6

Anticura

ANTICURA lies 22km east of Aguas Calientes, just off the main Ruta 215 to Argentina. There's an information centre where you pay the fee to walk the short trails and arrange accommodation, and a Conaf ranger post across the road. The information centre has an exhibition on the 2011 volcanic eruption, complete with mind-blowing photographs.

Short trails

You'll find a number of short **hikes** here; the prettiest is the 850m walk to El Salto del Indio, a half-hour loop through a forest of ancient *coigüe* to some thundering **waterfalls** amid dense greenery. From the Conaf side, a 1.3km track leads to the single gushing fall of Salto de Pudú, while from the other side of the office, an easy 1.5km ramble leads you to the Miradór del Puma, where you get a great view of Salto Anticura and the Volcán Puyehue beyond.

Sendero de Chile

More adventurous is the 50km trail that goes to Antillanca as part of the Sendero de Chile. The track is reasonably well maintained and signposted and runs through lush *ulmo*, *coigüe* and *lenga* forest, skirting the eastern flank of Volcán Casablanca and affording great views of the neighbouring volcanoes. Some parts of the trail are quite steep, though not technical. Halfway along, on the Pampa Frutilla, the trail passes by two pretty little lagoons harbouring a wealth of waterfowl. The trail starts behind the Conaf office in Anticura and takes approximately two days to complete.

Volcán Puyehue trail

Another adventurous hike is the 32km return trail to Volcán Puyehue (2–3 days), which starts 2km west of Anticura, at the El Caulle restaurant (☎09 9920 3180; follow the signposts). The beginning of the trail crosses private land belonging to the restaurant owners, so you have to pay a CH$10,000 entrance fee. The fee pays for trail maintenance and entitles you to use the basic *refugio*, which sleeps fourteen; it's a three-hour walk along the trail from the Conaf office. You can also stow any excess luggage at the restaurant and treat yourself to a grilled meat feast upon return.

Shortly past the *refugio*, the trail forks; the right-hand route goes up the volcano; from the crater there are views over Lagos Puyehue and Rupanco. The left-hand path leads to a thermal spring next to an icy stream, half a day's walk from the *refugio*. You can mix the waters and bathe – an amazing experience at night, cooking yourself gently in the waters underneath the stars.

ARRIVAL AND INFORMATION	**PARQUE NACIONAL PUYEHUE**

By bus Expreso Lago Puyehue runs several daily buses from Osorno to Aguas Calientes between 7am and 7pm. There is no public transport from Osorno to Antillanca, but private transfers can be arranged via the *Antillanca Hotel* (CH$70,000 for up to 4 people; CH$80,000 for up to 10 people).

By car Take Ruta 215 from the Panamericana towards the Argentinian border. The road to Antillanca is unpaved and rough in places.

Information The Conaf office at Aguas Calientes (Mon–Fri 9am–noon & 1.30–5pm) is the most helpful one.

ACCOMMODATION AND EATING

Aguas Calientes Turismo & Cabañas Camino a Antillanca, Km 4 ☎65 223 6988, ⓦterm asaguascalientes.cl. At the popular hot springs site (see p.292), these cute, chalet-style *cabañas* sleep four to ten people and are well equipped with fridges, cookers, *parrillas* on the balcony for barbecuing, terraces and hot tubs ('superior' only), but they are arranged in a military-style row that offers little privacy. There's also a campsite and 2-/4-person geodomes. Camping/person CH$19,000, domes CH$65,000, *cabañas* CH$109,000

Antillanca Hotel Camino a Antillanca ☎65 261 2071, ⓦskiantillanca.cl. The only option for skiers, this hotel has a sauna, gym and shops; the rooms are rather overpriced for what they are, though. A new *refugio* under the same management was being built at research time. CH$35,000

Camping No Me Olvides 6km east of Entre Lagos along Ruta 215 ☎65 237 1633, ⓦnomeolvides.cl. Excellent campsite en route to the national park, with tree-shaded hedges separating individual sites, hot showers, a supply shop and a restaurant. Camping/person CH$6000

★**Donde Armin** Km10, Ruta 215 ☎09 8294 1818. Hidden behind some trees en route from Osorno to Parque Nacional Puyehue is this fantastic German-owned microbrewery where you can sample the Bock, Doppeldock and Märzen, accompanied by the likes of bratwurst and other meaty German goodies, in the attractive *biergarten*. Mon–Sat noon–10pm.

★**Lodge El Taique** Ruta 215, Km76 ☎65 297 0980, ⓦlodgeeltaique.cl. A tranquil wooded location, beautiful wooden lodge with eye-catching purple sheets in the five sparcely furnished but luxurious rooms, two fully-equipped *cabañas* with volcano views and hot tub access – this French-run retreat has a lot going for it. To top it all, there's an excellent on-site restaurant (open to non-guests), serving the likes of steak with quinoa, wild boar goulash and profiteroles. To get here, drive south for 4km from El Taique, which is 12km east of Entre Lagos, and then follow the signposted road east for another 4km. Doubles CH$63,000, *cabañas* CH$70,000

Lago Llanquihue and around

Located just off the Panamericana, **LAGO LLANQUIHUE** is an immense inland sea of 870 square kilometres, a backdrop for one of the icons of the Lake District, the Mount Fuji-like **Volcán Osorno** (2661m), in all its stunning, symmetrical perfection, surrounded by gently rolling pastures. The little towns and villages around Lago Llanquihue have a shared German heritage, but differ greatly in character. **Puerto Varas** is a bustling adventure tourism centre to rival Pucón. **Frutillar** is a summer holiday resort beloved by Chileans, while **Puerto Octay** is a neat little Bavarian-looking town. By the time you come to the village of **Ensenada**, on the far eastern shore of the lake, forest has overtaken dairy fields and the land begins to rise as you enter the foothills of the Andes. This forest extends to the border, and is protected by the **Parque Nacional Vicente Pérez Rosales**. The national park is a favourite scenic route into Argentina via the magical green waters of **Lago Todos Los Santos**.

South of Ensenada the road winds its way down through isolated country to the placid calm of Chile's northernmost fjord, a branch of the **Estuario de Reloncaví**. Here you can horse-trek into South America's oldest rainforest – the famous *alerce* groves found in the valleys above the village of **Cochamó**.

Puerto Varas

Arguably the most appealing base along the shore of Lago Llanquihue, **PUERTO VARAS** is a spruce little town with wide streets, grassy lawns and exquisite views of two volcanoes, Osorno and Calbuco, particularly at sunset. Like Pucón, the reason you come to Puerto Varas is because it's a prime location for all manner of outdoor activities, with volcanoes, rivers and forests throwing down a gauntlet that few outdoor enthusiasts can refuse.

OPPOSITE LAGO LLANQUIHUE WITH VOLCÁN OSORNO >

6

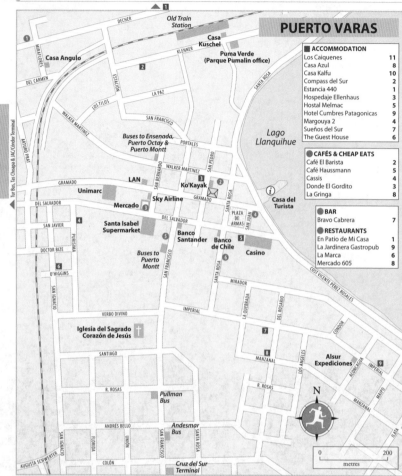

PUERTO VARAS

■ ACCOMMODATION
Los Caiquenes	11
Casa Azul	8
Casa Kalfu	10
Compass del Sur	2
Estancia 440	1
Hospedaje Ellenhaus	3
Hostal Melmac	5
Hotel Cumbres Patagonicas	9
Margouya 2	4
Sueños del Sur	7
The Guest House	6

● CAFÉS & CHEAP EATS
Café El Barista	2
Café Haussmann	5
Cassis	4
Donde El Gordito	3
La Gringa	8

● BAR
Bravo Cabrera	7

● RESTAURANTS
En Patio de Mi Casa	1
La Jardinera Gastropub	9
La Marca	6
Mercado 605	8

The town's German colonial architecture gives it a European feel, and notable early twentieth-century private residences include **Casa Kuschel**, on Klenner 299 (1910), Casona Alemana (1914) at Nuestra Señora del Carmen 788 and Casa Ángulo (1910) at Miraflores 96.

ARRIVAL AND DEPARTURE

PUERTO VARAS

By plane The nearest airport is near Puerto Montt, with flights to Santiago and Punta Arenas (see p.387). Most lodgings can organize airport transfers (CH$18,000).

Airlines LAN, Av Gramado 560 (ⓦlan.com); Sky Airline, San Bernardo 430 (ⓦskyairline.cl).

By bus All bus companies are scattered around the outskirts of Puerto Varas and no longer have offices in the town centre. Tur Bus (☎65 223 3787, ⓦturbus.cl), Tas Choapa (☎65 223 3787 ⓦtaschoapa.cl) and JAC/

Cóndor (☎65 238 3800, ⓦjac.cl) share a terminal at Del Salvador 1093; Cruz del Sur (☎65 223 6969, ⓦbusescruzdelsur.cl) is at San Francisco 1317; Pullman (☎65 223 4612, ⓦpullman.cl) is at San Francisco 1004 and Andesmar (☎65 223 4053, ⓦandesmar.com) is at San Francisco 1119. Tur Bus and Pullman serve all major destinations between Puerto Montt and Santiago, while JAC covers the Lake District. Tas Choapa runs to Argentina, while Cruz del Sur serves Chiloé. The efficient

THE LAND-AND-LAKE CROSSING INTO ARGENTINA

If you're Argentina-bound, **the land-and-lake crossing** between Puerto Varas and Bariloche allows you to experience the beauty of Chile's **Parque Nacional Vicente Perez Rosales**, and is an excellent alternative to a long bus journey. Starting out at 8am, you are first driven along the banks of Lago Llanquihue to **Petrohué**, before boarding the ferry that takes you across **Lago Todos Los Santos**, a spectacular expanse of clear blue-green. As you sail along the densely forested shores, skirting lovely Isla Margarita, the volcanoes Osorno (2660m) and Puntiagudo (2490m) loom to the north, with the majestic Tronador (3491m) to the east. You stop for lunch in Peulla, but since the only place to eat is a fairly pricey and mediocre restaurant at *Hotel Peulla*, it's worth packing a picnic lunch and going for a stroll to see the nearby waterfall instead. After going through **Chilean customs** at Peulla, you then cross the Argentine border at **Paso Pérez Rosales**, and get stamped in at tiny Puerto Frías. At this point you'll board the ferry again for the short crossing of Laguna Frías, then transfer by bus to your final nautical leg of the journey – a car ferry across the vast **Lago Nahuel Huapi**, arriving at your destination around 9pm. At CH$175,000, crossing by lake is significantly pricier than a bus journey, but the scenery is worth it. Book this popular trip in advance with **Turistour** (T 65 243 7127, W turistour.cl).

minibuses that connect Puerto Varas to Ensenada, Petrohué, Frutillar and Puerto Octay stop at a bus shelter at San Bernardo 240, while the Puerto Montt buses stop along San Francisco.

Destinations Ancud (8 daily; 2hr 30min); Castro (8 daily; 4hr); Ensenada (hourly; 1hr); Frutillar (4 daily; 40min); Puerto Montt (every 15min; 30min); Puerto Octay (2 daily; 1hr 15min); Santiago (6 daily; 16hr).

By boat There are daily boat crossings to Bariloche, Argentina (see box above).

INFORMATION AND TOURS

TOURIST INFORMATION

Casa del Turista On the wharf, Piedraplén s/n, Muelle de Puerto Varas (Mon–Fri 9am–6.30pm, Sat & Sun 10am–6.30pm; T 65 223 7956, W puertovaras.org).

TOUR OPERATORS

The main tours offered by the many companies in Puerto Varas are rafting on the Río Petrohué (grade 3 and 4; from CH$30,000/half-day); climbing Volcán Osorno (from CH$130,000); hiking in the Parque Nacional Vicente Pérez Rosales and Alerce Andino (day-trip around CH$30,000); and horseriding, generally on the slopes of Volcán Calbuco, through old *coigüe* forest (from CH$50,000/half-day).

Alsur Expediciones Aconcagua at Imperial T 65 223 2300, W alsurexpeditions.com. As well as offering standard trips, Alsur specialises in multi-day sea-kayaking to the northern part of Parque Pumalín (see p.354), rafting trips on the Ríos Petrohué, Puelo and Futaleufú, and hiking in Parque Nacional Vicente Pérez Rosales and Parque Nacional Alerce Andino (see p.351).

Campo Aventura T 09 9289 4314 or T 09 9289 43118, W campoaventura.cl. This experienced American operator runs multi-day horseriding adventures in the Cochamó Valley (see p.307) and the Río Puelo Valley (p.308), complete with stays at their two lodges.

Ko'Kayak San Pedro 311 T 65 223 3004, W kokayak.cl. Excellent French-run multilingual rafting and kayaking specialists who run half- to four-day rafting trips in the Lake District, as well as one- or three-day sea kayaking trips, with more challenging twelve-day expeditions to the southern fjords. New, adrenaline-filled options include rafting the Petrohué in smaller, 4-person rafts and riding a whitewater kayak as a passenger.

Yak Expediciones T 09 8332 0574 or 09 9299 6487, W yakexpediciones.cl. Long-standing operator running multi-day sea-kayaking adventures to the northern part of Parque Pumalín (see p.354), Chepu valley in Chiloé, and the Reloncaví Fjord (see p.306), as well as multi-day trekking and horseriding in Río Puelo valley.

ACCOMMODATION

HOTELS, B&B AND LODGES

★ **Los Caiquenes** Ruta 225, Km 9.5 T 09 8159 0489, W hotelloscaiquenes.cl. In a beautiful setting on the shores of Lago Llanquihue, this wood-shingled boutique hotel simply oozes tranquillity. All centrally heated, cream-coloured rooms are decked out in native woods, with king-size beds and Jacuzzis in the bathrooms. As for the food, you suggest to the chefs what you'd like to eat and they use locally sourced ingredients to make it happen. **US$300**

Casa Kalfu Tronador 1134 T 65 275 1261, W casakalfu.cl. With a warm colour scheme and weavings on the walls by celebrated local artists, this rambling, blue-hued, 1940s German mansion attracts a lively European, Argentine and Brazilian clientele. The bright, homely rooms are centrally heated and you can read on the terrace overlooking the lake. CH$69,000

★ **Estancia 440** Decher 440 ☎ 65 223 3921, ⓦ estancia440.cl. With one of the owners hailing from a farm in Patagonia, efforts have been made to give this boutique B&B an 'estancia' look – from huge sepia prints of *huasos* (Patagonian cowboys) to woolly bedspreads and baskets of yarn. The bathrooms of the artfully rustic en suites thoughtfully come with heated floors and the breakfast is ample and includes home-made cake. CH$55,000

Hotel Cumbres Patagónicas Imperial 561 ☎ 65 222 2000, ⓦ cumbrespuertovaras.com. Besides offering a pool and rooftop spa, this central hotel combines great lake views with the comfort of its spacious rooms, all with king-size beds and crisp linens. The buffet breakfast is a cut above most, with granola and locally produced jam among the offerings. US$179

★ **Sueños del Sur** Imperial 204 ☎ 65 271 1907, ⓦ suenosdelsur.com. With just four homely rooms, this cosy blue-shingled house is run by friendly *Santiagueños*. Cristina makes you feel extremely welcome and her home-made breads and jams are a real breakfast treat. As for the rooms, great emphasis is placed on quality: good mattresses, powerful showers, superior linen and towels. CH$55,000

The Guest House O'Higgins 608 ☎ 65 223 1521, ⓦ theguesthouse.cl. This characterful B&B is housed inside a beautifully restored 1926 mansion, the former Casa Kortmann. There are eleven big, sunny rooms, bathrooms with actual tubs, a living room with a wonderful collection of art books and extras including yoga classes and massage. CH$62,000

HOSTELS

Casa Azul Manzanal 66 at Rosario ☎ 65 223 2904, ⓦ casaazul.net. Slightly uphill from the centre, this blue house has been hosting international travellers for years without waning in popularity. The buffet breakfast (CH$3500) includes home-made muesli, the garden with the bonzai trees is a lovely spot for relaxation and the owners organize tours to Parque Alerces, Volcán Osorno and the Saltos de Petrohué. Dorms CH$10,000, doubles CH$26,000

★ **Compass del Sur** Klenner 467 ☎ 65 223 2044, ⓦ compassdelsur.cl. With new en-suite rooms added, this lovely three-storey hostel is popular with international travellers of all ages, who come to appreciate the creaky wooden floors, powerful showers and the communal vibe. The super-helpful staff or the friendly Chilean–Swedish owners can help you organize your stay. Dorms CH$12,000, doubles CH$35,000, camping/person CH$9000

Hospedaje Ellenhaus Walker Martínez 239 ☎ 65 223 3577, ⓦ ellenhaus.cl. The place may be dead as heaven on a Sat night, and service can be brusque, but this super-central labyrinth of compact rooms is your best bet for a cheap single (facilities shared) or double (some en suite). Breakfast CH$3000 extra. Doubles CH$17,000

Hostal Melmac Santa Rosa 608 ☎ 65 223 0863, ⓦ melmacpatagonia.com. Up a steep staircase, this self-proclaimed "hostel from another world" is in a new location now, and featuring a snug 3-bed dorm, two individually decorated doubles, a twin and plenty of *buena onda* (good vibes). The Argentinian-Colombian owner is good to share a beer with and he sometimes throws barbecues in the garden. Dorms CH$13,000, doubles CH$40,000

Margouya 2 Purísima 681 ☎ 65 223 7695, ⓦ margouya2.com. The sister hostel of the ever-popular *Margouya* (but quieter than the original) is housed in one of the town's restored 1930s mansions and doubles as a language school. Guests have use of the large garden and lounge with cinema-sized TV. Dorms CH$10,000, doubles CH$22,000

EATING AND DRINKING

CAFÉS AND CHEAP EATS

Café El Barista Walker Martínez 211 ☎ 65 223 3130, ⓦ elbarista.cl. A great spot for people-watching, this trendy café serves some of the best coffee for miles around, with large slices of tasty *kuchen* and a good *menú del día* (CH$8000) that might involve vegetable risotto and palm heart salad. Becomes the hottest bar in town come evening. Daily 9am–late.

Café Haussmann San Francisco 644 ☎ 65 223 7600. If you are hankering after *crudos* (Chilean-German special consisting of raw meat on toast with an accompaniment of seasonings and sauces; CH$1900) and *kuchen* (cake), this Valdivian export does them best. Daily 10.30am–9pm.

Cassis Santa Rosa at Gramado ☎ 65 244 1529. This large, perpetually busy café has something to satisfy all tastes: sweet and savoury crêpes, chunky sandwiches, *tablas* to share, good coffee, and a delectable array of cakes and ice-cream flavours for those with a sweet tooth. Daily 10am–10pm.

Donde El Gordito San Bernardo 560 ☎ 65 223 3425. Busy little local institution inside the market, its walls and ceilings covered in knick-knacks, and serving large portions of inexpensive fish and seafood to hungry locals. Squid in *pil-pil* sauce, clams baked with parmesan, grilled fish – it's all fresh and fantastic. Mains from CH$6000. Daily 11am–10pm.

★**La Gringa** Imperial 605 ☎65 223 1980. *La Gringa's* expat owner hails from Seattle and has done her best to recreate her home town's perfect rainy day café vibe, one that locals and travellers gravitate to. There are sticky, gooey cinnamon rolls and delectable chocolate chip cookies to go with your coffee, and come noon the place fills up with ladies that lunch, with imaginative soups, salads and the likes of pulled pork sandwiches gracing the menu. Mon–Sat 9am–8pm.

RESTAURANTS

En Patio de Mi Casa Decher 830 ☎65 223 1507. Located literally in the back patio of the chef's house in a quiet residential area, this intimate dining room has just eight tables, so reserve in advance. The focus is on local ingredients, with the likes of filet mignon with *merkén*-spiced potatos, or hake in seafood sauce gracing the menu, and the service is wonderful. Tues–Fri 1–3pm & 7–10pm.

La Jardinera Gastropub Blanco Encalada 1160 ☎65 223 1684, ⓦlajardinera.cl. Tucked away on a quiet street off the *costanera*, the menu at this welcoming restaurant convincingly spans the world. The *tabla árabe* features moreish hummus, stuffed vine leaves and more, while the Thai green curry adds some welcome spice and the sticky toffee pudding is a boon for homesick Brits. Mains from CH$7500. Daily noon–3pm & 7–11pm.

DIRECTORY

Hospital Clínica Alemana, Otto Bader 810 (☎65 258 2100).

Money and exchange There are several banks with ATMs around the Plaza de Armas and along Del Salvador,

★**La Marca** Santa Rosa 539 ☎65 223 2026, ⓦlamarca.cl. With gaucho music on the stereo and cowboy paraphernalia on the wall, this is one of the best steakhouses in the Lake District. The *bife de chorizo* is mouthwateringly juicy and the menu features a few less-common items, such as *criadillos* (bull's testicles). The succinct, well-chosen wine list is the icing on the cake. Mon–Sat 12.30–11pm, Sun 1–4pm.

★**Mercado 605** Imperial 605 ☎65 223 1980. This candlelit half-tapas bar, half-fusion restaurant is responsible for some of the most imaginative dishes in Puerto Varas. Start off with little bites such as home-made liver pate with onion marmalade or Catalan *sobrasada* with honey and smoked cheese (3 tapas CH$3500) and then proceed with duck confit with quinoa or steak with port sauce. Mains from CH$7900. Mon–Sat 8pm–midnight.

BAR

Bravo Cabrera Vicente Pérez Rosales 1071 ☎65 223 3441, ⓦbravocabrera.cl. This is still one of the "it" places and justifiably so: "BC" has an incomparable selection of around fifty beers, including many mircobrews from around Chile, as well as excellent wood-fired pizzas and *tablas* to share for the perpetually packed house. Occasional DJs liven up this already lively lakefront joint. Mon–Thurs 7pm–2am, Fri & Sat 12.30pm–3am, Sun 12.30–6pm.

including Banco de Chile, Del Salvador 210. For a *cambio*, try Inter, Del Salvador 257, Local 11 (in the Galería Real).

Post office San José 242 at San Pedro (Mon–Sat 9am–noon & 2–6pm).

Frutillar

The Panamericana first approaches Lago Llanquihue at Frutillar Alto, 4km west of **Frutillar Bajo**, and collectively known as Frutillar. Up until the 1980s, apartheid divided Frutillar, with Frutillar Bajo reserved for the German–Chilean population and the mestizo population restricted to Frutillar Alto, forbidden to use the lower town's beaches. That has all changed now, and because it's so popular it gets very crowded here in summer, especially during the last week of January and the first week of February, when the town hosts the **classical music festival Semanas Musicales** (ⓦsemanasmusicales.cl).

Teatro del Lago Sur

Av Philippi 1000 • ⓦteatrodellago.cl

A state-of-the-art music venue that would do any capital city proud, the cutting-edge, copper-roofed **Teatro del Lago Sur** rises above the waterfront, against a backdrop of volcanoes. Its 1178-seat concert hall and a smaller amphitheatre play host mostly to classical music performances and attract renowned orchestras and soloists from all over the world (the website has the full schedule). There's also an appealing café on the ground floor.

Museo Histórico Alemán

Pérez Rosales at Prat • Daily 9am–6pm • CH$2500

At the bottom of the hill leading from Frutillar Alto, this museum initiates you into the world of German settlers in the Lake District. Besides a beautifully tended garden, an old water mill and several other traditional wooden buildings, the museum features a wide variety of household objects used by the earliest immigrants to Llanquihue, but most interesting is a circular barn *campanario*; inside, pairs of horses were once tethered to the central pillar and driven round in circles, threshing sheaves of corn with their hoofs. Further up the hill is the **Casa del Herrero**, the blacksmith's house, and higher up still is the reconstruction of a typical early farmhouse filled with period furniture and decorated with old family photos.

ARRIVAL AND INFORMATION   FRUTILLAR

By bus Minibuses from Puerto Montt and Puerto Varas stop on the corner of Montt and Av. Philippi in Frutillar Bajo. Other buses arrive in Frutillar Alto, connected to Frutillar Bajo by *colectivo* shuttle services (CH$600).
Tourist information Av Philippi at O'Higgins (daily 8.30am–1pm & 2–5pm; ⓦfrutillar.com).

ACCOMMODATION AND EATING

Hotel Aycara Philippi 1215 ☎65 242 1550, ⓦwww .hotelayacara.cl. This beautifully renovated mansion dating back to 1910 has just eight bright wood-panelled rooms with antique furnishings, crisp linens and crimson accents. The restaurant, specializing in dishes made from fresh local ingredients, comes highly recommended. US$170

Hotel Frau Holle Varas 54 ☎65 242 1345, ⓦfrauholle -frutillar.cl. Recently renovated, this historic home cum boutique hotel has won a lot of fans with its top-notch service, its quaint rooms with embroidered pillowcases (and thoroughly modern bathrooms) and its central location. Dining at the on-site restaurant is worth every penny, too. CH$105,000

Se Cocina 2km from Frutillar ☎09 8972 8195, ⓦsecocina.cl. Two kilometres out of town, this wood-shingled restaurant is one of the best in Frutillar, with a menu that changes monthly, and relies on locally sourced produce; treat yourself to the likes of crab-filled semolina ravioli and chocolate crepes flambéed in rum. There's also excellent beer produced on the premises. Mains CH$9500. Daily 12.30–4pm & 7.30pm–midnight.

Puerto Octay

Twenty-eight kilometres northeast of Frutillar, also on the shores of Lago Llanquihue, lies **PUERTO OCTAY**, the first German settlement on Lago Llanquihue. Dating to 1852, it's a friendly little place with a needle-steepled church and balconied houses with ornate eaves.

Museum "El Colono"

Independencia 591 • Tues–Sun 9.30am–1pm & 1.45–6.30pm • CH$1000

The small and well-organized Museum "El Colono" shares the 1920 Casa Niklitschek with the local library and its exhibits span the history of the area, from the earliest human settlement to the founding and growth of Puerto Octay, They comprise bilingual (Spanish/English) accounts, old photographs and period objects – from stone arrowheads to nineteenth-century household objects, agricultural machines and stills for making the sweet alcoholic *chicha* drink, a local speciality.

ARRIVAL AND DEPARTURE   PUERTO OCTAY

By bus Hourly departures from Osorno on Buses Via Octay and buses (up to 5 daily) from Frutillar and Puerto Montt.

ACCOMMODATION AND EATING

Hotel Haase Montt 344 ☎65 239 1302, ⓦhotelhaase .cl. Centrally located, this late nineteenth-century mansion with a wraparound upstairs terrace and polished wooden floors makes for an atmospheric stay. The on-site restaurant is popular with locals and serves German-style *onces* as well as solid regional dishes. CH$17,000

Rancho Espantapájaros 6km from Puerto Octay towards Frutillar ☎65 233 0049,

ⓦespantapajaros.cl. Local families and travellers alike head to this (now expanded) family-run restaurant for the great all-you-can-eat barbecue buffet (CH$15,000). The spit-roasted goat is excellent, as is the *jabalí* (wild boar). Mon–Sat 1–4pm & 7.30–11.30pm, Sun 1–4pm.

★**Zapato Amarillo** 2km north of town ☎65 221 0787, ⓦzapatoamarillo.cl. This well-signposted backpacker and cyclist favourite consists of a homely main lodge with grass roof and an eight-bed dorm, kitchen and communal area in a separate building. Canoe, bike, sailing boat, climbing gear and a scooter are available for guest hire, and the breakfast spread is extensive. The owners speak German and English and can organize a series of excursions to Vicente Pérez Rosales National Park, to Volcán Osorno or around Lake Rupanco. Dorms CH$12,000, doubles CH$32,000

Ensenada

The paved road continues around Lago Llanquihue from Puerto Octay, passing the turnoff to Volcán Osorno (see p.304) shortly before you arrive in **ENSENADA**, a small village in a lovely lakeside location with a smattering of *hospedajes*, campsites and restaurants stretching pretty much all the way to Puerto Varas.

ARRIVAL AND DEPARTURE   ENSENADA

By bus There are frequent minibuses (weekdays at least 1 hourly; weekends somewhat fewer) running to Ensenada from Puerto Varas and Puerto Montt, most continuing on to Petrohué.

ACCOMMODATION AND EATING

Biosfera Volcánica Lodge Ruta 225, Km 39.5 Cruce Navarro ☎09 7668 5266, ⓦbiosferavolcanicalodge.cl. Keep an eye out for the modest sign at the turnoff that leads you into the forest. In the clearing, you find three luxurious, natural-light-filled 2-person geodomes, each with a wood-stove-heated hot tub (CH$16,000), stargazing terrace and comfortable beds. All the furnishings are made of native woods, modern bathrooms include rain showers and there's even a separate guest kitchen if you don't feel like seeking out a restaurant along the Ruta 225. CH$78,000

Casa Ko Ruta 225, Km 37 (3km up the dirt road that branches off Ruta 225) ☎09 7703 6477, ⓦcasako.com. This rambling wooden house is run by the delightful French expats Rafael and Pauline; Rafael is an outdoor enthusiast who can arrange for you to hike up the surrounding volcanoes (visible from the house) and advise on other outdoor adventures. His breakfasts are legendary and guests end up socialising over the homecooked dinners. CH$45,000

Fox Hill Ruta 225, Km 37 ☎09 8461 3005, ⓦfoxhillchile.com. The hospitable American-Russian owners built their gorgeous stone-and-wooden-beamed lodge with their own hands and there's a great emphasis on quality: imported towels, superb showers, underfloor heating and an excellent breakfast that includes organic eggs and local honey. All rooms have a view of either Volcán Osorno or Calbuco, and on top of that, Irina bakes delicious bread and is an excellent cook: meals besides breakfast can be arranged on request, but you have to give a couple of days' notice. CH$71,000

Latitude 42 At the Yan Kee Way Lodge, Ruta 225, Km 42 ☎65 221 2030. This hotel restaurant – the best this side of the lake – offers perfectly executed dishes made from local and organic ingredients, such as in-house cognac-smoked salmon and beautifully seared steak, all complemented by a comprehensive wine list. Daily 12.30–3.30pm & 7–11pm.

Parque Nacional Vicente Pérez Rosales and around

PARQUE NACIONAL VICENTE PÉREZ ROSALES, Chile's first national park, was established in 1926, and covers an area of 2510 square kilometres. It is divided into three sectors: Sector Osorno, Sector Petrohué and Sector Peulla, and comprises some of the most sensational scenery in the Lake District: the emerald lago Todos los Santos, the thundering turquoise waters of the Saltos de Petrohué, and the imposing peaks of the area's main volcanoes: Osorno, Tronadór and Puntiagudo. Coupled with the fact that this vast chunk of wilderness provides numerous excellent hiking opportunities, it's little wonder that it's the most visited park in the whole of Chile. If you are planning to

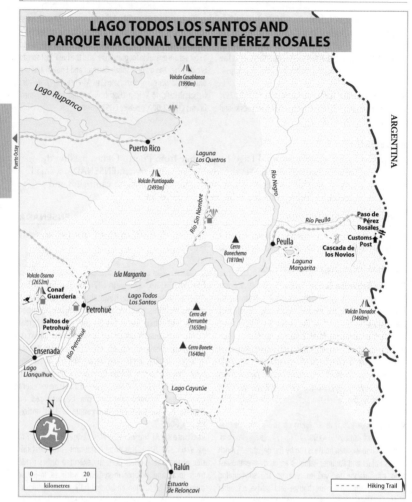

LAGO TODOS LOS SANTOS AND PARQUE NACIONAL VICENTE PÉREZ ROSALES

do any extensive hiking here, you'll find it useful to have a copy of the water-resistant *Llanquihue* map published by Trekking Chile (ⓦtrekkingchile.com).

Volcán Osorno

Ski season mid-June to early Nov • Ski lift passes CH$19,000/CH$24,000 for a half/full day • ⓦvolcanosorno.com

From the turnoff just short of Ensenada, a paved 14km road snakes up to the picture-perfect conical peak of **VOLCÁN OSORNO**. While it has erupted on many occasions in the past, the lava spewed from the craters around its base and this mighty volcano is yet to blow its top. About halfway up the slope you'll come across the signposted Sendero El Solitario (6km; 2hr) that leads east through dense forest before emerging on the road to Petrohué, about 1km away from the Saltos de Petrohué.

The Centro de Ski & Montaña Volcán Osorno (ⓦvolcanosorno.com) has two chairlifts and seven runs open to skiers, as well as a 'snow park' for snowboarders, a tubing park, a snowshoe route from the top of the first chairlift to a overlooking Cráter Rojo and several off-piste possibilities. Condition windy, but on the upside, you'll find skiers and snowboarders up he November and equipment is available for rent.

Incidentally, November and December are also the better (and sa the volcano; while many tour groups in Puerto Varas run half-day hiking Osorno's base (CH$50,000), the ascent of the peak is the region's toughest volcano-bagging challenge (CH$200,000) involving a 5am start, snow- and ice-climbing gear and roping up towards the end. It's about five hours to the summit (two to the snowline, three more to the top), and there are many crevasses; a guide is mandatory and it's never more than two hikers per guide. Several outfits are authorised to guide people up (see p.306). Conaf bans ascents once much of the snow melts in February, as the risk of rockslides increases dramatically.

In January and February, the ski runs turn into a downhill bike park and the two connected chairlifts stay open all year (CH$10,000/14,000 for one/two chairlifts); you can ride all the way to Estación Glaciar at the top of the second chairlift for the best view of the area. To the west you can see across Lago Llanquihue, the central plain and across to the sea, and dominating the skyline to the south are the jagged peaks of Volcán Calbuco.

Lago Todos los Santos and around

The volcanic rock in the area was part of a tongue of lava sent this way by Volcán Osorno in 1850, an eruption that diverted the Petrohué river from its old course into Lago Llanquihue. At the end of the riverside road lies **LAGO TODOS LOS SANTOS**, deep green and stunningly clear, one of the most beautiful in the Lake District – it's also known as Lago Esmeralda (Emerald Lake) because of the intense colour of its water. First Patagonia (☏09 9444 4339, ⍰firstpatagonia.cl) offers **tours** on the lake, which provide unsurpassed views of Volcán Osorno, the spiked peak of Volcán Puntiagudo, and, highest of all, the glacier-covered Monte Tronador.

Petrohué

Accessible by partially paved road from Ensenada, the sleepy hamlet of **PETROHUÉ** sits on the western shore of Lago Todos los Santos. The settlement dates from the early twentieth century, when one Ricardo Roth began taking tourists across the lakes between Puerto Varas and Bariloche.

In Petrohué there's a currently dug-up black-sand beach, **Playa Larga** – the start of two good hiking trails. A 5km trail skirts the lakeshore, while **Sendero Los Alerzales** makes for a two-hour (7km return) enjoyable hike through dense local forest, at one point crossing paths with the **Sendero Paso Desolación**, a tough 10km trek (6hr) which climbs up the northeast side of Volcán Osorno to a height of 1100m and offers a fantastic view of Volcán Tronador and the lake below.

The Termas de Callao trail

To reach the trailhead, you'll need to rent a boat from the dock at Petrohué (CH$55,000–65,000 for up to six people)

The 18km **Termas de Callao** trail (approximately 8hr) starts from the northern shores of Lago Todos los Santos, by the Río Sin Nombre (No-Name River). Head up the river – the path is reasonably clear but be sure always to head upwards to the source – and after about three or four hours' climbing you reach the namesake hot springs (free and safe to bathe in) and a basic *refugio*. From here you can either go back down to Lago Todos los Santos, having asked the boatman to pick you up again, or carry on up to the Laguna los Quetros (where there's a basic campsite) and then over the pass – another two hours' hike – and then descend to Lago Rupanco, which takes another three hours. From the shores of Lago Rupanco, it's about another hour (west) to Puerto Rico, from where there are buses to Osorno.

6

e Petrohué

...neast of Ensenada, off the gravel road that leads towards Petrohué • Daily: summer 8.30am–9pm; winter 9am–6pm • CH$1500
...1000 parking fee

...ne **Saltos de Petrohué**, a series of immense falls formed by an extremely hard layer of lava that has been eroded into small channels by the churning water of Río Petrohue. There's a brand-new visitor centre with shops selling woollen and *raulí* wood goodies and gourmet foodstuffs, as well as a basic café and a First Patagonia office (see below) where you can arrange all manner of outdoor activities on the spot.

The CH$1500 entrance fee only applies if you take the short Sendero Saltos to the viewpoints, though there's no other way to see the falls. Here you can watch the incredibly turquoise water roar and swirl below and the waterfalls are particularly impressive on a fine day when Volcán Osorno rises directly above them.

Peulla

Boat excursions depart at 10am (CH$34,000/person including transportation from Puerto Varas or Puerto Montt, or CH$24,000 from Petrohué), run by First Patagonia (see below) and TurisTour (see p.299)

Those staying overnight in **PEULLA**, a small scattering of houses spread out along the road at the far end of the lake, have time to do the moderately difficult yet rewarding 8km climb to **Laguna Margarita** (4hr) or take a stroll to the beautiful **Cascada de Los Novios** waterfall nearby.

ARRIVAL AND INFORMATION

By bus Buses run from Puerto Montt via Puerto Varas to Petrohué (peak season at least hourly, weekends less frequently; rest of the year 2 daily; 1hr 15min).

By boat For details of the Petrohué to Bariloche bus-and-boat journey, see p.299.

Tours From its office at the Saltos de Petrohue visitor centre, First Patagonia (☎09 9444 4339, ⊛firstpatagonia.cl)

PARQUE NACIONAL VICENTE PÉREZ ROSALES

arranges rafting on Río Petrohue (CH$29,000), kayaking on Lago Todos los Santos (CH$10,000/2hr), full-day catamaran outings on the lake from Petrohue or Puerto Varas/Puerto Montt (CH$24,000/34,000), ziplining (CH$25,000), jaunts on the giant Vuelo del Pionero swing (CH$6000), bicycle rent (CH$12,000/2hr) and guided hikes in the park (from CH$25,000/person for minimum of three).

ACCOMMODATION AND EATING

VOLCÁN OSORNO

Refugio Teski ☎09 9078 3360, ⊛teski.cl. This ski-adorned rustic lodge has compact dorms (bring own sleeping bag), a cosy little café with vibrant photographs of Volcán Osorno's deep-blue ice caves and the one touch of luxury – two outdoor hot tubs (CH$40,000), to be enjoyed with pisco sour in hand while looking down over Lago Llanquihue. Dorms CH$15,000, doubles CH$38,000

PETROHUÉ

Camping Playa Petrohué ☎65 221 2036. Shaded

Conaf-run campsite near the beach, with cold showers and firepits. Camping/person CH$7000

Petrohué Lodge Ruta 225, Km60, Petrohué ☎65 221 2025, ⊛petrohue.com. Besides the appealing lakeside location, this handsome stone-and-wood lodge features a tower, roaring fireplace in the guest lounge, skylights throughout, fully equipped lakeside *cabañas* (sleeping 4–8) and candle-dotted rooms, perfect for canoodling with your sweetie. Breakfast, packed and regular lunch, *onces* and dinner available at the decent on-site restaurant (open to non-guests). Doubles US$264, *cabañas* US$250

Estuario de Reloncaví

On the way back to Ensenada from Parque Nacional Vicente Pérez Rosales, a southern fork, 1km before the town, will take you 33km along a paved road, fringed with large bushes of wild fuchsia and giant rhubarb plants, to the tranquil **ESTUARIO DE RELONCAVÍ**. Your first view of the bay comes as you descend to the village of **Ralún**, from which a partially paved road leads you through wild, dramatic scenery deeper into pioneer country and the village of **Cochamó**.

TREKKING IN THE RÍO COCHAMÓ VALLEY

With the temperate rainforest's gnarly trees 'clothed' in lichen, towering *alerces* and granite mountains rising above the forest, it's easy to see how the Río Cochamó Valley acquired its "**Yosemite of the South**" moniker. The valley is bisected by the remnants of a nineteenth-century logging road (little more than a muddy footpath in places) that now serves as a popular 12km hiking trail (4–5hr) to the valley of La Junta, surrounded by mountains that are hugely popular with rock climbers. The trail is mostly easy to follow, but can be extremely muddy, as the horses bringing supplies to the two guesthouses (see below) churn up the path in rainy weather. If you're not a climber, there is plenty of scope for day hikes in the valley and more adventurous travellers can even continue on foot to Argentina. The **trailhead** for the Río Cochamó valley is at the end of an 8km dirt road that branches off the main road through Cochamó 4km south. Enterprising locals offer lifts up to the trailhead for CH$3000 in the summer months.

6

Cochamó

Sitting on the gorgeous Estuario de Reloncaví, against the backdrop of snow-tipped mountains, the appealing fishing village of Cochamó is a good place to go hiking or horse-trekking into the **Cochamó Valley**, 'Chile's Yosemite', home to the some of the oldest standing trees in South America and rife with opportunities for rockclimbing, particularly in the **La Junta Valley**. From there, adventurous hikers can continue on foot into Argentina.

ARRIVAL AND INFORMATION

COCHAMÓ

By bus Buses Río Puelo pass through daily en route from Puerto Montt to Río Puelo and vice versa.
By car Route V-69 is paved up to Ralún and beyond; the 12 or so km to Cochamó consists of a fairly potholed gravel road. If approaching the village from the south, the pitted gravel road from Puelo can be rough after heavy rains; navigable in a regular car but with caution.
Tourist information The municipal office (Mon–Sat 9am–6pm; ☎ 65 235 0271) on the main street, close to the entrance of town, has surprisingly good maps of the Río Puelo region.
Tours Southern Trips (☎ 09 8407 2559 or 9919 8947, ⓦ southern-trips.com), run by the friendly Fabian and Tatiana, offer some fantastic horseriding in the area, from half-day jaunts to multi-day treks. *Campo Aventura* (see below) specialises in multi-day horse treks in the region.

ACCOMMODATION AND EATING

Camping La Junta 24km west of Cochamó, ⓦ cochamo .com. Run by the owners of Refugio Cochamó (see below), this appealing campsite has solar-heated showers and composting toilets. Camping/person CH$3500
Campo Aventura Around 4km south of Cochamó proper, near the turnoff for Río Cochamó Valley ☎ 09 9289 4314 or 9289 4318, ⓦ campoaventura.cl. This beautiful, rustic, American-run lodge sits amidst a vast riverside property. It accommodates adventurers in its cluster of compact rooms and lets them camp by the river; full board available. *Campo Aventura* specialises in horse-riding adventures in the region, particularly multi-day explorations (see above). Camping/person CH$5000, doubles CH$38,000
Campo Aventura Mountain Lodge 24km west of Cochamó, ⓦ campoaventura.cl. *Campo Aventura*'s (see above) even more rustic outpost in the La Junta valley, this is a converted farmhouse with bunkrooms, simple rooms and camping spots; *asados* can be organised for guests. There are plans to build a new lodge nearby. Camping/person CH$4000, dorms CH$12,000, doubles CH$45,000

Eco Hostal Las Bandurrias Sector El Bosque s/n ☎ 09 9672 2590, ⓦ hostalbandurrias.com. High up on a hill above Cochamó (arrange pickup in advance), this gorgeous little hostel consists of a single 4-bed dorm, a twin and a double (shared bath), all with down duvets and run by a friendly and knowledgeable Swiss-Chilean couple. The excellent breakfast includes Sylvie's home-made bread and your hosts have luggage storage for those who want to travel light when hiking the Río Cochamó Valley. Dorms CH$14,000, double CH$32,000
La Ollita Calle Principal s/n. Right on the main street, and unusually for the region, this local favourite tends to stick to its opening hours, and serves simple dishes such as grilled *congrio* or *lomo a lo pobre*. Mains from CH$5500. Daily 12.30–10pm.
Refugio Cochamó 24km west of Cochamó ⓦ cochamo .cl. Run by effusive Argentinian-American hosts, this appealing guesthouse in the La Junta Valley has long been a haven for climbers. There's no phone so contact them via email in advance to book accommodation/request meals. Dorms CH$12,000, doubles CH$34,000

Río Puelo Valley

A 27km road runs south from Cochamó to the scattering of houses that is Río Puelo, straddling its namesake river. From here, an unpaved, narrow ribbon of road heads east, skirting the base of craggy peaks, before it culminates at Punta Canelo, on the shores of Lago Tagua-Tagua. This lake, surrounded by mountains clad in dense greenery and flecked with waterfalls, separates Chile as you know it from Chile that's still off-the-grid, *huaso* country where there is no phone signal and locals get about on horseback as much as on wheels. Yet this traditional way of life is under threat from a proposed dam project and increased traffic from Argentina once the road is paved from the main village of Llanada Grande (see p.309) to the Río Puelo border crossing, so many locals offer rural tourism in the shape of horseriding, homestays, fishing and hiking in a bid to fend off the dam. There is no phone signal in the valley, though some lodgings in Llanada Grande, by Lago Totoral and around Puerto Urrutia offer slow wi-fi.

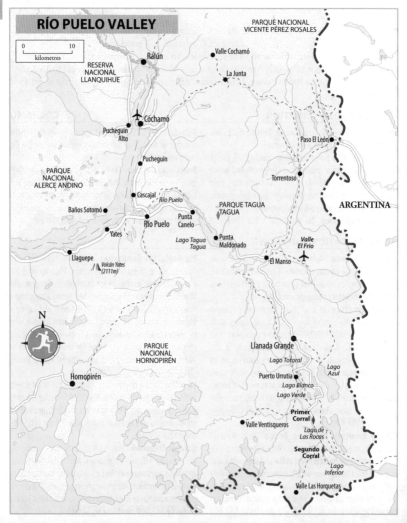

Llanada Grande and around

From Punta Maldonado, the dock on the side of the lake opposite Punta Canelo, it's a bumpy 32km drive to the one-street main settlement of Llanada Grande. Beyond, a 7km road skirts pretty Lago Totoral before reaching a fork in the road; the 3km left fork leads west to Puerto Urrutia, sitting alongside an aquamarine river (and from where fishing excursions can be arranged), while the 13km right fork continues to a lookout over a wide glacial river (you can pass through a gate to go down to the tiny settlement of Primer Corral). At the time of research, cars were not allowed beyond here, even though the 14km horse track (from the end of the 13km right fork) to Segundo Corral, a tiny scattering of houses, was being paved at the time of writing. If you do make it to Segundo Corral on foot (or horseback), another 4km horse track takes you from Segundo Corral to Lago Inferior, where it may be possible to catch a boat all the way across the lake that connects with Argentina's Lago Puelo, and then across Lago Puelo to its namesake settlement where it's possible to find public transport to El Bolsón.

In addition to that, adventurous hikers can attempt the 47km trek from El Manso, 12km south of Punta Maldonado, all the way to La Junta in the Río Cochamó Valley (see p.307) via the Río Manso Valley, the settlement of Torrentoso and along the west bank of Lago Vidal Gormaz, camping wild en route and buying supplies from isolated farmhouses.

Parque Tagua-Tagua

CH$5000 • ☎ 65 223 4892 • ⓦ parquetaguatagua.cl

This 3000-hectare slice of Valdivian rainforest is a private park that sits along the south shore of Lago Tagua-Tagua, with 18km worth of well-maintained trails, kayaking alongside lakeside waterfalls and rock climbing on offer, and the possibility of spotting pudú, pumas and other shy fauna. If you want to visit for the day or stay in the park, make arrangements over the phone before leaving Punta Canelo in order for the speedboat to meet you at the Punta Maldonado dock for the ten-minute ride to the park.

ARRIVAL AND INFORMATION   RÍO PUELO VALLEY

By bus A single bus runs from Puerto Montt daily at 7.45am all the way to Primer Corral, and there's a daily 9am departure from Primer Corral to Puerto Montt.

By ferry A ferry runs daily from Punta Canelo (at 7.30am,

9am & 1pm, returning from Punta Maldonado at 8.15am, noon & 4.30pm; outside Dec–Feb the earliest ferry on each leg does not run; CH$1050/7000/passenger/car). If driving, get to the dock 1hr before departure to queue up.

ACCOMMODATION AND EATING

Campo Eggers En route to Primer Corral, in front of the El Salto waterfall. The pioneer home of hospitable Blanca Eggers is a fantastic place to delve into local *huaso* culture. Price includes room with shared facilities, home-cooked meals and wine, and Blanca has numerous contacts in the valley and can help organise homestays in Primer Corral and Segundo Corral if you're thinking of trekking into Argentina. CH$50,000

Hospedaje Titina Just south of Llanada Grande. Friendly wood-panelled guesthouse with simple, homely rooms. The friendly owner can help organise horseriding outings in the valley and is happy to recommend a fantastic local 'restaurant' that consists of a neighbour's kitchen and solid home-cooking. CH$24,000

Mítico Lodge ☎ 65 223 4892, ⓦ parquetaguatagua.cl. The plushest accommodation inside Parque Tagua-Tagua consists of the handsome, secluded *Mítico Lodge* on the north side of the lake, complete with hot tub and swimming pool, spacious wood-panelled rooms and gourmet cuisine. CH$136,000

Refugio Quetrus & Refugio Alerce ☎ 65 223 4892, ⓦ parquetaguatagua.cl. On the south side of Parque Tagua-Tagua there are the rustic, wood-fire-heated two-person *Refugio Quetrus* and the eighteen-person *Refugio Alerce*, reachable via a 5hr 30min hike and 4hr hike, respectively, from the dock. *Refugio Alerce* dorms CH$12,000, *Refugio Quetrus* dorms CH$60,000

Puerto Montt

At the southern end of the Lake District and seventeen kilometres south of Puerto Varas, the Panamericana approaches a large bay – the Seno de Reloncaví – with snowcapped Volcán Calbuco (see box, p.273) and Volcán Osorno towering beyond. On its edge lies the administrative and commercial capital of the Lake District – **PUERTO MONTT**, founded by the same influx of German colonizers that settled Lago Llanquihue to the north. The city is strung out along the bay, with the central part of town located on a narrow flat area along the main Avenida Diego Portales, and much of the city crowding the hills behind it.

Puerto Montt is an important transportation hub and a busy port, with its formerly billion-dollar-a-year salmon farming industry slowly recovering from the major blow it had taken in recent years, and the embarkation point for long-distance ferry trips (see box, p.312). Gritty "Muerto Montt" has few attractions of its own beyond the graffiti-blighted promenade crowned with a redundant steam engine, but it's a worthwhile overnight stop if you want to catch a boat, a plane, or the latest blockbuster at the Mall Paseo Costanera.

Casa del Arte Diego Rivera

Quillota 116 • Mon–Fri 9am–8pm, Sat & Sun 11am–6pm • Free

Just off the Plaza de Armas, the Casa del Arte Diego Rivera is the product of a Chilean–Mexican collaboration, with works by local and international artists and photographers displayed inside the Sala Hardy Wistuba on the first floor. It also hosts film festivals and dance performances.

Angelmó

The fishing neighbourhood of **ANGELMÓ** sits at the western end of the bay, around 1km west of the bus terminal. Here the *costanera* (coastal road) features an extensive **feria artesanal**, its numerous stalls laden with carved wooden earrings, woven baskets and figures from Chilote mythology, woollen ponchos, sweaters and lapis lazuli jewellery.

Just west of the *feria artesanal* lies a thriving **fish market**, a combination of many fish retailers and various eateries operated by ebullient local ladies whose steaming vats of *curanto* (see p.322) and delicious smells of fish cooking attract numerous visitors, particularly at lunchtime. Next to the fish market are stalls selling country cheeses, honey, bottles of powerful *licor de oro* and strings of smoked shellfish.

ARRIVAL AND DEPARTURE

PUERTO MONTT

BY PLANE

Aeropuerto El Tepual (☎ 65 229 4161) is located 16km northwest of the city. Buses Andestur run to and from the airport hourly and meet flights. Daily flights serve Santiago, Punta Arenas and Balmaceda (Coyhaique). Cessna flights with Aerocord and two other small operators serve Chaitén from the Aeródromo La Paloma, off Camino A. Alerce.

Airlines Aerocord (☎ 65 226 2300, ⒲ aerocord.cl); LAN, O'Higgins 167 at Urmeneta (⒲ lan.com); Sky Airline, San Martín 189 at Benavente (⒲ skyairline.cl).

Destinations Balmaceda/Coyhaique (2 daily; 1hr); Chaitén (2–3 daily; 40min); Concepción (1 daily; 1hr 45min); Punta Arenas (2 daily; 2hr 10min); Santiago (8 daily; 1hr 30min); Temuco (1 daily; 45min).

BY BUS

The large, well-organised Terminal de Buses (⒲ terminalpm.cl) is at Av Diego Portales 1001 on the waterfront, six blocks west of the town centre. It is served by both long-distance buses to many points north and south, and frequent minibuses to regional destinations such as Puerto Varas, Frutillar and Ensenada.

Companies All of the main companies have offices in the terminal (☎ 65 228 3000), including Tur Bus (☎ 65 227 3979, ⒲ turbus.cl) and Pullman (☎ 65 225 4399, ⒲ www .pullman.cl), serving all major destinations between Puerto Montt and Santiago, with connections to the north of Chile. Cruz del Sur (☎ 65 225 2872, ⒲ busescruzdelsur .cl) has the most frequent departures to Chiloé; Queilén Bus

6

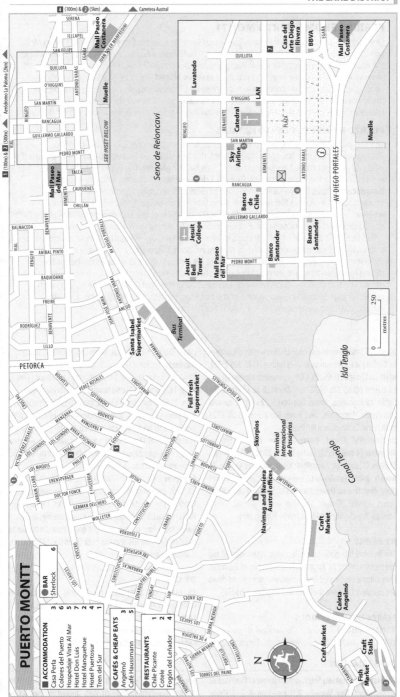

PUERTO MONTT

ACCOMMODATION
Casa Perla	3
Colores del Puerto	6
Hospedaje Vista Al Mar	7
Hotel Don Luis	5
Hotel Manquehue	4
Hotel Puertosur	2
Tren del Sur	1

CAFÉS & CHEAP EATS
| Angelmó | 3 |
| Café Haussmann | 5 |

RESTAURANTS
Chile Picante	1
Cotele	2
Fogón del Leñador	4

BAR
| Sherlock | 6 |

Seno de Reloncaví

Isla Tenglo

Canal Tenglo

0   250
metres

Map labels:
Carretera Austral
Mall Paseo Costanera
Casa del Arte Diego Rivera
BBVA
Lavatodo
Catedral
LAN
Sky Airline
Jesuit College
Jesuit Bell Tower
Mall Paseo del Mar
Banco de Chile
Banco Santander
Muelle
Av Diego Portales
Santa Isabel Supermarket
Bus Terminal
Full Fresh Supermarket
Skorpios
Terminal Internacional de Pasajeros
Navimag and Naviera Austral offices
Craft Market
Caleta Angelmó
Craft Market
Craft Stalls
Fish Market

PETORCA

6

FERRIES FROM PUERTO MONTT

One of the main reasons people travel to Puerto Montt is to catch a **ferry** south. From Puerto Montt you can sail to Chaitén and Puerto Chacabuco on the Carretera Austral, the Laguna San Rafael far in the southern fjords, Puerto Natales in Patagonia and Quellón in Chiloé. These ferry trips are almost always fully booked in summer, and you must **reserve ahead**. The quality of your experience will largely depend on the weather. The seas on these ferry rides are usually calm as most of the time the ferries are sailing through sheltered fjords, though it can still be windy. The exception is the trip to Puerto Natales, when the ship heads out to the Pacific across the often-turbulent Golfo de Penas.

PUERTO MONTT TO PUERTO NATALES

The Navimag trip from Puerto Montt to Puerto Natales is an incredible introduction to Patagonia. Lasting four days and three nights, the trip takes you through pristine and deserted waterways, past uninhabited islands and Chile's largest **glacier**, the Piu XI, with frequent sightings of marine life. It passes by **Puerto Edén**, the last remaining settlement of the **Kawéscar** people, before sailing into the cold and little-explored fjords of the south, and finally docking in Puerto Natales on the Seno Última Esperanza. If you're lucky with the weather, you'll not want to leave the deck for the duration of the trip, except to drink at the bar and to take part in a raucous game of bingo on the last night with a crowd of new friends.

The flipside is a cruise entirely shrouded in mist and fog, topped with a sleepless night as the ship navigates the turbulent waters of the open ocean, followed by the equally sickness-inducing waves of the **Golfo de Penas**, while you spend your trip stuck in the bar or the dining room, watching re-runs of films with people of whom, by trip's end, you may well have grown tired. In the off-season, you will also be sharing the boat (if not the main deck) with cattle. Though it could be worse; one of the Navimag ferries struck some rocks and sank in August 2014 (no passengers were injured). For ferry operators, see below.

(☎ 65 225 3468) also serves Chiloé and has weekly departures for Coyhaique via Argentina, as does Turibus (☎ 65 225 2872), while Tas Choapa (☎ 65 225 4828, ⓦ www.taschoapa.cl) and Igi Llaima (☎ 65 225 9320, ⓦ igillaima.cl) head across the border to Argentina. Kemel Bus (☎ 65 225 6450) runs to Chaitén via Hornopirén, and Buses Río Puelo (☎ 09 9123 0838) serve Cochamó and Río Puelo.

Destinations Ancud (every 30min; 2hr); Bariloche, Argentina (4 daily; 6hr); Castro (every 30min; 3hr 30min); Chaitén (1 daily at 7am; 9hr); Coyhaique via Osorno (4 weekly; 24hr); Futaleufú (2 weekly; 12hr); Hornopirén (3 daily; 4hr); Osorno (every 30min; 1hr 30min); Puerto Varas (every 15min; 30min); Santiago (every 30min; 14hr); Temuco (hourly; 5hr); Valdivia (every 30min; 3hr).

BY FERRY

The Terminal Internacional de Pasajeros, 700m west of the bus terminal along Av. Angelmó, is home to two of the major ferry companies. Shared taxis (*colectivos*) run up and down the *costanera* between the Plaza and Angelmó (CH$450).

FERRY CRUISE OPERATORS

Naviera Austral Terminal Internacional de Pasajeros ☎ 65 227 0430, ⓦ navieraustral.cl. Serves Chaitén

INFORMATION

Tourist information Southeastern corner of the Plaza de Armas (April–Nov Mon–Fri 8.30am–1pm & 3–5.30pm,

(Mon, Thurs & Fri; 9hr; seat/berth CH$16,000/35,000).

Navimag Terminal Internacional de Pasajeros ☎ 65 243 2360, ⓦ navimag.com. Sails to Puerto Chacabuco (Wed & Sat at 11.59pm) and Puerto Natales (1–2 weekly at 4pm; 3-4 days; US$450 for shared Class C cabin, US$1050/person for AAA cabin). Class C accommodation consists of a bunk with bedding, a locker for storage and a curtain for privacy; bring your own towel. Class AAA gives you your own room with sea view, en-suite bathroom and private dining with the captain; there are several categories in between.

Skorpios Av Angelmó 1660 ☎ 65 225 5050, ⓦ skorpios .cl. This luxury cruise company runs two routes: Ruta Chonos, the six-day/five-night voyage to Laguna San Rafael (from US$2200/person if sharing a double) and Ruta Kawéskar, a four-day/three-night fjord cruise from Puerto Natales to remote glaciers and back (from US$1850/person if sharing a double).

BY CAR

All major car companies (Hertz, Avis, Europcar) are represented at the airport. If you wish to drive the Carretera Austral (see box, p.352) and are thinking of dropping the car off elsewhere, bear in mind that one-way dropoff fees can be crippling (an additional CH$300,000 or more).

Sat 9am–2pm; Dec–March daily 9am–9pm; ☎ 65 226 1823; ⓦ puertomonttchile.cl). Well-stocked and helpful.

Hospital Hospital Base, Seminario s/n (☎ 65 226 1100).

Money and exchange AFEX exchange, Av Diego Portales 516. There are many banks with ATMs along Guillermo Gallardo and Urmeneta.

ACCOMMODATION

Casa Perla Trigal 312 ☎ 65 226 2104, ⓦ casaperla .com. Simple rooms and dorms with shared bathrooms in a yellow-shingled Chilean home, packed with antiques and knick-knacks and ruled over by Perla the matriarch. It's an uphill hike to the quiet residential neighbourhood, but pluses include a warm family atmosphere and camping out back; English and German spoken. Dorms CH$10,000, doubles CH$24,000, camping/person CH$7000

Colores del Puerto Schwerter 207 ☎ 65 248 9360, ⓦ coloresdelpuerto.cl. Run by the wonderfully friendly and helpful Tomás, this informal hostel is only a 5min walk from the port and a 10min walk from the bus station, down a quiet street in Puerto Montt's historic neighbourhood. Three twin rooms share facilities and your host can fix up a simple breakfast; let him know in advance what time you're arriving. CH$30,000

Hospedaje Vista Al Mar Vivar 1337 ☎ 65 225 5625, ⓦ hospedajevistaalmar.cl. Justly popular guesthouse overlooking the city from a high vantage point and offering excellent value, especially for single travellers, with cosy en-suite rooms. Owner Eliana offers a really good breakfast that includes eggs and even home-made bread. CH$25,000

Hotel Don Luis Quillota 146 ☎ 65 220 0302, ⓦ hoteldonluis.cl. Central, efficient hotel catering largely to business travellers. Rooms are modern, carpeted and come with queen-size beds or twins, with modern bathrooms and a buffet breakfast included in the price. CH$55,000

Hotel Manquehue Av Seminario 252 ☎ 65 233 1000, ⓦ hotelmanquehue.cl. A few blocks uphill from the *costanera*, this bright, contemporary hotel welcomes you with the grand fireplace in the slate-covered lounge and appealing rooms equipped with all mod cons, livened up with splashes of colour. The service aims to please, and there's a good breakfast buffet. CH$55,000

Hotel Puertosur Huasco 143 ☎ 65 235 1212, ⓦ hotelpuertosur.cl. Resembling a Piet Mondrian work from the outside, this smart four-star hotel is a great choice for its location and its comfortable rooms (the ones on the 4th floor come with a terrace). You can also sample a good mix of Chilean and international cuisine while looking out to sea from *Restaurant Barlovento*. CH$60,000

Tren del Sur Santa Teresa 643 ☎ 65 234 3939, ⓦ www .trendelsur.cl. Uphill from the port you'll find this train-themed boutique hotel, where guests are referred to as "passengers" and where much of the furniture is made from railway trestles. The 16 en-suite rooms are comfortable (if a little dark) and centrally heated, and the on-site restaurant is decent, but you may find yourself waiting a while for the hot water. CH$45,000

EATING AND DRINKING

Angelmó Next to the fish market, Av Angelmó. By far the best spot for an inexpensive seafood meal, this collection of no-frills eateries serves such goodies as *picorocos* (barnacles), *curanto* (see p.322), *almejas* (razor clams), *erizos* (sea urchins) and *chupe de locos* (abalone chowder). Daily noon–8pm.

Café Haussmann San Martín 185 ☎ 65 223 7600. This branch of the Valdivia original is the place to sample *crudos* (steak tartare on toast with lemon juice, capers and minced onion; CH$1900), tuck into smoked meat with spuds and sauerkraut or indulge in some of the delicious cakes on display. Mains from CH$6000. Mon–Sat 9.30am–8.30pm, Sun 11am–8.30pm.

★**Chile Picante** Vicente Pérez Rosales ☎ 09 8454 8923, ⓦ chilepicanterestoran.cl. There's been a conspicuous lack of good restaurants in this residential neighbourhood. Until now, that is. All bright colours and bay views, the six tables at this compact restaurant fill up quickly, so reserve on weekends. The succinct, three-course menu is remarkably good value (CH$8500) and you might be treated to such temptations as salmon tartare, crab cannelloni and wild mushroom risotto. Mon–Sat 12.30–3.30pm & 7.30–11pm.

★**Cotele** Manfredini 1661, Pelluco ☎ 65 227 8000, ⓦ cotele.cl. You have to travel out of the centre for these exceptional steaks. Choose between the fillet, sirloin and the ultra-popular rib-eye, complemented by the extensive menu of Chilean reds, and observe the chef in action as he cooks your cut of meat to the desired degree. Mains from CH$10,000. Mon–Sat 1–4pm & 7.30pm–midnight.

Fogón del Leñador Rancagua 245 ☎ 65 248 9299. The wrought-iron chandeliers, cow-hide seats and blazing fireplace set the scene for this carnivorous experience. You're warned that your steak will take at least 30min to cook to perfection, and while you wait, you can tuck into home-made *sopaipillas* with an assortment of fresh salsas. Steak from CH$8000. Mon–Sat 12.30–3.30pm & 7.30–11pm.

Sherlock Rancagua at Antonio Varas ☎ 65 228 8888. Whether or not you believe the story that Sherlock Holmes once visited the city, this restobar is a place to investigate. The food is only so-so, but the wide selection of Chilean beers (including the Kunstmann range) and the congenial atmosphere make this a linger-worthy evening spot. Daily noon–1am.

Chiloé

316 Ancud

324 Around Ancud

326 Quemchi

327 Dalcahue

328 Around Dalcahue

331 Castro

335 Parque Nacional Chiloé
and around

338 Chonchi

339 Isla Lemuy

339 Queilén and around

340 Quellón

342 Parque Tantauco

PALAFITOS, CASTRO

Chiloé

Located immediately to the south of the Lake District, the fascinating Chiloé archipelago – part of a mountain range that sank below the waves following the last Ice Age – is a haven of rural tranquillity. The main island, Isla Grande, is South America's second largest island. Sliced in half lengthways by the Panamericana, it connects the two main towns, Ancud and Castro, with the port of Quellón and is easily explored by bike, car or bus. The densely forested Parque Nacional Chiloé and Parque Tantauco offer great opportunities to explore unique Chilote wilderness, while coastal villages and islands off Isla Grande's east coast – the most accessible being Isla Quinchao and Isla Lemuy – provide glimpses into traditional Chilote life.

7

Chiloé was originally populated by the native Chonos and Huilliche (southern Mapuche), who eked out a living from fishing and farming before the Spanish took possession of the island in 1567. For over three hundred years, Chiloé was isolated from mainland Chile owing to the fierce resistance of the mainland Mapuche to European colonists. As a result, the slow pace of island life saw little change. Ancud, in fact, was the last stronghold of the Spanish empire during the wars of Independence, before the final defeat by pro-independence forces in 1826. In spite of being used as a stopover during the California Gold Rush, Chiloé remained relatively isolated until the end of the twentieth century, though now it draws scores of visitors with its unique blend of architecture, cuisine and famous myths and legends.

More than 150 eighteenth- and nineteenth-century **wooden churches** and **chapels** dot the land. Chiloé is also one of the few places in the country where you can still see **palafitos**, precarious but picturesque timber houses on stilts, which were once the traditional dwellings of most of the fishermen of southern Chile. Much of the old culture has been preserved, assimilated into Hispanic tradition by a profound mixing of the Spanish and indigenous cultures that occurred here more than in other parts of South America, making today's Chiloé more "pagan Catholic" than Roman Catholic.

ARRIVAL AND DEPARTURE
CHILOÉ

By ferry There are regular ferry services from Pargua, 59km southwest of Puerto Montt on the mainland (daily every 30min, 6am–1.20am; 35min; CH$600, cars CH$10,700) to the village of Chacao on Isla Grande's northern shore; the ferry price is included in the price of the bus ticket to either Ancud or Castro. Scheduled ferry services also crisscross the gulf, linking Puerto Montt, Chaitén, Castro and Quellón.

Ancud

ANCUD is a pretty little seaside town and a lively fishing port, its comparatively relaxed pace of life an antithesis to the hustle and bustle of grittier Castro. Built on a small,

Maquí – The wonder berry p.319
Chilote mythology p.321
Hot rocks: the culinary secrets of curanto p.322
Chilote churches p.329

Castro: the indestructible city p.331
Festival Costumbrista p.333
Hiking in Parque Nacional Chiloé p.336
The bridge to nowhere p.337
Sendero de Chile p.338

MARINE OTTERS, PARQUE NACIONAL CHILOÉ

Highlights

❶ Curanto Dig into Chiloé's traditional dish, a savoury hotchpotch of meat, seafood and potato dumplings, cooked either in a pit in the ground or in a cast-iron pot. **See p.322**

❷ Magellanic penguins Go penguin- and sea-otter-spotting on a boat trip from Puñihuil, easily reachable from Ancud. **See p.325**

❸ Chepu Valley Stay at Chiloé's self-sufficient ecolodge and explore this tranquil valley's sunken forest in a kayak at dawn. **See p.326**

❹ Isla Quinchao A soothing spot to experience the slow pace of Chiloé's lesser isles and see one

of the island's most celebrated wooden churches. **See p.329**

❺ Palafitos in Castro Undeniably picturesque, Castro's traditional fishermen's houses on stilts are the sole remaining examples in the country. **See p.331**

❻ Parque Nacional Chiloé Hike through this region's once vast forests, home to foxes, pygmy deer and marine otters (*chungungo*). **See p.335**

❼ Parque Tantauco A vast private nature reserve with a well-designed infrastructure offering access to pristine and remote corners of southern Chiloé. **See p.342**

HIGHLIGHTS ARE MARKED ON THE MAP ON P.318

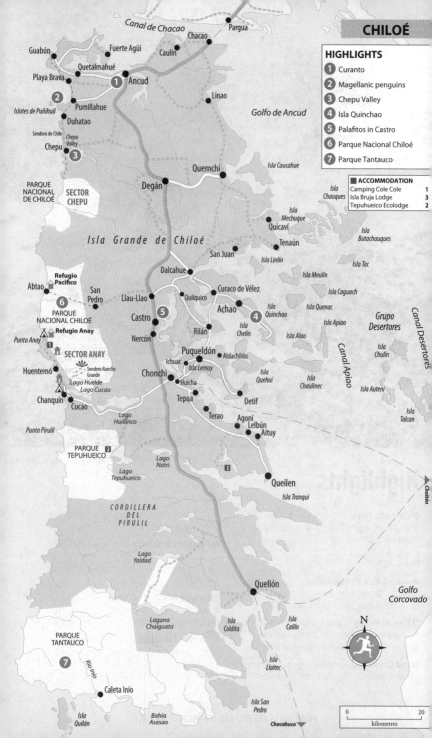

CHILOÉ

HIGHLIGHTS

1. Curanto
2. Magellanic penguins
3. Chepu Valley
4. Isla Quinchao
5. Palafitos in Castro
6. Parque Nacional Chiloé
7. Parque Tantauco

ACCOMMODATION

Camping Cole Cole	1
Isla Bruja Lodge	3
Tepuhueico Ecolodge	2

Canal de Chacao
Pargua
Chacao
Guabún
Fuerte Agüi
Caulín
Quetalmahué
Playa Brava
Ancud
Linao
Islotes de Puñihuil
Pumillahue
Duhatao
Golfo de Ancud
Sendero de Chile
Chepu Valley
Chepu
Quemchi
Isla Caucahue
Isla Chauques
PARQUE NACIONAL DE CHILOÉ
SECTOR CHEPU
Degán
Isla Mechuque
Quicaví
Tenaún
Isla Butachauques
Isla Grande de Chiloé
San Juan
Isla Linlín
Isla Tac
Dalcahue
Isla Meulín
Refugio Pacífico
Abtao
San Pedro
Curaco de Vélez
Isla Caguach
Llau-Llao
Quilquico
Achao
Isla Quenac
Grupo Desertores
PARQUE NACIONAL CHILOÉ
Castro
Isla Quinchao
Isla Apiao
Isla Chulín
Refugio Anay
Rilán
Isla Chelin
Isla Alao
Punta Anay
Nercón
Isla Aulén
SECTOR ANAY
Puqueldón
Aldachildo
Canal Apiao
Isla Auteni
Huentemó
Ichuac
Isla Lemuy
Isla Quehui
Sendero Rancho Grande
Chonchi
Isla Chaulinec
Lago Huelde
Huicha
Lago Cucao
Isla Talcan
Chanquín
Tepua
Detif
Cucao
Terao
Lago Huillinco
Agoní
Lelbún
Punta Pirulil
Aituy
PARQUE TEPUHUEICO
Lago Natri
Lago Tepuhueico
Queilen
Isla Tranqui
CORDILLERA DEL PIRULIL
Quellón
Golfo Corcovado
Lago Yaldad
Laguna Chaiguata
Isla Coldita
Isla Cailín
PARQUE TANTAUCO
Isla Llaitec
Río Inío
Caleta Inío
Isla San Pedro
Isla Quilán
Bahía Asasao
Chacabuco

N

Chaitén

0   20
kilometres

square promontory jutting into the Canal de Chacao and the Golfo de Quetalmahue, the town centres on the appealing **Plaza de Armas**, decorated with figures from Chilote mythology and abuzz with craft stalls and street musicians in the summer. The colourful **Mercado Municipal**, one block to the north, is the place to grab a cheap meal or pick up fresh produce and some local crafts, though there's also the new, attractive temporary produce and crafts market, **Feria Municipal**, a few blocks east of the centre along Arturo Prat.

Brief history

Ancud was founded in 1769 as a Spanish stronghold and, after Peruvian independence in 1824, became the crown's last desperate foothold in South America. Its forts resisted one attempt at capture, but finally fell in January 1826 when the lonely and demoralized Spanish garrison fled into the forest in the face of a small *criollo* attack. The remains of these Spanish forts – **Fuerte San Antonio** in the town and lonesome, cannon-studded **Fuerte Agüi** on Península Lacuy to the northwest – can still be visited today.

7

Fuerte de San Antonio and around

Mon–Fri 8.30am–9pm, Sat & Sun 9am–8pm • Free

From the harbour, a crushed-shell promenade heads south past half a dozen intriguing pieces of **sculpture**, while Calle Lord Cochrane follows the coast to the north to the reconstructed walls of the Spanish **Fuerte de San Antonio**. The fort affords a sweeping view over the Golfo de Quetalmahue and out to the Pacific Ocean, while its sixteen cannon, combined with the fifteen in Fuerte Agüi (on the Península Lacuy across the water), could sink any ship entering the Bahía de Ancud.

Calle Bellavista, parallel to Cochrane, leads further north to the **Playa Arena Gruesa**, a popular swimming beach in summer, sheltered by high cliffs.

Museo Regional de Ancud

Libertad 370 • Jan & Feb Mon–Fri 10.30am–7.30pm, Sat & Sun 10am–7.30pm; March–Dec Tues–Fri 10am–5.30pm, Sat, Sun & holidays 10am–2pm • CH$600

The outside patio of the **Museo Regional** houses an exact replica of the *Goleta Ancud*, a **schooner** with which the first Chilean settlers took possession of the Magellan Strait in September 1843. It was the culmination of a great tradition of Chilote boat-building, which included boats made from rough planks lashed together with vines and caulked with *alerce* bark. Also outside is an entire skeleton of a blue whale.

The permanent collection consists of partly interactive Spanish-language exhibits, covering various aspects of life in the archipelago, including traditional industries such

---

MAQUÍ – THE WONDER BERRY

Stronger than a blueberry. More powerful than the açai berry. Able to battle ageing and neurodegenerative diseases. Look! In the evergreen tree! It's Maquí the Wonder Berry! The **maquí berry** (*Aristotelia chilensis*), also known as the Chilean wineberry, is native to Chile's Valdivian rainforests and has been used by the Mapuche for centuries, both as a foodstuff and as a means of preparing *chicha* (an alcoholic drink made from fermented berries). In recent years, scientific studies have discovered that the maquí berry has far higher antioxidizing properties than its nearest competing "superfoods" – blackberries, açai berries and blueberries. While studies are still limited, it is believed that the consumption of antioxidants helps to prevent degenerative diseases such as cancer and Alzheimer's, and over the last three years the fame of this small, dark blue berry has spread far and wide. Maquí berry products can be found at ⓦ islanatura.com.

as fishing, textiles and pottery, Chiloé's natural environment and wildlife, European conquest, archaeology and religious art, with striking photographs illustrating the impact of the 1960 earthquake which devastated much of the island, and a vaguely menacing stone Trauco (see p.321)

The basement houses temporary exhibitions, such as a recent one on textiles by the artisans belonging to the Fundación Artesanías de Chile, an organisation dedicated to promoting traditional handicrafts around the country.

Centro de Visitantes de las Iglesias de Chiloé

Federico Errázuriz 227 • Daily 9.30am–7pm • ⓦ iglesiasdechiloe.cl • Suggested donation CH$500

If you are planning to visit Chiloé's spectacular **churches** (see p.329), this excellent museum/visitor centre makes an excellent starting point. Exhibits inside this church building include antique doors and other fragments, hung in the

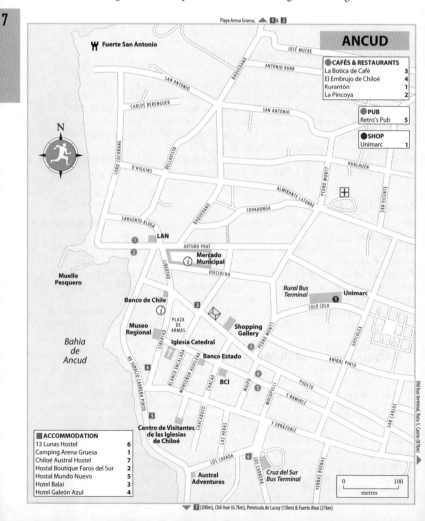

CHILOTE MYTHOLOGY

The Chiloé islands have long been rife with myths and legends, especially in the remote rural regions, where tradition and superstition hold sway, with colourful supernatural creatures cropping up in stories throughout the archipelago.

Basilisco A snake with the head of a cockerel, the Basilisco turns people to stone with its gaze. At night, the Basilisco enters houses and sucks the breath from sleeping inhabitants, so that they waste away into shrivelled skeletons. The only way to be rid of it is to burn the house down.

Brujo This is the general term for a witch; in Chiloé, there are only male witches and their legendary cave is rumoured to be near the village of Quicaví. To become a witch, an individual must wash away baptism in a waterfall for forty days, assassinate a loved one, make a purse out of their skin in which to carry their book of spells and sign a pact with the devil in their own blood, stating when the evil one can claim their soul. Witches are capable of great mischief and can cause illness and death, even from afar.

Caleuche This ghostly ship glows in the fog, travels at great speeds above and below the water, emitting beautiful music, carrying the witches to their next stop. Journeying through the archipelago, it's crewed by shipwrecked sailors and fishermen who have perished at sea.

Fiura An ugly, squat woman with halitosis, she lives in the woods, clothed in moss. The coquettish Fiura bathes in waterfalls, where she seduces young men before driving them insane.

Invunche Stolen at birth by witches, and raised on the flesh of the dead and cats' milk, the Invunche was transformed into a deformed monster with one leg crooked behind his back. He feeds on goats' flesh and stands guard at the entrance to the legendary witches' cave, the Cueva de Quicaví, grunting or emitting bloodcurdling screams. If you're unlucky enough to spot him, you'll be frozen to that spot forever.

Pincoya A fertility goddess of extraordinary beauty, Pincoya personifies the spirit of the ocean and is responsible for the abundance or scarcity of fish in the sea. She dances half-naked, draped in kelp, on the beaches or tops of waves. If she's spotted facing the sea, the village will enjoy an ample supply of seafood. If she's looking towards the land, there will be a shortage.

Trauco A deformed and ugly troll who dwells in the forest, Trauco dresses in ragged clothes and a conical cap and carries a stone axe or wooden club, a *pahueldœn*. His breath makes him irresistible to women, and he is blamed for all unexplained pregnancies on the island.

Voladora The witches' messenger, the Voladora is a woman who transforms into a black bird by vomiting up her internal organs. The Voladora travels under the cover of night and can only be detected by her terrible cries, which bring bad luck. If the Voladora is unable to recover her innards at the end of the night, she is stuck in bird shape forever.

7

centre of the room and illuminated to great effect by the light from the stained-glass windows. Diagrams along the walls show each stage of construction of a typical Chilote church, but the biggest draw here are the incredibly detailed scale models of the island's most spectacular churches, giving you a taste of the real thing.

ARRIVAL AND INFORMATION | ANCUD

By bus The majority of long-distance buses – Cruz del Sur and its affiliates – arrive at the Terminal de Buses on Los Carrera 850, a 5min walk from the Plaza de Armas. Queilén Bus still uses the largely abandoned and inconveniently located old bus terminal 1.5km along Arturo Prat.

Destinations Castro (every 15min; 1hr 15min); Puerto Montt (every 30min; 1hr 30min–2hr); Quellón (16 daily; 4hr).

The rural bus terminal, serving numerous villages, is on Colo Colo, above the supermarket Unimarc; note there are no Sun departures.

Destinations Caulín (Mon–Sat 1–4 daily; 30min); Chacao (every 15min; 30min); Chepu (3 weekly on Mon, Wed & Fri at 4pm; 1hr); Península Lacuy and Fuerte Agüi (Mon–Sat 1–2 daily; 45min); Puñihuil (2–3 daily; 1hr); Quemchi (up to 12 daily; 1hr); Quicaví (1–2 daily Mon–Sat; 1hr 45min).

Sernatur office Plaza de Armas at Libertad 665 (Dec–Feb Mon–Fri 8.30am–7pm, Sat & Sun 9.30am–7pm; March–Nov Mon–Thurs 8.30am–6pm, Fri 8.30am–5pm; ☎ 65 262 2800, ✉ infochiloe@sernatur.cl). Offers information on the entire archipelago. Very helpful staff.

Websites ⓦ chiloe.cl and ⓦ interpatagonia.cl also useful.

TOURS

Austral Adventures Av Costanera 904 ☎ 65 262 5977, ⓦ austral-adventures.com. Established American–run outfit catering to travellers wanting to see Chiloé off-the-beaten-track, leading expertly guided trips that may include visits to the penguin colonies, rugged hikes, kayaking in a sunken forest, and immersion into Chilote culture. Tailor-made trips available.

ACCOMMODATION

★**13 Lunas Hostel** Los Carrera 855 ☎ 65 262 2106, ⓦ 13lunas.cl. The young, English-speaking owner of this beautifully renovated, shingled wooden house gets full marks for backpacker-luring facilities: spacious rooms with large, comfortable beds and lockers, ample common spaces with guitars, cable TV and table football, BBQ area, spacious guest kitchen and outdoor terraces. A basement double lacks windows but bonus points for extras such as bike rentals, tour info and spirit of camaraderie. Dorms CH$10,500, doubles CH$33,000

Camping Arena Gruesa Constanera Norte 292 ☎ 65 262 3428, ⓦ hotelarenagruesa.cl. At this great cliff-top location, a few minutes' walk from the Arena Gruesa beach, there are three choices of accommodation: a large campsite with excellent sea views, hot water and individual shelters with lights for each site; several fully equipped *cabañas* for 2/4/6/8 people; and well-kept rooms in the white-shingled budget hotel. Camping/person CH$4500, doubles CH$26,000, *cabañas* CH$38,000

Chiloé Austral Hostel Yungay 282 ☎ 65 262 5818. Its snug, wood-panelled rooms overlooking the Bay of Ancud, this blue-shingled Chilote house sits just half a block up from the *costanera*. While little English is spoken, Roberto and his family go out of their way to make guests feel welcome, and his mum whips up home-made bread for breakfast. Dorms CH$10,000, doubles CH$22,000

Hostal Boutique Faros del Sur Costanera Norte 320 ☎ 65 262 5799, ⓦ farosdelsur.cl. Decked out in placid creams and with homely touches such as locally woven bedcovers, the thirteen rooms at this cliff-top guesthouse all have sea views; for the best views, snag the corner suite. The most striking feature, however, is the splendid wood-panelled guest lounge with tall ceilings, chunky stone fireplace and light streaming in from the vast windows. Guest kitchen available. CH$35,000

★**Hostal Mundo Nuevo** Costanera 748 ☎ 65 262 8383, ⓦ newworld.cl. Longtime favourite of international travellers, this guesthouse along the *costanera* offers bright, top-notch dorms and rooms with polished wooden floors, a great ratio of guests per bathroom, guest kitchen and handy folders full of info on the surrounding area. Sit down to a good breakfast (which includes home-made bread), ask helpful Swiss owner Martin for help with arranging excursions, or simmer in the hot tub (CH$12,000/ hour) overlooking the waves. Dorms CH$13,000, doubles CH$34,000

HOT ROCKS: THE CULINARY SECRETS OF CURANTO

Chiloé's signature dish, **curanto**, has been prepared for centuries using cooking methods very similar to those used in Polynesia, testimony to the legendary sailing prowess of the Polynesians. First, extremely hot rocks are placed at the bottom of an earthen pit; then, a layer of shellfish is added, followed by chunks of smoked meat, chicken, *longanisa* (sausage), potatoes, *chapaleles* and *milcaos* (potato dumplings). The pit is then covered with *nalca* (Chilean wild rhubarb) leaves; as the shellfish cooks, the shells spring open, releasing their juices onto the hot rocks, steaming the rest of the ingredients.

Traditional *curanto* (*curanto en hoyo*) is **slow-cooked in the ground** for a day or two, but since traditional cooking methods are only used in the countryside, most end up sampling *curanto en olla*, also known as *pulmay*, oven-baked in cast-iron pots. The dish comes with hot shellfish broth, known to the locals as "liquid Viagra", to be drunk (and used for dipping your shellfish) during the meal.

Good bets for *curanto en hoyo* are *Al Norte del Sur* (p.326) and *Agroturismo San Antonio* (p.326), while *Kurantón*, *La Pincoya* and some of the *palafito* restaurants behind the craft market in Castro whip up some of the best *curanto en olla* on the island.

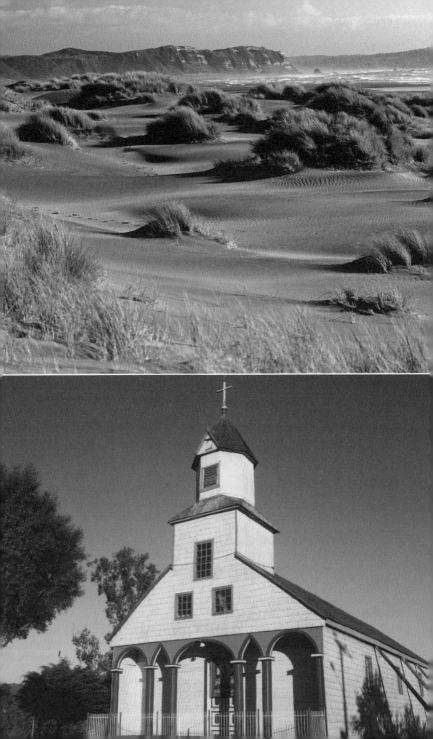

Hotel Balai Pudeto 169 ☎ 65 262 2966, ⓦ hotelbalai .cl. 'Quirky' and 'whimsical' are two adjectives that come to mind when you're confronted with ye olde diving suits, mermaid figureheads and other knick-knacks that clutter the common spaces. The rooms are not too bright, the bathrooms are of the swing-a-cat variety, and the breakfast is basic, but the location couldn't be more central. **CH$30,000**

Hotel Galeón Azul Libertad 751 ☎ 65 262 2567, ⓦ hotelgaleonazul.cl. A nautical theme prevails throughout this handsome hilltop hotel – from model boats and porthole windows to ship-shape, high-ceilinged rooms which shudder atmospherically during high winds. Boons include splendid views across the Golfo de Quetalmahue and a greenery-bedecked restaurant that serves seafood. **CH$62,000**

EATING AND DRINKING

La Botica de Café Pudeto 277. Cheerful café that brews excellent coffee to go with the home-made cheesecake and other sweet offerings. Inexpensive sandwiches and a few Chilean staples also on the menu if you're after something more substantial. Mains from CH$4000. Mon–Sat 9.30am–8pm, Sun 11am–4pm.

El Embrujo de Chiloé Maipú 650. This wood-panelled café, popular with local regulars, is another good option for coffee, cake and chunky sandwiches. Mains from CH$2500. Daily noon–8pm.

★ **Kurantón** Prat 94. The legend reads: "Curanto: helping people to have good sex since 1826". Tuck into this veritable mountain of shellfish and potato dumplings amidst photos of old Ancud, carvings of Chilote mythical creatures and nautical paraphernalia and wonder whether those people had to wait for their digestion to settle first. *Curanto* CH$7700. Daily 12.30–3pm & 7–11.30pm.

La Pincoya Prat 61 ☎ 65 262 2613. Overlooking the harbour, this family-run restaurant with an old-school, bow-tied waiter, is a good bet for excellent fishy offerings, such as *curanto en olla* and salmon *cancato* (CH$7700). Daily noon–3pm & 7–11pm; erratic hours in the off-season.

Retro's Pub Ramírez 317. Whether you come to this intimate pub to ward off homesickness with their monster burgers, home-made gnocchi, overflowing burritos or immense pizzas, or to court oblivion by knocking back potent Green Demon cocktails at the bar, you're in good company: you're surrounded by images of Bob Marley, Jim Morrison, James Dean and other live-hard, die-youngs. Pizzas CH$9000–12,300. Daily noon–11.30pm.

DIRECTORY

Car rental Salfa Sur, Arturo Prat at Pedro Montt (ⓦ salfasur.cl).
Hospital Almirante Latorre 301 (☎ 65 262 2356).
Money and exchange There are ATMs at Banco de Chile, 621 Chorillos, on the Plaza, as well as BCI, Chacao at Ramírez.
Post office Pudeto at Blanco Encalada (Mon–Sat 9am–noon & 2–5pm).

Around Ancud

West of Ancud lies Península Lacuy, its clifftop **Fuerte Agüi** famous as Spain's last stronghold in Chile, while south of the town you find **Islotes de Puñihuil**, a thriving penguin colony that's home to both Magellanic and Humboldt penguins.

Further south still, **Chepu Valley**, formed by the powerful tsunami after the earthquake of 1960, is a top destination for birders, its wetlands home to an abundant wealth of bird life. East of Ancud, a turn-off leads to **Caulín**, one of the best spots in Chile for oysters.

Caulín

Nine kilometres along the Panamericana on the way to Ancud from Chacao, a turn-off to the right leads to the hamlet of **Caulín** on the edge of a windswept, 1km-wide sandy beach, where you can often see locals collecting and laying out a stinking grey seaweed to dry. Called *pelillo* ("fine hair") because it resembles human hair, this alga has a dual purpose: agar-agar, a gelatinous substance used in the food and cosmetics industries can be extracted from it, or the seaweed can be woven into a fibre.

Caulín is famous for its specific type of small, sweet **oysters**, the likes of which are only otherwise found in New Zealand.

Península Lacuy

A paved road leads west out of Ancud, passing the turn-off towards Pumillahue and the Islotes de Puñihuil at 14km, and bisecting the tiny fishing community of **Quetalmahue** before reaching the **Península Lacuy**. The road forks: the left (and as yet unpaved) branch leads to the wind-whipped sand dunes and cliffs of **Playa Guabún**; if you have your own wheels, you can follow the picturesque loop of a dirt road past the beach, through Chilote countryside, to where you started from. Chiloé's northernmost section of the Sendero de Chile (see box, p.338) also starts at Guabún, though much of the trail consists of dirt roads. The right branch continues to **Faro Corona**, an isolated lighthouse on a remote promontory, with yet another (unpaved) fork splitting off to the right after 13km, depositing you below **Fuerte Agüi** (no set hours; entry CH$250), the last toehold of the Spanish Empire in South America. The forlorn cannons are still in place, and from the ruins you get great views of the bay of Ancud and beyond.

Pingüineras de Puñihuil

Puñihuil • Sept–March daily 10.30am–5.45pm • CH$8000 • ☎ 09 8317 4302 • ⓦ pinguineraschiloe.cl • Driving to Pumillahue is straightforward enough; you can also catch a bus (see below) or share a taxi (CH$16,000–20,000 one-way)

Reachable from Ancud along a mostly paved 28km road is the seaside village of Pumillahue. Just off the coast lies the rocky outcrop of the **Islotes de Puñihuil**, a **penguin colony** monitored by Ecoturismo Puñihuil, a local organization dedicated to the protection of the penguins. This thriving colony is unique to Chile in that it is visited by both Magellanic and Humboldt penguins in the breeding and rearing season, between December and March. The adults fish most of the day, so the optimum visiting time is either in the morning or mid-to-late afternoon.

Three companies based in the guesthouse and restaurants on the beach pool their customers and run well-explained trips in twenty-person boats to see the penguins and other marine fauna, including the sleek *chungungos* (marine otters). The excursions depart directly from the beach (at least hourly; 40min); it's best to reserve in advance during peak season.

The Chepu Valley

Heading south towards Castro, Ruta 5 (the main road that traverses the island) passes two gravelled turnoffs to Chepu – one at 12.5km south and the other at 25km south, both leading through farmland to the **Chepu Valley**. You'll see plenty of undulating pastureland and, making up the scattered settlement of Chepu, a few farmhouses spread out along the gravel roads. The main attraction is a large stretch of **wetlands**, created in 1960 when the tsunami caused by the most powerful earthquake ever recorded flooded a section of coastal forest. Today, the sunken forest provides a thriving habitat for over a hundred different bird species, as well as ground for **kayaking** and fishing.

ARRIVAL AND DEPARTURE   **AROUND ANCUD**

CAULÍN

By bus Buses Caulín (☎ 09 9222 8223) run to Caulín (Mon–Sat 1–4 daily; 30min) from Ancud's Terminal de Buses Rurales.

PENÍNSULA LACUY

By bus Minibuses Ahuí depart from Ancud's rural bus terminal for Fuerte Agüi (Mon–Sat 1–2 daily; 1hr).
By car Take Av Costanera south out of Ancud and follow the signposted road.

PUMILLAHUE & ISLOTES DE PUÑIHUÍL

By bus Buses Mar Brava (☎ 65 262 2312) runs a regular service from Ancud's rural bus terminal (Mon–Sat 3 daily; last bus returning at 3pm; 30min).
By tour Most tour companies in Ancud and Castro offer trips to the penguin colony.
By car Take Av Costanera south out of Ancud and follow the signposts to Pumillahue.

7

THE CHEPU VALLEY

By bus Buses Peter runs from Ancud's rural bus terminal to Chepu (Mon, Wed & Fri at 4pm; 1hr).

By car Take the Panamericana from Ancud and then either the gravel road to Chepu from Km25; or take another gravel road from the Km12 turnoff, though this route is longer and rougher.

ACCOMMODATION AND EATING

CAULÍN

Ostras Caulín Seafront ☎ 09 9643 7005. Oysters come in many guises at this fine restaurant: fried; in a cocktail; as a cream-of-oyster soup; and, the most popular choice, as an oyster platter featuring one of three types of oysters on the half shell (from CH$8000). Daily during daylight hours.

PENÍNSULA LACUY

★**Chil-hue** Km 6.4 Camino Lechagua ☎ 09 9644 2578, ⓦ chil-hue.com. Three unique living spaces – the open-plan, wooden-beamed *Beach House* and the wood-shingled *Tower* and the *Studio* beckon travellers who come to this deserted beach in search of silence, communion with nature and dolphin sightings from their window. Fresh, gourmet meals (breakfast CH$3500, four-course dinner CH$12,000) are conjured up from fresh local ingredients by Peruvian gourmet chef Sandra and yoga classes are on offer. CH$60,000

Al Norte del Sur 300m up the road to Guabún from the road fork ☎ 09 9919 5445, ⓦ alnortedelsur.cl. This homely little restaurant is a rising star of the *agroturismo* movement, and there's no menu; you'll get whatever's been cooked up on the day, such as *pastél de papas* with seafood, accompanied by organic greens from their own garden and a fresh herbal tea. Rustic accommodation also available. *Menú del día* CH$5500. Daily 10am–10pm. CH$24,000

Restaurant Quetalmahue Quetalmahue, 12km west of Ancud en route to Península Lacuy ☎ 09 8791 9410, ⓦ restaurantequetalmahue.es.tl. Located in the tiny village of Quetalmahue, with wooden carvings of mythological Chilote figures on the patio and its grounds covered in discarded mussel shells, this rural restaurant is an excellent bet for *curanto en hoyo*. Daily from around 2pm till around 9pm; call ahead to doublecheck opening hours.

ISLOTES DE PUÑIHUÍL

Restaurant El Rincón. On the beach. A good seafront eatery with a fishy menu. Avoid consuming *locos* (abalone) as it is endangered and tends to get fished illegally out of season. Daily noon–5.30pm.

THE CHEPU VALLEY

Agroturismo San Antonio Camino a Chepu Km2 ☎ 09 9643 7046, ⓔ agroturismosanantonio @gmail.com. Set amidst beautiful flowering gardens, the rural home of the Dimter Maldonado family welcomes you into its fold, largely thanks to the efforts of super-friendly hostess María Louisa. The rooms are simple yet comfortable, there's wi-fi out here in the countryside and if there are enough takers, this family cooks up a fantastic *curanto en hoyo*. Only Spanish spoken. Take the first turnoff to Chepu from Ancud for 2km. CH$24,000

★**Chepu Adventures** Camino a Chepu, Km13.2 ☎ 09 9227 4517 or 65 284 0543, ⓦ chepuadventures .com. This wonderful, award-winning ecolodge has become a destination in its own right through the efforts and warmth of Fernando and Amory, a Santiago couple who gave up city life to live self-sufficiently on a gorgeous bluff overlooking the river, all their energy needs supplied by solar panels and a wind turbine. There's room for nine guests in total in the snug, en suite two to three-person *cabañas* and cheaper *dormis* (mini-cabañas with bunk beds; bring your own sleeping bag), and there's a new campsite in the offing. Accommodation packages include the self-guided "Kayaking at Dawn" in the sunken forest below, plus meals, and must be booked in advance; you can arrange kayaking here even if not staying. If you don't have your own transport, pickup from "Cruce de Chepu", Km25 can be arranged. *Dormi* package CH$25,000, *cabañas* package CH$161,000

Quemchi

East from the Panamericana, 41km south of Ancud, a pictureque coastal road leads along the coast to **Quemchi**, an attractive little fishing town with narrow, irregular streets sloping down to the water's edge. On a sunny day, the sight of snow-tipped volcanoes beyond the village makes for an impressive sight. A couple of kilometres south, there's a tiny wooded island, **Isla Aucar**, only accessible by a 500m-long footbridge. Nestled on the island is a small wooden **church** with a duck-egg-blue roof and white walls.

ARRIVAL AND DEPARTURE

QUEMCHI

By bus Quemchi is served by up to ten buses per day by four different bus companies from Ancud's Terminal de Buses Rurales; the most frequent services are run by Buses Aucar (5 daily, 9am–7pm; 1hr) and Expreso Quicaví (2 daily; 1hr). There are also buses from Castro (Mon–Sat 18 daily, 3 on Sun, 7am–7.30pm; 1hr 15min).

EATING

El Chejo Diego Bahamonde 251 ☎65 269 1490. Wander into the kitchen at this wonderful family-run restaurant and peer into the pots to see what Elsa is cooking on any given day; the menu ranges from grilled fish to *casuela Chilote* (Chilote stew with *cochayuyo* seaweed) and *curanto*. It is the opinion of many that Elsa's seafood *empanadas* are the best on the island. Daily 1–3.30pm & 7.30–10.30pm.

Dalcahue

The bustling, historical town of **DALCAHUE** lies 20km northeast of Castro via the turn-off at Llau-Llao. It is famous for its thriving traditional boat-building industry and the Sunday **Feria Artesanal**, when artisans come from nearby islands to sell woollen crafts, wood carvings and hand-woven baskets, making it a better bet than Castro if you're shopping exclusively for Chilote goods. Dalcahue also provides the only link with nearby **Isla Quinchao** (see p.329), the second largest in the Chiloé archipelago.

Most of the action is centred around the attractive Plaza de Armas and the open-sided market building on the waterfront. On the plaza rises the imposing, UNESCO-listed Iglesia de Nuestra Señora de Los Dolores, which dates to 1893 and boasts a unique nine-arched portico (under extensive renovation at research time).

ARRIVAL AND DEPARTURE

DALCAHUE

By bus Buses Dalcahue Expreso run daily from Castro (Mon–Sat every 15min, Sun every 30min; 30min).

TOURS

Altué Expeditions ☎09 9419 6809, ⊛seakayakchile .com. Excellent outfit based near Dalcahue that offers multi-day trips around the Chiloé archipelago, as well as multi-activity trips in the Lake District and Patagonia; pick-up from Castro available.

ACCOMMODATION

Hostal Encanto Patagón Montt 146 ☎65 264 1651 ⊛hostalencantopatagon.blogspot.com. Sitting right on the *costanera*, this venerable 120-year-old house with sloping wooden floors accommodates travellers in a clutch of singles, doubles and triples named after locations on the Carretera Austral. The owners, Carlos and Cecilia, whip up delicious home-cooked meals and can help you if you're planning an adventurous getaway to some of the far-flung islands of the Chiloé Archipelago. **CH$24,000**

Hostal Lanita O'Higgins 50 ☎65 264 2020, ⊛lanitahostal.blogspot.com. Mother-hen-like Anita fusses over her guests and makes them feel like part of the family. Besides the snug five-bed dorm there's a double and a twin, and breakfast includes freshly-baked bread. The only downside is the occasional queue for the two bathrooms. Dorms **CH$10,000**, doubles **CH$32,000**

EATING

★ **Café Artesanías Casita de Piedra** Montt 144 ☎09 9489 9050. Bringing urban sophistication to Dalcahue's *costanera*, this split level boutique/café kills two birds with one stone. Purchase your woollen goodies downstairs (credit cards accepted) and then head up to the cheerful yellow café upstairs for a hit of espresso or a ristretto, summoning the waitress with the press of a handy button on each table. Tues–Sat 10.30am–2pm & 3.30–8pm, Sun 10.30am–2pm.

Las Cocinera Dalcahue Next to the Feria Artesanal. This indoor collection of food stalls inside an establishment that resembles an upside-down boat is an excellent place to try inexpensive Chilote specialities. Shop around as local women dish up *curanto*, *empanadas*, *milcaos* (flat potato dumplings studded with smoked pork) and sweet baked twists knows as *calzones rotos* (lit: "torn underpants"). *Doña Lula*, Puesto 8, does fabulous *empanadas*; *Tenchita*, Puesto 2, is a favourite for *canacato* and other substantial

7

mains, while *La Nenita*, Puesto 4, offers very fresh salmon ceviche. Daily 8am–9pm.

Refugio de Navegantes San Martín 165 ☎65 264 1128. With its vast slate fireplace and stellar location right on the plaza, this shingled house surrounded by monkey puzzle trees is a port in a storm for travellers in search of comfy seats to sink into and a menu full of delicious light bites. Their chocolate cheesecake is superb. Mains from CH$4500. Daily 9am–11pm; shorter hours outside Jan & Feb.

Around Dalcahue

For those who wish to witness traditional Chilote life in settlements where time seems to stand still, there are few better places to do so than Chiloé's east coast. If you have your own vehicle, take the gravel roads to tiny, sleepy coastal villages, where on a grey and misty day you can almost imagine the characters from Chiloé's mythology (see box, p.321) coming to life. Those without their own wheels can cross over to the island of Quinchao, characterized by its rolling farmland, small towns with striking traditional churches and the daily market in Achao, attended by sellers from neighbouring islands.

Península Rilán

Between Dalcahue and Castro, this tranquil rural peninsula has grown in popularity in recent years. Besides its Iglesia de Santa María de Rilán, one of the UNESCO churches, the peninsula boasts rich bird life thanks to its extensive wetlands, as well as several upmarket boutique hotels.

Tenaún

From Dalcahue, an attractive gravel road heads northeast towards Quemchi, following the coast. Thirty-seven kilometres along, a small bumpy road with two forks (first take the left, then the right) heads down to the somnolent coastal village of **TENAÚN**. Smiling down at the attractive waterfront and quaint little fishermen's cottages is arguably Chiloé's most extraordinary **church**. Founded in 1734 but rebuilt in 1861, and recently spruced up, it's dazzling to look at: painted white with two huge pale blue stars daubed onto the wall above the entrance, and topped off by three vibrant blue and red towers.

Quicaví

Six kilometres beyond Tenaún on the main road, a turn to the east leads, after 7km, to the tiny seafront village of **QUICAVÍ**, whose sleepiness belies its importance in Chilote mythology. It's said that somewhere along the nearby coast lies the legendary **Cueva de Quicaví**, where a Spanish warlock left a powerful book of spells for the resident *brujos* after being defeated in a magic duel. The Spanish Inquisition, and many others besides, have searched for the cave in vain. Perhaps because of this wealth of superstition, the missionaries built a larger than usual **church** in Quicaví.

Isla Mechuque

Small launches depart from the jetties at Tenaún and Quicaví for the beautiful island of **ISLA MECHUQUE**, the largest and most easily accessible of the Chauques subgroup. Since a quorum of passengers is required, the surest way of making this magical trip past unspoiled island scenery is to go on an organized excursion from Castro in the summer (see p.333). The highlight of such trips to the tiny village of Mechuque with its shingled *palafitos*, is a genuine *curanto en hoyo* prepared before your eyes in an outdoor pit (needs to be organized in advance).

CHILOTE CHURCHES

It is impossible to visit Chiloé and not be struck by the sight of the archipelago's incredible **wooden churches**. In the early nineteenth century these impressively large buildings would have been the heart of a Chilote village. Several of the churches have been declared national monuments, an honour crowned in 2001 when UNESCO accepted sixteen of them on its prestigious World Heritage list. In case you're a church completist, of these sixteen churches (Colo, Tenaún, San Juan, Dalcahue, Achao, Quinchao, Caguach, Rilán, Chelín, Nercón, Chonchi, Ichuac, Aldachildo, Detif, Vilupulli and Castro; see p.331) only fourteen are on Chiloé Island proper; Chelín and Caguach are found on tiny islands off the east coast, with the latter particularly far-flung and difficult to reach.

The churches generally face the sea and are built near a beach with an open area, plaza or *explanada* in front of them. The outside of the churches is almost always bare, and the only thing that expresses anything but functionality is the three-tiered, **hexagonal bell tower** that rises up directly above an open-fronted portico. The facades, doors and windows are often brightly painted, and the walls clad with *tejuelas* (wooden tiles or shingles). All the churches have three naves separated by columns, which in the larger buildings are highly decorated, supporting barrel-vaulted ceilings. The ceilings are often painted, too, with allegorical panels or sometimes with golden constellations of stars painted on an electric blue background.

HISTORY

Only the *pueblos* with a priest had a main church, or *iglesia parroquial*. If there was no church, the missionaries used to visit once a year, as part of their so-called *misión circular*. Using only native canoes, they carried everything required to hold a mass with them. When the priest arrived, one of the eldest Chilotes would lead a procession carrying an image of Jesus, and behind him two youths would follow with depictions of San Juan and the Virgin. They would be followed by married men carrying a statue of San Isidro and married women carrying one of Santa Neoburga.

If the *pueblo* was important enough there would be a small *capilla* (bell tower) with altars to receive the statues. The building where the missionaries stayed was known as a *residencia*, *villa*, *casa ermita* or *catecera*, and was looked after by a local trustee called a *fiscal*, whose function was somewhere between that of a verger and lay preacher. This honorary position still exists and, in Chiloé's remoter areas, the *fiscal* commands great respect in his community. For more information on Chiloé's churches, check out the informative ⓦ interpatagonia.com /iglesiaschiloe.

Isla Quinchao

For some, **ISLA QUINCHAO** is the cultural heart of the whole of Chiloé. Rich in traditional wooden architecture, this island is a mere ten-minute ferry ride from Dalcahue. A paved road runs across Isla Quinchao through the only two towns of any size, **Curaco de Vélez** and **Achao**, both of which offer a taste of traditional Chilote life and both of which can be seen on an easy day-trip from Castro or Dalcahue.

Curaco de Vélez

Twelve kilometres from the ferry terminal, **Curaco de Vélez** comprises a couple of streets of weather-beaten shingled houses set around a beautiful bay and bordered by gently rolling hills. The Plaza de Armas features an unusual sight – a decapitated **church steeple**, docked from the top of an old church, and a bust of locally born hero Almirante Riveros, who commanded the fleet that captured the Peruvian, ironclad *Huáscar* during the War of the Pacific (see p.478). From November to March, the kiosks just off the plaza play host to a Feria Artesanal (daily Jan & Feb, weekends only the rest of the time), with Chilote crafts for sale and *empanadas* for sustenance.

Achao

Fifteen kilometres southeast of Curaco lies the fishing village of **ACHAO** with its scattering of houses clad in colourful *tejuelas* (shingles), set against a backdrop of snowcapped volcano peaks across the gulf. It is famous both for its church and two simultaneous festivals in early February: *Encuentro Folklórico de las Islas del Archipiélago*, a folk festival that draws musical groups from all over Chiloé, and *Muestra Gastronómica y Artesanal*, which gives you a chance to both sample traditional Chilote cuisine and pick up the handiwork of the archipelago's artisans.

Iglesia Santa María de Loreto

Plaza de Armas • Tues–Sun 11am–12.45pm & 2–4pm • Free

Dominating the Plaza de Armas and dating back to 1764, **Iglesia Santa María de Loreto** is a prime example of a typical Chilote church and is thought to be the oldest one in the archipelago. The main framework is made from *ciprés de las Guaitecas* and *mañío*, a tree still common in southern Chile. The original *alerce* shingles which covered the exterior have mostly been replaced with *ciprés* boarding. Restoration work is a constant and expensive necessity – if you look around the *luma* wood floorboards, you can see the church's foundations, a rare glimpse into the way these old buildings were constructed. All the joints have been laboriously fixed into place with wooden plugs and dowels made from *canelo*, another type of Chilean wood.

ARRIVAL AND DEPARTURE

PENÍNSULA RILÁN

By bus Several daily buses run from Castro's rural bus terminal to the village of Rilán (1hr 15min), but it's best to have your own wheels.

TENAÚN

By bus There are regular buses to Tenaún (at least 4 daily; 1hr 15min) from Castro with Expresos Catalina and Expresos Tenaún.

QUICAVÍ

By bus Buses Expreso Quicaví (✆ 09 9248 4362) has

AROUND DALCAHUE

services from Ancud (Mon–Sat 1–2 daily; 1hr), as does Buses Rony Velásquez (Mon–Fri 1 daily).

ISLA QUINCHAO

By boat Ferry services run from the Dalcahue dock (every 30min, 7am–11pm; foot passengers free, cars CH$4000 return).

By bus Achao's Terminal de Buses (Miraflores at Zañartu), a couple of blocks east of the Plaza, has daily departures for Dalcahue (every 20min, 7.15am–8.30pm; 40min) via Curaco de Vélez. Note that bus tickets include the ferry journey.

ACCOMMODATION AND EATING

TENAÚN

Hospedaje Mirella Tenaún ✆ 09 9647 6750, ✉ mirellamontana@gmail.com. Part of the *Agroturismo* network, this friendly family-run guesthouse has room for seven guests in a few basic but comfy rooms and is run by the hospitable Mirella and the Soto family. *Curanto en hoyo* is sometimes on offer; otherwise Mirella does wonders with the catch of the day. CH$28,000

PENÍNSULA RILÁN

Hotel Parque Quilquico Quilquico ✆ 65 297 1100, ✇ hotelparquequilquico.cl. Overlooking a peaceful valley near the namesake village, this horseshoe-shaped, *alerce*-shingled hotel is the recipient of the hard-to-get 'sustainable' award. It's visually stunning, too, with grass growing on the roofs of its corridors, its *palafito*-style rooms on stilts, and indoor pool and hot tub. Even if not staying here, the restaurant alone is worth the trip, and guests have access to walking trails

that cross the property. Substantial discounts on single rooms for solo travellers. US$302

★ **Rucaluf Putemún** Km3.6 Camino de Rilán ✆ 09 9579 7571, ✇ rucalafputemun.cl. A short drive out of Castro, en route to the Rilán peninsula, this roadside treasure has won accolades for some of the most imaginative fusion cuisine on the island. Surrounded by colourful modern prints, you can treat yourself to the likes of *centolla* tartare, hake in blue cheese sauce with pears and Chilote-style paella, coupled with a succinct but well-chosen selection of wines, Chilean beers and cocktails (try the *murta* sour). Mains CH$7000–9000. Daily noon–5pm & 8–11pm.

Tierra Chiloé San José Playa ✆ 2 2207 8861, ✇ tierrachiloe.com. This luxurious, visually stunning bunker, constructed from a fusion of native woods and concrete, has privileged views of the waterfowl-rich estuary from each of its vast windows. There are only twelve rooms here, adding to the intimate feel of this boutique getaway, and rates include all meals, horseriding, sailing and kayaking excursions, and use of pools and Jacuzzi. Two-night minimum stay. US$2300

ISLA QUINCHAO
Hospedaje Sol y Lluvia Ricardo Jara 9, Achao ☎ 65 266 1383. The nicest guesthouse in town, with a burnt-orange exterior that hides spacious, comfortable rooms, some with shared bathrooms. The owners offer breakfast above and beyond the usual bread-and-instant-coffee combo and solo travellers pay exactly half. CH$24,000
Mar y Velas Serrano 2, Achao ☎ 65 266 1375.

Inexpensive fish and seafood dishes overlooking the sometimes busy boat ramp. Try the *cancato*, fish steamed with cheese, sausage and shellfish. Mains from CH$5500. Mon–Sat 12.30–11pm, Sun 12.20–3.30pm.
Ostras Los Troncos Francisco Bohle s/n, Curaco de Vélez. Follow the road downhill from the Plaza de Armas to the coastal road and look out for the sign that'll direct you to the garden, festooned with fishing nets and lined with rough-hewn wooden tables and seats – a superb spot for slurping a dozen or two local oysters (CH$300–400/oyster); bring your own wine. Summer daily 11am–7pm.

Castro

7

Built on a small promontory at the head of a 20km fjord, lively **CASTRO** occupies an unusual position both physically and historically. Founded in 1567, it's the third-oldest city in Chile, but it never became strategically important because it's a terrible harbour for sailing ships, only flourishing because the Jesuits chose to base their mission here. Today, little remains of old Castro, though some buildings have miraculously survived, such as the groups of brightly coloured **palafitos** – shingled fishermen's houses on stilts – on the waterfront to the north and south of town, many of which have now been revamped and turned into some of Chiloé's best lodgings and cafés. Castro is as cosmopolitan as Chiloé gets, with a clutch of innovative restaurants and excellent transport connections to all corners of the island.

Iglesia San Francisco de Castro

On the northeast corner of the central Plaza de Armas • Daily 8am–7pm

The national monument of **Iglesia San Francisco de Castro** is one of Chiloé's sixteen UNESCO-recognised churches, its ironclad wooden structure a mix of Classical and neo-Gothic styles, designed in 1906 by the Italian Eduardo Provasoli. The church's impressive interior is a harmonious blend of the island's native hardwoods and rows of stained-glass windows, while the exterior is currently a violent clash of yellow and purple.

Palafitos

Though deemed unsanitary by some locals, Chiloé's famous **palafitos** are still found at several locations around Castro. Perched precariously on stilts above the water, these brightly painted, *alerce*-shingled, traditional wooden fishermen's dwellings are an unforgettable sight. The idea was that you could moor your boat at your back door and walk out onto the street through the front one. The most impressive examples are found at the north end of town, off Pedro Montt, where

---

CASTRO: THE INDESTRUCTIBLE CITY

Castro has had its fair share of difficulties through the centuries. It was sacked by the Dutch both in 1600 and then in 1643, destroyed by earthquake in 1646, by fire in 1729, by earthquake again in 1739, by fire again in 1890, by fire once more in 1936, and most recently by earthquake and tidal wave in 1960. Anyone else would have given up and moved long ago, but the Chilotes keep hanging on.

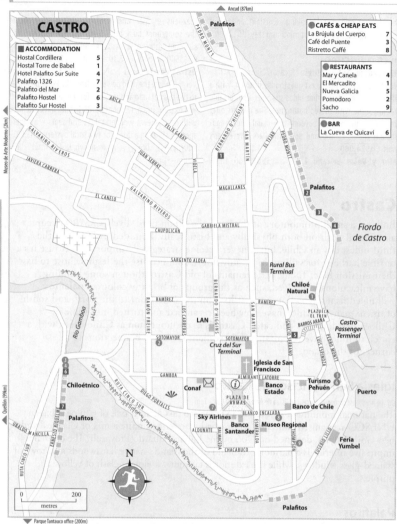

CASTRO

ACCOMMODATION

Hostal Cordillera	5
Hostal Torre de Babel	1
Hotel Palafito Sur Suite	4
Palafito 1326	7
Palafito del Mar	2
Palafito Hostel	6
Palafito Sur Hostel	3

CAFÉS & CHEAP EATS

La Brújula del Cuerpo	7
Café del Puente	3
Ristretto Caffé	8

RESTAURANTS

Mar y Canela	4
El Mercadito	1
Nueva Galicia	5
Pomodoro	2
Sacho	9

BAR

La Cueva de Quicaví	6

they are perfectly reflected in the grubby mini-lake by the roadside. More **palafitos** are found slightly south along the same street, while others are used as restaurants at the southern end of town, by the Feria Artesanal. A final batch can be seen from the western end of Lillo, across the Río Gamboa and a number have now been converted into luxurious lodgings (see p.334) and stylish cafés (see p.334).

Museo Regional

Calle Esmeralda • Mon–Sat 9.30am–5pm, Sun 10.30am–1pm • Donations welcome

The small but well-laid-out **Museo Regional** displays Huilliche artefacts and traditional farming implements, as well as black-and-white photographs of the town, before and after it was devastated by the 1960 earthquake.

FESTIVAL COSTUMBRISTA

At the northwest end of Castro lies the **Parque Municipal**. In mid-February the park hosts an enormous feast, the culmination of the **Festival Costumbrista**, a celebration of traditional Chilote life, when *curanto* is cooked in great cauldrons, *chicha* (cider) flows freely and balls of grated potato – *tropón* – are baked on hot embers. The inevitable burnt fingers and resultant hot-potato juggling that results from picking them up is known as *bailar el tropón* (dancing the *tropón*). From early January until the end of February, the Festival Costumbrista is held every weekend in a different part of Chiloé, with events organised by both the Castro and Ancud municipalities; if you're well-organised, you can attend more than one festival in a single weekend.

Feria Yumbel

Down by the water on Eusebio Lillo is the **Feria Yumbel**, a large covered market housed in a brand-new wooden building, selling woolly sweaters, wall hangings and other woolly goodies that the region is famous for. There are also some Peruvian and Bolivian offerings mixed in with genuine Chilote sweaters, so mind what you purchase. Next door is the produce market, where you can buy anything from necklaces of dried mussels to fresh fruit.

Museo de Arte Moderno

Pasaje Diaz 181 • Mid-Jan to mid-March daily 10am–6pm • Donation

A fair walk northwest of downtown, you'll find the **Museo de Arte Moderno** (MAM) housed inside a group of five restored wooden barns. Open in summer only, this modern art complex inside a park displays edgy contemporary works by Chilean artists.

ARRIVAL AND DEPARTURE

CASTRO

By plane Castro is now connected to Santiago and Puerto Montt by several LAN flights weekly, with an office at O'Higgins 412 (☎600 526 2000; ⓦlan.com). Sky Airline also has an office in town at Blanco Encalada 388 (☎600 600 2828). Transfers to the airport can be organised by your accommodation and cost CH$4000.

By bus Castro's long-distance bus terminal is at San Martín 486, a block north of the Plaza de Armas, while the rural bus terminal is at San Martín 667, down an alley two and a half blocks north of the Plaza.

Destinations (long distance bus terminal): Ancud (hourly; 1hr 15min); Chonchi (every 30min; 30min); Puerto Montt (12 daily; 3hr); Punta Arenas, via Argentina (3 weekly; 28hr); Quellón (hourly; 2hr 15min); Santiago (4 daily; 18hr).

Destinations (rural bus terminal): Achao (every 30min; fewer on Sun; 1hr 50min); Chonchi (every 30min; 30min); Cucao and the Parque Nacional Chiloé, sector Anay (up to 15 daily; 1hr 15min); Curaco de Vélez (every 30min, fewer on Sun; 1hr 30min); Dalcahue (every 30min; 30min); Puqueldón (2–3 daily, 1 on Sun; 1hr 15min); Queilén (12 daily; 1hr 30min).

By boat Naviera Austral (ⓦnavieraustral.cl) runs one weekly boat to Chaitén from Castro's passenger terminal (Sat at midnight; 5hr 30min). Time and date is subject to change, so check in advance. Book tickets via Turismo Pehuén (see p.334).

INFORMATION AND TOURS

Information Plaza de Armas (daily 10am–8pm; ⓔturismo@municastro.cl). A large and well-stocked office (though the brochures are hidden behind the information desk and you need to know what to ask for) that keeps erratic hours in spite of set timetable.

Conaf office Gamboa 424 (Mon–Fri 10am–12.30pm & 2.30–4pm; ☎65 253 2503). Limited information about Parque Nacional Chiloé (see p.335).

TOURS

Chiloé Natural Montt 201B ☎65 297 1878, ⓦchiloenatural.com. An experienced, English-speaking outfit offering day-trips and multi-day treks in Parque Tantauco, as well as trips to Parque Tepuhueico, Parque Nacional Chiloé, *curanto*-eating outings to Chelín by catamaran, and day visits to seven churches on the Ruta de las Iglesias. Tailor-made trips arranged and kayaks, mountain bikes and camping equipment available for rent.

Chiloétnico Riquelme 1228 ☎65 263 0951, ⓦchiloetnico.cl. Juan Pablo is an experienced and enthusiastic English-speaking guide who arranges anything from trips to Parque Tantauco, Tepuhueico and Parque Nacional Chiloé to multi-day cultural immersion in traditional Chilote culture, half-day horseback riding in Nercón and mountain bike rental (CH$12,000/day).

Turismo Pehuén Latorre 238 ☎65 263 5254, ⓦturismopehuen.cl. Established company specialising in day-trips – from boat outings to Isla Mechuque, complete with *curanto*, to gastronomic tours, church tours and outings to the Pingüineras de Puñihuil.

ACCOMMODATION

In recent years Castro has seen an explosion in boutique-y **accommodation** inside converted, renovated *palafitos*. *Palafito* hotels, guesthouses and hostels are found along the east side of Pedro Montt and Ernesto Riquelme, down the hill and across Río Gamboa. A short drive from Castro, tranquil Península Rilán (see p.328) is home to several luxury hotels.

Hostal Cordillera Barros Arana 175 ☎09 9512 2667, ⓦhostalcordillera.cl. The seemingly inexhaustible energy and warmth of the mother-hen owner translates into any language in spite of her speaking little English. The remodelled rooms (some en suite) are centrally heated, solo travellers pay exactly half the price of a double and there's a useful rent-a-car service available. CH$37,000

Hostal Torre de Babel O'Higgins 965 ☎65 253 4569, ⓦhostaltorredebabel.com. Contrary to the name, travellers from all over the world are able to find a common language in the vast, wood-stove-heated, beanbag-strewn lounge of this welcoming hostel. Young, helpful owner Louis is happy to give advice, and the wood-panelled rooms are simple but comfortable. Breakfast included. Dorms CH$15,000, doubles CH$30,000

Hotel Palafito Sur Suite Av Pedro Montt 231 ☎65 263 2121, ⓦpalafitosur.com. Consisting of just four simple yet luxurious, wood-panelled rooms, the design of this boutique hotel owes everything to its architect owners. The adjoining café (open to non-guests), *Patio Palafito*, is all floor-to-ceiling windows, sea terrace and a dream of descending white umbrellas. Café Dec–March daily roughly 9am–7pm. CH$60,000

★Palafito 1326 Riquelme 1326 ☎65 253 0053, ⓦpalafito1326.cl. This boutique *palafito* hotel combines traditional Chilote design (walls made of native cypress and *tepú* wood, thick woollen throws and pillows) with floor-to-ceiling windows, subtle lighting, immaculate, modern bathrooms and a first-rate café upstairs with estuary views. Tours around the islands can be arranged. CH$62,000

★Palafito del Mar Av Pedro Montt 567 ☎65 263 1622, ⓦpalafitodelmar.cl. With just six suites and a double, this homely yet elegant boutique *palafito* hotel is run by a friendly young couple. All rooms have terraces with sea views and the gorgeous common area, flooded with natural light and sporting quirky furniture, was instrumental in securing architectural awards. You can kayak right off the sea terrace out back, too. The same couple also run the four-person apartments at *El Palacito* next door. Doubles CH$50,000, apartments CH$95,000

★Palafito Hostel Riquelme 1210 ☎65 253 1008, ⓦpalafitohostel.com. Its curved wooden walls reminiscent of a ship, this revamped *palafito* has just eight beautiful rooms (two with sea view balconies, all en suite bar the dorms), an appealing common space upstairs, adorned with contemporary art and woollen hangings, and an outdoor deck overlooking the water. Breakfast includes home-made bread and the staff can help organize horseriding in Parque Nacional Chiloé (see p.335). Dorms CH$15,000, doubles CH$42,000

Palafito Sur Hostel Pedro Montt 465 ☎65 253 6472, ⓦpalafitosur.hostel.com. With its hard-earned 'sustainability' credentials and *alerce*-shingle-clad exterior, this *palafito* hostel comes with many thoughtful touches. Snug 4-bed dorms come with individual reading lights, the guest kitchen is fully equipped, the waterfront lounge is full of light, and you can kayak right off the waterfront deck. The simple doubles are a tad overpriced for what they are, though. Dorms CH$14,000, doubles CH$35,000

EATING AND DRINKING

CAFÉS AND CHEAP EATS

La Brújula del Cuerpo O'Higgins 308 ☎65 263 3229. Travellers and locals alike gravitate to "The Body's Compass" – a busy café on the main square specializing in inexpensive Chilean takes on fajitas, burgers, salads and sandwiches. Burgers CH$4500. Daily 11am–midnight.

Café del Puente Riquelme 1180B ☎65 263 4878. This great little café overlooking the water attracts a grateful international clientele with its generous American breakfasts, muesli, good (if not very strong) coffee and

thirty types of tea including the odd 'Mums Bums'. Homesick Brits will appreciate the tea with scones (CH$3100) and proper high tea served from 5pm onwards. Mon & Wed–Sun 8am–9pm.

★Ristretto Caffé Blanco 264 ☎65 263 4821. In a country where real coffee is becoming easier to find, this dark wood-panelled café, with 57 different coffees on the menu, still holds its own against the competition. You can join the rest of the laptop-toting clientele for some great foccacias, fresh fruit juices and an extensive range of teas, including the likes of Italian Almond. Mon–Sat 8am–9pm.

RESTAURANTS

★**Mar y Canela** Riquelme 1212 ☎65 253 1770, ⓦmarycanela.cl. The homely, bright, cookbook-stacked interior of this cute *palafito* restaurant and café leads you to expect good things and the short but sweet menu tantalises with such imaginative offerings as smoked pork loin with plums and sheep's cheese or conger eel with crab curry. The coffee and cakes are a great bet too, if you're looking for something light. Mains CH$7000–9000. Daily noon–10pm.

★**El Mercadito** Montt 210 ☎65 253 3866, ⓦelmercaditodechiloe.cl. You may find yourself cackling with childlike glee when you reach for the crayons and drawing paper placed on every table to entertain diners while they are waiting for the picture-perfect trio of ceviche, the choriburger, the crab 'bombs' or any of the other imaginative, playful fusion creations conjured up from local, seasonal ingredients. The decor is as whimsical as the food, with a colourful, shingle-covered bar, wacky light fixtures and knitted jellyfish. Mains from CH$6500. Daily 1–4pm & 8–11pm.

Nueva Galicia Montt 38 ☎65 253 2828. Inside this nautically-themed, white-linen restaurant, young, smartly attired waiters serve up Chilote standards such as *curanto* and *cancato* (salmon steamed with sausage and cheese), as well as more imaginative fusion dishes such as king crab lasagne. Accompaniments may include quinoa as well as Chilote potatoes. Mains from CH$7000. Daily 1–3.30pm & 7.30–11pm.

Pomodoro Sotomayor 520 ☎65 263 4141, ⓦpomodorotrattoria.cl. Castro's answer to an Italian trattoria particularly shines when it comes to home-made pastas; choose from the likes of home-made gnocchi with pesto Genovese and *agnolotti* with spinach and ricotta, and don't be shy to ask about off-the-menu specials, which sometimes include king crab cannelloni. The thin-and-crispy pizzas are more authentic than any other pizzas on the island, too. Mains from CH$6500. Mon–Sat 12.30–3.30pm & 7–11.30pm, Sun 1–4pm.

Sacho Thompson 213 ☎65 263 2079. The upstairs dining area of this local institution offers excellent views across the fjord and the menu focuses on Neptune's subjects. It's difficult to go wrong with anything clam-based, and while the choice of fish often seems to be limited to salmon and *congrio* (conger eel), all the dishes are well prepared. The *cancato* stands out. Mains from CH$7000. Daily noon–midnight.

BARS

La Cueva de Quicaví Encalada 55. With its demon keeping watch over the garishly painted entrance, this is actually Castro's most happening nightspot barring the nightclub at the casino. Live music is luck of the draw – local death metallers one night, reggae the next – but there's usually a lively crowd after midnight and there's a good beer selection. Daily 6.30pm–2.30am.

DIRECTORY

Car rental Salfa Sur, Mistral 499 (☎65 263 0422, ⓦsalfasur.cl); *Hostal Cordillera* (see p.334) also offers a selection of cars for rent.

Hospital Hospital Augusta Rifat, on Freire 852 (☎65 263 2445), has basic medical facilities.

Money and exchange There are ATMs around the Plaza de Armas, and a money exchange at Chacabuco 286.

Post office Plaza de Armas, O'Higgins 388 (Mon–Sat 9am–noon & 2–6pm).

Parque Nacional Chiloé and around

59km southwest of Castro • Daily 9am–7pm • CH$1500

On the island's western coast, the **PARQUE NACIONAL CHILOÉ** comprises over 420 square kilometres of native evergreen forest, covering the slopes and valleys of the **Cordillera de Piuchén**, largely unexplored by man and harbouring flora and fauna unique to the archipelago, as well as wide deserted beaches and long stretches of **rugged coastline**, home to dozens of seabird species, penguins and sea lions. The park is divided into three sectors.

The most accessible of the three, Sector Anay, is reached by a 25km paved road that shoots west from a junction on the Panamericana, 20km south of Castro. At the end of the road is the gateway to the park, Chanquín – a scattering of guesthouses across the bridge from the ramshackle village of **Cucao**, where you can buy last-minute provisions. Due to the somewhat limited trail system, you can see the park's highlights in a couple of days, staying overnight in Chanquín (see box, p.336).

7

HIKING IN PARQUE NACIONAL CHILOÉ

A couple of short **hikes** start from the visitor centre at the Conaf ranger post. Besides two ultra-short interpretative trails, one is the circular, 770m "**El Tepual**", running through an area of *tepu* forest, a tree which thrives in this humid bogland; there are log walkways across the wetter sections of these enchanted-looking woods, with twisted moss-covered trunks intertwined with other native species. The second hike is the **Sendero La Playa**, which leads you through patches of *nalca* (native rhubarb) and tunnels of dense vegetation before emerging on the regenerating scrubland that takes you via sand dunes to the exposed Pacific coast. A little more taxing is the 3km (one-way) walk along the beach to Lago Huelde, where you pick up a 9km trail known as **Sendero Rancho Grande**, along the Río Deñal up to the edge of the tree line, revealing beautiful views below.

The park's longest hike is the beautiful 25km (6hr) **Sendero Chanquín**, which alternates between stretches of coastline, pounded by the fierce Pacific surf, and dense, native evergreen forest, before finishing up by the rustic Conaf *refugio* and campsite at Cole Cole (overseen by the Huentemó community). There's also a Conaf ranger post that is only open in the summer. The trail then technically continues another 8km north to the *Refugio Anay*, though there's a river that has to be crossed and hiking further than the Huentemó community can be difficult; due to tensions between the villagers and Conaf (and the villagers and some unscrupulous home-grown backpackers stealing chickens after they'd run out of camping supplies), whether or not you're allowed to pass through depends on the whim of the villagers. Some days you may be waved on, while on others they may demand an exorbitant CH$20,000 'entry fee'.

Sector Anay

Every summer, backpackers descend on the park's **Sector Anay**, keen to camp on its 20km of white-sand beach and to explore the dense forest. This section of the national park covers 350 square kilometres of the Cordillera de Piuchén, rising up to 800m above sea level, and comprises vast chunks of native flora, including *coigüe* and *mañío* woodlands, and the magnificent *alerce*. Besides potentially catching glimpses of the shy Chilote fox, the elusive *pudú* (pygmy deer), *chungungo* (marine otters) and a wealth of native birds, the depths of primeval Chiloé forest allow you to experience a sense of true wilderness.

Sector Chepu

Thirty kilometres **south** of Ancud and to the north of Sector Anay is the northernmost section of the Parque Nacional Chiloé, **sector Chepu**, noted for its birdlife-rich **wetlands**. Though the Chiloé section of the Sendero de Chile (see box, p.338) technically starts from the village of Guabún on Península Lacuy (see p.325), it's not well-marked, so it's best to start from the bridge at the village of Duhatao, south of Pumillahue. From here, a trail combining coastal footpaths, stretches of beach and wooden walkways runs all the way to Chepu Valley (see p.325). Take the trail to the beach which can be crossed at low tide; at high tide, take the first trail up the hill, and follow the power lines. There are some nice little detours with great sea views. It's a six- or seven-hour walk that's as rugged as it is beautiful; be prepared for mud during the two-hour stretch that runs through the forest, and bear in mind that when crossing Chepu Beach, you'll have to ford a stream. The trail finishes at Río Chepu, and a road runs uphill from the coast through Chepu Valley; it's another 45-minute walk to the hamlet of Chepu and the bridge that the bus leaves from three times weekly (Mon, Wed and Fri). Given that departures are early morning only, however, you have no choice but to stay in Chepu overnight (see p.326).

THE BRIDGE TO NOWHERE

Reachable via a rough, unpaved 45-minute drive south from Cucao, the privately owned headland of **Punta Pirulil** is the stage for a beautiful, wind-whipped walk over the hills and along wave-battered cliffs. Indigenous Huilliche legends have it that this part of the island acts as a bridge between this world and the next, with the souls of the dead calling out to the boatman to ferry them across. The story goes that one day, a foreigner who was very much alive summoned the boatman; the boatman turned him away. The following year, the foreigner died and his soul tried to summon the boatman, but the boatman assumed that it was another trick, so the restless soul of this foreigner is said to still wander these hills, emitting eerie cries (which you'll get to hear). A symbolic **Muelle de las Almas**, a bridge to nowhere that ends halfway, has been built here to illustrate the legend, facing the bay, and the walk to and from the bridge takes a couple of hours.

The trailhead is accessible only by 4WD and to unlock the gate you have to call at the farmhouse directly before the only bridge you cross en route to the trailhead. This is where you pay the entry fee (CH$1500); Don Carmelo will then hand you a key and can show you his extensive collection of fossils and his personal contribution to the demise of endangered endemic fauna in the shape of pelts lining the wall. It's easiest to get to Punta Pirulil via half-day tour with Palafito Trip (see below).

7

Parque Tepuhueico

Reachable via a well-signposted, bumpy gravel road that branches off the road to Cucao at around Km9, **Parque Tepuhueico** is a 200km-square private nature reserve that sits between the Pacific coast and Lago Tepuhueico and consists largely of dense cypress, *tepué*, *canelo* and *coigue* forest, home to over a hundred bird species and native fauna such as Darwin's fox, the *pudú* and *monito del monte* – a tiny marsupial whose species are over forty million years old. At the heart of the reserve sits *Tepuhueico Ecolodge* (see p.338), and two beautiful walking trails run near the property, making a loop of sorts. The most spectacular is the **Catedral de Arrayanes** trail, a slippery twenty-minute ramble through an enchanted-looking, lichen-covered tangle of gnarly trees. The prize at the end is a gorgeous thicket of red-gold myrtle trees that reach for the sky. This trail joins up with the riverside trail that skirts the rushing river, where guests can go kayaking. Parque Tepuhueico is accessible either for guests of the hotel or those taking a tour (see p.338).

ARRIVAL AND INFORMATION

By bus Buses Ojeda and Buses Interlagos both run services from Castro to Cucao (up to 15 daily between them in peak season between 8.30am–5pm; last bus from Cucao leaves at 6.30pm).

Conaf At the park entrance (daily 9am–7pm; visitor centre daily: Jan & Feb 9.30am–8pm; March–Dec 9am–1pm & 2–6pm; ☎09 9644 2489). Pay the park fee at the Conaf ranger post, where there's also an interpretative centre.

PARQUE NACIONAL CHILOÉ AND AROUND

TOURS

Palafito Trip ☎09 8849 5522, ⓦpalafitotrip.cl. Based out of *Palafito Cucao* (see p.338), this reliable operator offers outings in Parque Nacional Chiloé on foot or horseback, as well as half-day trips to the Muelle de las Almas (see box above). The owner, Pato, only speaks Spanish, but if contacted in advance can round up an English-speaking guide.

ACCOMMODATION AND EATING

All Parque Nacional Chiloé **accommodation** options are situated in and around Chanquín. The *refugios* in the park are not in a great state of repair and are only open in peak season. They are not always staffed and you must bring own sleeping bags.

El Arrayán Near the park entrance. This is the only reliable restaurant around, with rough-hewn wooden furniture, friendly service and a menu full of simple but well-executed meat and seafood dishes. Mains from CH$5500. High season daily noon–10pm; low season restricted hours.

SENDERO DE CHILE

The **Sendero de Chile** (www.senderodechile.cl) is a hugely ambitious project, aimed at creating the **world's longest continuous hiking trail** to span the entire length of Chile, allowing hikers to traverse the country's varied landscapes and interact with local communities en route. The 8,500km-long trail was officially completed in 2010; much of the work revolved around linking existing trails within national parks with each other, as a result of which the route comprises some secondary roads as well as bona fide hiking trails. **Maintenance** has proved to be an enduring problem; while sections that pass through national parks are properly maintained and signposted, other sections of the Sendero are not.

Camping Chanquín 200m past the Conaf visitors' centre ☎09 9507 2559. This campsite offers 25 camping spots with fire pits, showers and picnic tables provided. There are also four refurnished, fully equipped *cabañas* for up to six guests each. Camping/person CH$2500, *refugio* CH$4000

Camping Cole Cole North end of Sendero Chanquín. This basic campsite is run by the Huentemó community and could be cleaner. Cold water showers only and also a *refugio* on-site (bring own bedding). Camping/person CH$2000, dorms CH$4000

Cucao Love Entrance just after the bridge In Chanquín ☎09 9675 1322, ⓦcucaolove.com. You'll spot the large geodome before you cross the river to Chanquín. Run by expats from the Canary Islands, this new option consists of basic bunkrooms and camping spots dotted about amid the shrubbery, as well as a dinner option (CH$4000). The geodome serves as a cavernous hangout area, complete with internet, bar and kayaks, mountain bikes and paddleboards for rent. Dorms CH$10,000, camping/person CH$4500

★**Hostel Palafito Cucao** 200m from the park entrance ☎65 297 1164 or ☎09 8403 4728 ⓦhostel palafitocucao.cl. Under the same management as Castro's *Palafito Hostel* and *Palafito 1326* (see p.334), this shingled guesthouse is ideally situated, boasting views of Lago Cucao from its centrally heated rooms and dorm. Guests congregate in the cosy lounge, heated by a wood-burning stove, watch the sunset from the deck or simmer in the hot tub. Nab the corner room for the best views. Palafito Trip (see p.337) is based out of here. Dorms CH$13,000, doubles CH$48,000

Tepuhueico Ecolodge Parque Tepuhueico, about 25km inside the park ⓦparquetepuhueico.cl. The wood-shingled keep that is *Tepuhueico Ecolodge* sports a circular, split-level dining and lounge area with vast ceilings. The two secluded, triple-level *cabañas* for up to six people carry on with the innovative architecture theme, with open-plan bedrooms, terraces overlooking the lake, huge windows and wood-burning stoves. The rooms inside the main hotel building are plush but darker, with powerful showers and cute touches in the form of Chilote woollen dolls and wall hangings. Doubles CH$139,000, *cabañas* CH$149,000

Chonchi

Twenty-three kilometres south of Castro lies the attractive working town of **CHONCHI**. Founded in 1767, the town was home to the wood baron Ciriaco Alvarez, who earned the name *El Rey de Ciprés* (The Cypress King) by stripping the archipelago of almost all of its native forest. The most sheltered harbour on the island is lined with beautiful old wooden buildings, and during low tide you can see local women digging for razor clams on the beach.

In February the town comes alive during the *Semana Verano Chonchi* – a folkloric festival featuring dancing, music, art and rodeo skills. Chonchi is also the home of the golden *licor de oro*, a potent concoction combining saffron, vanilla, milk, lemons, cloves, cinnamon and other ingredients to storm your palate.

Otherwise, the attractions of this sleepy town are limited to the **Iglesia San Carlos de Borromeo** (1900) on the main Calle Centenario (daily 9am–7pm), with its attractive yellow exterior and blue tower; its Neoclassical facade is one of the island's finest. The **Museo de las Tradiciones Chonchinas** lies further down the street and has never been open whenever we've visited. Rumour has it that it contains furniture, fittings and a large collection of photographs from the tree-felling heyday of *El Rey de Ciprés*.

ARRIVAL AND DEPARTURE CHONCHI

By bus There are frequent departures with operators such as Cruz del Sur, Transchiloé, Expresos Interlagos and Queilén Bus. Larger buses stop alongside the Plaza, while minibuses stop along the little triangular *plazuela* along Centenario.
Destinations Castro (14 daily; 30min); Quellón (14 daily; 1hr 45min).

ACCOMMODATION AND EATING

Hostal La Turtuga Pedro Montt 241 ☏09 9098 2925, ⓦhostallatortuga.com. Conveniently located in a historic wood-shingled house right next to the Cruz del Sur bus station, this rambling central guesthouse is run by a friendly proprietress. Rooms (some with own bathroom) are spartan and positively vast, their crooked floors testimony to the building's 120-plus years of existence.

Breakfast costs CH$2500 extra and consists of whatever the hostess happens to rustle up. CH$24,000
El Trebol Irarrázaval 187 ☏65 267 1203. At the southern end of the waterfront above the local market, this is a beloved local institution, serving primarily fish and seafood dishes to satisfied clientele. Mains from CH$5500. Daily noon–3pm & 7–11pm.

Isla Lemuy

On the coast, a 4km walk south of Chonchi at **Huicha**, a ferry heads to **ISLA LEMUY** – a quiet island, though this is changing, thanks to the newly paved road and the presence of no less than three of Chiloé's sixteen UNESCO churches (see box, p.329). It's dotted with traditional rural settlements, each boasting just a few houses, with the celebrated churches found in the villages of Ichuac, Aldachildo and Detif. **Detif** is the remotest of them all, on an isolated, bleak headland at the far eastern end of the island, about 20km from Puqueldón, the island's main settlement. The drive to Detif is particularly picturesque as you get to cross a precipitously narrow strip of land leading to the headland, with the ocean on both sides of the road.

ARRIVAL AND DEPARTURE ISLA LEMUY

By bus Buses Gallardo (☏65 264 3541) runs to Puqueldón from Castro (4 daily Mon–Fri, 7.40am–5.30pm, 2 on Sat at 9.30am & 5.30pm, 1 on Sun at 2.30pm); 1hr); the bus crosses to the island on the ferry.

By boat Ferry departs from a terminal 3km south of Chonchi (Mon–Sat every 30min, 8am–8pm; Sun hourly, 8am–8pm; 20min; free for passengers, CH$4500/car).

ACCOMMODATION AND EATING

El Castaño Aldachildo ☏09 7445 0886, ⓦautentico chiloe.com. Rural life needs no better introduction than a stay at this rustic *Agroturismo* guesthouse run by a friendly Italian–Chilean couple. There are just three doubles with neither TVs nor internet to distract you from your spectacular natural surroundings. Witness sheep-shearing or cider making, go horseriding with Silvio or sample Rosanna's delectable cakes and enjoy an *aperetivo italiano* with your hosts. CH$30,000
Parque Yayanes 1.5km from Puqueldón en route to

Lincay ☏09 8861 6462, ⓦparqueyayanes.cl. The best place to stay on the island consists of three adorable *cabañas* (think polished wooden floors, wood-burning stoves and carved headboards). The two six-person *cabañas* and the sole two-person *cabaña* come fully equipped with kitchenettes and satellite TV. Jamie and Perla – the hospitable owners – bake pies and can cook meat, fish and vegetarian dishes to order (CH$5000/meal), and sometimes hold impromptu barbecues. CH$55,000

Queilén and around

The paved road to Queilén runs above a string of pretty little villages down by the sea. **Tepua** in particular is worth a visit to see its graveyard filled with *mausoleos*, traditional shelters that protect mourners from the elements when they visit the graves of the dead, some of which are splendidly ornate. You'll either need a sturdy vehicle to tackle the steep dirt paths leading to the villages, or be prepared for a lot of walking.

Forty-six kilometres from Chonchi, the road pulls into **Queilén**, a sleepy little fishing town whose two main streets, Pedro Aguirre Cerda and Alessandri, bisect the neck of a long, sandy peninsula. The western end of town is very pretty, lined with fishermen's houses built on a long beach sheltered by the nearby **Isla Tranqui**. In February the town hosts a craft fair in which all types of local products are sold, from handicrafts and farming equipment to traditional medicines.

ARRIVAL AND DEPARTURE   QUEILÉN AND AROUND

By bus Queilén Bus (☎ 65 263 2173) runs services to Queilén from Castro (8–15 daily, 7.30am–8.15pm; 1hr 15min).

ACCOMMODATION AND EATING

Espejo de Luna Ruta Chonchi a Queilén, Km 35 ☎ 09 7431 3090 or 09 7431 3091, ⓦ espejodeluna.cl. Difficult to miss due to the distinctive shape of its restaurant, which resembles a boat on its side, this nature retreat combines thoughtful design (mesh-covered walkways to prevent slippage, lift down to the private beach for disabled guests) with somewhat overpriced flair – spacious, light rooms in the lodge and private *cabañas* (holding up to five people) hidden in the greenery. Non-guests can stop by for lunch or dinner; the dining room serves well-prepared meat and fish dishes with an emphasis on local ingredients. Doubles <u>CH$175,000</u>,

cabañas <u>CH$205,000</u>

★ **Isla Bruja Lodge** Overlooking an isolated bay near Pailldad (get directions if driving) ⓦ islabrujalodge .com. This beautiful lodge is the picture of rural tranquillity, with delightful antique touches throughout, such as a genuine Singer sewing machine. The luxurious en suites are presided over by the wonderfully welcoming and attentive Marie and Francisco, the friendly American-Chilean owners, as well as Lana the dog and Torpe the pet sheep. Room price includes full board and use of hot tub, the food (meals CH$15,000) is gourmet and you can kayak off the back porch. <u>CH$68,000</u>

Quellón

If you follow Route 5 south from the turn-off for Chonchi, after 70km you reach **QUELLÓN** – the official end of the Panamerican Highway, which starts in Alaska, and the end of Chiloé. Formerly a logging port and more recently the centre of a major salmon-farming industry, Quellón is now beginning to recover from Infectious Salmon Anaemia (ISA), the blight that affected Chile's salmon between 2005 and 2010, with salmon production falling by three-quarters. Unemployment is still the highest on the island, the port area is dodgy at night and the main reason to come here is to catch a **ferry** across to Chaitén (see p.357) or down to Chacabuco (see p.368). You can also organize transport to Parque Tantauco (see p.342), though that can equally be done in Castro (see p.333).

ARRIVAL AND INFORMATION   QUELLÓN

By bus Hourly Cruz del Sur and Transchiloé buses run to Castro (17 daily; 2hr) and Puerto Montt (13 daily; 6hr) via Chonchi (1hr 20min) from the terminal a block west of the Plaza on Pedro Aguirre Cerda.

By boat The Don Baldo ferry – operated by Naviera Austral at Montt 457 (CH$12,000/6000–$15,500/8875 per passenger/bicycle; ☎ 65 268 2207, ⓦ navieraustral.cl) – calls at the harbour a block south. Ferries may be subject to delays and cancellations, so check the exact departure time with the Naviera Austral

office in advance. Outside peak season there are fewer services.

Destinations Chaitén (Thurs evenings; 5hr); Puerto Chacabuco (Mon, Wed & Sat evenings; 28hr).

TOURS

Excursiones Quellón Av Vivar 382B ☎ 65 268 0234, ⓦ excursionesquellon.cl. Tour operator that runs buses to Parque Tantauco (see p.342) in Jan and Feb, and can help with other logistics.

ACCOMMODATION AND EATING

Hostería Romeo Alfa Leo Montt 554 ☎ 09 8858 0232. This restaurant sits right on the water and is a

good bet for fish and seafood dishes, which include ceviche and grilled fish with a variety of sauces. Mains

from CH$6500. Daily 12.30–3.30pm & 7.30–11.30pm.

Hotel Chico Leo Montt 325 ☎65 268 1567. The pick of a mediocre waterfront lot, this budget hotel offers (mostly) spick-and-span rooms, some with shared facilities. The water in the showers is reliably hot, but the restaurant's been getting a mixed response lately. **CH$22,000**

Hotel Patagonia Insular Ladrilleros 1737 ☎65 268 1610, ⊛hotelpatagoniainsular.cl. Swish and airy, Quellón's most modern hotel enjoys an enviable hilltop location just to the west of the centre. The large, comfortable rooms have porthole windows in the bathrooms and all the mod cons you'd expect from a four-star hotel, and the restaurant serves fine Chilean and international dishes. **CH$56,000**

Isla Sandwich Ladrilleros 190 ☎65 268 0683. Trendy, popular café offering a vast array of imaginative sandwiches (from CH$3500), as well as cakes, coffee and fresh fruit juices. Mon–Sat 11am–11pm.

Parque Tantauco

To the south of Isla Grande and 30km to the northwest of Quellón • Dec–March daily 9am–8pm • CH$3500 • Access by bus, boat or plane can be arranged via the Castro-based Parque Tantauco office (see p.344), or via Chiloé Natural or Chiloétnico (see p.333)

Parque Tantauco (⊛parquetantauco.cl) is Chiloé's largest natural attraction with nearly 1200 square kilometres of unspoiled wilderness, making it at least double the size of Parque Nacional Chiloé. The park, funded by the Fundación Futuro, is the brainchild of **Sebastián Piñera**, Harvard-educated politician, billionaire owner of LANChile, and Chile's former president.

After Doug Tompkins unveiled Parque Pumalín (see p.354), Piñera was inspired to start his own conservation project on Isla Grande. The project's goal is to "protect and conserve vulnerable ecosystems and species, and those at risk of extinction", as well as to restore a large chunk of the park's territory that was devastated by a forest fire in the 1940s, by replanting native species in the affected area. The park is located in one of the world's 25 "biodiversity hotspots", with unique ecosystems and wildlife habitats, and home to such species as the Chilote fox, the *pudú*, the *huillín* (otter) and the blue whale.

Consisting of Zona Sur and Zona Norte, Tantauco boasts over 130km of well-signposted, meticulously maintained hiking trails of varying length and difficulty, encompassing both the coastal areas and Chilote rainforest. These trails are part of an **excellent infrastructure** that also includes fully equipped campsites and unmanned basic *refugios*. Owing to the park's remoteness, moreover, it's not overrun by visitors in the summer, and away from Laguna Chaiguata and Caleta Inío, the gateways to Zona Norte and Zona Sur, respectively, you can hike practically in solitude for a week or more.

There are **two long trails** in the park which form a T-shape: the east-west Ruta Caleta Zorra from Lago Chaiguata (41km one-way; 7 days return), and the north-south Ruta Transversal (52km; 5 days one-way) from Lago Chaiguata to Caleta Inío, which turns south halfway along to Caleta Zorra. The longest hike you can do is Ruta Tantauco (94km; 8–9 days one-way), basically the two aforementioned routes combined: Lago Chaiguata to Caleta Zorra and Caleta Zorra to Caleta Inío, though inevitably the T-shape of this route entails some retracing of steps.

Zona Sur is accessible on foot from Zona Norte, as well as by boat and Cessna flight. Bring all the necessary gear, including waterproof clothing.

Zona Norte

It's possible to visit Zona Norte in a day, as Chiloé Natural and Chiloétnico (see p.333) both run day-trips there and there are a couple of nice short hikes, such as the **Sendero Siempreverde**, an interpretive walk leading through evergreen forest, or the **Circuito Muelle**, which goes from *Camping Chaiguata* along the banks of Lago Yaldad. Alternatively, the **Sendero Lagos Occidentales** is a 6km walk of moderate difficulty,

7

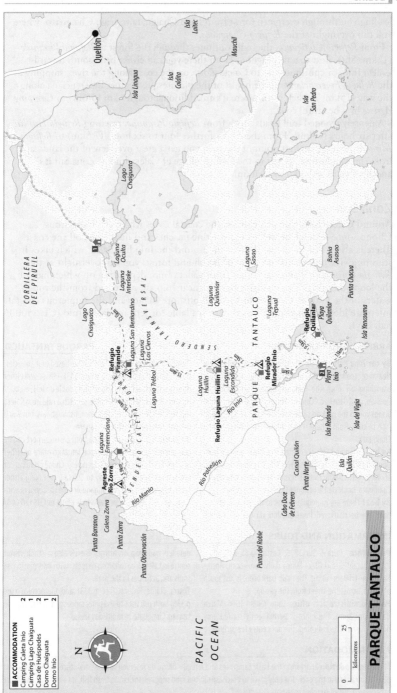

PARQUE TANTAUCO

ACCOMMODATION	
■ Camping Caleta Inío	2
Camping Lago Chaiguata	1
Casa de Huéspedes	2
Domo Chaiguata	1
Domo Inío	2

PACIFIC OCEAN

Quellón

Isla Laitec

Mauchil

Isla Coldita

Isla Linagua

Isla San Pedro

Lago Chaiguata

CORDILLERA DEL PIRULIL

Laguna Oculta

Laguna Interlake

Lago Chaiguaco

Laguna San Bernardino

Laguna Sasao

Bahía Asasao

Punta Chacua

Laguna Quilanlar

PARQUE TANTAUCO

Refugio Piramide

Laguna Los Ciervos

SENDERO TRANSVERSAL

Laguna Tepual

Laguna Quilanlar

Refugio Quilanlar

Playa Quilanlar

Isla Yencouma

15.1km

Laguna Trébol

Refugio Laguna Huillín

Laguna Huillín

Laguna Escondida

15.4km

Refugio Mirador Inío

13.2km

Río Inío

1.5km

Playa Inío

5.3km

2.5km

Río Pabellón

PARQUE TANTAUCO

0.6km

SENDERO CALETA ZORRA

Laguna Emerenciana

Agreste Río Zorra

5.9km

Río Manío

Punta Barranca

Caleta Zorra

Punta Zorra

Punta Observación

Punta del Roble

Cabo Doce de Febrero

Canal Quilán

Punta Norte

Isla Quilán

Isla del Vigía

Isla Vigía

Isla Redonda

N

0 25
kilometres

leading you through evergreen forest from Lago Chaiguata to Lago Chaiguaco, where you can overnight at the *Refugio Chaiguaco*.

From *Refugio Chaiguaco*, the trail continues through the forest to *Refugio Pirámide* (15km; 5hr), next to a tiny lagoon. From there you can either head south towards Caleta Inío, or continue west to Caleta Zorra on the coast along the river, stopping at the *Refugio Emerenciana* on the banks of the picturesque Laguna Emerenciana along the way (15km; 7–9hr), from where it's an additional tough 6km (5-6hr) to *Camping Agreste* by a beautiful cove.

A densely wooded trail heads south from *Refugio Pirámide*, reaching *Refugio Huillín* after six hours (14km). From there it's a further four to six hours (7.5km) to *Refugio Miradór Inío*, the highest point of the trek; you get a great overview of the landscape from the watchtower. To get to the fishing village of Caleta Inío in Zona Sur it's another five to seven hours (9.6km).

Zona Sur

Around Caleta Inío, you can explore the coastal caves where the indigenous Chonos once resided, as well as the pristine beaches and little islets off the coast. There is also a beautiful two-day circuit around the Inío headland, which takes in stunning viewpoints and stretches of beach and forest; you can overnight at the *Refugio Quilanlar* (13km or 9.5km from Caleta Inío, depending on which half of the loop you take). The extensive beaches near Inío are protected from the rough waters of the Gulf of Corcovado by small offshore islands and the numerous coastal inlets are ideal for **kayaking**. Kayaks are available for rent in Caleta Inío (CH$5000/half day).

ARRIVAL AND DEPARTURE   PARQUE TANTAUCO

By car Zona Norte can be accessed by vehicles with high clearance (pickup trucks or 4WDs) along a dirt road branching off from the Panamericana, 14km north of Quellón, and labelled "Colonia Yungay". The 18km drive brings you to the park administration office by Lago Yaldad (see below), from where it's an additional 20km to Lago Chaiguata.

By bus In Jan and Feb, there are three buses weekly from Quellón to Zona Norte (Mon, Wed & Sat at 9am, returning at 4pm; CH$15,000/25,000 return to Lago Yaldad/Lago Chaiguata; book via Excursiones Quellón – see p.340).

By boat There are no regular boats to the park. A private boat can be chartered from Quellón via Castro's Parque

Tantauco office or either of the Castro-based tour agencies, Chiloé Natural or Chiloétnico (see p.333) – these will either drop people off at Caleta Inío or pick people up (CH$60,000/person). It's sometimes possible to catch a ride from Caleta Inío to Quellón with one of the local fishing boats, but you'll need to have plenty of time to spare.

By plane A four-person Cessna from Castro airport can be chartered through Castro's Parque Tantauco office or either of the Castro-based tour agencies, Chiloé Natural or Chiloétnico (see p.333), to fly to Caleta Inío, taking either three passengers and no luggage or two passengers with luggage (CH$360,000 for the whole plane or CH$120,000/person for a day-trip).

INFORMATION AND TOURS

Park office Ruta 5 Sur 1826, Castro ☎ 65 263 3805, ⦿ parquetantauco.cl (Dec–March daily 9am–6pm; April–Nov Mon–Fri 9am–6pm). The main park office is just south of Castro, across the street from the casino.

Park administration office Lago Yaldad (Dec–March daily 9am–8pm). The office is permanently staffed only during the months indicated. The park entry fee includes a

detailed trail map on arrival. There's also a small visitor centre in Caleta Inío (open on request) with information on trails and activities in the park.

Tours Chiloé Natural (see p.333) and Chiloétnico (see p.333) both run trips to the park, ranging from day-trips to Laguna Chaiguata to multi-day treks.

ACCOMMODATION

All **accommodation** apart from the basic campsites and *refugios* has to be reserved via the park offices (see above) and paid for on arrival at the park. The only place to purchase limited food supplies, including fresh fish, is Caleta Inío; you must otherwise bring all supplies with you.

Camping and refugios Basic campsites and *refugios* are deliberately arranged with a day's hike between each site, and drinking water is found at every site apart from *Refugio Mirador Inío*, the highest of the sites; bring two days' worth of water from either *Camping Inío* or *Refugio Laguna Huillín*. Camping wild is not allowed. There's a standard camping price per night throughout, with the exception of the fully equipped campsites at Lago Chaiguata and Caleta Inío (see below). Smaller campsites along the trails consist of 4–6 camping spots each. Basic *refugios* are equipped with 8 bunk beds each (bring own bedding) and are also priced at a standard rate. Camping/person ‾CH$5000‾, dorms ‾CH$8000‾

Camping Caleta Inío Caleta Inío. Large campsite consisting of 24 spaces, complete with showers, fully equipped indoor cooking area, a large *fogón* for barbecue and even a *curanto* pit. Camping/person ‾CH$15,000‾

Camping Lago Chaiguata Lago Chaiguata. Camping site with 15 spaces, some with sheltered picnic tables. Access to showers and *quincho*. Ranger station nearby. There's also a restaurant and visitors can book a hot tub (CH$35,000) in advance to soak with up to seven of their closest friends. Sites with sheltered picnic table cost slightly more. Camping/person ‾CH$20,000‾

Casa de Huéspedes Caleta Inío. Attractive guesthouse offering six homely, wood-panelled rooms with down duvets: three en-suite twins, a standard double and two doubles with shared facilities. There's a guest kitchen and a large lounge for pre- and post-hike relaxation, and breakfast is included in the room price. ‾CH$50,000‾

Domo Chaiguata Lago Chaiguata. Six geothermal domes with central heating and four or eight beds each for those who prefer glamping to camping. Facilities (including restaurant and hot tub) shared with the adjacent campsite (see below). Bring own sleeping bag. ‾CH$65,000‾

Domo Inío Caleta Inío. A cluster of geothermal domes for three or five people, complete with beds but more basic than the ones at Chaiguata (see above). ‾CH$25,000‾

7

Northern Patagonia

351 Parque Nacional Alerce Andino

352 Hornopirén and around

354 Parque Pumalín

358 The Futaleufú Valley

361 Parque Nacional Queulat and around

365 Coyhaique and around

368 West of Coyhaique

370 Around Lago General Carrera

375 South of Lago General Carrera

FLOWER MEADOW, CARRETERA AUSTRAL

Northern Patagonia

From Puerto Montt, the Carretera Austral, or "Southern Highway", stretches over 1000km south through the wettest, greenest, wildest and narrowest part of Chile, ending its mammoth journey at the tiny settlement of Villa O'Higgins. Carving its path through tracts of untouched wilderness, the route takes in soaring, snowcapped mountains, Ice Age glaciers, blue-green fjords, turquoise lakes and rivers, and one of the world's largest swathes of temperate rainforest. Most of it falls into Aysén, Chile's "last frontier", the final region to be opened up in the early twentieth century. A hundred years on, the region remains very sparsely populated, and still has the cut-off, marginal feel of a pioneer zone.

With the 2008 eruption of the Chaitén volcano (see p.358) now in the past, you can once again begin your exploration of the region from the north. Leaving Puerto Montt, you can travel through both **Parque Nacional Alerce Andino** and **Parque Nacional Hornopirén**, before taking the boat over to Caleta Gonzalo, where the Carretera cuts a passage through virgin temperate rainforest of **Parque Pumalín,** and finally emerging in the volcano-ravaged town of **Chaitén**.

South along the Carretera from Chaitén is the nondescript settlement of Villa Santa Lucía. From here, one branch of the road heads east, to the border village of Futaleufú, one of the world's top destinations for **whitewater rafting**. Continuing south, the Carretera emerges at the **Parque Nacional Queulat**, whose extraordinary hanging glacier and excellent trails make for one of the most rewarding places to get off the road. Don't miss the chance to luxuriate in the secluded hot pools of the luxurious **Termas de Puyuhuapi**.

The main town of **Coyhaique** marks the centre of the Carretera; to the west, **Puerto Chacabuco** is one of the starting points for boat excursions to the sensational **Laguna San Rafael glacier**, the other being **Puerto Río Tranquilo** further south, a jumping-off point for kayaking, boating and hiking on a nearby glacier. Here, the road skirts South America's second largest lake, **Lago General Carrera**, with a branch shooting off towards **Chile Chico** and the Argentinian border. The final stretch of the Carretera passes by the turnoff to **Parque Patagonia,** the region's newest and most exciting protected area with ample hiking opportunities, before connecting the ranching town of **Cochrane** to the isolated hamlet of **Villa O'Higgins**, with another road branching off en route to the highly unusual logging settlement of **Caleta Tortel**.

Brief history

The original inhabitants of this rain-swept land were the nomadic, hunter-gatherer **Tehuelche** of the interior, and the canoe-faring **Kawéshkar**, who fished the fjords and

Alerce trees p.351
"Doing" the Carretera Austral p.352
Douglas Tompkins and the Pumalín project p.355
Whitewater rafting on the Futa p.359
Fly-fishing and lodges on the Carretera Austral p.364

Visiting the San Rafael Glacier p.369
Hiking in Parque Patagonia p.376
Death in the forest p.378
Glaciers around Caleta Tortel p.379
Argentina the hard way: the El Chaltén Crossing p.380

Highlights

❶ **The Carretera Austral** Drive Chile's most spectacular – and still most challenging – road. **See p.352**

❷ **Parque Pumalín** Hike the trails and sail the fjords of Chile's largest private nature reserve. **See p.354**

❸ **Whitewater rafting at Futaleufú** "Purgatory", "Hell" and "Terminator" are just three of the world-class rapids you can hurtle down on the "Futa". **See p.359**

❹ **Ventisquero Colgante** Gawk at the suspended glacier that seems to defy gravity in Parque Nacional Queulat. **See p.362**

❺ **Termas de Puyuhuapi** Soak your bones while gazing at the southern night skies in Chile's premier spa resort. **See p.363**

❻ **Puerto Río Tranquilo** Kayak to otherworldly marble formations, go ice hiking on Glaciar Exploradores and take a boat ride to Laguna San Rafael to see its namesake glacier – it may be gone by 2030. **See p.369**

❼ **Parque Patagonia** Hike past dazzling highland lagoons, drive what may be Chile's most gorgeous road and marvel at the almost-tame guanacos. **See p.375**

❽ **Villa O'Higgins border crossing** Take up the challenge of crossing the border into Argentina both on foot and by boat through spectacular scenery. **See p.380**

HIGHLIGHTS ARE MARKED ON THE MAP ON P.350

NORTHERN PATAGONIA

HIGHLIGHTS

1. The Carretera Austral
2. Parque Pumalín
3. Whitewater rafting at Futaleufú
4. Ventisquero Colgante
5. Termas de Puyuhuapi
6. Puerto Río Tranquilo
7. Parque Patagonia
8. Villa O'Higgins border crossing

0 — 40 kilometres

PACIFIC OCEAN

ARGENTINA

MAR CHILENO

N

PARQUE NACIONAL ALERCE ANDINO
La Arena
Puelo
Caleta Puelche
Hornopirén
PARQUE NACIONAL HORNOPIRÉN
Cholgo
Ancud
Isla Llancahue
PARQUE PUMALÍN
Castro
Caleta Gonzálo
PARQUE PUMALÍN
ARGENTINA
Isla de Chiloé
Santa Barbara
Termas de Amarillo
Esquel
Chaitén
El Amarillo
Quellón
Puerto Cárdenas
Futaleufú
Trevelin
Villa Santa Lucia
Puerto Ramírez
Corcovado
Tecka
Golfo Corcovado
Palena
Puerto Raúl Marín Balmaceda
Lago Palena
Lago General Vintter
Melinka
La Junta
Sendero de Chile
RESERVA NACIONAL LAGO PALENA
Lago Risopatrón
Lago Verde
Puyuhuapi
Ventisquero Colgante
Termas de Puyuhuapi
PARQUE NACIONAL QUEULAT
Lago Verde
Isla Magdalena
Villa La Tapera
Puerto Cisnes
Villa Amengual
Lago La Plata
Lago Fontano
Puerto Gaviota
Mañihuales
Alto Río-Sénguer
Puerto Aysén
RESERVA NACIONAL COYHAIQUE
PARQUE NACIONAL LAS GUAITECAS
Puerto Chacabuco
RESERVA NACIONAL RÍO SIMPSON
Coyhaique
PARQUE NACIONAL CERRO CASTILLO
Villa Cerro Castillo
Balmaceda
Bahía Exploradores
Puerto Ibáñez
Puerto Murta
Valle Exploradores
Lago Buenos Aires
Perito Moreno
Exploradores Glacier
Puerto Río Tranquilo
Lago General Carrera
Chile Chico
Los Antiguas
PARQUE NACIONAL LAGUNA SAN RAFAEL
Laguna San Rafael Glacier
RESERVA NACIONAL LAGO GENERAL CARRERA
Capilla de Mármol
Puerto Guadal
RESERVA NACIONAL LAGO JEINIMENI
Lago Bertrand
Parque Patagonia
Puerto Bertrand
Cruce El Maitén
PARQUE PATAGONIA
Golfo de Peñas
Cochrane
Lago Cochrane
Lago Pueyrredón
CAMPO DE HIELO NORTE
RESERVA NACIONAL TAMANGO
Caleta Tortel
Puerto Yungay
ARGENTINA
RESERVA NACIOANL KATALALIXAR
PARQUE NACIONAL BERNARDO O'HIGGINS
PARQUE CERRO SANTIAGO
Lago Villa O'Higgins
Villa O'Higgins

Archipelago de Los Chonos
Canal Moraleda

channels of the coast, though now only a handful of the latter remain. In 1903, the government initiated a colonization programme that ultimately handed over thousands of hectares of land to three large livestock companies. At the same time, a wave of individual pioneers – known as **colonos** – came down from the north to try their luck at logging and farming, resulting in massive deforestation and destruction of the natural environment.

Faced with Argentina's encroaching influence, the government set out to actively "Chileanize" this new zone. Over the years, the perceived need for state control of the region did not diminish, explaining the rationale behind the construction of the Carretera Austral, initiated by earlier governments but with the greatest progress achieved under **General Pinochet**. Building the road was a colossal and incredibly expensive undertaking: the first section was finished in 1983 and engineers completed the final 100km in 2000, from tiny Puerto Yungay to the frontier outpost of Villa O'Higgins, by the Argentine border.

Northern Patagonia today

In spite of the Carretera Austral, the settlements in Northern Patagonia still have a frontier feel to them and the people who live here reflect the area's intrepid settler spirit. Their resourcefulness allows them to overcome major natural disasters such as volcanic eruptions, and every spring, they celebrate their *huaso* (cowboy) heritage in a series of rodeos, pitting their equestrian skills against one another.

Parque Nacional Alerce Andino

47km south of Puerto Montt • CH$1500 • Take southbound Ruta 7 until Chaica (35km from Puerto Montt); the park entrance is to the left

Heading out of Puerto Montt, the Carretera Austral hugs the shore of the Reloncaví fjord, skirting wide mud flats and empty beaches. Some 40km down the road – just beyond the Puente de Lenca – a signed track branches left and leads 7km to the southern entrance of **PARQUE NACIONAL ALERCE ANDINO**, where you'll find a small **Conaf** hut (daily 8am–5pm), a ranger station and a basic **camping** area. The park was created in 1982 to protect the region's ancient and rapidly depleting *alerce* forests, threatened with extinction by intense logging activity. Almost 200 square kilometres – half the park's land area – are covered by the massive, millenia-old *alerces*, mixed in with other native species like *coigüe* and *lenga*. This dense covering is spread over a landscape of steep hills and narrow glacial valleys dotted with dozens of lakes.

ALERCE TREES

The famed **alerce** trees – accorded national monument status by the government in 1976 – are endemic to southern Chile and Argentina and grow in high, soggy soil, usually on mountainsides between 600m and 800m above sea level. Among the **largest and oldest trees in the world**, they can rise to a height of 45m, with a trunk diameter of up to 4m, and live for over three thousand years. After shooting up rapidly during their first hundred years, they slow down dramatically, their diameter increasing just 1mm every three years. As they grow, they lose their lower branches, keeping only their top crown of dark-green, broccoli-like leaves. The lighter, lower leaves belong to parasite trees, which often prove useful to the ancient *alerces*, supporting them when they topple and keeping them alive. The trees' grey, papery bark conceals a beautiful, reddish-brown and extremely **valuable wood**; a large tree is worth tens of thousands of dollars. In the late-nineteenth and early twentieth centuries, the trees were chopped down at random by early colonizers – sometimes to be used for telegraph poles or shingles, but often just to clear land which was later found to be useless for agriculture. Today, it's illegal to chop down an *alerce* owing to their protected status, but it's not forbidden to sell the wood of dead trees, hence the untimely death of many *alerces*.

Hikes in Parque Nacional Alerce Andino

There's a good, long **day-hike** from the Conaf hut (at the southern entrance); the path follows the Río Chaica for 5km as far as the pretty **Laguna Chaiquenes**, surrounded by steep, forested hills. On the way, about an hour from the hut, you pass some impressive waterfalls and, twenty minutes later, a huge, 3000-year-old *alerce* tree. From Laguna Chaiquenes, the now deteriorating path heads north for a further 4km, as far as the long, thin **Laguna Triángulo**, where it peters out. Count on taking around three hours to get to Laguna Chaiquenes, and another three hours to get to Laguna Triángulo.

Hornopirén and around

The sheltered, sandy cove of **La Arena** lies 13km south of the turn-off to Parque Nacional Alerce Andino; it's the departure point of a thirty-minute **ferry** crossing (see p.353) to tiny **Caleta Puelche**, from where the road winds through 58km of thickly

---

"DOING" THE CARRETERA AUSTRAL

"Doing" the Carretera Austral requires a certain amount of forward planning, and time should be allowed for unexpected delays such as landslides, which tend to affect the northern half of the Carretera Austral from the Puerto Cisnes turnoff onwards during rainy weather. At the time of writing, two sections of the Carretera Austral – the road from the Puerto Cisnes turnoff to Puyuhuapi and the road from Puyuhuapi to La Junta – were closed to all traffic between 1 and 5pm daily due to paving operations; roadworks should finish in 2016.

BY PUBLIC TRANSPORT

The Carretera Austral is perfectly doable by bus, but plan ahead since stretches such as Coyhaique–Chaitén and Villa O'Higgins–Cochrane are served only twice-weekly. In peak season, the villages are covered by a combination of minibuses, ferries and local flights, but outside the December–March period there may be fewer services between some destinations; call and enquire in advance.

BY BICYCLE

Cycling the Carretera Austral is a challenge. While stretches of the northern half of the Southern Highway are now paved, equally there are steep, narrow and unpaved sections (Paso Queulat; see opposite) and long stretches of washboard-type gravel road, particularly south of Villa Cerro Castillo. Always cycle defensively to avoid the reckless drivers and be particularly careful south of Cochrane, as the road is frequently narrow and with blind turns. You will need to carry all necessary spare parts and supplies, because of the challenging road conditions and absence of bike shops (barring Coyhaique) and be prepared for plenty of rain.

BY CAR

The words "Carretera Austral" or 'Southern Highway' conjure up images of a smooth, paved, multi-lane road, right? Wrong. The Carretera Austral is still very much a "triumph" of man over nature; though parts of the road are being "tamed" through paving as we type, it is still a challenging – not to mention spectacularly scenic – drive.

What type of car do I need?

Some car rental agencies may insist that you rent a 4WD or a pickup truck for the journey, but while certain sections may be easier to drive in a high-clearance vehicle, the whole of the Carretera Austral is perfectly doable in a regular car. A pickup truck is mandatory for some side trips, such as the road that passes through Parque Patagonia (see p.376) en route to the Argentinian border.

What are the road conditions like?

The question you should be asking yourself is not "Will there be potholes?" It is: "Which of the following potholes should I hit to minimize the damage to my vehicle?" Some sections are more challenging than others; see below for a brief guide to the different stretches of road.

forested hills before arriving at the village of **HORNOPIRÉN**. Here you catch another (Naviera Austral) ferry to Caleta Gonzalo, where the Carretera continues.

Perched on the northern shore of a wide fjord, at the foot of **Volcán Hornopirén**, the village enjoys a spectacular location.

ARRIVAL AND DEPARTURE   HORNOPIRÉN

By bus Kemel Bus (☎ 65 225 3530) runs to Puerto Montt (3 daily; 3hr 30min) and passes through en route to Chaitén at around 10.30am (1 daily; 5hr).

By car The road from Puerto Montt is largely paved, but if you're looking to drive from Hornopirén towards Cochamó (see p.307) via the V-69 that leads east from Caleta Puelche, allow yourself at least 1hr to cover the 36km to Puelo, as the road is not very well maintained.

By ferry The La Arena–Caleta Puelche ferry is operated by Naviera Puelche (every 45min, 6.45am–12.30am; CH$9500/car, passengers CH$600; ☎ 65 227 0761, ⓦ navierapuelche.cl). Naviera Austral (☎ 65 227 0431, ⓦ navieraustral.cl) covers the two-stage ferry crossing between Hornopirén and Caleta Gonzalo, with daily ferries from Hornopirén departing for Leptepú at 11am, and ferries sailing from Caleta Gonzalo, at the north end of Parque Pumalín, at 2pm. There's an extra daily departure from both ends in Jan and Feb. Rates are CH$5000 for passengers and CH$30,000 for cars; book the Hornopirén–Caleta Gonzalo leg well in advance.

8

Will there be anywhere to buy petrol?
The vast majority of settlements along the Carretera Austral have petrol stations, so you needn't worry about running dry.

What essentials should I bring?
Bring a spare tyre (*neumático*), and all equipment necessary to change said tyre, as you'll only be able to rely on yourself and passing motorists for roadside assistance. Carry food, water and a sleeping bag, just in case.

What about crossing the border into Argentina?
You'll need to have the required paperwork from your car rental company as well as relevant insurance.

Any other precautions?
Try to avoid driving when it's dark, as not all curves in the road are marked with reflectors. Driving too close to other cars is a bad idea as the loose gravel flying out from under the wheels of the vehicle in front of you can crack your windscreen. Do not take corners at high speeds on the *ripio* (dirt and gravel) sections of the road, as you can skid right off the side of the road. If travelling via Hornopirén and Caleta Gonzalo, and if you wish to take the ferry between Puerto Ibañez and Chile Chico, book ferry tickets a week in advance (see p.371).

ROAD CONDITIONS BY SECTION
Chaitén to Villa Santa Lucia Paved up to Puerto Cárdenas, otherwise heavily potholed and prone to landslides in rainy conditions.

Villa Santa Lucía to Futaleufú Valley Somewhat potholed, mostly good gravel road; some landslide-prone sections.

Villa Santa Lucía to Puyuhuapi Partially paved, but the section between La Junta and Puyuhuapi is prone to landslides.

Puyuhuapi to Puerto Cisnes crossroads The most challenging section is the Paso Queulat – narrow, steep, deeply rutted and with tight curves. Sections were being paved at the time of writing.

Parque Nacional Queulat to the turn-off for Puerto Aysén Completely paved.

Coyhaique to Puerto Aisén Completely paved but with some blind turns.

Coyhaique to Cochrane Paved between Coyhaique and Cerro Castillo; otherwise mostly good gravel road with few potholes and some narrow sections.

Cruce El Maitén to Chile Chico Mostly good gravel road, but narrow and with precipitous drop on one side.

Cochrane to Villa O'Higgins Mostly good gravel road, steep in parts; ferry crossing required at Puerto Yungay; some sections are narrow with blind turns and sheer drop to one side.

ACCOMMODATION AND EATING

Hostería Catalina Av Ingenieros Militares s/n ☎ 65 221 7359. Attractive B&B with wood-panelled en-suite rooms, very attentive hosts and good home-cooked meals on offer. On the downside, the thin walls can make you feel as if you're in bed with your neighbours. **CH$40,000**

Hotel Termas de Llancahué Isla Llancahué ☎ 09 9642 4857 or 09 8529 9771, ⓦ termasdellancahue.cl. Located on Isla Llancahué, a 20min/1hr boat ride from Hornopirén depending on which boat you take (and with departures according to demand), this simple resort features pools fed by water from the hot springs with fabulous ocean views. **CH$70,000**

Parque Nacional Volcán Hornopirén

16km east of Hornopirén

To the east of Hornopirén unfold the 500 square kilometres of protected wilderness that make up **PARQUE NACIONAL VOLCÁN HORNOPIRÉN**. The park's namesake and centrepiece, 16km along a muddy track from the village, is the perfectly conical **Volcán Hornopirén**. Five kilometres further along the track lies the seldom-visited **Lago General Pinto Concha**, with excellent fishing and stunning views onto the 2111m **Volcán Yate** (1hr hike one-way). From Lago General Pinto Concha, another track leads to the base of Volcán Yate (2hr hike one-way).

Back towards the village, a turn-off from the track leads south around the end of the fjord to a modern bridge over the **Río Blanco**, with a short trail to your left leading up to the impressive Salto del Río Blanco waterfall. An 8km path follows the river upstream, passing through alternating patches of pastureland and grand stands of *alerce*, *coigüe*, *tepa* and *lenga*; above the tree line, you'll enter a landscape of ice-covered peaks and glaciers. Bear in mind that the trails are not very well marked.

Parque Pumalín

30km north of Chaitén • ⓦ www.parquepumalin.cl

South of Hornopirén, connected to it by two ferries, lies **PARQUE PUMALÍN**, the world's largest privately owned conservation area, covering 2900 square kilometres of land. The Pumalín Project, founded by North American billionaire philanthropist Douglas Tompkins to protect one of the world's last strongholds of temperate rainforest, originally generated a considerable amount of controversy, yet few would deny that the park represents a magnificent environmental achievement. It's a place of overwhelming natural beauty, with calm lakes reflecting stands of endangered *alerce* trees, ferocious waterfalls gushing through chasms of dark rock, and high, snowy-peaked mountains. Parque Pumalín consists of three sectors, with the southern sector being the most-visited one.

The northern sector

The largely inaccessible **northern sector** features the gloriously isolated **Termas de Cahuelmó**: a series of natural hot pools, carved out of the rock at the end of a steep, narrow fjord, reachable only by private boat from Hornopirén. There's a manned campsite there also. Though there are several other remote hiking trails in the northern section, they are difficult and expensive to reach, so visitors to this less-explored part of the park do so by kayak (see p.356) or by hiring a boat.

The southern sector

The **southern section** has the most infrastructure geared towards visitors, with trails and campsites branching off the 58km of the Carretera Austral. Near the ferry ramp at Caleta Gonzalo, the **Sendero Cascadas** climbs steeply through a canopy of overhanging foliage up to a 15m waterfall (3hr round-trip). Other trails have been carved out of the

DOUGLAS TOMPKINS AND THE PUMALÍN PROJECT

In 1995 it was publicly announced that a North American billionaire, **Douglas Tompkins**, had used intermediaries to buy a 3000-square-kilometre chunk of southern Chile – marking the beginning of a five-year national soap opera that transformed Tompkins into one of the most controversial public figures in the country. In 1991, the 49-year-old Californian, increasingly committed to environmental issues, sold his share in the North Face and Esprit clothing empire, bought an abandoned ranch on the edge of the **Reñihué fjord**, 130km south of Puerto Montt, and moved there with his wife Kris. Inspired by the "deep ecology" movement pioneered by the Norwegian environmentalist **Arne Naess**, Tompkins set out to acquire more of the surrounding wilderness, with the aim of protecting it from the threat of commercial exploitation. As he did so, he was seized with the idea of creating a massive, privately funded national park, which would ensure permanent protection of the **ancient forest** while providing low-impact facilities for visitors.

THE MEDIA BACKLASH

Over the next four years Tompkins spent more than US$14 million buying up adjoining tracts of land, in most cases hiding his identity to prevent prices from shooting up. His initial secrecy was to have damaging repercussions, however, for once his land acquisitions became public knowledge, he was engulfed by a wave of suspicion and hostility, fuelled by several right-wing politicians and the press, with his motives questioned by everyone. The biggest cause for alarm, it seemed, was the fact that Tompkins' land stretched from the Argentine border to the Pacific Ocean, effectively "cutting Chile in two". Tompkins appeared on national television, explaining his intentions to create **Parque Pumalín**, a nature sanctuary with free access, slowly winning over some of the public.

SUCCESS WITH STRINGS

Eventually, the government agreed to support Tompkins' aims to establish the park – on the condition that for one year he would not buy more than 7000 contiguous hectares (17,250 acres) of land in the south of Chile. Tompkins was also prevented from purchasing Huinay, a 740,000-acre property owned by the Catholic University of Valparaíso, separating the two separate chunks of his land, which was instead sold to ENDESA, Chile's largest energy corporation.

Tompkins, determined to save a little more unspoiled terrain from development, purchased another chunk of land in 2001 near the Termas del Amarillo, south of Chaitén, while in 2005, Parque Pumalín, by this point managed by the Chilean Fundación Pumalín (whose board includes Tompkins and his wife), was finally declared a **santuario de la naturaleza** (nature sanctuary), which gave it additional protection.

Pumalín was only the start of the Tompkins' environmentalist legacy in Chile and Argentina; to date, Douglas and his wife Kristine have been involved in numerous conservation projects in both Chile and Argentina, purchasing tracts of land, restoring the original ecosystems and donating them to the respective countries as national parks. In Chile, these include Estancia Yendegaia (see p.425) and the most exciting current project is **Parque Patagonia** (see p.375), Kris Tompkins' major initiative.

8

forest, branching off from the Carretera Austral as it heads south through the park, passing the splendid Lago Blanco and other numerous natural highlights. Twelve kilometres south of Caleta Gonzalo, **Sendero Laguna Tronador** is the most challenging, crossing a narrow gorge filled with a rushing, whitewater stream, and climbing steeply up a series of wooden stepladders to a look-out point with fabulous views onto Volcán Michinmahuida, and ending at the pristine lake with a camping area alongside (3hr round-trip).

One kilometre south, across the Río Blanco, **Sendero Los Alerces** is an enjoyable twenty-minute circular route, dotted with information panels, through a grove of ancient, colossal *alerces*. Another kilometre down the road, the **Sendero Cascadas Escondidas** is an easy walk through the forest to three high, slender waterfalls; you reach the first one after 25 minutes or so, and the other two, half an hour after that.

Closer to Chaitén there are two other trails: the **Sendero Volcán Michinmahuida**, a 12km ramble to the base of the eponymous volcano, and the **Sendero Volcán Chaitén**, a popular trail that climbs up to the rim of the cantankerous volcano that wreaked so much recent havoc in the area (2hr 30min roundtrip).

The El Amarillo sector

Next to the village of the same name, 24km south of Chaitén, the **El Amarillo sector** is the newest part of the park. Just over 4km from the entrance is the start of the 2.5km **Sendero Darwin**, an interpretative loop that runs through dense forest. From the Ventisquero campsite, the flat 10km **Sendero El Amarillo Ventisquero** runs to the base of the Michimahuida glacier, with superb views en route, making it a really good, easy day hike. Another ambitious trail is in the planning, due to connect this trail to the southern sector of the park via the mountain pass that lies between the Michimahuida and Chaitén volcanoes in 2016; it will include a *refugio* halfway along.

Not strictly in the El Amarillo sector, 2km uphill from the park entrance are the **Termas El Amarillo**, some relaxing hot-spring-fed outdoor pools (CH$4000).

ARRIVAL AND DEPARTURE   PARQUE PUMALÍN

THE NORTHERN SECTOR

By organized tour One option is to join a multi-day kayaking adventure trip with either Alsur Expediciones (☎65 223 2300, ⓦalsurexpeditions.com) or Yak Expediciones (☎09 9299 6487, ⓦyakexpediciones.cl). It's also possible to charter a boat in Hornopirén.

THE SOUTHERN SECTOR

By bus Kemel Buses (☎65 225 3530) pass through the southern section en route from Puerto Montt to Chaitén (1 daily) and can drop you off along the way.

By car In peak season, there are daily car ferries from Hornopirén to Caleta Gonzalo (see p.353), the entry

point to the park. Book well in advance.

By organized tour Chaitur and Chaitén Nativo (see p.357) both run tours to the park in summer months from Chaitén.

THE AMARILLO SECTOR

By bus Any bus between Chaitén and destinations south can drop you off at El Amarillo village.

By car If driving into the park, the Ventisquero El Amarillo campsite can only be reached by pickup truck or 4WD, but the other dirt roads are fine.

By organized tour Chaitur and Chaitén Nativo (see p.357) both run tours to the Termas El Amarillo (CH$25,000) and can drop you by the park entrance en route.

INFORMATION

Park information There are two Centros de Visitantes: one at Caleta Gonzalo and the other at El Amarillo, across the road and uphill from the park entrance (Dec–Feb Mon–Sat 9am–7pm, Sun 10am–4pm; ⓦwww.parquepumalin.cl). There's also Casa Puma at Klenner 299 in Puerto Varas (Mon–Fri 9am–5pm; ☎65 225 0079), where you can get advance info on the park.

ACCOMMODATION AND EATING

SOUTHERN SECTOR

Cabañas Río Gonzalo Caleta Gonzalo ☎65 225 0079. At Caleta Gonzalo, these seven *cabañas* (sleeping 2–5) are the epitome of rustic luxury, each individually designed, with comfy loft beds and ocean views. There's also a good camping spot nearby with cold showers and sheltered cooking spaces. Camping/person CH$2500, *cabañas* CH$85,000

Café Caleta Gonzalo Caleta Gonzalo ☎65 225 0079. This appealing restaurant with massive fireplace serves Chilean dishes cooked with organic vegetables, and the delicious bread is home-made. Large groups can book in advance for an *asado* (barbecue) and there are picnic boxes to take away. Summer daily 9am–10pm.

Camping Cascadas Escondidas 14km south of Caleta Gonzalo. Small campsite with showers and sheltered cooking area. Camping/person CH$7500

Camping Lago Blanco 36km north of Chaitén. This campsite has fantastic views of Lago Blanco from the covered sites, as well as hot showers and fire pits. Camping/person CH$7500

Camping El Volcán Halfway between Chaitén and Caleta Gonzalo. Large, tree-fringed campsite; each site comes with own cooking area, barbecue and drinking water access. Camping/person CH$2500

AMARILLO SECTOR

Camping Grande 3.3km from park entrance. Attractive

campsite with sites scattered around giant *nalca* patches and surrounded by trees. Comes with bathrooms and *quinchos* for cooking. Camping/person CH$2500

Camping Ventisquero 8km from park entrance. Dubbed "The most beautiful campsite in Chile", albeit the furthest from the park entrance. this tree-fringed spot comes with spectacular views of the hanging glacier, as well as cooking shelters and bathrooms. Camping/person CH$2500

Camping Vuelta del Rio 600m from park entrance.

Creekside campsite that's the closest to the park entrance, with bathrooms and a communal cooking shelter. Camping/person CH$2500

Yelcho En La Patagonia Puerto Cárdenas, 19km south of El Amarillo ☎ 65 257 6005, ⓦ yelcho.cl. This luxurious retreat consists of a boutique hotel with eight intimate rooms, and fishing and horseriding on the menu. Nearby is a large lakeside campsite; each of its sites comes with a cooking shelter, firepit and firewood, and hot shower access. Doubles CH$90,000, camping/person CH$2000

SHOPPING

Puma Verde Carretera Austral s/n. By the El Amarillo petrol station, this is an excellent store selling varied foods as well as camping supplies and even outdoor gear. Mon–Sat 9am–6pm.

Chaitén

On May 2, 2008, **Volcán Chaitén**, at the foot of which nestles its namesake town, **erupted** for the first time in over nine thousand years, taking the local residents completely by surprise, as the volcano was thought to be dormant. The town, and much of the surrounding area, had to be evacuated as the 30km plume of ash and steam from the volcano affected the local water sources and a mudslide caused floods which devastated the town. While the Bachelet government ordered the town to be abandoned, the Piñera administration subsequently reversed the decision and, with vital services now reinstated and the town largely rebuilt (though you still see a number of eerie, wrecked houses half-buried in volcanic detritus), Chaitén is once again connected to Puerto Montt and other destinations along the Carretera Austral by frequent boat, bus and plane.

ARRIVAL AND DEPARTURE   CHAITÉN

By bus Buses Becker (☎ 67 223 2167) run to Coyhaique via La Junta and Puyuhuapi, Buses Cardenas (☎ 67 272 1214) serve Futaleufú, Buses Cumbres Nevadas (☎ 09 8597 6405) run both to Futaleufú and Palena, while Kemel Bus (☎ 65 225 3530) runs to Puerto Montt via Hornopirén.

Destinations Coyhaique (Wed & Sun at noon; 9hr); Futaleufú (2–3 daily at 1pm, 4pm & 6pm; 2hr 30min–4hr); Hornopirén (daily at noon; 4hr 30min); La Junta (2 weekly; 3hr); Palena (daily at 4pm & 6pm; 2hr 30min); Puerto Montt (daily at noon; 7hr).

By boat The Naviera Austral office at Av Corcovado 466 (☎ 65 273 1011, ⓦ navieraustral.cl) sells tickets for ferries to Quellón, Castro and Puerto Montt; double-check timetables as they're prone to change.

Destinations Castro (Jan & Feb Sat at noon; 5hr 30min); Puerto Montt (Fri & Sun at 10am; 8hr); Quellón (Mon at 10am; 5hr).

By car From the north, you can drive via Hornopirén, booking the Caleta Gonzalo ferry in advance (see p.353). It's possible to take the car ferry from Quellón but prices are steep.

By air Pewen Air Services (☎ 65 222 4000, ⓦ pewenchile .com), CieloMarAustral (☎ 65 226 4010) and Aerocord (☎ 65 226 2300, ⓦ aerocord.cl) all have scheduled flights to Puerto Montt from the Santa Barbara airstrip (CH$40,000 one way, CH$80,000 return).

Destinations Puerto Montt (Mon–Sat at 11am; 8hr)

INFORMATION AND TOURS

There's a tourist information kiosk on the *costanera*, but it's rarely staffed or open.

Chaitur O'Higgins 67 ☎ 65 273 1429 or ☎ 09 7468 5608, ⓦ chaitur.com. The HQ of the indomitable American expat Nicolas La Penna – a treasure trove of local information – doubles as the local bus terminal and is the place for organizing both onward travel and day tours to Parque Pumalín and Termas de Amarillo. If Nicolas is not at the office, locals can point out his house

so you can go and knock on his door.

Chaiten Nativo Libertad 253 ☎ 65 273 1333 or ☎ 09 7764 5891, ⓦ chaitennativo.cl. Besides outings to Termas de Amarillo, kayaking and mountain biking excursions, this knowledgeable, local one-man show also leads varied tours to different parts of Parque Pumalín. Bikes available for rent.

ACCOMMODATION AND EATING

Hostal Don Carlos Riveros 53 ☎ 65 273 1287. Popular family-run guesthouse a block from the waterfront, with compact, functional rooms. En-suite rooms with cable TV are more expensive. Hosts won't win many congeniality prizes and breakfast is not worth writing home about. CH$24,000
Hostería Llanos Corcovado 387 ☎ 09 8826 0448. Seafront residence run by a friendly elderly lady, with wood-panelled en-suite rooms and frilly bedspreads. Breakfast includes a hefty slice of cake. CH$24,000
Pizzeria Reconquista Portales at O'Higgins. Returning to reconquer Chaitén after years of volcanic-eruption-induced absence, this locally-beloved pizzeria is now in a

new location, with a cute little bar dispensing Espumalín and two other local brews, and walls hung with photos of ye olde Chaitén and the spectacular eruption. Pizzas are solidly Chilean (very little tomato sauce) but thin-and-crispy, large and sporting some exotic ingredients. Mains from CH$7000. Daily 12.30–3.30pm & 7–10pm.
El Quijote O'Higgins s/n ☎ 09 7654 9841. Half a block from the *costanera*, this cheery, family-run restaurant serves heaped portions of super-fresh grilled fish or chicken and chips. Owner Javier has several basic but comfortable rooms for rent, too. Daily 12.30–3.30pm & 7–10pm. CH$24,000

DIRECTORY

Money and exchange A Banco Estado on the plaza has an ATM which accepts some foreign cards, but not others, though it does change dollars, Euros and Argentinian pesos.

The Futaleufú Valley

The 80km trip up the **FUTALEUFÚ VALLEY** is one of the most enjoyable diversions off the Carretera Austral. Heading east from the drab crossroads settlement of Villa Santa Lucía, south of Chaitén, you first skirt the southern shore of Lago Yelcho for 30km, before arriving at a fork in the road. The right turn goes to the quiet border village of **Palena**, while the left branch follows the turquoise **Río Futaleufú** for 17km through towering gorges, lush forests and snow-streaked mountain peaks to its namesake town.

Futaleufú

Sitting on the Río Futaleufú, near its confluence with the Rio Espolón, and surrounded by forested, snowy peaks, Futaleufú more than earns the grandiose slogan – "A landscape painted by God" – coined by its early inhabitants. With its big "explosion waves" and massive "rodeo holes", the Río Futaleufú is regarded by many professional rafters and kayakers as one of the most challenging whitewater rivers in the world, with sections of the river known as "Hell" and "The Terminator", though the toughest Class V rapids are "Trono" and "Zeta". A number of Chilean and US operators offer **rafting** trips down the river, a body of water which runs through a basalt gorge known as the Gates of Hell, and boasts over forty class IV–V rapids; to run the whole river you need 3–4 days,

An attractive little town, Futaleufú serves as a popular summer base for rafting, kayaking, hiking and horseriding. Since it's very close to the Argentinian border, it also makes for an easy transfer to Esquel and Trevelín.

ARRIVAL AND INFORMATION

By bus Buses Transaustral (☎ 67 272 1360) runs to Osorno and Puerto Montt via Argentina, while Transporte Internacional runs across the border to Esquel, leaving from Cerda between Prat and Aldea. Buses Becker (☎ 67 223 2167) runs to Coyhaique, while Buses Cardenas (☎ 09 9545 4891) heads to Chaitén and Cumbres Nevadas (☎ 67 272 1208) serves Palena and Chaitén. All buses apart from those to Esquel depart from the corner of Prat and Balmaceda.
Destinations Chaitén (2–3 daily, one of which departs at 6am, Sun excepted; 2hr 30min); Coyhaique (Fri at 11.45am;

10hr); Esquel (Argentina; Mon, Wed & Fri 2 daily at 9am & 6.45pm; 30min); Osorno (Sun & Wed at 7.30am; 14hr); Puerto Montt (Sun & Wed at 7.30am; 12hr).
Tourist office O'Higgins 536, south side of the Plaza de Armas (summer daily 9am–8pm).

TOUR OPERATORS

Expediciones Chile Mistral 296 ☎ 65 272 1386, ⓦ exchile.com. With their own riverfront camp, this American-Chilean outfit specializes in multi-day rafting on the Futa. Occasional half-day and full-day outings, whitewater kayaking lessons, and also offers small-group, multi-day trekking and ranch stays, combining cultural immersion with spectacular mountain scenery.

Patagonia Elements Cerda 549 ☎ 09 7499 0296, ⓦ patagoniaelements.com. Right on the plaza, this reputable, safety-conscious Chilean operator is your best bet for half- and full-day rafting on the Futa.

ACCOMMODATION

Camping Puerto Espolón next to the bridge, just south of town ☎ 65 272 1509. This tree-dotted riverfront campsite is a 10min walk from the plaza, and has its own little beach, as well as accommodation inside two geodomes (up to 8 people in each). As an extra nice touch, owner Arturo brews his own FutaAlhue pale ale and stout which he's happy to sell to campers. Camping/person `CH$5000`. domes/person `CH$12,000`

Cara del Indio 35km from Futaleufú ☎ 2 1962 4240, ⓦ caradelindio.cl. This riverfront adventure camp makes a great base for whitewater enthusiasts, who can choose between camping, staying in a basic *refugio* or sharing one of the fully equipped *cabañas*. The on-site restaurant serves Chilean favourites such as *cazuela* (stew) and if there's a group of you, you can opt for barbecued Patagonian lamb. Camping/person `CH$5000`, refugio `CH$5000`, cabañas `CH$35,000`

H20 Patagonia Km2 en route to Argentinian border ☎ 888 426 7238, ⓦ h2opatagonia.com. Brian and the rest of this established American–Chilean outfit offers seven-day all-inclusive packages based at their luxurious riverfront camp, 2km east of Futa. The week revolves around three days of rafting (see box below), with canyoning, horseriding and kayaking, and Patagonian *asados* also on the menu. Guests can enjoy their downtime in the hexagonal lounge with massive fireplace. Per person `US$3600`

★**La Gringa Carioca** Aldea 498 ☎ 65 272 1260 ⓦ hostallagringacarioca.cl. South African Adriana is the effusive hostess at this intimate cottage sitting in the middle of a large garden on the edge of Futa. The four light, bright,

spacious doubles may all be individually decorated but have in common the high-quality beds and linens. A delicious American-style breakfast seals the deal and après-adventure cheese-and-wine soirees are in the planning. CH$25,000 discount for solo travellers. `CH$60,000`

Hostal Las Natalias O'Higgins 302 ☎ 09 9631 1330, ⓦ hostallasnatalias.info. A 10min walk from town (follow Cerda west until it dips downhill and then heads up again), this rambling hostel is run by hospitable American-Argentinian Nate. The huge open-plan communal area/kitchen is a very sociable place with occasional barbecues for guests. People find themselves extending their stay, seduced by the easy-going vibe. Dorms `CH$10,000`, doubles `CH$25,000`

Hostería Río Grande O'Higgins 397 ☎ 65 272 1320, ⓦ pachile.com. Favoured by rafting gringos, this hotel with its chic-rustic decor and narrow doorways is still one of the most popular places to stay. The carpeted rooms are bright and comfortable, the bar makes a good hangout spot and the owner can help you organise your rafting adventure. `US$110`

Lodge El Barranco Bernardo O'Higgins 172 ☎ 65 272 1314, ⓦ elbarrancochile.cl. The hospitable owners of this lodge on the outskirts of town go out of their way to welcome you and can help organise fishing, rafting and horseriding excursions. The spacious, wood-panelled rooms may be on the dark side, but they have comfortable beds with crisp linens and there's even a small swimming pool for guest use. `CH$130,000`

WHITEWATER RAFTING ON THE FUTA

Most people come to Futaleufú for the **whitewater rafting and kayaking**, though you needn't stop there: the area around Futa lends itself to a range of **outdoor activities** including hiking, horse-trekking, mountain biking, fly-fishing, drifting down the tamer Río Espolón on an inner tyre tube, canyoning (abseiling down waterfalls) and canoeing. Expect to pay around CH$25,000 for a relatively simple run down the Río Espolón, CH$50,000 for a half-day excursion on the Río Futaleufú and CH$90,000 for a full day on the Futa, which includes tackling numerous Class V rapids. A number of experienced local outfits offer these activities (see p.358).

The standard half-day outing on the river is the "Bridge to Bridge" section, which comprises around twelve rapids, mostly Class III+ and IV, and one V ("Mundaca"). You don't have to have prior rafting experience, because you'll be taught all the safety instructions and commands, but you do have to be reasonably fit and a decent swimmer. Futa is a serious river and even a half-day excursion (1.5–2hr on the water) will expose you to some drenching, **heart-stopping fun** amidst raft-battering turquoise waves. Tour operators take safety seriously and a raft or two is accompanied by a rescue cataraft and two rescue kayaks. Occasionally people fall out of rafts, and sometimes a raft will flip; you will be taught what to do in each situation and rescuers will be nearby.

★**Uman Lodge** Fundo La Confluencia s/n, 4km south of Futaleufú ☎65 272 1700 🔊umanlodge.cl. Reachable via a steep, bumpy road that branches off from the Carretera Austral south of town, this shingled wonder of a hotel sits on a bluff overlooking the river far below. Besides its covered outdoor terrace that sports a telescope and fireplace, the hotel's many enticing features include a library/lounge with immense ceilings, a first-class restaurant that's worth the gnarly drive (even if you're not staying here) and infinity pool, Turkish sauna and Jacuzzi. The open-plan rooms with free-standing tubs are both luxurious and stylish, and trekking, ziplining and other outdoor activities are available to guests. Half- and full-board options available. Breakfast included. U̲S̲$̲4̲4̲0̲

EATING

Martín Pescadór Balmaceda 603 ☎65 272 1279. One of the best restaurants in town, serving the likes of grilled salmon with honey and ginger, carpaccio and inventive meat dishes in a mountain lodge, living room-style atmosphere, with a fire roaring on colder days. The wine list is extensive. Mains from CH$8000. Daily 7–11.30pm.

Siete Siete Aldea 346 ☎09 5980 1039. This newcomer on the scene is poised to win fans with its innovative takes on fish, pasta and meat dishes. Mains from CH$6500. Mon–Fri noon–3pm & 7–10pm, Fri & Sat 11am–10pm.

SurAndes Cerda 308 ☎65 272 1405. Real coffee, freshly squeezed juice and numerous vegetarian options contribute to the popularity of this tiny café, which also offers good omelettes, lentil and chorizo stew, home-made pastas and hefty burgers. Mains CH$5000. Daily 9am–11pm.

DIRECTORY

Money and exchange There's a single ATM at Banco Estado, on the Plaza de Armas, but it doesn't accept some foreign cards so bring plenty of cash.

8

Raul Marín Balmaceda

Around 75km south of the crossroads settlement of Villa Santa Lucía – where the road to the Futaleufú Valley branches off from the Carretera Austral – a westbound, 53km-long gravel road splits off from the Carretera, running along the banks of Río Palena to **Raúl Marín Balmaceda** – a fishing village with the most attractive setting along the whole of the Carretera Austral. The cluster of houses, hiding behind greenery along several streets, sits on an island in the river delta, reachable by car ferry (see below) and boasting attractive white sand beaches; note that you have to drive an additional 21km post-ferry to get to the village. The bay is full of marine life, such as seals and cormorants, and it's possible to see dolphins and even blue whales if you do a boat excursion (see below).

ARRIVAL AND DEPARTURE RAUL MARÍN BALMACEDA

By bus Buses run to Raúl Marín Balmaceda from La Junta (Mon, Wed & Fri at 8.30am; 2hr); check with the tourist office (see p.361) for up-to-date timetables.

By ferry The car ferry to and from the village runs several times daily (passengers free, cars CH$4000). Naviera Austral ferries (🔊navieraustral.cl) stop here en route between Puerto Chacabuco and Quellón.

TOURS

Kawelyek Expediciones ☎09 5742 9056, 🔊kawelyek.cl. Local guide Patricio runs three different tours: a 2hr boat tour that takes you dolphin- and sea bird-spotting, a 4hr wildlife-watching boat tour that runs up the Estuario Pitipalena and a 6hr tour up Canal Garrao, which can be done in a boat or sea kayak.

ACCOMMODATION AND EATING

Fundo Los Leones ☎09 7898 2956, 🔊fundo losleones.com. You'll find this delightful retreat, reachable by boat from the village, just on the outskirts of Raúl Marín Balmaceda. The wood-panelled, wi-fi-equipped *cabañas* (sleeping 2) are bright, individually decorated and named after sea mammals, while the lodge offers a variety of boat trips and fishing excursions and there's an outdoor hot tub for relaxation. Meals extra. C̲H̲$̲9̲0̲,̲0̲0̲0̲

Residencial Los Lirios Central s/n ☎09 6242 0180. Snug family-run option in the village proper; rooms share facilities and meals can be provided on request. C̲H̲$̲2̲6̲,̲0̲0̲0̲

La Junta and Reserva Nacional Lago Rosselot

South of the turn-offs for Raúl Marín Balmaceda and Lago Verde, and just before the northern boundary of Parque Nacional Queulat, the Carretera Austral passes through **La Junta**, a collection of tin houses established in 1983 as one of General Pinochet's "new towns", and home to a controversial unauthorized monument to the dictator. La Junta is the access point to the **Reserva Nacional Lago Rosselot**, whose namesake lake has gained popularity with the fly-fishing set.

ARRIVAL AND INFORMATION LA JUNTA

By bus Transportes Terraustral (☎67 225 4335) run to Coyhaique and Chaitén. Buses Becker also serve Chaitén, as well as Futaleufú. Most buses depart from the plaza. Destinations Chaitén (1 daily Mon at 7am, Tues around 3pm, Fri at 7am & Sat around 3pm; 3hr 30min); Coyhaique (several times weekly; 6hr); Futaleufú (1 weekly Thurs, returning the following day; 3hr)

Tourist information Plaza de Armas (Dec–March daily 9am–9pm; shorter hours rest of year ☎65 272 1239, ⓦcamaralajunta.cl).

ACCOMMODATION

★**Alto Melimoyu Hotel & Patagonia** Carretera Austral 375 ☎67 231 4320, ⓦaltomelimoyu.cl. The young owners of this beautiful guesthouse offer numerous excursions to active travellers, from hiking in Reserva Nacional Lago Rosselot to kayaking and mountain biking. Bright rooms come with all manner of creature comforts (including satellite TV) though some share facilities. CH$48,000

Espacio y Tiempo Hotel de Montaña Carretera Austral 399 ☎67 231 4141, ⓦespacioytiempo.cl. With appealing rustic interior, friendly staff and just nine spiffy, centrally-heated rooms, this wood-and-stone mountain lodge just off the Carretera Austral allows easy exploration of the Río Palena watershed on horseback, or just lets you curl up by the fireplace in the cosy guest lounge. The on-site restaurant serves good Chilean staples. CH$88,000

Hostería Valderas Varas s/n ☎67 231 4195. One of several centrally located guesthouses of comparable quality, the Lagos family home sits a couple of blocks from the plaza. Rooms are clean and basic, facilities are shared and the proprietress can cook up simple meals on request. CH$24,000

EATING

Mi Casita de Té Carretera Austral at Patricio Lynch ☎67 231 4206. A bright, welcoming café with wool hangings and an inexpensive menu of Chilean standards, with friendly Eliana and her daughters serving large portions of grilled fish, *lomo a lo pobre* (cut of meat with fried egg on top) and *cazuela* (stew). Mon–Sat 12.30–10pm, Sun 12.30–3.30pm.

Parque Nacional Queulat and around

22km south of Puyuhuapi • CH$4000, payable only if you enter Sector Ventisquero Colgante

Consisting of rugged, mountains, dense forest, raging glacial rivers and its namesake hanging glacier, the 1540-square-km **PARQUE NACIONAL QUEULAT** is one of the region's most impressive natural attractions, as beautiful as it is remote and as rainy as it is beautiful. It is divided into three sectors. The Carretera Austral enters the park's northern boundary 15km north of the village of Puyuhuapi and crosses its southern limit 55km further south, just beyond the Portezuelo de Queulat pass. The park's main entrance lies 2.5km along a signposted turn-off from the Carretera Austral, and that's where you find most accommodation and trails.

Sector Angostura

Beyond Puyuhuapi, in the northern sector of the park, a track pulls off the road to the Conaf *guardería*, on the shores of the long, thin **Lago Risopatrón**. The lake, flanked by steep mountains jutting abruptly out of its deep-blue waters, is a lovely spot, and the **camping** area (see p.362) near the Conaf hut is one of the prettiest along the entire road. By the *guardería*, the **Sendero Laguna Los Pumas** (13km return; 5hr) starts with a steep ascent, climbing to 1100m. From the plateau at the top, you get sweeping views onto surrounding mountains and out to the fjord. The trail then descends through a pass, leading to the shimmering Laguna Los Pumas.

Sector Ventisquero Colgante

The central and most popular section of the park is named after the incredible **Ventisquero Colgante**, or "hanging glacier". Wedged between two peaks, forming a V-shaped mass of blue-white ice, the glacier indeed seems to hang suspended over a sheer rock face above a glacial lake. From the parking area 2km beyond the ranger post, follow the signposted 250m **Sendero Mirádor Panorámico**, a muddy fifteen-minute roundtrip up to a viewpoint overlooking the raging glacial river. For a closer look at the glacier, cross the suspension bridge over the river, and turn right, taking the 600m **Sendero Laguna Témpanos**, a non-strenuous trail (15min one-way) through overgrown woods that skirts the river and leads to the glacial emerald lagoon, fed by two thundering waterfalls plummeting down from the glacier.

At the ranger station it's possible to organise a boat outing on the lagoon (CH\$3500/person) for a closer peek at the Ventisquero Colgante. Left of the bridge, the steep **Sendero Ventisquero Colgante** climbs 3.2km (2hr return) to a higher viewpoint overlooking the glacier.

Sector Portezuelo Queulat

Just beyond the southern entrance to the park, a short trail leads west to a mighty waterfall, the 40m-high **Saltos del Cóndor**. Five kilometres beyond, the Carretera Austral narrows and zigzags its way down the steep **Cuesta de Queulat**, through sheer-sided mountains crowned with glaciers. A signposted 2km trail, **Sendero Bosque Encantado**, makes for an easy but exhilarating hike (3hr 30min return), branching off to the left from the road just before the Portezuelo de Queulat, and leading 1.7km through moss-covered ancient trees before ending at the Río Cascadas.

From here, follow the river up the hill for another 800m, and you'll arrive at its source – a jade-green lake at the foot of a granite cliff, topped by a glacier and streaked by waterfalls. Just beyond the Portezuelo de Queulat pass is Sendero Padre García, with a 100m-staircase leading down to the **Salto Padre García**, a powerful waterfall dropping 30m into the Río Queulat.

ARRIVAL AND INFORMATION

PARQUE NACIONAL QUEULAT

By bus From Coyhaique, you can get any northbound bus that goes to Puyuhuapi or beyond, or any Coyhaique-bound bus from any destination north of Parque Nacional Queulat to drop you off by the main entrance to the park. Book a bus seat in advance for the day you plan to leave the park.

By organized tour Several tour companies run day-trips

to the Ventisquero Colgante from Coyhaique during the summer months (see p.365).

National park information The Centro de Información Ambiental (daily: April–Nov 9am–6pm; Dec–March 9am–8pm), with its detailed displays on the park's flora and glacier, is located at the main entrance.

ACCOMMODATION

Camping Angostura Sector Angostura. Beautiful campsite on the shores of Lago Risopatrón near the Conaf ranger hut; each site comes with its own picnic table and *fogón*. Cold showers only. Camping/person CH\$6000

Camping Ventisquero Sector Ventisquero Colgante. Though the ground is rocky and hard, the ten emplacements are attractive and come equipped with picnic tables and *fogones* (barbecue areas). You'll need to make use of the firewood to get over the

freezing cold showers. Camping/person CH\$6000

★ **Eco Camping Los Arrayanes** Carretera Austral Norte Km 227 ☎ 09 8549 3679, ⓦ campingarrayanes.com. Located 5km north of Puyuhuapi, this is a gorgeous waterfront campsite surrounded by a myrtle grove. It's clean, orderly, with its own beach and access to hot showers, *fogones* for cooking and kayaks and canoes for rent. For an extra CH\$4000 you can also visit the volcanic caves on the property – a worthwhile ramble. Camping/person CH\$5000

Puyuhuapi and around

Sitting at the head of the narrow Ventisquero fjord, surrounded by steep, wooded hills and frequently shrouded in low-hanging mist, **PUYUHUAPI**, founded in 1935 by four young German immigrants from Sudetenland who married Chilean women, is a great place to break your journey along the Carretera Austral in either direction – not only for the wild beauty of its setting, but also for its proximity to the **Termas de Puyuhuapi** and its convenience as a base for exploring **Parque Queulat**. The town's historic **textiles factory** is sometimes open to visitors.

Termas Ventisquero

Dec–Feb 7am–9pm, shorter hours rest of year • CH\$17,000 • ☎ 09 7666 6862, ⓦ termasventisqueropuyuhuapi.cl

The town's premier attraction is the **Termas de Puyuhuapi** – an upmarket hot springs resort (see p.364) that can be visited on a day-trip. A cheaper alternative to the plush *termas* is the more easily accessible **Termas Ventisquero**, 6km south of town along the Carretera, with two simple outdoor pools fed by thermal springs (temperature tends to vary) and a beautiful view over the fjord.

Termas de Puyuhuapi

17km south of Puyuhuapi and across the bay • Day visit CH\$50,000 for outdoor pools, indoor pool and Jacuzzis; price includes round-trip boat ride • ☎ 09 7966 6862, ⓦ puyuhuapilodge.com • Boat departs from a signposted wooden jetty 15km south of Puyuhuapi (Dec–March 4 daily, typically at 10am, 1pm, 3.30pm & 7pm; less frequently off-season; call for updated schedule; 10min)

The luxurious thermal baths, lodge and spa at ★TERMAS DE PUYUHUAPI enjoy a fantastic location, marooned on the edge of a peninsula on the opposite side of the fjord from the Carretera Austral. You don't need to be an overnight guest (see p.364) to visit, but you should phone ahead to book.

The thermal baths used to be a handful of ramshackle cabins that were transformed into a series of low-lying, beautifully designed buildings made of reddish-brown *alerce* timber and lots of glass by the East German shipbuilding magnate Eberhard Kossman in the late 1980s. Apart from its spectacular location, the main reason to come here is to soak in the steaming **hot springs**, channelled into three outdoor pools reached by a short walk through the forest. Two of the pools are large enough to swim in, and sit right on the edge of the fjord, while the third one, containing the hottest water, is a small pond enclosed by overhanging ferns and native trees. There's a state-of-the-art **spa**, specializing in a range of treatments and massages, an indoor pool with 'waterfall', a cold water pool and two Jacuzzis.

ARRIVAL AND INFORMATION   PUYUHUAPI

By bus Buses Terraustral (☎67 225 4335) serves Coyhaique while Buses Becker (☎67 272 1248) serves Chaitén and Futaleufú.
Destinations Chaitén (Tues & Sat around 1–2pm, returning the following day in the afternoon; 4hr 30min); Coyhaique (1 daily at 6am, returning in the afternoon; 5hr);

Futaleufú (Thurs around 1–2pm, returning the following day in the afternoon; 4hr).
Tourist information Av Übel (daily 10.30am–1pm & 3–8pm; ⓦ puertopuyuhuapi.cl). This small but well-stocked and helpful tourist office is located in the centre of town.

ACCOMMODATION

★**Casa Ludwig** Otto Uebel 202 ☎67 232 5220, ⓦ casaludwig.cl. The most popular option with international travellers, this rambling yellow chalet has comfortable singles and doubles (some en suite), polished wooden floors, excellent breakfast, a library and great views. It's run by English- and German-speaking Louisa, a descendant of the original colonists, who is a wealth of information on the area. CH\$26,000
Hostal Augusto Grosse Camilo Henriquez 4 ☎67 232

5150, ⓦ hostalaugustogrosse.cl. An excellent choice for backpackers, this tiny hostel consists of a couple of dorms and doubles, all decked out with beautiful wooden furniture hand-carved by the owner. Guests gather in the tiny wood-stove-heated living area and are welcome to use the kitchen. Breakfast costs an extra CH\$1000. Dorms CH\$10,000 doubles CH\$24,000
Hostería Aonikenk Hamburgo 16 ☎67 232 5208. An ultra-helpful hostess presides over this collection of rooms

and *cabañas* (sleeping up to 5) with something to suit everyone, from compact doubles to fully equipped cabins with balconies. Meals are served in the cheery dining area of the main house, and there's a lounge area upstairs for chilling out. Doubles CH$40,000, *cabañas* CH$45,000

★**Puyuhuapi Lodge & Spa** Bahía Dorita ☎2 2225 6489, ⓦpuyuhuapilodge.com. If you're after secluded relaxation and a good soak, then this elegant, wood-shingled lodge that sits right on the tranquil fjord offers a melange of the two. The spacious, carpeted rooms come with king-sized beds and terraces overlooking the water and guests can choose whether to have access just to the outdoor hot springs or the indoor spa/pool complex. The restaurant serves delicious three-course meals made with fresh local produce, and the inclusive breakfast buffet is the best in the region. Half-board and full-board available. **$300**

EATING

El Muelle Otto Uebel ☎09 7654 3598. This fjordside restaurant is the only place in the village that's reliably open for meals and its wonderfully fresh catch-of-the-day dishes do not disappoint. Their grilled hake is a winner and the home-made *kuchen* with wild berries really hits the spot. Mains from CH$6000. Daily 12.30–3.30pm & 7–10pm.

Isla Magdalena

A remote 1580-square-kilometre expanse of densely forested mountains and icy rivers with hot springs, home to Chile's rare and shy pygmy deer and forest cat, **ISLA MAGDALENA** is one of the least visited of Chile's national parks. If you wish to hike the pristine wilderness or delve into the local culture by heading out at dawn with local fishermen, you can stay overnight (see p.365) in the tiny fishing village of Puerto Gaviota at the island's southern tip.

ARRIVAL AND DEPARTURE

By boat Getting to Isla Magdalena is part of the adventure; Naviera Austral (ⓦnavieraustral.cl) boats stop here twice weekly en route between Puerto Chacabuco (CH$24,550) and Quellón (CH$38,450). Since the boat also calls at Puerto Cisnes, connected by daily Terraustral bus to Coyhaique (see p.365), it's easiest to catch the ferry to Puerto Gaviota from there (CH$8050).

FLY-FISHING AND LODGES ON THE CARRETERA AUSTRAL

Aysén is the most exciting fly-fishing region in Chile and is internationally renowned, drawing serious anglers, including a number of Hollywood stars. The **season** varies slightly according to the area, but in general lasts from October or November to May. You need a **licence** to fish (CH$15,000), widely available in sport-fishing shops. A number of first-class fishing lodges have sprung up around the region; week-long packages cost US$1200–3900 and typically include accommodation, fishing guide, all meals and an open bar. Below, we have listed the pick of the bunch.

Cinco Ríos Lodge Km 5, Camino a Balmaceda ☎67 224 4917, ⓦcincorios.cl. On the banks of the Río Simpson, a short drive from Coyhaique, this luxurious lodge with owners from Montana caters to up to twelve guests and offers gourmet takes on Chilean dishes as well as an extensive wine list. There's easy access to an astounding twelve rivers, such as Paloma, Blanco and Nireguao, as well as countless creeks and the small Pollux, Frio and Castor lakes. Guests fish mainly for trout, along with king and coho salmon, accessed by a combination of wading and floating. Oct–April.

Nomads of the Seas ☎2 2414 4600, ⓦnomads.cl. Taking a unique approach to fly fishing, this exciting operator bases all its fishing itineraries out of its 150-foot luxury mothership, complete with a helicopter and its own fleet of jet boats, which enable it to penetrate little-explored corners of Aysén for an experience of unparalleled diversity. Non-fishing guests can engage in whale- and bird-watching, and there's an on-board spa available to all, as is the gourmet Chilean cuisine. Mid-Oct to April.

Patagonia Baker Lodge Puerto Bertrand ☎67 241 1903, ⓦpbl.cl. *The* place for fly-fishing enthusiasts, sitting on the waterfront of the world-renowned Río Baker, which is teeming with brown and rainbow trout as well as good-sized salmon. Deluxe rooms have electric heating and private bathrooms as well as a stunning view of the Río Baker's rushing turquoise waters. The lodge also boasts two halls with open fireplaces and a gourmet restaurant. Horseback riding, boat trips along the Río Baker and bird-watching excursions also on offer. Late Oct to April.

ACCOMMODATION

Cabaña Amparo Puerto Gaviota ☎09 7530 1984, ⓦislamagdalena.blogspot.com. Run by the effusive Señora Morrás, the village's unofficial tourism ambassador, this snug guesthouse can accommodate up to five guests in basic but comfortable rooms. Your hostess can cook for you on request or send you to eat at the neighbours. **CH$20,000**

Coyhaique and around

After the smattering of small villages scattered along the Carretera Austral, Aysén's lively regional capital, **COYHAIQUE**, can be a welcome change. The city's fifty or so thousand inhabitants make up half the region's population, and it's the only place along the Carretera that offers a wide range of services. It's also a good launch pad for some great **day-trips** (see p.368). Coyhaique's most unusual feature is its large, five-sided **Plaza de Armas**, from which the main streets radiate like a spider's web; even with map in hand, travellers often find themselves wandering around in circles (or pentagons).

ARRIVAL AND DEPARTURE   COYHAIQUE

BY PLANE

Sky and LAN flights to and from Santiago, Puerto Montt and Punta Arenas land at the Aeropuerto de Balmaceda, 55km south of Coyhaique, and are met by three minibus transfer companies that take passengers to their hotels (CH$5000). Charter flights over the San Rafael glacier with Aerocord, as well as weekly flights to Villa O'Higgins and charter flights to Chile Chico, take off from the Aeródromo Teniente Vidal, 5km west of town.

Airlines Aerocord (General Parra 21 ☎67 224 6300, ⓦaerocord.cl); LAN, Parra 402 (☎600 526 2000, ⓦlan.com); Sky Airline, Prat 203 (☎600 600 2828, ⓦskyairline.cl).

Destinations (airport) Puerto Montt (2 daily; 1hr 15min); Punta Arenas (5 weekly; 1hr 45min); Santiago (2 daily; 3hr).

Destinations (aerodrome) San Rafael glacier (on demand in season; 2hr); Villa O'Higgins (Mon & Thurs at 10am; 1hr 15min).

BY BUS

Most buses pull in at the central terminal on the corner of Lautaro and Magallanes, though a few arrive at, and depart from, their respective company offices. Companies are listed after the destinations they serve.

Destinations Caleta Tortel (Mon at 8.30am; 10hr; Buses Patagonia ☎09 7521 9478); Castro via Ancud, Puerto Montt & Osorno (Mon & Fri at 4pm; 28hr; Queilen Bus ☎67 224 0760); Chaitén via La Junta (Tues & Sat at 8am; 12hr; Buses Becker, General Parra 335 ☎09 8465 2959, ⓦbusesbecker.com); Cochrane via Villa Cerro Castillo, Puerto Río Tranquilo, Cruce El Maitén and Puerto Bertrand (1–2 daily at 9am & 9.30am; Buses Acuario 13 ☎67 252 2143, Buses Don Carlos ☎67 252 2150 and Buses Sao Paolo ☎67 225 5726); Comodoro Rivadavia, Argentina (Mon & Fri at 8–9am; 9hr; Transaustral ☎67 223 2067); Futaleufú (Sat at 8am; 12hr; Buses Becker); Puerto Aysén & Puerto Chacabuco (every 30min; Buses Suray, Prat 265 ☎67 223 8387); Puyuhuapi (1–2 daily; 4hr 30min; Buses Becker and Buses Terraustral ☎67 225 4335); Puerto Ibáñez (1–2 daily; 2hr 30min; Miguel Acuña ☎67 225 1579 and Buses Carolina ☎09 8952 1592).

BY FERRY

Navimag, Horn 47 (☎67 223 3306, ⓦnavimag.com) runs to Puerto Montt from nearby Puerto Chacabuco (see p.368) frequently during summer, less often in winter. Naviera Austral, Horn 40 (☎67 221 0727, ⓦnavieraustral.cl) connects Puerto Chacabuco with Quellón via Puerto Cisnes and Raul Marín Balmaceda (see p.360).

GETTING AROUND

Car rental To make the most of the surrounding area, you may need to rent a car; reserve in advance, particularly in peak season. Driving the Carretera Austral requires a certain amount of forward planning (see box, p.352).

Reputable car rental companies include Traeger, Baquedano 457 (☎67 223 1648, ⓦtraeger.cl); Hertz, General Parra 280 (☎67 224 5780, ⓦhertz.cl); and Europcar, Errázuriz 454 (☎67 225 5171, ⓦeuropcar.cl).

INFORMATION AND TOURS

Conaf Los Coigües s/n (Mon–Fri 8.30am–12.30pm & 2.30–4pm; ☎67 221 2225).

Sernatur Bulnes 35 (Jan & Feb daily 8.30am–8.30pm; March–Dec Mon–Fri 8.30am–5.30pm; ☎67 227 0290, ⓦsernatur.cl). You can pick up a wealth of brochures on the region at this ultra-helpful office.

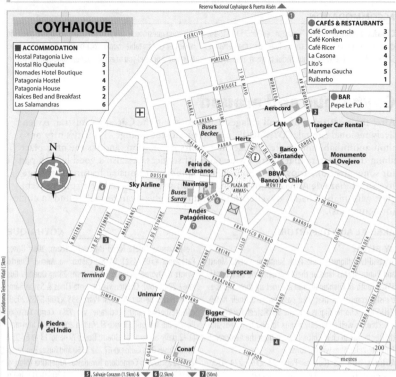

COYHAIQUE

ACCOMMODATION

Hostal Patagonia Live	7
Hostal Río Queulat	3
Nomades Hotel Boutique	1
Patagonia Hostel	4
Patagonia House	5
Raíces Bed and Breakfast	2
Las Salamandras	6

CAFÉS & RESTAURANTS

Café Confluencia	3
Café Konken	7
Café Ricer	6
La Casona	4
Lito's	8
Mamma Gaucha	5
Ruibarbo	1

BAR

| Pepe Le Pub | 2 |

Salvaje Corazon (1.5km) & 6 (2.5km) 7 (50m)

Tour operators Salvaje Corazón, Casilla 311 (☎67 221 1488, wsalvajecorazon.com), is a recommended operator offering expeditions to the Southern Icefields, trekking in the San Lorenzo Massif, photo safaris across Patagonia, and multi-day trips along the northern half of the Carretera Austral that take in Parque Pumalín, Futa and Parque Nacional Queulat.

ACCOMMODATION

Hostal Patagonia Live Lillo 826 ☎67 223 0892, ⓔhostalpatagonialive@gmail.com. In a quiet residential area south of the plaza, this secure guesthouse consists of a handful of cream-coloured, spacious rooms with modern bathrooms and powerful showers. A quiet retreat rather than a place to meet people. CH$30,000

Hostal Río Queulat Errázuriz 39 ☎67 223 3200, ⓔhostalrioqueulat@gmail.com. The singles, doubles and triples may be snug, bordering on tiny, and you may have to step over the toilet to wrap yourself in the clammy embrace of the shower curtains, but the location is central, the wi-fi is reliable, the owner is super helpful, and the price is right. Microwave, fridge and kettle for guest use downstairs. CH$25,000

★Nomades Hotel Boutique Av Baquedano 84 ☎67 223 7777, ⓦnomadeshotel.com. This handsome edifice of rough-hewn stone chunks slotted together hides just seven luxurious rooms, all with rain showers and some with splendid terrace views of Río Coyhaique down below. The decor pays homage to Coyhaique's pioneer heritage, with wool throws, cowboy lassos and deer antler chandeliers, and the massive slate fireplace keeps the lounge toasty warm. US$175

★Patagonia Hostel Lautaro 667 ☎09 6240 6974, ⓦpatagonia-hostel.com. Given that it's the only proper backpacker/cyclist hostel in town, with only ten beds, it's little wonder this place is always booked up. The beds and bunks are large and comfortable, with a personal reading light above each one; the lounge encourages socializing and the young, energetic German owners, Thomas and Sandra, run their own tour agency and can assist with kayaking trips and more. Dorms CH$14,000, doubles CH$34,000

★Patagonia House Camino Campo Alegre, Quinta 18 de Julio ☎67 221 1488, ⓦpatagonia-house.com. Set on a hillside above Coyhaique, the large panoramic windows of this boutique three-storey lodge offer splendid views of the Coyhaique Valley. The four rooms make great use of natural light, the chef cooks up gourmet dishes in the kitchen and the attention that owner Ruth gives her guests is difficult to fault. CH$65,000

Raíces Bed and Breakfast Av Baquedano 444 ☎67 221 0490, ⓦraícesbedandbreakfast.com. This B&B has some of the most attractive rooms in town – wood-panelled, full of light, decorated in whites and creams with woollen accents (the owner sells high-quality knitwear).

The inclusive breakfast is above par. CH$69,000

Las Salamandras Carretera Teniente Vidal, Km 2.5 ☎67 221 1865, ⓔinfo@salamandras.cl. Set in a wood by a river 2.5km along the road to Teniente Vidal, this hostel, popular with backpackers and cyclists, offers the use of a kitchen, ample common spaces, mountain-bike rental and a range of excursions, including one to Parque Nacional Queulat and cross-country skiing trips. Dorms CH$10,000, doubles CH$25,000, camping/person CH$7000

EATING AND DRINKING

Café Confluencia 21 de Mayo 548 ☎67 224 5080. This trendy café serves dishes as diverse as *ajís rellenos* (stuffed hot peppers), tacos and Spanish-style *tortilla*. The selection of teas and coffees is extensive and evening tipples that accompany the live weekend music include the signature mint pisco sours. Mains from CH$6000. Mon–Thurs & Sun daily 10am–11pm, Fri & Sat 10am–2am.

Café Konken Prat 340. This café is so tiny there isn't even any room to sit down, but that doesn't stop customers from filing in for the excellent freshly ground coffee, giant smoothies and fresh fruit juices. Mon–Sat 10am–6pm.

Café Ricer Horn 48 ☎67 221 6709. This favourite with cyclists and backpackers doesn't wow you with its culinary offerings, which tend to be carbfests of the quantity-over-quality variety, but it's central, one of the very few places open on Sun, and has a few outdoor tables for sipping the local microbrew. Mains from CH$4500. Daily 11am–10pm.

La Casona Vielmo 77 ☎67 223 8894. Set on a quiet street, this homely, family-run restaurant is a decent, upscale dining option, with a menu full of steaks and seafood dishes. The *filete casona* is a top choice for the carnivorously inclined, and the service is attentive, but consistency can be an issue. Mains from CH$7000. Mon–Sat 12.30–3.30pm & 7.30–10.30pm, Sun 12.30–3.30pm & 8–10.30pm.

Lito's Lautaro 147 ☎67 225 4528. A block from the bus station, this local joint looks like a dive from the outside but inside it's one pleasant surprise after another. They serve a humungous *lomo a lo pobre*, but the focus is mostly fish

and seafood, including the less typical steamed barnacles. Very popular with locals, so get here before 1pm for lunch to be guaranteed a seat. Mains from CH$5000. Mon–Sat 12.30–3pm & 7.30–10pm.

★**Mamma Gaucha** Horn 47 ☎67 221 0712. At this trattoria-meets-Patagonia, efficient staff serve you wood-fired pizzas, lamb-filled ravioli, baked Camembert with calafate berry jam, vast salads and imaginative desserts (try the blueberry *crème brulée*), all under the watchful eye of Mamma, looking down from the large black-and-white photos. The only downside is that the drinks machine that makes the signature mint lemonades sounds like an industrial drill. Mains from CH$7000. Mon–Sat 12.30–11.30pm.

Pepe Le Pub Parra 72 ☎67 224 6474. Pretty much the only bona fide bar in town, this friendly watering hole is a good place to try the local microbrew or the strong cocktails mixed by the sociable barman. Things tend to really pick up on weekends after midnight, and the locals take karaoke seriously. Mon–Sat 8pm–late.

★**Ruibarbo** Av Baquedano 208 ☎67 221 1826. This intimate restaurant may look unassuming from the outside, but the fusion dishes are undoubtedly Coyhaique's best, from the trio of ceviche and quinoa salad with Calafate dressing, to the lamb's tongue and wild mushroom risotto, and sesame-encrusted salmon. The menu is succinct, the wine list well-chosen and the service is attentive. Mon–Sat 1–3.30pm & 7.30–10.30pm.

DIRECTORY

Hospital The regional hospital is at Jorge Ibar 168 (☎67 221 9100).

Laundry Lavandería All Clean, General Parra 55 (Mon–Sat only).

Money and exchange The following banks have ATMs:

Banco Santander, Condell 184, Banco de Chile, Condell 298, and BBVA, Condell 254. *Cambios* include Emperador at Freire 171.

Post office Cochrane 202, near Plaza de Armas (Mon–Sat 9am–6pm).

Reserva Nacional Coyhaique

5km north of Coyhaique • CH$2500 • Any bus from Coyhaique towards Puerto Aysén can drop you near the entrance

About an hour and a quarter's hike from Coyhaique, the **RESERVA NACIONAL COYHAIQUE**, huddled at the foot of towering Cerro McKay, is an easily accessible slice

8

of wilderness, featuring areas of native forest, a couple of lakes and fantastic views down to Coyhaique and the Río Simpson valley. **Sendero Los Leñeros** leads 2.5km from the *guardería* by the entrance through native *lenga* and *ñire* trees to the Casa Bruja sector, where you'll find fully-equipped campsites and an appealing 4km trail to **Laguna Verde**.

From here, you pick up with a jeep track which, if you follow it north for a couple of hundred metres, will take you to the trailhead of **Sendero Las Piedras**, the best (and steepest) hike in the reserve, leading 13km up to and across a ridge, and giving breathtaking views for miles around; allow four hours to complete. After descending at the other end, a side path branches off to **Lago Venus**, an attractive lake 1km beyond, reached by walking through dense native forest. Alternatively, keep on going another couple of hundred metres and you'll join up with **Sendero El Chucao**, which leads 2.6km back to the *guardería*.

West of Coyhaique

From Coyhaique, a paved section of the Carretera Austral runs west towards the coast, past a modest nature reserve, to the port of Puerto Aysén, 65km away – a small town you have to pass through on the way to the even more nondescript Puerto Chacabuco, one of the gateways to Parque Nacional Laguna San Rafael.

Reserva Nacional Río Simpson

Road to Puerto Aysén, Km 37 • Daily 8.30am–5.30pm • CH$1000 • Any bus from Coyhaique towards Puerto Aysén can drop you by the entrance

The scenic route holds fast to the Río Simpson as it rushes through the **Reserva Nacional Río Simpson**, sandwiched between tall, craggy cliffs. Thirty-seven kilometres out of Coyhaique, a small wooden sign by the road points to the reserve's Conaf office. The reserve's main attractions are conveniently located right by the road: 1km on from the Conaf office, you'll pass the **Cascada de la Virgen**, a tall, graceful waterfall that drops in two stages, separated by a pool of water with a shrine to the Virgin Mary next to it. A further 8km east thunders another waterfall, the **Velo de la Novia**, or "bride's veil", so named for its diaphanous spray.

Puerto Aysén & Puerto Chacabuco

Sixty-five kilometres west of Coyhaique, the former cattle-shipping port of **Puerto Aysén** literally became a backwater when its harbour silted up, forcing commercial vessels to use nearby **Puerto Chacabuco** from 1960. Puerto Chacabuco is a one-road town lined with ugly fishmeal-processing factories emitting a nauseating smell of fish. Your only reason for coming here would be to take a boat to the Laguna San Rafael glacier or to catch a Navimag or Naviera Austral ferry.

ARRIVAL AND DEPARTURE   PUERTO AYSÉN & PUERTO CHACABUCO

By bus Buses Suray, Eusebio Ibar 630 (☏ 67 233 6231), serves neighbouring Puerto Chacabuco, as well as Coyhaique.
Destinations Coyhaique (every 30min; 45min); Puerto Chacabuco (at least 20 daily; 20min).
By ferry Chacabuco is the arrival and departure point for Naviera Austral ferries (ⓦ navieraustral.cl) to Quellón (CH$14,950), Navimag (ⓦ navimag.com) ferries to Puerto

Montt (from CH$48,000) and catamarans operated by Catamaranes del Sur (ⓦ catamaranesdelsur.cl) to Laguna San Rafael.
Destinations Laguna San Rafael (2 ferries weekly; 16hr); catamaran several weekly in season; 5hr one-way); Puerto Montt (Tues & Fri; 24hr); Quellón via Puerto Cisnes, Puerto Gaviota and Raúl Marín Balmaceda (Mon & Fri; 28hr).

ACCOMMODATION

Hotel Loberías del Sur JM Carrera 50 ☎67 235 1112, ⓦ loberiasdelsur.cl. Just uphill from the port, the only upmarket option in Puerto Chacabuco looks impressive from the outside, and amenities include a gym, sauna and a good restaurant with a focus on seafood. The rooms are seriously overpriced for what they are, though staying at the hotel does give you free access to the attractive, private 2.5-square-kilometre nature reserve nearby and the hotel runs all-day catamaran excursions to Laguna San Rafael (CH$190,000), also open to non-guests. Minimum stay three days. <u>US$1396</u>

Parque Nacional Laguna San Rafael

125 nautical miles south of Puerto Chacabuco • CH$6000, payable only if you land

Almost half of the remote 12,000-square-km **Parque Nacional Laguna San Rafael** is covered by the immense ice field known as the **Campo de Hielo Norte**; it feeds eighteen other glaciers on top of the San Rafael Glacier and contains over 250 lakes and lagoons. The 4058m **Monte San Valentín**, the highest peak in the southern Andes, towers over the frozen plateau. A handful of visitors who opt to fly over the glacier touch down here with barely enough time to take the 7km trail from the Conaf *guardería* to a breathtaking viewpoint platform over the sprawling, icy tongue (allow around 2hr up and slightly less coming down).

Laguna San Rafael

A boat ride either from Bahía Exploradores or Puerto Chacabuco through the labyrinthine fjords of Aysén brings you to the dazzling San Rafael glacier, spilling into the broad Laguna San Rafael. The journey is a spectacle in itself, as boats edge their way through channels hemmed in by precipitous cliffs dripping with vegetation, passing the odd sea lion colony along the way. After sailing down the long, thin Golfo de Elefantes, the boat enters the seemingly unnavigable Río Témpanos, or "Iceberg River", before emerging into the Laguna San Rafael. Floating in the lagoon are dozens of **icebergs**, fashioned by wind and rain into monumental sculptures, with such a vibrant electric-blue colour that they appear to be lit from within.

San Rafael glacier

Sailing around icebergs, you approach the giant **San Rafael glacier** at the far end of the lagoon. Over 4km wide, and rearing out of the water to a height of 70m, it really is a dizzying sight. While the cruise boat keeps at a safe distance, you'll be given the chance to get a closer look from an inflatable motor dinghy – but not too close, as the huge blocks of ice that calve off into the water with a deafening roar create dangerous waves. What you can see from the boat is in fact just the tip of the glacier's "tongue", which extends some 15km from its source.

The glacier is retreating fast, however, frequently by as much as 100m a year. Early explorers reported that in 1800 the glacier filled three-quarters of the lagoon, and

---

VISITING THE SAN RAFAEL GLACIER

The glacier is currently accessible *only* by boat or plane, though as of 2011 you can drive up Valle Exploradores from Puerto Río Tranquilo (see p.371) and take a three-hour boat ride to reach the lagoon from Bahía Exploradores, with three hours at the glacier itself. During high season *Hotel Loberías del Sur*'s (see above) own **Catamaranes del Sur** (☎22 231 1902, ⓦ catamaranesdelsur.cl; CH$190,000) do day-trips to the glacier (check website for dates; 5hr each way). Trips include three meals and operate an open bar – it is a tradition to drink a whisky or cocktail containing "thousand-year-old ice cubes" chipped from an iceberg. Cessna **flights** from Coyhaique are operated by **Aerocord**, Gral Parra 21 (☎67 224 6300, ⓦ aerocord .cl), and usually require the full quota of five passengers (90 min each way; around CH$170,000/person).

archive photographs from the beginning of the twentieth century show it as being far longer than it is today. It is estimated that by the year 2030, the glacier will be gone.

Reserva Nacional Cerro Castillo

75km south of Coyhaique along the Carretera Austral • CH$1500 • Take any southbound bus from Coyhaique

About an hour's drive south of Coyhaique, the Carretera Austral crosses the northern boundary of the **RESERVA NACIONAL CERRO CASTILLO**, a 445,000-acre protected area that's home to the elusive *huermúl* deer. Spread out below you is a broad river valley flanked by densely forested lower slopes that rise to a breathtaking panorama of barren, rocky peaks. Dominating the skyline is the reserve's eponymous centrepiece, **Cerro Castillo** (2700m) whose needlepoint spires loom over the valley like the turrets of a Transylvanian castle. Further north, 67km from Coyhaique, by Laguna Chaguay, you pass the *guardería* on your left, which has a basic **camping** area (see below). Just south of Reserva Nacional Cerro Castillo, Villa Cerro Castillo (see p.371) is the ending/starting point for the **Sendero Cerro Castillo.**

Sendero Cerro Castillo

75km south of Coyhaique along the Carretera Austral • Take any southbound bus from Coyhaique

The rewarding 40km Sendero Cerro Castillo, which takes four days to complete, starts at Km75, branches right (west) from the road 6km south of the *guardería*, and follows the Río La Lima upstream to a 1450m pass on the east side of Cerro Castillo (2300m) through *coigüe* and *ñire* forest. On the way, you pass the stunning **Laguna Cerro Castillo**, at the foot of a glacier suspended from the mountainside, before descending to the village of **Villa Cerro Castillo** (see p.371). Note that the trail is poorly marked; you should buy an IGM map in advance in Coyhaique and get more detailed route advice from Conaf, whose staff should be informed before you set off. It may be easier to start at the Villa Cerro Castillo trailhead and hike the trail in reverse order, especially since it means fewer uphill stints. This trek is the antidote to the "W" in Torres del Paine (see p.408); the mountain scenery is almost equally spectacular and you have it almost to yourself.

ACCOMMODATION   RESERVA NACIONAL CERRO CASTILLO

Camping Laguna Chaguay This Conaf-maintained campsite at the start of the Sendero Cerro Castillo (with six other basic campsites spaced out along the trail) has basic sites and access to hot showers. Camping/person CH$4500

Around Lago General Carrera

Just beyond the southern boundary of **Reserva Nacional Cerro Castillo**, a 31km side road shoots southeast from the Carretera Austral to the tiny village of **Puerto Ibáñez**, on the northern shore of **Lago General Carrera**. This lake, encircled by rocky, sharp-peaked mountains, is the second largest in South America, and stretches east into Argentina. Regular ferries connect Puerto Ibáñez with the sunny, cherry-growing town of **Chile Chico**, on the opposite shore, making this an attractive alternative to following the Carretera Austral around the lake. From Chile Chico, a 128km road skirts the lake's southern shore, joining the Carretera just beyond the village of **Puerto Guadal**.

Puerto Ibáñez

Sitting in a green, fertile plain, divided up by rows of soldier-like poplars, in sharp contrast with the barren hills around it, **PUERTO IBÁÑEZ** is a shrinking village. Once an important port, connecting Coyhaique with Chile Chico and the remote *estancias* on the Lago General Carrera's southern shore, it fell into decline with the construction of the Carretera Austral bypass.

Chile Chico

Sitting on the southern shore of Lago General Carrera, the small agricultural town of **CHILE CHICO** is a sunny place with an attractive Plaza de Armas, lined with apricot trees and pines, and is famous for its fruit festival at the end of January, as well as Chile's best cherries. The town was settled by farmers who crossed over from Argentina in 1909, causing a conflict known as the "Chile Chico war" when they refused to hand over land to the concessionaires given grants by the government. The new settlement depended entirely on Argentina until a road was built between Coyhaique and Puerto Ibáñez in 1952, after which Chile Chico's orchards became Coyhaique's main source of fresh fruit. You get a great view of the town and the lake from the hill viewpoint opposite the dock, and Chile Chico makes a good base for the exploration of the gorgeous **Reserva Nacional Jeinemeni.**

Reserva Nacional Jeinemeni

52km southwest of Chile Chico • CH$2500 • Accessible by 4WD only

This beautiful, seldom-visited nature reserve comprises Patagonian steppe and azure lakes, covers a vast area of 1610 square kilometres and is home to guanacos, vizcachas (a cross between a bunny and a squirrel), puma and a smaller forest cat, among others. There are several trails here including a 6km steep uphill hike to the Cueva de los Manos – a cave with Tehuelche cave paintings en route to the reserve, around 25km south of Chile Chico; the Sendero Escorial del Silencio, an ascent of 1650m passing five viewpoints along the way with sweeping views of the park; and Sendero Lago Verde, a three-hour roundtrip to the eponymous lake.

The most ambitious hiking trail, however, is the three-day, 50km **Sendero La Leona**, which starts at the Conaf ranger station, skirts the southern shore of Lago Jeinemeni, climbs up to the Cordón La Gloria before touching the northern tip of Lago Verde and then follows Valle Hermoso and Valle Áviles all the way to Casa Piedra in Parque Patagonia (see p.375), with the latter part of the trail following Río Áviles. If driving to the park, you need a high-clearance vehicle to get over Río Jeinemeni that floods part of the road. Trips to the park are run by Expediciones Patagonia (see p.374).

Villa Cerro Castillo

Looping around Lago General Carrera along the Carretera Austral offers spectacular panoramas of the grey-and-pink mountains west of the road, plus a few glimpses of the Campo de Hielo Norte (see p.369). Nine kilometres on from the turn-off to Puerto Ibáñez, you pass **Villa Cerro Castillo**, a rather bleak pioneer settlement whose sole draw is the rugged hiking around Cerro Castillo (see p.370).

Monumento Nacional Manos de Cerro Castillo

Just across the bridge outside Villa Cerro Castillo, up a signed 2km track • Dec–April • CH$1500

A track leads steeply uphill to **Monumento Nacional Manos de Cerro Castillo**, a dense collection of over one hundred handprints (some belonging to children), in three separate panels at the foot of a sheer basalt rock face. The images, mostly negative prints against a red background, are thought to have been left by the Tehuelche people between five thousand and eight thousand years ago.

Puerto Río Tranquilo

Some 25km south of the turn for Puerto Murta, a tiny cattle-farming community, you'll reach **Puerto Río Tranquilo**, a picturesque village on the shore of Lago General Carrera. Puerto Río Tranquilo has been a popular traveller stop for many years due to its proximity to the **Capilla de Mármol** ("Marble Chapel"), an impressive limestone cliff looming out of the water, streaked with blue-and-white patterns and gashed with caves which can be entered by boat. Numerous companies with kiosks by the shore offer trips; for something more adventurous, you can opt for a kayaking trip instead (see p.374). In the last three years, the village's appeal has skyrocketed due to the opening of **Valle Exploradores**, a stupendously scenic, narrow road that snakes its way past glacial lakes and mountains for 82km to Bahía Exploradores, the launchpad for boat trips to Laguna San Rafael. Since Puerto Río Tranquilo is considerably closer to Glaciar San Rafael than Puerto Chacabuco, the three-hour boat trip to the icy lagoon is an enticing alternative for those who don't wish to spend all day on a boat. That's not all: 55km west along the Valle Exploradores road is the starting point for the guided trek and ice hike (see p.374) on the vast **Glaciar Exploradores**, the northern tongue of ice that extends from the Campo de Hielo San Valentín.

Cruce El Maitén

Thirty-five kilometres south of Puerto Tranquilo lies the outlet of **Lago General Carrera**, which drains into the adjacent Lago Bertrand. Shortly afterwards, you'll reach **Cruce El Maitén**, a fork in the road with a couple of lodges. The eastern fork skirts the southern edge of Lago General Carrera to Puerto Guadal, a picturesque little village with an excellent stretch of beach, before the precipitous and sometimes narrow road continues to Chile Chico (see p.371)

Puerto Bertrand

Twenty-five kilometres south of Cruce El Maitén you arrive at the charming little village of **Puerto Bertrand**, sitting pretty much on top of the turquoise waters of Lago Bertrand. Besides the fishing lodges in the vicinity of the village, Puerto Bertrand is a base for rafting adventures on the Río Baker and multi-day trekking expeditions on the Campo de Hielo Norte.

ARRIVAL AND DEPARTURE   AROUND LAGO GENERAL CARRERA

PUERTO IBÁÑEZ

By bus Miguel Acuña (☏ 67 225 1579) and Buses Carolina (☏ 09 8952 1592) run minibuses to Puerto Ibáñez from Coyhaique, timed to coincide with the arrival and departure of the ferry to Chile Chico. Book in advance to be picked up from your place of residence.

By ferry The Sotramin office in Puerto Ibáñez is at Carrera 202 (☏ 67 252 6992, ⊕ sotramin.cl). For more info, see the By Ferry section for Chile Chico (p.372).

CHILE CHICO

By bus Buses Baker (☏ 09 8464 1067) and Buses Malfer (☏ 09 7756 8234) run to Cochrane via Puerto Guadál, Cruce El Maitén and Puerto Bertrand. Buses Baker also run to Puerto Río Tranquilo. There are also daily departures to Los Antiguos in Argentina (CH$5000), where you can connect to Ruta 40; these leave from O'Higgins 426. Alternatively, you can take a taxi to the border (CH$10,000).

Destinations Cochrane (Mon at 8am, Wed at 9.30am, Fri at 8am & 9.30am, Sun at 9.30am; 5hr); Los Antiguos

(3 daily, 30min); Puerto Río Tranquilo (Mon, Thurs & Sat at 9.30am, returning at 4pm; 5hr).

By ferry Transbordador *La Tehuelche* run by Sotramin (☏ 67 241 1003, ⊕ sotramin.cl) crosses Lago General Carrera from Chile Chico to Puerto Ibáñez (passengers CH$2100, vehicles CH$18,650); book tickets a week in advance in peak season if you want to transport your car, otherwise a couple of days in advance. Check times well ahead because they are subject to change; reservations are a must. When buying your ticket in Chile Chico it's a good idea to buy an onward minibus ticket to Coyhaique from Puerto Ibañez.

Destinations Puerto Ibañez (1 daily: Mon, Tues & Wed at 8am, Thurs, Fri & Sun at 4pm, Sat at 9am; 2hr 30min)

VILLA CERRO CASTILLO

By bus Buses Acuario 13 (☏ 67 252 2143), Buses Don Carlos (☏ 67 252 2150) and Buses Sao Paolo (☏ 67 252 2143) all stop along the main street of Villa Cerro Castillo en route between Coyhaique and Cochrane.

Destinations Coyhaique (at least 2 daily; 1hr 15min); Cochrane (at least 2 daily; 4hr).

INFORMATION & TOURS

CHILE CHICO

Tourist office O'Higgins at Egaña (Mon–Fri 9am–5pm; ☎67 241 1338, ⍵chilechico.cl). You can pick up a town map here.

Expediciones Patagonia O'Higgins 333 (☎09 8464 1067). Fernando runs trekking trips to Jeinemeni as well as mountaineering excursions.

PUERTO RIO TRANQUILO

Boats to Capilla de Mármol leave throughout the day; just approach any of the kiosks on the *costanera* (promenade). It's CH$5000–8000 per person or CH$40,000–45,000 if you want the whole boat to yourself.

★**El Puesto** Lagos 258 ☎09 6207 3794, ⍵elpuesto.cl. The only operator in town to offer kayaking trips to the Capilla de Mármol (CH$35,000) and to the less visited and gorgeous Isla Panchini (CH$70,000). They also organise trekking on Glaciar Exploradores (with/without transport CH$50,000/40,000). They also have an office near the *costanera*.

Río Exploradores ☎09 8259 4017, ⍵exploradores-sanrafael.cl. This operator offers full-day excursions (CH$140,000) and multi-day excursions to Laguna San Rafael from Km75 (you need own wheels to get there), as well as boat transfers to the Laguna San Rafael National Park (Jan & Feb only, CH$90,000) for those planning to camp there for at least two nights.

PUERTO BERTRAND

Baker Patagonia Aventura Costanera s/n, ☎09 8817 7525, ⍵bakerpatagonia.com. Río Baker rafting trips, ranging from Class III half-day floats (CH$25,000–33,000/person) to multi-day expeditions.

Patagonia Adventure Expeditions ☎09 8182 0608, ⍵adventurepatagonia.com. Pioneering operator that offers superb multi-day treks, such as the challenging 10-day Aisén Glacier Trail, the two-week trekking-and-rafting Ice to Ocean expedition and multi-activity adventures in the Soler Valley.

ACCOMMODATION AND EATING

CHILE CHICO

Café Loly y Elizabeth González 25 ☎09 9085 5091. Facing the plaza, and serving basic meat and fish dishes, as well as *empanadas*, this is the only place open on Sun. Mains from CH$7500. Daily 12.30–3.30pm & 7–10.30pm.

Camping Reserva Nacional Jeinemeni By the shores of Lago Jeinemeni. There's a decent campsite in the park with a gorgeous location, cold water showers and fire pits for cooking. Camping/person CH$6000

Casa Quinta No Me Olvides Camino Internacional Chacra 3-A ☎09 8847 8510. Popular with backpackers, and offering seven basic, good-value rooms and space to camp in the large orchard. Doubles CH$20,000, camping/person CH$4500

Hostería de la Patagonia Camino Internacional Chacra 3-A ☎67 241 1337, ⍵hosteriadelapatagonia.cl. A charming Belgian–Chilean-owned house with comfortable en-suite rooms, camping spots with access to hot showers, good home-cooked food and outdoor excursions on offer, tucked away in a large garden on the eastern edge of town. As of 2015, guests will also be able to simmer in the garden hot tub. Doubles CH$50,000, camping/person CH$4000

VILLA CERRO CASTILLO

Cabañas El Tropero Carretera Austral 305 ☎09 7759 5766 ⍵eltropero.cl. This friendly, family-run place offers two two-storey cabins for up to six people each. Both come fully equipped with wood-burning stove for heating, cable TV and small kitchen, as well as simple, wood-panelled rooms. Owners charge according to number of people. CH$30,000

Camping Baqueanos de la Patagonia O'Higgins s/n, sector El Bosque ☎09 7898 8550, ⍵baqueanosdelapatagonia.cl. Besides basic camping spots, this friendly outfit offers recommended horseriding excursions in the area (2–6 hr), and has mountain bikes for rent. Camping/person CH$5000

El Puesto Huemul Camino Estero del Bosque ☎09 9218 3250. An unexpected treat in this small pioneer town, this homely restaurant really delivers when it comes to imaginative dishes such as lamb ravioli, freshly baked *empanadas* and gnocchi with wild mushrooms. Mains from CH$6500. Daily 8am–10pm.

PUERTO RÍO TRANQUILO

Camping Pudú 1km south of Puerto Río Tranquilo ☎67 257 3003, ⍵puduexcursiones.cl. Attractive lakeside campsite with hot showers and even access to laundry service. Owners are happy to organise excursions to the Capilla de Mármol, into Valle Exploradores and more. Camping/person CH$5000

Campo Alacalúf Valle Exploradores Km44 ⍵campoalacaluf.com. In the nearby Valle Exploradores, this secluded, German-owned rustic house offers a handful of rooms and home-cooked meals (CH$7000 for lunch or dinner), as well as a few camping spots with access to a *quincho* for cooking. Katrin and Thomas, your gracious hosts, can help organise trips to Laguna San Rafael. Doubles CH$24,000, camping/person CH$4000

★**El Puesto** Lagos 258 ☎09 6207 3794, ⍵elpuesto.cl. Specializing in multi-activity itineraries which include hiking on the Glaciar Exploradores and kayaking to the Capillas de Mármol, this boutique guesthouse consists of nine beautiful, light en-suite singles, doubles, triples and quads with crisp linens and down duvets. Packed lunch and other meals available on request and there are bikes and kayaks for rent. CH$82.000

Restaurant Costanera Carretera Austral 243 ☎09 5743 2175. The simple menu at this central restaurant includes grilled fish and *lomo a lo pobre*. Menu *del día* CH$8000. There are also single and double rooms for rent. Daily 8am–9pm. CH$50,000

CRUCE EL MAITÉN AND PUERTO BERTRAND

Green Baker Lodge Camino a Cochrane, Km 3 ☎09 9159 7757, ⓦgreenlodgebaker.com. This attractive wooden lodge on the bank of Río Baker, 3km south of Puerto Bertrand, caters to anglers and other outdoor enthusiasts with seven comfortable *cabañas* (2–4 people) and a mini-hotel. Non-fishing guests can enjoy horseback riding, rafting on the Río Baker and ice trekking, among other adventures. Doubles CH$60,000, *cabañas* CH$75,000

★**Hacienda Tres Lagos** Km 274 ☎67 241 1323, ⓦhaciendatreslagos.com. In an idyllic location on the banks of Lago Negro, right by the Cruce Maitén, this hacienda is the recipient of the Calidad Turística seal, and boasts sumptuous, modern rooms with plenty of light, iPod docks, satellite TV, their own zip line and a restaurant serving gourmet takes on Patagonian cuisine. Trilingual guides lead kayaking, trekking, horseback riding and fly fishing excursions, and relaxation options include outdoor hot tubs and Jacuzzi at the lakeside spa, plus telescopes for stargazing. US$316

PUERTO GUADÁL

Terra Luna Patagonia Camino a Chile Chico, Km 1.5 ☎09 8449 1092, ⓦterra-luna.cl. Two kilometres along the road to Puerto Guadal, this lodge specializes in multi-activity programmes which couple kayaking, trekking, cross country skiing and mountaineering with relaxation in the on-site outdoor hot tubs and sauna. They also run Patagonia Jet speedboats to the Leones, Fiero, Soler and Nef glaciers that branch off the Northern Ice Field. You can stay in either one of the lodge's comfortable doubles, fully equipped *cabañas* or a more basic camp hut. Doubles CH$63,000, *cabañas* CH$69,000, camp huts CH$38,000

★**Un Destino No Turístico** Camino Laguna La Manga, Km1 ☎09 8756 7545, ⓦdestino-noturistico.com. Sustainability is the watchword at this eco-hostel and campsite: these guys recycle and reuse anything they can and grow their own organic food. There's a sun cooker in the guest kitchen and even the shower runs on solar power. Even if you're not staying here, they're happy to show you their energy-saving techniques (CH$5000). Camping/person CH$5500, dorms CH$12,000, doubles CH$28,000

8

South of Lago General Carrera

South of the great lake, a gravel road winds its way along the river towards **Cochrane**, the last settlement of any size and the gateway to the **Reserva Nacional Tamango**. Seventeen kilometres north of Cochrane, one of the most gorgeous roads branches off east to **Parque Patagonia** before crossing the Argentinian border beyond. South of Cochrane, the road snakes its way through a dense carpet of evergreens and giant *nalca*. After just over 100km south, you come to the embarcadero de Río Vagabundo, the launching spot for boats to the tiny, remote logging village of **Caleta Tortel**, also reachable by the gravel road that forks west from the Carretera. Further south, at Puerto Yungay, a car ferry crosses Fiordo Mitchell and a precarious road leads to the Carretera's final stop – the pioneer settlement of **Villa O'Higgins**.

Parque Patagonia

17km north of Cochrane

The 690-square-kilometre private nature reserve that lies and stretches along the little-travelled X-83 all the way to the Argentinian border is a triumph for ecologists in general and for the non-profit foundation Conservación Patagónica (ⓦconservacionpatagonica.org) in particular. The ten-year Kris-Tompkins-led initiative (see box, p.355) has seen incredibly hard work from scores of volunteers as they laboured to restore the heavily damaged steppe from damage caused by sheep from the historic Estancia Valle Chacabuco. Invasive non-indigenous plants were ripped out by hand and replaced by endemic species, and today the park is home to diverse fauna such as the endangered *huemúl*, as well as guanacos, puma and the four-eyed

---

HIKING IN PARQUE PATAGONIA

Of the three existing trails in the park, two are readily accessible. The 21km-**Sendero Lagunas Altas** starts by the *Westwinds Campground* (see below), climbing gently uphill through scrubland and then snow-brushed forest to a lagoon-dotted plateau with snowy mountains in the distance. The trail meanders between the lagoons, with some splendid views of the valley below along the way, before descending along scrubland-covered hill slopes to a spot near the park headquarters. The 50km **Sendero Avilés** starts at the *Casa Piedra* campsite (see below). Taking around three days to hike, much of the trail meanders through the Avilés valley before turning east into Valle Hermoso, skirting the northern shore of Lago Verde, traversing the Cordón la Gloria and coming to an end by the ranger headquarters of Lago Jeinemeni. There are plans to connect the two trails via another trail in 2016, resulting in a week's continuous hike from Reserva Nacional Tamango (see p.377) all the way to Reserva Nacional Jeinemeni (see p.371).

Patagonian frog. Parque Patagonia currently provides a wildlife corridor between Reserva Nacional Tamango and Reserva Nacional Jeinemeni; the aim is to donate Parque Patagonia to Chile in 2020, making it a national park, which, together with the other two national parks, will rival Torres del Paine in size. In the meantime, visitors are welcome to hike the reserve's trails and if you have your own (4x4) wheels, the gravel road that bisects the park is one of the most gorgeous drives in the country, passing through a varied landscape of snow-tipped mountains, icy highland lakes, shallow lagoons teeming with flamingos, and wind-battered steppe and scrubland.

ARRIVAL AND INFORMATION

PARQUE PATAGONIA

By car There's currently no public transport to Parque Patagonia. To get to the main lodge/administration area a city car will suffice, but to proceed any further towards the Argentinian border, a vehicle with high clearance (pickup truck) is essential.

By foot A hiking trail (8hr) connects Reserva Nacional Tamango (see p.377), adjacent to Cochrane, to the Lagunas Altas trail in Parque Patagonia.

Administration office 17 km east of the park entrance, at Park Headquarters (Mon–Fri 8.30am–12.30pm & 2–6pm, Sat 8.30am–1pm; ☏65 297 0829; ⓦ patagoniapark.org). Register and pay for camping here and pick up a basic map. Detailed maps of the park are for sale at the gift shop of nearby *El Rincón Gaucho*.

ACCOMMODATION AND EATING

Casa Piedra Around 25km east of the park headquarters along the X-83. Sheltered campsite in a splendid location, due to open in Feb 2015. Camping/person <u>CH$5000</u>

★ **El Lodge** 17km east of the park entrance, by the Administration office ☏65 297 0829. The six rooms at this handsome, *estancia*-style stone lodge combine original wildlife photography and antique furniture with thoroughly modern rain showers heated by solar power. In the lounge you can sink onto the leather sofas and peruse the collection of coffee-table books on Patagonia's wild spaces, or else sip a glass of wine by the fireplace. If you're travelling with family or friends, the quad is a very good deal. <u>US$500</u>

★ **El Rincón Gaucho** Park headquarters, 17km east of the park entrance. All high beams and stone, the park restaurant serves fantastic food, making full use of greens from the on-site greenhouses, local lamb, and more. The menu changes seasonally and you can expect anything from a Patagonian-style *asado* buffet in the evenings to goat's cheese and caramelised onion sandwiches for lunch. Choose from set menu or à la carte. Lunch CH$12,000, dinner buffet CH$17,000. Daily 12.30–3pm & 7.30–10pm.

Westwinds Campground 2km from the administration area (see above). This tree-shaded campsite has sheltered areas for cooking and bathrooms with solar-power-heated showers. Oct to late April. Camping/person <u>CH$5000</u>

Cochrane

The last major stop on the Carretera Austral if you're southbound, the ranching settlement of **COCHRANE** lies 50km south of Puerto Bertrand. The town's paved, orderly grid of streets spreading out from the neat Plaza de Armas, and array of limited services, make this a prime spot to rest up after the wildness of the Carretera Austral, to fill up on fuel if heading south or to pick up provisions if you're looking to hike to Parque Patagonia (see p.375).

ARRIVAL AND INFORMATION COCHRANE

By bus Buses depart from the northwest corner of the Plaza. Buses Acuario 13 (☎ 67 252 2143), Buses Don Carlos (☎ 67 252 2150) and Buses Sao Paolo (☎ 67 252 2143) run services to Coyhaique; Buses Katalina (☎ 09 7961 3358) serve Villa O'Higgins, while Buses Aldea (☎ 09 6232 2798) runs to Caleta Tortel, as does Buses Patagonia (☎ 09 7521 9478). Chile Chico via Puerto Bertrand and Puerto Guadal is served by Buses Baker (☎ 09 8464 1067) and Buses Malfer (☎ 09 7756 8234).

Destinations Caleta Tortel (Tues, Thurs & Sun at 9.30am, Wed at 6am, Fri at 6am & 4pm; 3hr); Chile Chico via Puerto Bertrand and Puerto Guadal (Mon, Wed, Fri & Sun at 4pm;

5hr); Coyhaique (1–2 daily at 8am; 6–7hr); Villa O'Higgins (Thurs & Sun at 8am; 7hr).

Tourist information Plaza de Armas (Dec–March Mon–Sat 9am–1pm & 2.30–8pm; ⊛ www .cochranepatagonia.cl).

Conaf Río Nef 417 (Mon–Fri 10am–5pm; ☎ 67 252 2164). This is a good place for information on the nearby Reserva Nacional Tamango; trail maps sometimes available.

Money and exchange Bring plenty of cash. The Banco Estado ATM on the plaza accepts some foreign cards but not others and is not to be relied on.

ACCOMMODATION

Hotel Ultimo Paraíso Lago Brown 455 ☎ 67 252 2361, ⊛ hotelultimoparaiso.cl. As close as you get to paradise in Cochrane, this hotel is split into six spacious wood-panelled rooms with wood-burning stoves and cable TV. Breakfast is included and in summer there's a restaurant for guests only. CH$57,000

Latitud 47 Sur Lago Brown 564 ☎ 09 8829 0956. Located by and within a hunter's house decorated with antlers and other assorted paraphernalia, this place comprises an annexe block of several en suite rooms boasting the best power showers in Aisén as well as fridges

and kitchenettes. There are also cheaper rooms in the house proper which share facilities and cause tall people to stoop. No wi-fi (yet). House CH$25,000, annexe CH$20,000

Residencial Cero a Cero Lago Brown 464 ☎ 67 252 2158. This rambling family home caters to backpackers and cyclists with their clutch of small, unheated twins and doubles (though plenty of woolly blankets are provided). It's run by a friendly family, breakfast is basic and wi-fi works in the tiny lounge area by the stove. CH$24,000

EATING AND DRINKING

Ada's Café Restaurant Teniente Merino 374 ☎ 09 8399 5899. Cochrane's big splurge, this large, family-run restaurant attracts hungry cyclists and locals with their nicely cooked steaks, standard fish dishes, strong signature cocktails and pints of beer. Mains from CH$6000. Daily 7–11pm.

Café Tamango Esmeralda 464 ☎ 09 9158 4521. Just off

the main square, this light and bright café dishes up hearty burgers, more-ish crêpes with sweet fillings and even fresh fruit juice. Mon–Sat 9am–8.30pm.

Nacionpatagonia Steffens at Las Golondrinas. Adorable little café with hospitable owners serving real coffee as well as sandwiches and delicious home-made cakes. Daily 10am–9pm.

Reserva Nacional Tamango

6km east of Cochrane • CH$4000 • No public transport, but it's possible to walk to the park entrance from Cochrane by taking Pasaje 1 north and then east from San Valentín and Colonia

Reserva Nacional Tamango sits on the banks of **Lago Cochrane**, a skinny, twisting lake that straddles the Argentine border. The eight rewarding trails from the entrance vary in difficulty and range (40min to 6–8hr); the longest trail leads to Laguna Tamanguito, seamlessly connecting Reserva Nacional Tamango with Parque Patagonia's Lagunas Altas trail (see box, p.376); bring windproof clothing. The reserve is notable for its population of around eighty *huemúl* (native deer); if you're lucky, you may spot one, particularly along the Sendero Los Huemules from the ranger station to Refugio El Húngaro (5km; 2hr).

> ## DEATH IN THE FOREST
> Caleta Tortel's nearby island assumed its grisly moniker after dozens of employees involved in a timber-felling scheme a century ago suddenly died in **unexplained circumstances**. Officially the cause was an epidemic of some kind, possibly scurvy, but rumours suggested they were poisoned, maybe deliberately so that the company didn't have to pay their wages.

Caleta Tortel

Perhaps the most unusual village in Chile, Tortel consists of a scattering of houses on forested slopes surrounding a pale emerald bay. Located at the mouth of the Río Baker between the northern and southern ice fields and a logging spot for a lumber company, Tortel soon grew into a scattered settlement, each house with its own jetty, linked by a network of walkways and bridges made of fragrant cypress. There are no streets here, and even the police car and the fire engine are boats. Until very recently, Tortel didn't even have telephones, though with the Entel mobile network and widespread wi-fi it has now joined the digital world.

The village is divided into five sections: Rincón Alto (closest to the car park), Rincón Bajo (below Rincón Alto), Rincón Base (the centre of the village), Playa Ancha (further up along the coast from Rincón Base) and Junquillo, uphill from Playa Ancha.

Isla de los Muertos

Expediciones Patagonia Landeros (☎ 09 7704 2651) and Steffen Aventura (☎ 09 5696 5000) run boats from Tortel (CH$45,000 for up to six passengers)

Made famous in Britain when Prince William worked on an Operation Raleigh project here during his gap year, Tortel is also renowned for a mysterious incident (see box above) that gave its name to a nearby island, the **Isla de los Muertos**. You can visit this morbid but beautifully unspoiled place on a forty-minute boat-trip.

ARRIVAL AND INFORMATION

CALETA TORTEL

By bus Buses stop in the car park in Rincón Alto, the upper section of the village, next to the tourist office. Buses Aldea (☎ 09 6232 2798) runs to Cochrane, as does Buses Patagonia (☎ 09 7521 9478). The latter also runs directly to Coyhaique.

Destinations Cochrane (Tues, Thurs, & Sun at 3pm, Wed & Fri at 4pm, Fri at 6pm; 3hr); Coyhaique (Wed at 8.30am; 10hr).

Tourist information The very helpful office with plenty of info on Tortel is in the car park at the upper entrance to the village (daily 10am–8pm in peak season).

Money and exchange There are no banks or ATMs, so you have to bring plenty of cash.

ACCOMMODATION AND EATING

There's a free camping ground with no facilities at Playa Ancha.

Hospedaje Brisas Del Sur Playa Ancha ☎ 09 5688 2723. Sparkling, simple rooms, most with shared bathrooms, colourful bedspreads and sea views, presided over by hospitable Señora Landeros. Meals available on request. CH$24,000

Hospedaje Hielo Sur Rincón Bajo ☎ 09 5634 6080. Wood-shingled guesthouse run by friendly Señora Ortega; compact rooms share facilities and home-cooked meals available on request. Don Ortega operates a water taxi and does trips to Isla de Los Muertos. CH$24,000

Lodge Entre Hielos Rincón Bajo ☎ 09 9579 3779, ⊛ entrehielostortel.cl. Beautiful wooden lodge uphill from the boardwalk, decorated in neutral tones with attractive woollen detail in the six plush rooms. The restaurant serves fine Patagonian cuisine with emphasis on local ingredients, while staff organize boat trips and glacier hikes. US$150

Residencial Porvenir Junquillo ☎ 09 7652 1937. The welcoming Iñiguez family offers several wood-stove-heated twins and doubles with colourful bedspreads and home-cooked meals on request. CH$24,000

★**Sabores Locales** Sector Rincón Bajo. The indomitable Maritza cooks up large portions of ultra-fresh fish dishes, hearty shellfish soup and more, and is a great source of local info. She also has a guidebook of particular interest to cyclists. Daily 12.30–9pm.

GLACIERS AROUND CALETA TORTEL

Within easy reach by boat are two glaciers: **Ventisquero Steffens**, which originates in the northern ice field (3hr north by boat; speedboat CH$220,000; *lancha* CH$250,000), and **Ventisquero Jorge Montt**, an enormous bluish ice-wall that comes from the southern ice field (5hr by *lancha*; CH$280,000; 2hr by motorboat; CH$250,000), best done in a group of 8–10 people, as the trip is charged per vessel. Expediciones Patagonia Landeros (☏ 09 7704 2651) runs boat trips to both, as do Steffen Aventura (☏ 09 5696 5000).

Puerto Yungay

Dec–Feb 3 free ferries south daily at 10am, noon & 6pm; rest of year 2 ferries daily each way; return trips 1hr later; double-check timetable locally; 45min

Villa O'Higgins is reached via the very final – and particularly spectacular – 100km stretch of the Carretera beyond the small military camp of Puerto Yungay, 20km beyond the turn-off to Caleta Tortel, where you must cross the Fiordo Mitchell via ferry. If driving, confirm departure times in Cochrane and arrive at least half an hour early to guarantee a space. Here the Carretera Austral narrows in places to a single lane, ribboning its way through hilly terrain, with sheer drops on the side of the track revealing spectacular vistas of glacial rivers cutting through endless forest, wind-whipped lakes and distant mountains shrouded in mist.

Villa O'Higgins and around

Tiny **VILLA O'HIGGINS** was built on a simple grid, with the Carretera Austral running along the western side all the way down to the Bahía Bahamondez on the enormous glacial **Lago O'Higgins**, 7km away.

Most of the earliest settlers – who came at the beginning of the twentieth century, when it was most easily accessible from Argentina – were British. The first Chilean settlers did not arrive until the 1920s, and the town wasn't officially founded and given its present name until 1966. Until 1999, this orderly collection of wooden houses huddled against a sheer mountain face was reachable only by a small prop plane from Coyhaique or by boat from Argentina; a ten-minute hike up to the **Miradór Cerro Santiago** gives you a bird's eye view; a longer, two-hour hike carries on up to the even higher **Miradór La Bandera**.

In the not-too-distant future Villa O'Higgins may be connected to Argentina's Ruta 40; a road is already pretty much completed on the Chilean side and is worth driving for the views alone; on the Argentinian side, a road exists on paper but not in reality. Cosmopolitan Villa O'Higgins is not, but it is a starting and finishing point for cyclists "doing" the Carretera Austral, as well as a springboard for reaching some of the area's remote glaciers. Surprisingly, for a village of around five hundred people, there are quite a few accommodation options.

ARRIVAL AND INFORMATION

VILLA O'HIGGINS

By bus Buses Katalina (☏ 09 7961 3358) serve Cochrane (arriving in O'Higgins the day before), departing from Calle Río Mayer, between Calle Lago O'Higgins and Calle Lago Christie (buy your ticket in advance at the little office).
Destinations Cochrane (Mon & Fri at 8am; 7hr).

By plane Aereocord (☟ aerocord.cl) serves Coyhaique (CH$36,000 one way).
Destinations Coyhaique (Mon & Thurs; 1hr 15 min).

Tourist information On the plaza (summer Mon–Fri 10am–2pm & 3–7pm; ☟ villaohiggins.com). The staff at the small tourist office are very friendly and helpful, and provide plenty of information on the town and the surrounding area.

Hielo Sur Next to *Robinson Crusoe* (see p.380). ☟ hielosur.com. Runs boat trips to the Ventisquero O'Higgins (see p.381) and Ventisquero Chico, as well as single and multi-day hikes, and provides info for self-guided ventures.

Money and exchange Since there are no banks or ATMs, you'll have to bring plenty of cash. If you've just crossed the border from Argentina and have a surplus of Argentine pesos but no Chilean currency, you can change a limited amount of cash on the *Quetru* boat (see p.380); some lodgings can unofficially change Argentinian pesos at a poor rate.

8

ACCOMMODATION AND EATING

Camping Los Ñires Hernan Merino s/n ☏ 67 243 1811, ✉ campinglosnires@gmail.com. This centrally-located campsite is spacious and tree-lined with a cooking hut for campers and hot showers, though the ground can be muddy. Camping/person CH$4000

Hospedaje Patagonia Río Pascua 191 ☏ 61 243 1818. Friendly, family-run guesthouse just off the Plaza with simple but clean rooms with shared facilities and without central heating. The lady of the house is happy to provide home-cooked meals, which are not terribly memorable but perfectly adequate. CH$20,000

★ **El Mosco** Carretera Austral Km 1240 ☏ 67 243 1819. With its hammock-festooned porch and guitars in the snug living area, the town's only hostel acts as a hiker and biker magnet. Having been taken over by owner Jorge's brother following the former's untimely death, it has lost none of its warmth. Campers can use the hot showers and kitchen; the dorms are spacious; and there are doubles upstairs for those wishing to splurge. Breakfast CH$3000 extra. Dorms CH$10,000, doubles CH$32,000, camping/person CH$5000

Restaurante Entre Patagones Carretera Austral 1 ☏ 67 243 1810. This large wooden lodge dining hall fills up nightly with locals and travellers; food is simple and portions are large. Expect the likes of noodle soup and grilled hake; if you're lucky, you'll be there on *asador patagónico* (spit-roasted lamb) night. Mon–Sat 7.30–11pm, Sun 1–3.30pm.

★ **Robinson Crusoe Deep Patagonia** Carretera Austral Km 1240 ☏ 67 243 1821, ⌨ robinsoncrusoe .com. The only high-end option, this beautiful wooden lodge is distinguished by its twelve spacious, light-filled, centrally heated rooms set apart from the main building, with excellent beds, rain showers, and a high-ceilinged, wood-stove-heated guest lounge. A good breakfast is included, the outdoor hot tubs are great for a post-hike soak and there's glacier ice for your cocktails on excursion days. US$230

ARGENTINA THE HARD WAY: THE EL CHALTÉN CROSSING

The crossing between Villa O'Higgins and Argentina's El Chaltén is still remote and challenging, yet more and more travellers are prepared to take the boat, followed by a 20km hike over the border and then another lake crossing. The sixty-passenger *Quetru*, connected to Villa O'Higgins by the 7.50am transfers run by *Robinson Crusoe Deep Patagonia* lodge (CH$2500), leaves Bahía Bahamóndez at 8.30am (Jan & Feb Mon, Wed & Sat; Nov, Dec & March Sat only; CH$44,000) and arrives at the hamlet of **Candelario Mancilla** at around 11am. Just beyond the dock a signposted dirt track leads to the only accommodation option – a **campsite** with no facilities (US$4000) and two or three basic rooms available in the owner's house (CH$8000/person); the latter can provide meals on request. Get your passport stamped by **Chilean border control** further up the main road before you set off for Argentina.

TO THE BORDER

Beyond, a gravel road winds uphill through patches of woodland to the international border. Beyond the border, marked by signs welcoming you into Chile and Argentina, the 7.5km stretch of trail to the **Argentine Gendarmería** (no set hours) on the banks of the **Lago del Desierto** becomes a narrow, muddy footpath snaking its way through hilly forest and scrubland; cyclists have to push and sometimes carry their bikes. After getting stamped into Argentina, you can either pitch a tent at *Camping Lago del Desierto* (US$6), or stay in the basic *cabaña* run by the gendarmes (US$15). The next day, you can catch the motor launch *Huemul* across the lake (late Dec to late Feb Tues, Thurs & Sun at 6.30pm; early to mid-Dec & early March Thurs & Sun; mid-March to early April Sun only; 30–45min; AR$251) or hike the remaining 16km (5hr) along a steep, thickly forested path on the left side of the lake, emerging at the *guardería* by the pier on the south side.

Minibuses to **El Chaltén** meet the arriving motor launches (1.30pm, 4pm & 8pm; AR$270). If crossing from El Chaltén to Villa O'Higgins, bring enough food for at least three days as boat schedules are weather-dependent and you can get stuck for a day or two at Candelario Mancilla. To book a guide and packhorses (CH$20,000/packhorse, two-horse minimum), visit ⌨ villaohiggins.com.

Glaciers around Villa O'Higgins

A footpath from Calle Lago Cisnes runs through Parque Cerro Santiago up to two viewpoints (see p.379); from the second viewpoint, the path continues on towards the ice "tongue" of the **Ventisquero Mosco**, the nearest hanging glacier. It's a nine-hour round-trip hike; you can camp wild en route. Several glaciers, including Ventisquero O'Higgins, spill into Lago O'Higgins from the massive Campo de Hielo Sur – a titanic ice cap that blocks any further progress southwards for the Carretera. These can be visited by boat (see p.399).

From here, in the spring and summer months (November–March), a cross-lake ferry travels to the Argentine side, from where it's possible to walk to Argentina's **El Chaltén** along a route that's become very popular with intrepid hikers and particularly with bikers (see box, p.380). The boat crosses over to the hamlet of Candelario Mancilla – the starting point for the rewarding 7km Sendero de Chile hike that climbs steeply through *lenga* forest to the Dos Lagunas pass, where you get sweeping views of the O'Higgins, Chico and Pirámide glaciers, before descending to the *refugio* by Lago O'Higgins' Brazo Sur. You can arrange to be picked up here by the boat that runs tours to the glaciers.

8

Southern Patagonia

387 Punta Arenas and around

397 Puerto Natales and around

402 Parque Nacional Torres del Paine

410 Parque Nacional Los Glaciares

GAUCHOS, PARQUE NACIONAL TORRES DEL PAINE

9

Southern Patagonia

Patagonia lies tucked away right at the southernmost tip of the Americas – indeed of the world's landmass, not counting Antarctica. While the very name holds a fascination for many travellers, the reality can be harsh: the place is cursed by a persistent wind, the *Escoba de Dios* (God's Broom); trees grow horizontally here, sculpted by the gales; winters are long and summers short. Geographically ill-defined, "Patagonia" usually refers to the narrow triangle of land south of a line between Puerto Montt, in Chile, and Argentina's Península Valdés. In Chile the term is actually usually reserved for Southern Patagonia, where the Andes take a last, dramatic breath before plunging into the ocean.

While much of Argentine Patagonia is flat rolling **pampa**, the land rises in the western sliver of land shared by both countries; it is said that people on both sides of the border think of themselves as Patagonians first, and Chileans or Argentinians second, united by a common ranching culture that has long been in decline. These days, large numbers of Chileans and non-Chilean visitors alike come to Patagonia to hike – in Chile's most famous and stunning national park, **Parque Nacional Torres del Paine**, a massif crowned with otherworldly granite towers, and accessed from the superbly located gateway town of **Puerto Natales**. Others come to follow in the footsteps of the region's famous travellers: navigator Ferdinand Magellan, naturalist Charles Darwin and author Bruce Chatwin; to gaze at the region's many spectacular **glaciers**; or to visit the **penguin colonies** from the lively provincial capital of **Punta Arenas** – a port city sitting on the shore of the stormy Magellan Strait. The broad expanse of frigid grassland between the two towns stretches to the Atlantic coast, taking in the desolately beautiful **Parque Nacional Pali Aike**. Fewer visitors make it to the remote **islands** of the Pacific coast.

Since the whole of this region is physically cut off from the rest of Chile by two vast ice caps, the only links with territory to the north are by air, water or through **Argentina**. The last option allows you to visit traditional **estancias** and some of Argentina's finest landscapes, including the **Parque Nacional Los Glaciares**, where the **Fitz Roy Massif**, near the tiny town of El Chaltén, offers incredible hiking and climbing opportunities, while **Glaciar Perito Moreno**, accessible from the tourist hub of El Calafate, is visually arresting, not to mention the most accessible of all South American glaciers.

Brief history

Chilean Patagonia, the site of the some of the continent's oldest human habitation, was originally populated by Tehuelche hunter-gatherers, who stalked roaming guanacos in the interior, and the sea-faring Kawéscar who dived naked for shellfish in the frigid

Magellan, pioneer of global exploration p.389
It's a dog's life p.390
Hiking to Cabo Froward p.395
The strange case of the giant sloth skin p.402

Fire in the park p.403
Beyond the W: Torres del Paine alternatives p.408
Patagonian estancias p.413
Trekking in Parque Nacional Los Glaciares p.414

MAGELLANIC PENGUINS, ISLA MAGDALENA

Highlights

❶ Cemetery at Punta Arenas Visit this moving – and beautiful – memorial to the pioneers from Britain and Spain, Croatia and Italy. **See p.391**

❷ Penguins at Isla Magdalena Watch the birds' comic antics on this island sanctuary – the second largest colony of Magellanic penguins in South America. **See p.396**

❸ Hiking Parque Nacional Torres del Paine Set aside at least a few days to trek through Chile's most popular, spectacular park. **See p.403**

❹ Parque Nacional Los Glaciares Hike and boat your way to the remotest corner of the park and watch glaciers crumble into a pristine, ice-filled lagoon. **See p.410**

❺ Glaciar Perito Moreno Admire Argentine Patagonia's most spectacular glacier from afar, take a boat right up to its face or go ice-hiking on its surface. **See p.413**

❻ Laguna de Los Tres Complete the most demanding and scenic of hikes in the Fitz Roy mountain range of Argentina's Parque Nacional Los Glaciares. **See p.414**

HIGHLIGHTS ARE MARKED ON THE MAP ON P.386

waters around the southern fjords. The first European to discover the area was **Ferdinand Magellan**, a Portuguese navigator who sailed through the strait now bearing his name. Spanish colonization attempts failed catastrophically and no European tried to settle the place again for another two hundred and fifty years.

The voyages of the *Beagle*, from 1826 to 1834, the second one bearing young Charles Darwin, renewed interest in the area, prompting continued Chilean and Argentine attempts to colonize the area. In the 1870s the two narrowly avoided war over the

SOUTHERN PATAGONIA

HIGHLIGHTS

1. Cemetery at Punta Arenas
2. Penguins at Isla Magdalena
3. Hiking Parque Nacional Torres del Paine
4. Parque Nacional Los Glaciares
5. Glaciar Perito Moreno
6. Laguna de Los Tres

Villa O'Higgins

Lago O'Higgins

CAMPO DE HIELO SUR

PARQUE NACIONAL BERNARDO O'HIGGINS

El Chaltén

Lago Viedma

Upsala Glacier

PARQUE NACIONAL LOS GLACIARES

Spegazzini Glacier

Punta Bandera

Lago Argentino

El Calafate

Estancia Cerro Fortaleza

Perito Moreno Glacier

Lago Roca

El Cerrito

PARQUE NACIONAL BERNARDO O'HIGGINS

La Esperanza

Cuernos del Paine (2600m)

Cerro Paine Grande (3248m)

PARQUE NACIONAL TORRES DEL PAINE

Cerro Castillo

ARGENTINA

Serrano Glacier

Lago del Toro

Cueva del Milodón

Seno Ultima Esperanza

Puerto Bories

Río Gallego

RESERVA NACIONAL ALACALUFES

Puerto Natales

Puerto Ramírez

Monte Aymond

PARQUE NACIONAL PALI AIKE

Punta Delgada

CHILE

Lago Blanca

Estancia San Gregorio

Mt Burney (1750m)

Seno Skyring

Río Verde

Estrecho de Magallanes

Bahía Azul (Puerto Espora)

Cerro Atalaya (1850m)

Isla Riesco

Mt Pirámide (1200m)

Cerro Ladrillero (1665m)

Penguin Sanctuary

Seno Otway

Isla Magdalena (Penguin Sanctuary)

Punta Arenas

TIERRA DEL FUEGO

Porvenir

RESERVA NACIONAL MAGALLANES

Peninsula Cordova

Cutter Cove

RESERVA NACIONAL LAGUNA PARRILLAR

Río Amarillo
Puerto Hambre

Bahía Inútil

Camerón

PACIFIC OCEAN

Estancia San Juan

Isla Dawson

Canal Whiteside

Isla Santa Inés

Cabo Froward

Puerto Yartau
Puerto Condor
Puerto Arturo

N

0   40
kilometres

territory, not for the last time. From 1849, Punta Arenas was boosted by sea traffic enroute to the California Gold Rush; while it didn't last long, the introduction of sheep farming created sprawling **estancias** (ranches) and brought great wealth to their owners – and misery to the indigenous populations – in the late nineteenth century.

Wool has now been replaced by **oil**, commercial salmon farming and tourism as the region's main resources. The Chileans call the area the province of **Magallanes**, in the explorer's honour; it has its own flag and is one of the least inhabited areas in Chile.

Punta Arenas and around

Seen from above, **PUNTA ARENAS**, 2190km south of Santiago, is a sprawling patchwork of galvanized tin roofs climbing up from the shores of the Magellan Strait. On the ground, however, the city is substantial and largely modern, especially in the centre where glass and concrete office buildings sit cheek by jowl alongside the grand nineteenth-century stone mansions of the wool barons.

Brief history

Punta Arenas started life 60km south of where it is today, at a place called **Fuerte Bulnes**, the first Chilean settlement along the Magellan Strait. It was founded in 1843 by Captain John Williams, a seaman from Bristol in the service of the Chileans, with the aim of forestalling any other country's attempts at colonization. In 1848 the new settlement moved to a more suitable location to the north, named by an English sailor "Sandy Point", loosely translated into "Punta Arenas" in Spanish. Punta Arenas blossomed in the nineteenth-century sheep boom which, in turn, attracted immigrant communities from Croatia, Germany, Ireland, Spain, England and elsewhere, all of whom left their marks. Prior to the creation of the Panama Canal, Punta Arenas was an important port of call for all ships bound for the western coast of the USA from Europe, as well as a stopover for Antarctica-bound explorers, which it remains to this day. The visitor contingent these days is also comprised of travellers bound for Tierra del Fuego and Torres del Paine. The recent petrol boom has left the city with a legacy of duty-free shops and huge shopping malls on the city's outskirts.

Plaza Muñoz Gamero

The tranquil **Plaza Muñoz Gamero**, featuring shady pathways under magnificent hundred-year-old Monterey cypresses, teems with strolling families and vendors selling souvenirs from their carts. In the middle rises an imposing **monument to Ferdinand Magellan**. Below Magellan sits a Selk'nam Indian – one of only two references to the now extinct people that you'll find in the city (see p.391). If you touch (some say kiss) the Indian's polished toe, tradition has it that you'll return to Punta Arenas. The two blocks of Magallanes running from the square's northeast corner are all that remains of the city's oldest original street, originally named Calle María Isabel.

Palacio Sara Braun

Plaza Muñoz Gamero • Mon–Fri 10.30am–1pm & 4pm–midnight, Sat 10.30am–1pm & 8–10pm • CH$1000

Around the plaza rise several grand houses dating from the wool boom, but the only one you can visit is the **Palacio Sara Braun**, on the northwestern corner, designed by a French architect, Numa Mayer, for Sara Braun, widow of the great sheep baron José Nogueira. While it is now divided between the *Club de la Unión* and the *Hotel José Nogueira* (see p.392), visitors can stroll through the elegant, period furniture-lined rooms of the *Club de la Unión* section, and marvel at the opulence of the frescoes.

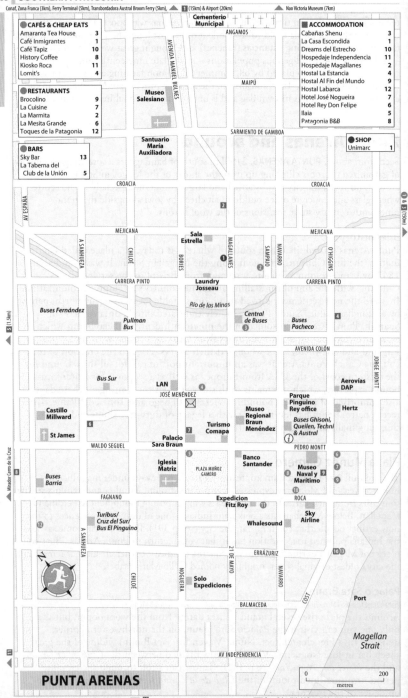

Conaf, Zona Franca (3km), Ferry Terminal (5km), Transbordadora Austral Broom Ferry (5km), ▲ 🚽 (15km) & Airport (20km) ▲ Nao Victoria Museum (7km)

CAFÉS & CHEAP EATS
Amaranta Tea House	3
Café Inmigrantes	1
Café Tapiz	10
History Coffee	8
Kiosko Roca	11
Lomit's	4

RESTAURANTS
Brocolino	9
La Cuisine	7
La Marmita	2
La Mesita Grande	6
Toques de la Patagonia	12

BARS
Sky Bar	13
La Taberna del Club de la Unión	5

ACCOMMODATION
Cabañas Shenu	3
La Casa Escondida	1
Dreams del Estrecho	10
Hospedaje Independencia	11
Hospedaje Magallanes	2
Hostal La Estancia	4
Hostal Al Fin del Mundo	9
Hostal Labarca	12
Hotel José Nogueira	7
Hotel Rey Don Felipe	6
Ilaia	5
Patagonia B&B	8

SHOP
Unimarc	1

Fuerte Bulnes (51km) & Puerto Hambre (51km)

PUNTA ARENAS

0   200
metres

Museo Regional Braun Menéndez

Magallanes 949 • Mon & Wed–Sat: May–Sept 10.30am–5pm; Oct–April 10.30am–2pm • ⓦ museodemagallanes.cl • CH$1000

Half a block north of the square sits the **Palacio Braun Menéndez** – the former family residence of the marriage that united the two wealthiest and most powerful families in Punta Arenas, and now housing the **Museo Regional Magallanes**. The beautifully preserved private quarters of this early twentieth-century family home offer a window onto a wealthy middle-class lifestyle achieved by few who came to Patagonia in search of it: a dining room and bedrooms, lavishly decorated and filled with superb French Art Nouveau furnishings and the billiard room where men discussed affairs of state.

Several rooms are devoted to a permanent exhibition detailing the colonization of Patagonia and Tierra del Fuego, with pioneer articles, historical photos and bilingual displays on the maritime and farming history of the region, as well as the region's **indigenous peoples** – the Kawéscar and the Selk'nam. Dusty old account books and documents reveal that the founding families controlled not only the sheep trade, but an immense range of other commercial activities. In effect, they *were* the city.

Museo Naval y Marítimo

Pedro Montt 981 • Tues–Sat 9.30am–12.30pm & 2–5pm • CH$1200

Housed in the former naval headquarters, the engaging **Museo Naval y Marítimo** focuses on Chile's naval history and the exploration of the southern waters. The ground floor

---

MAGELLAN, PIONEER OF GLOBAL EXPLORATION

Fernão de Magalhães, known to English-speakers as **Ferdinand Magellan**, was born in about 1480 in northern Portugal, and had an adventurous early life: in his 20s he saw service with the Portuguese fleets in their wars against the Muslims of the Indian Ocean, and by 1515 he was a veteran of the campaigns in Morocco. In 1516, after being refused a rise in his pension by the king of Portugal, Magellan took his services to the Spanish crown.

Those days were the beginning of European exploration, prompted mainly by the desire to seek out **new routes** to the East and its valuable **Spice Islands** (the Moluccas of Indonesia). Magellan believed that the answer lay to the west, under or through the newly discovered American continents, and he asked the king of Spain, Carlos I, to fund his search. Charles agreed, eager to prove that the Spice Islands lay in the half of the New World that the pope had just assigned to Spain.

THROUGH THE STRAITS TO THE PACIFIC

On September 20, 1519, Magellan sailed west as admiral of a fleet of five ships. They crossed the Atlantic Ocean, and started to search the coast of South America for the elusive passage. It was a long and hard hunt, and not all Magellan's fleet believed there was a strait: on Easter Day 1520, Magellan had to quash a mutiny by his Spanish captains. But on October 21, 1520, his flagship, the *Trinidad*, finally rounded Cabo Virgenes and entered the **strait** that now bears his name. Thirty-six days later the open seas of an ocean were sighted; they named the new ocean "**the Pacific**" for its calmness after the storms of the strait, and set out across it, not expecting it to be so wide. Seeing the smoke from countless fires of the Selk'nam and the Yamaná people on the coast of the immense island on the southern side of the Strait, Magellan gave it its present name: Tierra del Fuego (Land of Fire).

BACK TO SPAIN

They sailed for four months without seeing land. When Magellan himself was **killed** in a fight with the natives of Mactán Island, the fleet didn't turn back; petrified of attempting to go through the straits at the bottom of South America for a second time, they took the longer route round the Cape of Good Hope. Three years after they'd set out, just one of Magellan's original five ships finally limped back to Spain. It was loaded with spices (cloves and nutmeg) and manned by only eighteen of the original crew, men wasted and half-dead. The voyage's chronicler said he could not imagine the journey ever being repeated.

9

IT'S A DOG'S LIFE

One thing many visitors notice when they arrive in Punta Arenas (and other large Chilean cities) is the large number of **stray dogs** on the streets. Most tend to be tame – many of them are abandoned pets – but there are occasional incidents of dog bites, car accidents and attacks on wildlife, not to mention sickness, injury and starvation on the part of the dogs, exacerbated by the city's large stray population.

The Chilean federal and local governments do not regularly provide animal control services, but Punta Arenas has a bone fido (!) **Centre Rescate Canino** (☎61 220 0604, ⓦwww.puntaarenas.cl/perritos) that gathers up strays, nurses them back to health, neuters them and tries to find them a new home. This animal shelter welcomes volunteers and visitors (call in advance) and can be visited at Km 9.5, Ruta 9, just outside Punta Arenas.

features a collection of minutely detailed scale models of ships, including Sir Ernest Shackleton's *Endurance* and the *Yelcho* that ended up rescuing Shackleton's crew, as well as a block of Antarctic ice. Upstairs you can play around in the area decked out as a ship, complete with nautical equipment, maps, charts and interactive displays of sailing routes and Chile's southernmost lighthouses.

Castillo Millward

España 959

In the nineteenth century when sterling was still a widely accepted currency, a leading member of the community was one **Charles Milward**, great-uncle of the author **Bruce Chatwin**. Chatwin wrote his celebrated part-travelogue, part-fiction, *In Patagonia,* about his trip here to learn more about Milward, ex-sea captain and adventurer, and the man who helped discover a chunk of a deep-frozen prehistoric ground sloth in the Cueva del Milodón (see box, p.402).

Milward's old house, a red brick tower with Gothic windows, is now owned by the local daily newspaper, *El Pinguino*, and not open to the public. It was here, in 1914, that the famous explorer Sir Ernest Shackleton stayed and planned the rescue of his stranded crew after his ship, the *Endurance*, was crushed by ice in the Antarctic.

Mirador Cerro La Cruz

Across Avenida España, and a block along Fagnano, some steps lead up to the **Mirador Cerro la Cruz**, where you can enjoy a sweeping view of the city's multicoloured roofs and the wind-whipped Magellan Strait.

Museo Salesiano Maggiorino Borgatello

Av Manuel Bulnes • Tues–Sun 10am–12.30pm & 3–5.30pm • CH$2500

Besides a plethora of taxidermied local wildlife, the exhibits at this absorbing museum focus largely on the indigenous peoples of Southern Patagonia and Tierra del Fuego and their evangelization by the Salesian religious order. The exhibits suggest that the missionaries acted as mediators between the locals and the settlers, failing to point out the evangelizers' roles in the demise of native culture.

The best displays among the natural history samples vividly depict the daily life of the Kawéscar Indians and the weapons they used for hunting and fishing. Another choice exhibit is the unparalleled collection of photographs of the region and its inhabitants, taken by the Italian mountaineering priest, Alberto de Agostini, who spent many years among the native people of Patagonia and Tierra del Fuego.

Cementerio Municipal

Av Bulnes • Daily: summer 7.30am–8pm; winter 8am–6pm • Free

The city's magnificent **Cementerio Municipal** extends over four city blocks. Crisscrossed by a network of footpaths lined with immaculately clipped cypresses, this eclectic necropolis reflects the turbulent history of Patagonia. The monumental tombs of the city's ruling families – some made of the same Italian marble as Michelangelo's *David* and elaborately engraved with the English and Spanish names – mingle with the Croatian and Scandinavian names of immigrant labourers, etched on more modest gravestones and locker-sized funerary urn receptacles.

A monument depicting a **Selk'nam Indian** is surrounded with plaques conveying the gratitude of those whose wishes it allegedly granted. See if you can spot the onion-domed crypt of the Braun family – one of the city's founding dynasties – and the simple gravestone of Charles Milward (there's a map inside the main entrance that highlights some of the more famous graves).

Nao Victoria Museum

Río Seco, Km 7 north • Daily 9am–7pm • ⓦ naovictoria.cl • CH$3000 • Buses run to Río Seco from the corner of Carrera Pinto and Chiloé.

Well worth the 7km drive north of town, this new interactive space by the sea consists of three full-size replicas of famous nautical vessels associated with the history of the area, with a fourth – the replica HMS *Beagle* that carried Charles Darwin to Patagonia – being constructed at research time. You can climb down into the hold of Magellan's *Nao Victoria* carrack that took him around Cape Horn, view the surprisingly compact *Goleta Ancud* that brought the original colonists to Punta Arenas and check out Shackleton's lifeboat, *James Caird*. The latter carried him and five crew members to South Georgia through the most violent stretch of ocean on earth after the *Endurance* was crushed by ice.

ARRIVAL AND DEPARTURE | PUNTA ARENAS

BY PLANE

Most travellers arrive at the user-friendly Aeropuerto Presidente Ibañez, 20km north of town. Scheduled LAN and Sky Airline flights leave Punta Arenas for Coyhaique (Balmaceda), Puerto Montt and Santiago. In summer, Aerovías DAP runs flights to Porvenir (CH$26,000–29,000 one way), Puerto Williams (CH$67,000–75,000 one way) and Antarctica (US$5500/6500 for full day/overnight stay; Nov–March only). Taxis to the centre charge CH$6,000, minibuses CH$4000 and Buses Fernández (ⓣ 61 224 2313) runs airport transfers for CH$3500; they all meet incoming flights. Buses heading to Puerto Natales also stop at the airport.

Airlines Aerovías DAP, O'Higgins at Menéndez (ⓣ 61 261 6100, ⓦ www.dap.cl or dapantartica.cl); LAN, Menéndez at Bories (ⓣ 61 224 1100, ⓦ www.lanchile.cl); Sky Airline, Roca 935 (ⓣ 61 271 0645, ⓦ skyairline.cl).

Destinations Antarctica (Nov–March several monthly; 6hr round-trip); Balmaceda (several daily; 1hr); Porvenir (Mon–Sat 2–3; 12min); Puerto Montt (2 daily; 2hr); Puerto Williams (summer Mon–Sat 1 daily at 10am; winter 3 weekly; 40min–1hr 20min); Santiago (several daily; 4hr).

BY BUS

Each bus company has its own terminal in the centre of Punta Arenas.

Companies Buses Tecni Austral, Navarro 975 (ⓣ 61 261 3420), Buses Pacheco, Av Colón 900 (ⓣ 61 224 2174, ⓦ www.busespacheco.co.cl), Buses Barria, Av España 264 (ⓣ 61 224 0646) and Bus Sur, Menéndez 552 (ⓣ 61 261 4224, ⓦ bussur.com) serve Ushuaia via Río Grande; book ahead in peak season. Bus Sur, Buses Fernández, Sanhueza 745 (ⓣ 61 224 2313, ⓦ www.busesfernandez.com) and Buses Pacheco go to Puerto Natales. Bus El Pingüino, Sanhueza 745 (ⓣ 61 222 1812), Buses Ghisoni, España 264 (ⓣ 61 261 3420) and Buses Pacheco serve Río Gallegos. Buses Queilén, Navarro 975 (ⓣ 61 222 2714, ⓦ queilenbus. cl), Turibus/Cruz del Sur, Sanhueza 745 (ⓣ 61 222 7970, ⓦ busescruzdelsur.cl) and Pullman, Av Colón 568 (ⓣ 61 222 3359, ⓦ www.pullman.cl) run to Osorno, Puerto Montt, Ancud and Castro. Bus journeys to Ushuaia involve a 40min ferry crossing and don't always include a meal stop, so bring food with you.

Destinations Ancud and Castro via Puerto Montt & Osorno (5 weekly at 8/9am; 27hr); Puerto Natales (16 daily; 3hr); Río Gallegos, Argentina (1–2 daily; 4hr); Ushuaia, Argentina, via Río Grande (daily at 8.30/9am; 12hr).

BY FERRY

The ferry terminal at Tres Puentes, 5km north of town, is a short *colectivo* (CH$1000) or taxi ride (around CH$4000)

9

from downtown, along the Natales road to the north. Transbordadora Austral Broom ferries, Juan Williams 6450 (☎61 272 8100, ⌨tabsa.cl), serves Porvenir in Tierra del Fuego and Puerto Williams on Isla Navarino, as well as the Primera Angostura crossing between Punta Delgada on the Patagonian mainland and Bahía Azul (Puerto Espora) in Tierra del Fuego. Timetables are weather-dependent; if

taking a car to Porvenir, book a space in advance.
Destinations Porvenir (Tues–Sat 1 daily; 2hr 30min; passenger CH$6200, car CH$39,800); Primera Angostura (summer every 45min, 8.30am–11pm; less often in winter; 20min; passenger CH$1700, car CH$15,000); Puerto Williams (Nov–March weekly Thurs at 6pm; 30hr; Pullman seat CH$98,000, berth CH$137,000).

INFORMATION AND TOURS

TOURIST INFORMATION
Conaf Bulnes 309, fourth floor (Mon–Thurs 8.30am–5pm, Fri 8.30am–4pm; ☎61 223 8554). Information on the area's national parks and reserves.
Parque Pingüino Rey office Navarro 975 (☎61 261 3420 ⌨pinguinorey.cl). Info on the small king penguin colony in Tierra del Fuego (see p.425).
Sernatur Navarro 999 (Mon–Fri 8.30am–8pm, Sat 10am–6pm; ☎61 224 1330, ⌨patagonia-chile.com). Lots of information on the city and the region.

TOUR OPERATORS
Most tour companies offer trips to the Seno Otway penguin colony (CH$19,000), Fuerte Bulnes (CH$28,000) and Parque Nacional Pali Aike (CH$55,000). Below are reputable operators offering standard and specialized excursions.
Expedición Fitz Roy Roca 825 ☎61 261 3932, ⌨expedicionfitzroy.com. Overnight trips aboard the M/V *Forrest* (accommodation onboard): either whale-watching, glacier-viewing on D'Agostini Sound or exploring Skyring Sound. From US$930.
Kayak Agua Fresca ☎09 9655 5073, ⌨kayakagua fresca.com. Highly recommended outfit specializing in sea

kayaking trips – from a half-day paddle along the Magellan Strait (CH$55,000) to a serious four-day kayaking expedition to Cabo Froward (CH$550,000). They also offer dolphin-watching trips aboard Zodiac boats (which can also take you to Cabo Froward in 12 hours; CH$250,000).
Solo Expediciones Nogueira 1255 ☎61 271 0219, ⌨soloexpediciones.com. With their fast, covered speedboat, these guys whisk passengers off on half-day-trips to Isla Magdalena, stopping at the sea lion colony of Isla Marta. They sail from Laredo pier, rather than Punta Arenas itself, which means far less time on the water than with Comapa (see below), though their boat is more weather-dependent.
Turismo Comapa Magallanes 990 ☎61 220 0200, ⌨comapa.com. Longstanding operator offers ferry excursions to Isla Magdalena (see p.364; CH$30,000) that involve four hours on the boat in total. Land excursions to Fuerte Bulnes and Reserva Magallanes also on offer.
Whalesound Navarro 1191 ☎09 9887 9814, ⌨whalesound.com. Responsible operator offering humpback whale-watching trips in Coloane Marine Park (Dec–May), ranging from two to four days and overnighting on Carlos III island or Faro San Isidro (2 day, 2 night, all-inclusive trip US$1100).

ACCOMMODATION

HOTELS AND B&BS
Dreams del Estrecho O'Higgins 1235 ☎61 220 4648, ⌨www.mundodreams.com. This shiny glass tower may look more at home in Dubai than Punta Arenas, but *Dreams* is indisputably the city's most modern, luxurious business hotel. Its rooms and suites come equipped with king-size beds and every convenience you'd expect, and other perks include a lofty swimming pool with sea views, massage spa, international restaurant, swanky bar (see p.394) and casino. And if you don't know how to gamble, their special TV programme will teach you. US$260
Hostal Labarca Chiloé 1581 ☎61 224 2979, ⌨hostallabarca.cl. A few blocks north of the plaza, a friendly, helpful hostess presides over a clutch of homely, frilly, comfortable doubles and twins (some with own bathroom). Some rooms are rather compact, but a good breakfast is included and she goes out of her way to make you feel welcome. A little English spoken. CH$35,000
Hotel José Nogueira Bories 959 ☎61 271 1000,

⌨hotelnogueira.com. This historic hotel boasts a prime location on the plaza, inside the Palacio Sara Braun, former home to the city's most powerful family. Here's your chance to reside in the style of nineteenth-century wool barons (with the added benefit of central heating and cable TV); bear in mind that not all rooms are the same size. US$215
Hotel Rey Don Felipe Sanhueza 965 ☎61 229 5000, ⌨hotelreydonfelipe.com. The handsome mock-Tudor façade is a fitting introduction to a luxury hotel (quality-certified by Sernatur) that gets all the important details right: all rooms are spacious, with classic decor and king-size or twin beds, rain showers in the modern bathrooms and a very good restaurant. A gym, sauna and Jacuzzi are nice extras and service is very attentive. US$202
★**Ilaia** Carrera Pinto 351 ☎61 222 3592, ⌨ilaia.cl. This small, whimsical boutique hotel places emphasis on the rejuvenation of body and spirit, with playful messages to be discovered, and individually decorated rooms with plenty of space and light, bright woolly touches and an

absence of TVs. You can take part in hatha yoga, reiki and meditation, and nourishment at breakfast consists of home-made muesli, chapatis, fruit and yogurt. CH$82,000

Patagonia B&B España 1048 ☎61 222 7243, ⓦpatagoniabb.cl. Set back from the main street and thus shielded from the noise, this beautiful, modern B&B is more like a hotel; all twins and doubles are bright, spacious, en suite, come with cable TV and bright splashes of colour. The CH$20,000 discount for solo travellers makes this a great bargain; the only thing that lets the side down is the mediocre breakfast. CH$50,000

CABAÑAS

Cabañas Shenu Quillota 658 ☎61 237 1573, ⓦshenu patagonia.cl. These four gorgeous, compact-yet-luxurious stone-and-wood *cabañas* sit in a quiet residential neighbourhood several blocks from the plaza. All come with brand-new fittings, bathtubs and rain showers, a cosy double, a sofa-cum-double-bed and a folder full of info on the city. Cribs are provided for young children and there's even a little playground on the property. *Cabañas* CH$60,000

★**La Casa Escondida** Parcela 26, Sector Ojo Bueno ☎61 222 3023, ⓦlacasaescondida.cl. The family-run "*Hidden House*" makes a wonderful retreat from the bustle of the city. Located 15km north of Punta Arenas, it consists of adorably rustic rooms and *cabañas* with handmade furniture, down duvets and guest sauna. Traditional Patagonian barbecue and evening meals available on request and prices include airport transfer and breakfast. Doubles CH$42,000, *cabañas* CH$84,000

HOSTELS

Hospedaje Independencia Independencia 374 ☎61 222 7572, ⓦchileaustral.com/independencia/camping .html. Friendly young owners allow camping in the yard and can rent out equipment and organize tours of the area. Dorms and rooms are too small to swing a cat but the warmth of the owners and generous breakfast (CH$1000) makes up for it. Camping/person CH$2000, dorms CH$6000, doubles CH$12,000

★**Hospedaje Magallanes** Magallanes 570 ☎61 222 8616, ⓦaonikenk.com. Just four simple doubles (one windowless) and a six-bed dorm on offer at this family home which you'll share with a gregarious German– Chilean couple and Emma the dog. Sebastian is a wilderness expert who's happy to impart his advice, there's plenty of *buena onda* (good vibes) and socialising between guests is fuelled by the occasional impromptu barbecue. Dorms CH$14,000, doubles CH$34,000

Hostal La Estancia O'Higgins 765 ☎61 224 9130, ⓦestancia.cl. Many travellers end up using this restored 1920s house as a home away from home, attracted by its high-ceilinged dorms and bright rooms with cable TV. The large common area features table football and small book exchange and the owner is happy to assist with onward travel. Dorms CH$12,500, doubles CH$38,000

Hostal Al Fin del Mundo O'Higgins 1026 ☎61 271 0185. The rooms here are basic, of varying sizes and some are windowless, and it's not always easy to tell who's staff and who's a guest. However, perks include pool table, book exchange and a comfy lounge with massive TV. The location is super central and opposite three good restaurants. Dorms CH$14,000, doubles CH$37,000

EATING AND DRINKING

CAFÉS AND CHEAP EATS

Amaranta Tea House Av Colón 822B ☎61 237 1132, ⓦteamaranta.cl. Amid flowery seats, colourful mandalas and pastel-coloured walls, this cute café serves eleven types of loose-leaf tea, tempting cakes and a great-value daily menu that typically involves veggie lasagne or the like. Only the loud and funky soundtrack is slightly out of sync with the peaceful ambience. Mon–Fri 10am–10pm, Sat 10am–9pm.

Café Inmigrantes Quillota 559 ☎61 222 2205, ⓦinmigrante.cl. Located on a corner in the quiet Croatian neighbourhood, this homely café is filled with knick-knacks and sports sepia prints of historic Punta Arenas. Come here for chunky sandwiches overflowing with locally-smoked salmon, meats and more, and don't leave without sampling the home-made cakes. Mains from CH$5500. Mon–Sat 12.30–10pm.

Café Tapiz Roca 912 ☎09 8730 3481. This wood-shingled café has been drawing locals and travellers alike with its salads, sandwiches (try the smoked salmon with capers and cream cheese), grilled cheese toasties, real coffee and excellent home-made cake selection. The fruit juices are not watered down and will give you that vitamin boost you've been lacking. Mon–Sat 10.30am–6pm, Sun 11am–5pm.

History Coffee Navarro 1065 ☎61 222 0000. At this aptly-named café you're surrounded by history (ye olde photos of Punta Arenas, antique coffee grinders) and coffee (beans embedded in your table). The brew is decent, there's a good selection of sweet and savoury crepes, *churrascos* and burgers (CH$3200–4000), and the service is sweet and prompt. Mon–Sat 9am–9pm.

Kiosko Roca Roca at Navarro. To get at this hole-in-the-wall's specialities – banana milk, *choripan* (mini grilled sandwich with chorizo) or *choripan con queso* (the same but with cheese) – you have to push through the rows of locals propping up the bar. But it's worth it. Daily 8am–4pm.

Lomit's José Menéndez 722 ☎61 224 3399. Locals and travellers alike pack this American diner-style burger and

9

hot dog joint and it's a good spot for striking up a conversation with fellow diners. But in the name of all that is holy, why are there no French fries??? Daily 10am–2.30am.

RESTAURANTS

Brocolino O'Higgins 1049 ☏ 61 222 4989. With a menu showcasing the whimsical creations of zany chef Hector, *Brocolino* is a Punta Arenas institution, found inside an unassuming-looking historic wooden building. Read the stories behind the dishes, and tuck into lamb sweetbreads in champagne sauce, perfectly-seared steak 'in the style of Paris Hilton' or kick-start your libido with "Aphrodisiac soup". On the downside, consistency can be a problem. Mains CH$4600–8500. Daily 1–3pm & 7–11.30pm.

La Cuisine O'Higgins 1037 ☏ 61 222 8641. With his good-value lunch menu (CH$5500), French chef Eric has earned himself a loyal local clientele. While the set menu is not bad, his cooking shines on a la carte choices such as boeuf bourguignon, scallop gratin and crème brulee....if you're prepared to ignore the clichéd 'French' decor and the somewhat erratic service. Mains around CH$7000. Mon–Sat 12.30–3pm & 7.30–11pm, Sun 1–3.30pm.

★**La Marmita** Plaza Sampaio 678 ☏ 61 222 2056. Among the colourful rugs, weavings, collections of teapots and other eclectica you'll find some of the best flavours for miles around and attentive service from the young staff. The pisco (and berry) sours are the best in town, and you can feast on the likes of ceviche, vegetable risotto and hare casserole with beer. The chef's signature chocolate pyramid with calafate berry mousse should be compulsory. Mains CH$6000–9000. Mon–Sat 12.30–3pm & 6.30–11.30pm.

La Mesita Grande O'Higgins at Montt ☏ 61 224 4312. This Puerto Natales transplant has taken this city by storm, the inadequate competition unable to withstand the onslaught of its beautiful thin-and-crispy pizzas and the lively, communal ambience, encouraged by the long wooden tables and benches. Pizzas from CH$8500. Daily 12.30–3pm & 7–11.30pm.

★**Toques de la Patagonia** España 1175 ☏ 09 8534 8690. An unassuming façade hides this little gem. The hard-working chef whips up the likes of smoked salmon and scallop skewers with pineapple chutney and hare stew with polenta, and just wait till you see what he can do with chocolate! The Mon–Sat lunchtime *menú* is an absolute steal at CH$4000; mains from CH$7000. Reserve ahead. Daily 12.30–3.30pm & 7–10pm.

BARS AND PUBS

Sky Bar O'Higgins 1235 ☏ 61 292 2900. Occupying a lofty spot inside the *Dreams del Estrecho* (see p.392) this luxury glass-and-chrome bar has a wide selection of spirits and cocktails, sushi on the menu and views of the Magellan Straits. Daily 7pm–3am.

La Taberna del Club de la Unión Plaza Muñoz Gamero 716 ☏ 61 224 1317. In the basement of the Palacio Sara Braun (see p.387), you can nurse a whisky or cocktail at this atmospheric former gathering spot for the city's most powerful men, decorated with black-and-white maritime photographs. Daily 7pm–2am.

SHOPPING

Unimarc Magallanes and Carrera Pinto. This branch of Unimarc is the largest and best-stocked in town, offering an extensive range of meat, cheese, fruit, vegetables, cereals, non-alcoholic bevarages and wines. Non-edible goods include toothpaste, toilet paper and deodorant. Daily 8am–9pm.

DIRECTORY

Car rental Europcar at the airport, O'Higgins 964 (☏ 61 220 2720, ⊚ www.europcar.cl); Hertz, O'Higgins 931 (☏ 61 261 3087, ⊚ hertz.cl). Reserve in advance in peak season.

Hospital Hospital Regional, Angamos 180, between Señoret and Zenteno (☏ 61 224 4040).

Money and exchange Most of the banks, including

BBVA and Banco Santander, are clustered around the plaza, especially on its eastern side, and numerous *cambios* are found on Pedro Montt and Navarro; try Sur Cambio de Moneda, Navarro 1070.

Pharmacy There are several well-stocked pharmacies along Bories.

Post office Bories 911 (Mon–Sat 10am–1pm & 3–7pm).

Reserva Forestal Magallanes

8km west of Punta Arenas • Daylight hours • Free • To get here, you can walk, cycle, or take a taxi (around CH$10,000)

The pretty **RESERVA FORESTAL MAGALLANES** comprises 196 square kilometres of protected Magellanic forest. Several short trails lead from the main entrance, including the two-hour loop of **Sendero Mirador**, which offers panoramic views of the Strait and Tierra del Fuego beyond, and the **Sendero de Chile Tramo Bocatoma-Las Minas** (3km; 1hr), both of which meander through native *coigüe*, *lenga* and *ñirre* trees.

HIKING TO CABO FROWARD

Ninety kilometres south of Punta Arenas lies **CABO FROWARD**, the southernmost mainland point on the continent, marked with an enormous cross, erected in honour of the 1987 visit by Pope John Paul II. The cape can be reached via a starkly picturesque two-day wild hike on pristine beaches, through forest, scrambling among rocks and following weather-beaten cliffs by any reasonably fit individual. The **50km trail** is much better signposted than it used to be, but the trail is still not always obvious and this is a challenging hike that requires you to ford or even swim across several narrow but deep rivers along the way (having your gear in a waterproof canoe bag is best), depending on the tides. You can either join a guided expedition with Erratic Rock (see Puerto Natales tour operators, p.399) or with a hiking partner (it is not advisable to go it alone), taking all necessary supplies with you, as well as a good map: *SIG Patagon* maps of the Cabo Froward trail are the most up-to-date. To get to the trailhead, arrange a lift or check the schedule for the thrice-weekly municipal bus from Punta Arenas that goes almost to the start of the trail along the road to the extreme right of the obelisk near Fuerte Bulnes (see below). There are very basic camping facilities en route, as well as a rustic *refugio* (bring own bedding).

Hostería San Isidro ☎ 09 9349 3862, ⓦ hosteriafarosanisidro.cl. The southernmost guesthouse on the South American continent, located at the hilltop San Isidro lighthouse, halfway along the trail, with six bright, centrally heated doubles. Great location for kayaking, trekking or wallowing in the on-site hot tubs. Reserve in advance. **CH$70,000**

Puerto Hambre

Fifty-eight kilometres south from Arenas along the beautiful, shore-hugging road, you'll see a large **white obelisk** – a monument to the "navel of Chile": the country's geographical centre, which takes into account Chilean Antarctic territory right down to the South Pole. The road to the left of the obelisk leads 2km south to **Puerto Hambre** ("Port Famine"). One of the first two Spanish colonies on the Magellan Strait, Puerto Hambre is the site of the ambitious 1584 colony founded by Pedro Sarmiento de Gamboa – "Ciudad del Rey Don Felipe" – which ended in the starvation of most of its 337 colonists. Two remaining men were rescued by English privateer Thomas Cavendish, one of whom then died on board the ship. All that's left on a little promontory is a plaque, together with a palpable sense of desolation.

Fuerte Bulnes

62km south of Punta Arenas along the Y-621 and 4km from Puerto Hambre • Nov to mid-April daily 8.30am–8pm • CH$12,000 • Many tour companies run half-day tours from Punta Arenas to Fuerte Bulnes and Puerto Hambre

The road to the right of the obelisk near Puerto Hambre leads to **Fuerte Bulnes**, a 1940s reconstruction of the first Chilean settlement in the area. Fuerte Bulnes was founded in September 1843 (and named after President Manuel Bulnes) by a boatload of sailors from Chiloé who arrived in the *Goleta Ancud*, captained by one John Williams. They came to pre-empt colonization from Europe, and only just made it: a few hours after they arrived, a French warship, the *Phaeton*, turned up and planted the tricolour on the shore. After Williams protested, the French moved off and annexed Tahiti in the Pacific instead. The location was less than ideal for a settlement owing to a lack of drinking water and pasture land, which prompted Williams to move the colony to the site of present-day Punta Arenas.

The fort

A restored stockade surrounds a number of old cannons, sturdy log cabins, a gaol building, a lookout tower, the governor's house and a small wooden chapel. The history of the fort and the story of its reconstruction is immortalised in the new display in the former barracks and there are several short **walking trails** with viewpoints overlooking the sea. We're not sure this justifies the twelvefold increase in entrance price, though.

9

Monumento Natural Isla Magdalena

35km northeast of Punta Arenas • Get here either with Solo Expediciones (see p.392) or Turismo Comapa (see p.392)

One of the largest penguin colonies in southern Chile, **MONUMENTO NATURAL ISLA MAGDALENA** is home to more than 120,000 Magellanic penguins. The small island, just one square kilometre in size and topped by a pretty red lighthouse, is two hours away from Punta Arenas by boat. The penguins dig their burrows under the tufts of grass covering the 15m-high cliffs.

In October each year, the birds migrate back here and find their mate – they're monogamous and remain faithful to one partner all their lives. The female lays two eggs in the nest and when the chicks hatch, in November, both parents nurture the young, one adult remaining with the chick, the other going fishing. In late January, the chicks shed their baby feathers and get ready for their first trips into the ocean. By the end of March the penguins have returned to sea again.

Viewing the penguins

You can get very close to the birds as they half hide in the waving grass, and lounge by the sea. If they start to cock their heads from side to side, it's a sign that you're disturbing them. Both Solo Expediciones and Turismo Comapa give you just over an hour on the island, with an additional stop at the Isla Marta sea lion colony with the former. During the boat ride you may spot Commerson's dolphins and other marine mammals.

Seno Otway penguin colony

47km north of Punta Arenas along Ruta 9 and Y-510 • Mid-Oct to April 8am–6.30pm • CH$6000 • Ⓦ turisotway.cl • No public transport; many tour agencies run half-day tours daily (CH$16,000)

An hour's drive north of Punta Arenas across open pampa lies the small **Seno Otway penguin colony**. Hosting around five thousand or so Magellanic penguins at its peak, the nesting ground is best seen in the morning before 10am or evening after 5pm, before or after they go fishing. The breeding site is fenced off and you're not allowed on the beach, but beachfront hides strung along an 1800m walkway that runs between the penguin burrows let you watch the birds frolic in the frigid waves just a few metres away.

Parque Nacional Pali Aike

146km north of Punta Arenas • Oct–April daily 9am–6pm • CH$2500 • No public transport; several companies run full-day tours from Punta Arenas (CH$30,000/person)

Eleven kilometres beyond the turning for the Punta Arenas ferry (see p.391) is the small town of Punta Delgada, from which a good gravel road heads 28km north to Chilean Patagonia's seldom-visited **PARQUE NACIONAL PALI AIKE**. The park's entrance looms up out of the barren rolling plains, green roof first; the sight explains its Tehuelche name, meaning "desolate place of bad spirits". There's a strange magic to the otherworldly volcanic formations that dot the heath and the small lagoons ringed by white tidemarks; this seemingly barren place is home to a surprising amount of smaller wildlife – from well-camouflaged lizards and owls, which may be mistaken for rocks, to the guanacos feeding on the hardy *coirón*.

Cueva Pali Aike and around

From the *guardería*, the main gravel road runs north to the remote, picturesque **Laguna Ana**, where you can occasionally spot flamingos, and the start of the park's longest hike: a 9km (2hr 45min) **walk** across flat, windy, exposed terrain to **Cueva Pali Aike**, a 17m-deep cave in a tall ridge of congealed lava. It was excavated by the famous archaeologist Junius Bird in 1937, and was found to contain evidence of prehistoric inhabitation, including bones of a *milodón* and the *Onohippidium*, an extinct American horse, dating from nine thousand years ago.

An 8km gravel road branches off from the main one, heading east to the cave via the starting point for the park's other two hikes: a 1700m (30min) wander through the largely flat old lava beds to the volcano rim of the **Crater Morada del Diablo** ("Dwelling of the devil"), followed by a 2000m (45min) ascent through the fields of jagged volcanic rock to the **Pozos del Diablo** ("The devil's wells") – dozens and dozens of somewhat sinister craters; sturdy footwear is a must.

Puerto Natales and around

Chilean Patagonia's second-largest settlement, **PUERTO NATALES**, 250km north of Punta Arenas, is the gateway to the **Parque Nacional Torres del Paine**. In spite of its popularity, Natales retains a pioneer feel, its history reflected in its simple wood-and-tin buildings, and it makes a useful base for visiting the nearby **Cueva del Milodón**, the glaciers of the **Parque Nacional Bernardo O'Higgins**, and, across the border in Argentina, the **Parque Nacional Los Glaciares**. Natales is also a good transport hub, home to the terminal of the **Navimag** ferry from Puerto Montt in the Lake District, and linked to Punta Arenas, Torres del Paine and Argentina by regular bus services.

Puerto Natales sits on the wind-whipped Seno Ultima Esperanza ("Last Hope Sound"), fringed by tall peaks, with the powerful wind stirring up waves on the turquoise channel where the remnants of a wooden pier bedecked with cormorants stretch into the distance. The channel's name comes from the 1557 explorer, Juan Ladrilleros, who came upon it when he was at the end of his tether while searching for the western entrance to the Magellan Strait. He found the strait, but almost all his crew died in the attempt.

Plaza de Armas

Natales centres on the Plaza de Armas, which has an old locomotive engine formerly used in the nearby Puerto Bories abattoir as its centrepiece – an evening magnet for lovers and drunken teenagers.

Museo Histórico Municipal

Bulnes 285 • Mon–Fri 9am–7pm, Sat 10am–1pm & 3–7pm • CH$1000

A couple of blocks west of the plaza is the small **Museo Histórico Municipal**, with attractively laid-out bilingual exhibits on the region's European settlement, natural history, the Milodón's cave and the indigenous Aonikenk and Kawéshkar tribes who dwelled in this inhospitable land, illustrated with black-and-white photos. Besides displays on Aonikenk funeral customs and Kawéshkar harpoons, a highlight is the room dedicated to the region's first settler, a rather fierce-looking German called Herman Eberhard; look out for his ingenious collapsible boat that turns into a suitcase.

ARRIVAL AND DEPARTURE | **PUERTO NATALES**

BY PLANE

There's a tiny airport just north of Puerto Natales that was on private loan at the time of writing; flights to Santiago with Sky Airline (Manuel Bulnes 682; ☎61 241 0646, ⓦskyairline.cl) may resume during peak season.

BY BUS

There's a new main bus terminal, Rodoviario Puerto Natales, at Av. España 1455. It's a 10–15min walk from the centre; taxis cost CH$1000 within town. Note that the various bus companies have kept their offices in town, and while you can buy tickets in these offices, buses depart from the main terminal. Services to El Calafate and Torres del Paine only operate Oct–April.

Companies Buses Cootra, Baquedano 244 (☎61 241 2785) runs to El Calafate; Buses Fernández, Ramírez 399 (☎61 241 1111, ⓦbusesfernandez.com) and Buses Magallanes (☎61 241 0101) serve Punta Arenas; Buses Pacheco, Ramírez 224

9

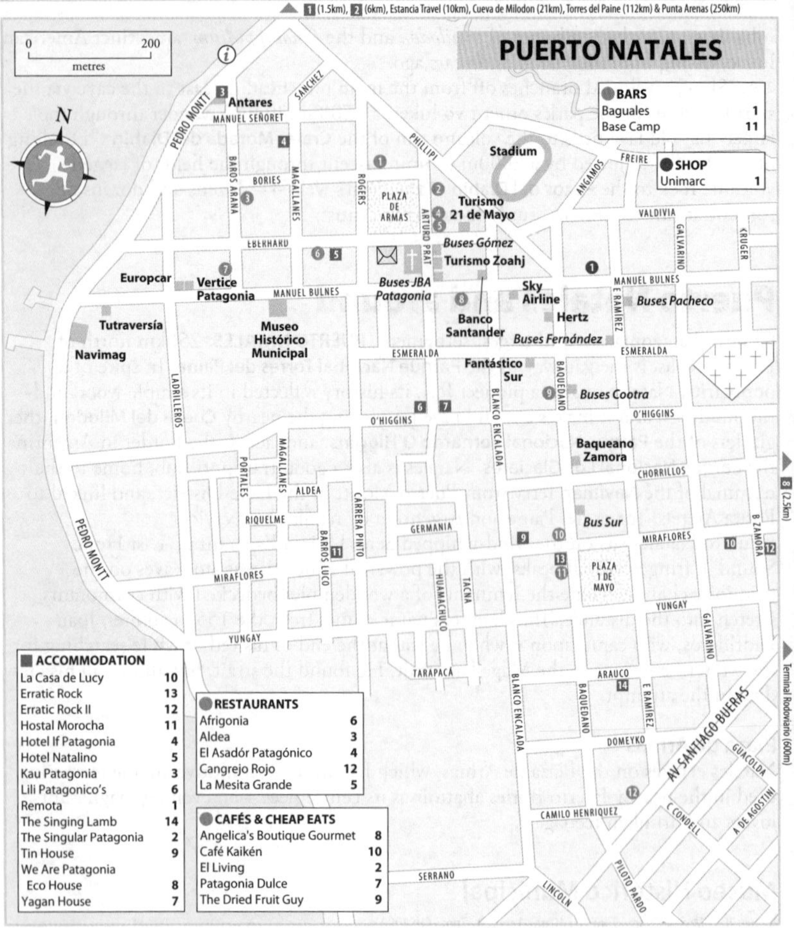
1 (1.5km), 2 (6km), Estancia Travel (10km), Cueva de Milodon (21km), Torres del Paine (112km) & Punta Arenas (250km)
PUERTO NATALES
0 200
metres
N
BARS
Baguales 1
Base Camp 11
SHOP
Unimarc 1
ACCOMMODATION
La Casa de Lucy 10
Erratic Rock 13
Erratic Rock II 12
Hostal Morocha 11
Hotel If Patagonia 4
Hotel Natalino 5
Kau Patagonia 3
Lili Patagonico's 6
Remota 1
The Singing Lamb 14
The Singular Patagonia 2
Tin House 9
We Are Patagonia Eco House 8
Yagan House 7
RESTAURANTS
Afrigonia 6
Aldea 3
El Asadór Patagónico 4
Cangrejo Rojo 12
La Mesita Grande 5
CAFÉS & CHEAP EATS
Angelica's Boutique Gourmet 8
Café Kaikén 10
El Living 2
Patagonia Dulce 7
The Dried Fruit Guy 9
Antares
Stadium
Turismo 21 de Mayo
Buses Gómez
Turismo Zoahj
Buses JBA Patagonia
Europcar
Vertice Patagonia
Sky Airline
Hertz
Buses Pacheco
Banco Santander
Buses Fernández
Tutraversía
Navimag
Museo Histórico Municipal
Fantástico Sur
Buses Cootra
Baqueano Zamora
Bus Sur
PLAZA DE ARMAS
PLAZA 1 DE MAYO
PEDRO MONTT
SANCHEZ
MANUEL SEÑORET
PHILLIPI
FREIRE
ANGAMOS
BORIES
BAROS ARANA
MAGALLANES
ROGERS
ARTURO PRAT
EBERHARD
MANUEL BULNES
VALDIVIA
GALVARINO
KRUGER
E RAMIREZ
ESMERALDA
LADRILLEROS
BLANCO ENCALADA
BAQUEDANO
O'HIGGINS
PORTALES
ALDEA
CHORRILLOS
RIQUELME
CARRERA PINTO
GERMANIA
BARROS LUCO
MIRAFLORES
HUAMACHUCO
TACNA
YUNGAY
B ZAMORA
TARAPACÁ
ARAUCO
DOMEYKO
AV SANTIAGO BUERAS
GUACOLDA
CAMILO HENRIQUEZ
C CONDELL
A DE AGOSTINI
SERRANO
LINCOLN
PILOTO PARDO
8 (2.5km)
Terminal Rodoviario (600m)

(☎ 61 241 4800, ⓦ busespacheco.com) runs to Punta Arenas, El Calafate, Ushuaia and Río Gallegos; Bus Sur, Baquedano 668 (☎ 61 241 0784, ⓦ bussur.com) runs to Punta Arenas, Río Gallegos and Ushuaia; Turismo Zaahj, Arturo Prat 236 (☎ 61 241 1355, ⓦ www.turismozaahj.co.cl), Buses JB, Prat 258 (☎ 61 241 0242, ⓦ busesjb.cl) and Buses Gómez, Prat 234 (☎ 61 241 1971, ⓦ busesgomez.com) run to Torres del Paine, while Turismo Zaahj also serves El Calafate. Pullman Baquedano 668 (☎ 61 241 3203, ⓦ www.pullman.cl) is the only company to run weekly trips to Castro via Puerto Montt and Osorno.

Destinations Castro via Puerto Montt and Osorno (1 weekly; 38hr); El Calafate, Argentina (2–3 daily; 5hr); Parque Nacional Torres del Paine (numerous daily; 2hr 30min; departures at 7.30am & 2.30pm); Punta Arenas (hourly; 3hr); Río Gallegos, Argentina (3 weekly; 5hr); Ushuaia, Argentina (1–2 daily; 12hr).

BY FERRY

The Navimag ferry terminal is on Pedro Montt 308, five blocks west and one block south of the Plaza de Armas (☎ 61 241 1421).

Destinations Puerto Montt (summer 1 weekly, less often in winter; around 70hr).

INFORMATION AND TOURS

TOURIST INFORMATION

Tourist office Pedro Montt s/n (Mon–Fri 8.30am–8pm, Sat & Sun 9am–1pm & 3–6pm; ☎ 61 241 2125). The small office by the water has basic maps of town and brochures on attractions. There's another information kiosk at the bus terminal. Visitors heading to Torres del Paine National Park (see p.402) shouldn't miss the daily 3pm informative talk at Base Camp, next door to Erratic Rock (see below), where experienced local trekkers will give you the lowdown on what to expect and how best to tackle the park.

TOUR OPERATORS

Antares/Bigfoot Montt 161 ☎61 241 4611, ⓦantarespatagonia.com. Operating out of *Refugio/ Campamento Grey* in Torres del Paine (where you have to overnight to take part; see p.406), this longstanding operator offers 5hr ice hikes on Glaciar Grey as well as kayaking amidst the house-sized chunks of ice.

Baqueano Zamora Baquedano 534 ☎61 261 3531, ⓦbaqueanozamora.cl. Horse-trekking in Torres del Paine (CH$25,000/45,000 for half-/full-day-trip) arranged by this longstanding operator; they also run a ranch and a hotel in, and near, Torres del Paine, respectively.

Erratic Rock Baquedano 719 ⓦerraticrock.com. Experienced operator with an excellent reputation runs multi-day trekking trips to Cabo Froward (see p.395) and in Torres del Paine, as well as rock climbing ascents of Torre Norte and dog sledding jaunts in Ushuaia.

Estancia Travel Puerto Bories 13B ☎61 241 2221, ⓦestanciatravel.com. Highly recommended horseriding trips, from half-day rides to the Cueva de Milodón to 12-day estancia expeditions by an English-Chilean outfit.

Fantástico Sur Esmeralda 661 ☎61 261 4184 ⓦfantasticosur.com. Makes bookings for the Torre Norte, Torre Central, Chileno and Los Cuernos *refugios* and campsites, as well as *Campamento Serón* and *Camping Francés*, the latter new as of December 2014.

Turismo 21 de Mayo Eberhard 560 ☎61 261 4420, ⓦturismo21demayo.cl. Organizes sailing excursions to see the Balmaceda and Serrano Glaciers in Parque Nacional Bernardo O'Higgins on their private cutter, *21 de Mayo*, and combo sailing day-trips that include a tour of Torres del Paine. Multi-day adventures include yachting, horseriding and a stay at the *Estancia Perrales*.

Tutravesia Bulnes 47 ☎61 241 5747, ⓦtutravesia .com. Established kayaking outfit offers multi-day-trips for beginner and advanced kayakers alike – from a gentle paddle along the Río Serrano to the spectacular 4-day Ice Route, which ends in a lake filled with icebergs.

Vertice Patagonia Bulnes 100 ☎61 241 2742, ⓦverticepatagonia.com. Makes bookings for Paine Grande, Lago Grey, Los Perros and Dickson *refugios*, as well as campsites in Torres del Paine.

ACCOMMODATION

HOTELS

Hotel If Patagonia Magallanes 73 ☎61 241 0312, ⓦhotelifpatagonia.com. The light-filled atrium of this excellent mid-range hotel puts you in mind of an M.C. Escher work, leading up as it does to a rooftop terrace with superb views of Last Hope Sound. The rooms are bright (though with little luggage space), characterised by warm touches of woven art, and the superior doubles have Jacuzzis. CH$110,000

Hotel Natalino Eberhard 371 ☎61 241 4345, ⓦhotel natalino.com. In keeping with the bunker-like entrance (complete with water feature steps), the rooms at this ultra-central, modern hotel are minimalist but with a strong emphasis on creature comforts. Guests choose from 'standard', 'loft' or 'suite' and have access to the gym, indoor pool and Jacuzzi. A good buffet breakfast seals the deal. US$255

★**Remota** Ruta 9 Norte, Km 1.5 ☎2 2387 1500, ⓦremotahotel.com. Drawing on the area's estancia heritage, this award-winning piece of architecture combines the comfort of the king-sized beds and rain showers with deliberate sparseness of decor – a single gaucho's woollen poncho gracing a wall. The two grass-roofed corridors are an aesthetic representation of a sheep yard and huge windows let in the wilderness beyond. There's wi-fi in the lobby, but the rooms and the glass-walled 'beach' appeal to those seeking silent contemplation. Breakfast included. Full board options available. US$350

★**The Singular Patagonia** Puerto Bories ☎61 272 2030, ⓦthesingular.com. This former-meatpacking-factory-cum-5-star-hotel is unique in concept and design. Lovingly restored by the descendants of two pioneer families, it has kept its original machinery in vast, stripped-down brick halls. Living museum aside, a funicular whisks you to the rooms (note how the corridor is half-spaceship, half-estancia in feel) with immense floor-to-ceiling windows gazing out over Last Hope Sound. Besides the tranquil spa and indoor/outdoor pool, the restaurant is one of the best in Patagonia and all-inclusive rates include 25 excursions to choose from. Breakfast included. Full board also available. US$370

B&B AND GUESTHOUSES

La Casa de Lucy Miraflores 969 ☎61 241 3792, ⓦcasalucypuertonatales.com. The simple exterior of this wooden house hides several spacious, beautifully decorated rooms with king-size beds that take tall foreigners into account, tasteful woollen wall hangings and plasma-screen TVs. Hostess Lucy speaks little English but dishes up ample breakfasts. CH$55,000

Erratic Rock II Zamora 732 ☎61 241 4317, ⓦerraticrock2.com. An upmarket offshoot of the original hostel, this warm, family-run guesthouse is a popular option with couples wanting a quiet stay with all the creature comforts. The ten centrally-heated en-suite

9

doubles have cable TV and compact bathrooms, and breakfast is ample. Oct–March. CH$40,000

Hostal Morocha Barros Luco 688 ☎09 9708 1250, ⓦhostalmorocha.com. With just five individually decorated rooms (expect James Dean quotes!), a most satisfying breakfast spread, and welcoming, knowledgeable owners (Pablo is a Sherpa in Torres del Paine), this is an excellent choice for those who want some privacy without breaking the budget. If you want a private bathroom, you'll need to ask for one of the doubles, as both the twin and the single rooms are not en-suite. CH$35,000

★**Kau Patagonia** Montt 161 ☎61 241 4611, ⓦwww .kaulodge.com. The sparse decor and design of these luxurious rooms seems to reflect Patagonia as a theme: plenty of space, light and views of the Sound from all windows; creams, blues and a single wooden wall reminiscent of forests. Four of the nine rooms have generous bunk beds. If the Patagonian weather is getting you down and you fancy a pick-me-up, the *Coffee Maker* cafe downstairs is the place to hide from the wind and rain with a potent espresso and home-made cakes. Standard doubles CH$68,000, bunk doubles CH$56,000

We Are Patagonia Eco House Huerto 82B ☎09 7389 4802, ⓦwearepatagonia.com. Run by a young, friendly local couple, this gorgeous guesthouse sits right on the outskirts of Natales. There's immediate appeal to the common space with wicker hammock seat and the warm, light-filled rooms decked out in tranquil creams, with eye-catching woollen touches. To get here, take Av España from the bus terminal all the way out of town and onto the unpaved rural road. If you want to actually stay in Natales proper, note that there's a central branch at Galvarino 745; the rooms are just as appealing but most have shared facilities only. CH$37,000

HOSTELS

★**Erratic Rock** Baquedano 719, ⓦerraticrock.com. The self-styled "burnt-out hippie from Oregon" got it exactly right: the atmosphere is laidback, hostel cats Bonnie and Clyde wander in and out, dorms and rooms are snug and there's a real sense of camaraderie between the trekkers who bunk here. Bill's early morning breakfast

– one of the best in town – provides the hikers heading to Torres del Paine with nourishment while the daily 3pm talk gives them the low-down on trekking in the park; onward transport and tours can now also be booked here. The hostel operates a walk-in only policy. Dorms CH$10,000, doubles CH$25,000

Lili Patagónico's Arturo Prat 479 ☎61 241 4063, ⓦlilipatagonicos.com. This brightly painted backpacker magnet has a cavernous dining and lounge area and nice extras such as an indoor climbing wall, equipment for rent and good breakfast. Owners organise half- and full-day tours of the surrounding area. More expensive doubles come with their own bathroom. Dorms CH$8000, doubles CH$22,000

★**The Singing Lamb** Arauco 779 ☎61 241 0958, ⓦthesinginglamb.com. Popular with international travellers of all ages, this newly-redesigned hostel is a cut above the rest: nine-/six-/four-bed dorms with comfortable beds rather than bunks, homely common area, well-designed showers and a new block of private doubles with windows that open into the corridor. At breakfast, guests can fill up on fresh porridge, home-made bread and jam, and scrambled eggs, a fortifying feast for the rigours of trekking in Torres del Paine. Dorms CH$15,000, doubles CH$52,000

Tin House Miraflores 616 ☎61 261 4201, ⓦtinhousepatagonia.com. This snug eight-bed hostel is run by friendly young hosts: David, a trekking guide in Torres del Paine, and his wife Laura. The two cosy doubles share a bathroom, and while the four-bed dorm is on the small side, there's plenty of space to hang out and socialise in the lounge. If you don't fancy eating out, or are up early the next day for a trek, you're in luck: the kitchen is a boon for self-caterers. Dorms CH$11,000, doubles CH$25,000

Yagan House O'Higgins 584 ☎61 241 4137, ⓦyaganhouse.cl. Excellent beds with down duvets, warm red-and-cream decor, eco-friendly practices and a guest lounge with a roaring fire distinguish this popular hostel. The owners throw a great Patagonian barbecue and other great extras are gear rental and an on-site restaurant and bar and laundry service to take care of your dirty post-Torres togs. Dorms CH$12,000, doubles CH$30,000

EATING AND DRINKING

CAFÉS AND CHEAP EATS

Angelica's Boutique Gourmet Bulnes 501. Next door to the eponymous restaurant, this bakery-cum-coffee shop serves real coffee, gooey brownies, home-made cheesecake (try the chocolate orange) and inexpensive daily specials, such as calzones, Greek salad and pizza with goat's cheese (from CH$5800). Daily 9am–4pm & 5–10pm.

Café Kaikén Baquedano 699 ☎09 8295 2036. This small café is showered with praise by travellers for its

wonderful home-made food – from lamb with gnocchi and heaped portions of ceviche to chunky sandwiches. There are only half a dozen tables, so reservations are a good idea in the evenings. Mains from CH$5000. Daily 9am–11pm.

★**El Living** Arturo Prat 156 ☎61 241 1140. An excellent vegetarian restaurant and lounge cafe, with chillout music in the background and comfortable sofas to sink into. Treats include pumpkin and walnut ravioli, Caribbean pepperpot and bean tacos with guacamole, and their cakes and home-made honeycomb ice cream are equally good. Mains from CH$5500. Jan–March & Dec Mon–Sat 11am–10pm.

Patagonia Dulce Barros Arana 233 ☎ 61 241 5285. For home-made chocolate, cookies, excellent *kuchen* and home-made ice cream, head to this gingerbread-house-like café. They say that if you eat *calafate* berries, you'll return to Patagonia; you can find out if the same is true of *calafate*-flavoured ice cream. Mon–Sat 10am–6pm, Sun 11am–3pm.

The Dried Fruit Guy Baquedano 443. This shop is *the* place to stock up on trail mix and all manner of dried fruit before heading to Torres del Paine. Mon–Sat 10am–8pm.

RESTAURANTS

★**Afrigonia** Eberhard 343 ☎ 61 241 3609. Natales's most imaginative restaurant serves delectable African–Patagonian fusion dishes. Standout dishes include ceviche with mango, melt-off-the-bone Patagonian lamb and spicy seafood curry with *wali* (rice with almonds and raisins). Be prepared for a leisurely dinner. Mains from CH$8000. Daily 12.30–3pm & 7.30–11.30pm.

★**Aldea** Barros Arana 132 ☎ 61 241 4027. The menu at this intimate, vegetarian-friendly spot changes daily according to the whim of chef Pato and consists of just a few beautifully executed dishes. Choose from the likes of hare loin with *plátano* puree and vegetable tajine, and finish off with a sublime *arroz con leche*. Mains CH$7000–8000. Daily 12.30–3pm & 7–11pm.

El Asador Patagónico Arturo Prat 158 ☎ 61 241 3553. The signature *asado Patagónico* – lamb roasting on a spit in the barbecue pit by the window – acts as a magnet for the carnivorously inclined. The expertly grilled steaks at this established *parrilla* are just as good, and portions are ample. Daily 12.30–3pm & 7.30–11pm.

Cangrejo Rojo Santiago Bueras 782 ☎ 61 241 2436. Strategically hung with fishing nets, buoys, snorkelling masks and other nautical paraphernalia, this cute little restaurant specialises in Neptune's subjects. Among the likes of super-fresh ceviche and grilled conger eel you'll nevertheless find more unusual items, such as sheep's testicles. Mains from CH$7000. Tues–Sun 10am–3pm & 5.30–10.30pm.

La Mesita Grande Eberhard 508 ☎ 61 241 1571. Hordes of hungry hikers stage a daily invasion of the best pizzeria in Patagonia, drawn by the generous portions of superb thin-crust pizzas (from CH$6500), home-made pasta and interesting desserts (including sweet pizza with *dulce de leche*). The two long wooden tables make for a communal dining experience and encourage mingling. Daily 12.30–3.30pm & 7–11.30pm.

BARS

Baguales Bories 430 ☎ 61 241 1920. If the one thing that would make your Patagonian hiking experience complete is returning to a cosy microbrewery serving ample platters of fiery Buffalo wings, quesadillas, tacos and other assorted Tex-Mex food, accompanied by a home-made light or dark brew, then you're in luck: look no further than this new Californian–Chilean pub on the Plaza de Armas. Beers CH$2500; mains from CH$6000. Mon–Sat noon–late.

Base Camp Baquedano 719. Next door to the most popular hostel in town, this former-brothel-cum-lively-pub (which doubles as an equipment rental centre) is often full to the brim with pre- and post-Torres hikers, contentedly drinking local brews and eating thin-and-crispy pizzas. Sat is taco night! Expect occasional performances by local bands, themed nights and spontaneous barbecues. Daily 5pm–1am.

DIRECTORY

Camping equipment rental Try Base Camp, next to Erratic Rock, Baquedano 732, or La Maddera, Bulnes at Prat, which also sells all manner of equipment, including fuel canisters.

Car rental Europcar, Manuel Bulnes 100 (☎ 61 241 4475, ⓦ www.europcar.cl) and Hertz, Blanco Encalada 353 (☎ 61 241 4519, ⓦ hertz.cl).

Hospital Hospital Puerto Natales, Ignacio Carrera Pinto 537 (☎ 61 241 1582).

Laundry ServiLaundry, Arturo Prat 357 (☎ 61 241 2869); promises to do your laundry within 2hr.

Money and exchange There's an ATM in Banco Santander, Manuel Bulnes 598, or Banco de Chile, Manuel Bulnes 544. There are several *cambios* along Blanco Encalada and Bulnes; try Mily at Blanco Encalada 266.

Pharmacy Farmacia Puerto Natales, Esmeralda 701.

Post office Eberhard 429 (Mon–Sat 10am–1pm & 3–7pm).

Cueva del Milodón

21km from Puerto Natales • Daily 8am–8pm • CH$4000

From Natales, a bumpy 150km gravel road runs through flat Patagonian scrubland to Torres del Paine national park, with the **Cueva del Milodón** a standard stop. The vast cave is impressive enough – 30m high, 80m wide and 200m deep. In 1895, the German settler Herman Eberhard, who owned the land bordering the cave, discovered

> ## THE STRANGE CASE OF THE GIANT SLOTH SKIN
>
> In 1900 an **expedition** sponsored by London's *Daily Express* arrived to investigate the rumours of a **giant sloth** in a cave near Puerto Natales, but no live creatures were found. The skin, it turned out, was so well preserved because it had been deep-frozen by the frigid Patagonian climate. Shortly after the 1900 expedition an unscrupulous gold prospector together with **Charley Milward** (see p.390) dynamited the cave's floor, uncovering and then selling the remaining skin and bones. Two pieces made their way to Britain: one to the Natural History Museum in London, and the other to Charley Milward's family, the very same which was to fire the imagination of a young **Bruce Chatwin**.

a large piece of skin from an unidentifiable animal, which was eventually traced to a giant sloth called a milodón. This creature was thought to be long extinct, but the excavated skin looked so fresh that rumours began to circulate that it might still be alive. An expedition was mounted (see box above), though no live sloth was ever found. Along the short boardwalk leading to the cave there are displays on Patagonia's (mostly) extinct prehistoric animals, such as the sabre-tooth tiger, the panther and the ancestor of a horse. Inside the cave, a small display features part of a young milodón femur and some skin and hair, as well as a life-size plastic replica of the creature.

The Balmaceda and Serrano glaciers

136km northwest of Puerto Natales

To the northwest of the Cueva del Milodón, the Seno Ultima Esperanza continues on for about 100km until it meets the Río Serrano, which, after 36km, arrives at the **Balmaceda** and **Serrano glaciers**. A boat trip here (see p.399) is one of the most beautiful in the entire area. It takes seven hours and you pass a colony of cormorants and a slippery mass of sea lions. The glaciers themselves make an impressive sight, especially when a chunk of ice the size of a small house breaks off and crashes into the water. They form the southern tip of **Parque Nacional Bernardo O'Higgins** (see p.397), the largest and least visited national park in the whole of Chile. The east of the park is almost entirely made up of the Campo de Hielo Sur (the Southern Ice-Field); the west comprises fjords, islands and untouched forest.

Parque Nacional Torres del Paine

102km north of Puerto Natales via Ruta 9 • Summer CH$18,000, winter CH$5000 • ⓦ torresdelpaine.com

Nothing really prepares you for your first sight of **PARQUE NACIONAL TORRES DEL PAINE**. The **Paine Massif**, the unforgettable centrepiece of the park, appears beyond the turquoise lakes long before you get close to it. The finest views of the massif are from the south bank of Lago Nordenskjöld, whose waters act as a great reflecting mirror. If driving through the park, take the southern entrance to constantly have the best views in front of you.

The centrepiece is made up of the twin peaks of **Cerro Monte Almirante Nieto** (2668m and 2640m). On the northern side are the soaring, unnaturally elegant **Torres del Paine** ("Paine Towers"), the icon of the park, and further west the sculpted, dark-capped **Cuernos del Paine** ("Paine Horns"). To the west of the park is the broad ice river of **Glaciar Grey**, and on the plains at the mountains' feet, large herds of **guanacos** and the odd *ñandú* (rhea) still run wild; you're more likely to spot these than the park's more elusive fauna: pumas and the rare *huemul* deer.

In January and February the park is crammed with holidaymakers, so the best months to visit are October, November and December or March and April. Although in winter (June–Sept) temperatures can fall to -10°C (14°F) or even lower, freezing lakes and icing over trails, the small numbers of visitors, lack of wind and often clear visibility can also make this another good time to come – just wrap up warmly.

Hiking routes

This may not be the place to taste true wilderness, but there are still plenty of places to lose the crowds. The two most popular hikes are the "**W**", so-called because the route you follow looks like a "W", up three valleys, taking you to the "stars" of the park – Las Torres, Valle del Francés and Glaciar Grey, and the "**Circuit**", which leads you around the back of the park and encompasses the "W"; allow seven to ten days for the "Circuit" and at least four for the "W".

The Circuit

The best way to tackle the "Circuit" is anticlockwise, as it also means you'll have excellent views of Glaciar Grey in front of you rather than behind you when you come to tackle the most challenging part of the hike – the Paso John Gardner.

Hostería Las Torres to Las Torres

From *Hostería Las Torres*, go southwest along the foot of the massif. Just after a bridge, the track veers to the north up Valle Ascencio along a dirt trail strewn with scree; after a relatively steep two-hour climb it's possible to spend the first night at the *Refugio y Camping Chileno*. From *Chileno*, the trail continues up and down exposed inclines (beware of sudden gusts of wind), and then through *lenga* brush, crossing a stream, to the wooded *Campamento Torres*; allow ninety minutes. *Campamento Torres* is a free campsite by another stream at the foot of the track up to the **Torres** themselves. You can camp overnight here, leave your gear and then tackle the knee-popping 45-minute climb up uneven boulders in order to reach Las Torres just before daybreak. If the weather is clear you are treated to a stunning postcard view across Laguna Torres up to the three strange statuesque towers that give the park its name – **Torre Norte Monzino** (2600m), **Torre Central** (2800m) and **Torre Sur D'Agostini** (2850m), at their most gorgeous when bathed in the first rays of the sun.

Hostería Las Torres to Refugio Lago Dickson

From *Hostería Las Torres*, *Campamento Serón* is an easy four-hour walk northwards up and down gentle inclines and vast fields. From *Campamento Serón*, it's a five- or

---

FIRE IN THE PARK

On December 27, 2011, Torres del Paine suffered from its second major **fire** in less than a decade; it was started by human negligence in the southern section of **Torres del Paine** and quickly spread, exacerbated by the bone-dry conditions and strong winds. The Chilean government was criticized for its slow and inadequate response; by the time the blaze was finally brought under control, over 130 square kilometres of forest had been destroyed. The tourist accused of accidentally starting the fire was made to pay a US$10,000 fine, even though he denied responsibility

In a bid to protect the park from future damage, trekkers coming to Torres del Paine via the Laguna Amarga entrance are now subjected to a 3-minute **video on park safety** which mainly warns you that the penalty for accidentally starting a fire is US$16,000 and up to five years in prison; arson carries the same fine but up to twenty years in prison. Neither ranger patrols nor volunteer patrols in the park have materialised, though volunteers are welcome to help out with the reforestation programme.

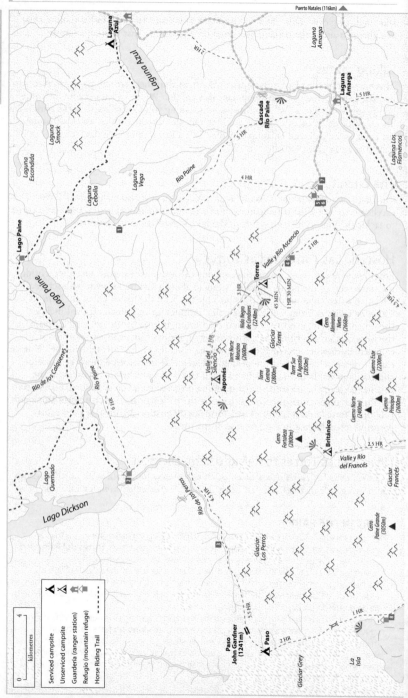

Puerto Natales (116km)

Laguna Azul

2 HR

Laguna Amarga

Laguna Amarga

1.5 HR

Cascada Río Paine

Laguna Escondida

Laguna Smock

Laguna Cebolla

Laguna Vega

Río Paine

5 HR

Laguna Los Flamencos

4 HR

5 6 7

1

Valle y Río Accencio

Lago Paine

Torres

2 HR

Lago Paine

4

4.5 HR

3 HR

Nido Negro de Condores (2248m)

Cerro Almirante Nieto (2668m)

45 MIN

1 HR 30 MIN

Valle del Silencio 3 HR

Torre Norte Monzino (2600m)

Glaciar Torres

Río Paine

Japonés

Torre Central (2800m)

Torre Sur Di Agostini (2850m)

Cuerno Este (2200m)

Río de los Calquenes

6 HR

Cuerno Norte (2400m)

Cuerno Principal (2600m)

Cerro Fortaleza (2800m)

Británico

2.5 HR

Valle y Río del Francés

Lago Quemado

Glaciar Francés

2

4.5 HR

Río de los Perros

Lago Dickson

Cerro Paine Grande (3050m)

3

Glaciar Los Perros

5.5 HR

1 HR

Paso John Gardner (1241m)

8

La Isla

Paso

2 HR

Glaciar Grey

0   4
kilometres

Serviced campsite
Unserviced campsite
Guardería (ranger station)
Refugio (mountain refuge)
Horse Riding Trail

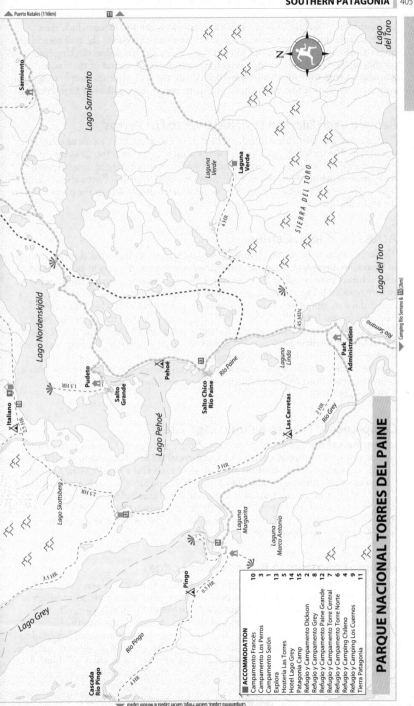

PARQUE NACIONAL TORRES DEL PAINE

Puerto Natales (116km)

Lago del Toro

Lago Sarmiento

Sarmiento

Laguna Verde

Laguna Verde

SIERRA DEL TORO

Lago del Toro

4 HR

Lago Nordenskjöld

45 MIN

Pudeto

Salto Grande

Pehoé

Salto Chico Rio Paine

Rio Paine

Laguna Linda

Park Administration

Rio Serrano

Camping Río Serrano & (2km)

Italiano

2.5 HR

1.5 HR

Las Carretas

Rio Grey

2.1 HR

Lago Pehoé

Lago Skottsberg

2.5 HR

3 HR

Laguna Margarita

Laguna Marco Antonio

3.5 HR

Pingo

0.5 HR

Lago Grey

Rio Pingo

4 HR

Cascada Rio Pingo

Campamento Zapata, Glacier Pingo, Glacier Zapata & Mirador Zapata

ACCOMMODATION

Campamento Francés	10
Campamento Los Perros	3
Campamento Serón	1
Explora	13
Hostería Las Torres	5
Patagonia Camp	14
Refugio y Campamento Dickson	15
Refugio y Campamento Grey	2
Refugio y Campamento Paine Grande	8
Refugio y Campamento Torre Central	12
Refugio y Campamento Torre Norte	6
Refugio y Camping Chileno	7
Refugio y Camping Los Cuernos	4
Tierra Patagonia	9
	11

9

six-hour hike to *Refugio Dickson*, with a flat trail along the Río Paine, which then climbs steeply uphill as you pass a small horseshoe-shaped lagoon. The trail meanders on west, with sweeping views of Lago Paine on your right-hand side, ducking into patches of vegetation and crossing several streams. A boggy section of the trail is partially covered with wooden boardwalks. Finally, the trail descends steeply to *Refugio Lago Dickson* in its scenic setting at the southern end of iceberg-flecked Lago Dickson.

Refugio Lago Dickson to Campamento Los Perros

Campamento Los Perros lies a four-hour hike from *Dickson* southwest along a largely uphill trail that snakes through dense forest for most of the way. You cross two bridges over large glacial streams and pass a pretty waterfall, before emerging at an exposed, rocky section, which treats you to a fabulous view of Glaciar Los Perros above a round lagoon, before continuing to a patch of forest which partially shields the campsite from icy blasts of wind.

Across Paso John Gardner

The weather has to be in your favour before you start on a three-hour climb to the top of **Paso John Gardner** (1241m). It is too dangerous to cross the pass in gale-force wind; several hikers have lost their lives this way. From *Los Perros* you cross a stream using a rickety wooden bridge, followed by an hour's muddy trudge. Above the tree line, it's a straightforward uphill slog along the rock-strewn slope before reaching the exposed pass. The reward for all this is the sudden, staggering view over the icy pinnacles of **Glaciar Grey**, more than 7km wide at its largest point, and the vast immaculate expanse of the **Campo del Hielo Sur** – over ten thousand square kilometres of ice cap and one of the largest ice-fields outside the polar regions.

On the other side of the pass crude steps descend steeply into *lenga* forest. It takes a couple of hours from the top of the pass to reach the small and unserviced *Campamento Paso*.

Campamento Paso to Refugio Lago Grey

It takes around three hours to descend to *Refugio y Camping Lago Grey*. In two places, you have to ascend or descend along metal ladders attached to vertical slopes. The campsite is beautifully sited on the beach at the foot of Glaciar Grey, while the *refugio* building is just uphill from it. It's possible to catch a boat to *Hotel Lago Grey* in summer; the boat sails alongside the glacier before making its way along the length of the lake (CH$55,000). If staying overnight at *Refugio y Camping Lago Grey*, it's also possible to go ice hiking on the glacier or kayaking around it with Antares/Bigfoot (see p.399).

Refugio Lago Grey to Paine Grande Lodge

From *Refugio y Camping Lago Grey*, the path runs alongside the lake, before the largely exposed trail almost doubles back on itself, climbing steeply, after which it runs mostly uphill through the **Quebrada de los Vientos** ("Windy Gorge"), with several viewpoints from which to admire the lake. It then ducks into the burnt remains of *ñire* glen – a relic of the 2011 forest fire – passing the small Laguna Los Patos on the right-hand side, and descends to the *Paine Grande Lodge* and campsite, situated on the bank of the stunning glacial Lago Pehoé, three and a half hours later. From here you can continue along the "Circuit"; this is also the ideal place to start the "W".

9

The "W"

Like the "Circuit", it's best to do the "W" anti-clockwise, leaving the steepest hike to Las Torres until last, by which time you will have consumed most of your supplies. The first leg of the "W" is the hike there and back from *Paine Grande Lodge* to Glaciar Grey, described above.

Paine Grande Lodge to Valle Francés

Take the signposted trail that runs along the southern side of the Paine Grande massif along Lago Skottsberg and a couple of smaller lagoons on the right-hand side, before crossing a suspension bridge across Río Francés to *Campamento Italiano*; it takes around two and a half hours to get here and you can leave your gear here before heading north up the Valle del Francés.

It's a rather steep two-hour hike with great views of the **Glaciar Francés** to *Campamento Británico*. It's another hour up to the viewpoint (sometimes closed due to excessive amounts of snow) from which you can admire **Paine Grande**, the massif's highest peak at 3050m, to your west, and the **Cuernos del Paine**, a set of incredibly carved towers capped with dark rock peaks, guarding the entrance to the valley to the southeast.

Valle del Francés to Refugio Los Cuernos

From *Campamento Italiano*, it's a mostly steep downhill ascent (allow two and a half hours) along the pale blue waters of the icy Lago Nordenskjold to the bustling *Refugio y Camping Los Cuernos*, which nestles in a clearing in the shadow of Los Cuernos.

BEYOND THE W: TORRES DEL PAINE ALTERNATIVES

There is more to Torres del Paine than just the "Circuit" and the "W"; numerous shorter hikes can be just as spectacular.

MIRADOR LAGO GREY AND MIRADOR FERRIER

From the Lago Grey ranger station near *Hotel Lago Grey*, a short trail leads through the forest to the lake's vast windswept beach, where you can watch house-sized chunks of bluish ice bobbing on the pale waters. To the left of the beach, by the jetty, a fairly steep unmarked trail skirts around the cliff before giving you an unobstructed view of Glaciar Gray. The most spectacular viewpoint of them all, **Mirador Ferrier**, lies a stiff two-hour hike up from behind the ranger station. From up there, you get a jaw-dropping vista over the park's many lakes, their colours ranging from aquamarine to greyish white. At the top, you make your way through forest before emerging among exposed rocks; bring warm clothes as the icy wind can be ferocious.

LAGUNA AZUL

There's a three-and-a-half-hour signposted walk from the *guardería* at Laguna Amarga to **Laguna Azul**, a secluded and little-visited lake in the northeast. From there, a mostly gentle four-hour trail leads past Laguna Cebolla to **Lago Paine**. It used to be possible to hike to Lago Dickson and cross the narrowest part of the lake to *Refugio Dickson*, but the boat is no longer functioning, though if you are on horseback, you can wade across Río Paine and continue along this trail to a viewpoint overlooking Glaciar Dickson.

MIRADOR ZAPATA

Another seldom-trod path takes you up to **Mirador Zapata**, a steep six-to-seven-hour climb from *Guardería Lago Grey* at the southern tip of Lago Grey, itself a four-and-a-half-hour walk from the park administration building, rewarding you with views of the ice cap and the magnificent Glaciar Pingo. *Campamento Pingo* is half an hour into the trek, and *Campamento Zapata* an hour and a half from the *mirador*, making it an ideal overnight stop.

Refugio Los Cuernos to Hostería Las Torres

From *Los Cuernos*, it takes around four and a half hours to reach the *Hostería Las Torres*; the trail runs along gentle inclines through low shrubbery and then along green hills. You will pass two shortcuts to Las Torres, and shortly before reaching the *Hostería Las Torres*, you will see the signposted trail leading up Valle Ascencio (see p.403). Depending on whether or not you have already paid a visit to the park's last highlight, you either head uphill, or complete your trek up ahead.

ARRIVAL AND DEPARTURE

By bus The only entrance to the park for those coming by bus from Puerto Natales (daily at 7.30am & 2.30pm; 3hr) is 117km from the town at Laguna Amarga, where you pay the park fee at the Conaf station. From here, minibuses meet bus arrivals from Natales for the transfer to *Hostería Las Torres* (see below; CH$2000). The buses from Natales continue along Lago Nordenskjöld for another 19km to the *guardería* at Pudeto, the departure point for the catamaran to *Paine Grande Lodge*; the morning buses arrive in time for the noon boat. The bus continues beyond here, past *Hostería Pehoé, Camping Pehoé* and *Explora* (see below), opposite Salto Chico, to reach the

PARQUE NACIONAL TORRES DEL PAINE

Park Administration 18km further on, where there's a visitor centre, a *refugio*, a grocery store and a *hostería*.

By car Driving up from Puerto Natales, you have a choice: to reach the southern entrance of the park, take the gravel Y-290 turn-off towards the Milodón Cave from the main, paved Ruta 9 towards Cerro Castillo; this route is picturesque but potholed. Ruta 9 from Natales continues to the park's north entrance; from there, a compacted gravel road leads to the Laguna Amarga entrance. A few kilometres before Laguna Amarga, you can turn off towards Lago Nordenskjöld.

GETTING AROUND

By catamaran From the *guardería* Pudeto, a Hielos Patagónicos catamaran (☎ 61 241 1380; mid-Nov to mid-March daily at 9.30am, noon & 6pm; first half of Nov and second half of March at noon & 6pm; Oct & April noon; 30min; CH$15,000 one-way, CH$24,000 return; tickets sold on board) runs across Lago Pehoé. Return trips from *Paine Grande Lodge* are 30min after the arrival times and are met

by buses heading back to Puerto Natales. From Laguna Amarga and the park administration there are daily buses to Puerto Natales, the last leaving at 4.30pm and 6pm, respectively.

By car The gravel road that runs through the park is reasonably well maintained. Take the bends slowly as loose gravel is a hazard.

INFORMATION

Tourist information The Park Administration Centre at the park's southern entrance (Dec–Feb daily 8.30am–8pm; ☎ 61 269 1931) has detailed displays on the park's fauna and flora. However, all the *guarderías* provide information about trail conditions and you'll be given a basic trail map when you pay your entrance fee and watch the park safety video.

Climbing To climb in the park, you'll need to get a permit from the Park Administration Centre; it costs CH$75,000 and covers any ascent.

Park rules Follow park guidelines regarding never lighting fires (human negligence in 2005 and in 2011 led to the destruction of a large chunk of the park) and carry *all* your rubbish back to Puerto Natales, including toilet paper.

ACCOMMODATION

Accommodation in the park is divided into unserviced (free) campsites, serviced campsites and *refugios* run either by Vertice Patagonia (see p.399) or Fantástico Sur (see p.399), as well as top end *hosterías* and hotels, and privately-owned campsites. *Refugios* provide hot meals for around CH$7000 for lunch and CH$11,000 for dinner.

HOSTERÍAS AND HOTELS

Explora ☎ 2 2395 2800, ⍟ explora.com. The most extravagant and exclusive five-star hotel in the park, this sleek white building overlooks Lago Pehoé, with incredible views from every room. A boardwalk leads down past nearby Salto Chico to the lakeside swimming pool and open-air hot tubs. The restaurant serves excellent fusion cuisine and you can choose from 25 different tours with knowledgeable bilingual guides, from day treks to horseriding. Obligatory four to eight-night all-inclusive packages. Four nights US$6000

Hostería Las Torres ☎ 61 261 7450, ⍟ lastorres.com. Convenient location at the foot of Cerro Paine, beautiful, comfortable (though compact) rooms and a good restaurant (open to non-guests as well) make this a good choice, if rather overpriced. Numerous excursions available in the all-inclusive package, such as horseriding trips of varying length and guided treks. There's also a spa in which to pamper yourself. US$284

Hotel Lago Grey ☎ 61 271 2190, ⍟ turismolagogrey .com. Sitting amid some beech trees, this *hostería* has a

9

number of good hiking trails nearby, including one overlooking the lake and the glacier. However, the location is rather isolated from the rest of the park unless you have your own wheels, and meals (except breakfast) are not included in the price. There are daily boat trips (CH$55,000; 3hr return) twice daily (8am & 3.30pm) to Glaciar Grey. US$350

★ **Patagonia Camp** ☎ 2 2334 9255, ⓦ patagonia camp.com. A short drive from the Administración entrance to the park, this supremely eco-conscious hotel overlooking Lago Toro consists of eighteen luxury yurts peeking through the trees, with boardwalks built around them. Each yurt is centrally heated, with a skylight for stargazing, bathtub and supremely comfortable beds. Dishes at the light-filled restaurant are beautifully executed, traditional Patagonian barbecues are held in the *quincho* and guests may choose from all-inclusive rates (complete with excursions) or B&B. Minimum two-night stay. US$860

Tierra Patagonia ☎ 2 2207 8861, ⓦ tierrapatagonia .com. Located by Lago Sarmiento, the spacious rooms and suites at this luxurious lodge are the ultimate in comfort, with wood-panelled walls, king-sized beds, quality linens and full-sized bathtubs. The floor-to-ceiling windows in the suites take in the surrounding steppe and the welcoming lounge centres around an enormous fireplace. Guided hikes and horse rides are on offer. Three-night minimum with obligatory full-board. US$4300

CAMPSITES AND REFUGIOS

Most campsites tend to be open Oct–April, though the ones on the Circuit open later in the season. Unserviced campsites including *Japonés* (climbers only), *Italiano*, *Británico* and *Paso* on the Torres del Paine Circuit are free and are basically just a flat patch of land and a *fogón* (some have pit toilets). All the serviced campsites are listed below. If camping, take your own food (the small shops attached to *refugios* and campsites have a limited selection and are overpriced); drinking water, however, can be collected from streams. Bring a sturdy waterproof tent – enough to withstand the Patagonian wind – and all necessary camping equipment. It is possible to rent tents and sleeping bags from most *refugios* but the costs will add up. Wild camping isn't permitted.

Campamento Francés (Fantástico Sur). Brand-new campsite overlooking Lago Nordenskjöld, a short, steep hike down from the trail between *Campamento Italiano* and *Refugio Los Cuernos*, with two multi-person geodomes

(bring own bedding or rent it here). Camping/person CH$7500, domes/person CH$34,000

Campamento Los Perros (Vértice Patagonia). Last campsite before the John Gardner pass, situated in a wooded area, with a small food shop, cold showers and a cooking hut. Camping/person CH$4300

Campamento Serón (Fantástico Sur). Partially shaded campsite beside the Río Paine with picnic tables, cold showers and a small shop in a pleasant meadow setting at the bottom of the massif's northeast corner. Camping/person CH$7500

Refugio y Campamento Dickson (Vertice Patagonia). On the shores of Lago Dickson on the northern part of the Circuit, this is the most remote refuge in the park. Staff are friendly and there's a well-stocked shop, though the campsite has basic facilities only. Camping/person CH$4300, dorms CH$18,400

Refugio y Campamento Grey (Vertice Patagonia). A popular *refugio* overlooking Lago and Glaciar Grey. Beachside campsite includes hot showers and a small on-site grocery store. Camping/person CH$4300, dorms CH$18,400

Refugio y Campamento Paine Grande (Vertice Patagonia). This modern structure has a scenic location and a café, restaurant and small store within the lodge. You can camp in the adjoining grassy fields and there are separate toilets and hot showers, as well as a cooking hut for campers. Camping/person CH$5200, dorms CH$28,400

Refugio y Campamento Torre Norte & Torre Central (Fantástico Sur). Near the entrance to the park and the *Hostería Las Torres*, this *refugio* is split between two buildings and has comfortable bunks, a small shop and gear rental. Hearty meals are served in the large dining room. Campsite has hot showers, picnic tables and fire pits. Camping/person CH$7500, *Refugio Torre Norte* dorms CH$26,000, *Refugio Torre Central* dorms CH$40,000

Refugio y Camping Chileno (Fantástico Sur). A popular stop halfway along the Valle Ascencio, this small *refugio* offers just 32 beds and has a small provisions shop as well as offering hot meals. Camping/person CH$7500, dorms CH$26,000

Refugio y Camping Los Cuernos (Fantástico Sur). This *refugio* sits in a clearing beneath the Cuernos del Paine, on the northern shore of Lago Nordenskjöld, with geodomes and private *cabañas* as well as a cafeteria, cooking room for campers, tree-shaded campsite with platforms and hot showers. Camping/person CH$7500, dorms CH$26,000, *cabañas* CH$86,500, domes/person CH$30,500

Parque Nacional Los Glaciares

The vast majority of travellers to Patagonia don't limit themselves to the Chilean side alone. Just over the easily crossed border lies Argentina's most spectacular national park – **Parque Nacional Los Glaciares** – home to two of the region's star attractions. The first is the craggy blue face of the **Glaciar Perito Moreno** – regularly cited as one of the world's natural wonders, and situated near the tourist hub of **El Calafate**. The second is the trekkers' and climbers' paradise of the **Fitz Roy mountain range** in the north of the park, accessed from the relaxed little town of **El Chaltén**.

El Calafate

Originally settled by wool traders in the 1920s and named after the edible purple berry that pops up on thorny bushes in summertime, **EL CALAFATE** expanded rapidly following the creation of Parque Nacional Los Glaciares in 1937. Perito Moreno glacier remains the main draw for visitors who flood the town particularly between December and March. The glacier aside, El Calafate makes an excellent base for other park-related activities: boat trips, ice trekking, hiking ventures into the remotest corners of this slice of wilderness, and visits to local *estancias*. The main drag, Avenida Libertador, is lined with tourism outfits, restaurants and supermarkets.

Glaciarium

6km from El Calafate along Ruta 11 • May–Aug 11am–8pm; Sept–April 9am–8pm • AR$180 • ⓦ glaciarium.com • Hourly free transfers (9am–6pm) from the car park in front of the Santa Cruz Province Touristic Bureau, 1 de Mayo between Libertador and Roca

El Calafate's main attraction is a superb interactive museum dedicated to glaciers – what they are, how they are created, the main features of different types of glaciers and where they are found. Illuminated displays in the strategic semigloom cover the discovery and research of the two Patagonian ice-fields and reveal the tiny creature that's adapted to live on the ice. The video presentations – the striking 3D documentary on the Parque Nacional Los Glaciares and one on environmental issues facing our planet – are particularly worthwhile. End the visit with a drink at the on-site *Glacio Bar Branca* – the first Icebar in Argentina.

ARRIVAL AND DEPARTURE
EL CALAFATE

BY PLANE

El Calafate's airport (ⓦ www.aeropuertoelcalafate.com) is 22km east of town; taxis (AR$200) and minibuses run by Ves Patagonia (☎ 02902 497355 ⓦ vespatagonia.com; AR$90) connect it with El Calafate. El Calafate is linked by frequent Aerolíneas Argentinas and LADE flights to Buenos Aires, Ushuaia, Bariloche, Puerto Madryn and Esquel, among other Argentine destinations.

BY BUS

Buses to and from Puerto Natales and various Argentine destinations arrive at the hilltop bus station along Av Roca,

one block above the main street, Av Libertador.

Companies Chaltén Travel (☎ 02902 492212, ⓦ www .chaltentravel.com), Taqsa (☎ 02902 491843, ⓦ taqsa .com.ar) and Cal-tur (☎ 02902 491842, ⓦ caltur.com.ar) all serve El Chaltén during high season, typically at 8am, 1pm and 6.30pm; Chaltén Travel and Taqsa also run buses up the Ruta 40 every other day Nov–April. Taqsa and Sportman (☎ 02902 492680) also run to Río Gallegos; change there for daily departures to Ushuaia.

Destinations Bariloche (summer only; 1 daily; 30hr); El Chaltén (up to 9 daily; 2hr 30min); Puerto Natales (Chile; 3–4 weekly; 6hr); Río Gallegos (4–5 daily; 4hr–4hr 30min).

INFORMATION AND TOURS

TOURIST INFORMATION

Tourist information The tourist office is on Coronel Rosales, just beyond the bridge (daily: summer 8am–10pm; winter 8am–8pm; ☎ 02902 49190, ⓦ elcalafate.tur.ar). There's also a kiosk in the bus terminal (same hours).

National park information The national park office, in a historic wooden cabin at Av Libertador 1302 (Mon–Fri 8am–6pm, Sat & Sun 9am–6pm; ☎ 02902 491005, ⓦ parquesnacionales.gov.ar), has maps, sells fishing licences and can provide up-to-date information.

BAFT (Backpacking Free Travel) Gregores at 9 de Julio (daily 9am–7pm; ⓦ baftravel.com). Excellent information centre aimed at backpackers and staffed by an energetic young team who can help book accommodation and onward travel.

Car rental Companies include Europcar, Av Libertador 1741 (☎ 02902 493606) and Hertz at the airport (☎ 02902 492525).

TOUR OPERATORS

Virtually every tour agency in El Calafate runs day-trips to

9

the Perito Moreno glacier, allowing around 4hr at the ice face. For more specialized excursions, try the established operators listed below.

Glaciar Sur 9 de Julio 57, Local 2 ☎ 02902 495050, ⓦ glaciarsur.com. The only operator allowed to take small groups of visitors into the pristine, remote southwestern corner of Parque Nacional Los Glaciares (see p.410).

Hielo y Aventura Av Libertador 935 ☎ 02902 492205, ⓦ hieloyaventura.com. Offers Mini Trekking and Big Ice ice-trekking trips on Glaciar Perito Moreno (from AR$640), and boat excursions to the glacier.

Solo Patagonia Av Libertador 867 ☎ 02902 491115, ⓦ solopatagonia.com. Runs full-day boat trips to Upsala, Spegazzini and Perito Moreno glaciers.

ACCOMMODATION

★**América del Sur** Puerto Deseado 153 ☎ 02902 493525, ⓦ americahostel.com.ar. A well-designed, spacious and friendly place with wonderful views of Lago Argentino and knowledgeable staff who can help you organize a wide range of trips. The four-bed dorms and private rooms are clean, bright and have under-floor heating. It's a 10min uphill walk from the centre. Dorms US$33, doubles US$81

Casa de Grillos Los Condores 1215 ☎ 02902 491160, ⓦ casadegrillos.com.ar. A peaceful B&B in a two-storey family home that's come under new management, with a handful of comfortable doubles and triples. It's a 15–20min walk from the centre, and some guests have complained that the owner is a bit overzealous when selling tours. US$79

EOLO – Patagonia's Spirit Ruta 11, Km 23 ☎ 02902 492042, ⓦ eolo.com.ar. The main draws of this luxurious lodge, set on a hillside amid a 7400-acre property, are isolation, incredible views of Lago Argentino, Torres del Paine and Valle Anita, all manner of creature comforts – from indoor swimming pool and sauna to gourmet Patagonian cuisine, and numerous excursions, all included in the daily rate. Late Sept to late April. US$950

Hostel del Glaciar Libertador Av Libertador 587 ☎ 02902 491792, ⓦ glaciar.com. This enormous (and somewhat anonymous) wooden house sleeps more than a hundred, has spotless dorms with private bathrooms, and

lovely private rooms. Walls are thin, so you may feel as if you're in bed with your neighbours, and the service is professional if impersonal. Dorms US$20, doubles US$84

Hostal Schilling Gobernador Paradelo 141 ☎ 02902 491453, ⓦ hostalschilling.com. Its vast lounge wall decorated by globetrotting guests of all ages, this professionally-run guesthouse offers spacious, comfortable but featureless en suite rooms and a single dorm. There's a bar on site, and the owner runs the excellent Glaciar Sur trips (see above). Dorms US$20, doubles US$51

★**Madretierra** 9 de Julio 239 ☎ 02902 498880, ⓦ madretierrapatagonia.com. The main draws of this family-run boutique hotel are the personal touches (your name on the door), the wonderfully attentive hosts, the snug, stylish rooms with excellent showers and beds, and a funky lounge with plenty of glossy books on Patagonia to leaf through. Effusive owner Mariano is an experienced guide happy to organise outdoor adventures to suit your taste. US$180

El Ovejero José Pantín 64 ☎ 02902 493422. Just a block from the main street, this clean campsite is protected from the wind by a row of trees and sits alongside a babbling brook and a *parrilla*. Price includes hot showers and there are picnic tables and *fogones* for cooking (firewood costs extra). Pitches across the stream are cheaper but a longer trek to the bathroom than the pricier ones. Camping/ person US$8

EATING AND DRINKING

Borges & Alvarez Libro-bar Av Libertador 1015 ☎ 02902 491464. This small, warm café-bar with a cave-like, book-covered lounge attracts bibliophiles and cocktail lovers alike. There's an extensive range of coffee-table books to flick through while perusing the long list of cocktails (AR$85–99), or sipping an Antares beer or coffee. Daily 10am–3am.

Casimiro Biguá Av Libertador 963 ☎ 02902 492590. With formally attired waiters and a Patagonian barbecue pit in the window, this is the town's most upmarket steakhouse. You can order unusual (at least for Argentina) sides such as sweet potato chips or grilled vegetables to go with the grilled meats, and their made-to-share plate of Patagonian appetizers, such as smoked trout and deer salami, is superb. Daily noon–4pm & 7.30pm–1am.

★**Mi Rancho** Gobernador Moyano at 9 de Julio ☎ 02902 490540. All exposed brick and homely touches,

this intimate little restaurant offers some wonderfully creative and surprisingly affordable dishes. Your taste buds will thank you for the king crab ravioli with Vermouth sauce and lamb T-bone with calafate reduction. Round off with a passion fruit parfait or apple crumble. Mains AR$120–175. Reserve ahead. Daily noon–3pm & 8pm–midnight.

Pura Vida Av Libertador 1876 ☎ 02902 493358. A 10min walk from the centre, this A-frame cabin is a godsend for vegetarians, though meat eaters can also enjoy the likes of "Granny's lentil stew", country chicken pie, lamb *empanadas* and gnocchi in saffron sauce. Save room for dessert. Mains AR$110–160. Mon, Tues & Thurs–Sun 7.30–11.30pm.

★**La Tablita** Rosales 28 ☎ 02902 491065. An El Calafate institution for over 25 years, this large hall heaves with discerning carnivores who come for the spit-roasted

---

PATAGONIAN ESTANCIAS

Patagonia's empty steppe is speckled with isolated *estancias* - the legacy of the first pioneers - and many of these open their doors to visitors. As lodgings, most cater to high-end tourists, but many are accessible on day visits if you wish to take part in hiking, horseriding, traditional *asados* and perhaps witness a sheep-shearing demonstration.

Estancia Cristina Near Brazo Norte of Lago Argentina ☎02902 491133, ⊕estanciacristina .com. Completely devoted to tourism these days, *Estancia Cristina* is one of the most popular day-trips from El Calafate, involving a boat ride across the northern arm of Lago Argentino and plenty of scope for hiking and horseriding.

Estancia El Cóndor By Lago San Martín, north of El Chaltén, off Ruta 40 ☎011 4152 5400, ⊕cielospatagonicos.com. Remote and difficult to get to (own wheels essential) but the scenery here is tremendous. You can go on multi-day horseriding expeditions, visit the local condor's nest and overnight in a simple homestead during multi-day treks. Visit for several days to make the most of it.

Estancia Nibepo Aike By Lago Roca ☎02902 492797, ⊕nibepoaike.com.ar. A working *estancia* where you can take a peek at the world of cattle ranching, go horseriding, cycle around the property and enjoy an evening barbecue.

Patagonian lamb, slabs of steak and traditional gaucho fare, such as lamb chitterlings and sweetbreads. If there's two of you, go for "Mix Carnes" (AR$400) and unless you're ravenous, half a steak (AR$110) is plenty. Daily noon–3.30pm & 7.30pm–midnight.

Viva La Pepa Amado 833 ☎02902 491880. Cheerful, whimsical café decorated with children's paintings and specialising in sweet and savoury crepes (think lamb with honey and rosemary, chicken with blue cheese and pear, and *dulce de leche* with chocolate-covered banana (AR$68–90), as well as soups, sandwiches, fresh juices and coffee. Daily noon–8pm.

Glaciar Perito Moreno

49 km from El Calafate along Ruta 11 • Daily 8am–7pm • AR$215

At the southern sector of the Parque Nacional Los Glaciares you'll find one of Argentina's leading attractions, the **GLACIAR PERITO MORENO**. The vast glacier – 30km long, 5km wide and 60m high – sweeps down off the ice cap in a great curve, a jagged mass of crevasses and towering, knife-edged obelisks of ice (seracs), almost unsullied by the streaks of dirty moraine; it's marbled in places with streaks of muddy grey and copper sulphate blue, while at the bottom the pressurized, de-oxygenated ice has a deep blue, waxy sheen.

When it collides with the southern arm of Lago Argentino, vast blocks of ice, some weighing hundreds of tonnes, detonate off the face of the glacier with the report of a small cannon and come crashing down into the waters of Canal de los Témpanos (Iceberg Channel) below. One of the world's few advancing glaciers, Perito Moreno periodically blocks off Lago Argentino, causing the waters to build up until they burst through the dam, creating a spectacular ice arch. The glacier tends to be more active in sunny weather and in the afternoon. You can admire it from a series of boardwalks or take one of the hourly boats up close to the face of the glacier for a greater appreciation of its vastness.

Upsala and other glaciers

45km west of El Calafate • Accessible by catamaran excursion along Lago Argentino's northern arm (boats leave from Puerto Bandera); tours run by Solo Patagonia (see p.412) • Full-day tours AR$1200, plus park entry fee (AR$215)

Although receding fast, **GLACIAR UPSALA** remains the longest glacier in the park and indeed in South America. The same height as Perito Moreno (60m), Upsala is twice as long (roughly 60km), 7km wide and known for calving huge translucent, blue-tinged icebergs that bob around Lago Argentino like surreal art sculptures. Tours (see p.411), usually called "All Glaciers", also take in the Spegazzini and Perito Moreno glaciers. Note that Upsala is occasionally inaccessible when icebergs block the channels.

9

Lago Roca and around

The southern arm of Lago Argentino, and also known as Brazo Sur, **LAGO ROCA** is fringed by dense forest and hemmed in by mountains. This is the least visited and the most serene corner of Parque Nacional Los Glaciares, where there are plenty of hiking opportunities. But to reach the most spectacular part – an unnamed glacial lagoon full of enormous chunks of ice, fed by two glaciers and with Glaciar Dickson peeping from the border of Parque Nacional Torres del Paine (see p.402) – you have to go via organised tour. At research time, Glaciar Sur (see p.412) was the only company allowed to bring a group of up to fourteen people three times weekly to this remote area. The tour involves a boat ride to the southern end of Brazo Sur, an hour's stiff hike to the smaller Lago Frías, a zodiac boat ride across and then a spectacular, mostly flat hike along a dried riverbed to the lagoon, with waterfalls cascading down the mountains on one side.

Fitz Roy Massif

The northernmost section of Argentina's **Parque Nacional Los Glaciares** contains the **FITZ ROY MASSIF**, boasting some of the most breathtakingly beautiful mountain peaks on the planet. Two concentric jaws of jagged teeth puncture the Patagonian sky, with the 3445m incisor of **Monte Fitz Roy** at the centre.

TREKKING IN PARQUE NACIONAL LOS GLACIARES

One of the beauties of this park is that those with limited time can still make worthwhile **day hikes**, using El Chaltén as a base. For those who enjoy sleeping in the wild, there are free basic campsites at Laguna Torre, Laguna Capri, Laguna Toro and Poincenot, with Río Blanco reserved for climbers only.

DAY HIKES

The most popular trail is the relatively flat hike to **Laguna Torre** (11km; 6hr round-trip), which follows the Río Fitz Roy to a silty lake resplendent with floating icebergs, overlooked by Cerro Torre. A more strenuous hike is to **Laguna de los Tres** (12.5km; 8hr), which ascends sharply to a glacial lake with in-your-face views of Fitz Roy; this is impassable in the winter. For the best panoramic views in the area – of both Monte Fitz Roy and Cerro Torre as well as Lago Viedma – hike uphill to 1490m-high **Lomo del Pliegue Tumbado** (12km; 8hr).

SHORT WALKS

For short hikes, from the north end of town, it's an hour's walk to Chorillo del Salto (waterfall). From the national park information centre, take the Los Condores or Las Aguilas trails; you will get a panoramic view of El Chaltén.

MULTI-DAY TREKS

A classic multi-day hike is the **Monte Fitz Roy/Cerro Torre loop** (3 days, 2 nights), which leaves either from El Chaltén or just beyond the park's boundaries at *Hostería El Pilar* (15km north of town). There are three free **campsites** (with latrines only) along the route. A tough five-day, anticlockwise loop takes in Laguna Toro, Paso del Viento, amazing views of Glaciar Viedma, and Paso Huemul, before skirting Lago Viedma on the way back to town. Tougher still, and requiring a guide, is the multi-day trek from Río Eléctrico that crosses Glaciar Marconi and involves overnighting at least twice on the Southern Ice-Field.

HIKES AROUND LAGO DEL DESIERTO

If you exhaust your hiking options in the immediate vicinity of El Chaltén, take one of the daily transfers to Lago del Desierto (37km away); there's an easy roundtrip hike (2hr) to Glaciar Huemul and a trek (5hr) that skirts the side of the lake, heading towards the border with Chile (see box, p.380). There's also a 25km network of beautifully-maintained trails at the private Reserva Los Huemules (AR$100; ⓦloshuemules.com), 17km north of El Chaltén (Lago del Desierto transfers pass it by).

El Chaltén

Argentina's trekking capital, **EL CHALTÉN**, sits at the confluence of two pristine rivers, with a healthy contingent of hikers and climbers flocking to this surprisingly cosmopolitan town of just over one thousand inhabitants for the summer season. El Chaltén means "smoking mountain", a name given to Monte Fitz Roy by the Tehuelche, who probably mistook the wisps of cloud around its summit for volcanic activity.

ARRIVAL AND DEPARTURE   EL CHALTÉN

BY BUS

All buses stop at the national park information centre before arriving at the large new bus terminal at the south end of town. In peak season, buy your bus ticket out of town in advance, as demand outstrips supply. You have to return to El Calafate for all onwards connections to most other Argentine destinations.

Companies Chaltén Travel (☎02962 493092, ⓦwww .chaltentravel.com), Taqsa (☎02962 493068, ⓦtaqsa. com.ar) and Cal-tur (☎02962 493801, ⓦcaltur.com.ar) all run up to three buses daily to El Calafate. Chaltén Travel and Taqsa also run buses up the Ruta 40 every other day Nov–April. Las Lengas (☎02962 493023, ⓦtransportelaslengas.com) runs shuttle services to El Calafate Airport, Lago del Desierto, Río Eléctrico and

Hostería El Pilar. Buy tickets at least a day in advance for all services.

Destinations Bariloche (1–2 daily; around 27hr); El Calafate (3–9 daily, typically at 8am, 1pm & 6pm; 3hr); El Calafate Airport (1–3 daily; 3hr); Perito Moreno (1–2 daily; 11hr).

BY CAR

From El Calafate, head east along Ruta Nacional 11 for 30km, then turn left on Ruta 40 north, then northwest onto Ruta 23. The 220km road is completely paved.

BY BOAT

For the most direct route possible to Chile – boat/hike or hike/boat (see box, p.379).

INFORMATION AND TOURS

TOURIST INFORMATION

Tourist office There's a helpful tourist office (daily 8am–8pm; ☎0292 493370) inside the bus terminal.

Park office At the village entrance (daily 9am–8pm in peak season, shorter hours rest of the year; ☎02962 493004, ⓦelchalten.com). Climbers *must* register here, as should anyone planning to stay at the Laguna Toro *refugio* and campsite to the south. Visitors are given an informative talk on hiking in the park and receive trail maps.

TOUR OPERATORS

Parque Nacional Los Glaciares has more to offer than just trekking. Those looking for alternative adventure activities can try the following reputable operators.

El Chaltén Mountain Guides San Martín 187 ☎02962 493320, ⓦecmg.com.ar. These certified guides run ice climbing and rock climbing trips – from half-day introductions to multi-day ventures.

Estancia Cerro Fitzroy Around 2km south of town, across the river ☎02966 1534 4540, ⓔestancia cerrofitzroy@gmail.com. Fitzroy Madsen, the great-grandson of the first Danish settler in the area, combines an easy, scenic walk with a tour of the newly restored Andreas Madsen House, telling you the story of his settler family, showing you the family graveyard and treating you to *mate* and biscuits afterwards. This tour departs at 3pm from the bridge at the end of Calle Trevisan (US$20).

Patagonia Aventura San Martín 56B ☎02964 436424, ⓦpatagonia-aventura.com. Offers boat excursions across the lake to the snout of Glaciar Viedma, and ice-trekking on the glacier itself (ARS$1200).

Walk Patagonia Antonio Rojo 62 ☎02962 493275, ⓦwalkpatagonia.com. This energetic Argentinian–British husband and wife team organizes anything from tailor-made treks with an emphasis on local fauna, flora and history to onward travel all over Argentina.

ACCOMMODATION

HOTELS AND GUESTHOUSES

★**Aguas Arriba Lodge** Lago del Desierto ☎011 4512 5697, ⓦaguasarribalodge.com. This dream of a 'hometel' (intimate, eco-conscious five-room lodge that's also the home of South African-Argentinian owners Ivor and Pato) sits in splendid isolation halfway along Lago del Desierto. Access is by speedboat or 3hr hike only, its five unadorned, spacious, luxurious rooms look out over Fitz Roy or the

Vespionani glacier (or both!) and rates include all gourmet meals and hikes led by a bilingual guide. Guests currently have exclusive access to the Vespionani glacier, while rainy days find them by the immense stone fireplace in the lounge. Oct–April. U̲S̲$̲9̲0̲0̲

Cabañas Aires del Fitz Ricardo Arbilla 124 ☎02962 493134, ⓦairesdelfitz.com.ar. An effusive hostess runs four split-level *cabañas* sleeping either two to three or six

9

9

people; each beautiful living space comes with a fully-equipped kitchen, satellite TV in the common area, lofty bedrooms and nice touches such as blackout curtains and drying racks in bathrooms. No breakfast. *Cabañas* US$105

Hostería Senderos Perito Moreno 35 ☎02962 493336, ⓦsenderoshosteria.com.ar. Catering to hikers who appreciate their creature comforts, this attractive lodge comes with 21 spacious rooms, most with king-sized beds, all with bathtubs and half with views of Fitz Roy (US$30 extra). The attentive hostess goes out of her way to be helpful, prices include an extensive buffet breakfast and there are occasional wine tastings in the evenings. Sept–April. US$170

Kaulem Av Antonio Rojo at Commandante Arrua ☎02962 493267, ⓦkaulem.com.ar. With just four doubles and a two-person *cabaña*, this intimate hotel with Monte Fitz Roy views holds great appeal for couples. Supported by a rough-hewn tree trunk, the lounge is full of light, with splashes of colour courtesy of the owner's artwork; king-size beds and bathtubs are the norm and breakfast includes freshly baked bread. Doubles US$175, *cabañas* US$150

Nothofagus Bed & Breakfast Hensen at Riquelme ☎02962 493087, ⓦnothofagusbb.com.ar. A bright and homely B&B with wooden furnishing and a rustic feel; three rooms are en suites, while the other four share a bathroom; some have views of Monte Fitz Roy. Besides the good breakfast, there's a small library and book exchange. Nov–April. US$81

HOSTELS

Condor de los Andes Av Río de las Vueltas, at Halvorsen ☎02962 493101, ⓦcondordelosandes.com. A well-run HI hostel that provides all the services backpackers have come to expect: tour and transport booking, laundry, guest kitchen and lunch boxes for hikers. The four- and six-bed dorms and doubles are all en-suite and in the evenings guests congregate in the appealing lounge with stone fireplace. Mid-Sept to April. Dorms US$23, doubles US$76

Hostel Pioneros del Valle San Martín 451 ☎02902 492217, ⓦcaltur.com.ar. Located more centrally on the main street, the Cal Tur-affiliated behemoth is *Rancho Grande's* biggest competition. Service is similarly impersonal yet professional, there's a large range of backpacker amenities including currency exchange and bus pickup and dropoff, friendly staff and large, sparsely-decorated en suite and good-value private rooms. Dorms US$17, doubles US$58

★**Patagonia Travellers' Hostel** San Martín 493 ☎02962 493019, ⓦpatagoniahostel.com.ar. With its slate walls, a beautiful, airy common space with plasma screen TV and well-equipped guest kitchen, this chalet-like hiker refuge is the most appealing of the town's hostels. Downsides are lockers located outside the simple four-person dorms and school-gym-like communal bathrooms, though private rooms are en suite. Their biking tours from Lago del Desierto are justifiably popular. Mid-Sept to mid-April. Dorms US$20, doubles US$87

Rancho Grande San Martín 520 ☎02962 493005, ⓦranchograndehostel.com. Yes, this large Chaltén-Travel-affiliated hostel is a backpacker factory, but they're good at what they do. Pluses include snug four-bed dorms, appealing, two-tiered dining/hangout area, on-site café/bar, small kitchen and a designated member of staff who helps you plan your stay. They also change currency, accept credit cards and sell onward bus tickets. Dorms US$17, doubles US$83

EATING AND DRINKING

La Cervecería San Martín 564 ☎02962 493109. One of the most sociable spots in town, with locals and hikers perching on rough-hewn wooden seats to savour pints of bock or pilsner microbrews or tuck into ample portions of stew, pizza or pasta. Daily 11am–midnight.

★**Estepa** Cerro Solo at Antonio Rojo ☎02962 493069. Revamped and featuring snug booths and posters of Warhol and Che Guevara, *Estepa* has lost none of its culinary creativity. Treat yourself to lamb sweetbreads with lemon butter, smoked trout ravioli (AR$145) and slow-cooked lamb in calafate sauce with gnocchi (AR$250). Tues–Sun 11.30am–midnight.

El Muro San Martín 948 ☎02962 493248. Steak with peppers and bacon, sweet and sour ribs, salmon *sorrentinos* and slow-cooked lamb with mint are just some of the tempting creations dished up at this hungry hiker haven. There's a climbing wall out back to help you work up an appetite. Mains from AR$130. Daily 7.30pm–midnight.

Patagónicus Güemes at Madsen ☎02962 493025. Consistently the best pizza in town (twenty types, to be precise, include plenty of vegetarian ones), served to hungry diners at big wooden tables. The good range of beers includes their very own Chaltén and Patagónicus brews. Small/large pizza from AR$40/80. Mon & Wed–Sun noon–11pm.

Prana San Martín. Indian wall hangings decorate the salmon-pink walls of this snug vegetarian bistro and delicious smells lure you in to try the likes of brown rice risotto, lentil stew and beetroot gnocchi stuffed with sheep's cheese. Fantastic selection of gourmet teas, too. Mains AR$100–130. Daily noon–11pm.

La Tapera Av Antonio Rojo ☎02962 493195. Adorable, split-level log cabin with a roaring fire, packed full of hungry punters tucking into pork shoulder cooked with beer, beautifully-seared steak, salmon with spring onion and ginger, a smattering of tapas and a couple of cold weather warmers: *locro* (classic lamb/chorizo/bacon stew) and lamb and lentil stew. Mains AR$97–192. Daily 12.30–3pm & 7.30–11.30pm.

Techado Negro Av Antonio Rojo at Riquelme ☎ 02962 493268. Amidst psychedelic murals and collages of the Stones, Gandhi and Bowie, you'll find a very reasonable *menú* that might feature the likes of chicken cannelloni (AR$85), as well as steak, large bowls of *locro* and a range of Argentinian beers. Mains AR$110–150. Daily noon–midnight.

Verdelimon Cabo García 38. Besides its wide selection of fruit and veg, this greengrocer also offers freshly baked muffins, salads, granola with home-made yogurt, fruit smoothies and honey. Daily 10am–2pm & 5–10pm.

★**La Vineria** Av Lago del Desierto 265 ☎ 02962 493301. This busy, buzzy little joint is the place to sample a couple of dozen craft beers as well as wines from all over Argentina, accompanied by sharing platters (AR$330) of cold cuts (think smoked venison, trout, black pudding) and local and imported cheeses, as well as gourmet sandwiches (AR$120). Hugely popular, so you'll have to queue. Daily 4pm–midnight.

La Wafflería San Martín. Colourful, snug and run by two friendly guys, *La Wafflería* sates your cravings for waffles. Toppings vary from calafate ice cream with *dulce de leche* to blue cheese, black olives and nuts (AR$49–75), and tipples range from seven types of hot chocolate to El Chaltén's very own Supay brew. Daily 11am–9pm.

DIRECTORY

Camping equipment Pick up any camping gear that you're missing at Camping Center, San Martín 56, or Patagonia Hikes, Lago del Desierto at Rojo.

Hospital El Puesto Sanitario (☎ 02962 493033) is extremely basic; for medical emergencies, go to El Calafate.

Laundry Wash your dirty camping gear at the *lavandería* on the corner of Lago del Desierto and Av Güemes.

Money and exchange El Chaltén has one ATM at the bus station but don't rely on it; bring plenty of cash to cover your stay. Dollars, euros and Chilean pesos are widely accepted. If planning on crossing the border to the Chilean village of Villa O'Higgins (see box, p.380) and travel up the Carretera Austral, stock up on plenty of Chilean pesos.

Telephone As of mid-2014, El Chaltén has mobile phone reception.

Tierra del Fuego

420 Porvenir

424 Around Porvenir

426 Isla Navarino

430 Ushuaia

438 Around Ushuaia

CROSSING THE BEAGLE CHANNEL

Tierra del Fuego

At the bottom end of the South American continent, and split between Chile and Argentina, Tierra del Fuego ("Land of Fire") holds nearly as much fascination for travellers as Patagonia, from which it is separated by the Magellan Strait. In fact, it was Magellan who dreamed up the dramatic and somewhat unlikely name, after sighting dozens of fires lit by the native Yámana. Though comprising a number of islands, it's more or less the sum of its most developed part, the Isla Grande, the biggest island in South America. Argentina possesses the easternmost half of Isla Grande, plus Isla de los Estados (Staten Island) and a smattering of tiny islets to the south; the rest is Chilean territory.

On the **Chilean side**, you'll find the isolated main town of **Porvenir**, which huddles on the Magellan Strait. Flat and dusty plains cover much of northern and central Isla Grande, but further south, the countryside becomes less barren, with thick woodland and crystalline rivers near **Camerón** stretching southeast towards a number of pristine lakes, including **Lago Blanco**, and the largely inaccessible 2000m peaks of the Cordillera Darwin in the far south. South of Isla Grande, across the Beagle Channel, lies **Isla Navarino**, home to tiny **Puerto Williams**, the southernmost permanently inhabited settlement in the world, plus one of the most challenging hiking trails in South America, the **Los Dientes Circuit**. Beyond Navarino is **Cabo de Hornos** (Cape Horn), the land's end of the Americas, accessible only by sea or air.

In the Argentine sector, the leading attraction is the city of **Ushuaia** on the south coast of **Argentine** Tierra del Fuego. It is *the* base for visiting the **Beagle Channel**, rich in **marine wildlife**, the lakes, forests and tundra of nearby **Parque Nacional Tierra del Fuego**, the historic **Estancia Harberton**, and, of course, **Antarctica**. It is also Tierra del Fuego's main tourist destination, with winter skiing and summer trekking high on the list of activities. Also in Argentine Tierra del Fuego, you'll find the scenic **Lago Fagnano**; from the lake to the 2985m **Paso Garibaldi**, the gateway to Ushuaia by road, you'll travel through patches of low, transitional, lichen-festooned **Fuegian woodland**.

Porvenir

A collection of brightly painted corrugated-iron houses lining a narrow bay, **PORVENIR** (optimistically meaning "future") is order stamped on nature, with neat topiary leading down the main street, Philippi, from an immaculate Plaza de Armas, overflowing with native vegetation. The seafront Parque del Recuerdo sports a curve of flagpoles, the painted skeleton of a steam engine, the mounted stern of a boat and a statue of a Tehuelche man – a rare reminder of a culture made extinct by the gold rush. A twenty-minute walk along the coast takes you to **Cerro Mirador**, from where you get an excellent view of the town.

A plague [of beavers] on both your houses p.423
Exploring Tierra del Fuego on four wheels p.424
King penguins in Tierra del Fuego p.425
The Yámana, the Selk'nam, the Mánekenk and the Kawéshkar p.427

Los Dientes de Navarino circuit p.428
Round the Horn by sea and air p.430
How the Cape found its Horn p.432
Antarctica – the remotest continent p.434
Winter sports around Ushuaia p.439

PARQUE NACIONAL TIERRA DEL FUEGO

Highlights

❶ Porvenir and around Visit Chile's Fuegian capital and explore the harsh land around it, which includes gold mine remains and a small king penguin colony. **See p.420**

❷ Isla Navarino Fly or sail to Puerto Williams, the most southerly town on earth, or tackle one of the toughest hiking circuits in South America – the Dientes de Navarino. **See p.426**

❸ Cape Horn Even if you don't kayak around it, consider rounding the tip in a ship or viewing its harsh beauty from the air. **See p.430**

❹ Boat trip along the Beagle Channel Spot sea lions and penguins, cormorants and albatrosses, and maybe even killer whales. **See p.438**

❺ Winter sports around Ushuaia Zip down the slopes of the winter sports resort dramatically located at the end of the world or go sledging with huskies. **See p.439**

❻ Parque Nacional Tierra del Fuego Explore this fascinating and little-visited chunk of jagged mountains, beech forest, bogs, tundra and beautiful coast on foot or in a 4WD. **See p.424 & p.438**

HIGHLIGHTS ARE MARKED ON THE MAP ON P.422

Porvenir cemetery

Esmeralda at Damian Riobo • Daily 8am–6pm

Porvenir started life in 1883 as a police outpost during the Fuegian gold rush and has since been settled by foreigners: first came the British managers of sheep farms, and then refugees from Croatia after World War II. You can read the history of the town in the names of the dead at the **cemetery** four blocks north of the plaza, a smaller version of Punta Arenas' Cementerio Municipal (see p.391), where grand

TIERRA DEL FUEGO

HIGHLIGHTS

1. Porvenir and around
2. Isla Navarino
3. Cape Horn
4. Boat trip along the Beagle Channel
5. Winter sports around Ushuaia
6. Parque Nacional Tierra del Fuego

A PLAGUE [OF BEAVERS] ON BOTH YOUR HOUSES

As you travel around Tierra del Fuego, the sight of dead trees and beaver dams is depressingly common, a situation that owes everything to the crackpot decision made by the Argentine military in the 1940s to import 25 pairs of **Canadian beavers** in a bid to start a lucrative fur trade. This bid backfired catastrophically: the beavers multiplied like wildfire in the absence of natural predators, the fur trade never took off and today more than over half a million buck-toothed descendants of the original beavers plague the whole of Tierra del Fuego as well as the neighbouring islands, wreaking environmental havoc, infecting lake and river water with giardia and threatening to spread to Patagonia.

At one point, the Chilean government offered US$5 per tail, but it didn't have the desired result of curbing the beaver population, so other options are being looked into. In the meantime, sightings of beavers have been confirmed in the Cabo Froward area (see p.395), meaning that they have now made landfall in mainland Patagonia. The Chilean and Argentinian governments must act, and fast, if they are to prevent an **ecological disaster** on Tierra del Fuego's scale.

10

---

marble tombs intermix with modest stone slabs amid meticulously pruned cypresses.

Museo de Tierra del Fuego Fernando Cordero Rusque

Padre Mario Zavattaro 402 • Mon–Thurs 8am–5.30pm, Fri 9am–4pm, Sat & Sun 10am–1.30pm & 3–5pm • CH$500

On the north corner of the plaza, with a 1928 Ford-T parked outside, this intriguing museum ushers you into the harsh world that shaped Porvenir. A mixture of evocative black-and-white photos, dioramas and period objects introduce the visitor to the Fuegian gold rush, the lives of the now-extinct Tehuelche and the conquest of Patagonia by Europeans. The Selk'nam skulls and mummies are a standout exhibit.

ARRIVAL AND INFORMATION

PORVENIR

By plane The aerodrome sits 5km north of town. Taxis charge around CH$4000 to take you to Porvenir; Aerovías DAP runs a cheaper door-to-door shuttle (CH$2500). DAP's office, in the same building as Tabsa on Calle Señoret, sells plane tickets to Punta Arenas (CH$21,000 one way; maximum 10kg luggage). Destinations Punta Arenas (Mon–Fri 3 daily, Sat 2; around 15min)

By ferry New, faster Transbordadora Austral Broom ferries from Punta Arenas arrive at Bahía Chilota, 5km to the west of Porvenir. A taxi costs CH$3500 and a *colectivo* CH$1000. Check schedule well ahead and purchase ferry tickets from Tabsa on the seafront at Calle Señoret s/n (Mon–Fri 9.15am–12.15pm & 2.30–6.30pm, Sat 9am–12.15pm; passengers CH$6200; ☏ 61 258 0089, ⓦ tabsa.cl).

Destinations Punta Arenas (Tues–Sun 1 daily; 2hr 30min).

By car The turn-off for Porvenir is 16km south of the Punta Delgada ferry crossing (see p.391). The gravel road has a few potholes, but the section near Porvenir is paved.

By bus While there are no buses from Punta Arenas to Porvenir, there are services from Porvenir to Camerón departing from the DAP office.

Destinations Camerón (Tues & Fri at 6am & 4pm, returning at 8.30am & 6pm on the same days; 2hr); Vicuña (2nd and 4th week of the month Wed & Thurs at 6am, returning at 10am the same day; 3hr 30min).

Tourist information The tourist office is at Zavatarro 434 (Mon–Fri 9am–5pm, Sat & Sun 11am–5pm; ☏ 61 258 0094), next to the museum.

ACCOMMODATION

Hostal Los Canelos Croacia 356 ☏ 61 258 1949. Opposite the Catholic church, you'll find a handful of swing-a-cat rooms with private bathrooms. Breakfast includes *kuchen* and home-made bread, and singles cost exactly half of a double – a rarity in Chile. CH$24,000

★**Hostería Yendegaia** Croacia 702 ☏ 61 258 1919, ⓦ hosteriayendegaia.com. Large, attractive, creaky wooden house run by congenial owners who specialise in

birding and penguin-watching tours in Tierra del Fuego. The spacious rooms have high ceilings, appealing splashes of colour and cable TV, and the inclusive breakfast is the best in town. CH$30,000

Hotel Barlovento John Williams 2 ☏ 61 258 0046, ⓦ hotelbarlovento.cl/index1.html. Located on the outskirts of town, Porvenir's plushest hotel gives you access to a unique gym and indoor football field, the staff are friendly and helpful and the centrally heated rooms are tastefully decorated in neutral tones. Anything exotic-sounding at the restaurant is bound to disappoint, though, so stick to Chilean standards. **CH$70,000**

Hotel España Croacia 698 ☎61 258 0160, ⊛hotelespana.cl. This deceptively large old building, run by a friendly, formidable hostess, features large, centrally heated rooms with TV. Prices include breakfast and the downstairs restaurant serves bargain set lunches and good à la carte seafood dishes, such as the ever popular *palta Porvenir* (avocado stuffed with king crab). **CH$30,000**

EATING

Club Croata Señoret 542 ☎61 258 0053. There's a Croatian coat of arms above the doorway and the menu at this grand old gentlemen's club focuses mainly on fresh fish and seafood. The house special is the *trilogia austral*: crêpes with *centolla* (king crab), oysters and mussels, and the service is bow-tied and old-school. Mains from CH$7000. Tues–Sun 12.30–3.30pm & 7–11pm.

Hotel Rosas Croacia 698 ☎61 258 0088. Generous portions of well-prepared seafood and fish dishes are to be had at this informal restaurant popular with locals. The lunchtime set menu is a bargain at CH$5000 and the owner is extremely knowledgeable about the mining history of the area. Daily 12.30–3pm & 7–11pm.

Restaurant La Chispa Señoret at Riobo ☎61 258 0054. Inside the historic fire station, *La Chispa* is popular with locals who come for the no-nonsense grilled fish and other simple home cooking. Mains from CH$5500. Tues–Sat noon–3pm & 7–10.30pm, Sun 12.30–3.30pm.

DIRECTORY

Hospital Carlos Wood between Av Manuel Señoret and Guerrero (☎61 258 0034).
Money and exchange Bring plenty of cash as the single

Banco Estado ATM only accepts Chilean MasterCard.
Post office On the plaza at Philippi 176 (Mon–Fri 9am–noon & 2–6pm).

Around Porvenir

The exploration of Porvenir's environs is about driving the island's virtually empty roads and taking in the rolling pampas, the lakes teeming with birdlife, and the rusting hulks of old machinery that hint at Tierra del Fuego's gold rush past.

Bahía Azul

Ferry summer every 45min, 8.30am–11pm; less often in winter; 20min

The first 20km out of Porvenir heading north is lined with large shallow lakes, ranging in colour from turquoise to sapphire and often adorned with dazzling pink flamingos. Forty-three kilometres north of the oil settlement of Cerro Sombrero (139km from Porvenir), the **ferry** that connects Tierra del Fuego with Patagonia crosses the Primera Angostura from a place known locally as **BAHÍA AZUL** (Puerto Espora). During the crossing you may see schools of black-and-white Commerson's dolphins.

EXPLORING TIERRA DEL FUEGO ON FOUR WHEELS

Visitors with their own **vehicles** get far more out of a trip to Chilean Tierra del Fuego than those limited to Porvenir. Cars can be rented in Punta Arenas and brought over to the island on the car ferry. Most of the roads – with the exception of the stretch from Onaisín to Cerro Sombrero, which is newly paved – are unpaved, but can be tackled without a 4WD if driving carefully. You'll need a high-clearance vehicle for the coastal road south of Camerón to Puerto Arturo, though.

Fuegians rely only on themselves and on each other when it comes to **breakdowns** and all motorists will stop should you come to grief. Nevertheless, you should come prepared with a sleeping bag, food, water, a torch, warm clothes, a spare tyre and all necessary equipment. Always stop to help other motorists in need and plan your journey carefully: there are only two petrol stations – one in Porvenir and the other in Cerro Sombrero. If you wish to head south to Lago Blanco, you must take a spare can of petrol with you.

The Baquedano Hills

A little-used road heads east from Porvenir across the **BAQUEDANO HILLS**, where most of the region's gold was discovered; you pass the rusted remains of dredges along the way. The road meets the main Porvenir–San Sebastián road and, after another 84km of rolling pampas, reaches the **San Sebastián frontier** (see p.426). Ten kilometres southeast of San Sebastián lies "Las Onas" hill, the site of the oldest inhabited place on the island, estimated to be 11,880 years old.

10

Bahía Inútil

A pretty road follows the coast from **Bahía Inútil**, a wide bay that got its name by being a useless anchorage for sailing ships. After 99km you reach a crossroads; turn south, and a little past the village of Onaisín you pass a little **English cemetery**. The gravestones have inscriptions in English that suggest tragic stories: "killed by Indians", "accidentally drowned" and "died in a storm".

When the tide's out, you can see an ancient way of catching fish – underwater stone *corrales* (pens) built by the Selk'nam Indians to trap fish when the tide turned. Just before the village of Camerón, the road turns inland and leaves the bay, while a rough track carries on south along the coast to Puerto Arturo, a small stockbreeding settlement.

Camerón and around

From **CAMERÓN**, a former Scottish sheep farm settlement, a road leads through Magellanic forest, occasionally interspersed with open grassland, to a fork in the road: north to San Sebastián, and south to Río Grande.

Lago Blanco and beyond

Twenty-one kilometres south of Río Grande lies **Lago Blanco**, surrounded by steeply forested hills and snow-covered mountains. From Lago Blanco the road continues further south, past Lago Deseado, currently ending just beyond the majestic Lago Fagnano, part of Parque Nacional Tierra del Fuego. The Chilean government plans to build a new settlement on the shores of the lake, thus providing easier access to the natural attractions on the Argentinian side. A rough gravel road now reaches the western shore of Lago Fagnano (4WD only) and it may be possible to cross over to Argentina via Paso Bellavista (Dec–March only); check with local *carabineros*.

Yendegaia National Park

A former Doug and Kris Tompkins' conservation project (see p.355), Estancia Yendegaia is a 385-hundred-square-kilometre swathe of native Fuegian forest, native grasslands, snow-tipped crags and icy waters, sitting by the Beagle Channel amid the Cordillera

---

KING PENGUINS IN TIERRA DEL FUEGO

A number of **king penguins**, whose colonies have previously not been found further north than the South Georgia islands and Antarctica, have made Chile's Tierra del Fuego their home. The originally sixteen or so penguins have now increased in number, making this a permanent little colony. The location, 15km south of the crossroads with the turn-off for Onaisín along the coastal road, is accessed via Estancia San Clemente, which is doing its best to protect the penguins.

The owners of San Clemente are working together with a Punta Arenas-based interest group (see p.392) keen to study the penguins' behaviour. Visitors coming by car will see the sign for **Parque Pingüino Rey** (Tues–Sun 11am–6pm; CH\$12,000). Tours are run by *Hostería Yendegaia* in Porvenir (p.423).

10

Darwin. Originally a cattle ranch, this piece of land had been turned into a nature reserve and great efforts have been made to restore its original ecosystem, in spite of the presence of feral horses and cows. In January 2014, Yendegaia was donated to the Chilean government as a new national park and its location directly between Chile's Parque Nacional Alberto de Agostini and Argentina's Parque Nacional Tierra del Fuego (see p.438) acts as a wildlife corridor. Though it is conceivable that visitors to the latter may eventually be able to cross over to Yendegaia, at research time Yendegaia was only accessible by boat (you can ask the weekly ferry between Puerto Williams and Punta Arenas to drop you off); you have to bring all your supplies with you and camping wild is the only option.

The horse trail that runs south from Lago Fagnano to Yendegaia is due to be turned into a proper road, ostensibly to connect the rest of Tierra del Fuego to Puerto Williams by regular ferry and to give visitors easier access to the southern fjords. The construction of the road is yet to commence.

CROSSING THE ARGENTINE BORDER

Via San Sebastián Note that there are two San Sebastiáns, one being the Chilean border post (daily 8am–10pm) with a fast-food stall and not much else, and the other being a fully fledged village further on in Argentina.

AROUND PORVENIR

ACCOMMODATION AND EATING

Estancia Camerón Lodge Near Camerón ☎2 2520 2024 & ☎61 221 5029, ⓦestanciacameronlodge.com. This cosy lodge, built of native wood and stone overlooking the Río Grande, was designed with serious anglers in mind; Lu, the host, is an extremely knowledgeable fishing guide, the four rooms are comfortable and centrally heated and the cuisine emphasizes fresh local produce. Price includes land/air transfer from Punta Arenas or Río Grande, Argentina, as well as all meals and alcoholic bevarages, lodging, fishing licences and guided angling excursions. Obligatory seven-day packages only. Jan to mid-April. US$9000

Lodge Deseado on Lago Deseado ☎09 9165 2564, ⓦlodgedeseado.cl. This intimate lodge consists of four cosy *cabañas* for a total of twelve guests and excursions ranging from brown trout fishing on Lago Fagnano and Deseado to snoeshoeing and cross-country skiing in winter. *Cabañas* CH$160,000

Isla Navarino

Apart from compact **Puerto Williams** and the even tinier fishing village of **Puerto Toro**, **ISLA NAVARINO**, the largish island to the south of Isla Grande, is an uninhabited wilderness studded with barren peaks and isolated valleys. Navarino is dominated by a dramatic range of peaks, the **Dientes del Navarino**, through which weaves a 70km hiking trail called the **Los Dientes Circuit**. What has spoiled some of the landscape, especially the woodland, however, is the devastation brought about by feral **beavers** (see box, p.423).

ARRIVAL AND DEPARTURE

ISLA NAVARINO

By plane Aerovías DAP has frequent flights from Punta Arenas to Puerto Williams (summer Mon–Sat 10am; winter less frequent; around CH$56,000 one way).

By boat The Transbordadora Austral Broom (ⓦtabsa.cl) ferry, *Yaghan*, sails between Punta Arenas and Puerto Williams (departing Punta Arenas Wed 6pm, returning from Puerto Williams Sat 4pm; 30hr; Pullman seat CH$98,000, berth CH$137,000). COMAPA (ⓦcomapa.com/

es/) also runs a four-day luxury cruise on the *Mare Australis* and the *Via Australis* (cheapest cabin from US$1420/person; ⓦaustralis.com), dropping anchor in Isla Navarino's Wulaia Bay. From Ushuaia, Ushuaia Boating (see p.434) and Piratour (see p.439) run daily eight-person Zodiac boats in summer (US$125 one way). You might also be able to catch a ride on a private yacht from Ushuaia's Yacht Club.

Puerto Williams and around

Although Ushuaia loudly proclaims its "end of the world" status, it suffers from geographical envy when it comes to **PUERTO WILLIAMS** that nestles in a small bay on the north shore of Isla Navarino, 82km due east and slightly south of Ushuaia along

THE YÁMANA, THE SELK'NAM, THE MÁNEKENK AND THE KAWÉSHKAR

Tierra del Fuego and Isla Navarino were originally home to the **Yámana (Yaghan),** the **Selk'nam (Ona),** the **Kawéshkar (Alacalúf)** and the Mánekenk (Haush). The Kawéshkar inhabited the Magellan Strait and the western fjords, the Selk'nam dominated Tierra del Fuego, the Mánekenk favoured Tierra del Fuego's southeastern tip, while the Yámana resided in the southern fjords and Isla Navarino. Unlike the hunter-gatherer Selk'nam and Mánekenk, the Yámana and the Kawéskar were both nomadic "Canoe Indians", living off fish, shellfish and marine animals. European sealing and whaling activities from the nineteenth century onwards tremendously depleted their main sources of nourishment and European-borne diseases decimated the indigenous population. The last Yámana speaker, Cristina Calderón, lives on Isla Navarino while the remote Puerto Edén is populated by the remaining Kawéshkar, and the descendants of the Selk'nam survive in Tolhuin and Río Grande in Argentina.

Though dismissed by European explorers as savages, the indigenous peoples had complex rituals. The Selk'nam performed a sophisticated **male initiation ceremony**, the *Hain*, during which the young male initiates, or *kloketens*, confronted and unmasked malevolent spirits that they had been taught to fear since their youth, emerging as *maars* (adults). Father Martín Gusinde was present at the last *Hain* ceremony in 1923, and managed to capture the event in a series of remarkable photographs, copies of which circulate as postcards today. Italian mountaineering priest and photographer, Alberto de Agostini, also sustained a long and fruitful relationship with the indigenous peoples of Tierra del Fuego.

10

the Beagle Channel, home to just over two thousand people. Originally founded as a military outpost, it's officially the capital of Chilean Antarctica. The compact, windblown settlement has a somewhat desolate quality to it even in the height of the brief summer, but the people are exceptionally warm and welcoming and you get a real sense of a close-knit community, brought together by isolation from the rest of Chile. Most businesses are concentrated in the **Centro Comercial**, by the Plaza O'Higgins.

Museo Antropológico Martín Gusinde
Aragay at Gusinde • Mon–Fri 9am–1pm & 2.30–7pm • Donations

In a smart blue building with a skeleton of a whale by the entrance, this excellent museum, named after the clergyman and anthropologist who spent a great deal of time among the indigenous peoples of Tierra del Fuego, you'll find a host of beautifully presented displays on the history, fauna and flora of the area. These include exhibits on Yámana life, complete with artefacts, photographs and accounts of their legends; an obligatory stuffed Fuegian fauna section; and maps that chart the exploration of the region, from the days of the Fuegian Indians, through the gold rush, to the commercial shipping of today. The spiral staircase is decorated with stunning close-ups of local wildlife.

Villa Ukika
A five-minute coastal walk east from Puerto Williams' new ferry ramp brings you to the hamlet of **Villa Ukika**, home to Cristina Calderón, the last Yámana speaker, aged 87. In 2005 she published a book of Yámana stories with the help of her granddaughter. The only object of note in Villa Ukika is the replica of a traditional dwelling – the **Kipa-Akar** (House of Woman); in summer it's open to visitors who can purchase traditional handicrafts – from miniature canoes to whalebone harpoons; ask around if you find it closed.

ARRIVAL AND DEPARTURE   **PUERTO WILLIAMS**

By plane On arrival at the tiny Aeródromo, you're met by a transfer van (CH$2500). Aerovías DAP has its office at the Centro Comercial Sur 151 (☎61 262 1114, ⊚aeroviasdap .cl); double-check flight departure times here. One-way flights to Punta Arenas cost around CH$50,000; book well ahead for the Dec or Feb peak season.

Destinations Punta Arenas (Nov–March 1 daily Mon–Sat at 11.30am; otherwise 3 weekly; 1hr 20min).

10

LOS DIENTES DE NAVARINO CIRCUIT

Many travellers come to Puerto Williams to complete the **Los Dientes de Navarino Circuit** challenge, a strenuous four- to seven-day hike in the Isla Navarino wilderness, where there is no infrastructure whatsoever, and you are faced with unpredictable weather as well as the rigours of the trail. This is for experienced hikers only and not to be attempted alone.

THE TRAIL

Follow Vía Uno west out of town; the trail starts behind the statue of the Virgin Mary in a grassy clearing. The road leads uphill to a waterfall and reservoir, from where a marked trail climbs steadily through the *coigüe* and *ñire* forest. It is a two-hour ascent to **Cerro Bandera**, a *mirador* with a wonderful view of the town, the Beagle Channel and the nearby mountains. The rest of the trail is not very well marked; there are 38 trail markers (rock piles) spread out over the 53km route, which entails crossing four significant passes and negotiating beaver dams in between.

Once past the starkly beautiful **Laguna El Salto**, you can either cross a fairly steep pass and make a detour to the south, to the remote expanse of Lago Windward, or head west to **Laguna de los Dientes**. Continue west past Lagunas Escondido, Hermosa and Matrillo before reaching the particularly steep and treacherous descent of **Arroyo Virginia**; beware of loose rocks. The trail markers end before Bahía Virginia, and you have to make your own way over pastures and through scrubland to the main road. The trail officially finishes 12km out of town, behind a former *estancia* owned by the MacLean family, which has been developed into a *centolla*- and shellfish-processing factory. From here you can follow the main road back to Puerto Williams or hitch a lift.

MAPS AND ESSENTIALS

The best map is the *Tierra del Fuego & Isla Navarino* satellite map by Zagier & Urruty Publications, available in Ushuaia in conjunction with GPS. Make sure you have plentiful food and water supplies (water on the island is not drinkable owing to the giardia carried by the beavers), sunscreen and warm and waterproof outdoor gear, and inform people in town of your plans before leaving.

GUIDED TREKS

If you prefer to have the benefit of a professional guide and logistical support, Fueguia & Co (see below) can advise on trail conditions and offer guided four-day treks for around CH$350,000 per person.

By boat Coming from Punta Arenas, you'll arrive at the ferry ramp on Av Costanera. Zodiac boats run by Ushuaia Boating (p.434) and Piratour (p.435) from Ushuaia disembark at Puerto Navarino on the west side of the island, where you pass through Chilean customs before an hour's ride in a minibus to Puerto Williams. The Puerto Williams ferry continues to Puerto Toro once a month. The Transbordadora Austral Broom office at Costanera 435 (☎61 262 1015, ⌨tabsa.cl) sells tickets for the Punta Arenas-bound ferry (CH$98,000/137,000 for *semi-cama/cama* seats). A minibus picks up passengers at their *hospedaje* to take them to Puerto Navarino in time to catch a boat to Ushuaia (weather permitting).

Destinations Punta Arenas (1 weekly on Sat; 30hr); Ushuaia (Dec–Feb 1 daily, weather permitting; 45min–1hr).

INFORMATION AND TOURS

TOURIST INFORMATION

Tourist information Inside the Municipalidad on O'Higgins (Mon–Fri 8.30am–1pm & 2–5pm; ☎61 241 2125). The helpful tourist information desk offers brochures on Puerto Williams and Cape Horn, but not maps of the Dientes de Navarino circuit. The Turismo Aventura Shila shop stocks basic maps of the Dientes de Navarino and camping equipment is available for rent.

TOUR OPERATORS

Fuegia & Co Patrullero Ortiz 49 ☎61 262 1251. Guided treks and logistical support in the Dientes de Navarino.

SIM Expeditions Casilla 6 ☎61 262 1150, ⌨simexpeditions.com. This intrepid German–Venezuelan operator runs highly recommended 2–3 week sailing trips to Cape Horn, South Georgia and Antarctica, as well as short jaunts on the Beagle Channel.

Victory Adventure Expeditions Teniente Muñoz 118 ☎61 222 7098, ⌨victory-cruises.com. Sailing expeditions around Cape Horn, along the Beagle Channel and even to Antarctica in schooner-style ships, run by Californian Ben Garrett.

ACCOMMODATION

With the exception of *Hotel Lakutaia* (see below) in an isolated location next to the airport, **accommodation** in Puerto Williams consists of private rooms and dorms inside family homes. Jan–March is peak season for hikers, so booking in advance is wise. Phoning is best, as most hostel owners do not have instant access to email.

Hostal Akainij Austral 22 ☎61 262 1173, ⓦturismoakainij.cl. Cosy en-suite rooms with down duvets, a cheerful living room filled with plants and friendly owners happy to arrange a plethora of excursions, make this an ideal midrange guesthouse to base yourself in. CH$35,000

Hostal Paso McKinlay Piloto Pardo 213 ☎61 262 1124. Though you can touch the walls of the corridor with both elbows if you stand with your hands on your hips, the six centrally heated doubles and singles at this friendly guesthouse are bright, comfortable and come equipped with cable TV. Bikes are available for rent and owners can pick you up from the airport. CH$35,000

Hotel Lakutaia ☎61 262 1721, ⓦlakutaia.cl. Near the airport and somewhat isolated from Puerto Williams proper as it's 2km west of town, the island's only hotel attracts active, well-heeled tourists with its multi-day wilderness excursions around the island, which include heliskiing in winter, guided hikes in the Dientes de Navarino and sailing around Cape Horn. Rooms are comfortable and the restaurant is decent; guests may also stay without participating in the all-inclusive programmes. US$250

Refugio El Padrino Av Costanera 276 ☎61 262 1136 or ☎09 8438 0843, ⓔceciliamancillao@yahoo.com.ar. A snug backpacker haven, this colourful hostel has a sign on the door inviting you to let yourself in and decide if you wish to stay. Most do; Cecilia, the owner, may not speak much English, but her genuine warmth transcends language barriers. Dorms CH$12,000

Residencial Pusaki Piloto Pardo 222 ☎61 262 1116, ⓔpattypusaki@yahoo.es. A perpetual traveller favourite with a warm family atmosphere and excellent home-cooked food. Even if you are not staying here, you can arrange to come for dinner, provided you give Patty a couple of hours' warning; *centolla* night is best. Dorms CH$10,000, doubles CH$30,000

EATING AND DRINKING

For those who wish to do their bit for the environment, Cecilia of *Refugio El Padrino* (see above) can organize a beaver-eating experience at a family home. Note that none of the below establishments is contactable by phone.

Mikalvi Av Constanera. Docked at the west end of the *costanera*, this ex-Navy supply ship with a markedly "old salt" atmosphere, flags of different countries covering the walls and a well-stocked bar often plays host to an eclectic mix of hikers, Antarctic explorers, international yachtsmen and local navy personnel. Sept–May Mon–Sat 9pm–2am.

La Pica de Castór Centro Comercial. Red brick walls hung with black-and-white photos and friendly staff dishing out hearty home-style cooking, such as roast chicken with mash and peas, attract locals and travellers alike. Mon–Sat 10am–10pm.

El Resto del Sur Ricardo Maragano 146. This is as close as Puerto Williams gets to dining sophistication, with pizzas sitting side by side on the menu with king crab dishes, locally-caught trout and more. Mon–Sat noon–10pm.

La Trattoria de Mateo Centro Comercial. Mellow reggae on the stereo, cheery lime green decor and chef Mattías's imaginative creations make this the nicest place to eat in town. Mains from CH$5500. Tues–Sat 1–3.30pm & 7–11pm.

DIRECTORY

Internet Some guesthouses offer excruciatingly slow internet. Your best bet is one of the computers at the museum (see p.427).

Money and exchange Banks Banco de Chile, located down a narrow passageway from the Centro Comercial towards the seafront, has an ATM, but it's best to bring plenty of cash.

Post office The post office is located in the Centro Comercial (Mon–Fri 10am–noon & 4–6pm).

Parque Etnobotánico Omora

Daylight hours • Donation • ⓦ omora.org

Near the start of the Los Dientes trail, 3km west of Puerto Williams, is the entrance to the experimental part-state, part-private enterprise **Parque Etnobotánico Omora**, named for the world's southernmost hummingbird. The park plays an educational and environmental role, protecting the *ñire* and *lenga* forest by, among other things, encouraging locals to cull beavers for their meat. Native birds, including the red-headed Magellanic woodpecker (*lana*) and the ruffed-legged owl (*kujurj*), are monitored, along with other endangered species of flora, fauna and plants along the trails, and labelled in Latin, Spanish and Yámana.

Puerto Toro

On the east side of the island lies **Puerto Toro**, a tiny fishing post inhabited by around seventy *centolla* fishermen and their families, complete with a school for all seven children and a police station. It is reachable only by boat; visitors can come here on a day-trip by taking the monthly ferry (see p.428) from Puerto Williams.

Cabo de Hornos (Cape Horn)

Directly south of Isla Navarino lies a cluster of islands, part of the **Cabo de Hornos biosphere reserve** – a staggering five million hectares of native forest, tundra, glaciers, fjords and tall black cliffs. This pristine marine habitat is set aside for strict conservation only; overnight stays are not permitted.

Ushuaia

Meaning "westward-looking bay" in the indigenous Yámana tongue, **USHUAIA** lies hemmed in between the Sierra Venciguerra range and the deep blue of the icy **Beagle Channel** – arguably the most dramatic location of all Argentine cities, with colourful houses tumbling down the hillside to the wide, encircling arm of land that protects its bay from the southwesterly winds. San Martín is the town's main thoroughfare, and most visitors without their own transport stick to the compact grid of streets in Ushuaia's centre.

Brief history

In 1869, Reverend Waite Stirling became Tierra del Fuego's first white settler when he founded his **Anglican mission** among the Yámana here. Stirling stayed for six months before being recalled to the Falklands Islands to be appointed Anglican bishop for South America. Thomas Bridges, his assistant, returned to take over the mission in 1871, after which time Ushuaia began to figure on mariners' charts as a place of refuge in the event of shipwreck. In 1896, in order to consolidate its sovereignty and open up the region to wider colonization, the Argentine government used a popular nineteenth-century tactic and established a **penal colony** here, eventually closed by Perón in 1947.

ROUND THE HORN BY SEA AND AIR

For centuries the treacherous icy waters surrounding the islands of **Cape Horn** captured the imagination of sailors and adventurers, not least because they constitute the biggest ship graveyard in the Americas: on old nautical maps, the waters around the islands are littered with tiny pictures of sunken ships. Today, Cape Horn still presents a sizeable challenge for experienced sailors and travellers alike, many of whom, having come this far south, can't resist going all the way round.

SIM (see p.428) and Victory Adventure Expeditions (see p.428) are good places to enquire about **sailing trips**. Weather permitting, you disembark on a shingle beach, climb a rickety ladder and visit the tiny Chilean naval base, lighthouse and chapel; a statue of an albatross overlooks the stormy waters beyond. Aerovías DAP (see p.426) and the local flying clubs run fairly expensive (around CH$650,000 per small chartered plane) half-hour flights from both Punta Arenas and Puerto Williams that do a loop and return without landing. These air excursions treat you to incredible views of Isla Navarino and the Darwin peaks. Weather is a vital factor.

HOW THE CAPE FOUND ITS HORN

In January 1616, the cape was christened Hoorn by the Dutchmen **Willem Schouten** and **Jacob Le Maire** who passed by aboard the *Unity*, in honour of another ship of theirs that got shipwrecked off the coast of Argentina. In time, the Spanish changed the name to **Cabo de Hornos**, which was corrupted in turn to Cape Horn.

10

Plaza Islas Malvinas

Maipú, between Sarmiento and Patagonia

Created to commemorate the thirtieth anniversary of the Falklands War, this memorial square honours, by keeping an eternal flame burning, the 649 Argentinian military personnel who died in the conflict that was started by Argentina invading the islands on 5 April, 1982. It also reinstates the dubious Argentinian claim on the Falkland Islands – British Crown territory since 1841 – as well as South Georgia and the South Sandwich Islands. Dramatic, blown-up black-and-white photographs of the conflict and emotional moments between Argentinian soldiers and their families fringe the square.

Museo Yámana

Rivadavia 56 • Daily: summer 9am–8pm; winter noon–7pm • AR$60

A small gem, **Museo Yámana** explores the remarkable lifestyle, classless society and gender equality practised by the Yámana people who have lived along the Tierra del Fuego coast for over seven thousand years, getting by through fishing, hunting for seals and whales, and diving for shellfish. Intricate dioramas recreate scenes from their harsh lives and there are some original bone harpoons on display. The last part of the display deals with the founding of the 1869 Anglican mission, which led to a rapid decrease in the native population through the introduction of European-borne diseases.

Museo del Fin del Mundo

Maipú 175 • Mon 2–7pm, Tues–Fri 10am–7pm, Sat & Sun 2–8pm • AR$90

Along the seafront you'll find this small museum, with exhibits on the region's native peoples – the Yámana, Selk'nam, Kawéshkar, and the arrival of the missionaries. There's a thorough section on birdlife, complete with dozens of stuffed specimens, and a rare example of the Selk'nam–Spanish dictionary written by the Salesian missionary, José María Beauvoir. The ghostly figurehead of the *Duchess of Albany*, a ship wrecked on the eastern end of the island in 1893, looks on overhead.

Museo Marítimo & Museo del Presidio

Yaganes at Gobernador Paz • Daily 10am–8pm • AR$150 • Ⓦ museomaritimo.com

The star attraction within the town itself is undoubtedly the imposing former
between 1902 and 1920 and home to the **Museo Marítimo**
exhibits, ranging from Antarctic wildlife and exploration of
ryday life in the prison and its most notorious inhabitants,
cells along three of the five wings that radiate from the
kes from a half-wheel. Most engaging are the scale models
e island's history; spot a ship made entirely out of
he inmates. The most celebrated prisoner to stay here was
anarchist Simón Radowitzky, whose miserable incarceration
scape in 1918 are recounted by Bruce Chatwin in *In*

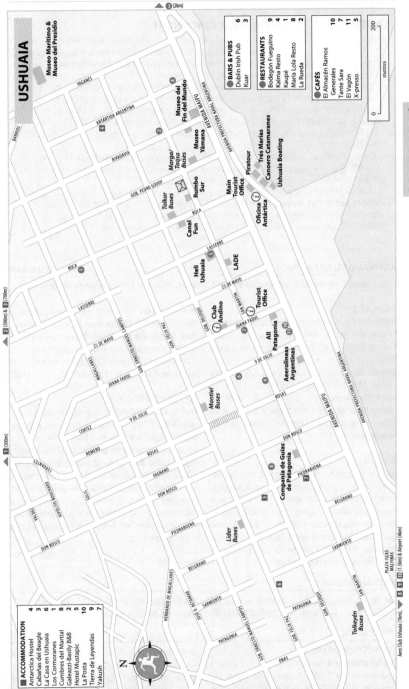

USHUAIA

Museo Marítimo &
Museo del Presidio

(2km)

BARS & PUBS
Dublin Irish Pub 6
Kuar 3

RESTAURANTS
Bodegón Fueguino 9
Kalma Resto 4
Kaupé 1
María Lola Resto 8
La Rueda 2

CAFÉS
El Almacén Ramos
Generales 10
Tante Sara 7
El Vagón 11
X-presso 5

0   metres   200

10

ACCOMMODATION
Antarctica Hostel 4
Cabañas del Beagle 3
La Casa en Ushuaia 6
Los Cormoranes 1
Cumbres del Martial 8
Galeazzi-Basily B&B 2
Hotel Mustapic 5
La Posta 10
Tierra de Leyendas 9
Yakush 7

10

ANTARCTICA – THE REMOTEST CONTINENT

Every year, over 35,000 people pass through Ushuaia en route to Antarctica's floating, mountain-sized "ice cathedrals" and glaciers spilling from pristine mountains to observe killer and minke whales, elephant and leopard seals and emperor, king and macaroni penguins.

The **Antarctic tourist season** runs from November until mid-March and cruises last between 10 and 21 days. Typical destinations include the Antarctic continent, the South Georgia Islands and the Falkland Islands. When choosing the length of the cruise and type of vessel, bear in mind that the crossing of the Drake Passage alone takes at least two days one-way. The smaller the ship and the fewer the passengers, the more shore landings there are per passenger, though smaller vessels are more vulnerable to the notoriously stormy Drake Passage crossing.

Cruise prices start from US$4300 (the last-minute bargain price) and run into six figures, depending on the length of the trip and the level of comfort. Those trying to get a last-minute bargain need to have weeks of free time at their disposal.

Check at the Antarctica office for last-minute cruise deals. A hugely experienced operator, Alicia Petiet of **Antarctica Travels** at San Martín 1306, Ushuaia (☎02901 586016, ⌨antarcticatravels .com) and other members of IAATO (International Association of Antarctica Tour Operators; ⌨iaato.org) specialize in safe and environmentally responsible travel to Antarctica.

ARRIVAL AND DEPARTURE   USHUAIA

In peak season it's a good idea to book your bus or plane ticket well in advance, as demand frequently outstrips supply.

BY PLANE

From Ushuaia there are frequent flights to Río Gallegos, El Calafate and Buenos Aires. The international airport, Malvinas Argentinas, sits 4km southwest of town; a taxi to the centre costs about AR$55–75.

Airlines Aerolineas Argentinas, Maipú 823 (☎02901 436586); LADE, San Martín 542 (☎02901 421123).

Destinations Buenos Aires (2–3 daily; 3hr 30min); El Calafate (1–2 daily; 2hr 15min, longer if stopover at Río Gallegos); Puerto Madryn, Argentina (3 weekly; 2hr); Río Gallegos (4 weekly; 1hr).

BY BUS

Frequent bus services run via Chile to both Argentine and Chilean destinations, setting off either at 5am or 8am daily. All long-distance bus rides entail a short ferry ride at Primera Angostura (see p.391). Buses arrive and depart from their companies' respective offices. Buses Pacheco, Bus Sur and Tecni Austral run to Punta Arenas, Bus Sur carries on to Puerto Natales; Río Gallegos is served by Taqsa; change there for buses to El Calafate.

Bus companies Tecni Austral – book through Tolkar at Roca 157 (☎02901 431408); Buses Pacheco and Bus Sur – book through Tolkeyen at San Martín 1267 (☎02901 437073); Marga/Taqsa, Gob. Godoy 41 (☎02901 435453).

Destinations Río Gallegos (1 daily; 12hr); Punta Arenas (1–2 daily; 12hr); Puerto Natales (1 daily via Punta Arenas; 15hr).

BY FERRY & BOAT

Cruceros Australis (⌨australis.com) runs scheduled luxury cruise ships (at least 1 weekly) to Punta Arenas, with trips lasting 4 days/3 nights. To cross from Ushuaia to Puerto Williams, Isla Navarino, the only option is to take an eight-person zodiac boat with Ushuaia Boating (☎02901 436193) or Piratour (☎02901 424834, ⌨piratour.com.ar). One-way tickets cost US$125 and the zodiac boats are notoriously weather-dependent; crossings can be a rollercoaster ride and if it's too windy, they can be delayed for hours and sometimes days. Both companies have kiosks at the Muelle Touristico.

Destinations Puerto Williams (Nov–April daily; 45min–1hr).

GETTING AROUND

Car rental Alamo Rent a Car, Belgrano 96 (☎02901 431131); Hertz, San Martín 409 (☎02901 437529); Patagonia Sur Rent a Car, 9 de Julio 423 (☎02901 440385). Rental rates, including insurance, start at AR$590/day.

INFORMATION AND TOURS

TOURIST INFORMATION

Tourist office The main tourist office is at Av Prefectura Naval Argentina 470 (Mon–Fri 9am–10pm, Sat & Sun 9am–8pm; ☎02901 437666, ⌨turismoushuaia.com), by the passenger boat terminal. The smaller office at Martín 674 (☎02901 424550) was closed for refurbishment at the time of writing. There's also an information kiosk at the airport, which opens to meet incoming flights.

Oficina Antártica Maipú 505, opposite the Muelle Turístico (Mon–Fri 8am–4pm, weekends if there is a boat that day; ☎02901 421423). This ultra-helpful office specializes in information on Antarctica and Antarctic cruises, and provides a list of approved International Association of Antarctica Tour Operators (ⓦiaato.org).

Club Andino Fadúl 50 (Mon–Fri 10am–noon & 3–8.30pm; ☎02901 422335, ⓦwww.clubandinoushuaia .com.ar). Trekking and climbing information office. Skiing and snowboarding also offered.

TOUR OPERATORS

Ushuaia is Tierra del Fuego's outdoor activity centre and there are a number of companies which offer everything from conventional city tours and boat outings on the Beagle Channel to rock climbing, 4WD adventures, horseriding and diving. Recommended operators listed below.

Aero Club Ushuaia Luis Pedro Fique 151 ☎02901 421717, ⓦaeroclubushuaia.com.ar. Two spectacular six-seater plane circuits on offer: the 30min circuit takes in Parque Nacional Tierra del Fuego and the Faro Les Éclaireurs, while the hour-long flight covers the length of the Beagle Channel up to Estancia Harberton as well as part of Lago Fagnano and Lago Escondido.

Canal Fun Roca 136 ☎02901 435777, ⓦcanalfun .com. Runs 4WD trips to Lago Fagnano, complete with barbecue, as well as kayaking trips. Excellent horseriding centre with free transfers from town. Choose from half- and full-day excursions (the latter with *asado*); multi-day trips also available on request.

Canoero Catamaranes Ushuaia Muelle Turístico ☎02901 433893, ⓦcatamaranescanoero.com.ar. High-quality, standard 5hr trips on a two-tiered catamaran along the Beagle Channel, taking in the bird life of Isla de Pájaros, a sea-lion colony, the Magellanic and Papua penguins of Isla Martillo, and the Faro Les Éclaireurs.

Chimango ☎02901 1560 5673. Take to the streets of Ushuaia as part of a morning bike tour, or else join the night-biking-and-barbecue combo.

Compañía de Guías de Patagonia San Martín 628 ☎02901 437753. Experienced agency that runs multi-day trekking trips in Tierra del Fuego and arranges ice- and rock-climbing.

Heli Ushuaia San Martín at Lasserre ☎02901 444444, ⓦheliushuaia.com.ar. Scenic helicopter circuits (7–45min), the shortest covering the city highlights, and the other three taking in various combinations of natural highlights around Ushuaia.

Piratour Muelle Turístico ☎02901 424834, ⓦpiratour .net. The only boat company authorized to offer a walk with the Magellanic penguins on Isla Martillo, which allows you to see the birds from up close.

Tres Marías Muelle Turístico ☎02901 436416, ⓦtresmariasweb.com. The only boat company allowed to land on Isla H, taking only eight passengers at a time on hiking/birding excursions.

Ushuaia Divers Muelle Turístico ☎02901 444701, ⓦtierradelfuego.org.ar/divers. Reputable operator runs diving trips in the frigid Beagle Channel to see shipwrecks, sea lions and king crabs.

ACCOMMODATION

Ushuaia offers a good range of hotels and hostels, most on the first four streets parallel to the bay, with the more exclusive options up in the foothills or further out of town along the waterfront. Dec to Feb is peak season for Antarctica-bound travellers and backpackers alike, so book all **accommodation** well in advance.

HOTELS AND B&BS

La Casa en Ushuaia Gob Paz 1380 ☎02901 423202, ⓦlacasaenushuaia.com. Run by the helpful, trilingual Silvia, this set of comfortable, cream-coloured doubles benefits from its central location, good breakfast and plenty of city-related info on hand. Solo travellers get an AR$160 discount and the only downside is the ratio of rooms per shared bathroom. U̲S̲$̲8̲1̲

★**Galeazzi-Basily B&B** Gob Valdéz 323 ☎02901 423213, ⓦwww.avesdelsur.com.ar. This guesthouse, run by the warm and hospitable, English- and French-speaking Frances and Alejandro, is an excellent place to meet fellow travellers without sacrificing comfort or privacy. Besides the twin and a double there are two fully equipped *cabañas* which sleep up to four people. Doubles U̲S̲$̲8̲1̲, cabañas U̲S̲$̲1̲6̲0̲

Hotel Mustapic Piedrabuena 230 ☎02901 423557, ⓦushuaiamustapic.com. This venerable hotel is showing its age; its rooms are rather spare and compact compared to the large bathrooms and the wi-fi comes and goes as it pleases. On the upside, it's central, warm, with friendly and helpful service, and all-encompassing views of the Beagle Channel from its light-filled breakfast area. U̲S̲$̲1̲1̲0̲

★**Tierra de Leyendas** Tierra de Vientos 2448 ☎02901 446565, ⓦtierradeleyendas.com.ar. Southwest of the centre, this small boutique hotel gives you a choice between two views: the sea or the mountains. Besides the splendid location, the deluxe rooms all come with Jacuzzis and the superb on-site restaurant (not just for guests) serves a buffet breakfast (included in the price) and fusion dishes. Airport pickup available. U̲S̲$̲2̲0̲8̲

LODGES AND CABAÑAS

★**Cabañas del Beagle** Las Aljabas 375 ☎02901 432785, ⓦcabanasdelbeagle.com. These three luxurious split-level *cabañas*, lovingly constructed from local stone

10

and wood by the indomitable Alejandro, are a perfect retreat from the downtown hustle and bustle. Each self-catering *cabaña* sleeps up to four people and comes equipped with underfloor heating, enormous fireplace, kitchenette and Jacuzzi bathtub, and your attentive hosts are always on hand to make your stay more comfortable. Two-night minimum stays; discounts for longer stays. *Cabañas* US$580

Cumbres del Martial Luis F. Martial Km5 ☎02901 424779, ⓦcumbresdelmartial.com.ar. At this secluded mountain lodge, you can reside either in one of the six luxurious rooms, complete with king-sized beds and state-of-the-art bathrooms, or retreat with your loved one to one of the four deluxe split-level *cabañas*, built out of native wood and stone, and equipped with large fireplaces. Non-guests can also stop by the *Tea House* for a wide range of teas and sumptuous cakes. Doubles US$332, *cabañas* US$477

HOSTELS

Antarctica Hostel Antártida Argentina 270 ☎02901 435774, ⓦantarcticahostel.com. This hostel's best feature is the huge, light-drenched lounge with colourful wall hangings, mini-library, guitars for guest use and a bona fide bar serving a range of beers and cocktails. However, the plain upstairs dorms are a bit of a hike from the downstairs bathrooms. Dorms US$20, doubles US$57

Los Cormoranes Kamshen 788 ☎02901 423459, ⓦloscormoranes.com. A stiff hike (or short cab ride) uphill from the city, this hostel has plenty *buena onda* (good vibes), a traveller-magnet lounge for swapping stories from the road and lovely, helpful staff. The facilities are a bit worn and could use refurbishing, but some rooms have great city views and breakfast includes make-your-own eggs and fresh oranges for squeezing. Dorms US$21

La Posta Perón Sur 864 ☎02901 444650, ⓦlapostahostel.com.ar. A flat 30min walk (or AR$15 cab ride) from downtown, this lovely family-run hostel has facilities more akin to a hotel than a backpacker joint: two kitchens, free laundry, well-scrubbed dorms, private rooms and self-contained apartments. There's a tangible sense of guest camaraderie and Lucas the owner is a treasure trove of local knowledge. Dorms US$24, doubles US$72, apartments US$125

Yakush San Martín at Piedrabuena ☎02901 435807. Spacious and with good guest chillout areas, this central hostel gets high marks for the helpfulness of its staff. The dorms are roomy enough to spread out in, one of the doubles is en suite and breakfast is good if unexceptional. Dorms US$23, doubles US$73

EATING AND DRINKING

CAFÉS

El Almacén Ramos Generales Av Maipú 749 ☎02901 424317. At this half-museum, half-café/bakery, the antique-dotted surroundings are as much of a draw as the hearty soups, sandwiches, cakes and *picadas* (shared platters; from AR$170). See if you can spot the porcelain chamber pots, the splendid antique bank till and the harlequin doll peeking out of a chest. Daily 9am–midnight.

Tante Sara San Martín at Fadúl ☎02901 423912. Aunt Sara must be a busy woman, judging from the perpetually full interior of this spacious, shiny *confitería* and *panadería*, which does a fine line in cakes, sandwiches and salads, as well as decent coffee (AR$24). Skip the mediocre pasta, though. Mon–Thurs & Sun 8am–8.30pm, Fri & Sat 8am–9pm.

El Vagón Av Maipú 771. Decked out like an antique, wood-panelled train carriage, with glimpses of labouring convicts out of the 'windows', this café offers its 'passengers' an inexpensive menu of burgers, *milanesas* and *picadas* (mains from AR$80). Or else you just sip your *mate* or coffee while making use of the free wi-fi. Mon–Fri 8am–1am, Sat 10am–1am.

X-presso San Martín at Lasserre. Grab a cupcake, quiche, good coffee, salad or hefty sandwich at this spacious modern café which shares the premises with Heli Ushuaia (see p.435). Daily 9.30am–6pm.

RESTAURANTS

Bodegón Fueguino San Martín 859 ☎02901 431972. Park yourself down on a sheepskin-draped wooden bench in this historic wooden house (built in 1896) and order the likes of lamb with orange and honey sauce or pork leg with mustard and sweet potato croquettes. Good home-brewed beer too. Mains AR$105–186. Tues–Sun 12.30–3pm & 8pm–midnight.

★**Kalma Resto** Antártida Argentina 57 ☎02901 425786, ⓦkalmaresto.com.ar. Still the culinary king of Ushuaia, young chef Jorge comes out to explain the dishes to diners at this intimate, black linen-draped restaurant. His menu changes depending on seasonal availability of local ingredients, but you may be treated to the likes of crab and roast pumpkin ravioli with saffron sauce, his signature *merluza negra* (black hake) and the 'deconstructed' *chocotorta*. The presentation and service is flawless, dishes are often adorned with edible flowers and delicate sauces; if you're going to splurge on a meal in Argentina, do it here. Mains from AR$140. Reservations essential. Mon–Fri 12.30–3pm & 7–11.30pm, Sat 7–11.30pm.

10

★**Kaupé** Roca 470 ☎02901 422704, ⦿kaupe.com.ar. This stylish, well-established hilltop restaurant still holds its own against the newcomers thanks to the efforts of chef Ernesto, who works wonders with *centolla* and *merluza negra* dishes, and the extensive wine list. Non-pescetarians can opt for steak flambéed in cognac whereas seafood lovers are treated to the likes of king crab crepes in saffron sauce. Reservations recommended. Mon–Sat 1–3pm & 7.30–11.30pm, Sun 1–3.30pm.

María Lola Resto Deloqui 1048 ☎02901 421185, ⦿marialolaresto.com.ar. Besides its superlative hilltop views of the bay, this slick, professional restaurant really delivers when it comes to creative and classic dishes. Feast yourself on the likes of pumpkin ravioli with blue cheese, southern sea bass with ginger and Fuegian lamb (mains from AR$150); each dish is thoughtfully paired with a wine. Mon–Sat 12.30–2.30pm & 8–11.30pm.

★**La Rueda** San Martín at Rivadavia ☎02901 436540. This all-you-can-eat *parrilla* gets our vote as the best place in Ushuaia to get your fill of spit-roasted lamb, chorizo, beef, chicken, *morcilla* (black pudding) and *chinchulines* (crispy lamb chitterlings), with bottomless salads thrown in (AR$230), and a la carte meaty choices if you're too famished. Daily noon–11pm.

BARS AND PUBS

Dublin Irish Pub 9 de Julio at Deloqui. This traveller favourite draws Guinness drinkers by the dozen. Lively spot for meeting people and the occasional performance by local bands. Daily 8pm–late.

★**Kuar** Perito Moreno 2232 ☎02901 437396. Set in an attractive stone-and-timber building right on the seafront, on the road to Río Grande, this resto-bar has stupendous views and a blazing fire, as well as imaginative fish and pasta dishes, locally-smoked meaty and fishy delights, their own delicious home-brewed pale ale, amber ale and dark porter (each around AR$55), and an extensive wine list. Daily 3pm–4am.

DIRECTORY

Hospital The regional hospital is at Maipú and 12 de Octubre (☎02901 423200).

Money and exchange ATMs at most banks, most of which are along San Martín; there's also the HSBC at Maipú and Godoy.

Pharmacy Several pharmacies are located along San Martín.

Post office San Martín at Godoy (Mon–Fri 9am–noon & 2–7pm, Sat 9am–1pm).

Around Ushuaia

Beyond the city limits, the nature trails of Parque Nacional Tierra del Fuego, the spectacular Beagle Channel, the historic Estancia Harberton and the snow-covered slopes of Cerro Castor beckon travellers.

Cerro Martial and Glaciar Martial

Chairlift closed indefinitely for maintenance at the time of writing • Minibuses depart from the corner of Fadúl and Maipú (every 30min, 8.30am–6.30pm)

There are lofty views of Ushuaia and the Beagle Channel from the base of **Glaciar Martial**, a receding glacier that's accessed from the top of the 7km road that winds up **Cerro Martial** from the city. From the car park at the top, it should be possible to take the chairlift part of the way; it's then a further one-hour-thirty-minute uphill hike (or a two-hour hike up without the chairlift) and scramble to the base of the glacier. Views of the channel below are even better than the glacier itself. A charming mountain *refugio* sells snacks, coffee and mulled wine at the bottom of the chairlift and canopy tours are on offer in peak season, consisting of eleven zip lines (⦿canopyushuaia.com.ar; AR$230–320).

Beagle Channel

Boats depart from Ushuaia's Muelle Turístico; several companies run tours of the channel (see p.435)

No visit to Ushuaia is complete without a journey on the **BEAGLE CHANNEL**, the majestic, mountain-fringed sea passage to the south of the city. Most **boat trips** start and finish in Ushuaia, and you can enjoy the best views of the town looking back at it

WINTER SPORTS AROUND USHUAIA

To ski at the end of the world, come sometime between June and early September (though not in July if you wish to avoid the holidaying crowds) and head for **Cerro Castór** (full-day tickets AR$470), the only Alpine ski resort in the area, located 26km away from Ushuaia along the RN3 and boasting powder snow as well as 24km of ski runs. The fifteen slopes feature a good mix of runs catering to beginners, advanced and everything in between, and you can rent skis, boards and cross-country skis at the resort; equipment costs between AR$90 and AR$200 per day. Ask at the tourist office about transport to and from Ushuaia. If cross-country skiing is your passion, you won't want to miss the annual **Marcha Blanca** (w marchablanca .com), the ski marathon that symbolically recreates General San Martín's crossing of the Andes.

If you have your own transport there are a couple of other nearby attractions: **Nunatak Adventure** (t 02901 430329, w nunatakadventure.com/index.htm) runs a host of winter activities from the Tierra Valle Mayor centre, 20km from Ushuaia, which include cross-country skiing, short husky sledding trips, and Snow Cat safaris. In the same valley you'll come across the **Valle de Lobos** (t 015 612319, w valledelobos.com), 18km out of Ushuaia. This breeding centre for seventy or so huskies (husky rides available in the winter; open for visits in the summer) was part of owner Gato Cruchet's dream to take part in Alaska's challenging 1800km Iditarod race; he was the first South American contestant to do so.

10

from the straits. Most tours visit Les Éclaireurs Lighthouse – previously thought to be the Lighthouse at the End of the World from Jules Verne's namesake novel. Other popular destinations include Isla de los Pájaros, Isla de los Lobos, Estancia Harberton, the penguin colony on Isla Martillo and Parque Nacional Tierra del Fuego. The main draw of these excursions is the chance to spot the **marine wildlife** that lives along the channel, including albatrosses, giant petrels, skuas, cormorants, South American terns and Magellanic penguins; resident sea mammals are sea lions, Peale's dolphins, minke whales and, if you're lucky, killer whales. Tours returning by land from Estancia Harberton stop by the **árboles banderas** – trees bent sideways by the fierce Patagonian wind, known as the *Escoba de Díos* (God's Broom).

Estancia Harberton

85km east of Ushuaia along the scenic RN3 then Route J (Ruta 33) **Estancia** Daily mid-Oct to mid-April 10am–7pm; guided tours daily at 11am, 1.30pm, 3pm & 5pm • AR$150 • w estanciaharberton.com **Museo Acatushún** Daily 10am–7pm; five tours daily • w acatushun.com

The first ranch to be founded in Tierra del Fuego, **ESTANCIA HARBERTON** is an ordered assortment of whitewashed buildings on the shores of a sheltered bay, named after Bridges' home village of Harberton in Devon, near Totnes. The estancia was built in 1886 by the Reverend Thomas Bridges, author of the Yámana–English dictionary, and served as a voluntary refuge for groups of Yámana, Selk'nam and Manékenk. Its location was immortalized in the *Uttermost Part of the Earth*, the evocative memoir written by Thomas's son Lucas.

It is now run as a museum by his great-grandson, Tommy Goodall, and bilingual tours of the grounds include sampling and identification of local flora and viewing the estancia's cemetery. If you're staying as a guest at the estancia, you can take part in a number of tours, including trekking in the Harberton and Cambaceres Peninsulas (see website for more details) and full-moon barbecues. If you come to Harberton by boat, you stop at Reserva Yécapasela on Isla Martillo, also known as **Penguin Island**, along the way, home to Magellanic and gentoo penguins and a large shag colony; only Piratour customers are allowed to disembark on the island (see p.435).

Museo Acatushún

Tommy Goodall's wife, Nathalie, is a renowned biologist responsible for the impressive marine mammal museum, **Museo Acatushún**. The museum features murals and

10

skeletons of large marine fauna – whales, dolphins, and more, their remains recovered after the animals were left stranded at Bahía San Sebastián, the pride and joy of the collection being the rare Hector's beaked whale. You can wander around the museum by yourself, learning about the behaviour and anatomy of the animals, or you can take one of the excellent tours in English.

ARRIVAL AND DEPARTURE	ESTANCIA HARBERTON

By bus Daily buses run from the corner of Maipú and 25 de Mayo in Ushuaia (departing at 9am and coming back around 3pm); the return fare is around AR$450.

By boat Several tour companies (see p.435) run boat tours of the Beagle Channel, which include a stop at Estancia Harberton.

ACCOMMODATION AND EATING

Estancia Harberton ⓦ estanciaharberton.com (reservations by Skype or email). It's possible to stay on the estancia itself, in semi-rustic but comfortable accommodation, either private rooms inside the *Old Shepherd's House* or a hostel bed in the shared *Foreman's House*. Those staying in the private rooms have a choice of either half-board (which includes the cost of some

activities) or full board. Dorms US$50, doubles half-board US$260, doubles full board US$290

The Tea House Incredibly popular with visitors, this café serves afternoon tea with large helpings of rhubarb, lemon and chocolate cake, scones and home-made jams. Daily 9.30am–6.30pm.

Parque Nacional Tierra del Fuego

12km west of Ushuaia • Summer daily 8am–8pm; reduced hours in winter • AR$140

The **PARQUE NACIONAL TIERRA DEL FUEGO** protects 630 square kilometres of jagged mountains, intricate lakes, southern beech forest, swampy peat bog, sub-Antarctic tundra and verdant coastline. The park stretches along the frontier with Chile, from the Beagle Channel to the **Sierra de Injugoyen** north of Lago

PARQUE NACIONAL TIERRA DEL FUEGO

Fagnano, but only the southernmost quarter is open to the public, accessed by the RN-3 from Ushuaia.

There are three main sectors: Bahía Ensenada and Río Pipo in the east; Lago Roca further to the west; and the Lapataia area to the south of Lago Roca, which includes Laguna Verde and, at the end of RN-3, Bahía Lapataia on the Beagle Channel. Here you may see **birds** such as Magellanic woodpeckers, condors, torrent ducks, steamer ducks, upland geese and buff-necked ibises, and **mammals** such as guanacos, the rare sea otter, Patagonian grey foxes and their larger, endangered cousin, the native Fuegian fox once heavily hunted for its pelt. Introduced Canadian beavers (see box, p.423) and European rabbits also run amok, wreaking environmental havoc.

The park offers several beautiful **trails**, ideal for short excursions or day hikes.

Bahía Ensenada and Senda Costera

The small **BAHÍA ENSENADA**, 2km south of the crossroads by the Tren del Fin del Mundo train station, is where you'll find the jetty for boats (no fixed schedule) to Lapataia and the Isla Redonda. It's also the trailhead for one of the most pleasant walks in the park, the **Senda Costera** (8km; 4hr), which starts at the jetty and follows the shore of Bahía Ensenada through dense coastal forest of evergreen beech, winter's bark and *lenga*, meeting the RN3 near the Lapataia park administration centre. It affords spectacular views of the Beagle Channel, passing grass-covered mounds that were former campsites of the indigenous Yámana.

Cerro Guanaco

A more challenging trek is the climb up **CERRO GUANACO** (8km; 3hr), the 973m-high mountain ridge on the north side of Lago Roca. Take the Hito XXIV path from the car park at Lago Roca and after ten minutes you'll cross a small bridge over a stream. Immediately afterwards, the path forks: to the left, **Senda Hito XXIV** runs along the northeastern shore of Lago Roca to an obelisk that marks Argentina's border with Chile (3.5km, 1hr 30min one way). To the right, **Senda Cerro Guanaco** runs right up the slope to the summit of its namesake peak.

The path up the forested mountainside is steep, and parts are boggy. The view from the crest to the south is memorable: the tangle of islands and rivers of the Archipiélago Cormoranes, Lapataia's sinuous curves, the Isla Redonda in the Beagle Channel, and across to the Chilean islands, Hoste and Navarino, separated by the Murray Narrows.

ARRIVAL AND INFORMATION	**PARQUE NACIONAL TIERRA DEL FUEGO**

By bus Regular high season buses (every 30–40min, 9am–6pm; 20–30min) depart from the corner of Maipú and Fadúl in Ushuaia for various points in the park. Services are reduced during off-season.

By train El Tren del Fin del Mundo is a scenic ride on the narrow-gauge train that used to transport wood in the days of the penal colony, departing from its main station, 8km west of Ushuaia (3 daily at 9am, noon – conditional – & 3pm; 50min each way; AR$380 round trip; ticket office at the Muelle Turístico; ☎02901 431600,

ⓦ trendelfindelmundo.com.ar) and arriving at the park station, 2km from the main gate.

By taxi It's only worth taking a taxi from Ushuaia if there are four of you.

Park office By the park entrance (daily 8am–8pm in summer; reduced hours in winter.) Offers a map of the park in exchange for your entrance fee; if you're planning to come back the following day, let the staff know, and you won't have to pay the fee twice.

Easter Island and the Juan Fernández Archipelago

444 Easter Island

460 The Juan Fernández Archipelago

MOAI, AHU TONGARIKI, EASTER ISLAND

Easter Island and the Juan Fernández Archipelago

Chile's two remote island territories, enchanting Easter Island and the virtually unknown Juan Fernández Archipelago, are collectively referred to as the Islas Esporádicas ("Far Flung Isles"). Both are national parks and have been singled out by UNESCO for special protection. Neither is easy to get to, and most travellers never do, but those who make the journeys will find their efforts and expenditure richly rewarded with a set of tantalizingly enigmatic statues and one of the world's most precarious ecosystems, respectively.

11

Lost in the vastness of the ocean, tiny **Easter Island** (or, in Spanish, Isla de Pascua) remains a world unto itself, its closest inhabited neighbour being Pitcairn Island, 2250km northwest. Spanning just 23km at its longest stretch, the island is triangular, with low-lying extinct volcanoes rising out of each corner. Scattered between these points are dozens of **moai**, the intriguing monolithic stone **statues** that have made the island universally famous.

Much closer to the mainland, at a mere 675km west of Valparaíso, but still relatively unknown, the **Juan Fernández Archipelago** is, ironically, far more difficult to reach. With their sharp, jagged peaks, coated in lush, deep-green foliage, the islands boast a topography that is among the most spectacular in Chile.

The archipelago's largest and only permanently inhabited island – **Isla Robinson Crusoe** – started out as a pirates' refuge. In 1709 it was brought to public attention when Scottish seaman Alexander Selkirk was rescued from its shores after being marooned there for more than four years – his story was used as the basis for *The Adventures of Robinson Crusoe* (see p.507). Today the Juan Fernández Archipelago remains an adventurous destination, well off the beaten track.

Easter Island

One of the most remote places on earth, tiny **EASTER ISLAND** is home to some seven thousand people. Around half are indigenous (who generally refer to themselves as Rapa Nui; mainland Chileans call them *pascuenses*), with the rest being mainly *continentales* (mainland Chilean immigrants). The Rapa Nui have fine-boned Polynesian features and speak their own Polynesian-based language (also called Rapa Nui) in addition to Spanish. Virtually the entire population lives in the island's single settlement, **Hanga Roa**, and most islanders make their living from tourism, which has been growing steadily ever since an airstrip was built here in 1968.

Where did the Rapa Nui come from? p.447	**The Moai of Easter Island** p.456
Rongo rongo: Easter island's mysterious script p.448	**The myth of the "Long Ears" and the "Short Ears"** p.458
Outdoor activities and tours p.450	**The Birdman ceremony** p.460
Easter Island festivals p.452	**THE 2010 tsunami** p.461
Parque Nacional Rapa Nui p.453	**Alexander Selkirk** p.463
	Boat trips from San Juan Bautista p.464

TAPATI RAPA NUI FESTIVAL, EASTER ISLAND

Highlights

❶ Tapati Rapa Nui festival Discover the mysterious roots of Easter Island's ancient culture at its carnival (late Jan/early Feb), featuring everything from traditional dancing and singing to hurtling down volcanic slopes on banana trunks. **See p.452**

❷ Ahu Tongariki Fifteen impeccably restored *moai* (giant statues) line up to be admired against a backdrop of green cliffs and roaring waves. **See p.453**

❸ Rano Raraku This mighty mountain at the heart of Easter Island is where the *moai* were

quarried – and some, too big to move, never left the rock where they were hewn. **See p.454**

❹ Orongo Imagine the mindboggling rituals of the Birdman cult as you gaze out at craggy islets in a sapphire-blue ocean or inwards to a reed-filled crater at one of the island's most breathtaking natural sites. **See p.458**

❺ Juan Fernández flora and fauna Frolic underwater with fish and sea lions, watch the antics of hummingbirds and observe dozens of endemic species of plant on this treasure island of unique (and painfully fragile) wildlife. **See p.460**

HIGHLIGHTS ARE MARKED ON THE MAPS ON PP.446 & 462

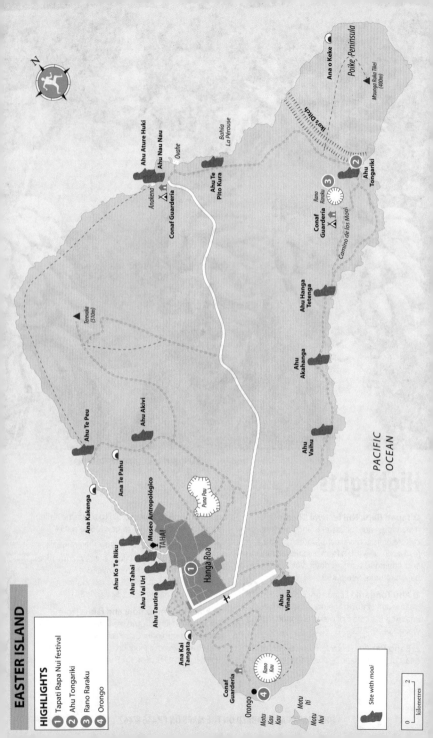

EASTER ISLAND

HIGHLIGHTS
1. Tapati Rapa Nui festival
2. Ahu Tongariki
3. Rano Raraku
4. Orongo

Poike Peninsula

Ana o Keke

Maunga Puka Tikei (400m)

Iko's Ditch

Ahu Ature Huki
Ahu Nau Nau
Ovahe
Bahía La Pérouse
Ahu Te Pito Kura

Anakena
Conaf Guardería

2 Ahu Tongariki

3 Rano Raraku

Conaf Guardería

Camino de los Moai

Terevaka (510m)

Ahu Hanga Tetenga

Ahu Te Peu

Ahu Akivi

Ahu Akahanga

Ana Te Pahu

Ana Kakenga

Ahu Vaihu

Ahu Ko Te Riku
Ahu Tahai
Museo Antropológico
TAHAI
Ahu Vai Uri
Ahu Tautira

Rano Kau
Pana Pau

1 Hanga Roa

PACIFIC OCEAN

Ahu Vinapu

Ana Kai Tangata

Rano Kau

Conaf Guardería

4 Orongo

Motu Iti
Motu Kau Kau
Motu Nui

Site with moai

0   1   2
kilometres

WHERE DID THE RAPA NUI COME FROM?

The islanders' oral history claims that Easter Island's original colonizer was **Hotu Matu'a**, a great *ariki henua* (chief) who lived possibly in Polynesia or the Marquesas. It had been revealed to Hotu Matu'a's tattooist, in a dream, that an island with craters and fine beaches awaited his master. The chief dispatched a reconnaissance party to find this promised land, following some time later with his family and fellow colonists. He arrived on Anakena beach, just as his wife was giving birth to their first son.

As *ariki henua*, Hotu Matu'a was not a political leader, but a revered and important person with great supernatural qualities (*mana*). Accordingly, he and his home were *tapu* (sacred and untouchable), and so Hotu Matu'a and his family lived at Anakena while the rest of his party dispersed around the island. Their families eventually grew into eight separate kin-groups, and as time passed, these groups became more sophisticated and stratified.

THOR HEYERDAHL AND THE SOUTH AMERICAN THEORY

Central to any discussion of Easter Island's settlement are the controversial theories of **Thor Heyerdahl**, the Norwegian explorer-archeologist whose widely publicized expeditions and books generated enormous interest in the island. Heyerdahl was convinced the island had been colonized by South American settlers and, in 1948, he proved, spectacularly, that such a voyage was possible when he and five companions successfully sailed a traditional balsa raft (the *Kon Tiki*) from Peru to an island east of Tahiti.

He backed up his theory with some persuasive but highly selective details, concentrating on the fact that Pacific winds and currents move in a westward direction; the presence in Polynesia of the sweet potato, indisputably of South American origin; the resemblance between the stonework of some Easter Island platforms and certain types of Inca masonry; and the ancient Peruvian custom of artificially extending the ear lobes, just like the islanders at the time of European contact. He failed to explain, however, the total absence of South American pottery and textiles in Polynesia, and the fact that no trace of any indigenous South American language had been found there.

WHAT THE EXPERTS SAY

The view of most experts is that Easter Island was colonized by Polynesians from the west – an opinion backed by linguistic evidence, physical anthropology and the proliferation on Easter Island of Polynesian plants. Which part of Polynesia these settlers came from is still open to debate, though the **Marquesas** is thought the most likely.

- As for the date of the settlers' arrival, all we can be sure of is that they were constructing *ahu* (ceremonial platforms) by 800 AD. No one knows for sure if this culture developed in complete isolation, or if another wave of colonists arrived later, as suggested in some of the oral traditions.

11

The key points of interest are found within **Parque Nacional Rapa Nui**, which comprises much of the island. Highlights include **Rano Kau**, a huge volcanic crater and site of the ceremonial village of **Orongo**; the **Rano Raraku** quarry, where almost all the *moai* were carved; and the largest *ahu* (platform) on the island, **Ahu Tongariki**, which boasts fifteen *moai*. Archeological treasures aside, Easter Island has much to offer outdoor enthusiasts, from diving in waters with arguably the best visibility in the world to surfing major waves off the island's south coast.

Easter Island is two hours behind mainland Chile. The weather is fairly constant year-round, with an average temperature of 23°C (73°F) in January and February, and 18°C (64°F) in July and August. Late January and early February is the busiest time, as the islanders stage the annual **Tapati Rapa Nui festival**.

Brief history

Easter Island was "discovered" and named by Dutch naval commander **Jacob Roggeveen** on Easter Sunday, 1722. In the absence of any written records left by the islanders, Roggeveen's **log** is the earliest written account of the island. His party spent only a single day on land, long enough to observe the "particularly high erected stone images". After their departure, it was another 48 years before Easter Island was revisited, this time by Spanish commander **Felipe González**, who mapped the island and claimed it for King Carlos III of Spain during a six-day stay.

Four years later, **Captain Cook** anchored here in the hope of restoring the health of his scurvy-ridden crew. He, too, observed with incredulity the "stupendous figures", though he noted that some lay strewn on the ground, toppled from their platforms. Later visitors reported an increasing number of **fallen statues**, and by 1825 all of the *moai* on Hanga Roa bay had been destroyed.

The arrival of the slave traders

In 1805, the island was raided by the first of the **slave traders**, when an American schooner captured 22 men and women to be used as seal hunters on the Juan Fernández Islands. After three days at sea, the prisoners were allowed onto the deck, whereupon they promptly threw themselves overboard and drowned in a desperate attempt to swim back to the island. Between 1862 and 1864, Peruvian sailors captured over two thousand five hundred islanders, who were shipped off to work as slaves in the guano mines.

After many of the islanders had died from disease and the appalling conditions in the mines, the Bishop of Tahiti finally managed to persuade the Peruvian government to repatriate the remaining prisoners – most of whom died on the voyage home. Tragically, the sixteen who made it back infected the rest of the islanders with smallpox and TB, reducing the population to around one hundred. Critically, the loss of life was accompanied by the loss of a crucial part of the island's culture and collective memory, for the last *ariki henua* (high chief), *moari* (keepers of sacred knowledge) and *tangata rongo rongo* (specialist readers) were among those who perished.

Missionaries and plantations

A certain degree of stability came when the first missionary, **Eugène Eyraud**, arrived in 1864 and set to converting the islanders to Christianity, a mission fully accomplished by the time of his death, four years later. The peace was disrupted, however, when a French plantation owner, **Jean-Baptiste Onésime Dutrou-Bornier**, bought up large tracts of land and proceeded to run the island as his personal ranch, paying the islanders a pittance for their hard labour and resorting to violence when they wouldn't cooperate. When the missionaries opposed Doutrou-Bornier's exploitation, he attacked their

---

RONGO RONGO: EASTER ISLAND'S MYSTERIOUS SCRIPT

In 1864, French missionary **Eugène Eyraud** wrote of "tablets or staff of wood covered with hieroglyphics" that he'd found in the islanders' homes. This was the first the outside world had heard of *ko hau motu mo rongo rongo* or "lines of script for recitation". The *rongo rongo* tablets remained firmly beyond the grasp of the scholars who came to study them, for none of the islanders knew how to read them. Almost one hundred and fifty years later, no one has succeeded in deciphering them.

The script consists of tiny, tightly packed symbols carved in straight lines across the wooden boards. The symbols, which include representations of people, animals, birds and plants, are upside down on each alternate line. Late nineteenth-century oral testimonies suggest the tablets contained records of genealogies, myths, wars, deaths and religious hymns.

POPULAR THEORIES

Some modern scholars believe the script was developed after the first European contact, inspired by the written documents the Spaniards made the chiefs sign in 1770; others believe it is only one of four written languages in the world to have developed entirely independently of outside influence. The most widely accepted theory is that the symbols were **mnemonics** for use in recitals and chanting.

Today, only 29 *rongo rongo* tablets remain in existence, all of them spirited off to overseas museums in Santiago, Rome, London and Washington, DC.

missions, forcing them to flee the island. He dealt a further blow to the island's slowly recovering population by sending all but a hundred islanders to Tahiti to work on his partner's plantation, before finally being murdered in 1877 by the oppressed islanders.

Annexation

The **Chilean government** acquired first Doutrou-Bornier's lands, and then most of the remaining land on the island, leaving only the village of **Hanga Roa** in the possession of the islanders. Then, on September 9, 1888, the Chilean Navy – apparently with the islanders' consent – officially **annexed** Easter Island, declaring it Chilean territory. Chile subsequently leased it to British wool-trading company Williamson Balfour, which virtually governed the island according to its own needs and interests.

In 1953, the company's lease was revoked and the Chilean Navy stepped in to resume command, though the islanders were given no say in the running of the island. It was not until 1964 that they were allowed outside Hanga Roa (let alone off the island), and granted full citizenship and the right to vote.

The drive towards autonomy

In recent years the management of some local affairs, including education (which is bilingual), has been transferred to the islanders. However, many continue to call for greater autonomy and even secession, expressing concern over the pace of development, the impact of the growing tourist industry (some eighty thousand people visit each year) and the increasing numbers of mainland Chileans settling on the island, as well as overfishing and a lack of adequate waste-disposal facilities.

11

ARRIVAL AND DEPARTURE   EASTER ISLAND

By plane LAN, currently the only airline serving Easter Island, has seven to eight weekly flights to/from Santiago (4hr 50min–5hr 40min), and one to two weekly to/from Papeete, Tahiti (5hr 50min). Return flights to/from Santiago cost around US$800–1500 if booked from outside Chile; cheaper deals are generally available if you buy your ticket at a LAN office in Chile, via a Chilean travel agent, or in conjunction with a long-distance LAN flight. Mataveri airport is on the southern edge of Hanga Roa, about 1km from the centre. The LAN office is also in Hanga Roa at Atamu Tekena and Pont (☎ 32 210 0279, ⌨ lan.com).

GETTING AROUND

The easiest way to get around is via a guided tour (see box, p.450), though some of the cheaper ones can feel a bit crowded and rushed.

By car or motorbike Many travellers hire a car (from around CH$45,000/day), motorbike (around CH$27,000/day) or even a quad bike (around CH$38,000/day) to explore the island. Book a vehicle as soon as you can after arrival (or even before). Outlets include Oceanic Rent a Car, Atamu Tekena s/n, Hanga Roa (☎ 32 210 0985, ⌨ rentacaroceanic.

cl). Note that there is no car insurance on the island.

By bike or on foot You can visit some sites on a mountain bike or on foot, though walking around the whole island would present quite a challenge. Several stores on Atamu Tekena, in Hanga Roa, as well as many hotels, have bikes for hire (generally CH$12,000–15,000/day).

Hanga Roa

Hanga Roa has been the island's only residential sector since the 1860s, when Catholic missionaries relocated the islanders here to facilitate their conversion. Its long, sprawling streets are lined with single-storey houses and fragrant eucalyptus trees, giving the place the feel of a recently settled frontier town.

Atamu Tekena is the main road, lined with small shops, restaurants and tour agencies. Most of the action is centred around the Caleta Hanga Roa harbour, overlooked by Ahu Tautira, the only *moai* in the town proper. Restaurants stretch from here along oceanside Policarpo Toro, parallel to Atamu Tekena. East–west Te Pito O Te Henua connects the two, ending at the church, where islanders still congregate every Sunday

OUTDOOR ACTIVITIES AND TOURS

There are innumerable ways to explore Easter Island's beautiful sites and terrain. Cabalgatas Pantu (☎32 210 0577, ⓦpantupikerauri.cl) offers horseback tours of the west and north coasts, including the ascent of Maunga Terevaka, the island's highest point, as well as traditional Rapa Nui meals. Piti Pont (☎32 210 0664 or 09 9574 0582), a renowned guide, also runs various horseriding excursions. A day-trip with either costs around CH$40,000–50,000. The established Orca Diving Center (☎32 255 0877 or 32 255 0375, ⓦorcadivingcenter.cl) and Mike Rapu Diving Centre (☎32 255 1055, ⓦmikerapu.cl), both with offices on the *caleta*, offer a range of scuba-diving (CH$30,000–50,000) and snorkelling (CH$15,000) trips. Hare Orca, next door and attached to the Orca Diving Center, rents out surfboards (CH$15,000/4hr), boogie boards (CH$10,000/4hr) and snorkelling gear (CH$10,000/8hr); the shop can put you in touch with surfing instructors. Mike Rapu Diving Centre also rents out kayaks (CH$15,000/3hr).

GUIDED TOURS

Aku Aku Turismo at Av Tu'u Koihu s/n (☎32 210 0770, ⓦakuakuturismo.cl), and Kia Koe Tour, Atamu Tekena s/n (☎32 210 0282, ⓦkiakoetour.cl), both offer bilingual archeological tours (from CH$25,000/full day, from CH$17,000/half day). ★Haumaka Archaelogical Tours on Puku Rangi Uka s/n (☎32 210 0274, ⓔhaumakatours@gmail.com) offers excellent, small-group tours in English, French and German, with extremely well-informed and friendly guides. Taura'a Tours, Atamu Tekena s/n (☎32 210 0463, ⓦtauraahotel.cl), also offers small-group trips.

morning. Just south of the pier lies tiny Playa Pea, where a rock pool safe for swimming is cordoned off from the stretch of ocean popular with surfers and body boarders.

INFORMATION   HANGA ROA

Sernatur Sernatur, Tu'u Maheke and Policarpo Toro (Mon–Fri 8.30am–1pm; ☎32 210 0255, ⓔipascua@sernatur.cl). **Conaf** has a small booth at the airport, a larger office at Mataveri s/n, on the outskirts of Hanga Roa (Mon–Sat 9am–3.45pm; ☎32 210 0236, ⓦwww.conaf.cl) and a visitors' centre at Orongo (see p.458).

ACCOMMODATION

Accommodation is more expensive than on the mainland, though there are some budget options. As many places don't accept credit cards, you should bring plenty of cash with you; US dollars are widely accepted. Book well in advance during busy times such as Tapati (see p.452). Most hotels offer a free airport pick-up and include breakfast in the rates.

HOTELS AND GUESTHOUSES

Aloha Nui Guest House Av Atamu Tekena s/n ☎32 210 0274, ⓔhaumakatours@gmail.com. Run by the couple behind the excellent Haumaka Tours (see box above), this tastefully decorated guesthouse has six clean and comfortable en suites, a tropical garden and a well-stocked library filled with books, music and pieces of artwork. CH$80,000

★**Explora Rapa Nui** 5.6km from Hanga Roa; reservations ☎2 2395 2800, ⓦexplora.com. The most luxurious hotel on the island, and one of the most memorable places to stay in Chile, the eco-friendly *Explora* has elegant, contemporary en suites with all the creature comforts you'd expect. There's also a wonderful pool, Jacuzzi and spa, delicious food and drinks, and expert guides to help you explore the island. Rates include full board and two daily excursions; minimum three-night stay. Three nights US$5100

Hostal Aukara Pont s/n ☎32 210 0539, ⓔaukararapanui@gmail.com. Follow the signs for the Aukara art gallery, which showcases the owner's pieces, to this small guesthouse, lost in the midst of a beautiful garden. The rooms are simple but comfortable; there's a small kitchen for guests and guided tours of the gallery are available. CH$80,000

Hotel O'Tai Av Te Pito Te Henua s/n ☎32 210 0250, ⓦhotelotai.com. The lush flower-filled garden at this hotel is a real highlight, as is the appealing pool. The rooms are clean and well kept: all have private bathrooms, indigenous artwork on the walls, fridges, safes and patio doors; superior ones also come with a/c. US$190

★**Hotel Taura'a** Av Atamu Tekena s/n ☎32 210 0463, ⓦtauraahotel.cl. This highly recommended hotel boasts spacious, airy a/c rooms and an attractive garden. Both English and French are spoken, and the congenial owners run a good tour agency (full-day tours cost US$100). CH$86,000

CABAÑAS

Mana Nui Inn Tahai s/n ☎32 210 0811, ⓦmananui.cl. Boasting a peaceful location away from the town centre and great sea views, *Mana Nui Inn* is a good mid-range option. There's a choice of rooms and *cabañas* with kitchenettes sleeping up to seven; all have private bathrooms, TVs and fridges

11

and fans. Guests can also use the kitchen, barbecue and laundry facilities. Doubles CH$60,000, *cabañas* CH$117,000

Te'ora Apina s/n ⓦ rapanuiteora.com. This friendly, good-value Canadian-run place has, amid its gardens, a handful of delightful, spotlessly clean *cabañas*; all come with kitchenettes, private patios and sea views. A laundry service (CH$5000/load) is also available. CH$40,000

HOSTEL

Residencial Kona Tau Avareipua s/n ☎ 32 210 0321, ⓔ konatau@entelchile.net. Hostelling International-affiliated hostel in a large and friendly family home, with comfortable dorms, as well as simple en-suite rooms and a mango-strewn garden. Close to the airport but somewhat inconvenient for the rest of town. Dorms CH$15,000, doubles CH$45,000

CAMPSITE

Camping Mihinoa Pont s/n ☎ 32 255 1593, ⓦ mihinoa.com. Large campsite with an excellent ocean view, run by a friendly family. Showers, kitchen facilities, dining room, and car, scooter and bike hire all available; the lack of shade is the only drawback. The adjoining guesthouse has basic rooms and a five-bed dorm; it's also possible to rent tents (CH$6500). Camping/person CH$6500, dorms CH$10,000, doubles CH$20,000

EATING AND DRINKING

Hanga Roa offers a good selection of cafés and **restaurants**, though prices are significantly higher than on mainland Chile. The **seafood** is a highlight. Keep an eye out for Mahina **beer**, produced by the island's microbrewery.

CAFÉ

Mikafé La Caleta. This tiny café, with just a handful of tables outside, serves delicious home-made ice cream (from CH$1800) – don't miss the *lúcuma* meringue flavour – as well as cakes, muffins, pastries and good coffee. Mon–Sat 9am–1.30pm & 4.30–9pm.

RESTAURANTS

Au Bout du Monde Av Policarpo Toro s/n ☎ 32 255 2060. A Belgian chef is at the helm at this restaurant, and the inventive menu features some excellent food (mains CH$10,000–20,000) such as prawn pesto salad, smoked salmon pâté, and chocolate mousse. There's live music and dance in the evenings; book ahead. Mon & Wed–Sun 1–2.30pm & 7–10.30pm.

Chez Ramon Av Te Pito Te Henua s/n ☎ 32 210 0833. Friendly little restaurant with an overgrown garden, friendly service and a short, straightforward menu. There are five dishes of the day – like fried fish or *cazuela* – for CH$5000 each, which is good value for Easter Island. Mon–Sat noon–3pm & 7.30–10pm.

Haka Honu Av Policarpo Toro ☎ 32 255 1677. This

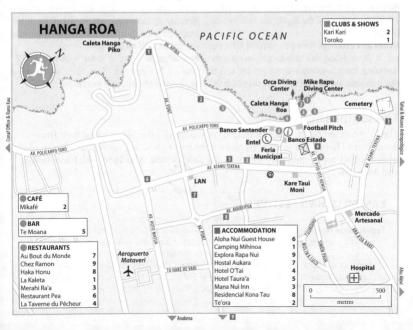

super-friendly, open-fronted restaurant has a breezy location looking out to sea. Excellent fish and seafood is on offer, including *pastel de jaiba* (crab gratin), ceviche, seafood salad and fish and chips. Mains CH$10,000–15,000. Daily 10.30am–11pm.

★**La Kaleta** La Caleta ☏ 32 255 2244. *La Kaleta's* wooden deck, right on the water, is a wonderfully romantic place for a meal, particularly around sunset. The menu is strong on seafood – try the octopus carpaccio or the scallops topped with Parmesan – and dishes are beautifully presented. Mains CH$8000–15,000. Daily 12.30–3.30pm & 7.30–11pm.

Merahi Ra'a Te Pito O Te Henua s/n ☏ 32 255 1125. This low-key joint is *the* place for large servings of expertly prepared fish and the local speciality of *rape rape* (spiny lobster), as well as melt-in-your-mouth tuna ceviche (mains CH$8000–25,000). Mon–Thurs, Sat & Sun noon–3pm & 7–10pm.

Restaurant Pea Policarpo Toro s/n, next to Playa Pea ☏ 32 255 1140. In a lovely seafront location, particularly appealing in the early evening, *Restaurant Pea* serves tasty sandwiches (CH$5000–7000) that are ideal for a snack or light meal, as well as decent mains (around CH$9000–15,000). Tues–Sun 12.30–3pm & 7–11pm.

La Taverne du Pêcheur Te Pito O Te Henua s/n ☏ 32 210 0619. The food is undoubtedly good at this restaurant – notably the steaks (which come direct from Argentina), the lobster dishes and the desserts. However, prices are high and the service leaves a lot to be desired. Mains CH$13,000–30,000. Mon–Sat noon–3pm & 6–11pm.

BAR

Te Moana Av Policarpo Toro s/n, near the caleta ☏ 32 255 1578. Sophisticated restaurant-bar, right on the front and perfect for a sundowner: there's a good range of cocktails (CH$4500–6500) and beers (CH$2500–4500), including the Tahitian lager, Hinano. The food (mains CH$10,000–20,000) is good too: try the shrimp tempura or the sesame-crusted, seared tuna. Mon–Sat 12.30–11pm/midnight.

NIGHTLIFE AND ENTERTAINMENT

Kari Kari Av Atamu Tekena s/n ☏ 32 210 0767. Entertaining traditional dance-and-music show (1hr), featuring talented young dancers and musicians in elaborate costumes. Entry from CH$12,000. Tues, Thurs & Sat 9pm.

Toroko Av Policarpo Toro s/n, near the cemetery. Popular disco with a mellow atmosphere that seems to draw all the young islanders on a Sat night; although it may initially seem a little daunting for travellers, it's a friendly place to hang out. Thurs–Sat 11pm–4/5am.

DIRECTORY

Hospital Hospital Hanga Roa on Simón Paoa s/n (☏ 32 210 0183), southeast of the church, has basic medical facilities.

Money and exchange There are a couple of ATMs: the one at Banco Estado, Tu'u Maheke s/n, only accepts MasterCard; Banco Santander, Policarpo Toro s/n, accepts Visa. Both banks also offer cash advances on credit cards.

Several places change cash and travellers' cheques (generally at poor rates), and US dollars are widely accepted. It's worth bringing a stash of pesos/dollars with you from the mainland to be on the safe side.

Post office Av Te Pito Te Henua, opposite *Hotel O'Tai* (Mon–Fri 9am–6pm, Sat 10am–1pm). You can get a novelty Easter Island stamp in your passport here.

The southeastern circuit

The loop formed by the 16km southern coast road and the 30km paved road from Anakena to Hanga Roa lends itself to a convenient sightseeing route that takes in some of the island's most impressive sights – including **Vinapu**, **Ahu Tongariki**, **Rano Raraku** and **Anakena**.

EASTER ISLAND FESTIVALS

To witness the island's culture at its best, time your visit to coincide with one of the festivals. **Tapati Rapa Nui** is a ten-day cultural celebration held in late January or early February. Famous for celebrating Rapa Nui culture, tradition and history, the festival features dancing, body painting, statue carving, choral recitals, surfing displays, canoe races, re-enactments of old legends and huge *curanto* feasts. **Semana Santa** (Easter week) features lively celebrations at Hanga Roa's church. The **Ceremonia Culto al Sol** is a feast that takes place on June 21 for the winter solstice, while **Día de la Lengua Rapa Nui**, a celebration of the Rapa Nui language, is held in late November.

Vinapu

From Hanga Roa, follow Avenida Hotu Matu'a down to the southern coast road then turn right, just after the white oil containers, and you'll reach **VINAPU**, the site of two large *ahus*, with *moai* lying in fragments behind the platforms. Anyone who's seen Machu Picchu or other Inca ruins will be amazed by the similarity of the masonry of Vinapu's main *ahu*, made of huge, mortarless blocks of stone "fitted carefully to one another without a crack or a hole". Close to this platform, known as Vinapu I, is another *ahu*, Vinapu II, whose stonework is vastly inferior to its neighbour.

Thor Heyerdahl's expedition was the first to excavate the site and, with radiocarbon dating, concluded that the precisely carved Vinapu I was among the earliest built on the island, and that Vinapu II was a much later construction, suggesting that the island's first settlers imported the highly specialized stone-carving techniques of Peru, and that later platforms were built by "far less capable architects, who were no longer masters of the complicated Inca technique". Modern archeologists, however, believe that this impressive masonry is simply a perfected example of a style developed locally on Easter Island, and more recent radiocarbon tests have given Vinapu I a new date of 1516 AD, and Vinapu II a date of 857 AD – the reverse of Heyerdahl's sequence.

11

Sites along the southern coast

East from Vinapu on the coast road, the first site you pass is **Vaihu**, where eight tall statues lie face-down on the ground, their red stone topknots strewn along the coast. Three kilometres further along, **Ahu Akahanga** presents an equally mournful picture of a row of fallen *moai*; according to some oral traditions, it's also the burial place of Hotu Matu'a. Further up the coast, **Ahu Hanga Tetenga** is the site of the tallest *moai* (9.94m) ever transported to a platform.

Just beyond Ahu Hanga Tetenga, the road forks. The left-hand branch (**Camino de los Moai**) leads to the quarry of Rano Raraku. It's thought to have been the main roadway along which the statues were transported from the quarry. The right-hand branch continues up the coast to the magnificent Ahu Tongariki.

Ahu Tongariki

The fifteen colossal *moai* lined up on **AHU TONGARIKI** make a sensational sight. This was the largest number of *moai* ever erected on a single *ahu*, which, at 200m long, was the largest built on the island. It was totally destroyed in 1960 when a massive tsunami, triggered by an earthquake in Chile, swept across this corner of the island, dragging the platform blocks and the statues 90m inland – a remarkable distance, given that the statues weigh up to 30 tonnes each.

In November 1988, Sergio Rapu, a former Governor of Easter Island, was being interviewed for a **Japanese television programme**, and said that if they had a crane they could save the *moai*; a Japanese man watching the show decided to act and a committee was set up in Japan. The restoration of the *ahu* involved Chilean archeologists Claudio Cristino and Patricia Vargas, a group of forty islanders, specialists from the Nara Institute of Japan and recognized international experts in stone conservation. The project took five years and was finally completed in 1995.

PARQUE NACIONAL RAPA NUI

There is a CH$30,000 fee to enter **Parque Nacional Rapa Nui**, which covers most of the island's archeological sites. You can buy your entry permit from the Conaf kiosk at the airport just after you land, or at the Conaf office on the outskirts of Hanga Roa (see p.450); most hotels and travel agencies will also purchase them for you. Along with the permit, you'll receive leaflets warning you not to touch or interfere in any way with the *moai* or the other archeological sites. These rules are not to be taken lightly: an idiotic Finnish tourist was arrested, fined and banned from Chile for three years after chipping off the earlobe of a *moai* in 2008.

Rano Raraku

North of Tongariki • Daily: April–Nov 9am–6pm; Dec–March 9am–7pm • Your entry permit will be checked at the ranger's office here

North of Tongariki, **RANO RARAKU** rises from the land in a hulking mass of volcanic stone. This crag is where almost all of the island's statues were produced, carved directly from the "tuff" (compacted volcanic ash) of the crater's outer slopes. The first surprise, on approaching the crater from the car park, are the dozens of **giant heads** sprouting from the ground. They are, in fact, finished *moai* brought down from the quarry, which were probably placed in shallow pits (that gradually built up) until they could be transported to their *ahu*. One of them bears an image on its chest of a three-masted sailing ship, suggesting that they were carved after European contact.

Among this mass of shapes, still attached to the rock face, is **El Gigante**, the biggest *moai* ever carved, stretching over 20m from top to bottom. Experts believe that it would have been impossible to transport, let alone erect.

The east end of the trail culminates in the kneeling, round-headed **Moai Tukuturi**, the only one of its kind, discovered by Thor Heyerdahl's expedition in 1955. To the west, the trail winds its way up between wild guava trees into the crater itself, with several dirt paths running through knee-high shrubbery alongside the large reed-strewn, freshwater lake. If you follow the trails all the way up to the crater's eastern rim (avoid treading on the toppled *moai* at the top) you are rewarded with unparalleled views of the bay and Ahu Tongariki in the distance.

The Poike Peninsula

East of Rano Raraku, the seldom-visited **POIKE PENINSULA** is a green, gently rounded plateau bounded by steep cliffs. You can walk round the edge of the peninsula in about four hours, but there's no shade and no path.

Ana o Keke

Poike's main interest lies in the myths and legends associated with it. One tells of the **cave of the virgins**, Ana o Keke, where a number of young girls were confined for months on end so that their skin would remain as pale as possible. Access to Ana o Keke is treacherous, however, and should only be attempted with a guide.

Iko's Trench

More famous than Ana o Keke is the myth of the battle of the **"Long Ears" and "Short Ears"** (see box, p.458). This battle is supposed to have taken place in the 3.5km-long ditch separating the peninsula from the rest of the island, known as Ko te Ava o Iko, or "Iko's ditch".

Ahu te Pito Kura

From the southern coast, the road turns inland, cutting past the Poike Peninsula, and leads directly to Ovahe and Anakena. On the way, look out for **Ahu te Pito Kura**, down by Bahía La Pérouse (signposted). This is the site of **Paro**, at 9.8m tall probably the largest *moai* successfully erected on a platform. Paro is thought to have been one of the last *moai* to be moved and erected, and is estimated to weigh a staggering ninety tonnes. No one has attempted to restore and re-erect the giant, which still lies face down before its *ahu*, surrounded by rubble.

Ovahe

Further north from Paro, **Ovahe** is a tiny, secluded and exquisitely beautiful beach, its white sands lapped by crystal-clear waters at the foot of a large volcanic cliff, very popular with locals who come here to picnic, swim and snorkel. It's best earlier in the day, before the cliff blocks the afternoon sun.

Playa Anakena

Up the coast from Ovahe, **Playa Anakena** is much larger, and presents a picture-postcard scene of powdery golden sands fringed by swaying palm trees, great for an afternoon of swimming or sunbathing. Several snack stands offer drinks and sandwiches, though they're not always open, so bring some food and water with you.

Anakena

ANAKENA has a special place in Rapa Nui oral history, which holds it to be the landing site and dwelling place of Hotu Matu'a, the island's first colonizer (see box, p.447). It's also home to the splendid *moai* of **Ahu Nau Nau**, which were so deeply covered in sand until their restoration, led by local archeologist Sergio Rapu Haoa in 1978, that they were largely protected from the effects of weathering.

Ahu Ature Huki

Just up the hillside by the beach you'll find the squat and rather corpulent *moai* of **Ahu Ature Huki**. This was the first *moai* to be re-erected on the island in the experiment carried out by Thor Heyerdahl in 1955, when twelve strong islanders showed they could raise a 25-tonne statue in eighteen days (see box, p.447).

11

The northern circuit

Although the triangle formed by Vinapu, Tongariki and Anakena contains the densest concentration of sites, the western and northern parts of the island are also well worth exploring. Attractions include the impressive *moai* of **Tahai** and **Ahu Akivi**, plus a network of underground **caves**.

Tahai and around

If you walk north from the *caleta* past the cemetery, taking the road that hugs the coast, after about ten minutes you'll reach the ceremonial centre of **TAHAI**, composed of three *ahus*, a favourite spot for viewing colourful sunsets. The first, **Ahu Vai Uri**, supports four broad, squat *moai*, two of which have badly damaged heads, and the stump of a fifth statue. In front of the *ahu* is the outline of a flattened esplanade, presumed to have been used as a ceremonial site.

Archeological remains suggest some individuals – possibly chiefs and priests – used to live near these ceremonial sites, in several locations on the island, in stone, oval houses called *hare paenga* that looked like an upturned canoe. You can see the foundations of one of these houses near Ahu Vai Uri. The second platform is **Ahu Tahai** itself, topped by a lone, weathered *moai*. Finally, **Ahu Ko Te Riku** is the site of a well-preserved *moai* fitted with white, glinting eyes and a red topknot.

Museo Antropológico Sebastián Englert

About 500m north of Tahai, set well back from the coastal path • Tues–Fri 9.30am–5.30pm, Sat & Sun 9.30am–12.30pm • CH$1000 • ☎ 32 255 1020, Ⓦ museorapanui.cl

The excellent **Museo Antropológico Sebastián Englert** is not to be missed. It gives a thorough introduction to the island's geography, history, society, **birdman cult** and the origins and significance of the *moai*. The well-labelled displays are in Spanish and English, and include an evocative collection of black-and-white photographs of islanders from about 1915 onwards, a rare female *moai* and replica *rongo rongo* tablets.

Dos Ventanas Caves

On the coastal road, around 3km north of the Museo Antropológico (see above), you reach the point where you're opposite two little islands out at sea. A stone cairn by the left-hand side of the road signals a track down towards the cliffs; it's

11

THE MOAI OF EASTER ISLAND

The enduring symbol of Easter Island always has been the *moai*. A **Neolithic statue cult** on this scale would impress in any location, but the fact that it developed in total isolation on a tiny island in the middle of the Pacific almost defies belief. There are some four hundred finished statues scattered around the island, and almost as many in the quarry, in varying stages of completion. The *moai* range in height from 2m to about 20m, and though styles evolved over time, all are carved in a **highly stylized** manner. Their bellies are gently rounded, and their arms are held tightly by their sides, with their strange, long-fingered hands placed across their abdomens. Their heads are long and rectangular, with pointed chins; prominent, angular noses; and thin, tight lips.

FUNCTION AND FORM

According to the islanders' assertions, which are consistent with widespread Polynesian tradition, these figures represented important **ancestors**, and were erected on the ancestral land of their kin-groups, which they would watch over and protect with their *mana* (almost all the *moai* face inland). Archeologists have proposed tentative dates of around 1000 AD for the carving of the early statues, and around the **fifteenth century** for the bulk of the statues, when production peaked. Rano Raraku's unfinished statues demonstrate how their forms were chiselled out of the rock face until they were attached to it by just a thin keel running down their spine. When all was completed but their eye sockets, they were freed from their keel and slid down the quarry's slope, then temporarily erected in a pit until they were transported to their *ahus*.

TRANSPORTATION

The island's oral histories offer no clues as to how the **20 to 25-tonne statues** were moved, claiming the statues' *mana* enabled them to walk short distances each day until they reached their platforms. Modern theories have included horizontal and vertical swivelling, but since it was established in the 1980s that the island was once densely covered by trees, it's been assumed that they were dragged on wooden sledges or on top of rollers.

RAISING THE MOAI

How the statues were **erected** onto their platforms in the absence of any type of machinery is another enigma, though in 1955, Thor Heyerdahl challenged the island's mayor to raise a fallen, 25-tonne statue at Anakena Beach and, under the mayor's supervision, twelve islanders raised the statue in eighteen days, using two levers and slipping layer after layer of stones

not easy to spot. At the end of the track, a tiny opening in the ground is the entrance to a pitch-black passage (take a torch), which continues 50m underground to the adjoining Ana Kakenga (**DOS VENTANAS CAVES**). Both caves are flooded with light streaming in from the "windows", or gaping holes, that open out of the cliff wall. Prepare for a rush of adrenaline as you approach the edges, as both drop vertically down to a bed of sharp rocks and pounding waves many metres below.

Ahu Te Peu

About 1km further up the coast from the Dos Ventanas Caves is **AHU TE PEU**. The *moai* that once stood on the *ahu* still lie flat on the ground, left as they were during the period of warfare. Scattered around are the remains of many boat-shaped *hare paenga*, including one that's 60m long. It's thought this was the site of the village of the Miru clan, the direct descendants of Hotu Matu'a.

At Ahu Te Peu, most people join up with the inland road and head back to Hanga Roa via Ahu Akivi. You can, however, continue north, either heading up the gentle volcanic cone of **Terevaka**, where you'll be rewarded with fine views across the island from its 510m summit, the highest point of the island (no path; 1hr up), or else follow the coastline round to Playa Anakena (4–5hr on foot; sunscreen is

underneath the horizontal statue. Little by little, it was raised on the bed of stones until it was level with its platform; at this point, the layers of pebbles were placed only under its head, until the statue was nearly vertical and could be slipped into place. Archeologists agree this method is highly likely to have been used to raise the statues. In contrast, no one has been able to demonstrate how the large, heavy "topknots" were placed on the raised statues' heads – a monumental feat, achieved only with a crane in modern times.

THE STATUE-CARVERS

Easter Island society was based around independent clans, or **kin-groups**, each with its own high-ranking members. The statue-carvers were highly revered members of a privileged class who were exempt from food production and were supported by farmers and fishermen. Such a system must have involved a great deal of economic cooperation, which appears to have been successfully maintained for hundreds of years.

THE BEGINNING OF THE END

Then, in the later stages of the island's prehistory, the system collapsed, and the island became engulfed by warfare. Archeological records reveal a sudden, dramatic proliferation of obsidian **weapons** during the eighteenth century, as well as the remains of violently beaten skulls, and evidence of the widespread use of caves as refuges. Archeologists have also found possible evidence of cannibalism – something featured prominently in the island's oral traditions. The most dramatic testimony of this period, however, is provided by the hundreds of fallen statues littering the island, deliberately toppled as enemy groups set out to desecrate each other's sacred sites.

SO WHAT WENT WRONG ON EASTER ISLAND?

It seems likely the seeds of social collapse lay in the extremes the statue cult was taken to by the islanders. As the impulse to produce *moai* required more and more hands, the delicate balance between food distribution and statue-carving was destroyed. This situation was profoundly aggravated by the growing scarcity of food brought about by overpopulation, and deforestation, following centuries of logging for boat-building, fuel consumption and statue-transportation. This must have had a catastrophic effect on the islanders' ability to feed themselves: deep-sea fishing became increasingly difficult, and eventually impossible, owing to the lack of wood available for new canoes, and even land cultivation was affected, as the deforestation caused soil erosion. In this climate of encroaching deprivation, the Easter Island civilization descended into anarchy, dragging its majestic monuments with it.

11

absolutely essential and you must take plenty of water). On the way, you'll pass many fallen *moai*, none of them restored, as well as the ruins of stone houses and chicken pens.

Inland to Puna Pau

From Hanga Roa, heading up the inland road to Ahu Akivi (first left from the paved road to Anakena) you'll pass a signed track branching left to **PUNA PAU**, a low volcanic crater made of rusty-coloured rock, known as *scoria*, where the islanders carved the **pukao** – the cylindrical "topknots" worn by up to seventy of the *moai* standing on *ahu*. No one knows for sure what these cylinders represented, though suggestions include topknots (of hair) and feather headdresses. Up in the quarry, and along the track to the top, you can see thirty or so finished *pukao* lying on the ground.

Ahu Akivi

On the inland road north of Puna Pau, you'll find **AHU AKIVI**, whose seven *moai* are the only ones to have been erected inland, and the only ones that look towards the sea. It's been discovered that they are oriented directly towards the rising summer solstice, along with several other *ahu*, suggesting that solar positions were of significance to the islanders. The Ahu Akivi *moai* were raised in 1960 by William Mulloy and Gonzalo

---

THE MYTH OF THE "LONG EARS" AND THE "SHORT EARS"

An oft-repeated oral tradition has it that the island's population, in the time just before the toppling of the statues, was divided into two principal groups, the **"Short Ears"** and the **"Long Ears"**. In fact, the whole myth is based on a mistranslation. It seems the two clans were really the *Hanau eepe* ("short and stocky") and the *Hanau momoko* ("tall and slim"); the strange mix-up came from mistranslating *eepe* – short and stocky – as "ear" ("*epe*" in Rapa Nui).

The "Long Ears", who saw themselves as more aristocratic, were extremely domineering, and the "Short Ears" resented them intensely. The "Short Ears" rebelled when forced to clear rocks off the land, forcing the "Long Ears" to retreat to the **Poike Peninsula**. Here they dug deep ditches, and filled them with branches and grass, intending to force their enemies inside and set them alight. However, a "Short Ears" woman who was married to one of the "Long Ears" alerted her people, and allowed them to surround their enemies while they were sleeping. When they attacked, the "Long Ears" ran straight into their own ditch, which was set alight. Most of the "Long Ears" burned to death, but three escaped. Two of them were caught and executed, but one, **Ororoina**, was allowed to live, and went on to father many children – whose descendants, to this day, are proud of their *Hanau momoko* heritage.

Figueroa, two of the archeologists recruited by Heyerdahl in 1955, both of whom devoted their careers to Easter Island.

Te Pahu Caves

From Ahu Akivi, the road turns towards the coast, where it meets Ahu Te Peu. On the way, a second path branches left from the main road, leading towards the **ANA TE PAHU CAVES**. If you clamber down, you'll see some tall bamboo trees growing in a magical underground garden, along with sweet potatoes, taro, avocados, lemons and sugarcane. This cave is connected to another huge cave (once used as a dwelling) by a long lava tube.

South of Hanga Roa: Rano Kau

South of Hanga Roa, a dirt road climbs steeply past a *mirador* offering an excellent view of Hanga Roa up to one of the most awe-inspiring spots on the island – the giant crater of the extinct **RANO KAU** volcano, and the ceremonial village of **ORONGO**, perched high on its rim. The dull waters of the volcano's reed-choked lake contrast sharply with the brilliant blue of the Pacific, stretching as far as the eye can see, visible where a great chunk of the crater wall is missing. Just before you reach Orongo, a path disappears into the lush vegetation around the crater's edge; it is possible to follow this around the crater as a leisurely day's walk, but bring plenty of water.

Orongo

Just west of Rano Kau • Daily: April–Nov 9am–6pm; Dec–March 9am–7pm • Your entry permit will be checked at the ranger's office here • Car or taxi from Hanga Roa (10min; the latter costs around CH\$18,000, including waiting time), or on foot (1hr)

Orongo, just beyond the Conaf visitors' centre, consists of the partially restored remains of some 48 low-lying, oval-shaped huts made of thin stone slabs, each with a tiny entrance just large enough to crawl through (don't try). A few steps from the houses, on the face of some basalt outcrops looking out to sea, you'll find a dense group of exquisitely carved **petroglyphs** depicting curled-up human figures with birds' heads and long curved beaks. These images honour an important annual ceremony dedicated to the **cult of the birdman**. A great deal is known about this ceremony, as it was practised right up to 1878.

11

THE BIRDMAN CEREMONY

The Birdman ceremony took place annually at the September **equinox**, when the chiefs of the various kin-groups assembled at Orongo to compete. The aim was to find the first egg laid by the sooty tern (a migratory bird) on Motu Nui, the largest of three islets sitting opposite Orongo, 2km out to sea. Each chief would choose a representative, or *hopu*, who would scale down the sheer cliff to the ocean and swim through shark-infested waters to the islet. It could take several weeks for the egg to be found; meanwhile, the chiefs would remain in Orongo, where they participated in ritual dances, songs and prayers.

Once the egg was finally found, its discoverer would bellow the name of his master, and then swim back to the island with the egg tucked into a headband. The victorious chief now became the new *tangata manu*, or **birdman**. The new birdman would first have all the hair shaved off his head; he would then live in strict seclusion for a whole year in a sacred house at the foot of Rano Raraku, eating only certain foods, and forbidden to bathe himself or cut his nails. His kin-group, meanwhile, was endowed with a special, high status, which was often taken as an excuse for members to dominate and bully their rival groups.

11

The Juan Fernández Archipelago

The **JUAN FERNÁNDEZ ARCHIPELAGO** is made up of three islands and numerous rocky islets. The archipelago is named after **João Fernandes**, the Portuguese sailor who discovered it on November 22, 1574, while straying out to sea to avoid coastal winds and currents in an attempt to shorten the journey between Lima and Valparaíso. The more easterly of the two main islands was originally called **Más a Tierra** ("Nearer Land"), while the other, 187km further west, was known as **Más Afuera** ("Farther Out").

Brief history

João Fernandes made a brief attempt to colonize the three uninhabited islands, introducing vegetables and goats, which multiplied in great numbers (the third, smallest, island was later known as Goat Island, officially as Isla Santa Clara). These were still flourishing when British buccaneers started making occasional calls here to stock up on water and fresh meat between their raids on the mainland.

Following Alexander Selkirk's much-publicized rescue (see p.463) buccaneers began calling at the islands more frequently, prompting the Spanish Crown to take official possession of the archipelago in 1742, building a series of forts around Más a Tierra. The island was then used as a **penal colony** for many years, and it wasn't until the mid-nineteenth century that a mixture of Chilean and European colonizers formed a permanent settlement. In 1966, with an eye on the islands' potential as a tourist destination, the Chilean government changed Más a Tierra's name to **Isla Robinson Crusoe**, while Más Afuera became **Isla Alejandro Selkirk**, seasonal home to lobster fishermen and very difficult to reach.

Today, few tourists make it out here each year, arriving mainly between October and March, when the climate is warm and mostly dry, and the sea is perfect for swimming.

Isla Robinson Crusoe

Twenty-two kilometres long, and 7km at its widest point, **ISLA ROBINSON CRUSOE** is the archipelago's only permanently inhabited island. Most of the islanders – some of them descendants of the Swiss Baron de Rodt and his compatriots who settled the island at the end of the nineteenth century – live in the little village of **San Juan Bautista**, on the sheltered Bahía Cumberland. The main economic activity is trapping **lobsters**, and one of the highlights of a stay here is accompanying a fisherman out to haul in his catch (and later sample it).

THE 2010 TSUNAMI

In the early hours of February 27, 2010, a **tsunami** triggered by the 8.8 magnitude **earthquake** on mainland Chile struck the Juan Fernández Archipelago. A wave of around 20m in height swept 300m into Isla Robinson Crusoe, destroying much of San Juan Bautista and killing sixteen people. A mix-up between the Chilean Navy and the tsunami alert services meant that the islanders received no official warning, and the death toll would have been much higher but for a 12-year-old girl: awake at night, Martina Maturana spotted the fishing boats bobbing violently in the harbour, and ran from her home to ring the emergency bell in the town square to warn the island's six hundred or so inhabitants.

Following the disaster, the island's population fell by about a third, as many people left for the mainland. Islanders, angry at the lack of official warning, launched a court case against the government. Meanwhile, **rebuilding** attempts – the tsunami destroyed the island's library, town hall, civil registry office, museum, cultural centre, naval offices, post office, school and every single shop, as well as many homes and hotels – are ongoing.

To compound matters, on September 2, 2011, 21 passengers were killed after an air force plane crashed into the sea after twice failing to land in windy conditions on the island. Among those killed was TV presenter Felipe Camiroaga, who had been making a film on the reconstruction efforts.

The island is still getting back on its feet – and the money you spend will certainly help the rebuilding efforts.

11

    Lobsters aside, the island's two principal attractions are the sites associated with **Alexander Selkirk** and the richness of its flora and fauna. Of the 146 plant species that grow here, 101 are endemic or unique to the island (the second highest proportion in the world after Hawaii), which is both a national park and a UNESCO World Biosphere Reserve. Most prolific, and stunning, is the luxuriant rainforest that covers the island's higher slopes.

    The local fauna also comprises numerous endemic species, such as the **Juan Fernández fur seal**, which is making a comeback after being hunted to near-extinction in the eighteenth century, and the Firecrown hummingbird, as well as seabirds, such as the giant petrel. Meanwhile, diving at various sites around Isla Robinson Crusoe is an excellent way to appreciate the wealth and diversity of its abundant underwater life. **Mosquitoes** abound, so be sure to bring plenty of repellent.

San Juan Bautista

Huddled by the shores of Bahía Cumberland, at the foot of a green curtain of mountains, **SAN JUAN BAUTISTA** is the island's only settlement. A spread-out village with a few dirt streets lined with simple wooden houses, and an unfinished look to it, for most people "El Pueblo" is just a base from which to explore the island's interior and the coast. That said, there are several curious historical relics here.

Fuerte Santa Barbara

Fuerte Santa Barbara, a small stone fort, is perched on a hillside just north of the plaza. Heavily restored in 1974, it was originally built by the Spanish in 1749 in an attempt to prevent buccaneers from using the island as a watering point.

Cuevas de los Patriotas

A short walk north of Fuerte Santa Barbara takes you to the **Cuevas de los Patriotas**, a group of seven fern-covered caves allegedly inhabited by 42 independence fighters who were banished to Más a Tierra after the Battle of Rancagua in 1814.

Punta San Carlos

Down on the shore, follow the path to the north end of the bay and you'll reach the cliffs of the **Punta San Carlos**, embedded with unexploded shells fired by British

11

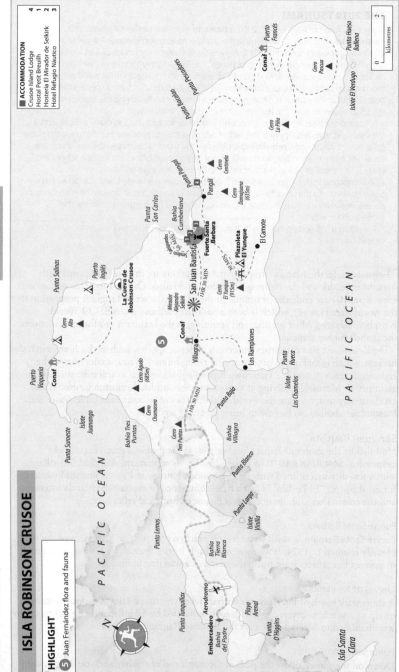

ISLA ROBINSON CRUSOE

	ACCOMMODATION	
Crusoe Island Lodge		4
Hostal Petit Breuilh		1
Hostería El Mirador de Selkirk		2
Hotel Refugio Náutico		3

HIGHLIGHT

5 Juan Fernández flora and fauna

ALEXANDER SELKIRK

Daniel Defoe's story of Robinson Crusoe, the world's most famous literary castaway, was inspired by the misadventures of the real-life Scottish mariner **Alexander Selkirk**, who was marooned on Isla Robinson Crusoe (then Más a Tierra) in 1704 while crossing the Pacific on a privateering expedition. Unlike Crusoe, who was shipwrecked, Selkirk actually asked to be put ashore following a series of quarrels with his captain. The irascible sailor regretted his decision as soon as he was deposited on the beach with a few scanty supplies, but his cries from the shore begging to be taken back onboard were ignored. Selkirk spent four years and four months on the island, with only his Bible and dozens of wild goats for company. During that time he was transformed into an extraordinary athlete, as he hunted the goats on foot, and a devout Christian.

Following his **rescue** by a British ship in 1709, however, Selkirk reverted to his buccaneering ways, joining in attacks on Spanish vessels all the way home. Back in Fife, the former castaway became something of a celebrity and threw himself into a life of drink and women. Fourteen years after his rescue, Selkirk finally met his end when he took up the seafaring life once more, set off on another privateering expedition and died of fever in the tropics.

11

warships at the German *Dresden* during World War I. The Germans surrendered, but sank their ship rather than let it go to the British, and the wreck still lies 70m under the sea, in Bahía Cumberland. Nearby you'll find the graves of the naval battle's casualties in the island's **cemetery**, next to the lighthouse.

Casa de la Cultura and El Palillo

At the **Casa de la Cultura**, there are some interesting historic **photos**, primarily of the World War I incident. The building was badly damaged in the tsunami, however, and was closed at the time of research. At the southern end of the bay, a 5min walk from the village, the small rocky beach of **El Palillo** is good for swimming and diving.

Hikes on Isla Robinson Crusoe

There are numerous good hikes around the island, though some are not marked; you will need local guides for all of those in the eastern half of the island, as well as between Bahía Inglés and Puerto Vaquería. Some destinations are reached by boat with a local fisherman, who can drop you off in the morning and pick you up at the end of their day's work.

Sendero Salsipuedes

Excellent short hikes from San Juan Bautista include the fairly steep **Sendero Salsipuedes** ("Get out if you can"), which leads from the village's Calle La Pólvora through pine and eucalyptus forest up to the *mirador* overlooking Bahía Cumberland from the northwest side. Allow an hour's roundtrip and beware of loose scree. The views of San Juan Bautista spread out below are excellent. From here, though, landslides render it dangerous to navigate.

Plazoleta El Yunque

A sometimes muddy 3km trail leads from the village (continuing from Calle Lord Anson; 1hr 30min return) through native forest to **Plazoleta El Yunque**, a lookout point and an attractive shaded campsite with picnic tables at the foot of Cerro El Yunque, the island's tallest mountain (915m). The nearby stone ruins are the remains of the house of Hugo Weber, the "German Robinson Crusoe", who spent twelve years living as a hermit here after escaping from the *Dresden* in 1915. From the campsite, the pleasant trail loops through native vegetation, including giant *nalca* (rhubarb) and ferns, before finishing back at the campsite. From the Plazoleta, it is possible to make the steep ascent through thick native forest to **El Camote**, a peak offering spectacular views of the island, though this requires a guide.

11

> ### BOAT TRIPS FROM SAN JUAN BAUTISTA
>
> A fifteen-minute boat ride from the village is **Puerto Inglés**, where you'll find a mock-up of the cave where Selkirk took refuge and a good camping spot. Other boat destinations include **Puerto Vaquería**, west of Bahía Inglés, a popular spot to snorkel with seals; **Puerto Francés**, in the eastern part of the island, where there are ramparts overlooking the sea, built by the Spanish to deter French pirates; and **Playa Arenal**, the island's only sandy beach with warm, transparent waters, which lies 2hr 30min by boat through islets and seal colonies, just south of the airstrip.

Cerro Centinela

A 45min walk south of San Juan Bautista, and then a 362m hike up a trail, takes you to the top of **Cerro Centinela**, which offers expansive views of Bahía Cumberland and Bahía El Pangál. From here, an unmarked trail zigzags its way along the coast to Puerto Francés, a route only to be attempted with a knowledgeable local.

The cross-island hike

The island's **best hike** runs from the airstrip to San Juan Bautista, via the Mirador Alejandro Selkirk; bring plenty of water and allow at least five hours. Arrange to be dropped off by a fisherman at the Bahía del Padre, the launching place for the boat that picks you up from the airstrip, and home to a large colony of fur seals. Outside breeding season, they are not dangerous and you can swim and snorkel with them. The largest fur seal colony lies at **Bahía Tierra Blanca**, the first bay you come to along the trail.

Follow the road uphill and take the well-marked trail running from the airstrip. The path skirts the zigzagging coastline, with turquoise bays appearing around every corner, the barking of sea lions echoing from below and the landscape gradually changing from arid desert-like hills with their vividly multicoloured soil to steep pasture land to jagged mountains covered in dense endemic vegetation. For the most part, it's wide enough to take a vehicle, ascending very gradually until you reach **Villagra**, a couple of houses with a corral for animals, where the rodeo is held in February.

Mirador Alejandro Selkirk

At Villagra, the cross-island track divides; take the rocky footpath overgrown with vegetation, which climbs steeply uphill until it reaches the **Mirador Alejandro Selkirk**, the famous lookout point where, according to a disputed story, Selkirk lit his daily smoke signals and scoured the horizon for ships. Here you'll be rewarded with stunning panoramic views of most of the island. Note the two metal memorial plaques set in the rocks, one donated by the officers of HMS *Topaze* in 1868, the other by one of Selkirk's descendants in 1983, pledging to remember his forefather "Till a' the seas gang dry and the rocks melt i' the sun".

If you don't have time to do a cross-island hike, you can reach the *mirador* from the village, though it's a steeper climb (around 90min); the path starts north of the plaza.

ARRIVAL AND DEPARTURE

ISLA ROBINSON CRUSOE

By plane Getting to Isla Robinson Crusoe is an adventure in itself, involving a bumpy flight on a seven-seater plane. Two airlines serve the island, usually once or twice weekly, depending on demand: ATA (☎2 2275 0363, ⓦ aerolineasata.cl) and LASSA (☎2 2273 5209, ⓔ lassa@ terra.cl), both based at Aeródromo Tobalaba, Av Larraín 7941, Santiago. Both firms have a 10-kilo luggage allowance and charge around CH$550,000 (US$955) return. It is a bit cheaper to organize a charter flight, if you

can get a group of at least six together; contact Santiago FBO (☎2 2674 4000, ⓦ santiagofbo.cl) for details. Flights are weather-dependent, so be prepared to spend an extra day or two on the island in case of inclement weather. The little airstrip is 13km from San Juan Bautista; a speedboat (included in the price of your flight) transfers you to the village; it can be a rough ride.

By boat Transmarko (☎09 6157 7480, ⓦ transmarko.cl) has irregular services from Valparaíso (return ticket, including full board, CH$154,500; 40–45hr); the boat spends 5–7 days on the island before returning. There is also a monthly navy supply boat from Valparaíso, which spends around 72hr on the island; a one-way ticket costs around CH$30,000. You can try and book passage with the Comando de Transporte at the Primera Zona Naval, Plaza Sotomayor 592, Valparaíso (☎ 32 250 6354), but bear in mind that departure dates change monthly, and preference is given to islanders.

INFORMATION AND TOURS

Tourist information The Municipalidad (☎ 32 270 1045, ⓦ comunajuanfernandez.cl) and Conaf (☎ 32 268 0381, ⓦ www.conaf.cl), next door to each other on Vicente González, can both provide information on the island; the latter also has a small kiosk near the plaza. National park entry permits (necessary for most of the activities on the island) cost CH$3000, and are valid for a week.

Tours *Crusoe Island Lodge* (see below) offers a range of activities, including hikes, historical tours, fishing trips (including for lobster), diving, surfing and birdwatching.

ACCOMMODATION

There is a full list of **accommodation** options on the municipal website (ⓦ comunajuanfernandez.cl). Most people eat at their hotel/guesthouse.

Crusoe Island Lodge 3km east of the village ☎ 09 9078 1301, ⓦ crusoeislandlodge.com. This stylish lodge has a wonderful location, in a tranquil spot overlooking a bay. The modern en suites – constructed from recycled materials and local wood – have wonderful sea views from their balconies. There's an excellent restaurant, plus a pool, spa, wi-fi access and plenty of activities to keep you busy. Breakfast included; full-board deals available too. US$270

Hostal Petit Breuilh Vicente Rozales 80 ☎ 09 9549 9033, ⓦ hostalpetit.cl. This guesthouse, 300m from the dock, has simple rooms with attached bathrooms, fridges and TVs, as well as a bar-restaurant and laundry service. The owners can help arrange local guides and excursions. Rates include full-board. CH$64,000

Hostería El Mirador de Selkirk Castillo 251 ☎ 09 8845 7024, ⓔ mfernandeziana@hotmail.com. Attractive B&B with good views and a handful of comfy rooms. The owner is a third-generation islander – she is happy to talk about her family history – and a good cook. Rates include full-board. CH$80,000

Hotel Refugio Náutico At the southeastern edge of the village ☎ 09 7483 5014, ⓦ islarobinsoncrusoe.cl. This mid-range choice boasts attractive, en-suite rooms, a good bar-restaurant (try the local lobster or golden crab) and a hot tub. Staff can arrange various excursions and activities, and guests can make use of kayaks and snorkelling gear. The rate here is for room only, but bed-and-breakfast and half- and full-board packages are available too. US$220

DIRECTORY

Hospital The Posta Rural, Vicente González s/n, deals with minor medical emergencies; anyone requiring serious treatment has to be flown to the mainland.

Money and exchange There are no banks or *cambios* on the island, so bring plenty of cash with you; bear in mind that poor weather may delay your flight by a day or two.

Isla Alejandro Selkirk

Travellers to Isla Robinson Crusoe with plenty of time and energy to spare may consider attempting to reach the even more remote and ruggedly mountainous **Isla Alejandro Selkirk**. During the October to May lobster season, it is home to around forty to fifty people, as well as a small team of conservationists and some feral goats. Bring all necessary food and gear with you, including a tent.

ARRIVAL AND DEPARTURE
ISLA ALEJANDRO SELKIRK

By boat An irregular supply boat (roughly 17hr; around CH$60,000), as well as fishermen, ply the waters between Isla Robinson Crusoe and Isla Alejandro Selkirk. Contact the Municipalidad about passage; if you don't arrange a return trip, you may find yourself marooned for some time.

EX-PRESIDENT SEBASTIÁN PIÑERA AT THE SAN JOSÉ MINE

Contexts

467 History

492 Landscape and the environment

498 Chilean music: nueva canción

504 Books

509 Chilean Spanish

History

Enveloped by the Andes, the Atacama Desert and the Pacific Ocean, Chile has evolved almost as an island, relatively undisturbed by the turbulence that has raged through much of South America's history. Though inhabited by indigenous groups for millennia, the country's actual recorded history dates from the sixteenth-century arrival of the Spaniards. The colonial society that emerged and the ensuing struggle for independence resemble that of the whole continent, but from its early days as a republic, Chile took on its own political shape, distinct from that of its neighbours. With its largely ordered, constitutional model of government, and a healthy respect for the law, Chile earned itself the sobriquet "the England of South America" in the nineteenth century, which is why it was so surprising when it returned to the attention of the outside world with the repressive military regime of General Augusto Pinochet in the 1970s and 1980s. Today, with democracy firmly back in place, Chile is an outward-looking nation boasting political and economic stability, albeit with some serious social inequalities and unresolved political legacies lurking beneath the surface.

The Ice Age and beyond

Chile's anthropological record, like that of all the Americas, began when the first groups of Asians crossed the land bridge connecting Siberia to Alaska before the end of the last Ice Age, when the sea level was 70–100m lower than it is today. Archaeologists are unable to tell us exactly when this **first migration** occurred, but it's generally thought to have been between 25,000 and 40,000 years ago.

What *is* known is that by 12,000 BC the descendants of these people, supplemented by further waves of migration from Asia, had spread down the whole of North and South America as far as the southern tip of Patagonia. While some devoted themselves to fishing, the majority were probably nomadic hunters living off the animals that inhabited the region at the time – mastodons (prehistoric elephants), mammoths, giant armadillos and wild horses. When the last Ice Age came to an end around 11,000 BC, the climate changed abruptly and many of these animals became extinct. The hunters were forced to adapt, supplementing their diet by gathering fruits and seeds. Eventually this led to the deliberate cultivation of foodstuffs and the domestication of animals; along with these incipient agricultural practices came more stable communities and important developments, such as pottery and burial customs. Slowly, distinct cultural groups emerged, shaped by their very different environments and the resources available to them.

12,500 BC	5000 BC	1463 AD	1520
Carbon dating places the first inhabited site in South America just outside Chile's Puerto Montt.	Mummification technique developed by the Chinchorro people.	The Incas conquer a huge part of Chile up to the Río Maule.	The first European to reach Chile, Ferdinand Magellan, sails through the strait now named after him.

The pre-Columbian cultures

In the absence of written records, archeologists have had to piece together information about Chile's **pre-Columbian cultures** from what these groups have left behind, principally funerary offerings found in burial sites and domestic objects left in former dwelling places. The strata in which the remains are buried (plus the use of radiocarbon dating) indicate the chronology in which these developments took place. However, variations in Chile's geography from north to south present unequal conditions for the preservation of artefacts and have led to a far greater knowledge of the cultures of the north than those of the south.

Mummies and hallucinogens: El Norte Grande

More is known about the pre-Columbian cultures of Chile's Norte Grande – the Far North – than of any other part of the country. The extreme dryness of the Atacama Desert preserved archeological remains for thousands of years. One of the earliest groups of people to leave its mark was the **Chinchorro culture**, a collection of nomadic fishing communities that lived along the desert coast some eight thousand years ago. By 5000 BC, the Chinchorro had developed the practice of **mummifying their dead** (see box, p.209) – two thousand years earlier than the Egyptians. Their technique, which involved removing internal organs and tissues and replacing them with vegetable fibres and mud, survived for four thousand years and is the oldest known in the world.

By around 500 BC, life in El Norte Grande was based largely on agriculture, supplemented by fishing in the coastal areas, and herding llamas and alpacas in the Andean highlands. Although vast tracts of the region are taken up by barren desert, a number of oases provided fertile land where agricultural communities were able to dedicate themselves to the cultivation of maize, beans, squash, chillies and potatoes. They lived in permanent dwellings, usually consisting of circular huts surrounding a shared patio, and often with a cemetery nearby.

Among the most important (and longest-lasting) of these early agricultural groups was the **San Pedro culture** (also known as the Atacameño culture), which settled along the salt-flat oases around San Pedro de Atacama in around 500 BC. They produced ceramics, textiles and objects in copper and stone, along with delicately carved wooden snuff tablets and tubes used for inhaling hallucinogenic substances – a custom probably introduced by the **Tihuanaco culture** in around 300 AD. This latter was a powerful religious state based near the southern shores of Lake Titicaca in present-day Bolivia, and its influence extended over most of northern Chile and much of Peru for many centuries. The Tihuanaco impact was most visible in the spread of its ceramics and textiles, often decorated with images of cats, condors and snakes, which probably had religious significance. The Tihuanaco also fostered an active trading system, encouraging the exchange of goods between regions, bringing about increased social stratification, with those at the top controlling the commercial traffic.

Sometime between 900 and 1200 AD, the Tihuanaco culture declined and collapsed, for reasons unknown today. The regional cultures of the Norte Grande were then free to reassert their individual authority and identity, expressing their independence with a series of *pukarás* (fortresses) dotted around the altiplano. This period of *desarrollo regional* ("regional development"), as it is known, was halted only by the arrival of the Inca in the late fifteenth century.

1535	1535–1880	1541
The first Spanish venture into Chile under the command of Diego de Almagro ends in failure.	The Arauco War: the Mapuche resist all attempts at conquest from their stronghold south of the Río Biobío.	Conquistador Pedro de Valdivia reaches the Mapocho Valley and founds the city of Santiago de Nueva Extremadura on February 12.

Llamas and ceramics: El Norte Chico

Around 300 AD, when the peoples of the Norte Grande had been living in fixed agricultural communities for several centuries, those of the Norte Chico were just beginning to abandon their lives of hunting and gathering, and turn to cattle herding and farming. The resulting **El Molle culture** was composed of communities that settled along the river valleys between Copiapó and Illapel, where they developed a system of artificial irrigation to cultivate maize, beans, squash and possibly cotton. They also herded llamas, a practice recorded in numerous petroglyphs, and produced the first ceramics of the Norte Chico. Between 700 and 800 AD the El Molle culture declined and was replaced by a new cultural group known as **Las Animas**, which probably originated in the Argentine highlands. The changes introduced by this culture included rapid developments in metalworking; new, more decorative, styles of pottery, and – most curiously – the custom of ritual sacrifice of llamas.

Towards 1000 AD, the important **Diaguita culture** appeared in the Norte Chico, dominating the region over the next five centuries until the Spanish invasion. The Diaguita tended to live in large villages along the river valleys, presided over by a chief and a shaman. Each valley was divided into two sections: a "lower" section, towards the coast, which was ruled by one chief, and a "higher" section, towards the mountains, ruled by another. Their economy was based on agriculture, herding, mining and metalworking, and was supplemented by fishing on the coast, aided by the invention of inflated sealskin rafts. The Diaguita's greatest achievement, however, was their outstandingly fine pottery, characterized by intricate white, black and red geometric patterns.

Burial urns and mud huts: central Chile

The first agricultural groups to settle in central Chile were the **El Bato** and **Llolleo** peoples, from around 300 AD. The El Bato group occupied the zone between the Río Choapa (near Illapel) and the Río Maipo (south of Santiago); its highly polished monochrome pottery indicates that it was strongly influenced by the El Molle culture from the Norte Chico. The Llolleo settlements were spread along the coastal plains between the Río Aconcagua (just north of Santiago) and the Río Maule (near Talca). One of the most striking characteristics of this culture was their custom of burying their dead under their own houses, with small children buried in clay urns.

Later, around 900 AD, the **Aconcagua** emerged as the dominant culture in Central Chile; these people lived in houses made of branches and mud and dedicated themselves to growing beans, maize, squash and potatoes; they also developed far more specialized ceramics than had previously existed in the region.

Nomads and hunters: Araucania

While relatively little is known about the development of the cultures in the south of Chile, owing to a paucity of archeological remains, it's generally agreed that the first group to adopt cultivation was the **Pitrén culture**, around 600 AD. This comprised small family groups spread between the Biobío and Lago Llanquihue, where they grew maize and potatoes on a small scale, as well as hunting and gathering. They also produced ceramics, often decorated with zoomorphic and anthropomorphic images, which they usually buried with their dead.

1553	1554	1561
Lautaro, a famous Mapuche chief, kills Pedro de Valdivia in a particularly gruesome manner during the Battle of Tucapel.	The first vines are brought to Chile by conquistadors, marking the beginning of wine production.	Governor Don García Hurtado de Mendoza is sent from Peru to subjugate the natives in central Chile.

LA LUCHA DE MAPUCHE

The **Mapuche**, or "people of the land" from "che" (people) and "mapu" (of the land), have been in constant conflict with invaders since the arrival of the Spanish, a conflict that continues today. Though they have put up the bravest resistance out of all the indigenous people of the Americas, the Mapuche have nevertheless seen their original homeland of over 100,000 square kilometres shrink to just 5000 square kilometres. While Chile's left-wing governments tried to address the **land issue**, any improvements made between 1965 and 1973 were reversed by Pinochet's government, which went a step further by signing into law an anti-terrorist act aimed squarely at any Mapuche attempts to assert themselves and pursue their rights, punishing crimes such as arson with excessively long prison sentences, torture and harassment of families of arsonists.

While some progress has been made in the dispute over their historical **ancestral territory** (known as *Wallmapu*) since the return of democracy, many Mapuche feel that the concessions made by the Chilean government fall far short and that their lands are under constant threat from powerful business interests. Today, the Mapuche lead a largely marginalized existence in Chile's Lake District; living mostly in cities – Temuco in particular – or rural *reducciones* (settlements) and making a living from small-scale agriculture and selling handicrafts. Though their language, *Mapundungun*, is no longer outlawed as it was under Pinochet, there is nevertheless constant pressure to assimilate.

Though not as actively endorsed by the Chilean government as under Pinochet, police persecution of Mapuche communities (and those sympathetic to the Mapuche cause, such as foreign journalists) has nevertheless been brought to the attention of various human rights organizations in recent years. **Clashes** between the Mapuche and the police are commonplace and abuses have ranged from harassment, such as tear gas grenades thrown into Mapuche houses, to holding the likes of 12-year-old Luis Marileo – accused of belonging to an "illegal terrorist organization" – in a detention centre and shooting 17-year-old Alex Lemun in the head during a violent eviction. In January 2012, indigenous Mapuche activists were accused of deliberately starting forest fires in the Biobío region, killing seven firemen and leading President Sebastian Piñera to invoke an **anti-terror law** to pursue those responsible; when coming home after attending the funeral of a fire fighter who died in the forest fire, one of the Mapuche leaders found his house had been deliberately burnt down.

For more information on the Mapuche's ongoing struggle check out ⓦmapuche-nation.org.

Around 1000 AD a new community, known as **El Vergel**, emerged in the region between Angol and Temuco. Its economy combined hunting and gathering with the cultivation of potatoes, maize, beans and squash, and it is likely that its people were the first to domesticate guanacos. Other practices these people brought to the region included burying their dead in ceramic urns, which they decorated with red and white paint. They also developed a very beautiful style of pottery, now known as Valdivia pottery, characterized by parallel zigzag lines and shaded triangles.

Sometime in the fourteenth century a group of nomadic hunters called the *moluche* ("people of war") arrived from Argentina and occupied the land between the Itata and Toltén rivers. They absorbed the existing Pitrén and El Vergel cultures to form a new entity called **Mapuche** ("people of the land"). While engaging in fishing, hunting and gathering, their lifestyle was based principally on herding and farming – labour was divided between the sexes, with men responsible for preparing the fields, and women for sowing and harvesting. The basic social unit was the family clan, or "lov", which were

1593	1598	1600s
The first Jesuit order arrives in Chile and sets about converting locals and appropriating large amounts of land.	The Great Uprising removes all Spanish presence south of the Río Biobío and the river becomes the Spanish–Mapuche frontier.	The *encomienda* system is established, which involves parcelling out land to settlers and using natives as slaves.

independent from each other and autonomous. Its isolation meant the Mapuche culture didn't develop any further until it was forced to unite in the face of the Spanish invasion.

Canoe fishermen and hunters: the far south

The narrow channels, fjords, impenetrable jungles and wild steppes of the far south have never encouraged communities to settle in one place. Accordingly, the peoples that inhabited this region led a more primitive lifestyle than those further north – they could not adopt agriculture as their main economy, and so maintained their tradition of hunting and fishing in nomadic groups. Groups like the **Selk'nam** and the **Tehuelche** hunted guanaco and rhea on the Patagonian steppes, and lived in temporary wigwam-like structures covered in guanaco skins. The **Yámana** and **Chono** people hunted seals, otters, birds and gathered shellfish in their canoes, constantly moving from place to place. None of the Patagonian or Fuegian groups produced ceramics, manufacturing instead bows, arrows, lassos, baskets and warm skin capes. Their understanding of the world was rich in mythology and symbolism – the Selk'nam, for instance, believed that many birds and animals were spirits that had once been human; they also practised elaborate initiation rites marking the passage from boyhood into manhood, involving physical tests and secret ceremonies. Unlike the other native peoples of Chile, these groups were never incorporated into Spanish colonial society, and their lifestyles remained virtually unchanged until the twentieth century, when the clash with seal hunters and sheep farmers led to their disappearance.

The Inca conquest

While the native peoples of Chile were developing relatively simple communities based on agriculture, herding and fishing, a great civilization was emerging further to the north – that of the **Inca**. These people arrived in Cusco around 1200 AD and by the fifteenth century had developed a sophisticated and highly organized society that boasted palaces, temples and fortresses of great architectural sophistication. In 1463, the Inca emperor, Pachacuti, initiated a period of massive **expansion** that saw the conquest of lands stretching north to modern-day Quito and south as far as the Río Maule in Chile, where its progress was halted by the fierce resistance of the Mapuche.

The Inca effect

The impact of the Inca in Chile was considerable: they constructed a breathtaking network of roads connecting conquered territory to the capital of the empire in Cusco (which later proved to be very useful to the Spanish conquistadors), and forced the subjugated peoples to pay tribute to the Inca ruler and to use **Quechua** as their official language. While the Inca tolerated indigenous cults, they required their subjects also to adopt the **cult of the sun**, a central tenet of the Inca religion. Sun worship usually took place at altars built on high mountain peaks where the sun's first rays were received; it sometimes involved human sacrifice, but more commonly animals or objects like silver figurines were offered as substitutes. Remains of Inca worship sites have been found on numerous mountains in Chile, the most famous being Cerro El Plomo, near Santiago, where the frozen body of a small child, undoubtedly offered as a sacrifice, was discovered in 1954. The Inca occupation of Chile spanned a relatively short period of

Late 1600s	1759–88	1767
Owing to the decimation of the native population, mestizos are used as hacienda labourers.	Charles III takes the Spanish throne and lifts trade restrictions in order to increase Chile's revenue and then tax it.	Believing them to be too powerful, the Spanish Crown expels the Jesuits from Chile and other Spanish colonies.

time – about seventy years in the Norte Grande and perhaps just thirty in Central Chile. It was interrupted first by civil war in Cusco, caused by the struggle between two rivals over succession to the throne. Then, in 1532, the Spanish arrived in Peru, marking the beginning of the end of the Inca empire.

Enter the Spanish

It was while seeking a westward route to Asia across the Atlantic that **Christopher Columbus** inadvertently "discovered" the Americas in 1492. His patron, Queen Isabella of Spain, supported him on two further expeditions, and sent settlers to colonize the Caribbean island of Hispaniola (site of today's Haiti and Dominican Republic). It gradually became apparent that the islands were not part of Asia, and that a giant landmass – indeed a whole continent – separated them from the East. After colonizing several other islands, the explorers and adventurers, backed by the Spanish Crown, turned their attention to the mainland, and the period of conquest began in earnest.

The conquest of Peru and venture into Chile

In 1521 **Hernán Cortés** defeated the great **Aztec Empire** in Mexico and then in 1524 **Francisco Pizarro** and his partner **Diego de Almagro** set out to find the rich empire they had been told lay further south. After several failed attempts, they finally landed on the coast of **Peru** in 1532, where they found the great **Inca Empire** racked by civil war. Pizarro speedily conquered the empire, aided by advanced military weapons and tactics, a frenzied desire for gold and glory and, most significantly, the devastating effect of Old World diseases on the indigenous population. Within a few years, Peru was firmly in Spanish hands.

Diego de Almagro was entrusted with the mission of carrying the conquest further south to the region named **Chile**, spoken of by the Peruvian natives as a land rich in gold and silver. In 1535, Almagro and his four hundred men set off from Cusco and followed an Inca road down the spine of the Andes as far as the Aconcagua Valley, suffering extreme deprivation and hardship along the way. To make matters worse, the conquistador found none of the riches the Peruvians had spoken of. Bitterly disappointed, Almagro returned to Cusco, where his deteriorating relations with Pizarro led to armed combat and death at the hands of Pizarro's brothers.

Colonization of Chile and clashes with the Mapuche

Three years later, **Pedro de Valdivia** (one of Pizarro's most trusted officers) was granted license to colonize Chile. Owing to its lack of gold and the miseries of the first expedition, Chile was not an attractive destination, and so it was with just ten compatriots, a group of native porters and his mistress, Inés Suarez, that Valdivia set off from Cusco in 1540. Almost a year later, having picked up 150 extra men en route, Valdivia reached the Río Mapocho in the Aconcagua Valley, where he founded **Santiago de la Nueva Extremadura** on February 12, 1541. The new "city" was hastily put together, with all the trappings of a colonial capital, including church, prison, court and *cabildo* (town council), which elected Valdivia as governor. It was a humble affair, regularly attacked and destroyed by local Picunche, but the new colonists were determined to stay and did not return to Peru.

1777–78	1810	1818
Chile's first general census indicates that the country's population consists of 259,646 inhabitants.	A national junta is established to govern Chile in place of the deposed King Ferdinand VII.	José de San Martín liberates Santiago and Bernardo O'Higgins becomes "supreme director" of the new Chilean republic.

Over the next decade, Valdivia attempted to expand the colony, founding the cities of **La Serena** in the north in 1544 and **Concepción** in the south in 1550, followed by a handful of other centres in the south. It was here that the Spaniards faced the fierce resistance of the **Mapuche** (known by the Spanish as the Araucanians), who successfully prevented the spread of colonization south of the Río Biobío, thereafter known as **La Frontera**. It was in a confrontation with the Mapuche that Valdivia met his death in 1553, at the hands of the famous chief **Lautaro**. The details of Valdivia's execution are believed to be particularly grisly – some versions claim he was forced to swallow molten gold, others that he was lanced to death by a crowd of warriors, one of whom sliced through his breast and ripped out his heart.

In the panic caused by Valdivia's death, the southern colonists retreated to Santiago, leaving only Concepción as a garrison outpost, occupied mainly by soldiers guarding La Frontera. A new governor – Don García Hurtado de Mendoza – was dispatched from Peru, and by the time his term of office ended, in 1561, the natives in the central region had been subjugated, though the south would remain a no-go area for another three centuries.

Colonial society

The new colony was a marginal, isolated and unprofitable addition to Spain's empire in the Americas, which revolved around the viceroyalties of Mexico and Peru. The need to maintain a standing army to guard La Frontera, and the absence of large quantities of precious metals to fund it, meant that Chile ran at a deficit for most of the colonial period. Administratively, it was designated a "**captaincy-general**", ruled by a governor with the help of an *audiencia* (a high court, whose function included advising the governor). All high officials were sent from Spain as representatives of the king, whose authority was absolute, and whose instructions were communicated via the *Consejo de Indias* (Council of the Indies). Chile, however, received little attention and, enclosed within the mighty barriers of the Atacama desert and Andean cordillera, was more or less left to its own devices.

Haciendas and encomiendas

Growth was very slow, amounting to no more than five thousand settlers by 1600. Most of these lived from the farming of land handed out by the governor in grants known as **mercedes de tierra**, spreading over the valleys near Santiago and in the Central Valley. At the same time, large "grants" of indigenous people were given to the colonists in what was known as the **encomienda** system – the *encomienda* being the group of natives allocated to an *encomendero* as a force of effectively slave labour (see box, p.474).

During the **seventeenth century** this pattern became more clearly defined with the emergence and economic dominance of the **hacienda**. Enclosed within thick, protective walls, haciendas were self-sufficient, self-contained entities, whose buildings – arranged around numerous courtyards – comprised workshops, wine *bodegas*, dairies, a chapel and the *casa patronal*, the landowner's home. Initially the workforce was provided by *encomiendas*, but, with tragic inevitability, the indigenous population rapidly decreased through exposure to Old World diseases. In its place there sprang up a new generation of **mestizos**, the result of miscegenation between the Spanish colonists (almost exclusively male in the early years) and indigenous women.

1821	1826	1833
Spanish troops around Valdivia are defeated by British privateer Thomas Cochrane who sails in under a Spanish flag.	The remaining Spanish troops on the island of Chiloé surrender, marking the end of the Spanish presence in Chile.	Diego Portales is the architect of Chile's first Constitution, which grants enormous powers to the president.

> ## THE LIE OF THE LAND
>
> In theory, the land-owning *encomenderos* of the colonial system were supposed to look after the wellbeing of their charges and convert them to Christianity in exchange for tribute (by means of work) offered to the Spanish Crown. In reality, the system simply provided the colonists with a large **slave workforce** that they could treat however they pleased, which was often appallingly. From the very beginning, then, the *mercedes de tierra* and *encomiendas* established a pattern that was to dominate Chile's rural society until modern times: namely, large estates owned by seignorial landlords at the head of a dependent, disempowered workforce.

In time, a more or less homogeneous mestizo population came to make up the bulk of the Chilean workforce, presided over by a ruling, land-owning elite made up of **peninsulares** (Spaniards born in Spain) and **criollos** (those of Spanish blood born in the colony). Most mestizos were incorporated into the haciendas either as peons or as **inquilinos** – labourers allowed to farm a small plot of land in return for year-round service (a practice that continued until the twentieth century).

The rise of the Catholic Church

Along with the haciendas, the other main shaping force in Chilean society was the **Catholic Church**. From the colony's earliest days, missionaries from most orders poured into Chile and embarked on a zealous programme of conversion in the farthest flung corners of the territory, which further helped to decimate the native population through the introduction of European-borne diseases. The missionaries' success was rapid and set the seal on the "pacification" of the indigenous people, who were less likely to cause trouble if they could be incorporated into the Hispanic culture and their sense of separate identity diminished. The Catholicism that emerged wasn't an altogether orthodox version, as many indigenous elements of worship – such as ritual dancing and sacrificial offerings – were incorporated into this new religion, and even now survive in Chile's more remote communities, especially in the north. Nonetheless, both *indígenas* and mestizos embraced the symbolic elements of the Catholic faith with enthusiasm, and several cults sprang up around supposedly miraculous icons, such as the **Cristo de Mayo** in Santiago, believed to have bled real blood after an earthquake in 1647.

The most influential element of the Church was the **Jesuit order** (Compañía de Jesús), which arrived in Chile in 1593 and quickly established itself as one of the colony's largest landowners (see box, p.475).

Expansion of trade

The reign of **Charles III**, from 1759 to 1788, brought great changes to the colony. The most progressive of the Bourbon monarchs (who had replaced the Habsburg dynasty in Spain in 1700), the king set about improving the management of the American colonies and increasing their productivity, so as to augment revenues. Among his reforms was the relaxation of the stifling trade restrictions that had hampered economic growth throughout much of Spanish America. Suddenly, the colonies were able to trade freely with each other and with Spain. There was no overnight miracle, but Chilean trade did expand considerably, particularly with neighbouring Río de la Plata (future Argentina).

1834–35	1848–58	1860
Charles Darwin sails along Chile's coast in the HMS *Beagle* and seizes three Fuegian natives.	The port of Valparaíso becomes a crucial supply stop for ships en route to California during the California Gold Rush.	Orélie-Antoine de Tounens, an eccentric Frenchman, befriends Mapuche leaders and is crowned King of Araucanía.

THE RISE AND FALL OF THE JESUITS

In a paternalistic arrangement, the **Jesuits** gathered hundreds of indigenous families to their **missions**, where they were fed, clothed, converted, taught Spanish and instructed in a diverse array of skills from weaving to glass manufacturing. As a result, the order's numerous **workshops** were the most productive and profitable in the country – as was the case throughout Spanish America – until the Jesuits were suddenly **expelled** from the Spanish Empire in 1767, when the Crown was persuaded that they had become too powerful to be tolerated.

At the same time, imports soared, and the need to pay for them in gold or silver stimulated a small **mining boom** in the Norte Chico. Settlements sprang up around the mining centres, and some, such as Copiapó, Vallenar and Illapel, were granted official city status. All in all, there was an emerging spirit of change and progress, which gave a sense of empowerment to Chile's *criollos*, who had always been barred from the highest colonial offices. But while Chile's commercial horizons were widening, the king's administrative shake-ups – which involved sending a number of *intendants* to the colonies to tighten up administration and eradicate abuses of local power – were experienced as unwanted interference. The resulting tension would soon find a more focused channel.

The struggle for independence

Chile entered the **nineteenth century** with a burgeoning sense of its own identity. The *criollo* elite (Chile-born Spanish), while fiercely loyal to the Spanish king, was becoming increasingly alienated from the *intendants* dispatched from Spain to administer the colony, and the gap between them was widening with each successive generation. *Criollo* aspirations of playing a more active role in government (and thus of looking after their own interests, not just the Crown's) were given a sudden, unexpected opportunity for fulfilment when Napoleon invaded Spain in 1808 and deposed Ferdinand VII. **Local juntas** sprang up in Spain's main cities to organize resistance to Napoleon, and they were soon followed by a number of locally elected juntas in the American colonies. In Chile, over four hundred leading citizens gathered in Santiago on September 18, 1810, and elected a six-man **junta**, made up of Chileans. It must be stressed that the junta's initial objective was to "preserve the sovereignty of Ferdinand VII" in the absence of legitimate authority, and few entertained thoughts of independence at this stage. The junta did, however, go on to implement several far-reaching reforms: trade was liberalized; a Congress was elected; and the *real audiencia* (royal court) was replaced by a tribunal with Chilean judges.

The first stirrings of independence

Soon, a minority of *criollos* began to seek a far greater degree of autonomy for the colony, and whispers of independence grew. This small tide was given dramatic impetus in November 1811, when **José Miguel Carrera**, a member of one of the wealthiest and most influential *criollo* families in Chile, seized power, dissolving Congress and appointing himself head of a new, more radical, junta. His actions were swift and bold, and included the creation of a Chilean flag and the drafting of a provisional constitution that declared all rulings issued outside Chile to be illegitimate. Greatly alarmed, the

1865	1879–84	1881–83
A wool boom heralds a prosperous new era in Patagonia after the introduction of sheep from the Falklands brings wealth.	Chile goes to war with Bolivia and Peru in the War of the Pacific and emerges victorious.	The last big Mapuche uprising is defeated in the "Pacification of Araucanía"; Mapuche children are enslaved.

viceroy of Peru – where the colonial machinery remained intact – sent troops in early 1813 down to the old-guard strongholds of Chiloé and Valdivia to prepare for an assault on Santiago. In response, Carrera charged down to confront them with Chilean troops (whose generals numbered one Bernardo O'Higgins, the son of a former viceroy of Peru), and war was effectively declared. Loyalties were now thrown sharply into focus with the **Royalists** on one side, made up of Spaniards and pro-Spanish Chileans, and the **Patriots** on the other, made up of *criollos* who supported some form of self-government.

The liberators: Bernardo O'Higgins and José de San Martín

When Carrera's military leadership did not produce impressive results, the junta voted to replace him with **Bernardo O'Higgins**, who proved far more adept at holding off the Royalist forces. In July 1814, the power-hungry Carrera returned to Santiago and overthrew the government once more, reinstating himself at its head and causing considerable upheaval. In October of that year, Royalist troops, taking advantage of the chaos, began to advance on Santiago and, after a showdown at Rancagua (see box, below), ultimately won out.

The victory coincided with the defeat of Napoleon in Spain and the restoration of Ferdinand VII, who immediately set out to crack down on all insurgent elements in his American colonies. In Chile, some forty Patriot *criollos* were exiled to the Juan Fernández Islands, where they were to live in caves, and every reform instigated by the junta was reversed. The Spanish Crown's attempt to turn back the clock and revert to a centralized, interventionist colonial government was felt as repressive and authoritarian by *criollos* throughout the continent.

Just as the great general **Simón Bolívar** was preparing anti-Spanish campaigns in Venezuela that would liberate the northern half of the continent, **José de San Martín**, the Argentine general, was drawing plans for South American emancipation from his base in Mendoza, near the Chilean border. San Martín knew that independence could never be assured until the Spanish were ejected from their heartland in Peru, which he planned to achieve by first liberating Chile, from where he would launch a naval attack on Lima.

The final push

With O'Higgins in command of the Chilean division, San Martín's army scaled the cordillera over four different passes in February 1817. On February 12, Patriot forces surprised the Spaniards and defeated them at the Battle of Chacabuco, just north of Santiago. The Royalists fled to the south, and the Patriots entered the capital in triumph. Fighting continued after Royalist reinforcements were sent from Peru, but when San Martín inflicted devastating losses on their army at the Battle of Maipú in

---

THE DISASTER OF RANCAGUA

As Royalist troops neared Santiago in the autumn of 1814, **Bernardo O'Higgins** mounted a desperate and heroic defence at Rancagua, but promised reinforcements never arrived and the Patriots were overwhelmingly defeated. The "**Disaster of Rancagua**", as it is known, marked the end of **La Patria Vieja** (the name given to the fledgling independent nation) and its leaders fled across the Andean border to Mendoza in Argentina, as the Royalist troops marched triumphantly into the capital.

1883–1909	1888	1890–91
Gold is discovered in Tierra del Fuego, prompting mass immigration by fortune seekers and abuse of the native Selk'nam population.	Chile claims Easter Island; the island is turned into a sheep farm and islanders are confined to Hanga Roa.	Civil war erupts when Congress revolts over President José Manuel Balmaceda's wealth redistribution reforms, resulting in 10,000 deaths.

April 1818, the Patriot victory was complete, setting the final seal on Chilean independence. Leadership of the new country was offered to San Martín, but he declined – instead, the job went to Bernardo O'Higgins, who was elected Supreme Director by an assembly of Chile's leading *criollos*.

O'Higgins' immediate task was to put together a national navy with which to clear the southern coast of remaining Royalist troublemakers and launch the seaborne attack on Peru. A flotilla was equipped and placed under the command of a British admiral, **Lord Thomas Cochrane**, who successfully captured Callao, the port of Lima, in 1820. With the colonial nerve centre effectively toppled, the days of the Spanish Empire in the Americas were numbered.

The building of a nation

The transition from colony to republic was not smooth. In its first thirteen years of independence, Chile got through five constitutions and eleven changes of government, marked by continual tussles between **Liberal** and **Conservative** factions. Then, in 1829, the Conservatives, with the support of the army, imposed an authoritarian-style government that ushered in a long period of political stability, making Chile the envy of Latin America. The chief architect of the regime was **Diego Portales**, who never stood for presidency, preferring to run the show from various cabinet posts. Convinced that Chile could only move forward under a strong, centralist government able to maintain rigorous order, Portales designed, in 1833, the **Constitution** that was to underpin Chilean government for 92 years. It granted enormous powers to the president, allowing him, for instance, to veto any legislation passed by Congress, and protecting him from impeachment until his term of office had expired (two five-year terms were allowed). Portales was not, however, without his detractors, and in 1837, in protest at the government's invasion of Peru (which had been forcibly annexed by the Bolivian president), he was brutally gunned down by political opponents. This atrocity led to increased support for the government, which went on to defeat the Peru–Bolivia Confederation – to the great pride of Chilean citizens.

Growth and prosperity

The growing self-confidence of the nation, together with the political and social stability within it, created conditions that were favourable to growth. Between the 1830s and 1870s international trade took off rapidly, with hugely increased wheat exports fuelled by the Californian and Australian gold rushes, and, more significantly, a silver- and copper-mining boom in the Norte Chico. At the same time, advances in technology and communications saw railways, roads, steamships and a telegraph network opening up the country. Its populated territory expanded, too: a government programme encouraged Europeans to come over and settle the lakeland region of the south, which was duly cleared and farmed by some four thousand German immigrants. Meanwhile, Santiago and Valparaíso were being transformed – with avenues, parks, palaces and mansions, and an ever-expanding population.

Rise of the Liberals

In time, the nation began to tire of the authoritarian model of government established by Portales, and the influence of Liberal politics began to gain ground. In 1871 the

1904	1907	1914
Neftalí Ricardo Reyes Basoalto, better known as Pablo Neruda, is born on July 12.	The Chilean army massacres over five hundred saltpetre miners, their wives and children in Iquique.	The creation of the Panama Canal deals a huge blow to Chile's economy. Punta Arenas goes into decline.

election of **Federico Errázuriz Zañartu** as president marked the beginning of twenty years of Liberal government. Many of the Liberals' reforms were aimed at reducing the undiminished power of the Church: they legalized free worship in private places; they introduced civil cemeteries, where persons of any faith could be buried; and they instituted civil marriages and registries. The Liberals also went some way towards reducing the individual power of the president, and giving Congress a stronger role in government. The breath of fresh air and sense of optimism produced by these reforms suffered a deathblow, however, when a world recession between 1876 and 1878 sent copper and silver prices tumbling and brought wheat exports to a virtual halt, plunging Chile into economic crisis.

The War of the Pacific

Rescue was at hand in what at first appeared to be yet another calamitous situation. Ever since the 1860s, when two enterprising Chileans started exploiting the vast nitrate deposits of the Atacama desert, Chilean capital and labour had dominated the region's growing **nitrate** industry (see box, p.194). Most activity took place on the pampas around Antofagasta, which Chile had formally acknowledged as Bolivian territory in 1874 – following lengthy border disputes – in exchange for an assurance from Bolivia that export tariffs would not be raised for 25 years. Many of Chile's most prominent politicians had shares in the nitrate companies, so when Bolivia flouted its agreement by raising export taxes in 1878 – directly hitting shareholders' pockets – they were up in arms, and determined to take action.

With tension mounting, Chilean troops invaded Antofagasta in February 1879 and soon took control of the surrounding coastal strip. Within two weeks Chile and Bolivia were at war, with Peru drawn into the conflict on Bolivia's side within a couple of months. It soon became clear that success would depend on **naval supremacy** – Bolivia did not have a navy, leaving Peru and Chile pitted against each other, and fairly evenly matched. Following a series of early losses, Chile secured an overwhelming maritime victory in August 1879, when it captured Peru's principal warship, the *Huáscar*. The coast was now clear for the invasion of Peru's nitrate territories, and the emphasis shifted to land fighting. Casualties were heavy on both sides, but by June 1880 Chile had secured control of these areas with a resounding victory at El Morro, Arica.

ARTURO PRAT – A NAVAL TRAGEDY

Nothing has captured the Chilean imagination like the heroic, and tragic, efforts of **Arturo Prat** in the Battle of Iquique. On the morning of May 21, 1879, the *Esmeralda* – an old wooden boat under Prat's command – found itself under attack from Peruvian artillery on one side, and from the ironclad warship, the *Huáscar*, on the other. The two vessels could not have been more unevenly matched: the *Huáscar* boasted 300lb cannon, while those of the *Esmeralda* were only 40lb. When the *Huáscar* rammed the *Esmeralda*, Prat refused to give in, instead leaping aboard the enemy's vessel, sword in hand, determined to fight to the end. The gesture was futile, and Prat was killed on the warship's deck, but the commander's dignity and self-sacrifice have made him Chile's favourite national hero, in whose honour a thousand avenues and squares have been named.

1924	1925	1927–31
President Arturo Alessandri appoints military figures to key cabinet positions and puts pressure on Congress to pass social reform laws.	The new Constitution is drafted, restoring authority to the president, and incorporating welfare measures to quell protests.	General Carlos Ibañez passes far-reaching reforms before being ousted on a wave of Great Depression-related discontent.

With the nitrate fields theirs, the Chilean government would doubtless have been happy to bring the war to a close, but the public was clamouring for blood: it wanted Peru brought to its knees with the capture of Lima. In January 1881 Peru's humiliation was complete when Chilean troops occupied the capital. Peru was still not ready to give up, though, and the war dragged on for two more years, exhausting both sides and resulting in heavy human loss. Eventually, Peru accepted defeat, sealed by the **Treaty of Ancón** in October 1883 (an official truce with Bolivia was not signed until April the following year).

By the conclusion of the war, Chile had extended its territory by one-third, acquiring the Peruvian province of Tarapacá, and the Bolivian littoral (thus depriving Bolivia of sea access). Its new, nitrate-rich pampas yielded enormous, almost overnight wealth, refilling government coffers and restoring national confidence.

Civil war

With the nitrate industry booming in earnest, by 1890 export taxes were providing over fifty percent of government revenue. With national confidence running high and the economy in such good shape, the government's position looked unassailable. Within a short time, however, cracks began to appear in the constitutional framework, expressed by mounting tension between the legislature (Congress) and the executive branch (chiefly the president).

The conflict came to a dramatic head under the presidency of **José Manuel Balmaceda** (1886–91), a Liberal but autocratic leader who believed passionately in the president's right to run a strong executive branch – an approach jarringly at odds with the political trend of the previous couple of decades. One of the unifying objectives of the various Liberal parties was the elimination of electoral intervention, and when Balmaceda was seen to influence Congressional elections in 1886, many Liberals were outraged and withdrew their support. Equally polarizing was the president's determination to insist on his right to pick and choose his cabinet, without the approval of Congress – whose response was to refuse to pass legislation authorizing the following year's budget until Balmaceda agreed to appoint a cabinet in which they had confidence.

Neither side would give way, and as the deadline for budget approval drew close, it became obvious that Balmaceda would either have to give in to Congress's demands, or act against the Constitution. When he chose the latter option, declaring that he would carry the 1890 budget through to 1891, Congress revolted, propelling the two sides into war. Balmaceda held the army's support, while Congress secured the backing of the navy. Operating out of Iquique, where they established a junta, Congress was able to use nitrate funds to recruit and train an army. In August that year, its troops landed near Valparaíso, where they defeated Balmaceda's army in two long, bloody battles. The president, whose refusal to give in was absolute, fled to the Argentine embassy, where he wrote poignant farewell notes to his family and friends before shooting himself in the head.

The Parliamentary Republic

The authoritarian model of government established by Diego Portales in the 1830s, already undermined over the previous two decades, had now collapsed. Taking its place was a system – dubbed the **Parliamentary Republic** – based on an all-powerful

1931	1938–46	1945
Mountaineering priest Alberto de Agostini is the first man to cross the Patagonian Ice Fields.	The unionized labour movement lends its support to the Popular Front – a coalition of socialists, communists and radicals.	Gabriela Mistral – poet, educator and diplomat – is the first Latin American to win the Nobel prize for literature.

legislature and an extremely weak executive. Now it was Congress who imposed cabinets on the president, not the other way round, with frequent clashes and constantly shifting allegiances seeing cabinets formed and dissolved with breathtaking frequency – between 1891 and 1915 the government got through more than sixty ministries. This chronic instability seriously hampered government action, although, ironically, the one arena where great progress was made was the public works programme vigorously promoted by Balmaceda, which saw rapid construction of state railways, roads, bridges, schools, hospitals, prisons and town halls.

Industrial development and unrest

All this was taking place against a background of momentous social and economic change that the government, bound up with its continual infighting, seemed scarcely aware of. One of the by-products of the nitrate industry was increased **industrialization** elsewhere in Chile, as manufacturing stepped up to service increased production in the north. This, combined with the growth of railways, coal mining, education, construction and banking, saw a period of rapid **social diversification**. A new group of merchants, managers, bureaucrats and teachers formed an emerging middle class, while the increasingly urban workforce – usually living in dire poverty – formed a new working class more visible than its counterpart on the large rural estates.

It was in the nitrate fields of the north that an embryonic **labour movement** began to take root, as workers protested against the appalling conditions they were forced to live and work in. With no political representation to voice these grievances, **strikes** became the main form of protest, spreading from the mining cities of the north to the docks of Valparaíso. The government's heavy-handed attempts to suppress the strikes – reaching a peak of brutality when almost two hundred men, women and children were shot dead in Iquique, in 1907 – were symptomatic of its inability to deal with the social changes taking place in the country. When the nitrate industry entered a rapid decline with the outbreak of World War I in 1914, leaving thousands of workers unemployed and causing inflation to soar, Chile's domestic situation deteriorated further.

Military intervention

The first leader committed to dealing with the republic's mounting social problems was **Arturo Alessandri**, elected in 1920 on the strength of an ambitious reform programme. The weakness of his position, however, in the face of an all-powerful and obstructive Congress, prevented him from putting any of his plans into action, and after four years hardly anything had been achieved. Then, in 1924, a strange set of events was set in motion when an army junta – frustrated by the lack of government action – forced the cabinet to resign and had Alessandri appoint military men to key cabinet positions. The president appeared quite willing to accommodate the junta, which used its muscle to ensure that Congress swiftly passed a series of social reform laws, including legislation to protect workers' rights. After several months, however, the relationship between the president and his military cabinet began to unravel and Alessandri fled to exile in Argentina.

More drama was to follow when, on January 23, 1925, a rival junta led by General **Carlos Ibáñez** staged a coup, deposed the government and invited Alessandri to return to

1947	1960	1964
Chile establishes its first permanent Antarctic research station – Captain Arturo Prat Base – on Greenwich Island.	The tsunami caused by the Great Chilean Earthquake, the most powerful ever recorded (9.5 on the Richter Scale) devastates Valdivia.	Easter Island citizens, the Rapa Nui, are finally granted Chilean citizenship and given the right to vote.

Chile to complete his term of office. With Ibáñez's weight behind him, Alessandri set about redrafting the Constitution, with the aim of restoring authority to the president and reducing the power of Congress. This was achieved with the **Constitution of 1925**, which represented a radical departure from the one of 1833, incorporating protective welfare measures among other reforms. Despite this victory, however, tensions between Ibáñez and Alessandri led to the president's resignation. The way was now clear for the military strongman, Ibáñez, to get himself elected as president in May 1927.

Boom to bust

Ibáñez's presidency was a curious contradiction, at once highly autocratic, with severe restrictions on freedom of expression, and refreshingly progressive, ushering in a series of badly needed reforms promoting agriculture, industry and education. His early years were successful, bringing about improvements in living standards across all sections of society, and stimulating national prosperity. But when the Wall Street crash of 1929 sparked off a worldwide depression, Chile's economy collapsed virtually overnight, producing deep social unrest. Faced with a wave of street demonstrations and strikes, Ibáñez was forced to resign in July 1931. The task of restoring stability to the nation fell to the old populist, Alessandri, who was re-elected in 1932.

The rise of the multi-party system

Military interference in government affairs was now at an end (for a few decades, at least), and the country settled down to a period of orderly political evolution, no longer held back by a weak executive. What emerged was a highly diverse multi-party system embracing a wide spectrum of political persuasions. After 1938, the government was dominated by the **Radical Party**, a centre-right group principally representing the middle classes. Radical presidents such as Pedro Aguirre Cerda, Juan Antonio Ríos and Gabriel González Videla took an active role in regenerating Chile's economy, investing in state-sponsored steelworks, copper refineries, fisheries and power supplies. In the 1950s, left-wing groups gained considerable ground as the voting franchise widened, but old-guard landowners were able to counter this by controlling the votes of the thousands of peasants who depended on them for their survival, thus ensuring a firm swing back to the right. Nonetheless, it was by a very narrow margin that the socialist Salvador Allende was defeated by the Conservative Jorge Alessandri (son of Arturo) in the 1958 elections, causing widespread alarm among the wealthy elite. As the next election approached in 1964, the upper classes, with the discreet backing of the USA (still reeling from the shock of the Cuban missile crisis), threw all their efforts into securing the election of **Eduardo Frei**, the candidate of the rising young **Christian Democrat Party**.

From right-wing to left

In power, Frei turned out to be a good deal more progressive than his right-wing supporters could have imagined, initiating – to their horror – bold **agrarian reforms** that allowed the expropriation of all farms of more than 1.8 square kilometres. The other memorable achievement of the Frei administration was the "Chileanization" of the **copper industry**, which had replaced nitrates as the country's dominant source of revenue, and which was almost exclusively in the hands of North American

1964	1970	1970–73
Christian Democrat Eduardo Frei is elected president; he initiates far-reaching social and economic reforms.	Salvador Allende becomes the first democratically elected Marxist president in the world, winning by a tiny margin.	Allende's radical reforms – the nationalization of industry and land redistribution – are crippled by overspending and uncontrollable inflation.

corporations. Frei's policy gave the state a 51 percent stake in all the major copper mines, providing instant revenues to fund his social reform programme. These included the introduction of a minimum wage and impressive improvements in education, and made Frei's government popular with the working classes, though his reforms were unable to keep pace with the rush of expectations and demands. At the same time, Conservative groups became increasingly alarmed at the direction in which Frei was steering the country, prompting Liberals and Conservatives to join forces and form the new **National Party**, aimed at putting a check on reform. As Chile approached the 1970s, its population grew sharply polarized between those who clamoured for further social reform and greater representation of the working class, and those to whom this was anathema and to be reversed at all costs.

Salvador Allende's rise to power

On September 4, 1970, **Salvador Allende** was elected as Chile's first socialist president, heading a coalition of six left-wing parties, known as the **Unidad Popular** (UP). His majority, however, was tiny, and while half the country rejoiced, full of hopes for a better future, the other half feared a slide towards communism. Allende was passionately committed to improving the lot of the poorest sectors of society, whose appalling living conditions had shocked him when he had encountered them in his training as a doctor. His government pledged, among other things, to nationalize Chilean industries, to redistribute the nation's wealth, to increase popular participation in government, and to speed up agrarian reform, though there were disagreements as to how fast these changes should be made.

Within a year, over eighty major companies had been nationalized, including the copper mines, which were expropriated without compensation. The following year, radical agrarian reform was enforced, with over sixty percent of irrigated land – including all haciendas with more than 0.8 square kilometres – taken into government hands for redistribution among the rural workforce. In one fell swoop, the *latifundia* system (a system where landed estate utilised forced indigenous labour) that had dominated rural Chile for more than four hundred years was irrevocably dismantled.

In the short term, Allende's government was both successful and popular, presiding as it did over a period of economic growth, rising wages and falling unemployment. But it wasn't long before strains began to be felt. For a start, government expenditure soon exceeded income by a huge margin, creating an enormous deficit. The looming economic crisis was dramatically accelerated when the world copper price fell by some 27 percent, cutting government revenue still further. Inflation began to rise uncontrollably, with wages unable to keep pace, and before long food shortages became commonplace.

The cracks appear

Part of the UP's failure stemmed from the sharp divisions within the coalition, particularly between those who, like Allende, were in favour of a measured pace of reform, and those pressing for rapid, revolutionary change. This internal disunity led to a lack of coordination in implementing policy, and an irreversible slide towards political chaos. Making matters worse were the extremist far-left groups outside the

1973	**1973**	**1973**
Military coup led by Augusto Pinochet overthrows Allende's government on September 11; Allende dies during the siege of La Moneda.	Pablo Neruda dies on September 23; thousands of people defy Pinochet by mourning in the streets.	In September and October, the Caravan of Death army death squad travels the length of Chile, murdering Pinochet's opponents.

THIS DARK AND BITTER MOMENT: ALLENDE'S LAST STAND

Refusing a safe passage to exile, Salvador Allende ordered his soldiers to drag away his daughter (who wanted to remain with him in the besieged presidential palace) and, in an emotional **speech** broadcast live on radio, vowed that he would never give up, and that he was ready to repay the loyalty of the Chilean people with his life. In this unique moment of history, citizens heard their president declare "I have faith in Chile and in its destiny. Other men will overcome this dark and bitter moment…You must go on, safe in the knowledge that sooner rather than later, the great avenues will open once more, and free men will march along them to create a better society…These are my last words, but I am sure that my sacrifice will not be in vain." Shortly afterwards, the signals were cut short, and jets began to drop their bombs. At the end of the day, Allende was found dead in the ruins of the palace, clutching a submachine gun, with which, it is widely believed, he had killed himself.

government – notably the Revolutionary Left Movement, or **MIR** – which urged the workers to take reform into their own hands by seizing possession of the haciendas and factories where they worked.

Opposition to the government rose sharply during 1972, both from political parties outside the coalition (such as the Christian Democrats, who had previously supported Allende) and from widening sectors of the public. Panic was fuelled by the right-wing press and reinforced behind the scenes by the CIA, who, it later emerged, had been given a US$8 million budget with which to destabilize the Allende government. Strikes broke out across the country, culminating in the truckers' stoppage of October 1972, which virtually paralysed the economy. By 1973, with the country rocked by civil disorder, it was clear to all that the government could not survive for much longer. On the morning of September 11, 1973, tanks rolled through the capital and surrounded the presidential palace, La Moneda, marking the beginning of the **military coup** that Chile had been expecting for months, and the end of both Salvador Allende's reign and his life (see box above).

The Pinochet years

The military coup was headed by a four-man junta of whom **General Augusto Pinochet**, chief of the army, quickly emerged as the dominant figure. Although Chile had seen military intervention in government affairs on two occasions in the past, these had been the exception to a highly constitutional norm. Nothing in the country's political history prepared its people for the brutality of this operation. In the days and weeks following the takeover, the **Caravan of Death** – a Chilean army death squad – travelled the length of Chile, executing 97 people. At least seven thousand people – journalists, politicians, socialists, trade union organizers and so on – were herded into the national football stadium, where many were executed; tens of thousands more were tortured. Curfews were imposed, the press was placed under the strict control of the junta, and military officers were sent in to take charge of factories, universities and other seats of socialist support. Before long, Congress had been dissolved, opposition parties and trade unions banned, and over thirty thousand Chileans had fled the country.

1973–89	1976–81	1980
Pinochet dissolves Congress, indefinitely suspends all political parties and rules by decree; thousands are tortured and 3065 killed.	The rapid growth of Chile's free-market economy, spurred on by elimination of price controls, is dubbed the "Chilean Miracle".	Controversial new constitution is passed, giving Pinochet extended powers and an eight-year term.

Death and the free market

At the same time as his henchmen were murdering the opposition (see box below), General Pinochet saw his mission – and it was one in which he was supported by a sizeable portion of the population – as being that of rescuing Chile from the Left and, by extension, from the economic and political chaos into which it had undoubtedly fallen. To achieve this, he planned not to hand the country over to a right-wing political party of his approval, but to take it into his own hands and rule it himself. His key strategy was to be the adoption of a radical **free-market economy**, which involved a complete reversal of Allende's policies and a drastic restructuring of government and society. In this he was influenced by a group of Chilean economists known as "the Chicago boys", who had carried out postgraduate studies at the University of Chicago, where they'd come into contact with the monetarist theories of Milton Friedman. Almost immediately, price controls were abolished, government expenditure was slashed, most state-owned companies were privatized, import tariffs were reduced, and attempts were made to liberalize investment and attract foreign capital.

Such measures would take time to work, and called for a period of intense austerity. Sure enough, unemployment soared, wages plummeted, industrial output dropped, and the lower and middle classes became significantly poorer. At the same time, as Pinochet strove to reduce the role of the state in society, social welfare became increasingly neglected, particularly health and education. By the late 1970s, the economy was showing signs of growth and inflation was finally beginning to drop – from an annual rate of nine hundred percent in 1973 to 65 percent in 1977 and down to a respectable 9.5 percent in 1981. Soon, there was talk of the Chilean "economic miracle" in international circles.

The boom did not last, and in 1982, Chile found itself, along with much of Latin America, in the grip of a serious **debt crisis** which swept away the previous advances: the country was plunged into recession, with hundreds of private enterprises going bankrupt and unemployment rising to over thirty percent. It wasn't until the late 1980s that the economy recovered and Pinochet's free-market policies achieved the results he sought, with sustained growth, controlled inflation, booming, diversified exports and reduced unemployment. This prosperity, however, did not benefit all Chileans, and 49 percent of Chile's private wealth remained in the hands of ten percent of its population.

STATE-SPONSORED TERROR

Pinochet's free-market experiment had only been possible with the tools of ruthless repression at his disposal. His chief instrument was the secret police known as the **DINA**, which carried out surveillance on civilian (and even military) society, brutally silencing all opposition. Although the wholesale repression that followed the coup diminished in scale after the first year, regular "disappearances", torture and executions continued throughout Pinochet's regime. The regime was actively, if clandestinely, supported by the US, through the CIA, which even helped with the elimination of dissidents. In the absence of any organized political opposition, only the Catholic Church spoke out against the government's human rights violations, providing assistance and sanctuary to those who suffered, and vigilantly documenting all reports of abuse.

1982	1988	1989
Isabel Allende's debut novel, *The House of the Spirits*, is published, giving her international prominence.	Fifty-six percent of the population vote against Pinochet's continuing presidency in the plebiscite, leading to a democratic election.	The first free elections since 1970 result in a victory for moderate Christian Democrat Patricio Aylwyn.

The beginning of the end

Pinochet held the country in such a tight, personal grip – famously claiming "there is not a leaf that stirs in Chile without my knowing it" – that it doubtless became difficult for him to conceive of an end to his authority. The Constitution that he had drawn up in 1980 – ratified by a tightly controlled **plebiscite** – guaranteed him power until 1988, at which point the public would be given the chance either to accept military rule for another eight years, or else call for elections.

From the mid-1980s, **public protest** against Pinochet's regime began to be voiced, both in regular street demonstrations and with the reformation of political opposition parties (still officially banned). Open repression was stepped down as international attention became increasingly focused on the Chilean government's behaviour, and the US (a major source of foreign investment) made clear that it favoured a return to democracy. In this climate, the opposition parties were able to develop a united strategy in their efforts to oust the dictator. As the referendum in which Chile would decide whether or not to reject military rule drew closer, the opposition forces banded together to lead a highly professional and convincing "no" campaign. Pinochet remained convinced of his own victory, and with control of all media, and the intimidation tactics of a powerful police state at his disposal, it is easy to see why. But when the plebiscite took place on **October 5**, **1988**, 55 percent of the nation voted "no" to continued military rule.

Pinochet goes quietly

After sixteen years in power, the writing was on the wall for Pinochet's dictatorship. Much to everyone's surprise, he accepted his defeat without resistance and prepared to step down. But the handover system gave him one more year in power before democratic elections would be held – a year in which he hastily prepared **amnesty laws** that would protect both himself and the military from facing any charges of human rights abuses levied by the new government, and that would make his constitutional model extremely difficult to amend. A year later, on December 14, 1989, the Christian Democrat Patricio Aylwin, at the head of a seventeen-party centre-ground coalition called the **Concertación de los Partidos por la Democracia**, became Chile's first democratically elected president in seventeen years.

Return to democracy

The handover of power was smooth and handled with cautious goodwill on all sides, including the military. **Patricio Aylwin** was in the fortunate position of inheriting a robust economy and an optimistic public. Yet he faced serious challenges, including the need to channel substantial funds into those areas neglected by the previous regime while sustaining economic growth, and to address human rights abuses without antagonizing the military and endangering the transition to democracy.

Pinochet's **economic** model was barely contested, and was vigorously applied in an effort to promote "growth with equity" (the Concertación's electoral slogan). Foreign investment poured into the country and exports continued to rise, keeping economic growth at high levels and allowing Aylwin to divert resources into health and education. He was also felt to be making genuine efforts to alleviate the problems faced by the poorest members of society.

1990	1998	2000
Pinochet steps down but not before obtaining immunity from prosecution for himself and his cronies in the military.	Pinochet arrested in Britain – the first former head of state arrested on the principle of universal jurisdiction.	Ricardo Lagos, a moderate leftist, is elected president – one of several leftist leaders in South America at the time.

JUSTICE FOR SOME

One of the new Patricio Aylwin government's first actions was the establishment of a **National Commission for Truth and Reconciliation** to investigate and document the abuses committed by the military regime. The commission's 1991 report confirmed 2279 executions, disappearances and deaths caused by torture, and listed a further 641 suspected cases. Although compensation was paid to the families of the victims, the few attempts made to bring the perpetrators to justice were unsuccessful, owing to the protective **amnesty laws** passed by Pinochet before he relinquished power.

By 1995, however, the courts were finally willing to find ways of getting round Pinochet's amnesty laws. There were breakthrough convictions of six former *carabineros*, two former DINA (secret police) agents and most significantly, of General Manuel Contreras and Brigadier Pedro Espinoza, both sentenced to **life imprisonment** in "Punta Peuco", a jail built purposely for high-profile human rights criminals. Several more cases resulted in prison sentences for violators, though the government controversially approved measures aimed at imposing a time limit on human rights investigations, which some claimed were dragging on excessively. In spectacular circumstances, former secret police chief **Manuel Contreras**, who had already served part of an earlier life sentence, was arrested in early 2005 on fresh charges – he allegedly tried to shoot the officers who went to his house to detain him.

Return of Eduardo Frei (Jr)

After a successful four-year term, the Concertación was in 1993 once again elected to power, headed by the Christian Democrat **Eduardo Frei** (son of the 1964–70 president). Frei's policies were essentially a continuation of his predecessors', with a firmer emphasis on tackling human rights issues (see box above) and eradicating severe poverty. His success was mixed. His National Programme for Overcoming Poverty, established in 1994, was seen as inconsistent and ineffective. In its last couple of years, Frei's government ran into unexpected problems. First, the Asian economic crisis of 1998 had serious repercussions on the Chilean economy, hitting exports, foreign investment (much of which came from Southeast Asia) and the value of the peso, which has been sliding gradually ever since. At the same time, the unresolved tensions over lack of justice for Pinochet erupted afresh when the general retired from his position of commander-in-chief of the army in early 1998 but immediately took up a seat in Congress as a life senator. More controversy followed later the same year as he was dramatically thrust into the international spotlight following his arrest in a London hospital on October 16, following a request for his **extradition** to Spain to face charges of murder and torture (see box, p.487).

The rise of the left

In December 1999, the first round of presidential elections left two front-runners neck and neck in the second round: the Concertación's candidate, socialist **Ricardo Lagos**, a former education minister under Aylwin who had famously voiced criticism of Pinochet in the late 1980s, and **Joaquín Lavín**, who had served under the general and was standing on a firmly right-wing platform. Lagos pulled off an eleventh-hour victory on January 16, 2000, beating his opponent narrowly – by 51 to 49 percent.

2000	2004	2005
Pinochet is released on medical grounds and sent back to Chile, disappointing those demanding justice for his victims.	In spite of being a predominantly Catholic country, Chile finally legalizes divorce; courts are flooded with thousands of cases.	Constitutional reforms fully restore democracy, dispensing with military commanders and senators-for-life (non-elected senators) such as Pinochet.

WILL HE OR WON'T HE: THE PINOCHET AFFAIR

On October 16, 1998, justice finally caught up with Augusto Pinochet who was arrested in a London hospital after Spain had requested his extradition. The arrest provoked strong reactions in Chile: families of Pinochet's victims rejoiced euphorically; supporters of the general were outraged, burning British flags in the streets; while the government, in a difficult position, denounced the arrest as an affront to national sovereignty and demanded Pinochet's immediate return to Chile – whereupon, they claimed, his alleged crimes would be dealt with in the Chilean courts. After a protracted and complex legal battle, during which the British judiciary ruled both in Pinochet's favour and against him, in April 1999 Britain's Home Secretary, **Jack Straw**, announced that proceedings could go ahead. They again got bogged down, this time over whether the former dictator was fit to stand trial.

Straw finally decided to send Pinochet back to Chile in early March 2000, just before Ricardo Lagos was sworn in at La Moneda. There was an international outcry when he was welcomed back with pomp and circumstance by the armed forces, and Congress granted all former heads of state **lifelong immunity** from prosecution. Even Lagos expressed support for such a move, to quell any stirrings in the military. Yet the former dictator was stripped of his immunity in June and by Christmas 2000 he had faced charges for kidnapping opponents. At the beginning of 2001 he was judged mentally fit for trial, and, at the end of January Chilean judge **Juan Guzmán** ordered Pinochet's house arrest. But within months the case fizzled out yet again, and in July 2001 all charges against Pinochet were dropped after a Santiago court decided he was, after all, unfit to stand trial. Nevertheless, like the former tyrant himself, the case would not lie down and die. Further appeals and counter-appeals meant that the affair dragged on for one more year. Finally the country's Supreme Court ruled, in early July 2002, that Pinochet was indeed unfit to stand trial on mental-health grounds. He responded by resigning as life senator from Chile's Congress and was reported as saying that he did so "with a clear conscience", unleashing a furore among his opponents.

CORRUPTION CHARGES

Spectre-like, Pinochet returned to the fore once more amid a **financial scandal** in 2005. Though the ex-dictator had always claimed that, unlike many of his peers, his only interest was the wellbeing of his country and not of his pocket, it transpired that he and/or his relatives had creamed off tens of millions of dollars in murky wheeling and dealing, and carefully stashed the laundered booty in US bank accounts, one of them at Riggs; cooperation with the US financial authorities revealed the existence of the funds, a very generous nest egg for his family. In February 2005, the Riggs Bank donated $8 million to a pension fund set up for the families of three thousand victims of human rights abuses under the general's regime. In June of the same year, the courts decided that he was fit to stand trial to answer the corruption charges yet mortality was to intervene before any sentence could ever be passed (see p.488).

Social and land reform

Determined to continue with his predecessors' overhaul of two main areas of social policy, namely **health and education**, the highly popular Lagos implemented an ambitious programme based on reforming the state. A push towards universal free medical care initiated by Lagos has now mostly been achieved, with free treatment for low-income earners and people over 60, and with the rest paying a contribution dictated by their earnings. Hospitals and other services, mostly in a pitiful state after years of neglect, were improved, too. After compulsory schooling, shortened to the bare

2006	2006	2007
In January, Chile elects its first female president, Michelle Bachelet, to lead the centre-left Concertación coalition.	Pinochet dies without ever standing trial for his crimes and is denied a state funeral. Bachelet does not attend.	The DNA of a Polynesian chicken is found at the Mapuche settlement of El Arenal, suggesting new human migration theories.

minimum by Pinochet, was dramatically lengthened, plans to recruit more teachers, improve their training and raise their salaries were implemented. **Divorce** was finally legalized in late 2004 (leaving only Malta and the Philippines divorce-free), despite opposition by the Church, which has said it will do all it can to obstruct the new, democratically enacted law. Abortion remains utterly taboo.

Lagos also tried to tackle the thorny issue of **indigenous peoples' rights**, handing back large tracts of land to the Mapuche and others early on in his presidency. This backfired somewhat, with emboldened *indígenas* demanding even more of their land back, resulting in some ugly clashes with the police in early 2002, when demonstrators tried to block the construction of a new road through land claimed by the Mapuche; there have been several similar incidents in recent years.

Trouble abroad

International relations, in particular with the country's neighbours, were decidedly rocky as Lagos headed towards the end of his term of office. His dismissive remarks plus chauvinistic Chilean media coverage following the arrest of two young Chileans accused of defacing an ancient wall in the Inca city of Cusco, did little to smooth relations with **Peru**, Chile's traditional rival to the north. Chile's refusal to negotiate a guaranteed ocean access for landlocked **Bolivia**, meanwhile, further soured relations with another long-time foe. And **Argentina**'s decision to prioritize its domestic gas demand, at the risk of cutting supplies to Chile, increased trans-Andean tensions.

South America's first female president

From March 2006, Chile had a woman president, socialist **Michelle Bachelet**, elected by a comfortable margin in the second-round run-off on January 15 of that year. She had stood against charismatic businessman and current president Sebastián Piñera, of the centre-right National Renewal Party, in the *balotaje* (decisive second round).

> ### JUSTICE DENIED: THE DEATH OF PINOCHET
>
> Chile was once more convulsed with polarized passions following **Pinochet's death** from a heart attack in December 2006, symbolically enough on International Human Rights' Day. At the time of his death, he was under house arrest and facing trial over charges in Chilean courts relating to one financial enquiry and five human rights cases. In October 2006, an appeal court had dropped corruption charges brought against his wife and five children who had been accused of sending state funds illegally to foreign bank accounts in the US. They say that for Chileans there's no middle ground on Pinochet – they either love him or hate him. This never appeared so true than in the days following his death. While jubilant opponents danced in the centre of the capital, his supporters mourned outside the military hospital where he died, loving the man they insisted had saved the country from Marxism and put Chile on the path of strong economic growth.
>
> Bachelet **refused to authorize** the type of state funeral normally granted to former presidents, saying it would be "a violation of my conscience" to do so and did not attend. Instead, he was allowed only military honours as a former head of the Chilean army. For many, there is still anger and frustration that the former dictator never faced trial for his crimes. Though it may be little solace, in the words of Uruguayan writer Mario Benedetti: "Formal justice may remain incomplete, but history has judged him and condemned him."

2010	2010	2010
On February 27, a powerful earthquake damages Concepción and the resulting tsunami devastates the island of Juan Fernández.	Sebastián Piñera comes to power in January's elections in the first democratic victory for Chile's right-wing movement since Pinochet's coup.	In August, the collapse of a copper-gold mine leaves 33 miners trapped underground for 69 days.

WOMEN'S RIGHTS IN THE NEW CHILE

In a country with fewer **women** in the workforce than anywhere else in Latin America, Bachelet promised to champion the woman's cause and, in her first year, delivered not only the breast-feeding law but also set up hundreds of nurseries and shelters for victims of domestic violence. By presidential decree, and to the disgust of the Catholic Church, she made the **morning-after pill** available free to girls as young as 14.

Furious at his decision to run and split the right-wing vote, Lavín supporters likened Piñera – billionaire owner of the TV channel Chilevisión, and president of LAN, the national airline – to Italy's Silvio Berlusconi. Bachelet, by contrast, was a physician who'd gone into exile in Australia and East Germany in the 1970s after her father, a moderate Air Force general, was assassinated under Pinochet. In her victory speech she said that a **feminine touch** was needed to smooth international relations and promised to work for greater friendship between Chile and its neighbours, particularly Argentina.

A woman's work

Michelle Bachelet's election as Chile's first female head of state also made her the first woman to be directly and democratically elected in South American history. Indeed, one of outgoing President Lagos' stated aims had been to reduce the acute **gender inequality** in the country, and he appointed Chile's first female ministers for defence (Bachelet herself) and foreign affairs (her erstwhile rival in the presidential race, Soledad Alvear). The number of women in the principal judicial bodies has also gone up while the House of Deputies had two woman speakers at the beginning of the millennium and during Bachelet's presidency the Cabinet of Chile had an equal number of male and female ministers.

Criticized during the campaign for her vague policies and indecision, Bachelet nevertheless started her presidency with a strong mandate, a supportive parliament and many expectations. She promised a new, participatory style of government that would continue pro-market economic policies begun under the dictatorship of Augusto Pinochet, but with an accent on empowering ordinary Chileans. The fact that she was detained and tortured, along with her mother, in the early Pinochet years before her family was allowed to leave the country, enhanced her popularity on the left; but her **progressive stance** on delicate issues such as divorce, human rights and religion (she is a professed agnostic) and the fact that she is separated from her husband and did not marry the father of her third child, put off many traditional voters even in her own camp. All that said, she was staunchly opposed to abortion and gay marriage (but not to some kind of official recognition of same-sex couples).

Although Bachelet enjoyed 62 percent approval shortly after taking office, it didn't take long for the inherited hangovers from the previous administrations to reassert themselves: labour protests, social unrest from students complaining about the poor quality of public education and a botched overhaul of Santiago's transport caused her public standing to plummet. During the first two and a half years of her presidency, Chile's economy ticked along nicely, thanks largely to Asian demand delivering booming revenues for Chile's chief export, copper. But amid the **global financial crisis** that took hold in mid-2008, the price of copper halved in the space of four months.

2011	2011	2011–12
Seven cyclists are arrested in Santiago over participation in Chile's first Naked Bike Ride.	The ALMA telescope – the most complex in the world – begins its quest to study the "Cosmic Dawn".	Chilean Education Conflict: thousands of students stage demonstrations and occupy universities and schools in protest against expensive, inadequate education.

Landscape and the environment

One of South America's smaller countries, Chile is roughly the same size as France and Britain combined – but stretched over the equivalent distance of Vancouver to Panama. This strange sliver of a country, on average just 180km across, spans 4350km from the desert of the north to the sub-Antarctic ice-fields in the south, and encompasses almost every kind of natural habitat along the way.

Geography

Geographically, Chile is divided into a number of latitudinal **zones**, each of which shows clear differences in climate, vegetation and fauna. These zones only tell part of the story, though, with Chile's three principal landforms – the Andes, the central depression and the coastal range, running the length of the country – all having a significant impact on the local ecology. The **Andes**, in particular, straddles all of Chile's disparate regions. Characterized by precipitous slopes with ravines cut deep into the rock, at points the range acts as a great, impenetrable wall dividing Chile from neighbouring Argentina and Bolivia. Scores of **volcanoes**, many topping 6000m, line these borders, where episodic eruptions and seismic activity are everyday realities. The country's highest peak, Ojos del Salado (6893m), is also the world's highest active volcano; Aconcagua (6959m), the globe's tallest peak outside the Himalayas, lies a few kilometres over the Argentine border.

Desert and volcanoes: Norte Grande

In the far north, the **Norte Grande** region stretches from the Peruvian border over 1000km south to the Copiapó river valley. Covering the central depression between the Andes and the coastal range lies the **Atacama Desert**, thought to be the driest place on earth. Surprisingly, the desert is unusually temperate, owing to the moderating influence of the Humboldt Current, a cold-water sea current just off the coast. While thick fog banks, known as *camanchaca*, accumulate along the coast where the cold water meets the warm air, a high-pressure zone prevents the cloud from producing rain and moving inland.

A search for wildlife is a pretty fruitless activity in these barren northern wastes. The frustrated ornithologist A.W. Johnson remarked that the desert was "without doubt one of the most completely arid and utterly lifeless areas in the whole world". It's a very different story, however, up in the Andes bordering the Atacama, where a high plateau known as the **altiplano** is home to a diverse wildlife population and an otherworldly landscape of volcanoes, lakes and salt flats.

Mining and exotic fruit: Norte Chico

The semi-arid **Norte Chico**, bounded roughly by the Copiapó Valley and the Aconcagua Valley, just north of Santiago, forms a transitional zone, where the inhospitable northern desert gives way to scrubland and eventually forests further south, as precipitation levels increase. The heat of the sun here is tempered by air humidity, making the land suitable for irrigation farming. The crops of tobacco and cotton that predominated in the colonial era have since been replaced by more lucrative exotic fruits, such as papaya and *chirimoya*. Throughout the north mining has also long been prevalent, thanks to the high levels of nitrates, copper, silver and other minerals in the soil.

Grapes and non-native trees: Central Valley

Beyond Santiago, the region known as the **Central Valley** extends south to the Río Biobío. Mineral-rich earth coupled with warm dry summers and short humid winters have provided ideal conditions here for growing grapes, peaches, pears, plums, mangoes, melons and apricots. As the country's primary agricultural zone, as well as a major centre of industry, it is no surprise that this region is home to around eighty percent of the country's population, almost half based in the capital.

Towards the southern end of the Central Valley, forests signal a marked increase in precipitation levels. Systematic **afforestation**, begun over a hundred years ago in Arauco province, has seen the introduction of a variety of foreign trees, such as eucalyptus and Australian myrrh. No species has flourished as well as the radiata pine, however, which far exceeded the rate of development normal in its native California; concern is mounting that its success is damaging Chile's fragile endemic forest habitats.

The Lake District, Patagonia and Tierra del Fuego

In the **Lake District**, between Temuco and Puerto Montt, precipitation reaches 2300mm a year, allowing luxuriant native forests to predominate over the rolling foothills of the coastal range. To the east, azure lakes, remnants of the last glacial age, are backed by conical, snowcapped **volcanoes**. Among the many volcanoes still active, both Villarrica and Llaima have erupted ten times in the last hundred years. On May 2, 2008, the Chaitén volcano, situated further south on the mainland across from Chiloé, began erupting for the first time in nine thousand years; a huge column of smoke and ash rose into the sky, coating the land around the volcano and reaching into neighbouring Argentina.

Beyond Puerto Montt, the central depression submerges into the sea, while the tops of the coastal mountains nudge through the water in a mosaic of **islands** and **fjords**. It is here, in this splintered and remote region, that continental Chile finally runs out of dry land: the Carretera Austral, the highway that runs south from Puerto Montt, is cut short after 1000km by two massive ice-fields, the largest in the southern hemisphere outside Antarctica. **Southern Patagonia** is a mostly inhospitable place, with continual westerly winds roaring off the sea and dumping up to seven metres of snow, sleet, hail and rain on the western slopes every year. Even so, the glaciated scenery, with its perfect U-shaped valleys and rugged mountains, has an indisputable grandeur. In stark contrast, the monotonous grasslands of the Patagonian pampa, which lies in the rain shadow on the eastern side of the Andes, describe the beginning of a quite different habitat.

Tierra del Fuego ("Land of Fire") is an archipelago separated from mainland Chile by the Magellan Strait. Mountains and forests dominate the south of the region, while the north hosts little more than windswept grasses. From Cape Horn, South America's southernmost point, Antarctica is a mere 1000km away.

Flora

Extraordinary diversity of altitude, latitude and precipitation inevitably leads to an extraordinary diversity of flora. Only humid tropical forest fails to feature in Chile's rich and varied ecology. The tropical area in the far north is stricken with aridity too severe to support most plant life, except at higher altitudes, where **xerophytes** ("dry growers"), such as **cacti**, begin to appear. Ninety percent of Chile's vascular plants are from the cactus family, many of them endemic and endangered. On the altiplano, **tough grasses** and **brush** associated with minimal rainfall support the herds of grazing alpaca.

Central Chilean flora

Moving south towards Central Chile, where the climate is more balanced and water less scarce, **sclerophyllous** ("rigid leaf") shrubs and trees feature leathery leaves that help them retain water. As rainfall increases towards the south, these plants begin to blend with **temperate rainforests**. In the heavily populated areas of this central region, such woodlands have suffered widespread deforestation as land has been cleared for farming and housing, and only patches remain. In Parque Nacional La Campana near Santiago, for example, stands the last forest of endangered **Chilean palm** (*Jubaea chilensis*), sole reminder of a time when millions of the trees covered the area, favoured as they were for the flavour of their sap.

Temperate tree species and Patagonian flora

Further south the **temperate rainforests** have fared a little better, constituting almost a quarter of this type of habitat worldwide. Over 95 percent of the fifty tree species found here are endemic, including the **araucaria** (*Araucaria araucana*), known in English as the **monkey puzzle**, Chile's national tree, and rare **southern beeches** (*Nothofagus*) – principally *coïgue*, *ñire*, *raulí* and *lenga* – which vie for sunlight, towering up to 40m into the air to break clear of the canopy. The **alerce**, or **Chilean false larch** (*Fitzroya cupressoides*), a relative of the North American sequoia, takes several hundred years to reach maturity and can live for four thousand years, providing the loggers don't get there first. The tree is best seen in the areas around Puerto Montt.

In Chilean Patagonia, **evergreen beeches** (*Nothofagus betuloides*) grow in the sheltered areas bordering the great fields of ice, while their **deciduous** cousins *Nothofagus pumilio* and *N. antarctica* prefer the drier eastern flanks of the Andes. Where the canopy is broken, dazzling scarlet *embothrium*, yellow *berberis* bedecked with mauve berries, and deep-red *Pernettya* emblazon the ground. Rare **orchids** and pink **oxalis** interweave in a tapestry of colour. Such brilliant displays are impossible on the coastal Magellanic **moorland**, where high levels of precipitation drown all but the sphagnum **bog** communities and **dwarf shrubs**. Here, the wind-beaten **Magellanic gunnera** grows only a few centimetres high, a tiny fraction of what its relatives are capable of in the Valdivian rainforest. Meanwhile, the rain shadow effect on the eastern Patagonian steppe supports little more than coarse tussocks of *festuca* grasses.

Environmental issues

The slow destruction of Chile's environment was set in motion by the Spanish in the sixteenth century, though it wasn't until the early twentieth century, with widespread settlement and increased industrialization, that the scale reached damaging levels. Today, although Chile has suffered less environmental degradation than most other countries with comparable resources, there are few habitats that have not been affected in some way by human activity, and it's debatable whether future governments will be prepared to prioritize protection over financial exploitation. While the current government has overruled the decision made by the previous administration to allow the damming of Patagonia's wildest rivers, there is no guarantee that governments in the future won't counter-reverse this ruling.

Pollution

There was little interest in environmental issues in Chile until large-scale disruption caused by the appalling **smog in Santiago**, considered by Greenpeace to be the third most polluted city in Latin America, mobilized public concern. Most years the capital's schools are suspended for days on end and people are warned to stay indoors as a dense cloud of toxic gases hangs over the capital, caught between the two surrounding mountain ranges. The problem is worsened in dry weather, when the concentration of contaminated air is not dissolved by rain. Pressure from the urban middle class has forced the government to introduce (many say weak) measures to lessen air pollution in Santiago and has encouraged politicians to include environmental elements to their policies.

The most important **environmental law**, following a guarantee in the 1980 Constitution that all Chileans have "the right to live in an environment free of pollution", was the Environmental Act of 1994, which has standardized procedures for assessing environmental damage, while encouraging public involvement by allowing citizens to bring charges against violators, even if they have not been directly affected by them. One successful application of this new law occurred in 1997, when the Chilean Supreme Court overturned a government-approved project involving the logging for woodchips of centuries-old, endangered forests of native *lenga*, a cherry-like beech found in Tierra del Fuego. In 2012 the creation of the new office of the Environment Superintendent, to the surprise and delight of environmentalists, promptly slapped a US$16 million fine on the Barrick Gold Corporation – the largest gold-mining company in the world – for water pollution and other violations, though inadequate funding for inspections and enforcement of its rulings is still an issue.

Forests under threat

Chile's precious **temperate rainforests** have been threatened for many years by intensive logging and the introduction of harmful foreign species, with large tracts razed in the free-for-all scramble to colonize remote areas. The worst damage occurred in the first half of the twentieth century, but illegal clearance is still common today. The *alerce*, an evergreen with a life span of four thousand years, has been a target of international campaigning as it continues to be logged because of the high commercial value of its wood, despite a law passed in 1976 making it illegal to cut live *alerces*. Yet landowners burn the trees or strip their bark to kill them first, thus evading the hands of the law. Many thousands of hectares of *alerce* forest are wiped out in this manner every year.

Meanwhile in the central regions native trees have been wiped out to make space for the commercial planting of more profitable foreign species. In many areas the practice has left only islands of indigenous forest in an ocean of introduced eucalyptus and radiata pine. The result is genetic isolation of both flora and fauna, leaving many mammals with distinct ecological needs imprisoned in small pockets of native woodland. The few thin strips that connect such pockets are the only way for many species to maintain communication with the rest of their population. If these corridors are destroyed, countless endemic organisms face extinction. However, efforts are made by the likes of Parque Tantauco and also the various Tompkins' foundations (see p.355) to preserve unique ecosystems and to restore local ecosystems by hand if need be, pulling up aggressive non-indigenous species and planting indigenous plants in their stead.

Mining

In the north **mining** is a major cause of environmental concern. Chuquicamata, near Antofagasta, is the biggest open-pit copper mine in the world and it continues to grow. Now visible from space, the giant pit has effectively swallowed up the town that grew with it, as 600,000 tons of rock are dug up every day, spewing arsenic-rich dust into the air. Workers at the mine and their families have now been relocated from Chuquicamata to nearby Calama. The plume from the smelting works carries 200km to San Pedro de Atacama, a pre-colonial village in the east. The country's mines consume vast quantities of water, often contaminating it in the process. In tandem with agricultural irrigation, reckless water usage is taking its toll on wildlife, as animals find the search for drinking places increasingly difficult. Even the human population has been put out, relying in some northern villages on an ingenious invention that turns fog into drinking water.

Overexploitation of resources

Overexploitation of the land and sea has brought further problems. Incompetent or negligent farming, either through overgrazing or the clearing of vegetation, has resulted in extensive **desertification**, particularly in the north. Meanwhile, careless practices in the fishing industry are upsetting the fragile balance of Chile's **marine life**. A leaked

THE EL NIÑO EFFECT

Nature's footnote to the end of the millennium, the **1997–98 El Niño** wreaked havoc with global climate patterns and brought chaos to the world. In parts of Chile, Peru and Ecuador, floods and landslides engulfed people, animals, houses, farms and factories, while torrents swept away bridges, roads and railways. Elsewhere, severe droughts scorched the earth, drying up forests and bushland and creating the tinderbox conditions that sparked off raging fires. Clouds of poisonous smoke billowed into the atmosphere, affecting seventy million people in Southeast Asia, while millions of others risked starvation following widespread crop failure. As the Pacific countries affected by El Niño picked up the pieces, conservative estimates of the cost of reparation put it at around US$20 billion.

In Chile, **flooding** was the worst it had been for a decade, as eighty thousand people were made homeless in June 1998 alone. The warm coastal water associated with El Niño drove fish stocks to cooler places, crippling the fishing industry and killing millions of marine animals. But while some watched their crops and livestock drown, the rains also filled irrigation basins that had been at a critically low level for years, and water surges saved the hydroelectric companies from having to ration their power output. In the Atacama Desert, freak rainfall woke up the barren soil, causing it to burst into blossom. A relatively mild El Niño in early 2002, meanwhile, meant that while the ski season was one of the best in the last ten years, torrential rains in central Chile left fifty thousand people homeless and killed nine. The last El Niño episode occurred in 2009, bringing with it an unusually cold and wet summer which affected Chile's busiest tourist season.

THE METEOROLOGY BEHIND THE MAYHEM

The El Niño phenomenon is no new thing and it occurs roughly every five years or so. Records document such events over four hundred years ago, but it was only in the 1960s that the Norwegian meteorologist Jacob Bjerknes identified the processes that lead to such an event. He saw that El Niño (meaning "the Little Boy" or "the Christ Child", a name given by Peruvian fishermen to the body of warm water that would arrive around Christmas) was intimately connected to extremes in the so-called **Southern Oscillation**, a feature where atmospheric pressure between the eastern equatorial Pacific and the Indo-Australian areas behaves as a seesaw, one rising as the other falls.

In "normal" years easterly trade winds blow west across the Pacific, pushing warm surface water towards Indonesia, Australia and the Philippines, where the water becomes about 8°C warmer and about 50cm higher than on the other side of the ocean. In the east, the displacement of the sea allows cold, nutrient-rich water, known as the Humboldt or Peru Current, to swell up from the depths along the coast of South America, providing food for countless marine and bird species.

An El Niño event occurs when the trade winds fall off and the layer of warm water in the west laps back across the ocean, warming up the east Pacific and cooling the west. Consequently, air temperatures across the Pacific begin to even out, tipping the balance of the atmospheric pressure seesaw, which further reduces the strength of the trade winds. Thus the process is enhanced, as warm water continues to build up in the eastern Pacific, bringing with it abnormal amounts of rainfall to coastal South America, while completely starving other areas of precipitation. The warm water also forces the cold Humboldt Current and its micro-organisms to deeper levels, effectively removing a vital link in the marine food chain, killing innumerable fish, sea-birds and mammals. Meanwhile, the upset in the Southern Oscillation disturbs weather systems all around the world, resulting in severe and unexpected weather.

EL NIÑO AND GLOBAL WARMING

Since 1980 or so, El Niño-Southern Oscillation (ENSO) events seem to have become stronger, longer and more frequent, leading many to suggest that human activity, such as the warming of the earth's atmosphere through the **greenhouse effect**, could well be having an influence. If this is true, failure to cut emissions of greenhouse gases may in the end cost the lives and livelihoods of millions of people across the world, though some schools of thought suggest that perhaps the stronger El Niño events occur only during the initial stage of global warming and that they will become weaker as the ocean becomes warmer. More research is required to provide a definitive answer.

government report shows that some fish stocks were depleted by as much as 96 percent between 1985 and 1993. On a global level, many believe human-induced climate change to be a leading cause of the **El Niño phenomenon**, which has badly damaged Chile's fisheries, agriculture and marine species (see box opposite). Moreover, the large hole in the ozone layer over Antarctica has put many people, especially in Patagonia, on guard against the harmful ultraviolet rays that seep through it. Chile has been more effective than most Latin American countries in its opposition to the damage brought about by the excesses of unfettered capitalism, and awareness of the delicacy of the country's habitats and its unique species is growing. However, environmentalists continue to bemoan the lack of concerted pressure, claiming that many merely respond occasionally and emotionally to images churned out in the media rather than pushing consistently for action and reform.

Droughts and forest fires

In March 2015, the southern region of Araucanía which had been experiencing years of **drought**, was hit by **forest fires**. As the fires raged out of control, threatening centuries-old monkey puzzle trees in China Muerta National Reserve, Nalca Lolco National Reserve and Conguillío National Park, Chile declared a **national emergency**. At the time of writing, forest fires were also threatening the port of Valparaíso, leading to the immediate evacuation of 4500 people and the proposed evacuation of a further 10,000 inhabitants. In response to the most recent forest fires, President Bachelet announced that Chile would be investing millions of dollars in desalination plants to provide drinking water and to improve access to underground water. Throughout its history, Chile has been affected by droughts on a fairly regular basis, but these have become more frequent and consistent in recent years, something that many feel is due to climate change.

Chilean music: nueva canción

Chile has produced a wide range of music genres, from cueca to bolero, but none has been as important or influential as nueva canción, the "new song" movement that developed in Chile in the 1960s, along with parallel movements in Argentina, Uruguay and Cuba. A music rooted in the guitar traditions of the troubadour, the songs could be love lyric or chronicle, lament or call to action, and, as such, they have played an important part in Latin America's political and cultural struggles. It was brought to international attention, above all, through the lyrical songs of Chilean theatre director and singer-songwriter Víctor Jara, who was murdered for his art by Pinochet's thugs during the 1973 coup d'état, while groups like Inti Illimani were forced into exile. For further detail it's worth checking out an extract taken from the *Rough Guide to World Music* in which Jan Fairley looks at the history and legacy of this music of "guitar as gun".

Pity the singer…

Nueva canción as a movement spans a period of over thirty years, from the early 1960s, when its musicians became part of the political struggle to bring about change and reform in their own countries. As a result of their activities, many of their number were arrested or forced into exile by dictatorships which through murder, torture and disappearance wiped out so much of a generation. The sense of a movement grew as the musicians involved met one another at festivals in Cuba, Nicaragua, Peru, Mexico, Argentina and Brazil, visited each other's countries, and occasionally sang each other's songs. At the end of the 1990s, with the return to democracy on the continent, the singers continued to pursue their careers in different ways, while maintaining long-term friendships and exchanges.

The 1960s was a time of politics and idealism in South America – far more so than in Europe or North America. There was a stark challenge presented by the continent's obvious inequalities, its inherited power and wealth, its corrupt regimes, and by the denial of literacy and education to much of the population. It is within this context that *nueva canción* singers and writers must be understood. With voice and guitar, they composed songs of their own hopes and experiences in places where many of those involved in struggles for change regularly met and socialized.

It is a music that is now, in some ways, out of date, though its spirit, in keeping with the 1960s rhetoric of guitar as gun and song as bullet, is, in other ways, entirely appropriate to the current climate of global upheaval, given the Arab Spring and other protest movements around the world. These particular songs, though – poems written to be performed – are classic expressions of the years of hope and struggle for change, their beauty and truth later nurturing those suffering under dictatorship, and those forced into exile. They are still known by heart by audiences throughout the continent and exiled communities in Europe.

Nueva canción was an expression of politics in its widest sense. It was not "protest song" as such. The musicians involved were not card-carrying members of any international organization and were often independent of political parties – although in the early 1970s the Chilean musicians were closely linked with the Popular Unity government of Salvador Allende, the first socialist president and government to be legitimately elected through the ballot box.

What linked these and other musicians of the movement was an ethical stance – a commitment to improve conditions for the majority of people in Latin America. To that end they sang not only in concerts and clubs but in factories, shanty towns, community centres and at political meetings and street demonstrations. People in protest the world over have joined in the Chilean street anthems *El Pueblo Unido Jamás Sera Vencido* (The People United Will Never Be Defeated) and *Venceremos* (We Will Win).

Yupanqui and Violeta Parra

The roots of *nueva canción* lie in the work of two key figures, whose music bridged rural and urban life and culture in the 1940s and 1950s: the Argentine **Atahualpa Yupanqui** (1908–92) and the Chilean **Violeta Parra** (1917–67). Each had a passionate interest in his or her nation's rural musical traditions, which had both an Iberian and Amerindian sensibility. Their work was in some respects paralleled by Cuba's Carlos Puebla.

Atahualpa Yupanqui spent much of his early life travelling around Argentina, collecting popular songs from itinerant *payadores* (improvising poets, Chile's indigenous rappers) and folk singers in rural areas. He also wrote his own songs, and during a long career introduced a new integrity to Argentine folk music – and an assertive political outlook which ultimately forced him into exile in Paris.

Violeta Parra's career in Chile mirrored that of Yupanqui. She travelled extensively, singing with and collecting songs from old *payadores* and preserved and popularized them through radio broadcasts and records. She also composed new material based on these rural song traditions, creating a model and repertoire for what became *nueva canción*. Her songs celebrated the rural and regional, the music of the peasant, the land-worker and the marginalized migrant.

Musically, Parra was also significant in her popularization of **Andean** or **Amerindian instruments** – the armadillo-shelled *charango* (small Andean lute), the *quena* (bamboo flute) and panpipes – and in her enthusiasm for the **French chanson** tradition. She spent time in Paris in the 1960s with her children Angel and Isabel, where they met Yupanqui, Edith Piaf and the flautist Gilbert Favre, who was to found the influential Andean band, Los Jaivas, and with whom Parra fell in love. Returning to Buenos Aires, she performed in a tent in the district of La Reina, which came to be called the Carpa de La Reina (The Queen's Tent). However, with a long history of depression, she committed suicide in 1967.

Parra left behind a legacy of exquisite songs, many of them with a wry sense of humour, including the unparalleled *Gracias a la Vida* (Thanks to Life), later covered by Joan Baez and a host of others. Even her love songs seem informed by an awareness of poverty and injustice, while direct pieces like *Qué dirá el Santo Padre?* (What will the Sainted Pope Say?) highlighted the Church's responsibility to take action. As Parra wrote (in the form she often used in her songs) in her autobiography:

I sing to the Chilean people
if I have something to say
I don't take up the guitar
to win applause
I sing of the difference there is
between what is certain
and what is false
otherwise I don't sing.

The movement takes off

Nueva canción emerged as a real force in the mid-1960s, when various governments on the continent were trying to effect democratic social change. The search for a Latin American cultural identity became a spontaneous part of this wider struggle for self-determination, and music was a part of the process.

The first crystallization of a *nueva canción* ideal in Chile emerged with the opening of a crucial new folk club. This was and is the legendary crucible of *nueva canción*, the **Peña de los Parra**, which **Angel and Isabel Parra**, inspired by the Paris *chanson* nightclubs, opened in downtown Santiago in 1965. Among the regular singer-songwriters who performed here were Víctor Jara and Patricio Manns. Their audiences, in the politically charged and optimistic period prior to the election of Allende's government, were enthusiastic activists and fellow musicians.

Víctor Jara

The great singer-songwriter and theatre director **Víctor Jara** took *nueva canción* onto a world stage. His songs, and his life, continue to reverberate, and he has been recorded by rock singers like Sting, Bruce Springsteen, Peter Gabriel and Jackson Brown, and (memorably) by the British singer Robert Wyatt. All have been moved by Jara's story and inspired by his example.

Jara was born into a rural family who came to live in a shanty town on the barren outskirts of Santiago when Víctor's father died; he was just 11. His mother sang as a *cantora* for births, marriages and deaths, keeping her family alive by running a food stall in the main Santiago market. It was from his mother and her work that Jara gained his intuitive knowledge of Chilean guitar and singing styles.

He began performing his songs in the early 1960s and from the beginning caused a furore. During the government of Eduardo Frei, for example, his playful version of a traditional piece, *La Beata* – a send-up of the desires of a nun – was banned, as was his accusatory *Preguntas por Puerto Montt* (Questions for Puerto Montt), which accused the minister of the interior of the massacre of poor landless peasants in the south of Chile. Working with Isabel Parra and the group **Huamari**, Jara went on to create a sequence of songs called *La Población*, based on the history and life of Santiago's shanty-town communities. His great gift was a deceptively simple and direct style applied to whatever he did.

One of Jara's best-loved songs, *Te recuerdo Amanda* (I remember you, Amanda), is a good example of the simplicity of his craft. A hauntingly understated love song, it tells the story of a girl who goes to meet her man, Manuel, at the factory gates; he never appears because of an "accident", and Amanda waits for him in vain. In many of his songs, Jara subtly interwove allusions to his own life with the experiences of other ordinary people – Amanda and Manuel were the names of his parents.

PLEGARIA AUN LABRADOR (PRAYER TO A LABOURER)

Stand up and look at the mountain
From where the wind comes, the sun and the water
You who direct the courses of the rivers
You who have sown the flight of your soul
Stand up and look at your hands
So as to grow
Clasp your brother's, in your own
Together we will move united by blood
Today is the time that can become tomorrow

Deliver us from the one who dominates us
through misery
Bring to us your reign of justice and equality
Blow like the wind the flower of the canyon

Clean like fire the barrel of my gun
Let your will at last come about here on earth
Give to us your strength and valour so as to fight
Blow like the wind the flower of the canyon
Clean like fire the barrel of my gun

Stand up and look at your hands
So as to grow
Clasp your brother's, in your own
Together we will move united by blood
Now and in the hour of our death
Amen.
Victor Jara

Jara's influence was immense, both on *nueva canción* singers and the Andean-oriented groups like **Inti Illimani** and **Quilapayún** (see below), whom he worked with often, encouraging them to forge their own new performance styles. Enormously popular and fun-loving, he was nevertheless clear about his role as a singer: "The authentic revolutionary should be behind the guitar, so that the guitar becomes an instrument of struggle, so that it can also shoot like a gun." As he sang in 1972 in his song *Manifiesto*, a tender serenade which with hindsight has been seen as his testimony, "I don't sing just for love of singing, but for the statements made by my guitar, honest, its heart of earth, like the dove it goes flying…Song sung by a man who will die singing, truthfully singing his song".

Like many Chilean musicians, Jara was deeply involved with the Unidad Popular government of Salvador Allende who, in 1970, following his election, had appeared on an open-air stage in Santiago surrounded by musicians under a banner saying "There can be no revolution without song". Three years later, on September 11, 1973 – along with hundreds of others who had legitimately supported the government – Jara was arrested by the military and taken to the same downtown stadium in which he had won the First Festival of New Chilean Song in 1969. Tortured, his hands and wrists broken, his body was found with five others, riddled with machine-gun bullets, dumped alongside a wall of the Metropolitan Cemetery; his face was later recognized among a pile of unidentified bodies in one of the Santiago mortuaries by a worker. He was just 40.

Jara left behind a song composed during the final hours of his life, written down and remembered by those who were with him at the end, called as a poem of testimony *Estadio Chile* (Chile Stadium). It was later set a cappella to music as *Ay canto, que mal me sales*, by his friend and colleague Isabel Parra.

Exiles and Andean sounds

After Pinochet's coup d'état anything remotely associated with the Allende government and its values came under censorship, including books and records, whose possession could be cause for arrest. The junta issued warnings to musicians and folklorists that it would be unwise for them to play *nueva canción*, or indeed any of the Andean instruments associated with its sound – *charangos*, panpipes and *quenas*.

It was not exactly a ban but it was menacing enough to force the scene well underground – and abroad, where many Chilean musicians lived out the junta years in exile. Their numbers included the groups Inti Illimani and Quilapayún and later Illapu (see p.503), Sergio Ortega, Patricio Manns, Isabel and Angel Parra, and Patricio Castillo. They were not the only Latin Americans forced from their country. Other **musician exiles** of the 1970s included Brazilian MPB singers Chico Buarque, Caetano Veloso and Gilberto Gil; Uruguay's *nueva canción* singer Daniel Viglietti; and Argentina's Mercedes Sosa.

In Chile, the first acts of musical defiance took place behind church walls, where a group of musicians who called themselves **Barroco Andino** started to play baroque music with Andean instruments within months of the coup.

It was a brave act, for the use of Andean or Amerindian instruments and culture was instinctively linked with the *nueva canción* movement. Chilean groups like **Quilapayún** and **Inti Illimani** wore the traditional ponchos of the peasant and played Andean instruments such as panpipes, bamboo flutes and the *charango*, and the maracas and shakers of Central America and the Caribbean. That these were the instruments of the communities who had managed somehow to survive slavery, resist colonialism and its aftermath had a powerful symbolism. Both the "*los Intis*" and "*los Quilas*", as they became familiarly known, worked closely with Víctor Jara and also with popular classical composers Sergio Ortega and Luis Advis.

DISCOGRAPHY

Nueva canción has had a raw deal on **CD** – it peaked in the decades before shiny discs – and for many classics, you'll need to search secondhand stores for vinyl. If you travel to Chile, you can also obtain **songbooks** for the music of Víctor Jara (the Fundación Víctor Jara publishes his complete works), while most other songs of the period are featured in *Clásicos de la Música Popular Chilena Vol 11 1960–1973* (Ediciones Universidad Católica de Chile).

NUEVA CANCIÓN CDS

Inti Illimani The foremost Chilean "new song" group, Inti Illimani (see p.501) began as students in 1967, bringing the Andean sound to Europe through their thousands of concerts in exile, and featuring the glorious-voiced José Séves. *Lejan'a* focuses on Andean themes in this celebration of the band's thirtieth anniversary and their original inspiration. *Arriesgaré la piel* is a celebration of the music the Intis grew up with, from creole-style tunes to Chilean *cuecas*, most lyrics by Patricio Manns with music by Salinas. This was the final album to be made with the core of the original band before Séves left. *Grandes Exitos* is a compilation of seventeen songs and instrumental pieces taken from the band's thirty-year history.

Llapu With a track record stretching back over 25 years, and a big following in Chile, this band plays Andean instruments – panpipes, *quenas* and *charangos* – along with saxophones, electric bass and Caribbean percussion. Their music is rooted in the north of the country where most of the band hails from. *Sereno* is an enjoyable collection, which gives a pretty good idea of what Illapu have got up to over the years and includes strongly folkloric material, as well as dance pieces influenced by salsa, romantic ballads and the earlier styles of vocal harmony.

Quilapayún This key Chilean new-song group worked closely in their early years with Víctor Jara and in 1973 – the year of the coup – they split into multiple groups in order to get their message across on as many stages as possible. They co-authored, with Sergio Ortega, the street anthem *El Pueblo Unido Jamás Sera Vencido* (the People United Will Never Be Defeated). Although they disbanded in the late 1990s, their influence lives on. *Santa María de Iquique*, Chilean composer Luis Advis's ground-breaking Cantata, composed for Quilapayún, tells the emblematic and heroic tale of the murder of unarmed nitrate workers and their families in 1907.

Various artists *Music of the Andes*. Despite the title, this is essentially a *nueva canción* disc, with key Chilean groups Inti Illimani, Quilapayún and Illapu to the fore. There is also an instrumental recording of *Tinku* attributed to Víctor Jara.

Víctor Jara *Manifesto* was reissued to mark the 25th anniversary of the death of Víctor Jara, the leading singer-songwriter of his generation (see p.500); this is a key disc of *nueva canción*, with *Te recuerdo Amanda*, *Canto libre*, *La Plegaria a un Labrador* and *Ay canto, que mal me sales*, the final poem written in the Estadio Chile before his death. The disc includes Spanish lyrics and English translations. *Vientos del Pueblo* is a generous 22-song compilation that includes most of the Jara milestones, including *Te recuerdo Amanda* and *Preguntas por Puerto Montt*, plus the wonderful revolutionary romp of *A cochabamba me voy*. Quilapayún provide backing on half the album. *Víctor Jara Complete* is a four-CD box that is the definitive Jara, featuring material from eight original LPs. Plane has also released an excellent single-disc selection of highlights. *La Población* is classic Jara: a project involving other musicians, but including most of all the lives and experiences of those celebrated here, who lived in various shanty towns (*poblaciones*) including the one where Jara himself grew up.

Violeta Parra *Canto a mi América* is an excellent introduction to one of South America's most significant folklorists and composers (see p.499), bringing you Parra's seminal songs. *Las Ultimas Composiciones* is a reissue of Parra's 1965 release which turned out to be her last as well as latest songs ("*Ultimas*" means both in Spanish).

European exile

In 1973 both groups travelled to Europe as official cultural ambassadors of the Allende government, actively seeking support from governments in Europe at a time when the country was more or less besieged economically by a North American blockade, its economy being undermined by CIA activity. On September 11 when General Pinochet led the coup d'état in which Salvador Allende died, the Intis were in Italy and the Quilas in France. For the Intis, the tour ("the longest in history", as Intis member Jorge Coulon jokes) turned into a fifteen-year-and-fifty-four-day European exile for the group, an exile which put *nueva canción* and Amerindian music firmly on Europe's agenda of Latin American music.

The groups were the heart and soul of a worldwide Chilean (and Latin American) solidarity movement, performing almost daily for the first ten years. Both also recorded albums of new songs, the Intis influenced by their many years in Italy, creating some beautiful songs of exile, including the seminal song *Vuelvo* (I return), with key singer-songwriter and musician **Patricio Manns**.

The impact of their high-profile campaigning against the military meant that the Intis were turned back on the airport tarmac long after politicians and trade union leaders were repatriated. They eventually returned on September 18, 1988, Chile's National Day, the day of one of the biggest meetings of supporters of the "No" vote to the plebiscite called by Pinochet to determine whether he should stay in office. Going straight from the airport to sing on a huge open-air stage and to dance the traditional *cueca* (Chile's National Day dance), the group's homecoming was an emotional and timely one. Though their line-up has somewhat changed over the years, the two groups are still going strong today: they've joined forces as Inti+Quila through various collaborative efforts over the last decade, including a tour of South America and Europe and a release of a CD and DVD of their joint concerts, and continue to perform together.

The Andean instruments and rhythms used by Quilapayún (who disbanded in the 1980s) and Inti Illimani have been skilfully used by many other groups whose music is equally interesting – groups like **Illapu**, who remained popular throughout the 1980s (with a number of years in forced exile) and 1990s, and who released their most recent album, *Con Sentido y Razón*, in 2014.

The future and legacy

Times have changed in Chile and in Latin America generally, with revolutionary governments no longer in power, democracy restored after dictatorships, and even Pinochet dead and buried. The *nueva canción* movement, tied to an era of ideals and struggle, and then the brutal years of survival under dictatorship, would seem to have lost its relevance.

Its musicians have moved on to more individual concerns in their (always poetic) songwriting. But the *nueva canción* form, the inspiration of the song as message, and the rediscovery of Andean music and instruments, continue to have resonance and influence. The more recent generation of singers inspired by the history of "new song" includes **Carlos Varela** in Cuba, **Fernando Delgadillo** in Mexico, El Salvador's **Cutumay Camones**, Nicaragua's **Duo Guardabarranco** and the Bolivian singer **Emma Junaro**.

And there will be others. For Latin America, *nueva canción* is not only music but history. As the Cuban press has said of the songs of Silvio Rodríguez: "We have here the great epic poems of our days." Or as the Dominican Republic's merengue superstar, Juan Luis Guerra, put it, "They are the master songwriters – they have influenced everyone."

Books

Unfortunately, a number of the best and most evocative books written on Chile have long been out of print, but we include some of them – mainly travel narratives or general accounts – below (marked by o/p in the parentheses after the title), as they can often be found in public libraries or on the internet. Modern publications are inevitably dominated by analyses and testimonies of the Pinochet years, much of which makes compelling reading. There are relatively few up-to-date general histories of Chile in English, with those available focusing more on the academic market than the general reader. Chilean fiction, meanwhile, is not very widely translated into English, with the exception of a handful of the country's more famous authors. Its poetry, or more specifically the poetry of its famous Nobel laureate Pablo Neruda, has been translated into many languages and is widely available abroad. Book marked ★ are particularly recommended.

TRAVEL: GENERAL INTRODUCTIONS

Stephen Clissold *Chilean Scrapbook* (o/p). Beautifully and evocatively written, this book takes you from the top to the bottom of the country via a mixture of history, legend and anecdote.

Augustin Edwards *My Native Land* (o/p). Absorbing and vivid reflections on Chile's geography, history, folklore and literature; particularly strong on landscape descriptions.

Benjamin Subercaseaux *Chile: A Geographic Extravaganza* (o/p). This seductive, poetic meander through Chile's "mad geography" is still one of the most enjoyable general introductions to the country, if a little dated.

TRAVEL: NINETEENTH- AND EARLY TWENTIETH-CENTURY

John Arons and Claudio Vita-Finzi *The Useless Land* (o/p). Four Cambridge geography students set out to explore the Atacama Desert in 1958 and relate their adventures along the way in this highly readable book.

Charles Darwin *Voyage of the Beagle*. This eminently readable (abridged) book contains some superb, evocative descriptions of nineteenth-century Chile, from Tierra del Fuego right up to Iquique.

Maria Graham *Journal of a Residence in Chile During the Year 1822* (o/p). The classic nineteenth-century travel narrative on Chile, written by a spirited, perceptive and amusing British woman.

Che Guevara *The Motorcycle Diaries*. Comic, picaresque narrative taken from the diaries of the future revolutionary as he and his friend, both just out of medical school, travelled around South America – including a large chunk of Chile – by motorbike.

Auguste Guinnard *Three Years Slavery Among the Patagonians*. This is the account of Guinnard's capture and often brutal enslavement by Tehuelche Indians at war with the European colonizers in 1859, his surprising enlightenment and eventual escape.

Bea Howe *Child in Chile* (o/p). A charming description of the author's childhood in Valparaíso in the early 1900s, where her family formed part of the burgeoning British business community.

W.H. Hudson *Idle Days in Patagonia*. Drawn by the variety of fauna and the remarkable birdlife, the novelist and naturalist W.H. Hudson travelled to Patagonia at the tail-end of the nineteenth century and wrote this series of charming, gentle observations.

George Musters *At Home with the Patagonians*. Remarkable account of time spent living with the Tehuelche Indians at the end of the nineteenth century that explodes the myth of the "noble savage" and provides a historically important picture of their vanishing way of life.

TRAVEL: MODERN AND CONTEMPORARY

Tim Burford *Chile and Argentina: The Bradt Trekking Guide*. Fantastically detailed account of how to access and climb the Andes from Atacama to Tierra del Fuego. Plenty of trail maps and practical advice.

★ **Bruce Chatwin** *In Patagonia*. The cult travel book that single-handedly enshrined Patagonia as the ultimate edge-of-the-world destination. Witty and captivating, this is essential reading for visitors to Patagonia, though unfortunately concentrates far more on the Argentine side.

Ariel Dorfman *Desert Memories*. Vivid depiction of desert life gleaned from Dorfman's travels through Chile's Norte Grande, which weaves past and present, memoir and meditation, history and family lore to provide an engaging chronicle of modern Chile.

Toby Green *Saddled with Darwin*. One hundred and sixty-five years after Charles Darwin embarked on the journey that produced the most radical theory of modern times, Green set out to retrace his footsteps on horseback. The result is an epic journey across six countries, including Chile, which paints an incisive portrait of change across the southern section of the continent.

Alistair Horne *Small Earthquake in Chile*. Wry description of a visit to Chile during the turbulent months leading up to Pinochet's military coup, written by a British journalist.

Brian Keenan and John McCarthy *Between Extremes: A Journey Beyond Imagination*. Five years after Keenan and McCarthy were released from captivity in Beirut, the pair

set off to fulfil a dream they'd shared as hostages to journey down the spine of Chile, from Arica to Tierra del Fuego. This account of their journey, told in alternating narratives, is as much a homage to their friendship as it is a description of the landscapes and people of Chile.

John Pilkington *An Englishman in Patagonia* (o/p). A fun-to-read and sympathetic portrayal of Patagonia and its people. This book includes some wonderful black-and-white photographs.

Rosie Swale *Back to Cape Horn* (o/p). An extraordinary account of the author's epic 409-day journey on horseback from the Atacama Desert down to Cape Horn – which she'd last visited while sailing around the world ten years previously in 1972.

★**Patrick Symmes** *Chasing Che*. The author undertakes an epic motorbike trip through South America – including hundreds of miles of Chile – following the route taken by a young Che Guevara back in 1952, as chronicled in *The Motorcycle Diaries* (see p.504). A great mix of biography, history, politics and travel anecdotes, this is a sharply written and highly entertaining read.

HISTORY, POLITICS AND SOCIETY: GENERAL

Leslie Bethell (ed) *Chile Since Independence*. Made up of four chapters taken from the *Cambridge History of Latin American History*, this is rather dry in parts, but rigorous, comprehensive and clear.

Nick Caistor *In Focus: Chile*. Brief, potted introduction to Chile's history, politics and society, highlighting the social problems bequeathed by Pinochet's economic model.

★**Simon Collier and William Sater** *A History of Chile, 1801–1994*. Probably the best single-volume history of Chile from independence to the 1990s; thoroughly academic but enlivened by colourful detail along with the authors' clear fondness for the country and its people.

John Hickman *News from the End of the Earth: A Portrait of Chile*. Written by a former British ambassador to Chile, this concise and highly readable book makes a good (if conservative) introduction to Chile's history, taking you from the conquest to the 1990s in some 250 pages.

Brian Loveman *Chile: the Legacy of Hispanic Capitalism*. Solid analysis of Chile's history from the arrival of the Spanish in the 1540s to the 1973 military coup.

Sergio Villalobos *A Short History of Chile*. Clear, concise and sensible outline of Chile's history, from pre-Columbian cultures through to the past decade, aimed at the general reader with no prior knowledge of the subject. Available in Santiago.

HISTORY, POLITICS AND SOCIETY: THE PINOCHET YEARS

★**Andy Beckett** *Pinochet in Piccadilly: Britain and Chile's Hidden History*. A fascinating political travelogue that connects the past to the present as it explores the relationship between the two nations.

Sheila Cassidy *Audacity to Believe* (o/p). Distressing account of the imprisonment and horrific torture of a British doctor (the author) after she'd treated a wounded anti-Pinochet activist.

★**Pamela Constable and Arturo Valenzuela** *A Nation of Enemies*. Written during the mid- to late 1980s, this is a superb look at the terror of everyday life in Chile at that time and the state apparatus used to annihilate free thinking and initiative. Essential reading if you want to understand contemporary Chile.

Marc Cooper *Pinochet and Me: A Chilean Anti-Memoir*. First-hand account of life under Pinochet in the early days of the coup, written by a young American who served as

Allende's translator and narrowly escaped the death squads. Followed up by accounts of his periodic visits to Chile over the next quarter century.

John Dinges *The Condor Years: How Pinochet and His Allies Brought Terror to Three Continents*. Exhaustively researched book that examines the creation and use of international hit squads by the Pinochet regime. The chilling accounts of multinational agreements to execute "enemies of the state" are recreated by author Dinges, an internationally recognized investigative reporter and professor at Columbia University.

Paul Drake (ed) *The Struggle for Democracy in Chile*. Excellent collection of ten essays examining the gradual breakdown of the military government's authority. The pieces, which offer contrasting views in support of and opposition to the regime, were written in 1988, during the months around the plebiscite.

Diana Kay *Chileans in Exile: Private Struggles, Public Lives*. Although written in a somewhat dry, academic style, this is nonetheless a fascinating study of Chilean exiles in Scotland, with a strong focus on women. The author looks at their attempts to reconstruct their lives, their sense of dislocation, and the impact exile has had on their attitude to politics, marriage and the home.

Hugh O'Shaughnessy *Pinochet: The Politics of Torture*. Covering everything from the arrest of Pinochet in London to Pinochet's secret plans to distribute sarin nerve gas to Chilean consulates abroad, this book provides an overview of the most influential man in Chilean politics in the years from 1973 to 1998.

Patricia Politzer *Fear in Chile, Lives Under Pinochet*. Award-winning account of the lives of Chileans during the dictatorship, and another insight into the repressive apparatus used to subdue Chileans.

Grino Rojo and John J Hasset (ed) *Chile, Dictatorship and the Struggle for Democracy*. A slim, accessible volume containing four essays written in the months approaching the 1988 plebiscite, in which the country would vote to reject or continue with military rule. Contains contrasting analyses of the impact of the dictatorship on the country and its people.

Jacobo Timerman *Chile: Death in the South* (o/p). Reflections on the Pinochet years by an Argentine journalist, written thirteen years into the military regime. Particularly compelling are the short personal testimonies of torture victims that intersperse the narrative.

Thomas Wright and Rody Oñate *Flight from Chile: Voices of Exile*. This is a detailed and affecting account of the exodus after the 1973 coup, when over 200,000 Chileans fled their homeland.

SPECIAL-INTEREST STUDIES

George McBride *Chile: Land and Society* (o/p). A compelling and exhaustively researched examination of the impact of the hacienda system on Chilean society, and the relationship (up to the mid-twentieth century) between landowners and peasants.

Colin McEwan, Luis Borrero and Alfredo Prieto (eds) *Patagonia: Natural History, Prehistory and Ethnography at the Uttermost End of the Earth*. Brilliant account of the "human adaptation, survival and eventual extinction" of the native peoples of Patagonia, accompanied by dozens of haunting black-and-white photographs.

★ **Nick Reding** *The Last Cowboys at the End of the World: The Story of the Gauchos of Patagonia*. A brutally honest and

at times brutal look at the end of the gaucho era in Patagonia. Excellent exploration of how in the mid-1990s the gaucho culture crashed headlong into the advance of modern society.

William Sater *The Heroic Image in Chile* (o/p). Fascinating, scholarly look at the reasons behind the near-deification of Arturo Prat, the naval officer who died futilely in battle in 1879, described by the author as "a secular saint".

Richard W Slatta *Cowboys of the Americas*. Exhaustively researched, highly entertaining and lavishly illustrated history of the cowboy cultures of the Americas, including detailed treatment of the Chilean *huaso*.

CHILEAN WOMEN

Marjorie Agosin (ed) *Scraps of Life: Chilean Arpilleras: Chilean Women and the Pinochet Dictatorship*. A sensitive portrayal of the women of Santiago's shanty towns who, during the dictatorship, scraped a living by sewing scraps of material together to make wall hangings, known as *arpilleras*, depicting scenes of violence and repression. The *arpilleras* became a symbol of their protest, and were later exhibited around the world.

Jo Fisher *Out of the Shadows*. Penetrating analysis of the emergence of the women's movement in Latin America, with a couple of chapters devoted to Chile.

Elizabeth Jelin (ed) *Women and Social Change in Latin America*. A series of intelligent essays examining the ways women's organizations have acted as mobilizing forces for social and political change in Latin America.

Alicia Partnoy (ed) *You Can't Drown the Fire: Latin American Women Writing in Exile*. Excellent anthology bringing together a mixture of short stories, poems and essays by exiled Latin American women, including Veronica de Negri, Cecila Vicuña, Marjorie Agosin and Isabel Morel Letelier from Chile.

FICTION

Marjorie Agosin (ed) *Landscapes of a New Land: Short Fiction by Latin American Women*. This anthology includes four short stories by Chilean women authors, including the acclaimed Marta Brunet (1901–67) and María Luisa Bombal (1910–80). Overall, the book creates a poetic, at times haunting, evocation of female life in a patriarchal world. Also edited by Agosin, *Secret Weavers: Stories of the*

Fantastic by Women of Argentina and Chile (o/p) is a spellbinding collection of short stories interwoven with themes of magic, allegory, legend and fantasy.

★ **Isabel Allende** *The House of the Spirits* is the baroque, fantastical and best-selling novel by the niece of Salvador Allende, which chronicles the fortunes of several generations of a rich, landowning family in an unnamed but thinly disguised Chile, culminating with a brutal military coup and the murder of the president. *Of Love and Shadows* is set against a background of disappearances and dictatorship, including a fictional account of the real-life discovery of the bodies of fifteen executed workers in a Central Valley mine. Allende's recent novel, *Maya's Notebook*, much of which is set in a remote community off the island of Chiloé, delves into traditional Chilote island life in the twenty-first century and the issues faced by the villagers.

Roberto Bolaño *Last Evenings on Earth*. The celebrated Chilean novelist's haunting first novel to be translated into English is set against the bleak backdrop of the Pinochet dictatorship, with its protagonists living on the fringes of society.

★**José Donoso** *Curfew*. Gripping novel about an exiled folk singer's return to Santiago during the military dictatorship, by one of Chile's most outstanding twentieth-century writers. Other works by Donoso translated into English include *Hell Has No Limits*, about the strange existence of a transvestite and his daughter in a Central Valley brothel, and *The Obscene Bird of Night*, a dislocated, fragmented novel narrated by a deaf-mute old man as he retreats into madness.

Ariel Dorfman *Hard Rain*. This complicated, thought-provoking novel is both an examination of the role of the

writer in a revolutionary society, and a celebration of the "Chilean road to socialism" – not an easy read, but one that repays the effort. Dorfman later became internationally famous for his play *Death and the Maiden*, made into a film by Roman Polanski. Dorfman has also written an account of the effort to prosecute Pinochet in *Exorcising Terror: The Incredible Unending Trial of Augusto Pinochet*.

Alberto Fuguet *Bad Vibes* (o/p). Two weeks in September 1980 as lived by a mixed-up Santiago rich kid. A sort of Chilean *Catcher In the Rye* set against the tensions of the military regime.

Luis Sepúlveda *The Name of a Bullfighter*. Fast-paced, rather macho thriller set in Hamburg, Santiago and Tierra del Fuego, by one of Chile's leading young novelists.

Antonio Skármeta *The Postman*, formerly *Burning Patience*. Funny and poignant novel about a postman who delivers mail to the great poet Pablo Neruda. Neruda, in turn, helps him seduce the local beauty with the help of a few metaphors. It was also made into a successful film, *Il Postino*, with the action relocated to Capri. Also by Skármeta, *I Dreamt the Snow Was Burning* is a tense, dark novel evoking the suspicion and fear that permeated everyday life in the months surrounding the military coup, while *Watch Where the Wolf is Going* (Readers International) is a collection of short stories, some of them set in Chile.

POETRY

Vicente Huidobro *The Selected Poetry of Vicente Huidobro*. Intellectual, experimental and dynamic works by an early twentieth-century poet, highly acclaimed in his time (1893–1948) but often overlooked today.

Gabriela Mistral *Selected Poems*. Mistral is far less widely translated than her fellow Nobel laureate, Neruda, but this collection serves as an adequate English-language introduction to her quietly passionate and bittersweet poetry, much of which is inspired by the landscape of the Elqui Valley.

Pablo Neruda *Twenty Love Poems and a Song of Despair*; *Canto General*; *Captain's Verses*. The doyen of Chilean poetry seems to be one of those poets people love or hate – his work is extravagantly lyrical, frequently verbose, but often very tender, particularly his love poetry. Neruda has been translated into many languages, and is widely available.

Nicanor Parra *Emergency Poems*. Both a physicist and poet, Parra pioneered the "anti-poem" in Chile during the 1980s: bald, un-lyrical, often satirical prose poems. A stimulating read.

BIOGRAPHY AND MEMOIRS

Fernando Alegría *Allende: A Novel*. Basically a biography, with fictional dialogue, of Salvador Allende, written by his former cultural attaché, who was busy researching the book while the president died in the coup. Also of note by Alegría is *The Chilean Spring*, a fictional diary of a young photographer coming to terms with the coup in Santiago.

Isabel Allende *My Invented Country – A Nostalgic Journey Through Chile*. A memoir that is an enthralling mix of fiction and biography and which describes the author's life in Chile up until the assassination of her uncle, president Salvador Allende. She provides a very personal view of her homeland and exhaustively examines the country, its terrain, people, customs and language.

Ariel Dorfman *Heading South, Looking North*. Memoir of one of Chile's most famous writers, in which he reflects on

themes such as language, identity, guilt and politics. Intelligent and illuminating, with some interesting thoughts on the causes of the Unidad Popular's failures.

★**Joan Jara** *Víctor: An Unfinished Song* (o/p). Poignant memoir written by the British wife of the famous Chilean folksinger Víctor Jara, describing their life together, the *nueva canción* movement (see p.498) and their optimism for Allende's new Chile. The final part, detailing Jara's imprisonment, torture and execution in Santiago's football stadium, is almost unbearably moving.

R.L. Mégroz *The Real Robinson Crusoe* (o/p). Colourful biography of Alexander Selkirk, who spent four years and four months marooned on one of the Juan Fernández Islands, inspiring Daniel Defoe to write *The Adventures of Robinson Crusoe*.

Luis Muñoz *Being Luis*. Account of a childhood spent growing up in 1960s–70s Chile that reflects recent history and leads to Muñoz's development as a left-wing activist, his arrest and torture by the military regime and eventual exile to England.

Pablo Neruda *Memoirs*. Though his occasional displays of vanity and compulsive name-dropping can be irritating, there's no doubt that this is an extraordinary man with a fascinating life. The book also serves as a useful outline of Chile's political movements from the 1930s to the 1970s.

PACIFIC ISLANDS

Paul Bahn and John Flenley *Easter Island, Earth Island* (o/p). Richly illustrated with glossy photographs, this scholarly but accessible book provides an up-to-date and comprehensive introduction to the island's history and archeology. Interestingly, it also suggests that Easter Island could be a microcosm representing a global dilemma – that of a land so despoiled by man that it could no longer support its civilization.

Sebastian Englert *Island at the Centre of the World* (o/p). Based on a series of lectures broadcast to the Chilean Navy serving in Antarctica, this is perhaps the clearest and most accessible (though now somewhat dated) introduction to Easter Island, written by a genial German priest who lived there for 35 years from 1935.

Thor Heyerdahl *Aku Aku* (o/p). This account of Heyerdahl's famous expedition to Easter Island in 1955 makes a cracking read, with an acute sense of adventure and mystery. Dubious as the author's archeological theories are, it's hard not to get swept along by his enthusiasm. In contrast, his *Reports of the Norwegian Archeological Expedition to Easter Island and the East Pacific* is a rigorous and respected documentation of the expedition's findings.

Alfred Métraux *Easter Island* (o/p). Key study of Easter Island's traditions, beliefs and customs by a Belgian anthropologist, based on exhaustive research carried out in

the 1930s. Métraux's *The Ethnology of Easter Island* was published in periodical format.

Catherine and Michel Orliac *The Silent Gods: Mysteries of Easter Island* (o/p). This pocket-sized paperback is densely packed with colour illustrations and surprisingly detailed background on the island's explorers, statues, myths and traditions.

★**Katherine Routledge** *The Mystery of Easter Island*. Recently back in print, this compelling book chronicles one of the earliest archeological expeditions to the island, led by the author in 1914. Routledge interviewed many elderly islanders and recounts their oral testimonies as well as the discoveries of her excavations.

★**Diana Souhami** *Selkirk's Island*. This gripping account of the misadventures of Alexander Selkirk – the real life Robinson Crusoe, who spent four years marooned on a Chilean Pacific island – includes some vivid and evocative descriptions of what's now known as Isla Robinson Crusoe. Deservedly won the Whitbread Biography Award in 2001.

Ralph Lee Woodward *Robinson Crusoe's Island* (o/p). There's a good deal more drama to the Juan Fernández islands' history than the famous four-year marooning of Alexander Selkirk, all of it enthusiastically retold in this lively book.

FLORA AND FAUNA

Sharon R. Chester *Birds of Chile* is a first-rate, easy-to-carry guide with over three hundred colour illustrations of the birds of mainland Chile. *A Wildlife Guide to Chile* is the first comprehensive field guide in English that covers Chile's fauna, both on the mainland and its far-flung territories, including Antarctica and Easter Island. It features 120 colour plates with illustrations of over 800 species.

Claudio Donoso Zegers *Chilean Trees Identification Guide/Arboles Nativos de Chile*. Handy pocket guide to Chile's main native trees, with commentary in Spanish and English. Produced for Conaf (Chile's national parks administration), and part of a series that includes *Chilean Bushes*, *Chilean Climber Plants* and *Chilean Terrestrial Mammals*. It may be available in Conaf's information office in Santiago.

Chilean Spanish

To get by in Chile, it's very helpful to equip yourself with a bit of basic Spanish. It's not a difficult language to pick up and there are numerous book/CD packs on the market, teaching to various levels – *Pimsleur Basic Latin American Spanish* is a very good starting point, the *Learn (Latin American) Spanish* Android app and similar iPhone equivalents leave you with essential words and phrases at your fingertips, while for an old-fashioned, rigorous textbook, nothing beats H. Ramsden's *An Essential Course in Modern Spanish*, published in the UK by Nelson.

The snag is that Chilean Spanish does not conform to what you learn in the classroom or hear on your iPod, and even competent Spanish-speakers will find it takes a bit of getting used to. The first thing to contend with is the dizzying **speed** with which most Chileans speak; another is **pronunciation**, especially the habitual dropping of many consonants. In particular, "s" is frequently dropped from the end or middle of a word, so *dos* becomes *do*, *gracias* becomes *gracia*, and *fósforos* (matches) becomes *fohforo*. "D" has a habit of disappearing from past participles, so *comprado* is *comprao*, while the "gua" sound is commonly reduced to *wa*, making the city of Rancagua sound like *Rancawa*. The *–as* ending of the second person singular of verbs (*estás*, *viajas*, and so on) is transformed into *–ai*: hence *¿cómo estás?* usually comes out as "comehtai"; the classic *"¿cachai?"* ("get it?") is the second person singular form of the slang verb *cachar*, meaning to understand.

Another way in which Chilean differs from classic Castilian Spanish is its borrowing of words from indigenous languages, mainly Quechua, Aymara and Mapuche, but also from German (*kuchen*, for cake) and even English ("plumber" in Chile is inexplicably *el gasfiter*). Adding to the confusion is a widespread use of **slang** and **idiom**, much of which is unique to Chile. None of this, however, should put you off attempting to speak Spanish in Chile – Chileans will really appreciate your efforts, and even faltering beginners will be complimented on their language skills.

Pronunciation

The rules of **pronunciation** are pretty straightforward and, once you get to know them, strictly observed. Unless there's an accent, words ending in d, l, r, and z are **stressed** on the last syllable, all others on the second last. All **vowels** are pure and short.

A somewhere between the A sound of back and that of father.

E as in get.

I as in police.

O as in hot.

U as in rule.

C is soft before E and I, hard otherwise: *cerca* is pronounced "serka".

G works the same way, a slightly guttural H sound (between an aspirate "h" and the ch in loch) before E or I, a hard G elsewhere – *gigante* becomes "higante".

H is always silent.

J is guttural: *jamón* is pronounced "hamón".

LL sounds like an English Y: *tortilla* is pronounced "torteeya".

N is as in English unless it has a tilde (ñ) over it, when it becomes NY: *mañana* sounds like "manyana".

QU is pronounced like an English K (the "u" is silent).

R is rolled, RR doubly so.

V sounds more like B, *vino* becoming "beano".

X is slightly softer than in English – sometimes almost SH – except between vowels in place names where it has an H sound – for example *México* (Meh-Hee-Ko).

Z is the same as a soft C, so *cerveza* becomes "serbessa".

Below we've listed a few essential words and phrases, though if you're travelling for any length of time a dictionary or phrase book is obviously a worthwhile investment. If you're using a **dictionary**, bear in mind that in Spanish CH, LL, and Ñ count as separate letters and are traditionally listed in a special section after the Cs, Ls, and Ns respectively, though some new dictionaries do not follow this rule.

WORDS AND PHRASES

The following should help you with your most basic day-to-day language needs; a menu reader and list of slang terms follows on.

BASICS

yes, no	sí, no	open, closed	abierto/a, cerrado/a
please, thank you	por favor, gracias	with, without	con, sin
where, when?	dónde, cuándo	good, bad	buen(o)/a, mal(o)/a
what, how much?	qué, cuánto	big	gran(de)
here, there	aquí, allí	small	pequeño/a, chico
this, that	este, eso	more, less	más, menos
now, later	ahora, más tarde	today, tomorrow	hoy, mañana
		yesterday	ayer

GREETINGS AND RESPONSES

Hello, Goodbye	Hola, adiós (ciao/ chau)	Do you speak English?	¿Habla (usted) inglés?
		I (don't) speak Spanish	(No) Hablo español
Good morning	Buenos días	My name is…	Me llamo…
Good afternoon	Buenas tardes	What's your name?	¿Cómo se llama (usted)?
Good evening/night	Buenas noches	I am English	Soy inglés (a)
See you later	Hasta luego	…Irish	…irlandés (a)
Sorry	Lo siento/discúlpeme (perdón)	…Scottish	…escocés (a)
		…Welsh	…galés (a)
Excuse me	Con permiso/perdón	…American	…norte-americano (a)
How are you?	¿Como está (usted)?	…Australian	…australiano (a)
I (don't) understand	(No) Entiendo	…Canadian	…canadiense
Not at all/You're welcome	De nada	…New Zealander	…neozelandés (a)

ACCOMMODATION AND TRANSPORT

I want	Quiero…	Don't you have anything cheaper?	¿No tiene algo más barato?
I'd like	Quisiera…		
Do you know…	¿Sabe…?	Can one…?	¿Se puede…?
I don't know	No sé	…camp (near) here?	…acampar aquí (cerca)?
There is (is there?)	(¿) Hay (?)	Is there a hotel nearby?	¿Hay un hotel aquí cerca?
Give me…	Deme…	How do I get to…?	¿Por dónde se va a…?
…(one like that)	…(uno así)	Left, right, straight on	Izquierda, derecha, derecho
Do you have…	¿Tiene…?		
…the time	…la hora	Where is…?	¿Dónde está…?
…a room	…una habitación	the bus station	el terminal de buses
…with two beds/ double bed	…con dos camas/ cama matrimonial	the train station	la estación de ferrocarriles
…with private bath	…con baño privado	the nearest bank	el banco más cercano
It's for one person (two people)	es para una persona (dos personas)	the post office	el correo
		the toilet	el baño
For one night (one week)	para una noche (una semana)	Where does the bus leave from?	¿De dónde sale el bus para…?
It's fine	Está bien	Is this the train for Santiago?	¿Es éste el tren para Santiago?
How much is it?	¿Cuánto es?		
It's too expensive	Es demasiado caro	I'd like a (return) ticket to…	Quisiera un pasaje (de ida y vuelta) para…

USEFUL TRANSPORT VOCABULARY

Ticket	Pasaje	**Non-4WD**	Tracción single or
Seat	Asiento		dos por dos
Aisle	Pasillo		(2x2)
Window	Ventana	**Unlimited kilometres**	Kilometraje libre
Luggage	Equipaje	**Insurance**	Seguro
Left luggage	Custodia	**Damages excess**	Deducible
Car	Auto	**Petrol**	Bencina
Car rental outlet	Rentacar	**Petrol station**	Estación de
To rent	Arrendar		bencina
4WD	Doble tracción or	**Jerry can**	Bidon
	cuatro por cuatro	**Highway**	Carretera
	(4x4)	**Pick-up truck**	Camioneta

CHILEAN ROAD SIGNS

Danger	Peligro	**Dangerous bend**	Curva peligrosa
Detour	Desvío	**Reduce speed**	Reduzca velocidad
Slippery surface	Resbaladizo	**No hard shoulder**	Sin berma
No overtaking	No adelantar		

What time does it leave (arrive in…)?	¿A qué hora sale (llega en…)?	What is there to eat?	¿Qué hay para comer?
		What's that?	¿Qué es eso?
How long does the journey take?	¿Cuánto tiempo demora el viaje?	What's this called in Spanish?	¿Como se llama esto en español?

NUMBERS AND DAYS

1	un/uno/una	50	cincuenta
2	dos	60	sesenta
3	tres	70	setenta
4	cuatro	80	ochenta
5	cinco	90	noventa
6	seis	100	cien(to)
7	siete	101	ciento uno
8	ocho	200	doscientos (as)
9	nueve	201	doscientos (as) uno
10	diez	500	quinientos (as)
11	once	1000	mil
12	doce	2000	dos mil
13	trece	**first**	primer(o)/a
14	catorce	**second**	segundo/a
15	quince	**third**	tercer(o)/a
16	dieciséis	**Monday**	lunes
17	diecisiete	**Tuesday**	martes
18	dieciocho	**Wednesday**	miércoles
19	diecinueve	**Thursday**	jueves
20	veinte	**Friday**	viernes
21	veintiuno	**Saturday**	sábado
30	treinta	**Sunday**	domingo
40	cuarenta		

FOOD: A CHILEAN MENU READER

BASICS		Ajo	Garlic
Aceite	Oil	Arroz	Rice
Ají	Chilli	Azúcar	Sugar

Huevos	Eggs
Leche	Milk
Mantequilla	Butter
Mermelada	Jam
Miel	Honey
Mostaza	Mustard
Pan	Bread
Pimienta	Pepper
Sal	Salt

SOME COMMON TERMS

A la parrilla	Grilled
A la plancha	Grilled
A lo pobre	Served with chips, onions and a fried egg
Ahumado	Smoked
Al horno	Oven-baked
Al vapor	Steamed
Asado	Roast or barbecued
Asado al palo	Spit-roasted, barbecued
Crudo	Raw
Frito	Fried
Pastel	Paste, purée, mince
Picante	Spicy hot
Pil-pil	Very spicy
Puré	Mashed (potato)
Relleno	Filled or stuffed

MEALS

Agregado	Side order
Almuerzo	Lunch
Cena	Dinner
Comedor	Dining room
Cuchara	Spoon
Cuchillo	Knife
Desayuno	Breakfast
La carta	The menu
La cuenta	The bill
Menú del día	Fixed-price set meal (usually lunch)
Once	Afternoon tea
Plato vegetariano	Vegetarian dish
Tenedor	Fork

MEAT (CARNE) AND POULTRY (AVES)

Bistec	Beef steak
Carne de vacuno	Beef
Cerdo	Pork
Chuleta	Cutlet, chop (usually pork)
Churrasco	Griddled beef, like a minute steak
Conejo	Rabbit
Cordero	Lamb steak
Escalopa Milanesa	Breaded veal escalope

Filete	Fillet steak
Jamón	Ham
Lechón, cochinillo	Suckling pig
Lomo	General term for steak of indiscriminate cut
Pato	Duck
Pavo	Turkey
Pollo	Chicken
Ternera	Veal
Vienesa	Hot-dog sausage

OFFAL (MENUDOS)

Chunchules	Intestines
Guatitas	Tripe
Lengua	Tongue
Patas	Feet, trotters
Pana	Liver
Picante de conejo	Curried rabbits' innards
Riñones	Kidneys

FISH (PESCADO)

Albacora	Albacore (a small, white-fleshed tuna)
Anchoveta	Anchovy
Atún	Tuna
Bonito	Pacific bonito, similar to tuna
Ceviche	Strips of fish marinated in lemon juice and onions
Congrio	A large, superior member of the cod family known as conger eel
Corvina	Sea bass (not the same as Chilean sea bass, which is under boycott)
Lenguado	Sole
Merluza	Hake
Reineta	Similar to lemon sole
Salmón	Salmon
Trucha	Trout
Vidriola	Firm-fleshed white fish from the Juan Fernández archipelago

SEAFOOD (MARISCOS)

Almeja	Clam, cockle
Calamar	Squid
Camarón	Prawn
Centolla	King crab
Choro, chorito	Mussel
Erizo	Sea urchin
Langosta	Lobster
Langosta de Isla de Pascua	Spiny lobster

Langosta de Juan Fernández	Rock lobster fished near the Juan Fernández islands
Langostino	Crayfish, red crab
Loco	Abalone
Macha	Razor clam
Mariscal	Mixed shellfish, served chilled
Mejillones	Mussels
Ostiones	Scallops
Ostras	Oysters
Paila marina	Thick fish and seafood stew
Picoroco	Giant barnacle with a single crab-like claw
Piure	Scarlet-red, kidney-shaped animal with hair-like strands that lives inside a shell
Pulpo	Octopus

VEGETABLES (VERDURAS)

Aceitunas	Olives
Alcachofa	Artichoke
Cebolla	Onion
Champiñón	Mushroom
Choclo	Maize, sweetcorn
Chucrút	Sauerkraut
Espinaca	Spinach
Lechuga	Lettuce
Palmito	Palm heart
Palta	Avocado
Papa	Potato
Papas fritas	Chips (French fries)
Poroto verde	Green, French, runner bean
Tomate	Tomato
Zapallo	Squash

SOUPS AND STEWS

Caldillo	Vegetables cooked in meat stock; between a stew and a soup
Caldo	Quite bland, simple meat stock with loads of added salt
Charquicán	Meat stew with lots of vegetables
Chupe	Thick fish stew, topped with butter, breadcrumbs and grated cheese
Crema	Creamy soup thickened with flour or egg yolks

Zarzuela	Seafood stew (like bouillabaisse)

SALADS (ENSALADAS)

Ensalada chilena	Tomatoes, shredded onion and vinaigrette
Ensalada primavera	Hard-boiled eggs, sweetcorn, peas, carrot and beetroot
Ensalada rusa	Diced vegetables and peas mixed in a thick mayonnaise
Ensalada surtida	Mixed salad
Palta reina	Avocado filled with tuna

SANDWICHES (SANWICHES)

Ave mayo	Chicken and mayonnaise
Ave sola	Chicken
Barros jarpa	Ham and melted cheese
Barros luco	Beef and melted cheese
Churrasco solo	Griddled beef, like a minute steak
Completo	Hot dog, sauerkraut, tomato and mayonnaise
Diplomático	Beef, egg and melted cheese
Especial	Hot dog with mayonnaise
Hamburguesa	Hamburger

FRUIT (FRUTAS)

Albaricoque	Apricot
Cereza	Cherry
Chirimoya	Custard apple
Ciruela	Plum
Durazno	Peach
Frambuesa	Raspberry
Frutilla	Strawberry
Higo	Fig
Limón	Lemon
Lúcuma	Native fruit often used in ice cream and cakes
Manzana	Apple
Membrillo	Quince
Mora	Mulberry
Naranja	Orange
Pera	Pear
Piña	Pineapple
Plátano	Banana
Pomelo	Grapefruit
Sandía	Watermelon
Tuna	Prickly pear
Uva(s)	Grape(s)

IDIOM AND SLANG

As you travel through Chile you'll come across a lot of words and expressions that crop up again and again, many of which aren't in your dictionary, or, if they are, appear to have a different meaning from that given. Added to these day-to-day **chilenismos** is a very rich, exuberant and constantly expanding vocabulary of slang (*modismos*). Mastering a few of the most common examples will help you get by and raise a smile if you drop them into the conversation.

EVERYDAY WORDS AND EXPRESSIONS

Some of the words and expressions listed below are shared by neighbouring countries, while others are uniquely Chilean. As well as these peculiarities, we've listed a few other expressions you're likely to encounter very frequently.

Al tiro "right away", "immediately" – though this can mean anything up to several hours.

Boleta as Chilean law requires that customers must not leave shop premises without their *boleta* (receipt), you will frequently hear "*su boleta!*" yelled at you as you try to leave without it.

Calefónt (pronounced "*calefón*") water heater; not a real Chilean word, but one you'll need every day if you're staying in budget accommodation, where you'll have to remember to light the *calefónt* with *fósforos* (matches) before you take a shower.

Carné identity card.

Cédula interchangeable with *carné*.

Ciao (chau) by far the most common way of saying "goodbye" among friends; in slightly more formal situations, *hasta luego* is preferred over *adiós*.

Confort (pronounced "*confor*") a brand name but now the de facto word for toilet paper (which is correctly *papel higiénico*).

De repente in Spain this means "suddenly"; in Chile it means "maybe", "sometimes" or "occasionally".

Flojo "lazy", frequently invoked by northerners to describe southerners and southerners to describe northerners.

Guagua (pronounced "*wawa*") baby, derived from Quechua.

Harto "loads of" (for example *harto trabajo*, loads of work); a more widely used and idiomatic alternative to *mucho*.

Listo literally "ready", and used as a response to indicate agreement, or that what's been said is understood; something like "sure" or "right".

Plata literally "silver" but meaning "money", used far more commonly than *dinero*, except in formal situations.

Qué le vaya (muy) bien "May everything go (very) well for you", frequently said when saying goodbye to someone you probably won't see again.

Rico "good", "delicious", "tasty", usually to describe food and drink.

Ya Chilean equivalent of the Spanish *vale*; used universally to convey "OK", "fine", "sure" or (depending on the tone) "Whatever", "Hmm, I see".

SLANG

The few examples we give below barely scrape the surface of the living, constantly evolving lexicon of Chilean slang – for a crash course, get hold of the excellent *How to Survive in the Chilean Jungle* by John Brennan and Alvaro Baboada, published by Dolmen and available in the larger Santiago bookshops.

Buena onda "cool!"

Cachar "to understand"; hence "*¿cachai?*", "are you with me?", scattered ad nauseam through conversations.

Cocido drunk.

Cuico yuppie (especially in Santiago).

Huevón literally "huge testicle", meaning something like "asshole" or "fucker", but so commonly and enthusiastically used it's no longer particularly offensive. More like "jerk" or "idiot".

Los pacos the police.

Pololo/a boyfriend, girlfriend.

¡Sale! emphatically used to mean, "bullshit!" or "not a chance!"

Sí, po abbreviation of *sí, pues*, meaning "yeah", "sure" ("po" is tacked onto the end of just about every phrase, hence "*no po*", "*no sé po*").

Taco traffic jam.

DESSERT (POSTRES)

When fruit is described as being "in juice" (*al jugo*) or "in syrup" (*en almíbar*), it will be out of a tin.

Flan	Crème caramel
Helado	Ice cream
Kuchen	Cake
Macedonia	Fruit salad
Manjar	Very sweet caramel, made from condensed milk
Panqueques	Pancakes
Torta	Tart

DRINKS AND BEVERAGES

Note that, owing to the Chileans' compulsive use of the diminutive (*ito* and *ita*), you'll hardly ever be asked if you want a *té* or *café*, but rather a *tecito* or *cafecito*, which tends to throw people at first.

ALCOHOLIC DRINKS

Cerveza	Beer
Champán	Champagne
Chicha (or sidra)	Cider
Vino (tinto/blanco/ rosado)	Wine (red/white/rosé)

HOT DRINKS

Café	Coffee
Descafeinado	Decaff (rarely available)
Chocolate caliente	Hot chocolate
Té	Tea
Té de hierbas	Herbal tea

SOFT DRINKS

Bebida	Fizzy drink
(en lata/botella)	(in a can/bottle)
(de máquina)	(draught)
Jugo natural	Juice (pure)
Néctar	Juice (syrup)
Agua	Water
Agua mineral	Mineral water
(con gas)	(sparkling)
(sin gas)	(still)

Small print and index

517 Small print

518 About the authors

520 Index

526 Map symbols

A ROUGH GUIDE TO ROUGH GUIDES

Published in 1982, the first Rough Guide – to Greece – was a student scheme that became a publishing phenomenon. Mark Ellingham, a recent graduate in English from Bristol University, had been travelling in Greece the previous summer and couldn't find the right guidebook. With a small group of friends he wrote his own guide, combining a highly contemporary, journalistic style with a thoroughly practical approach to travellers' needs.

The immediate success of the book spawned a series that rapidly covered dozens of destinations. And, in addition to impecunious backpackers, Rough Guides soon acquired a much broader readership that relished the guides' wit and inquisitiveness as much as their enthusiastic, critical approach and value-for-money ethos.

These days, Rough Guides include recommendations from budget to luxury and cover more than 120 destinations around the globe, as well as producing an ever-growing range of ebooks.

Visit **roughguides.com** to find all our latest books, read articles, get inspired and share travel tips with the Rough Guides community.

Rough Guide credits

Editors: Olivia Rawes, Brendon Griffin
Layout: Anita Singh
Cartography: Animesh Pathak
Picture editor: Aude Vauconsant
Proofreader: Stewart Wild
Managing editor: Andy Turner
Assistant editor: Sharon Sonam
Production: Jimmy Lao

Cover design: Nicole Newman, Chloë Stickland, Anita Singh
Photographer: Tim Draper
Editorial assistant: Freya Godfrey
Senior pre-press designer: Dan May
Programme manager: Gareth Lowe
Publisher: Joanna Kirby
Publishing director: Georgina Dee

Publishing information

This sixth edition published September 2015 by
Rough Guides Ltd,
80 Strand, London WC2R 0RL
11, Community Centre, Panchsheel Park,
New Delhi 110017, India
Distributed by Penguin Random House
Penguin Books Ltd,
80 Strand, London WC2R 0RL
Penguin Group (USA)
345 Hudson Street, NY 10014, USA
Penguin Group (Australia)
250 Camberwell Road, Camberwell,
Victoria 3124, Australia
Penguin Group (NZ)
67 Apollo Drive, Mairangi Bay, Auckland 1310,
New Zealand
Penguin Group (South Africa)
Block D, Rosebank Office Park, 181 Jan Smuts Avenue,
Parktown North, Gauteng, South Africa 2193
Rough Guides is represented in Canada by Tourmaline
Editions Inc. 662 King Street West, Suite 304, Toronto,
Ontario M5V 1M7
Printed in Singapore

MIX
Paper from
responsible sources
FSC™ C018179
www.fsc.org

Help us update

We've gone to a lot of effort to ensure that the sixth
edition of **The Rough Guide to Chile** is accurate and up-
to-date. However, things change – places get "discovered",
opening hours are notoriously fickle, restaurants and
rooms raise prices or lower standards. If you feel we've got
it wrong or left something out, we'd like to know, and if
you can remember the address, the price, the hours, the
phone number, so much the better.

Please send your comments with the subject line
"Rough Guide Chile Update" to @mail@uk.roughguides
.com. We'll credit all contributions and send a copy of the
next edition (or any other Rough Guide if you prefer) for
the very best emails.
  Find more travel information, connect with fellow
travellers and plan your trip on ⑩roughguides.com.

ABOUT THE AUTHORS

Anna Kaminski has been enamoured of this long, thin country ever since becoming hooked on Isabel Allende novels and Pablo Neruda's poetry while doing a degree on the history and literature of Latin America. Since then, she has travelled the entire length of Chile on several occasions – for research and pleasure – though it's the frozen south that entices her the most: she considers Patagonia her second home and finds herself returning year after year.

Shafik Meghji is a south London-based travel writer and journalist. He has travelled throughout Chile since his first visit in 2004. In total, he has worked on over 25 Rough Guides and writes regularly for publications around the world. Shafik is a fellow of the Royal Geographical Society, a member of the British Guild of Travel Writers and a trustee of the Latin America Bureau. See ⓦshafikmeghji.com; blog See ⓦunmappedroutes.com; Twitter @ShafikMeghji.

Rosalba O'Brien arrived in Latin America in the 1990s as a Comparative American Studies undergraduate. She has worked as a journalist, travel writer and tour leader in the region, including in Argentina, Peru, Brazil and, of course, Chile, where her favourite thing to do is go skiing for the day in Valle Nevado and be back in Santiago in time for dinner.

Acknowledgements

Shafik Meghji Thanks to all the locals and travellers who helped me out along the way. A special muchas gracias must go to: Mani Ramaswamy, Andy Turner and Olivia Rawes at RG HQ; Brendon Griffin for his sterling editing work; co-authors Anna Kaminski and Rosalba O'Brien; Mary Anne Nelson and Laura Rendell-Dunn at Journey Latin America for the all their help with travel bookings; Nicolas Fernandez of Chile Running Tours; Jaime for showing me Humberstone and Santa Laura; Janak Jani in Valpo; Antonietta Varlese of Accor; Odile Palustran of *The Singular*; Kristina Schreck of Azure PR; Jean, Nizar and Nina Meghji; and Sioned Jones, for all her love and support.

Rosalba O'Brien Thanks to Shafik, Anna, Olivia and Andy at RG; the splendid tourism office in Concepción; Franz and Kati at *Casa Chueca*; Patricia for Santiago bar knowledge; Gaby, Kate, Eric and Daniela, Mum and Mimi for their visits; and as always Esteban and Arwen for schlepping up and down Ruta 5 without complaining (well, not much).

Readers' updates

Thanks to all the readers who have taken the time to write in with comments and suggestions (and apologies if we've inadvertently omitted or misspelt anyone's name):

Ben and Izzy, Jan Brunotte, Scott Fitzgerald, Melissa Graham, Naomi Griffiths, Juan Leon, Barry Ress, Caroline Robertson, Duncan Smith, Frank Stermitz, Mark Stringer.

Photo credits

All photos © Rough Guides except the following:
(Key: t-top; c-centre; b-bottom; l-left; r-right)

p.1 Richard Cummins/Robert Harding Picture Library
p.2 Keith Levit/Design Pics/Corbis
p.4 Menno Boermans/Getty Images
p.7 Thomas Schmitt/Getty Images (tl); John Warburton-Lee/AWL Images (tr); Fridmar Damm/Corbis (b)
p.11 Konrad Jacob (t); Foxphotoruins/Alamy Images (b)
p.12 Momatiuk – Eastcott/Corbis
p.13 Fotografias Jorge Leon Cabello/Getty Images (t); Oliver Gerhard/SuperStock (b)
p.15 Matthias Clamer/Getty Images (tl); R. Ian Lloyd/Masterfile/Corbis (b)
p.16 Oriol Alamany/Alamy
p.17 Paul Harris/AWL Images (t); Aurora Photos/AWL Images (b)
p.18 Paolo Messina/4Corners (t); Martin Bernetti/Getty Images (b)
p.19 Frank Krahmer/Corbis (t); Francoise EMILY/Alamy Images (b)
p.20 Atosan/Dreamstime.com (c); Sven Creutzmann/Getty Images (b)
p.22 John W Banagan/Getty Images
p.52 Matt Mawson/Corbis
p.65 David A. Barnes/Alamy (b)
p.87 James Quine/Alamy (t); Jon Hicks/Corbis (b)
p.94 John W Banagan/Getty Images
p.97 Stefano Politi/Alamy
p.115 Breton West/Alamy (t); Bon Appetit/Alamy (b)
p.122 WIN-Initiative/Getty Images

p.139 Megapress/Alamy
p.169 Blaine Harrington III/Alamy Images
p.219 Paul Harris/AWL Images
p.251 Paul Harris/AWL Images RM/Getty Images
p.261 Aaron McCoy/SuperStock
p.297 Jochen Tack/Robert Harding Picture Library
p.317 Nature Picture Library/Alamy Images
p.323 Paul Harris/AWL Images (t)
p.341 Robert Harding/Alamy
p.346 Imagebroker/Alamy
p.373 Novarc Images/Alamy Images (t); Ric Ergenbright/Corbis (b)
p.382 Paul Harris/AWL Images
p.407 Jose Fuste Raga/Corbis (b)
p.418 LOOK Die Bildagentur der Fotografen/Alamy
p.431 Feargus Cooney/Alamy (t); Ken Gillham/SuperStock (b)
p.437 WorldFoto/Alamy
p.442 Ripani Massimo/4Corners
p.445 Bill Bachmann/Alamy
p.459 Ken Welsh/SuperStock (t); Svea Pietschmann/Alamy (b)
p.466 Government of Chile/Corbis

Front cover & spine *Moai* quarry, Easter Island © Jon Arnold/Alamy Images
Back cover Michele Falzone (t); Walter Bibikow/AWL Images (bl); Ugo Mellone/SIME/4Corners (br)

Index

Maps are marked in grey

A

accommodation.................30–32
   alternative................................30
   cabañas....................................31
   camping....................................32
   casas de familia....................31
   hospedajes 31
   hostels......................................32
   hotels..30
   prices...31
   refugios 32
   residenciales 31
Achao..329
addresses.....................................29
adventure tourism..... 10, 38–42
Aguas Calientes.........................293
Aguas Calientes (Parque
   Nacional Volcán Isluga) 198
Ahu Akahanga............................453
Ahu Akivi.....................................457
Ahu Ature Huki...........................455
Ahu Hanga Tetenga....................453
Ahu Te Peu..................................456
Ahu Tongariki.............................453
air passes......................................25
airlines..27
airport tax......................................25
Alcohuaz......................................149
Aldea Intercultural Trawupeyüm
....279
alerce trees.................................351
Allende, Salvador........................482
Alma Observatory 175
altiplano, crossing......................200
altitude sickness 43
Alto del Carmen.........................153
Anakena.......................................455
Ancud............................. 316–324
Ancud.. 320
Andacollo....................................131
Angelmó......................................310
Angol..256
Antarctica....................................434
Anticura.......................................295
Antillanca....................................294
Antofagasta............... 171–174
Antofagasta, Downtown ... 172
Argentine border crossing
   El Chaltén................................380
   Puerto Pirehueico....................286
   Puerto Varas.............................299
   San Sebastián...........................426
   Santiago.....................................88
Arica 203–209

Arica..203
Arica, beaches............................206
Arica tours...................................207
artesanía 50
ATMs..49
Aymara people...........................202
Azapa Valley 209

B

Bachelet, Michelle........... 488, 491
Bahía Azul 424
Bahía Ensenada..........................441
Bahía Inglesa...............................162
Bahía Inútil..................................425
Bahía Salada................................163
Balmaceda, José Manuel 479
Baños de Colina 90
Baños de Puritama......................186
Baños Morales 90
Baquedano Hills..........................425
bargaining.....................................50
Barrio Inglés 134
Beagle Channel..........................438
beavers..423
birdman ceremony 460
Bolívar, Simón.............................476
Bolivian border crossing............200
books 504–508
Buchupureo.................................244
buses in Chile................................27
buses to Chile 25

C

Cabo de Hornos...........................430
Cabo Froward 395
Cachagua......................................118
Cajón del Maipo..............89–91
Calama..176
Calama.. 176
Caldera....................... 160–162
Caldera....................................... 161
Caleta Puelche............................352
Caleta Tortel...............................378
calling cards..................................50
Camar...185
Camerón......................................425
Candelario Mancilla....................380

Cañete...253
Cape Horn...................................430
Capilla de Mármol.....................371
Captain Cook 448
car rental.......................................28
carbon offsetting..........................26
Cariquima....................................200
Carretera Austral............11, 348,
   352–353
Carretera Austral, driving 352
Casa del Arte...............................248
Casablanca Valley Wine Route
....112
Castillo de San Pedro de
   Alcántara..................................292
Castro............................ 331–335
Castro.. 332
Caulín..324
cell phones....................................50
Cementerio Municipal................391
Central Valley, The 216–257
Central Valley, The 220
Centro de Esqui Volcán Antuco
....256
Centro de Ski Pucón...................280
Centro de Visitantes de las
   Iglesias de Chiloé....................320
Cerro Castillo..............................370
Cerro Guanaco............................441
Cerro Mamalluca observatory
....146
Cerro Martial 438
Cerro Paranal Observatory.....175
Cerro Pintados............................195
Cerro Sombrero...........................424
Cerro Tololo observatory 140
Cerro Unitas...............................168
Chaitén..357
Chañaral......................................163
Chanco...240
Chapa Verde ski centre.............224
Chatwin, Bruce...........................390
Chepu...325
Chepu Valley 325
children, travelling with............51
Chile...5
Chile Chico..................................371
Chilean music 498–503
Chilean Spanish 509–515
Chillán.......................... 242–244
Chillán... 242
Chiloé........................... 314–345
Chiloé.. 318
Chilote churches.........................329
Chilote mythology 321

Chinchorro mummies..............210
Chonchi...................................338
Choshuenco.............................285
Chug Chug geoglyphs 176
Chuquicamata..........................178
churches, Chilote.....................329
climate...............................45, 46
climbing....................................39
Cocha Resbaladero 195
Cochamó...................................307
Cochiguaz................................150
Cochrane..................................376
Colchane..................................200
colectivos..................................27
Collowara observatory 132
colonial Chile 473
Coñaripe..................................283
Concepción 247–250
Concepción........................ 248
Concón....................................118
Constitución.............................240
Copiapó 154–158
Copiapó 154
copper mine, El Teniente........223
Coquimbo 134–136
Corral......................................291
Cortés, Hernán.........................472
costs..45
Coyhaique.................. 365–368
Coyhaique 366
crime.......................................45
crossing the altiplano 200
Cruce El Maitén........................372
Cucao......................................335
cueca..38
Cuernos del Paine 402
Cueva del Milodón...................401
Cuevas Volcánicas...................281
culture and etiquette................44
Curacautín...............................268
Curaco de Vélez.......................329
Curanipe..................................241
curanto....................................322
Curicó 232
Curicó 233
currency...................................49
cycling.....................................29

D

Dalcahue...................................327
dehydration 44
Del Pangue observatory 146
Detif...339
Dichato....................................250
Dientes de Navarino.................428
disabilities, travellers with........51
disabled access 51

discography..............................502
Dos Ventanas Caves.................455
drinking.....................................34
driving 28

E

earthquake, 2010 225
Easter Island 442–459
Easter Island....................... 446
eating.................................32–34
El Abanico.................................255
El Calafate................................411
El Chaltén.................................415
El Gigante.................................454
El Morro....................................204
El Niño......................................496
El Norte Chico............. 122–165
El Norte Chico 126
El Norte Grande 166–215
El Norte Grande 170
El Tatio geysers.........................186
El Teniente................................223
El Tren del Fin del Mundo.......441
El Volcán....................................90
electricity...................................45
Elqui Valley 143–151
Elqui, Hurtado & Limarí
  Valleys, the.................... 130
embassies, Chilean abroad......46
Enqelga....................................198
Ensenada..................................303
entry requirements 46
environmental issues....494
Estancia Harberton...................439
Estancia Valle Chacabuco........375
Estuario de Reloncaví..............306
extensions, tourist card...........46

F

Faro Corona..............................325
ferries 29
Festival Costumbrista 333
festivals....................................35
festivals, Easter Island.............452
Fitz Roy Massif.........................414
flights 25
  from Australia, New Zealand and
    South Africa......................25
  from the UK and Ireland................25
  from the US and Canada 25
  round-the-world 25
  within Chile...........................27
flora...493
flowering desert.......................155

fly-fishing..................................40
fly-fishing lodges......................364
food and drink 32–34
football 37
Frutillar....................................301
Fuerte Agüi 325
Fuerte Bulnes...........................395
Fuerte de Niebla 291
Fuerte Santa Barbara...............461
Futaleufú..................................358

G

gay and lesbian travellers 47
geoglyphs 202
geography................................492
giant sloth................................402
Gigante de Atacama.................198
Glaciar Balmaceda....................402
Glaciar Martial.........................438
Glaciar Perito Moreno..............413
Glaciar San Rafael....................369
Glaciar Serrano........................402
gold mining..............................153
González, Felipe........................448
Guallatire..................................214

H

Hacienda de Tiliviche...............201
Hacienda San Agustín de Puñal
 244
Hanga Roa.................... 449–452
Hanga Roa 451
health 43
hiking.......................................39
history........................... 467–491
hitching....................................29
Horcón......................................118
Hornopirén...............................352
horse racing..............................37
horse-riding..............................42
hot springs
  Aguas Calientes.....................293
  Isla Magdalena......................364
  Laguna Verde.........................159
  Mamiña.........................191, 196
  Nevados de Chillan 245
  Pica................................191, 195
  Pucón (around).....................277
  Reserva Nacional Altos del Lircay
   238
  Termas de Flaco....................277
  Termas de Puyuhuapi............363
  Termas de Socos....................129
Huáscar....................................248

Hurtado, Elqui & Limarí
     Valleys, the...................... 130
Huasco valley, upper...............153
huaso 37
Huicha 339
Humberstone............................193
Humberstone, James 193, 202
Hurtado....................................129
Hurtado Valley..........................127
hypothermia 44

I

Iglesia Catedral.........................137
Iglesia de San Marcos 204
Iglesia de San Pedro 179
Iglesia San Francisco (Castro)
    331
insurance 47
internet 47
Iquique 186–193
Iquique 187
Isla Alejandro Selkirk...............465
Isla de los Lobos.......................119
Isla de los Muertos 378
Isla Lemuy 339
Isla Mechuque 328
Isla Navarino................. 426–430
Isla Negra 111
Isla Quinchao 329
Isla Robinson Crusoe
     460–465
Isla Robinson Crusoe......... 462
Isla Santa María 252
Isla Teja 289
Islotes de Puñihuil...................325
Isluga.......................................199
Itata Valley, The 242
itineraries..................................22
itineraries 23

J

Jara, Victor...............................500
Juan Fernández Archipelago
     460–465

K

Kawéshkar people....................427
kayaking 38
King penguins 425

L

La Herradura............................135
La Junta....................................361
La Ligua 119
La Portada................................175
La Ruta del Vino del Valle de
     Colchagua 229
La Serena...................... 136–143
La Serena, Downtown 137
La Serena's churches 138
La Silla observatory 140
La Tirana...................................197
Lago Blanco..............................425
Lago Calafquén........................283
Lago Chungará.........................213
Lago Colbún.............................239
Lago del Desierto......................380
Lago General Carrera 370
Lago General Pinto Concha
    354
Lago Lanalhue...........................253
Lago Llanquihue.......... 296–303
Lago Neltume...........................285
Lago Panguipulli........................284
Lago Pellaifa.............................283
Lago Pirehueico 286
Lago Puyehue...........................293
Lago Rapel...............................224
Lago Riñihue............................283
Lago Todos Los Santos 305
Lago Todos Los Santos and
     Parque Nacional Vicente
     Perez 304
Lago Vichuquén.......................234
Lago Villarrica 270
Laguna Chaiquenes..................352
Laguna del Negro Francisco
    159
Laguna Lejía 186
Laguna Margarita 306
Laguna Miñeques.....................186
Laguna Miscanti.......................186
Laguna San Rafael....................369
Laguna Santa Rosa...................159
Laguna Torca 234
Laguna Triángulo......................352
Laguna Tuyajto.........................186
Laguna Verde (El Norte Chico)
    159
Lagunas de Cotacotani 213
Lake District, The 258–313
Lake District, The 262
language 509–515
lapis lazuli..................................50
Las Campanas observatory
    140
Lebu..253
Lican Ray...................................283

Limarí Valley 127
Limarí, Hurtado & Elqui
     Valleys, The 130
Liquiñe.......................................283
living in Chile 47
Llico..234
Longquimay..............................268
Los 33......................................158
Los Andes 91
Los Angeles 255
Los Vilos 119
Lota..252

M

Magalhães, Fernão...................389
Magellan, Ferdinand 389
mail..48
Maitencillo 118
Mamiña....................................196
Mánekenk people.....................427
maps..48
Mapuche people 470
Maquí berry..............................319
marea roja 44
Matilla......................................196
Maule Valley, The 235
media 35
medical resources 44
Melipeuco 267
Mercado Fluvial........................288
military coup, Pinochet...........483
Mirador Alejandro Selkirk 464
Mistral, Gabriela 150
moai 456–457
mobile phones 50
money...49
Montegrande 146
mountain biking........................42
Museo Arqueológico (Arica)
     210
Museo Arqueológico (La Serena)
    138
Museo Arqueológico Gustavo Le
     Paige...................................180
Museo de Arte Contemporaneo
     (Valdivia)............................289
Museo de Colchagua 228
Museo de la Exploración R. A.
     Philippi..............................289
Museo de las Tradiciones
     Chonchinas........................338
Museo Desierto de Atacama
    173
Museo Gabriela Mistral 144
Museo Histórico y
     Antropológico Maurice van de
     Maele 289

Museo Regional (Ancud) 319

Museo Regional de la Araucanía
....263

Museo Regional Magallanes
....389

mythology, Chilote 321

N

Naess, Arne 355

**national parks, reserves and
monuments 42**

Monumento Natural Isla
Magdalena..............................396

Parque de Aguas Nevados de
Chillán......................................245

Parque Nacional Alerce Andino
....351

Parque Nacional Bernardo
O'Higgins..................................397

Parque Nacional Chiloé 335

Parque Nacional Conguillío 266

Parque Nacional Fray Jorge 131

Parque Nacional Huerquehue.....278

Parque Nacional la Campana 120

Parque Nacional Laguna del Laja
....255

Parque Nacional Laguna San Rafael
....369

Parque Nacional Lauca 211

**Parque Nacional Lauca and
around 212**

Parque Nacional Llanos de Challe
....153

Parque Nacional Los Glaciares
....410

Parque Nacional Nahuelbuta 256

**Parque Nacional Nahuelbuta
....257**

Parque Nacional Nevado de Tres
Cruces.......................................159

Parque Nacional Pali Aike 396

Parque Nacional Pan de Azúcar
....164

Parque Nacional Puyehue 293

Parque Nacional Puyehue ... 294

Parque Nacional Quelat............361

Parque Nacional Rapa Nui........453

Parque Nacional Tierra del Fuego
....440

**Parque Nacional Tierra del Fuego
....440**

Parque Nacional Tolhuaca 265

Parque Nacional Tolhuaca 266

Parque Nacional Torres del Paine
....402

**Parque Nacional Torres del Paine
....404–405**

Parque Nacional Vicente Pérez
Rosales......................................303

**Parque Nacional Vicente Perez,
Lago Todos Los Santos and
....304**

Parque Nacional Villarrica ...279–283

Parque Nacional Villarrica &
Parque Nacional Huerquehue
....280–281

Parque Nacional Volcán Hornopirén
....354

Parque Nacional Volcán Isluga
....198

**Parque Nacional Volcán Isluga
and around 199**

Parque Pumalín 354

Parque Tantauco...........342–345

Parque Tantauco 343

Reserva Forestal Magallanes 394

Reserva Nacional Altos del Lircay
....238

Reserva Nacional Cerro Castillo
....370

Reserva Nacional Coyhaique.......367

Reserva Nacional Federico Albert
....241

Reserva Nacional Jeinemeni.......371

Reserva Nacional Lago Rosselot
....361

Reserva Nacional Laguna Torca...234

Reserva Nacional las Vicuñas.......214

Reserva Nacional Malalcahuello-
Nalcas 268

Reserva Nacional Pampa del
Tamarugal 195

Reserva Nacional Pinguino de
Humboldt.................................152

Reserva Nacional Radal Siete Tazas
....234

Reserva Nacional Río de Los
Cipreses....................................224

Reserva Nacional Río Simpson
....368

Reserva Nacional Tamango.........377

Yendegaia National Park 425

Neruda, Pablo.........71, 110–111

Nevados de Chillán...................245

newspapers 35

Ninhue.......................................244

nitrate boom 194

nitrate pampa 175

nueva canción 498–503

O

observatories near La Serena
....140

O'Higgins, Bernardo 476

Ojos de Caburgua 277

Olmué.......................................120

opening hours............................49

Orongo 458

Osorno.......................................292

outdoor activities 38–42

Ovalle.......................................127

Ovalle.......................................128

P

palafitos...................................331

Palena 358

Pali Aike 396

Panguipulli 285

Papudo 119

paragliding 189

Parinacota 212

Paro...454

Parque Etnobotánico Omora
....429

Parque Ross 231

parques nacionales..see national
parks

Parra, Violeta 499

Paso de las Raíces.....................269

Paso del Agua Negra................149

Paso Garibaldi..........................420

Patagonia, Argentine 410

Patagonia, Northern ... 346–381

Patagonia, Northern 350

Patagonia, Southern ... 382–417

Patagonia, Southern 386

Pedro de Valdivia......................136

Peine 185

Pelluhue 241

penguins...................................325

Peninsula Lacuy 325

Perito Moreno glacier 413

Petrohué 305

Peulla 306

phones 49

Pica 195

Pichasca 129

Pichidangui...............................119

Pichilemu...................................230

Piedra del Aguila.......................257

Pinguineras de Puñihuil...........325

**Pinochet, Augusto 67,
483–485, 487, 488**

Pisagua......................................201

pisco 148

Playa Aguas Blancas 118

Playa Cocholgue 250

Playa Grande 119

Playa Las Cujas 118

Plazoleta El Yunque 463

Poike Peninsula 454

police 45

Polloquere.................................215

Pomaire 91

Porvenir.....................................420

post...48

press 35

public holidays 49

Puchuldiza.................................198

Pucón 273–277

Pucón 274

Puerto Aysén.................................368
Puerto Bertrand.........................372
Puerto Chacabuco.....................368
Puerto Hambre...........................395
Puerto Ibáñez.............................370
Puerto Montt................ 310–313
Puerto Montt........................ 311
Puerto Montt, ferries.............312
Puerto Natales............. 397–401
Puerto Natales 398
Puerto Octay..............................302
Puerto Río Tranquilo................371
Puerto Toro 430
Puerto Varas 296–301
Puerto Varas........................ 298
Puerto Williams.........................426
Puerto Yungay 379
Pukará de Quitor.......................183
Puna Pau......................................457
Punta Arenas 387–394
Punta Arenas........................ 388
Putre...210
Puyehue hot springs.................294
Puyuhuapi...................................363

Q

Quebrada de Jérez.....................185
Queilén...339
Quellón...340
Quemchi..326
Quicaví..328
Quintay...110

R

rabies 43
radio 35
rafting 38
Ralún..306
Rancagua.....................................222
Rancagua................................ 222
Rano Kau.....................................458
Rano Raraku...............................454
Rapa Nui, origins.....................447
Rapel Valley, The 221–225
Raúl Marín Balmaceda.............360
Reñaca 117
rental cars.................................... 28
Riñihue...283
Río Biobío...................................247
Río Cochiguaz............................150
Río Copiapó Valley 159
Río Futaleufú.............................358
Río Maule....................................235

Río Puelo Valley..........................308
Río Puelo Valley 308
rodeo.....................................38, 221
rongo rongo...............................448
Ruinas de Huanchaca...............173
Ruta del Vino del Valle de
   Colchagua, La.........................229
Ruta del Vino del Valle del Maule
  237

S

Salar de Atacama.......................185
Salar de Surire............................215
Salto de la Princesa...................268
Salto del Huilo-Huilo................285
Salto del Indio............................268
Salto del Laja..............................254
Salto del Torbellino...................255
Salto las Chilcas.........................255
Salto Malleco..............................265
Saltos de Petrohué....................306
San Alfonso.................................. 90
San Fernando..............................226
San Gabriel.................................. 90
San Javier....................................240
San José de Maipo...................... 90
San José miners rescue 158
San Juan Bautista 461–463
San Juan Bautista boat trips
  464
San Martín, José........................476
San Pedro de Atacama
   178–183
San Pedro de Atacama 179
San Pedro, Around............. 184
San Rafael glacier 369
Sanctuario El Cañi 279
Santa Cruz..................................228
Santa Cruz 228
Santa Laura.................................194
SANTIAGO 52–89
Santiago and around 56
Bellavista 72
Santiago 58–59
Santiago, Downtown........... 62
Santiago metro 77
   accommodation 78, 80
   airports 75
   arrival... 75
   arts and entertainment 85
   banks..88
   Barrio Bellavista..........................71
   Barrio Brasil.................................69
   Barrio Concha y Toro 69
   Barrio Lastarria............................66
   Barrio París-Londres...................67
   bars 84
   Barrio Yungay..............................69

Biblioteca Nacional 66
bike rental....................................78
bus terminals..............................75
buses 75, 76
cafés..80
cambios......................................88
car rental......................................75
Casa Colorada............................60
cathedral......................................60
Cerro San Cristóbal.....................73
Cerro Santa Lucía.......................66
clubs...84
colectivos 76
Correo Central............................59
currency exchange......................88
drinking..84
eating....................................80, 84
Edificio Iñíguez...........................68
embassies.....................................88
emergencies.................................88
Estación Central..........................69
Estación Mapocho......................70
Ex-Congreso Nacional...............61
Fería Municipal La Vega.............70
gay Santiago...............................86
history...56
hospitals.......................................88
Huérfanos.....................................63
Iglesia San Francisco...................67
information 78
La Chascona..................................71
Las Condes...................................73
markets...86
Mercado Central..........................70
metro...76
Moneda, La...................................64
Museo Colonial............................67
Museo de Arte Contemporaneo....71
Museo de Arte Precolombino 61
Museo de la Memoria y los
   Derechos Humanos..................70
Museo de Santiago......................60
Museo Histórico Nacional..............60
Museo Nacional de Bellas Artes
  71
nightlife..84
Palacio Cousiño...........................68
Palacio de Bellas Artes................71
Palacios of the Alameda.............68
Parque Bernardo O'Higgins 68
Parque Quinta Normal................69
Paseo Ahumada...........................63
Peñalolén.....................................74
Plaza de Armas 57
police...88
post offices...................................89
Providencia...................................73
restaurants..............................81–84
shopping......................................86
taxis..76
tour operators..............................78
train station.................................76
transport.......................................76
Universidad de Chile...................68
Santuario Cuna de Prat 244
Santuario de la Naturaleza
   Carlos Anwandter.................292
Santuario de la Tirana.............196

Sector Ventisquero Colgante 362
Selkirk, Alexander.....................463
Selk'nam people 427
Seno Otway penguin colony 396
Sewell...................223
shellfish poisoning.....................44
shopping 50
Sierra Velluda.....................256
Siete Lagos, The 283–286
Siete Lagos, The 284
skiing....................40
Socaire....................185
souvenirs 50
sports 37
statues, Easter Island... 456–457
study and work programmes 48
sunburn....................44
surfing 40

T

Tahai...................455
Talca 235–238
Talca 236
Tapati Rapa Nui festival...........452
taxis 28
Te Pahu...................458
telephone numbers, emergency 46
telephones.....................49
television 35
Temuco 260–266
Temuco 264
Tenaún...................328
Termas de Cahuelmó 354
Termas de Puyuhuapi 363
Termas de Socos 129
Termas de Tolhuaca 266
Termas del Flaco 227
Termas Geométricas...............283
Termas Malleco 266
Tierra del Fuego........... 418–441
Tierra del Fuego.................. 422
Tierra del Fuego, driving........424
time 50
tipping....................34
Toconao 185
Tomé 250
Tompkins, Douglas 355
Tompkins, Kris.....................355
Tongoy.....................135
Torres del Paine........... 402–410

Parque Nacional Torres del Paine 404–405
torture 67, 483, 484
tour operation 26
tourist entry card........................ 46
tourist information......................50
trains in Chile 30
trains to Chile................................ 26
transport 25–30
travel insurance........................47
travelling with children.............51
trekking...................39
Tricahue Parque 239
tsunami, 2010 461
Tulor..................185
Túnel de las Raíces...................269

U

Universidad Austral de Chile 248
Ushuaia (Argentina) 430–438
Ushuaia (Argentina) 433
Ushuaia, winter sports.............439

V

Vaihu...................453
Valdivia 286–291
Valdivia 288
Valdivia, Pedro de....................136
Valle de Aguas Calientes........245
Valle de la Luna 185
Valle del Encanto 129
Vallenar.......................151–153
Vallenar 152
VALPARAÍSO 94–110
Valparaíso 100–101
Cerro Alegre & Cerro Concepción 105
Valparaíso, Viña & the central coast 98
accommodation...........................107
arrival............................106
Congreso Nacional.......................106
drinking................................108
eating................................108
entertainment..............................109
funiculars 104
information 107
La Sebastiana 104
shopping.................................109
tours....................107
transport 106

Ventisquero Mosco....................381
Vertiente del Radium..............197
Vichuquén.....................234
Victoria 265
Vicuña 144–146
Vicuña 144
Villa Allegre.....................240
Villa Cerro Castillo 371
Villa Cultural Huilquilemu 238
Villa O'Higgins 379
Villa Ukika...................427
Villarrica...................270
Viña del Mar................. 112–117
Viña del Mar 113
Vinapu 453
visas...................46
Volcán Antuco 256
Volcán Chaitén 357
Volcán Chillán 245
Volcán Copiapó 159
Volcán Llaima.....................266
Volcán Lonquimay 269
Volcán Ojos de Salado............160
Volcán Osorno 304
Volcán Parinacota.....................213
Volcán Tres Cruces 159
Volcán Villarrica.....................282
volcanic eruption 273, 357
volunteering.....................48

W

War of the Pacific.......................478
websites.....................51
whitewater rafting 359
wildlife.....................9
wine tours 89
women's rights.....................489
working.....................48

Y

Yámana people 427
Yupanqui.....................499

Z

Zapallar.......................118

Map symbols

The symbols below are used on maps throughout the book

✈ Airport		⛳ Immigration/border crossing	🌊 Waterfall		- - - - Path
✈ Domestic airport		🏠 Guardería (ranger station)	⚓ Port		— · — Ferry
★ Bus stop		🏠 Refugio (mountain lodge)	/⚊\ Volcano		▬▬▬▬ Funicular railway
Ⓜ Metro station		◓ Cave	▲ Mountain peak		═══ Railway
@ Internet café/access		◓ Observatory	⌃⌃ Mountain range		●─● Cable car
ⓘ Information office		⚑ Fortess	♟ Museum		▬ Building
✚ Hospital		♙ Castle	⛰ Rocks		⇆ Church (town maps)
✉ Post office		🏛 Monument	☼ Hill		◯ Stadium
Ⓒ Telephone office		‡ Church (regional maps)	▬▬▬ Motorway		☐ Market
♨ Spring/spa		⛱ Picnic area	─── Main road		Salt pan
⚔ Battlefield		⚐ Viewpoint	⬥⬥⬥ Unpaved road		Glacier
◆ Point of interest		⚠ Campsite	─── Minor road		☐ Beach
∴ Ruin		☷ Swimming pool	▬▬▬ Pedestrian road		☐◆ Park/reserve
🍇 Vineyard/winery		🏄 Surf beach	⊓⊓⊓ Steps		⊞ Cemetery
⌣ Bridge		🎿 Ski area			

Listings key

■ Accommodation

● Café/cheap eat/restaurant/bar

■ Club/live music

● Shop